Baseball America
2021 DIRECTORY

Baseball America
2021 DIRECTORY

Editors
J.J. Cooper, Josh Norris,
Chris Hilburn-Trenkle

Assistant Editors
Matt Eddy, Carlos Collazo,
Teddy Cahill, Kyle Glaser,
Ben Badler

Contributing
Paul Trap

Database & Application Development
Brent Lewis

Design & Production
James Alworth, Leah Tyner

Programming & Technical Development
Brent Lewis

Cover Photo
Joseph Gareri

Distributed by: Simon & Schuster **ISBN-13:** 978-1-7355482-3-4

Baseball America

TABLE OF CONTENTS

WILLIAM PURNELL/ICON SPORTSWIRE VIA GETTY IMAGES

BA Baseball America

HEAD OF THE CLASS

The best college programs and players from the past four decades

South Carolina exhibits Palmetto pride

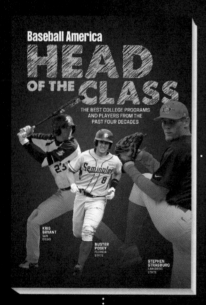

Head Of The Class collects 39 seasons—1981 through 2019—of college baseball reporting and analysis by Baseball America and its industry-leading voices.

New content exclusive to **Head Of The Class** analyzes the college game in the 1980s, 1990s, 2000s and 2010s.

Louisiana State ushers in era of SEC dominance

Includes the top 25 programs for each decade, the top storylines that shaped each decade and the top major league stars from each college class.

WHAT'S NEW IN 2021

The minor leagues saw the biggest shakeup in decades coming into the 2021 season. Major League Baseball has taken over governance and responsibility for administering the minor leagues, and minor league teams have signed 10-year licenses directly with MLB.

That means that Minor League Baseball, (legally known as the National Association), is winding down operations. MLB's takeover also brings with it the elimination of the league presidents and league offices that have long been a part of the minor leagues.

It also means that beginning in 2021, there will only be five levels of affiliated minor league baseball in North America—the Arizona and Gulf Coast rookie leagues as well as four full-season levels. The shuffling means that 43 teams that were affiliated going into 2020 are no longer in affiliated baseball. Three teams that had been part of independent baseball have now joined affiliated baseball as well.

MINOR LEAGUE MOVEMENT

TRIPLE-A
Added: Jacksonville (from Double-A), St. Paul (from independent American Association), Sugar Land (from independent Atlantic League).
Moved Out: Fresno (moved to Low-A), San Antonio (moved to Double-A), Wichita (moved to Double-A).
Moved: Pawtucket Red Sox move to Worcester, Mass.

DOUBLE-A
Added: San Antonio (from Triple-A), Wichita (from Triple-A), Somerset (from independent American Association).
Moved Out: Trenton (to MLB Draft League).
Dropped: Jackson.

HIGH-A
Added from Low-A: Dayton, Fort Wayne, Great Lakes, Lake County, Lansing, West Michigan, Beloit, Cedar Rapids, Peoria, Quad Cities, South Bend, Wisconsin, Jersey Shore, Asheville, Bowling Green, Greensboro, Greenville, Hickory, Rome.
Added from Short-Season: Aberdeen, Brooklyn, Hudson Valley, Eugene, Everett, Hillsboro, Spokane, Tri-City, Vancouver.
Moved to Low-A: Daytona, Jupiter, Palm Beach, St. Lucie, Bradenton, Clearwater, Dunedin, Fort Myers, Lakeland, Tampa, Carolina, Down East, Fayetteville, Lynchburg, Salem, Myrtle Beach.
Moved Out: Frederick (to MLB Draft League).
Dropped: Charlotte, Florida, Lancaster.
Name Change: Lakewood becomes Jersey Shore.

LOW-A
Added From High-A: Daytona, Jupiter, Palm Beach, St. Lucie, Bradenton, Clearwater, Dunedin, Fort Myers, Lakeland, Tampa, Carolina, Down East, Fayetteville, Lynchburg, Salem, Myrtle Beach.
Moved To High-A: Dayton, Fort Wayne, Great Lakes, Lake County, Lansing, West Michigan, Beloit, Cedar Rapids, Peoria, Quad Cities, South Bend, Wisconsin, Jersey Shore, Asheville, Bowling Green, Greensboro, Greenville, Hickory, Rome.
Added from Short-Season: Aberdeen, Brooklyn, Hudson Valley, Eugene, Everett, Hillsboro, Spokane, Tri-City, Vancouver.
Moved Out: Kane County (to American Association), Lexington (to Atlantic League), West Virginia (to Atlantic League), Clinton (to Prospect League), Burlington (to Prospect League).
Dropped: Hagerstown.

SHORT-SEASON/ROOKIE
Eliminated with exception of Arizona, Gulf Coast and Dominican Summer Leagues.

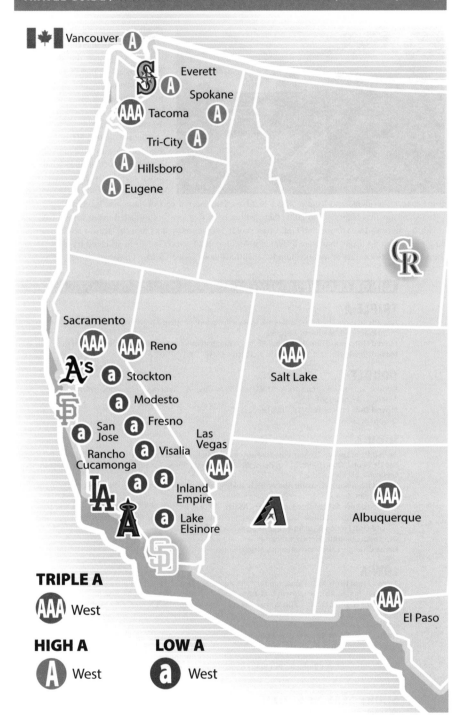

Vancouver

Everett

Spokane

Tacoma

Tri-City

Hillsboro

Eugene

Sacramento

Reno

Stockton

Salt Lake

Modesto

Fresno

San Jose

Las Vegas

Rancho Cucamonga

Visalia

Inland Empire

Lake Elsinore

Albuquerque

TRIPLE A

West

HIGH A

West

LOW A

West

El Paso

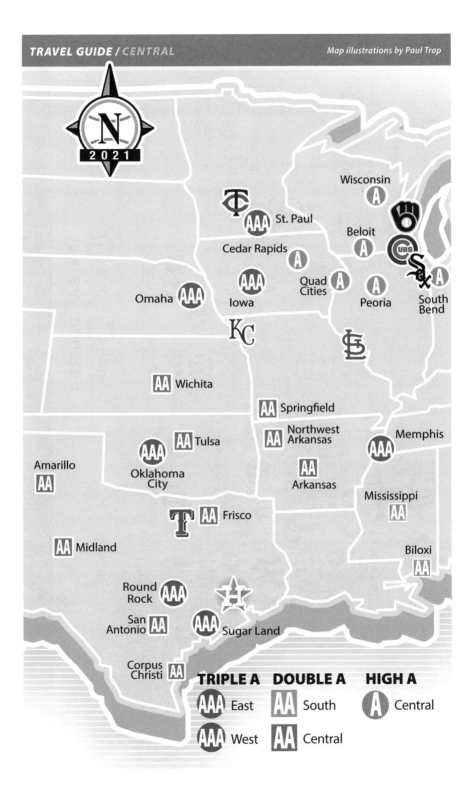

Map illustrations by Paul Trap

Wisconsin

Beloit

St. Paul

Cedar Rapids

Quad Cities

Peoria

South Bend

Omaha

Iowa

Wichita

Springfield

Amarillo

Oklahoma City

Tulsa

Northwest Arkansas

Memphis

Arkansas

Mississippi

Frisco

Midland

Biloxi

Round Rock

San Antonio

Sugar Land

Corpus Christi

TRIPLE A

AAA East

AAA West

DOUBLE A

AA South

AA Central

HIGH A

A Central

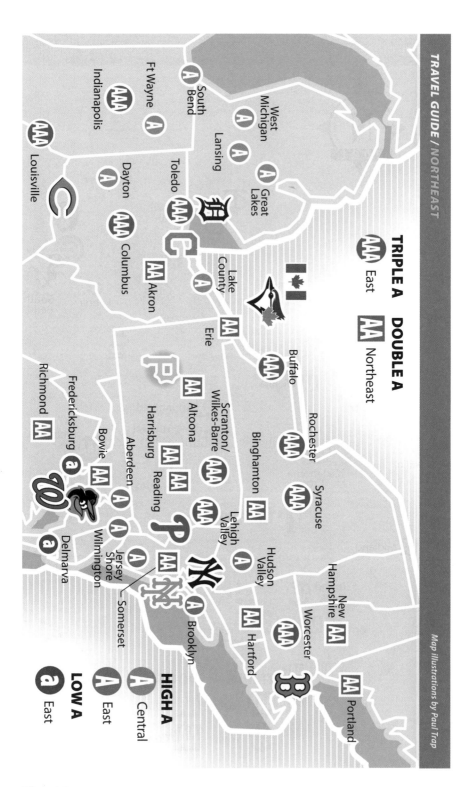

TRIPLE A
AAA East

DOUBLE A
AA Northeast

HIGH A
A Central
A East

LOW A
a East

Indianapolis
Ft Wayne
South Bend
West Michigan
Lansing
Louisville
Dayton
Toledo
Great Lakes
Columbus
Akron
Lake County
Erie
Buffalo
Rochester
Richmond
Fredericksburg
Bowie
Harrisburg
Altoona
Scranton/Wilkes-Barre
Binghamton
Syracuse
Aberdeen
Reading
Lehigh Valley
Hudson Valley
New Hampshire
Wilmington
Jersey Shore
Somerset
Brooklyn
Worcester
Hartford
Portland
Delmarva

Map illustrations by Paul Trap

 Columbus

 Bowie

Fredericksburg

Richmond

Delmarva

Louisville

 Bowling
Green

Salem

Lynchburg

Norfolk

Greensboro Durham

Carolina

Winston-
Salem

Tennessee Hickory

Kannapolis

Nashville

Asheville

Down East

Chattanooga

Charlotte

Fayetteville

Gwinnett

Greenville

Rocket
City

Rome

Columbia

Myrtle
Beach

Augusta

Birmingham

Charleston

Montgomery

N
2021

Pensacola

 Jacksonville

Dunedin

Daytona

Lakeland

Clearwater

TRIPLE A

 East

HIGH A

East

DOUBLE A

Northeast

South

LOW A

East

Southeast

St Lucie

Palm Beach/
Jupiter

Tampa
Bradenton

Ft Myers

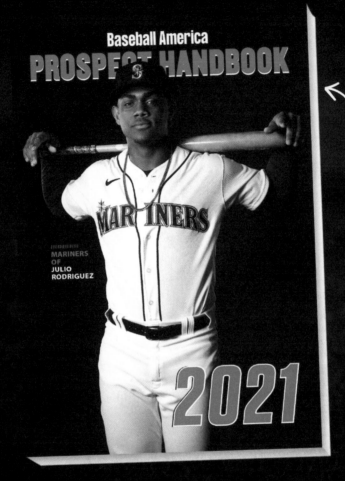

BA Baseball America

Baseball America
PROSPECT HANDBOOK

MARINERS
OF
JULIO
RODRIGUEZ

2021

AVAILABLE
NOW

PROSPECT HANDBOOK

The **2021 Prospect Handbook** is a must-have for superfans and fantasy players. You will find yourself returning to the book—now in its 21st edition—all year to see what we wrote. Get the scoop on big league callups, trade acquisitions or even prospective additions to your dynasty team.

GET YOURS AT:
BaseballAmerica.com

MAJOR LEAGUES

MAJOR LEAGUE BASEBALL

Mailing Address: 1271 Avenue of the Americas, New York, NY 10020.
Telephone: (212) 931-7800. **Website:** www.mlb.com.
Commissioner of Baseball: Rob Manfred.
Deputy Commissioner, Baseball Administration and Chief Legal Officer: Dan Halem.
Chief Communications Officer: Pat Courtney. **Chief People & Culture Officer:** Michele
Meyer-Shipp. **Chief Baseball Development Officer:** Tony Reagins. **Chief Financial Officer/
Sr. Advisor:** Bob Starkey. **Chief Operations & Strategy Officer:** Chris Marinak. **Chief Revenue
Officer:** Noah Garden. **Executive Vice President & General Counsel:** Lara Pitaro Wisch.

Rob Manfred

ON-FIELD OPERATIONS

Executive Vice President, Baseball Operations: Morgan Sword. **Senior Vice President,
On-Field Operations:** Michael Hill. **Senior Vice President, On-Field Operations:** Raul
Ibañez. **Senior VP, Minor League Operations & Development:** Peter Woodfork. **Vice
President, Amateur & Medical:** John D'Angelo. **Vice President, Baseball Economics:**
Reed MacPhail.**Vice President, Head Baseball Operations Counsel:** Paul Mifsud. **Vice
President, Instant Replay Operations:** Justin Klemm. **Senior Director, On-Field Operations:** Gregor Blanco. **Senior
Director, On-Field Operations:** Rajai Davis. **Senior Director, On-Field Operations:** Nick Hundley. **Senior Director,
International Operations:** Rebecca Seesel. **Senior Director, Player Programs:** Yenifer Fauche. **Senior Director,
Baseball Operations:** Jeff Pfeifer. **Senior Director, Umpiring Operations:** Matt McKendry. **Senior Director, Minor
League Operations & Affairs:** Freddie Seymour. **Senior Director, On-Field Strategy:** Joe Martinez. **Director, Draft
Operations:** Bill Francis. **Director, Umpire Development:** Rich Rieker. **Director, Sports Medicine:** Scott Sheridan.
Director, Player Development: Mike LaCassa. **Senior Manager, Baseball Economics:** Cameron Barwick. **Senior
Manager, Player Programs:** Ricardhy Grandoit. **Manager, Baseball Economics:** Travis Buck. **Manager, Baseball
Economics:** Kyle Krueger. **Manager, Medical & Equipment:** Kevin Ma. **Manager, Instant Replay:** Jeff Moody.
Manager, On-Field Operations: Chris Knettel. **Manager, Umpiring Operations:** Raquel Wagner. **Manager, Baseball
Operations:** Garrett Horan. **Senior Coordinator, International Operations:** Patrick Nathanson. **Senior Coordinator,
Umpiring Operations:** Chris Romanello. **Senior Coordinator, Video:** Freddie Hernandez. **Senior Coordinator,
Baseball Operations:** Gina Liento. **Senior Coordinator, Baseball Operations:** Elizabeth Benn. **Analyst, Baseball
Operations:** Josh Keen. **Coordinator, Medical Operations:** Dana Rowe. **Coordinator, Medical Operations:** Zack
Tenner. **Coordinator, Draft Operations:** Jalen Phillips. **Coordinator, Draft Operations:** Diego Delgado. **Coordinator,
Draft Operations:** Mark Nader. **Coordinator, International Operations:** Maritza Grillo. **Coordinator, On-Field
Operations:** Danielle Monday. **Coordinator, Umpiring Operations:** Alejandro Bermudez. **Coordinator, Player
Programs:** Lilah Drafts-Johnson.

LABOR RELATIONS

Senior Vice President, Deputy General Counsel, Labor Relations: Patrick Houlihan. **Vice President, Drug,
Health & Safety Programs:** Jon Coyles. **Senior Manager, Drug, Health & Safety Programs:** Lindsey Ingraham.
Senior Counsel: Kasey Sanossian. **Counsel:** Vanish Grover. **Counsel:** Justin Wiley. **Coordinator, Drug Health & Safety
Programs:** Isabel Caro.

BASEBALL & SOFTBALL DEVELOPMENT

Chief Baseball Development Officer: Tony Reagins. **Vice President, Baseball & Softball Development:** David
James. **Vice President, Youth & Facility Development:** Darrell Miller. **Vice President, Baseball Development:**
Del Matthews. **Senior Director, Baseball & Softball Development:** Chris Haydock. **Senior Director, Compliance:**
Katherine Anderson. **Senior Manager, Baseball & Softball Development:** Chuck Fox. **Senior Manager, Play
Ball & RBI:** Bennett Shields. **Manager, Baseball & Softball Development:** Henry Gonzalez. **Senior Coordinator,
Baseball Development:** Kindu Jones. **Senior Coordinator, Softball Development and Legal:** Sarah Padove. **Senior
Coordinator, Baseball Development, RBI:** Steven Smiegocki. **Coordinator, Softball Development:** Koely Kempisty.
Coordinator, MLB Compton Youth Academy: Kenneth Landreaux. **Coordinator, MLB Compton Youth Academy
Softball:** Eliza Crawford. **Senior Administrative Assistant:** Grace Carrasco.

COMMUNICATIONS

Telephone: (212) 931-7878. **Fax:** (212) 949-5654.
Chief Communications Officer: Pat Courtney. **Senior Vice President, Communications:** Matt Bourne. **Vice
Presidents, Communications:** John Blundell, Mike Teevan. **Senior Director, Business Communications & Youth
Engagement:** Steve Arocho. **Senior Director, Business Communications:** Ileana Peña. **Director, Communications:**
Donald Muller. **Manager, Communications:** Lydia Devlin. **Manager, Business Communications:** David Hochman.
Senior Coordinator, Communications & Scheduling: Paul Koehler. **Senior Coordinator, Communications:**
Yolayna Alvarez. **Coordinator, Business Communications:** Kerline Batista, Troy Watson. **Executive Assistant,
Communications:** Ginger Dillon. **Official Historian:** John Thorn.

AMERICAN LEAGUE

Year League Founded: 1901.
2021 Opening Date: April 1. **Closing Date:** Oct. 3.
Regular Season: 162 games.
Division Structure: East—Baltimore, Boston, New York, Tampa Bay, Toronto.
Central—Chicago, Cleveland, Detroit, Kansas City, Minnesota. **West**—Houston, Los Angeles, Oakland, Seattle, Texas.

Playoff Format: Two non-division winners with best records meet in one-game wild card. Wild card winner and three division champions meet in two best-of-five Division Series. Winners meet in best-of-seven Championship Series.

All-Star Game: July 13, Truist Park, Atlanta (American League vs. National League).

Roster Limit: 26, through Sept. 1, when rosters expand to 28. **Brand of Baseball:** Rawlings.

Statistician: MLB Advanced Media, 1271 Avenue of the Americas, New York, NY, 10020.

STADIUM INFORMATION

Team	Stadium	Dimensions			Capacity	2019 Att.
		LF	CF	RF		
Baltimore	Oriole Park at Camden Yards	333	410	318	45,971	1,307,807
Boston	Fenway Park	310	390	302	37,673	2,924,627
Chicago	Guaranteed Rate Field	330	400	335	40,615	1,649,775
Cleveland	Progressive Field	325	405	325	37,675	1,738,642
Detroit	Comerica Park	345	420	330	41,782	1,501,430
Houston	Minute Maid Park	315	435	326	40,976	2,857,367
Kansas City	Kauffman Stadium	330	410	330	37,903	1,479,659
Los Angeles	Angel Stadium	333	404	333	45,050	3,019,012
Minnesota	Target Field	339	404	328	39,504	2,294,152
New York	Yankee Stadium	318	408	314	50,291	3,304,404
Oakland	Oakland Coliseum	330	400	367	35,067	1,662,211
Seattle	T-Mobile Park	331	401	326	47,447	1,791,863
Tampa Bay	Tropicana Field	315	404	322	41,315	1,178,735
Texas	Globe Life Park in Arlington	332	400	325	48,114	2,132,994
Toronto	Rogers Centre	328	400	328	50,598	1,750,144

NATIONAL LEAGUE

Year League Founded: 1876.
2021 Opening Date: April 1. **Closing Date:** Oct. 3.
Regular Season: 162 games.
Division Structure: East—Atlanta, Miami, New York, Philadelphia, Washington.
Central—Chicago, Cincinnati, Milwaukee, Pittsburgh, St. Louis. **West**—Arizona, Colorado, Los Angeles, San Diego, San Francisco.

Playoff Format: Two non-division winners with best records meet in one-game wild card. Wild card winner and three division champions meet in two best-of-five Division Series. Winners meet in best-of-seven Championship Series.

All-Star Game: July 13, Truist Park, Atlanta (American League vs. National League).

Roster Limit: 26, through Sept. 1, when rosters expand to 28. **Brand of Baseball:** Rawlings.

Statistician: MLB Advanced Media, 1271 Avenue of the Americas, New York, NY, 10020.

STADIUM INFORMATION

Team	Stadium	Dimensions			Capacity	2019 Att.
		LF	CF	RF		
Arizona	Chase Field	330	407	334	49,033	2,135,510
Atlanta	Truist Park	335	400	325	41,500	2,655,100
Chicago	Wrigley Field	355	400	353	41,160	3,094,865
Cincinnati	Great American Ball Park	328	404	325	42,319	1,808,685
Colorado	Coors Field	347	415	350	50,499	2,993,244
Los Angeles	Dodger Stadium	330	395	330	56,000	3,974,309
Miami	Marlins Park	344	407	335	36,742	811,302
Milwaukee	Miller Park	344	400	345	41,900	2,923,333
New York	Citi Field	335	408	330	42,200	2,442,532
Philadelphia	Citizens Bank Park	329	401	330	43,647	2,727,421
Pittsburgh	PNC Park	325	399	320	38,496	1,491,439
St. Louis	Busch Stadium	336	400	335	46,681	3,480,393
San Diego	Petco Park	336	396	322	42,685	2,396,399
San Francisco	Oracle Park	339	399	309	41,503	2,707,760
Washington	Nationals Park	336	402	335	41,888	2,259,781

ARIZONA DIAMONDBACKS

Office Address: Chase Field, 401 E. Jefferson St, Phoenix, AZ 85004.
Mailing Address: P.O. Box 2095, Phoenix, AZ 85001.
Telephone: (602) 462-6500. **Fax:** (602) 462-6599. **Website:** www.dbacks.com

OWNERSHIP

Managing General Partner: Ken Kendrick. **General Partners:** Mike Chipman, Jeff Royer.

BUSINESS OPERATIONS

President/CEO: Derrick Hall. **Executive Vice President, Business Operations/Chief Revenue Officer:** Cullen Maxey. **Executive Vice President/Chief Financial Officer:** Tom Harris. **Executive Vice President, Chief Legal Officer:** Nona Lee. **Senior Advisor, President/CEO:** Luis Gonzalez.

Ken Kendrick

BROADCASTING

VP, Broadcasting: Scott Geyer. **VP, Game Operations/DBTV Productions:** Rob Weinheimer.

CORPORATE PARTNERSHIPS/MARKETING

VP, Corporate Partnerships: Judd Norris. **Senior Director, Corporate Partnership Services:** Kerri White. **VP, Marketing/Analytics:** Kenny Farrell. **Senior Director, Marketing:** Rayme Lofgren.

FINANCE/LEGAL

VP, Finance: Craig Bradley. **Senior Director, Financial Management and Purchasing:** Jeff Jacobs. **Director, Accounting:** Jeffrey Barnes. **General Counsel:** Caleb Jay.

COMMUNITY AFFAIRS

Senior VP, Corporate/Community Impact: Debbie Castaldo. **Senior Manager, Community/Foundation Operations:** Tara Trzinski. **Director, Strategic Community Partnerships & Programs:** Dustin Payne.

COMMUNICATIONS/MEDIA RELATIONS

Senior VP, Content/Communications: Josh Rawitch. **Senior Director, Communications:** Casey Wilcox. **Director, Player/Media Relations:** Patrick O'Connell.

TICKET SALES

Telephone: (602) 514-8400. **Fax:** (602) 462-4141. **Senior VP, Ticket Sales/Marketing:** John Fisher. **VP, Ticket Sales/Events:** Ryan Holmstedt.

BASEBALL OPERATIONS

Executive Vice President/General Manager: Mike Hazen. **Senior VP/Assistant GM:** Amiel Sawdaye. **VP/Assistant GM:** Michael Fitzgerald. **VP, Latin Operations:** Junior Noboa. **Special Assistants to GM:** Burke Badenhop, Craig Shipley. **Specialist Assistant to GM/Pitching Strategist:** Dan Haren. **Director, Baseball Operations:** Sam Eaton. **Assistant Director, Amateur Scouting & Baseball Administration:** Kristyn Pierce. **Coordinator, Baseball Operations:** Max Phillips. **Assistant, International Scouting:** Alex Lorenzo. **Manager, Baseball Systems:** John Krazit. **Baseball Systems Developer:** Thomas Johnson. **Analysts, Pro Personnel:** Matt Roffe, Connor Shannon. **Analysts, Research & Development:** Cody Callahan, Max Glick, Taylor Chloe. **Director of Pitching:** Ross Seaton. **Baseball Operations Fellow:** Carl Gonzalez.

Mike Hazen

MAJOR LEAGUE STAFF

Manager: Torey Lovullo. **Coaches: Bench**—Luis Urueta, **Pitching**—Matt Herges, **Hitting**—Darnell Coles, **First Base**—Dave McKay, **Third Base**—Tony Perezchica, **Bullpen**—Mike Fetters, **Assistant Hitting Coach**—Eric Hinske, **Quality Control/Catching**—Robby Hammock, **Bullpen Catcher**—Humberto Quintero. **Coordinator, Run Production**–Drew Hedman. **Coordinator, Run Prevention**–Alex Cultice. **Coordinator, Major League Video**–Allen Campbell.

MEDICAL/TRAINING

Club Physician: Dr. Gary Waslewski. **Director, Sports Medicine & Performance:** Ken Crenshaw. **Head Trainer:** Ryan DiPanfilo. **Assistant Trainer:** Ryne Eubanks. **Strength & Conditioning Coordinator:** Nate Shaw. **Assistant Strength & Conditioning Coordinator:** Matt Tenney. **Physical Therapist:** Ben Hagar. **Physical Therapist:** Junko Yazawa. **Analyst, Sports Medicine:** Patrick Sellas. **Team Performance Dietitian:** Michelle Riccardi.

PLAYER DEVELOPMENT

Director, Player Development: Josh Barfield. **Assistant Director, Player Development:** Matt Grabowski. **Assistant Director, Minor League Administration:** Shawn Marette. **Coordinator, Baseball Development Technology:** Cory Swope. **Coordinator, Latin American Baseball Operations:** Mariana Patraca. **Coordinator, Mental Skills:** Zach Brandon. **Assistant, Education & Cultural Development:** Chloe Medina. **Analyst, Baseball Operations Research & Development:** Micah Daley-Harris. **Coordinators:** Chris Cron (field), Dan Carlson (pitching), Bijan Rademacher (hitting), Jonny Gomes (outfield/baserunning), Gil Velazquez (infield), Mark Reed (catching/complex coach), Brad Arnsberg (rehab pitching), Orlando Hudson (assistant), Hatuey Mendoza (short-season pitching), Casey Chenoweth (short-season hitting), Jaime Del Valle (DSL field). **Medical Coordinator:** Max Esposito. **Director, Skills Development:** Vaughn Robinson. **Medical Administrator:** Jon Herzner. **Rehab and Performance Therapist:** Kelly Boyce. **Latin American Medical Coordinator:** Spencer Ryan. **Latin American Strength and Conditioning Coordinator:** Tim Queck.

FARM SYSTEM

Class	Club (League)	Manager	Hitting Coach	Pitching Coach
Triple-A	Reno	Blake Lalli	Rick Short	Jeff Bajenaru
Double-A	Amarillo	Shawn Roof	Travis Denker	Doug Drabek
High-A	Hillsboro	Vince Harrison	KC Judge	Shane Loux
Low-A	Visalia	Javier Colina	Micah Franklin	Barry Enright
Rookie	Diamondbacks (AZL)	Rolando Amedo	Mark Reed/Nick Evans	G. Hernandez

SCOUTING

Telephone: (602) 462-6500. **Fax:** (602) 462-6425.

Director, Amateur Scouting: Deric Ladnier. **Assistant Director, Amateur Scouting:** Ian Rebhan. **Director, Pro Scouting:** Jason Parks. **Coordinator, Pro Scouting:** Cory Hahn. **Vice President, Latin American Scouting & Player Development:** Cesar Geronimo. **Director, International Scouting:** Peter Wardell. **Director, Pacific Rim Operations:** Mack Hayashi.

National Crosscheckers: Greg Lonigro (Connellsville, PA), James Merriweather III (Glendale, AZ). **National Pitching Supervisor:** Jeff Mousser (Gilbert, AZ). **Regional Supervisors:** Steve Connelly (Emerald Isle, NC), Frank Damas (Miami Lakes, FL), Rick Matsko (Davidsville, PA), Steve McAllister (Chillicothe, IL), Doyle Wilson (Queen Creek, AZ). **Area Scouts:** Andrew Allen (Berkeley, CA), Hudson Belinsky (Smyrna, GA), Nathan Birtwell (St. Louis, MO), Eric Cruz (Pembroke Pines, FL), Jason Gallagher (Downingtown, PA), Pedro Hernandez (Vega Baja, PR), Kerry Jenkins (Nashville, TN), Jeremy Kehrt (Avon, IN), Jeremiah Luster (Oceanside, CA), Rick Matsko (Davidsville, PA), Matt Mercurio (Indialantic, FL), Mike Meyers (Houston, TX), Dan Ramsay (Spokane, WA), Mark Ross (Tucson, AZ), JR Salinas (Roanoke, TX), George Swain (Wilmington, NC), Garry Templeton (San Marcos, CA), Jake Williams (Kansas City, MO). **Developmental Scout:** Ryan Dobson (Los Angeles, CA).

Major League Advance Scout: Jeff Gardner (Scottsdale, AZ). **Special Assignment Scouts:** Todd Greene (Alpharetta, GA), Danny Haas (Madeira, OH), Alex Jacobs (Philadelphia, PA), Mark Snipp (The Woodlands, TX), Tim Wilken (Dunedin, FL). **Major League Scouts:** Bill Gayton (San Diego, CA), Jack Goin (Eagan, MN) Mike Piatnik (Winter Haven, FL).

Professional Scouts: Tucker Blair (Estero, FL), Diego Bordas (Santo Domingo, DR), Chris Carminucci (Scottsdale, AZ), Jacob Frisaro (Scottsdale, AZ), Matt Hahn (Tampa, FL), Brad Kelley (Scottsdale, AZ), Kelvin Kondo (Tokyo, Japan), Rob Leary (Melbourne, FL), Chris Slivka (Scottsdale, AZ), Brett West (Palm Harbor, FL). **Developmental Scout:** Aaron Thorn.

International Crosscheckers: Jon Lukens (Newport Beach, CA), Hector Otero (Miami, FL). **Crosschecker, Latin America:** Francisco Cartaya (Collierville, TN). **Supervisor, Dominican Republic:** Omar Rogers. **Coordinator, Dominican Republic:** Ronald Rivas. **International Scouts:** Luis Gonzalez Arteaga (Colombia); Bradley Stuart (Curacao); David Felida, Pedro Meyer, Jose Ortiz, Wilfredo Tejada (Dominican Republic); Kyle Lee (Korea); Limberth Marin, Ray Padilla (Mexico); Julio Sanchez (Nicaragua); Jose Luis Santos (Panama); TY Wei (Taiwan); Didimo Bracho, Gregory Blanco, David Chicarelli, Kristians Pereira, Ronald Salazar (Venezuela).

ATLANTA BRAVES

Office Address: 755 Battery Avenue, SE Atlanta, GA 30339-3017.
Mailing Address: PO Box 723009, Atlanta, GA 31139-2704.
Telephone: (404) 522-7630. **Website:** www.braves.com.

OWNERSHIP

Operated/Owned By: Liberty Media. **Chairman:** Terry McGuirk. **Vice Chairman, Emeritus:** John Schuerholz.

BUSINESS OPERATIONS

President/CEO: Derek Schiller. **Executive VP/Chief Legal Officer:** Greg Heller.

Terry McGuirk

MARKETING/SALES

Senior VP, Marketing: Adam Zimmerman. **Senior VP, Ticket Sales:** Paul Adams. **Senior VP, Corporate & Premium Partnerships:** Jim Allen. **Executive VP, Chief People Capital Officer:** DeRetta Rhodes.

FINANCE

Executive VP, Chief Financial Officer: Jill Robinson.

COMMUNICATIONS

Telephone: (404) 522-7630.
Vice President, Communications: Beth Marshall. **Director, Baseball Communications:** Jonathan Kerber. **Manager, Baseball Communications:** Jared Burleyson. **Bilingual Coordinator, Baseball Communications:** Franco García. **Coordinator, Baseball Communications:** Matt Grilli. **Coordinator, Corporate Communications:** Kara Zoellner.

STADIUM OPERATIONS

Senior Vice President, Facility Operations: Eric Perestuk. **Senior Director, Field Operations:** Ed Mangan. **VP, Fan Experience:** Scott Cunningham. **PA Announcer:** Casey Motter. **Official Scorers:** Guy Curtright, Richard Musterer, Mike Stamus.

TICKETING

Telephone: (404) 577-9100. **Email:** ticketsales@braves.com.
VP, Ticket Operations: Anthony Esposito.

TRAVEL/CLUBHOUSE

Director of Team Travel: Jim Lovell. **Director, Equipment & Clubhouse Service:** Calvin Minasian.
Visiting Clubhouse Manager: Fred Stone. **Assistant Equipment and Clubhouse Service Managers:** Eric Durban and Chris Hunter.

BASEBALL OPERATIONS

Telephone: (404) 522-7630. **Fax:** (404) 614-3308.

Alex Anthopoulos

President, Baseball Operations & General Manager: Alex Anthopoulos. **VP, Scouting:** Dana Brown. **Assistant GM/Research & Development:** Jason Paré. **Special Assistant to the GM:** Mike Fast. **Senior Director, Baseball Administration:** Dixie Keller. **Director, Baseball Operations:** Adam Sonabend. **Manager, Baseball Video Operations:** Rob Smith. **Executive Assistant to the President, Baseball Operations & General Manager:** Elizabeth Terán. **Manager, Major League Operations:** Doug Wachter. **Analysts, Major League Operations:** Caelan Collins, Nick Coppola, Tom O'Donnell. **Manager, Baseball Systems:** Garrett Wilson. **Data Architect & Systems Developer:** Mike Copeland. **Developer, Baseball Systems:** Dana Bennett & Isaac Lee. **Coordinator, Research & Development:** Josh Malek. **Machine Learning Engineer:** Kevin Song, PhD. **Analysts, Research & Development:** Scott Rapponotti, Kyle Sargent. **Data Scientist:** Evan Tucker, PhD. **Manager, Family Relations:** Rafael Becerra. **Assistant, Family Relations:** Seth Heizer, Bill Lucas. **Fellowship:** Jeremy Dorsey. **Advance Scouting Trainee:** Will Siskel & Matt Winn. **Research and Development Trainee:** Evan Olawsky.

MAJOR LEAGUE STAFF

Manager: Brian Snitker. **Coaches: Bench**—Walt Weiss, **Pitching**—Rick Kranitz, **Hitting**—Kevin Seitzer, **Assistant Hitting Coach**—Jose Castro and Bobby Magallanes, **First Base**—Eric Young, **Third Base**—Ron Washington. **Catching Coach:** Sal Fasano. **Bullpen Coach:** Drew French. **Bullpen Catchers:** Jimmy Leo & Jose Yepez. **Batting Practice Pitcher:** Tomas Perez.

MEDICAL/TRAINING

Director, Player Health/Head Athletic Trainer: George C. Poulis. **Head Team Physician:** Tim Griffith. **Senior Advisor, Athletic Training:** Jeff Porter. **Assistant Athletic Trainer:** Mike Frostad and Jeff Stevenson. **Head Strength & Conditioning Coach:** Bradford Scott. **Assistant Strength & Conditioning Coach:** Jordan Wolf. **Head Physical Therapist:** Pete Cicinelli. **Assistant Physical Therapist:** Nick Valencia. **Massage Therapist:** Nate Leet.

PLAYER DEVELOPMENT

Telephone: (404) 522-7630.

Assistant GM/Player Development: Ben Sestanovich. **Assistant Director of Minor League Operations:** Ron Knight. **Manager, PD Analytics:** Colin Wyers. **Assistant, Player Development:** Dylan Quantz. **Field Coordinator:** Doug Mansolino. **Pitching Coordinator:** Paul Davis. **Hitting Coordinator:** Mike Brumley. **Roving Coordinators:** Greg Walker (assistant hitting), JD Closser (catching), Nick Flynn (medical), Eric Hrycko (assistant medical), Jordan Sidwell (strength & conditioning), Ryan Driscoll (assistant strength & conditioning), Kyle Clements (video), Fernando Pineres (cultural development). **Coordinator, Florida Operations:** Jeff Pink. **Physical Therapist:** Johnny Passarelli.

FARM SYSTEM

Class	Club	Manager	Hitting Coach	Pitching Coach
Triple-A	Gwinnett	Matt Tuiasosopo	Carlos Mendez	Mike Maroth
Double-A	Mississippi	TBD	Einar Diaz	Dan Meyer
High A	Rome	Kanekoa Texeira	Danny Santiesteban	Bo Henning
Low A	Augusta	Michael Saunders	Mike Bard	Elvin Nina
Rookie	Braves (GCL)	Nestor Perez Jr.	B. Moore/C. Narron	Wes McGuire

SCOUTING

Telephone: (404) 522-7630. **Fax:** (404) 614-1350.

Special Assistants to Baseball Operations: Andruw Jones, Terry Pendleton, Eddie Perez. **Assistant Director, Pro Scouting:** Jonathan Schuerholz. **Professional Scouts:** Alan Butts, Jackson Lourie. **Special Assignment Scouts:** Ralph Garr, John Gibbons, Fred McGriff. **Advance Scouting Trainee:** Matt Winn. **Assistant Director, Amateur Scouting Operations:** Ronit Shah. **Administrative Assistant to Amateur Scouting:** Will Rich. **Ambassador to Amateur Scouting:** Smoke Laval (Reserve, LA). **National Cross Checkers:** Joe Jordan, Ron Marigny, Gary Rajsich, Deron Rombach. **Regional Cross Checkers: West/Southwest**—Joey Davis, **Southeast**—Reed Dunn, **Pacific Northwest**—Alan Hull, **Northeast**—Brian Sankey, **Midwest**—Terry Tripp Jr. **Area Scouting Supervisors:** Billy Best (Holly Springs, NC), Jon Bunnell (Tampa, FL), Travis Coleman (Trail Hoover, AL), Dan Cox (Huntington Beach, CA), JD French (Kennett, MO), Jeremy Gordon (Clinton Township, MI), Ted Lekas (Brewster, MA), Chris Lionetti (Rome, GA), Cody Martin (Vancouver, WA), Kevin Martin (Los Angeles, CA), Trey McNickle (Olive Branch, MS), Lou Sanchez (Miami, FL), Alan Sandberg (Hopatcong, NJ), Darin Vaughan (Kingwood, TX). **Video Coordinators:** Alex Burritt (St. Petersburg, FL), Anthony Flora (Katy, TX), Daniel Sabatino (Katy, TX). **Manager, Latin American Operations:** Jonathan Cruz. **Manager, International Scouting Administration:** Gerald Milanes. **Manager, Dominican Republic Administration & Operations:** Lothar Schott. **Scouting Supervisors:** Orlando Covo (South America), Chris Roque (Central America), Carlos Sequera (Venezuela). **International Scouts: Dominican Republic**—Reymond Nunez, Miguel Prestol, Luis Santos, Victor Torres. **Venezuela** — Richard Castillo, Raphachel Colatosti, Rafael Marcano, Edison Sanchez. **Video Coordinators**: Jaime Gil (Dominican Republic), Jesus Simancas (Venezuela).

BALTIMORE ORIOLES

Office Address: 333 W Camden St., Baltimore, MD 21201.
Telephone: (888) 848-BIRD. **Fax:** (410) 547-6272.
E-mail Address: birdmail@orioles.com. **Website:** www.orioles.com.

OWNERSHIP

Operated By: The Baltimore Orioles Limited Partnership Inc.
Chairman/CEO: John Angelos. **Ownership Representative:** Louis Angelos.

BUSINESS OPERATIONS

Peter Angelos

SENIOR LEADERSHIP TEAM

Executive Vice President and General Manager: Mike Elias. **Senior Vice President, Administration & Experience:** Greg Bader. **Senior Vice President, Chief Revenue Officer:** T.J. Brightman. **Senior Vice President, Community Development & Communications:** Jennifer Grondahl. **Senior Vice President, Finance:** Michael D. Hoppes, CPA. **Senior Vice President, Human Resources:** Lisa Tolson.

EXECUTIVE BUSINESS ADMINISTRATION

Vice President, Ticket Partnerships: Neil Aloise. **Vice President, Digital Marketing & Content Creation:** Tyler Hoffberger. **Senior Vice President, Business Development:** Lou Kousouris. **Vice President, Ballpark Experience & Operations:** Troy Scott. **Executive Vice President, Planning & Development:** Michael Shapiro. **Vice President, Corporate Partnerships:** Anthony Verni. **Executive Administrative Assistant:** Colleen Gellatly.

BALLPARK OPERATIONS & EXPERIENCE

Director, Ballpark Operations: Kevin Cummings. **Director, Ballpark Experience:** Kristen Schultz. **Director, Field Operations:** Nicole Sherry. **Director, Hospitality:** Tom Orszulak.

COMMUNICATIONS/ALUMNI

Telephone: (410) 547-6150. **Fax:** (410) 547-6272.
Senior Vice President, Community Development & Communications: Jennifer Grondahl. **Senior Manager, Baseball Communications:** Jim Misudek. **Senior Coordinator, Public Relations & Publications:** Kailey Adams. **Senior Coordinator, Baseball Communications:** Adam Esselman. **Senior Coordinator,Player & Family Relations:** Jackie Harig. **Public Relations Assistant:** Liam Davis. **Director, Orioles Alumni:** Bill Stetka. **Official Scorers:** Jim Henneman, Marc Jacobson, Ryan Eigenbrode.

DIGITAL MARKETING AND CONTENT CREATION

Vice President, Digital Marketing & Content Creation: Tyler Hoffberger. **Coordinator, Digital Marketing:** Kara Wagner. **Social Media Coordinator:** Kevin Hargrave. **Video Content Creator:** Johnny Douglas. **Team Photographer:** Todd Olszewski.

MARKETING/PRODUCTIONS

Senior Director, Marketing & Product Development: Jason Snapkoski. **Director, Orioles Productions:** Mike Stashik. **PA Announcer:** Ryan Wagner.

CORPORATE PARTNERSHIPS

Director, Strategy & Corporate Partner Relations: Cory Daniele. Director, **Suite Sales:** Matt Dryer.

INFORMATION TECHNOLOGY

Director, Information Technology: James L. Kline. Director, **Business Intelligence:** Doug Nickerson.

TICKET OPERATIONS, FAN SERVICES & PARTNERSHIPS

Telephone: (888) 848-BIRD. **Fax:** (410) 547-6270.
Director, Ticket Operations & Fan Services: Scott Rosier. **Director, Birdland Memberships:** Zach Brown. **Director, Group Events & Hospitality:** Mark Hromalik. **Director, Ticket Partnerships:** Ryan Kreissig.

BASEBALL OPERATIONS

Telephone: (410) 547-6107. **Fax:** (410) 547-6271.

Executive Vice President and General Manager: Mike Elias. **Director, Baseball Development:** Eve Rosenbaum. **Director, Baseball Administration:** Kevin Buck. **Manager, Team Travel:** Jeff Gillis. **Manager, Advance Scouting Operations:** Bill Wilkes. **Coordinator, Major League Video/Advance Scouting:** Ben Sussman-Hyde. **Coordinator, Major League Scouting:** Ryan Klimek. **Equipment Manager (Home):** Christopher Guth. **Equipment Manager (Road):** Frederick Tyler. **Umpire Room Manager:** James W. Tyler. **Assistant Equipment Manager:** Irving "Bunny" German.

Mike Elias

BASEBALL ANALYTICS

Vice President and Assistant General Manager, Analytics: Sig Mejdal.
Manager, Baseball Systems: Di Zou. **Analysts, Baseball Analytics:** Kevin Antonevich, Ryan Hardin, James Martin III, Hugh McCreery, Michael Weis. **Full-Stack Developers:** Peter Ash, James Daniels.

MAJOR LEAGUE STAFF

Manager: Brandon Hyde.
Major League Field Coordinator/Catching Instructor—Tim Cossins. **Major League Coach**—Fredi González. **Assistant Hitting Coach**—José Hernández. **Assistant Pitching Coach**—Darren Holmes.
Pitching Coach/Director of Pitching—Chris Holt. **Hitting Coach**—Don Long. **Third Base Coach**—Tony Mansolino. **First Base Coach**—Anthony Sanders.

MEDICAL/TRAINING

Team Physician: Dr. Sean Curtin.
Orthopedists: Dr. Michael Jacobs, Dr. Christopher Looze, Dr. Leigh Ann Curl, Dr. Derek Papp. **Primary Care:** Dr. Meyer Heyman, Dr. Jeff Mayer. **Dentist:** Dr. Gus Livaditis. **Optometrist:** Dr. Elliott Myrowitz.
Head Athletic Trainer: Brian Ebel. **Assistant Athletic Trainers:** Mark Shires, Pat Wesley. **Strength and Conditioning Coaches:** Joseph Hogarty, Ryosuke Naito. **Team Masseuse:** Adrian Pettaway. **Rehab Coordinator:** Kyle Corrick. **Mental Skills Coordinator:** Kathryn Rowe.

PLAYER DEVELOPMENT

Fax: (410) 547-6298.
Director, Player Development: Matt Blood. **Director, Minor League Operations:** Kent Qualls.
Director, Dominican Republic Academy: Felipe Rojas. **Senior Manager, Minor League and International Administration:** J. Maria Arellano. **Coordinator, Minor League Technology:** Joe Botelho. **Full Season Hitting Coordinator:** Ryan Fuller. **Complex Hitting Coordinator:** Anthony Villa. **Coordinator, Florida and Latin America Pitching:** Dave Schmidt. **Dominican Republic Field Coordinator:** Miguel Jabalera. **Minor League Medical Coordinator:** Dave Walker. **Minor League Strength and Conditioning Coordinator:** Nick White. **Administrator, Dominican Republic Academy:** Rancel Rosado. **Education Coordinator:** Anaíma García. **Minor League Equipment Manager:** Jake Parker. **Dominican Republic Equipment Manager:** Franklin Fajardo. **Spanish Translator and Coordinator, Latin American Operations:** Ramón Alarcón.

FARM SYSTEM

Class	Club	Manager	Hitting Coach	Pitching Coach
Triple-A	Norfolk	Gary Kendall	Tim Gibbons	Kennie Steenstra
Double-A	Bowie	Buck Britton	Ryan Fuller	Justin Ramsey
High A	Aberdeen	Kyle Moore	Tom Eller	Josh Conway
Low A	Delmarva	Dave Anderson	Patrick Jones	Robbie Aviles
Rookie	Orioles 1 (GCL)	Kevin Bradshaw	Anthony Villa	Adam Bleday
Rookie	Orioles 2 (GCL)	Alan Mills	Branden Becker	Joe Haumacher
Rookie	Orioles 1 (DSL)	Felipe Rojas	Josh Bunselmeyer	Andy Sadoski
Rookie	Orioles 2 (DSL)	Elbis Morel	Ramon Caraballo	Dioni Pascual

SCOUTING

Telephone: 410-547-6107. **Fax:** 410-547-6928.
Senior Director, International Scouting: Koby Perez. **Director, Pro Scouting:** Mike Snyder. **Supervisor, Domestic Scouting Operations:** Brad Ciolek. **Analysts, Scouting:** Hendrik Herz, Alex Tarandek, Chad Tatum. **Analysts, Pro Scouting:** Kevin Carter, Will Robertson. **Scouting Analyst Consultant:** Luke Siler.
Scouting Fellow: Chandler Couch.
Area Scouts: Rich Amaral (Huntington Beach, CA), David Blume (Elk Grove, CA), Quincy Boyd (Harrisburg, NC), Ryan Carlson (Chicago, IL), Thom Dreier (The Woodlands, TX), Trent Friedrich (Louisville, KY), Ken Guthrie (Sanger, TX), David Jennings (Spanish Fort, AL), Arthur McConnehead (Atlanta, GA), Donovan O'Dowd (Arnold, MD), Jim Richardson (Marlow, OK), Logan Schuemann (Scottsdale, AZ), Brandon Verley (Stuart, FL), Scott Walter (Manhattan Beach, CA).
Scouting Consultant: Christian Casanova (Caracas, VZ), Steven DiPuglia (Bradenton, FL), Anibal Zayas (San Lorenzo, PR). **Dominican Republic Scouting Supervisor (Santo Domingo):** Geraldo Cabrera.
Area Scouts: Rafael Belen (Santo Domingo), Michael Cruz (Santo Domingo), Luis Noel (San Pedro de Macorís), Francisco Rosario (Santiago). **Area Scout, Venezuela:** Adel Granadillo (Barquisimeto). **Administrative Consultant:** Scarlett Blanco (Caracas).

BOSTON RED SOX

Office Address: Fenway Park, 4 Jersey Street, Boston, MA 02215.
Telephone: (617) 226-6000. **Fax:** (617) 226-6416. **Website:** www.redsox.com

OWNERSHIP

Principal Owner: John Henry. **Chairman:** Thomas C. Werner. **President/CEO:** Sam Kennedy. **President/CEO Emeritus:** Larry Lucchino.

BUSINESS OPERATIONS

Sam Kennedy

EVP/COO: Jonathan Gilula. **SVP/Ballpark Operations:** Peter Nesbit. **SVP/Fan Services & Entertainment:** Sarah McKenna. **VP/Fan Services & Entertainment:** Stephanie Maneikis. **VP/Red Sox Productions:** John Carter. **VP/Fenway Park Tours:** Marcita Thompson. **VP/Facilities Management:** Jonathan Lister.

STRATEGY & BUSINESS DEVELOPMENT / FINANCE & ANALYTICS

EVP/Chief Strategy Officer: Dave Beeston. **EVP/Chief Financial Officer:** Tim Zue. **SVP/Finance:** Ryan Oremus. **VP/Financial Planning & Operations:** Ryan Scafidi. **VP/Data, Intelligence & Analytics:** Jonathan Hay.

HUMAN RESOURCES / INFORMATION TECHNOLOGY

EVP/Chief Human Resources Officer: Amy Waryas. **VP/Human Resources:** Mike Danubio. **VP/Information Technology:** Brian Shield. **VP/IT Operations:** Randy George

LEGAL

Executive Vice President of Corporate Strategy and General Counsel, FSG: Ed Weiss. **SVP/ Legal & Gov. Affairs & Special Counsel/FSG:** David Friedman. **VP/Senior Club Counsel:** Elaine Weddington Steward.

MARKETING/COMMUNICATIONS

EVP/Chief Marketing Officer: Adam Grossman. **VP/Corporate Communications:** Zineb Curran. **SVP/Marketing & Broadcasting:** Colin Burch. **VP/Media Relations:** Kevin Gregg.

PARTNERSHIPS/CLIENT SERVICES

EVP/Partnerships: Troup Parkinson. **SVP/Client and Sponsor Services:** Marcell Bhangoo. **SVP/Community, Alumni & Player Relations:** Pam Kenn.

TICKETING/SALES/EVENTS

EVP/Ticketing, Concerts, & Events: Ron Bumgarner. **SVP/Fenway Concerts & Entertainment:** Larry Cancro. **SVP/Ticketing:** Richard Beaton. **SVP/Ticketing Services & Operations:** Naomi Calder. **SVP/Ticket Sales:** William Droste. **SVP/Fenway Park Events:** Carrie Campbell.

RED SOX FOUNDATION

Honorary Chairman: Tim Wakefield. **Executive Director:** Rebekah Salwasser.

BASEBALL OPERATIONS

Chief Baseball Officer: Chaim Bloom
General Manager: Brian O'Halloran
EVP/Assistant GM: Raquel Ferreira, Eddie Romero. **Senior VP, Baseball Operations:** Ben Crockett. **Senior Director, Club Relations:** Jack McCormick. **Director, Team Travel:** Mark Cacciatore. **Director, Major League Operations:** Mike Regan. **Coordinator, Major League Operations:** Alex Gimenez. **Executive Assistant/Manager, Staff Support:** Erin Cox. **Director, Baseball Analytics:** Joe McDonald. **Director, Education and Process Analysis:** Greg Rybarczyk. **Senior Analysts, Baseball Analytics:** Spencer Bingol, Dan Meyer. **Analyst, Baseball Analytics:** Brad Alberts, Tyler Burch, Sam Larson, Dave Miller, Jonathan Waring. Assistant, **Baseball Analytics:** Kayla Mei, Jimmy O'Donnell, Scott Steinberg. **Coordinator, Major League Advance Information:** Mark Heil. **Analyst, Major League Advance Information:** Jeb Clarke.

Chaim Bloom

BILLIE WEISS/BOSTON RED SOX

MAJOR LEAGUE STAFF

Manager: Alex Cora
Coaches: Bench—Will Venable; **Pitching**—David Bush; **Bullpen**—Kevin Walker; **Hitting**—Tim Hyers; **Assistant Hitting**—Peter Fatse; **First Base**—Tom Goodwin; **Third Base**—Carlos Febles; **Quality Control Coach/Interpreter**—Ramon Vazquez; **Game Planning Coordinator**—Jason Varitek. **Bullpen Catchers:** Mani Martinez, Michael Brenly. **BP Thrower:** Matt Noone.

SPORTS MEDICINE SERVICE

Director, Sports Medicine Service/Head Athletic Trainer: Brad Pearson. **Medical Director:** Dr. Larry Ronan. **Head Team Orthopedist:** Dr. Peter Asnis. **Senior Physical Therapist/Clinical Specialist:** Jamie Creps. **Associate Head Athletic Trainer:** Brandon Henry. **Major League Assistant Athletic Trainers:** Masai Takahashi, Anthony Cerundolo. **Athletic Trainer/Major League Rehab Coordinator:** Jon Jochim. **Head Strength/Conditioning Coach:** Kiyoshi Momose. **Strength & Conditioning Coach:** Chris Messina. **Coordinator of Athletic Performance:** Mike Roose. **Assistant Strength & Conditioning Coordinator:** Kirby Retzer. **Sports Science Coordinator:** Mike Cianciosi. **Sports Scientist:** Shaun Owen. **Massage Therapists:** Russell Nua, Shinichiro Uchikubo. **Head Minor League Physician:** Dr. Brian Busconi.

PLAYER DEVELOPMENT

Director, Player Development: Brian Abraham. **Manager, Baseball Development:** Chris Stasio. **Coordinator, Minor League Operations:** Patrick McLaughlin. **Coordinator, Player Development:** Harry Roberson. **Assistant, Florida Baseball Operations:** Stephen Aluko. **Minor League Field Coordinator:** Ryan Jackson. **Assistant Field Coordinator/ Infield Coordinator:** Andy Fox. **Hitting Coordinator:** Greg Norton. **Catching Coordinator:** Chad Epperson. **Outfield/ Baserunning Coordinator:** Darren Fenster. **Senior Coordinator, Pitching:** Shawn Haviland. **Pitching Coordinator, Logistics:** Ralph Treuel. **Pitching Coordinator, Performance:** Chris Mears, Julio Rangel. **Assistant Hitting Coordinator:** Reed Gragnani. **Latin American Pitching Coordinator/Rehab Coordinator:** Walter Miranda. **Latin American Field Coordinator:** Jose Zapata. **Latin American Pitching Advisor:** Goose Gregson. **Assistant, Baseball Development:** Jordan Elkary. **Coach/Interpreter:** Mickey Jiang. **Minor League Equipment Manager:** Mike Stelmach.

FARM SYSTEM

Class	Club	Manager	Hitting Coach	Pitching Coach	Position Coach
Triple-A	Worcester	Billy McMillon	Rich Gedman	Paul Abbott	Bruce Crabbe
Double-A	Portland	Corey Wimberly	Lance Zawadzki	Lance Carter	
High-A	Greenville	Iggy Suarez	Nate Spears	Bob Kipper	
Low-A	Salem	Luke Montz	Nelson Paulino	Nick Green	
Rookie	Red Sox (GCL)	Tom Kotchman	J.Zamora/J. Prince	J. Blanton/B. Merritt	
Rookie	Red Sox (DSL)	Ozzie Chavez	Danny Ortega	Oscar Lira	Leonel Vasquez
Rookie	Red Sox (DSL)	Sandy Madera	Eider Torres	H. Sanchez	C. Sanchez

SCOUTING

VP/ Professional Scouting: Gus Quattlebaum. **VP/Scouting:** Mike Rikard. **Director, Professional Scouting:** Harrison Slutsky. **Director, Amateur Scouting:** Paul Toboni. **Assistant Director, Amateur Scouting:** Devin Pearson. **Assistant Director, Professional Scouting:** Andrew Mack. **Coordinator, International Scouting:** Marcus Cuellar. **Coordinator, Latin American Operations:** Alberto Mejia. **Assistant, Amateur Scouting:** Jake Bruml. **Special Assignment Scout:** Steve Peck. **Special Assistant, Player Personnel:** Mark Wasinger. **Professional Scouts:** Nate Field, Blair Henry, Steve Langone, Dana LeVangie, Matt Mahoney, Anthony Turco, Kyri Washington, JT Watkins. **Crosscheckers:** Chris Becerra, Justin Horowitz, Dan Madsen, John Booher, Paul Fryer, Fred Petersen, Jim Robinson, Tom Kotchman, Stephen Hargett. **Area Scouts:** JJ Altobelli, Lee Bryant, Matt Davis, Lane Decker, Raymond Fagnant, Kirk Fredriksson, Todd Gold, Josh Labandeira, Brian Moehler, Carl Moesche, Greg Morhardt, Edgar Perez, Chris Reilly, Dante Ricciardi, Willie Romay, Danny Watkins, Vaughn Williams, Alonzo Wright. **Part Time Scouts:** Rob English, Tim Martin, David Scrivines, Josh Tobias, Donovan May, Dick Sorkin, Terry Sullivan, Mark Sluys, Wallace Rios.

Co-Director, International Scouting: Todd Claus, Ronaldo Pino. **International Crosschecker:** Jason Karegeannes. **Latin American Crosschecker:** Hector Rincones. **Coordinator, Pacific Rim Operations:** Brett Ward. **Assistant Director, DR Academy:** Javier Hernandez. **Coordinator, DR Academy:** Martin Rodriguez. **Supervisor, Dominican Republic:** Manny Nanita. **Assistant Supervisor, Dominican Republic:** Jonathan Cruz. **International Scouts:** Domingo Brito (D.R.), Juan Carlos Calderon (D.R.), Alfredo Castellon (Colombia), Angel Escobar (Venezuela), Steve Fish (Australia), Cris Garibaldo (Panama), Ernesto Gomez (Venezuela), John Kim (Korea), Aneko Knowles (Bahamas), Matias Laureano (D.R.), Louie Lin (Taiwan), Wilder Lobo (Venezuela), Esau Medina (D.R.), Rafael Mendoza (Nicaragua), Ramon Mora (Venezuela), Cesar Morillo (Venezuela), Rafael Motooka (Brazil), Dennis Neuman (Aruba/Curacao), Alex Requena (Venezuela), Rene Saggiadi (Europe), Sotero Torres (Mexico). **International Pro Scouts:** Won Lee (Korea), Kento Matsumoto (Japan).

CHICAGO CUBS

Office Address: Wrigley Field, 1060 W. Addison St., Chicago, IL 60613.
Telephone: (773) 404-2827. **Website:** www.cubs.com.

OWNERSHIP
Chairman: Tom Ricketts. **Board of Directors:** Laura Ricketts, Todd Ricketts.

BUSINESS OPERATIONS
President, Business Operations: Crane Kenney. **Executive Assistant to Chairman:** Lorraine Swiatly. **Executive Assistant, President Business Operations:** Michele Dietz.

Tom Ricketts

BALLPARK/EVENT OPERATIONS
Senior Vice President, Operations: David Cromwell. **Director, Event Operations & Security:** Morgan Bucciferro. **Director, Guest Services:** Vanessa Ward. **Vice President, Facility & Supply Chain Operations:** Patrick Meenan. **Director, Facilities:** Ryan Egan.

LEGAL
EVP, Community & Gov't Affairs, Chief Legal Officer: Michael Lufrano. **Vice President, General Counsel:** Brett Scharback. **Counsel:** Amy Timm. **Counsel:** Shameeka Quallo. **Director, Community Affairs:** Alicia Gonzalez.

TICKET SALES/SALES & PARTNERSHIPS
Executive Vice President, Sales & Marketing: Colin Faulkner. **Senior Vice President, Marquee 360:** Cale Vennum. **Vice President, Partnerships, Marquee 360:** Alex Seyferth. **Vice President, Partnership Development:** Andy Blackburn.

MEDIA RELATIONS
Assistant Director, Media Relations: Jason Carr. **Media Relations Representative:** William Nadal.

BASEBALL OPERATIONS

Telephone: (773) 404-2827. **Fax:** (773) 404-4147.

Jed Hoyer

President, Baseball Operations: Jed Hoyer. **Assistant GMs:** Randy Bush, Jeff Greenberg. **Assistant GM/Vice President, Pitching:** Craig Breslow. **Senior Vice President, Player Personnel:** Jason McLeod. **Vice President, Special Projects:** Jared Banner. **Vice President, Research & Development:** Chris Moore. **Director, High Performance:** Adam Beard. **Director, Team Travel and Clubhouse Operations:** Vijay Tekchandani. **Director, Baseball Operations:** Greg Davey. **Director, Baseball Systems Development:** Ryan Kruse. **Director, Strategic Modeling:** Jeremy Greenhouse. **Assistant Director, Baseball Operations Administration and Strategic Initiatives:** Meghan Jones. **Assistant Director, Research & Development:** Chris Jones. **Special Assistants, President/GM:** Ryan Dempster, Ted Lilly, Kerry Wood. **Senior Biomechanist:** John Dewitt. **Senior Player Evaluation Analyst, Research and Development:** Garrett Chiado. **Analysts, Research & Development:** Bryan Cole, Jacob Eisenberg, Jennifer Gossels, Troy Mulholland, Eli Shayer. **Developers, Baseball Systems:** Zack Brusso, Kyle Chin, Dan Codos, Jonathan Robins. **Coordinator, Major League Data & Development:** Alex Smith. **Assistants, Baseball Operations:** Sam Abrams, Jackson New-Smith.

MAJOR LEAGUE STAFF

Manager: David Ross. **Coaches: Bench**—Andy Green, **Pitching**—Tommy Hottovy, **Hitting**—Anthony Iapoce, **Assistant Hitting**—Chris Valaika, **Third Base**—Willie Harris, **First Base/Catching**—Craig Driver, **Associate Pitching, Catching and Strategy**—Mike Borzello, **Bullpen**—Chris Young, **Quality Assurance Coach**—Mike Napoli. **Senior Director, Major League Data & Development:** Kyle Evans. **Staff Assistants:** Juan Cabreja, Jonathan Mota. **Bullpen Catcher:** Chad Noble. **Assistant Director, Run Prevention:** Brad Mills. **Assistant Director, Run Production:** Jim Adduci. **Coordinator, Major League Video/Pacific Rim Liaison:** Nao Masamoto.

MEDICAL/TRAINING

Team Physician: Dr. Stephen Adams. **Team Orthopedist:** Dr. Stephen Gryzlo. **Orthopedic Consultant:** Dr. Michael Schafer. **Major League Athletic Trainer:** P.J. Mainville. **Assistant Athletic Trainers:** Nick Frangella, Chuck Baughman. **Head Major League S&C Coach:** Shane Wallen. **Assistant Major League S&C Coach:** Keegan Knoll.

PLAYER DEVELOPMENT

Telephone: (773) 404-2827. **Fax:** (773) 404-4147.

Vice President, Player Development: Matt Dorey. **Senior Director, International Player Development:** Alex Suarez. **Director, Player Development:** Bobby Basham. **Director, Hitting:** Justin Stone. **Assistant Director, Baseball Development:** Jeremy Farrell. **Coordinator, Pitching Initiatives:** Ryan Otero. **Coordinator, Minor League Administration:** Allyson Darragh. **Coordinator, Minor League Operations:** Adam Unes. **Manager, Mesa Administration:** Gil Passarella. **Equipment Manager:** Dana Noeltner. **Minor League Coordinators:** Dustin Kelly (hitting), Casey Jacobson (pitching development), James Ogden (pitching performance), Mark Johnson (catching), Doug Dascenzo (outfield & baserunning), Dave Keller (Latin America field), Tom Beyers (asst. hitting development), Steven Pollakov (Dominican hitting analytics), Mike Mason (asst. pitching performance), Carlos Chantres (asst. pitching development), Josh Zeid (rehab pitching). **Minor League Medical Coordinator:** Mike McNulty. **Mental Skills Coordinators:** Dave DaSilva, Javier Guerrero. **Assistant, Pitching Development:** Danny Hultzen.

FARM SYSTEM

Class	Club (League)	Manager	Hitting Coach	Pitching Coach
Triple-A	Iowa	Marty Pevey	D. Wilson/W. Remillard	Ron Villone
Double-A	Tennessee	Mark Johnson	Chad Allen	Terry Clark
High-A	South Bend	Michael Ryan	Paul McAnulty	Tony Cougoule
Low-A	Myrtle Beach	Buddy Bailey	Dan Puente	Clayton Mortensen
Rookie	Cubs (AZL)	Lance Rymel	O. Melendez/R. Folden	D. Willey/A. Gambino
Rookie	Cubs 1 (DSL)	Carlos Ramirez	Enrique Wilson	Jose Zapata
Rookie	Cubs 2 (DSL)	D'Angelo Jimenez	Chris Pieters	Luis Hernandez

SCOUTING

Director, Pro Scouting: Andrew Bassett. **Special Assignment Scout:** Jason Cooper. **Major League Scouts:** Steve Boros, Jake Ciarrachi. **Pro Scouts:** Willie Fraser, Kyle Phillips, Aaron Sele, Thad Weber, Adam Wogan. **Pro Personnel Specialist:** Nate Halm. **Part-Time Pro Scouts:** Billy Blitzer, Robert Lofrano. **Vice President, Scouting:** Dan Kantrovitz. **Coordinator, Amateur Scouting:** Scottie Munson. **Analyst, Amateur Scouting:** Jasmine Horan. **Assistant, Amateur Scouting:** Ben Kullavanijaya. **National Supervisors:** Ron Tostenson, Jaron Madison. **Crosscheckers: West**—Alex Lontayo (Murrieta, CA), **Central**—Daniel Carte (McKinney, TX), **East**—Bobby Filotei (Mobile, AL). **Area Scouts:** Tom Clark (Lake City, FL), Trey Forkerway (Houston, TX), Todd George (Temple, TX), Edwards Guzman (Toa Baja, PR), Evan Kauffman (Irvine, CA), Alex McClure (Memphis, TN), Steve McFarland (Scottsdale, AZ), Tom Myers (Santa Barbara, CA), Ty Nichols (Broken Arrow, OK), John Pedrotty (Chicago, IL), Matt Sherman (Kingston, MA), Billy Swoope (Norfolk, VA), Jacob Williams (Lexington, KY), Gabe Zappin (Walnut Creek, CA), Ralph Reyes (Jupiter, FL), Zach Zielinski (Charlotte, NC), Greg Gerard (Acworth, GA). **Amateur Video Scout:** Garrett Tolivar (Baton Rouge, LA). **Part-Time Area Scout:** Keronn Walker (Chicago, IL). **Vice President, International Scouting:** Louie Eljaua. **Coordinator, International Scouting:** Kenny Socorro. **Director, Dominican Scouting:** Gian Guzman. **Coordinator, D.R. Scouting:** Miguel Diaz. **Scouting Supervisor, Central and South America:** Cirilo Cumberbatch. **Supervisor, Mexico:** Sergio Hernandez. **Coordinator, Colombian Operations:** Manny Esquivia. **International Scouts:** Hansel Izquierdo, Jaime McFarland, Brent Phelan. **Latin America Scouts: D.R.**—Alejandro Pena, Carlos Pellerano, Valerio Heredia, **Venezuela**—Julio Figueroa, Carlos Figueroa, **Mexico**—Salvador Hernandez, **Taiwan**—Po-chun Chang.

CHICAGO WHITE SOX

Office Address: Guaranteed Rate Field, 333 W. 35th St., Chicago, IL 60616.
Telephone: (312) 674-1000. **Fax:** (312) 674-5116.
Website: whitesox.com, loswhitesox.com.

OWNERSHIP
Chairman: Jerry Reinsdorf.
Board of Directors: Robert Judelson, Judd Malkin, Allan Muchin, Jay Pinsky, Lee Stern, Burton Ury, Charles Walsh.
Special Assistant to Chairman: Dennis Gilbert. **Assistant to Chairman:** Katie Hermle. **Coordinator, Administration/Investor Relations:** Elizabeth Anderson.

BUSINESS OPERATIONS
Senior Executive Vice President: Howard Pizer. **Senior Systems Analyst:** Stan Czyzewski.
Vice President, Human Resources: Moira Foy. **Senior Coordinator, Human Resources:** Leslie Gaggiano.

FINANCE
Senior VP, Administration/Finance: Tim Buzard. **VP, Finance:** Bill Waters. **Director of Accounting:** Mallory Penn.

MARKETING/SALES
Senior VP, Chief Revenue and Marketing Officer: Brooks Boyer. **Senior Director, Business Development/Broadcasting:** Bob Grim. **Director, Game Presentation:** Cris Quintana. **Sr. Manager, Scoreboard Operations/Production:** Jeff Szynal. **Sr. Manager, Game Operations:** Dan Mielke. **Sr. Director, Corporate Partnerships Sales Development:** George McDoniel. **Sr. Director, Corporate Partnerships Activation:** Gail Tucker. **Sr. Manager, Corporate Partnerships Development:** Jeff Floerke. **Coordinators/Managers, Corporate Partnership:** Ashley Sorenson, Kat Claeys, Drew Fischer, Krista Pulcini. **VP of Sales and Service:** Jim Willits. **Sr. Manager, Ticket Sales:** Rich Kuchar.

Jerry Reinsdorf

MEDIA RELATIONS/PUBLIC RELATIONS
Telephone: (312) 674-5300. **Fax:** (312) 674-5116.
Senior VP, Communications: Scott Reifert. **Senior Director, Media Relations:** Bob Beghtol. **Director, Public Relations:** Sheena Quinn. **Assistant Director, Media Relations:** Ray Garcia. **Coordinator, Public Relations:** Colin McGauley. **Coordinators, Media Relations/Services:** Joe Roti, Hannah Sundwall. **VP, Community Relations/Executive Director/CWS Charities:** Christine O'Reilly. **Director, Community Relations:** Sarah Marten, Lindsey Jordan. **Manager, Youth Baseball Initiatives:** Anthony Olivo. **Director, Digital Communications:** Brad Boron. **Director, Design Services:** Matt Peterson. **Manager, Online Communications:** Dakin Dugaw. **Manager of Social Media:** Jordan Doyle.

STADIUM OPERATIONS
Senior VP, Stadium Operations: Terry Savarise. **Senior Director, Park Operations:** Jonathan Vasquez.
Senior Director, Guest Services/Diamond Suite Operations: Julie Taylor. **Head Groundskeeper:** Roger Bossard.
PA Announcer: Gene Honda. **Official Scorers:** Don Friske, Allan Spear, Bill Sieple, Randy Liss.

TICKETING
Senior Director, Ticket Operations: Mike Mazza. **Manager, Ticket Operations:** Pete Catizone.

TRAVEL/CLUBHOUSE
Director, Team Travel: Ed Cassin. **Manager, White Sox Clubhouse:** Rob Warren. **Manager, Visiting Clubhouse:** Jason Gilliam. **Manager, Umpires Clubhouse:** Joe McNamara Jr.

BASEBALL OPERATIONS

Executive Vice President: Ken Williams.
Senior VP/General Manager: Rick Hahn. **Assistant General Manager:** Jeremy Haber.
Special Assistants: Bill Scherrer, Marco Paddy, Jim Thome, Nick Hostetler, Jose Contreras,
Todd Steverson. **Executive Assistant to GM:** Nancy Nesnidal. **Senior Director, Baseball
Operations:** Dan Fabian. **Director, Baseball Operations:** Daniel Zien. **Assistant Director,
Baseball Operations:** Jeff Lachman. **Director Baseball Analytics:** Matt Koenig. **Analyst,
Baseball Operations:** Emily Blady.

Rick Hahn

JON DURR/GETTY IMAGES

MAJOR LEAGUE STAFF

Manager: Tony La Russa. **Coaches: Bench**—Miguel Cairo; **Pitching**—Ethan Katz;
Hitting—Frank Menechino; **Assistant Hitting Coach**—Howie Clark; **First Base**—Daryl
Boston; **Third Base**—Joe McEwing; **Bullpen**—Curt Hasler. **Bullpen Catcher:** Miguel Gonzalez.
Mgr. of Cultural Development/Bullpen Catcher: Luis Sierra. **Instructor:** Jerry Narron.
Analytics Coordinator: Shelley Duncan.

MEDICAL/TRAINING

Senior Team Physician: Dr. Nikhil Verma. **Head Athletic Trainer Emeritus:** Herm Schneider. **Head Athletic Trainer:**
James Kruk. **Director of Rehabilitation:** Brett Walker. **Assistant Athletic Trainer:** Josh Fallin. **Director, Strength &
Conditioning:** Allen Thomas. **Assistant Director, Strength & Conditioning:** Ibrahim Rivera.

PLAYER DEVELOPMENT

Assistant General Manager/Player Development: Chris Getz.
Senior Director, Minor League Operations: Grace Guerrero-Zwit. **Assistant Director, Player Development:** Kenny
Williams, Jr. **Assistant Director, Baseball Operations:** Graham Harboe. **Assistant Director, Baseball Operations:** Rod
Larson. **Senior Biomechanical Engineer:** Ben Hansen. **Senior Coordinator, Minor League Administration:** Kathy
Potoski. **Coordinator, Baseball Information:** Devin Pickett. **Analyst, Player Development:** Zach Jones. **Assistant
Player Development:** Diego Francisco. **Rehab Pitching Coach:** Donnie Veal. **Education Coordinator:** Erin Santana.
Assistant, Player Development/Latin Education: Grant Flick. **Field Coordinator/Outfield and Baserunning:** Doug
Sisson. **Pitching Coordinator:** Everett Teaford. **Assistant Pitching Coordinator:** J.R. Perdew. **Hitting Advisor to Player
Development:** Andy Barkett. **Assistant Hitting Coordinator:** Ryan Johansen. **Catching Coordinator:** John Orton.
Director of Performance: Goldy Simmons. **Advisor to Performance:** Dale Torborg. **Medical Coordinator:** Scott Takao.
Physical Therapist: Brooks Klein. **Sports Psychologist:** Dr. Rob Seifer.

ARIZONA OPERATIONS

Facility Manager: Joe Lachcik. **Minor League Clubhouse and Equipment Manager:** Dan Flood. **Assistant Minor
League Clubhouse Manager:** Bryant Biasotti.

FARM SYSTEM

Class	Club (League)	Manager	Hitting Coach	Pitching Coach
Triple-A	Charlotte	Wes Helms	Chris Johnson	Matt Zaleski
Double-A	Birmingham	Justin Jirschele	Cam Seitzer	Richard Dotson
High-A	Winston-Salem	Ryan Newman	Mike Daniel	Danny Farquhar
Low-A	Kannapolis	Guillermo Quiroz	Charlie Romero	John Ely
Rookie	White Sox (AZL)	Ever Magallanes	Devin DeYoung	Drew Hasler
Rookie	White Sox (DSL)	Angel Rosario	Gerardo Olivares	Leo Hernandez

SCOUTING

Telephone: (312) 674-1000. **Fax:** (312) 674-5105.
Pro Scouts: Bruce Benedict (Atlanta, GA), Joe Butler (Long Beach, CA), Toney Howell (Darien, IL), Daraka Shaheed
(Vallejo, CA), Joe Siers (Wesley Chapel, FL), Keith Staab (College Station, TX), Chris Walker (Katy, TX), Bill Young
(Scottsdale, AZ). **Director, Amateur Scouting:** Mike Shirley. **Senior Advisor, Scouting Operations:** Doug Laumann.
Assistant Director, Amateur Scouting: Garrett Guest. **National Crosschecker:** Nathan Durst (Sycamore, IL),
National Pitching Crosschecker: Kirk Champion. **Regional Cross checkers: West**—Derek Valenzuela (Temecula,
CA), **Southeast**—Juan Alvarez (Miami, FL), **Midwest**—Rob Cummings (Chicago, IL). **Area Scouts:** Mike Baker (Santa
Ana, CA), Kevin Burrell (Sharpsburg, GA), Ryan Dorsey (Dallas, TX), Abe Fernandez (Miami, FL), Mike Gange (Portland,
OR), Phil Gulley (Morehead, KY), Jason Howell (Atlanta, GA), Warren Hughes (Mobile, AL), JJ Lally (Denison, IA), John
Kazanas (Phoenix, AZ), Steve Payne (Barrington, RI), Steffan Segui (St. Petersburg, FL), Noah St. Urbain (Stockton, CA),
John Stott (Charlotte, NC), Adam Virchis (Modesto, CA), Justin Wechsler (Niles, MI), Tyler Wilt (Wilus, TX), Torreon Woods
(Overland Park, KS). **International Scouts:** Amador Arias (Maracay, Venezuela). Marino DeLeon (Yamasa, Dominican
Republic), Robinson Garces (Maracaibo, Venezuela), Tomas Herrera (Saltillo, Mexico), Reydel Hernandez (Puerto La Cruz,
Venezuela), Ruddy Moreta, Supervisor Latin America (Santo Domingo, Dominican Republic), Miguel Peguero (Santo
Domingo, Dominican Republic), Guillermo Peralta (Santiago, Dominican Republic), Omar Sanchez (Valencia, Venezuela),
Fermin Ubri (Bani, Dominican Republic), Ricardo Ortiz (Colon, Panama).

CINCINNATI REDS

Office Address: 100 Joe Nuxhall Way, Cincinnati, OH 45202.
Telephone: (513) 765-7000. **Fax:** (513) 765-7342. **Website:** www.reds.com.

OWNERSHIP

Operated by: The Cincinnati Reds LLC. **Chief Executive Officer:** Robert H. Castellini. **Chairman:** W. Joseph Williams Jr. **Vice Chairman:** Thomas L. Williams. **President & Chief Operating Officer:** Phillip J. Castellini. Sr. **Advisor to President/COO:** Barry Larkin. **Executive Operations Manager:** Shellie Petrey. **Executive Advisor to the CEO:** Walt Jocketty. **Secretary & Treasurer:** Christopher L. Fister.

BUSINESS OPERATIONS

Senior Vice President, Business Operations: Karen Forgus. **Business Operations Assistant:** Teddy Siegel. **Business Operations, Assistant/Speakers Bureau:** Emily Mahle. **Exec. Asst. to Pres. of Baseball Ops. & GM:** Sarah Vedder.

Bob Castellini

FINANCE/ADMINISTRATION

Sr. Vice President of Finance and CFO: Doug Healy. **Chief Legal Counsel:** James A. Marx, Esq. **Assistant to CFO/CLO:** Teena Schweier. **Vice President of Finance, Controller:** Bentley Viator. .

TICKETING/BUSINESS DEVELOPMENT

Senior Director of Ticket Sales & Service: Mark Schueler. **Director of Ticketing New Business:** Patrick Montague. **Director of Season Ticket Membership:** Shelley Volpenhein. **Director of Premium Sales & Service:** Chris Bausano. **Director of Group Sales:** Carmen Alberini. **Season Sales Manager:** Chris Herrell. **Sr. Account Executive, New Business Dev.:** Blake Williams. **Account Executive, New Business Dev.:** Jake Eby. **Sr. Account Executive, Retention and Sales:** Eric Keller. **Account Executive, Retention and Sales:** Angel Gonzalez, Logan Grapenthien, Tiffany Huffman. **Premium Sales Manager:** Ryan Rizzo. **Sr. Premium Sales/Ownrshp Svcs. Exec.:** Megan Stuerenberg. **Suites and Premium Service Executive:** Kory Hetzer. **Premium Service Executive:** Craig Sample. **Premium Service Executive:** Jacob Swartz. **Group Account Executives:** Cardell Carter, Aly Gruber, Mason Smith, Drew Whitaker.

MEDIA RELATIONS

Vice President, Media Relations: Rob Butcher. **Director, Media Relations:** Larry Herms. **Director, Media Relations/Digital Content:** Jamie Ramsey. **Spanish Translator/Media Relations Assistant:** Jorge Merlos. **Japanese Translator/Media Relations Coordinator:** Luke Shinoda.

COMMUNICATIONS/MARKETING

Vice President of Communications & Marketing: Ralph Mitchell. **Director of Digitial Media:** Lisa Braun. **Director of Marketing:** Audra Sordyl. **Director of Communications & Web Content:** Jarrod Rollins. **Public Relations Manager:** Michael Anderson. **Promotional Purchasing/Broadcasting Admin.:** Lori Watt. **Communications Manager:** Brendan Hader. **Social Media Manager:** Chadwick Fischer. **Director of Creative Operations:** Jansen Dell. **Creative Services Manager:** Amy Calo. **Senior Designer:** Michael King. **Graphic Designer:** Sara Treash. **Social Media Design Coordinator:** Carter Kennedy.

COMMUNITY RELATIONS

Director, Community Relations: Lindsey Dingeldein. **Diversity Relations Coordinator:** Natalya Herndon.

BALLPARK OPERATIONS

Vice President, Ballpark Operations: Tim O'Connell. **Senior Director, Ballpark Operations:** Sean Brown.

BASEBALL OPERATIONS

Vice President & General Manager: Nick Krall. **Executive Assistant to Pres. of Baseball Ops/GM:** Sarah Vedder. **Vice President, Assistant General Manager:** Sam Grossman. **Vice President, Player Personnel:** Chris Buckley. **Senior Director, Player Personnel:** Jeff Graupe. **Manager, Baseball Operations:** Mark Edwards. **Director of Data Systems & Development:** Michael Mentzer **Sr. System Architect, Baseball Systems:** Brett Elkins. **Baseball Development Manager:** Ryan Barger. **Lead Data Scientist:** Michael Schatz. **Data Scientist:** Chris Jackson. **Major League Analytics Coordinator:** James Brand. **Sr. Developer, Baseball Systems:** Samantha Rack. **Data Quality Engineer, Baseball Systems:** Andrew Kyne. **Baseball Systems Developer:** Joe Delia. **Data Engineer, Baseball Systems:** Bryce Dugar. **Manager, Advance Scouting:** Bo Thompson. **Coordinator, Major League Video & Technology:** Gary Hall. **Baseball Operations Analyst:** Katie Krall. **Senior Director, Team Travel:** Gary Wahoff. **Sports Science Assistant:** Jesus Ramos. **Senior Director, Clubhouse Operations:** Rick Stowe. **Visiting Clubhouse Manager:** Josh Stewart. **Clubhouse Assistant:** Mark Stowe.

Nick Krall

MEDICAL/TRAINING

Senior Director, Health & Performance: Geoff Head. **Coordinator, Health and Performance, Program Integration:** Dan Adams. **Coordinator, Mental Skills:** Tyler Klein. **Coach, Mental Skills:** Andy Riise. **Coordinator, Minor League Nutrition:** Leah Reitmayer. **Minor League Rehabilitation Coordinator:** Marcus Ahrens. **Physical Therapist:** Eric Gonzalez. **Director, Sports Science Initiatives:** Charles Leddon. **Director, Strength & Conditioning:** Rob Fumagalli. **Coordinator, Strength & Conditioning:** Will Gilmore. Becky Schnakenberg. **Coordinator, Wellness:** Becky Schnakenberg. **Wellness Coach, Latin America:** Rafael Castillo. **Director, Athletic Training:** Patrick Serbus.

MAJOR LEAGUE STAFF

Manager: David Bell. **Coaches: Bench**—Freddie Benavides, **Hitting**—Alan Zinter, **Pitching**— Derek Johnson, **First Base**—Delino DeShields, **Third Base/Catching**—J.R. House, **Bullpen**—Lee Tunnell, **Game Planning/Outfield**—Jeff Pickler, **Assistant Hitting**—Joe Mather, **Assistant Pitching:** Eric Jagers, **Associate Coaches:** Rolando Valles, Cristian Perez. **Bullpen Catchers:** Jose Duarte, Nate Irving.

MEDICAL STAFF

Medical Director: Dr. Timothy Kremchek. **Head Athletic Trainer, ATC, CSCS:** Steve Baumann. **Assistant Athletic Trainer, ATC:** Jimmy Mattocks. **Assistant Athletic Trainer, ATC:** Tomas Vera. **Health & Performance Specialist:** Takeshi Yamamoto. **Director, Strength & Conditioning:** Rob Fumagalli. **Assistant Director, Str. & Cond.:** Morgan Gregory. **Director, Physical Therapy and Rehab:** Brad Epstein. **Major League Sports Dietician:** Ashley Meuser.

PLAYER DEVELOPMENT

Vice President, Player Development: Shawn Pender. **Senior Director, Player Development:** Eric Lee. **Special Assistant, Player Performance:** Eric Davis, Bill Doran, Mario Soto. **Coordinator, Baseball Administration:** Melissa Hill. **Coordinator, Minor League Video & Technology:** Mitchell Bonds. **Player Development Analytics Coordinator:** Harris Kingsley. **Manager, Arizona Operations:** Mike Saverino. **Arizona Operations Assistant:** Branden Croteau. **Manager, Minor League Equipment:** Jon Snyder. **Minor League Clubhouse Assistant:** John Bryk, Ryan Dammeyer. **Field Coordinator:** Chris Tremie. **Director of Pitching Initiatives/Pitching Coordinator:** Kyle Boddy. **Catching Coordinator:** Corky Miller. **Hitting Coordinator:** C.J. Gillman. **Academies Coordinator:** Luis Bolivar. **Latin American Field Coordinator:** Joel Noboa. **Infield Coordinator:** Jose Nieves. **Pitching Coordinator:** Bryan Conger.

FARM SYSTEM

Class	Club (League)	Manager	Hitting Coach	Pitching Coach
Triple-A	Louisville	Pat Kelly	Alex Pelaez	Seth Etherton
Double-A	Chattanooga	Ricky Gutierrez	Todd Takayoshi	Rob Wooten
High-A	Dayton	Jose Moreno	Daryle Ward	Brian Garman
Low-A	Daytona	Gookie Dawkins	Darryl Brinkley	Forrest Herrmann
Rookie	Reds (AZL)	Bryan LaHair	Jordan Stouffer	Elmer Dessens/Derrin Ebert
Rookie	Reds (DSL)	Luis Terrero	Jason Broussard	S. Matthews/L. Montano

SCOUTING

Director, Professional Scouting: Rob Coughlin. **Special Assistant to GM, Player Personnel:** Cam Bonifay. **Special Assistants to the General Manager:** "J" Harrison, Marty Maier, John Morris, Jeff Schugel. **Pro Scouts:** Gary Glover, Joe Jocketty, Ben Jones, Bruce Manno, Mick Mattaliano, Jeff Morris, Steve Roadcap. **Analyst, Pro Scouting:** Daniel Beattie. **Director, Amateur Scouting:** Brad Meador. **Assistant Director, Amateur Scouting:** Paul Pierson. **Assistant Director, National Crosschecker:** Joe Katuska. **National Crosscheckers:** Jerry Flowers, Mark McKnight. **Regional Crosschecker: East Coast/Canada**— Bill Byckowski, **West Coast**—Rex De La Nuez, **Midwest**—Will Harford, **Southeast**—Greg Zunino. **Scouting Supervisors:** Charlie Aliano, Rich Bordi, Jeff Brookens, Sean Buckley, John Ceprini, Dan Cholowsky, Andrew Fabian, Tyler Gibbons, Jerel Johnson, Mike Keenan, Brandon Marr, Mike Misuraca, Jim Moran, Mike Partida, Jonathan Reynolds, Paul Scott, Andy Stack. **Scouts:** Bill Killian, Denny Nagel, Juan Silva. **Director, International Scouting:** Trey Hendricks. **Assistant Director, International Scouting:** Greg McMillin. **Director, Latin America Scouting:** Richard Jimenez. **Assistant Director, Latin American Scouting:** Richard Castro. **Crosschecker, International Scouting:** David Espinosa, Matt Gaski, Boomer Prinstein. **Supervisor, South American Scouting:** Herman Albornoz. **Supervisor, Dominican Republic:** Enmanuel Cartagena. **Coordinator, Venezuela:** Richard Quintero. **Manager, Pacific Rim Scouting:** Rob Fidler. **Scout, Pacific Rim:** Jamey Storvick. **Video Scout, D.R:** Jenfry Del Rosario. **International Scouts:** Jose Valdelamar, Jose Diaz, Edgar Melo, Victor Nova, Samuel Pimentel, Alex Ahumada, Gustavo Martinez, Concepcion Rodriguez, Dan Kim, Sal Varriale, Ryan Schuman, Matt Everingham, Brian Ambrister, Aguido Gonzalez, Evert-Jan't Hoen, Victor Serrano, Fermin Coronel, Jose Valdelamar, Jean Tome.

CLEVELAND INDIANS

Office Address: Progressive Field, 2401 Ontario St., Cleveland, OH 44115.
Telephone: (216) 420-4200. **Fax:** (216) 420-4396.
Website: www.indians.com.

OWNERSHIP
Owner: Larry Dolan. **Chairman/Chief Executive Officer:** Paul Dolan.

BUSINESS OPERATIONS
President, Business Operations: Brian Barren. **Senior Vice President, Marketing/Strategy:** Alex King. **Executive Administrative Assistant:** Dru Kosik.

CORPORATE PARTNERSHIPS/FINANCE
Vice President, Corporate Partnership: Ted Baugh. **Senior Director, Corporate Partnership & Premium Hospitality:** Dom Polito. **Director, Corporate Partnership & Premium Hospitality:** Kevin Murphy. **Senior Sales Manager, Corporate Partnerships:** Bryan Hoffart. **Administrative Assistant:** Kim Scott. **VP/General Counsel:** Joe Znidarsic. **Vice President, Finance & Chief Financial Officer:** Rich Dorffer. **Controller:** Erica Chambers. **Manager, Accounting:** Karen Menzing. **Manager, Payroll Accounting/Services:** Mary Forkapa. **Concessions Accounting Manager:** Diane Turner.

Larry Dolan

HUMAN RESOURCES
VP, Human Resources/Chief Diversity Officer: Sara Lehrke. **Director, Human Resources Operations:** Jennifer Gibson. **Director, Talent Acquisition:** Mailynh Vu. **Manager, Talent Acquisition:** Valencia Kimbrough. **Manager, Talent Development:** Nate Daymut. **Coordinator, Talent Development:** Colleen Lynch. **Manager, Talent Development:** Sydney Merz.

MARKETING
VP, Marketing/Brand Management: Nicole Schmidt. **Director, Brand Management:** Jason Wiedemann. **Manager, Advertising/Promotions:** Anne Madzelan.

COMMUNICATIONS/BASEBALL INFORMATION
Telephone: (216) 420-4380. **Fax:** (216) 420-4430.
Senior VP, Public Affairs: Bob DiBiasio. **Vice President, Communications and Community Impact:** Curtis Danburg. **Director, Baseball Information & Player Relations:** Bart Swain. **Director, Communications & Player Relations:** Court Berry-Tripp. **Manager, Communications:** Austin Controulis. **Coordinator, Player Engagement & Family Relations:** Megan Ganser. **Team Photographer:** Dan Mendlik. **Coordinator, Communications & Team Historian:** Jeremy Feador.

BALLPARK OPERATIONS
VP, Ballpark Improvements: Jim Folk. **Senior Director, Ballpark Operations:** Jerry Crabb. **Senior Director, Facility Operations:** Seth Cooper. **Senior Director, Security:** Jonathan Wilham. **Head Groundskeeper:** Brandon Koehnke. **Director, Facility Maintenance:** Ron Miller. **Manager, Event Security:** Andy Finn. **Manager, Ballpark Operations:** Steve Walters. **Manager, Ballpark Operations:** Tyler Cochran. **Manager, Safety Policy and Training:** David Bonacci.

TICKETING
Telephone: (216) 420-4487. **Fax:** (216) 420-4481.
Director, Ticket Services: Matt Coppo. **Ticket Services Manager:** Eric Fronczek. **Manager, Ticket Operations:** Seth Fuller. **Ticket Services Coordinator:** Paige Selle.

TEAM OPERATIONS/CLUBHOUSE
Director, Team Travel: Mike Seghi. **Home Clubhouse Manager:** Tony Amato. **Asst. Home Clubhouse Manager:** Brandon Biller. **Director, Video Operations:** Bob Chester. **Goodyear Facility Manager:** Jared Jones.

BASEBALL OPERATIONS

President, Baseball Operations: Chris Antonetti. **General Manager:** Mike Chernoff. **Assistant GMs:** Matt Forman, Carter Hawkins, Sky Andrecheck. **Vice President, Baseball Operations—Strategy/Administration:** Brad Grant. **Vice President, Baseball Operations:** Eric Binder. **Director, Baseball Operations:** Alex Merberg. **Assistant Director, Baseball Research/Development:** Kevin Tenenbaum. **Principal Data Scientist:** Keith Woolner. **Baseball Analyst:** Max Marchi. **Director, Baseball Administration:** Wendy Hoppel. **Executive Administrative Assistant:** Marlene Lehky. **Assistant Director, Baseball Operations:** Sam Giller. **Assistant, Baseball Operations:** Zach Morton.

Chris Antonetti

MAJOR LEAGUE STAFF

Manager: Terry Francona. **Coaches: Bench**—DeMarlo Hale. **Pitching**—Carl Willis. **Hitting**—Ty Van Burkleo. **First Base**—Sandy Alomar Jr. **Third Base**—Mike Sarbaugh. **Bullpen**—Brian Sweeney. **Assistant Hitting Coach**—Victor Rodriguez. **Assistant Pitching Coach**—Ruben Niebla. **Assistants, Major League Staff:** Mike Barnett, Armando Camacaro, Justin Toole, Kyle Hudson, Ricky Pacione.

MEDICAL/TRAINING

Vice President, Medical Services: Lonnie Soloff. **Head Team Physician:** Dr. Mark Schickendantz. **Head Athletic Trainer:** James Quinlan. **Assistant Athletic Trainers:** Jeff Desjardins, Chad Wolfe. **Performance Coach (Triple-A/Major League):** Brian Miles.

PLAYER DEVELOPMENT

Vice President, Player Development: James Harris. **Special Assistants:** Travis Fryman, Travis Hafner, Tim Belcher, Tom Wiedenbauer. **Assistant Directors, Player Development:** Matt Cody Buckel, Rob Cerfolio, Andrew Bahnert. **Assistant Director, Player Development:** Rob Cerfolio. **Director, Administration:** Wendy Hoppel. **Advisor, Player Development:** Minnie Mendoza, Johnny Goryl. **Administrative Assistant:** Nilda Taffanelli. **Field Coordinator:** John McDonald. **Assistant Field Coordinator:** Anthony Medrano. **Coordinators:** Joe Torres (pitching), Joel Mangrum (pitching), Stephen Osterer (pitching resource), **Player Programs Coordinator:** Larry Day. **DR Academy Coordinator:** Jose Mejia. **Medical Coordinator:** Bobby Ruiz. **Performance Analyst, Player Development:** Todd Kubacki, Todd Tubbs, Josh Morrison. **Education & Language Coordinator:** Anna Bolton. **Mental Performance Coach:** Martin Rassamoff. **Performance Coordinator:** Ryan Faer (Arizona), Hasani Torres (Dominican Republic). **Rehab Coordinator:** Jeremy Harris. **Life Skills Coordinator:** Jen Wolf. **Nutrition Coordinator:** Grant Harris.

FARM SYSTEM

Class	Club	Manager	Hitting Coach	Pitching Coach
Triple-A	Columbus	Andy Tracy	Jason Esposito	Rigo Beltran
Double-A	Akron	Rouglas Odor	Junior Betances	Owen Dew
High A	Lake County	Greg DiCenzo	Grant Fink	Kevin Erminio
Low A	Lynchburg	Dennis Malave	Chris Smith	Tony Arnold
Rookie	Indians (AZL)	Jerry Owens	J.Becker/C. Massoni	M. Steele/K. Lindquist
Rookie	Indians 1(DSL)	Omir Santos	Odomar Valdez	Jesus Sanchez
Rookie	Indians 2(DSL)	Jesus Tavares	Ian Forster	Anderson Polanco

SCOUTING

Senior Director, Scouting Operations: John Mirabelli. **Director, Amateur Scouting:** Scott Barnsby. **Assistant Director, Amateur Scouting:** Clint Longenecker. **Assistant, Amateur Scouting:** Matt Czechanski. **Coordinators, Amateur Scouting:** David Compton (Newport Beach, CA), Jon Heuerman (Chandler, AZ), Ethan Purser (Dallas, GA). **Area Scouts:** Kyle Bamberger (Newport Beach, CA), CT Bradford (Pensacola, FL), Mike Bradford (Nashville, TN), Garrick Chaffee (Dallas, TX), Aaron Etchison (Dexter, MI), Conor Glassey (Bothell, WA), Mike Kanen (Brooklyn, NY), Andrew Krause (Jacksonville, FL), Jhonathan Leyba (Seminole, FL), Pete Loizzo (Durham, NC), Carlos Muniz (San Pedro, CA), Ryan Perry (Phoenix, AZ), Kyle Van Hook (Brenham, TX). **Amateur Scouting Fellows:** Michael Cuva, Matt Linder.
Vice President, Player Acquisitions: Victor Wang. **Special Assistant to President of Baseball Operations/GM:** Steve Lubratich (Lee, NH), Dave Malpass (Huntington Beach, CA), Don Poplin (Norwood, NC). **Special Assistant to Baseball Operations:** Tim Belcher (Marengo, OH). **Special Assignment Scouts:** Scott Meaney (Holly Springs, NC), Dave Miller (Wilmington, NC), Bo Hughes (Sherman Oaks, CA). **Senior Player Acquisitions Scouts:** Chris Calciano (Milton, DE), Kevin Cullen (Frisco, TX), Brad Tyler (Bishop, GA). **Professional Scouts**—Dan Budreika (Cleveland, OH), Doug Carpenter (North Palm Beach, FL), Jim Rickon (Seven Hills, OH). **Vice President, International Scouting:** Paul Gillispie. **Assistant Directors, International Scouting:** Richard Conway, Chris Gale. **Coordinator, International Scouting:** Junie Melendez (Avon, OH).

COLORADO ROCKIES

Office Address: 2001 Blake St., Denver, CO 80205.
Telephone: (303) 292-0200. **Fax:** (303) 312-2116.
Website: www.Rockies.com.

OWNERSHIP

Operated by: Colorado Rockies Baseball Club Ltd.
Owner/Chairman & Chief Executive Officer: Richard L. Monfort. **Executive Assistant to the Owner/Chairman & Chief Executive Officer:** Terry Douglass. **Owner/General Partner:** Charles K. Monfort.

BUSINESS OPERATIONS

Executive Vice President/Chief Operating Officer: Greg Feasel. **Assistant to Executive VP/Chief Operating Officer:** Kim Olson. **VP, Human Resources:** Elizabeth Stecklein. **Director, Diversity, Equity, Inclusion & Recruiting, Human Resources:** Dallas Davis.

MICHAEL MARTIN/GETTY IMAGES

Richard Monfort

FINANCE

Executive VP: Hal Roth. **Assistant to the Executive Vice President:** Tammy Vergara. **VP/CFO:** Michael Kent. **VP/General Counsel:** Brian Gaffney. **Senior Director, Procurement:** Gary Lawrence. **Coordinator, Purchasing:** Robert Wilkinson. **Senior Director, Accounting:** Phil Emerson. **Accountants:** Joel Binfet, Laine Campbell.

CORPORATE PARTNERSHIPS

VP, Corporate Partnerships: Walker Monfort. **Assistant to VP, Corporate Partnerships:** Nicole Ortiz. **Senior Director, Client Services & Events:** Kari Anderson. **Assistant Director:** Nate VanderWal. **Account Executives:** Sam Porter, Chris Zumbrennen. **Senior Director, In-Game Entertainment & Broadcasting:** Kent Krosbakken. **Public Address Announcer:** Reed Saunders.

COMMUNITY/RETAIL OPERATIONS

VP, Community & Retail Operations: James P. Kellogg. **Assistant to the VP, Community & Retail Operations:** Kelly Hall. **Senior Director, Retail Operations:** Aaron Heinrich.

MARKETING/COMMUNICATIONS

VP, Communications & Marketing: Jill Campbell. **Supervisor, Communications:** Cory Little. **Coordinator, Communications:** Nick Parson. **Brand Management & Social Media:** Julian Valentin. **Coordinator, Marketing**: Lauren Jacaruso. **Editor/Designer, Communications & Marketing:** Sarah Topf. **Team Photographer:** Matt Dirksen.

BALLPARK OPERATIONS

VP/Chief Customer Officer, Ballpark Operations: Kevin Kahn. **Assistant to the VP/Chief Customer Officer, Ballpark Operations:** Lenus Lucero. **Senior Director, Food Service Operations/Development:** Albert Valdes. **Senior Director, Guest Services:** Steven Burke. **Head Groundskeeper:** Mark Razum. **Assistant Head Groundskeeper:** Doug Zabinsky. **Senior Director, Engineering & Facilities:** Allyson Gutierrez.

TICKETING

Telephone: (303) 762-5437, (800) 388-7625. **Fax:** (303) 312-2115.
VP, Ticket Operations, Sales & Services: Sue Ann McClaren.

TRAVEL/CLUBHOUSE

Senior Director, Major League Operations: Paul Egins. **Manager, Major League Clubhouse:** Mike Pontarelli. **Coordinator, Major League Clubhouse:** Tyler Sanders.

BASEBALL OPERATIONS

Executive VP/General Manager: Jeff Bridich. **Assistant to Executive VP/GM:** Irma Castañeda. **Assistant GM, Baseball Operations/Assistant General Counsel:** Zack Rosenthal. **Assistant GM/Player Personnel:** Jon Weil. **Assistant GM/Player Development:** Zach Wilson. **Director, Baseball Operations:** Domenic Di Ricco. **Coordinator, Baseball Operations/Staff Counsel:** Matt Obernauer. **Full Stack Developer, Baseball Research & Development:** Bryce Leonard. **Baseball Operations Fellow:** Brittany Haby. **Special Assistant to the GM:** Danny Montgomery.

Jeff Bridich

MAJOR LEAGUE STAFF

Manager: Bud Black. **Coaches: Bench**—Mike Redmond, **Pitching**—Steve Foster, **Hitting**—David Magadan, **Assistant Hitting Coach**—Jeff Salazar, **Third Base**—Stu Cole, **First Base**—Ron Gideon, **Bullpen**—Darryl Scott, **Bullpen Catcher**—Aaron Munoz, **Director, Physical Performance**—Gabe Bauer, **Video**—Brian Jones. **ML Data & Game Planning Coordinator**—Doug Bernier.

MEDICAL/TRAINING

Senior Director, Medical Operations/Special Projects: Tom Probst. **Medical Director:** Dr. Thomas Noonan. **Club Physicians:** Dr. Allen Schreiber, Dr. Douglas Wyland. **Head Trainer:** Keith Dugger. **Assistant Athletic Trainer:** Scott Gehret.

PLAYER DEVELOPMENT

Assistant Director: Chris Forbes. **Manager:** Jesse Stender. **Camps and Fundamentals Coordinator:** Andy Gonzalez. **Director, Pitching Operations:** Mark Wiley. **Pitching Coordinator:** Doug Linton. **Catching Coordinator:** Mark Strittmatter. **Hitting Coordinator:** Darin Everson. **Rehab Coordinator:** Scott Murayama. **Assistant Rehab Coordinator/Manager, Scottsdale Operations, Scottsdale:** Andy Stover. **Physical Performance Coordinator:** Trevor Swartz. **Director, Mental Skills Development:** Doug Chadwick. **Assistant Mental Skills Coordinator:** Jerry Amador. **Coordinator, Cultural Education:** Angel Amparo. **Latin America Field & Pitching Coordinator:** Edison Lora. **Minor League Clubhouse and Equipment Manager:** Daniel Kleinholz. **Special Assistant, Player Development & Scouting:** Jerry Weinstein.

FARM SYSTEM

Class	Club (League)	Manager	Hitting Coach	Pitching Coach
Triple-A	Albuquerque	Warren Schaeffer	TBD	Blaine Beatty
Double-A	Hartford	Chris Denorfia	Tom Sutaris	Frank Gonzales
High A	Spokane	Scott Little	Zach Osborne	Ryan Kibler
Low A	Fresno	Robinson Cancel	Nic Wilson	Mark Brewer
Rookie	Rockies (AZL)	Jake Opitz	Burmeister/Ramirez	Burba/Rodriguez
Rookie	Rockies 1 (DSL)	Gonzalez/Jose	Samuel Deduno	Rosario/Nunez

SCOUTING

VP, Scouting: Bill Schmidt. **Special Assistant to the GM, Scouting:** Danny Montgomery. **Sr. Director, Scouting Operations:** Marc Gustafson. **Assistant Scouting Director:** Damon Iannelli. **Special Assistant, Scouting:** Rick Mathews. **Assistant Director, Scouting Operations:** Sterling Monfort. **Advance Scouts:** Chris Warren (Denver, CO), Peter Bourjos (Scottsdale, AZ). **Special Assistant, Player Personnel:** Ty Coslow (Louisville, KY). **Major League Scouts:** Kevin Bootay (Elk Grove, CA), Steve Fleming (Louisa, VA), Will George (Milford, DE), Jack Gillis (Sarasota, FL), Mark Germann (Denver, CO), Joe Housey (Hollywood, FL), John Corbin (Savannah, GA). **Professional Scout:** Joe Little (Arvada, CO). **National Crosscheckers:** Mike Ericson (Phoenix, AZ), Jay Matthews (Concord, NC). **Area Scouts:** Scott Alves (Phoenix, AZ), Brett Baldwin (Kansas City, MO), Julio Campos (Guaynabo, PR) John Cedarburg (Fort Myers, FL), Jermaine Clark (Fresno, CA) Scott Corman (Lexington, KY), Jordan Czarniecki (Greenville, SC), Jeff Edwards (Fresno, TX), Sean Gamble (Atlanta, GA), Mike Garlatti (Edison, NJ), Matt Hattabaugh (Westminster, CA), Matt Pignataro (Seattle, WA), Jesse Retzlaff (Dallas, TX), Rafael Reyes (Miami, FL), Ed Santa (Powell, OH), Zack Zulli (Hammond, LA). **Part-Time Scouts:** Norm DeBriyn (Fayetteville, AR), Dave McQueen (Bossier City, LA), Greg Pullia (Plymouth, MA). **VP, International Scouting/Player Development:** Rolando Fernandez. **Dominican Scouting/Development Coordinator:** Arnaldo Gomez. **Dominican Scouting/Development Assistant:** Enmanuel Frias. **International Crosschecker:** Marc Russo. **Supervisor, Latin America Scouting:** Orlando Medina. **International Scouting:** Martin Cabrera (Dominican Republic), Carlos Gomez (Venezuela), Raul Gomez (Cuba), Alving Mejias (Mexico), Frank Roa (Dominican Republic), Josher Suarez (Venezuela) Rogers Figueroa (Colombia).

DETROIT TIGERS

Office Address: 2100 Woodward Ave, Detroit, MI 48201.
Telephone: (313) 471-2000. **Fax:** (313) 471-2138. **Website:** www.tigers.com

OWNERSHIP

Operated By: Detroit Tigers Inc. **Chairman & CEO, Detroit Tigers:** Christopher Ilitch. **Group President, Sports & Entertainment, Ilitch Holdings, Inc.:** Chris Granger

BUSINESS OPERATIONS

FINANCE/ADMINISTRATION

Executive Vice President, Baseball Operations/General Manager: Al Avila. **Special Assistants to the GM:** Kirk Gibson, Willie Horton, Jim Leyland, Lance Parrish, Mike Russell, Alan Trammell. **VP/Assistant GM:** David Chadd. **VP, Player Personnel:** Scott Bream. **VP/Player Development:** Dave Littlefield. **Senior Director, Baseball Analytics/Operations:** Jay Sartori. **Director, Baseball Analytics:** Jim Logue. **Director, Baseball Operations/Professional Scouting:** Sam Menzin. **Assistant Counsel, Baseball Operations:** Alan Avila. Executive **Assistant to the Executive Vice President, Baseball Operations/General Manager:** Marty Lyon.

Chris Ilitch

PUBLIC/COMMUNITY AFFAIRS

Director, Player Relations & Authentics: Jordan Field. **Director, Promotions & Special Events:** Haley Kolff. **Manager, Promotions and Special Events:** Evan Novak. **Promotions & Special Events Coordinator:** Taylor Olson. **Content Producer:** Brent Brevak.

SALES/MARKETING

Director, Corporate Partnership Activation: Kaitlin Knutson. **Director, Corporate Partnership Business Strategy and Solutions:** Mike Singer. **Activation Manager, Corporate Partnerships:** Alex O'Connor, Krystal Wilson, Sydney Landers, Tiffany Harrington. **Coordinator, Corporate Partnership Activation:** Megan Malloy. **Solutions Managers, Corporate Partnerships:** Jacob Pnakovich, Max Klepper. **Sales Managers, Corporate Partnerships:** John Wolski, Donovan Powell, Matt Gay, Thomas Kappel.

MEDIA RELATIONS/COMMUNICATIONS

Telephone: (313) 471-21092. **Fax:** (313) 471-2138.
VP, Communications: Ron Colangelo. **Director, Communications:** Chad Crunk. **Coordinator, Media Relations:** Ben Fidelman. **Director, Broadcasting/In-Game Entertainment:** Stan Fracker.

BASEBALL OPERATIONS

Telephone: (313) 471-2000. **Fax:** (313) 471-2099.

VP, Player Development: Dave Littlefield. **Director, Minor League Operations:** Dan Lunetta. **Director, Player Development:** Kenny Graham. **Director, Pitching Development and Strategies:** Dan Hubbs. **Director, Performance Science:** Dr. Georgia Giblin. **Director, Minor League/Scouting Administration:** Cheryl Evans. **Director, International Operations:** Tom Moore. **Director, Latin American Operations:** Miguel Garcia. **Director, Latin American Player Development:** Rafael Martinez. **Administrators, Dominican Academy:** Wilfredo Crespo, Jimmy Ortiz. **Player Development Coordinators:** David Allende, Jim McKew. Coordinator, **International Operations:** Rafael Gonzalez. **Coordinator, International Player Programs:** Sharon Lockwood. **Minor League Field Coordinator:** Dave Owen. **Minor League Medical Coordinator:** Corey Tremble. **Minor League Strength/Conditioning Coordinator:** Francisco Rivas. **Assistant Medical Coordinator—International:** Manny Pena. **Minor League Clubhouse Manager:** Patrick Saenz. **Player Development Analytics Coordinator:** Jordan Wergiles. **Minor League Video Coordinators:** Cristian Crespo, Alex Gonzalez. **Player Development Assistant:** Daniel Crago. **Roving Instructors:** Jeff Branson (hitting), Joel McKeithan (hitting), A.J. Sager (pitching), Joe DePastino (catching), Jose Valentin (Infield), Kimera Bartee (outfield/baserunning), Jorge Cordova (assistant pitching), Brian Peterson (performance enhancement instructor), Bryan Taggett (Latin American performance coach).

Al Avila

MAJOR LEAGUE STAFF

Manager: A.J. Hinch. **Coaches: Pitching**—Chris Fetter, **Hitting** —Scott Coolbaugh, **First Base**—Ramon Santiago, **Third Base**—Chip Hale, **Assistant Pitching**—Juan Nieve, **Bench**—George Lombard, **Coach**—Jose Cruz, **Quality Control**—Josh Paul.

MEDICAL/TRAINING

Senior Director, Medical Services: Kevin Rand. **Head Athletic Trainer:** Doug Teter. **Assistant Athletic Trainers:** Chris McDonald, Matt Rankin. **Strength/Conditioning Coach:** Steve Chase. **Assistant Strength/Conditioning Coach:** Matt Rosenhamer. **Team Physicians:** Dr. Michael Workings, Dr. Stephen Lemos, Dr. Louis Saco (Florida). Coordinator, **Medical Services:** Gwen Keating.

PLAYER DEVELOPMENT

VP, Player Development: Dave Littlefield. **Director, Minor League Operations:** Dan Lunetta. **Director, Minor League/Scouting Administration:** Cheryl Evans. **Director, International Operations:** Tom Moore. **Director, Latin American Operations:** Miguel Garcia. **Coordinator, International Operations:** Rafael Gonzalez. **Coordinator, International Player Programs:** Sharon Lockwood. **Minor League Strength/Conditioning Coordinator:** Steve Chase. **Lakeland Clubhouse Manager:** Patrick Saenz. **Player Development Coordinators:** David Allende, Jim McKew. **Coordinator, Major League Advanced Scouting & International Pro Scout:** Kan Ikeda. **Minor League Video Coordinators:** Cristian Crespo, Alex Gonzalez. **Roving Instructors:** TBD.

FARM SYSTEM

Class	Club	Manager	Hitting Coach	Pitching Coach
Triple-A	Toledo	Tom Prince	Mike Hessman	Doug Bochtler
Double-A	Erie	Arnie Beyeler	Adam Melhuse	Mark Johnson
High A	West Michigan	Brayan Pena	Bill Springman	Willie Blair
Low A	Lakeland	Andrew Graham	John Murrian	Carlos Bohorquez
Rookie	Tigers West (GCL)	Ryan Minor	Tim Garland	Mike Alvarez
Rookie	Tigers East (GCL)	Gary Cathcart	Rafael Gil	Santiago Garrido
Rookie	Tigers 1 (DSL)	Ramon Zapata	Willians Moreno	Jose Ovalles
Rookie	Tigers 2 (DSL)	Marcos Yepez	Kely Ramos/Luis Mateo	Luis Marte

SCOUTING

VP, Assistant General Manager: David Chadd. **VP, Player Personnel:** Scott Bream. **Director, Amateur Scouting:** Scott Pleis. **Assistant Director, Amateur Scouting:** Eric Nieto. **Amateur Scouting Video Coordinator:** Sam Nasci. **Major League Scouts:** Ray Crone, Jim Elliott, Joe Ferrone, P.J. Jones, Paul Mirocke, Jim Olander, Jim Rough, John Stockstill, Bruce Tanner, Josh Wilson. **Special Assistant to the GM:** Mike Russell. **National Crosscheckers:** Tim Hallgren, Steve Hinton, James Orr. **Regional Crosscheckers: East**—Taylor Black, **Midwest**—Tim Grieve, **Central**—Justin Henry, **West**—Dave Lottsfeldt. **Area Scouts:** Nick Avila, Bryson Barber, Jim Bretz, Donald Brown, RJ Burgess, Austin Cousino, Dave Dangler, , Ryan Johnson, Joey Lothrop, Tim McWilliam, Steve Pack, George Schaefer, Mike Smith, Steve Taylor, Matt Zmuda, Harold Zonder. **Part-Time Scouts:** German Geigel, Deryl Horton, Mark Monahan, Clyde Weir. **Director, International Operations:** Tom Moore. **Director, Latin American Scouting:** Miguel Garcia. **Coordinator, Pacific Rim Scouting:** Kevin Hooker. **International Operations Coordinator:** Rafael Gonzalez. **International Crosscheckers:** Alejandro Rodriguez, Jeff Wetherby. **Dominican Scouting Supervisor:** Aldo Perez. **Dominican Republic Special Assignment Scouts:** Ramon Perez, Oliver Arias. **Venezuelan Scouting Supervisor:** Jesus Mendoza. **Venezuelan Academy Administrator/Area Scout:** Oscar Garcia. **International Area Scouts:** Edward Burgos, Rodolfo Penalo, Miguel Rodriguez, Carlos Santana, Raul Leiva, Delvis Pacheco, Jose Zambrano, Pedro Castellano, Luis Molina, Michael Hsieh, Kan Ikeda, Ho-Kyun Im.

HOUSTON ASTROS

Office Address: Minute Maid Park, Union Station, 501 Crawford, Suite 400, Houston, TX 77002.
Mailing Address: PO Box 288, Houston, TX 77001. **Telephone:** (713) 259-8000. **Fax:** (713) 259-8981.
Email Address: fanfeedback@astros.mlb.com. **Website:** www.astros.com.

OWNERSHIP
Owner/Chairman: Jim Crane.

BUSINESS OPERATIONS

Executive Assistant: Eileen Colgin. **Executive Assistant:** Adriana Moya. **Administrative Assistant:** Brittany Redeaux. **Senior VP, Business Operations:** Marcel Braithwaite. **Senior VP, Corporate Partnerships:** Matt Brand. **Senior VP, Community Relations/Executive Director, Astros Foundation:** Twila Carter. **Senior VP/ General Counsel:** Giles Kibbe. **Senior VP, Marketing/Communications:** Anita Sehgal. **Chief Financial Officer:** Michael Slaughter. **VP, Tax:** Vito Ciminello. **VP, Communications:** Gene Dias. **VP, Stadium Operations:** Bobby Forrest. **VP, Information Technology:** Chris Hanz. **VP, Foundation Development:** Marian Harper. **VP, Merchandising/Retail Operations:** Tom Jennings. **VP, Human Resources:** Jennifer Springs. **VP, Finance:** Doug Seckel. **VP, Event Sales/Operations:** Stephanie Stegall. **VP, Marketing:** Jason Wooden. **VP, Ticket Sales and Service:** Creighton Kahoalii. **VP, Corporate Partnerships:** Jeff Stewart.

Jim Crane

COMMUNICATIONS/COMMUNITY RELATIONS
Senior Manager, Communications: Steve Grande. **Manager, Communications:** Chris Peixoto. **Coordinator, Communications:** Meshach Sullivan. **Manager, Broadcasting:** Ginny Gotcher Grande. **Director, Astros Youth Academy:** Daryl Wade. **Manager, Astros Youth Academy:** Duane Stelly. **Coordinators, Community Relations/Astros Foundation:** Rachel Bubier, Andrew Remson. **Coordinator, Astros Youth Academy:** Megan Hays.

MARKETING/ANALYTICS
Senior Director, Ballpark Entertainment: Chris E. Garcia. **Senior Director, Business Strategy/Analytics:** Jay Verrill. **Senior Managers, Marketing Entertainment:** Kyle Hamsher, Richard Tapia. **Coordinator, Social Media:** Ryan Lasneske.

CORPORATE PARTNERSHIPS
Director, Corporate Partnerships: Melissa Hahn. **Director, Sales/Corporate Sponsorships:** Keshia Henderson. **Sales Managers, Corporate Partnerships:** Jimmy Comerota. **Account Managers, Corporate Partnerships:** Lauren Hill, Haleigh Sanders.

STADIUM OPERATIONS
Senior Director, Stadium Operations: Thomas Bell. **Director, Audio/Visual:** Lowell Matheny. **Director, Security/Parking:** Ben Williams. **Manager, Parking:** Gary Rowberry. **Manager, Engineering:** Michael Seighman. **Head Groundskeeper:** Izzy Hinojosa. **First Assistant Groundskeeper:** Chris Wolfe.

TICKETING
Senior Director, Ticket Sales: P.J. Keene. **Director, Box Office Operations:** Bill Cannon. **Director, Season Ticket Service:** Jeff Close. **Director, Ticket Operations:** Mark Cole.

BASEBALL OPERATIONS

Assistant GM, Player Development: Pete Putila. **Special Assistants:** Craig Biggio, Jeff Bagwell, Enos Cabell. **Sr. Director, Player Evaluation:** Ehsan Bokhari. **Sr. Director, Baseball Strategy:** Bill Firkus. **Sr. Director, Baseball Operations:** Armando Velasco. **Director, Minor League Operations:** Derrick Fong. **Director, Research/Development:** Sarah Gelles. **Director, Player Evaluation:** Charles Cook. **Director, Latin American Operations:** Caridad Cabrera.

James Click

MAJOR LEAGUE STAFF

Manager: Dusty Baker. **Coaches: Bench**—Joe Espada, **Pitching**—Brent Strom. **Pitching**—Josh Miller. **Assistant Pitching**—Bill Murphy. **Hitting**— Alex Cintron. **Second Hitting**—Troy Snitker. **First Base**—Omar Lopez. **Third Base**—Gary Pettis. **Quality Control**—Dan Firova. **Coach**—Michael Collins.

TEAM OPERATIONS/CLUBHOUSE

Director, Team Operations: Derek Vigoa. **Coordinator, Major League Advance Information:** Tommy Kawamura. **Manager, MLB Video and Technologies:** Antonio Padilla. **Clubhouse Manager:** Carl Schneider. **Visiting Clubhouse Manager:** Steve Perry.

MEDICAL/TRAINING

Head Team Physician: Dr. David Lintner. **Team Physicians:** Dr. Thomas Mehlhoff, Dr. James Muntz, Dr. Pat McCulloch, Dr. Vijay Jotwani. **Head Athletic Trainer and Head Physical Therapist:** Jeremiah Randall. **Massage Therapist:** Katsumi Oka. **Major League Strength/Conditioning Coach:** Brendan Verner.

PLAYER DEVELOPMENT

Assistant GM, Player Development: Pete Putila. **Director, Minor League Operations:** Derrick Fong. **Minor League Coordinators:** Jeremy Barnes (hitting), Jason Bell (fundamentals), Mark Bailey (catching).

FARM SYSTEM

Class	Club	Manager	Hitting Coach	Pitching Coach
Triple-A	Sugar Land	TBA	TBA	TBA
Double-A	Corpus Christi	TBA	TBA	TBA
High A	Asheville	TBA	TBA	TBA
Low A	Fayetteville	TBA	TBA	TBA
Rookie	Astros (GCL)	TBA	TBA	TBA
Rookie	Astros 1 (DSL)	TBA	TBA	TBA

SCOUTING

Senior Scouting Advisor: Charlie Gonzalez. **National Scouting Supervisor:** Kris Gross. **Supervisor, Area Scouting:** Landon Townsley, Andrew Johnson. **Domestic Crosscheckers:** Evan Brannon (St. Petersburg, FL), Gavin Dickey (Atlanta, GA). **Domestic Scouts:** Travis Coleman (Birmingham, AL), Tim Costic (Los Angeles, CA), Ryan Courville (Scottsdale, AZ), Ryan Leake (San Diego, CA), Bobby St. Pierre (Atlanta, GA), Jim Stevenson (Tulsa, OK), Joey Sola (San Juan, PR).

Manager, Pro Scouting Analysis: Matt Hogan. **Scouting Analysts:** Aaron DelGiudice, Will Sharp, Cam Pendino. **Assistant Director, International Scouting:** Roman Ocumarez. **Supervisors:** Alfredo Ulloa, Jose Palacios. **Dominican Republic:** Leocadio Guevara. **Dominican Republic:** Jose Lima. **Mexico:** Miguel Pintor. **Venezuela:** Enrique Brito.

VIDEO & TECHNOLOGY

Coordinator, Minor League Technology: Sam Visser. **Coordinator, International Technology, Assistant, Dominican Scouting:** Francisco Navarro. **Assistant, Dominican Scouting:** Carlos Vasquez. **Assistant, Venezuela Scouting:** Carlos Freites. **Amateur Video Technicians:** Aaron DelGuidice, Cam Pendino.

KANSAS CITY ROYALS

Office Address: One Royal Way, Kansas City, MO 64129.
Mailing Address: PO Box 419969, Kansas City, MO 64141.
Telephone: (816) 921-8000. **Fax:** (816) 924-0347. **Website:** www.royals.com.

OWNERSHIP
Operated By: Kansas City Royals Baseball Club, LLC. **Chairman & CEO: John Sherman.**

ADVISORS TO THE CHAIRMAN
Sr. Advisor, Business Processes: Brooks Sherman. **Sr. Advisor, Business Strategy:** Sarah Tourville.

BUSINESS OPERATIONS

GITTINGS PHOTOGRAPHY

John Sherman

FINANCE/ADMINISTRATION
VP, Finance/Administration: David Laverentz. **Director, Finance:** Whitney Beaver.
Director, Human Resources: Miriam Maiden. **Director, Accounting/Risk Management:**
Patrick Fleischmann. **Director, Payroll:** Jodi Parsons. **Sr. Director, Information Systems:** Brian
Himstedt. **Director, Information Systems:** Neil Sell. **Sr. Director, Ticket Operations:** Anthony
Blue. **Director, Ticket Ops:** Chris Darr.

COMMUNICATIONS/BROADCASTING
VP, Communications/Broadcasting: Mike Swanson. **Assistant Director, Media Relations:**
Mike Cummings. **Manager, Communications/Broadcasting:** Nick Kappel.

COMMUNITY IMPACT & URBAN YOUTH ACADEMY
VP, Community Impact: Kyle Vena. **Sr. Director, Community Investments & Exec.**
Director, Royals Charities: Amanda Grosdidier. **Director, Community initiatives:** Amanda Turk. **Director,**
Community Partnerships & Events: Chris Major. **Director, Alumni Relations:** Dina Blevins. **Director, Royals Hall of**
Fame: Curt Nelson. **Executive Director, Urban Youth Academy:** Darwin Pennye.

BALLPARK OPERATIONS
Sr. Director, Ballpark Operations: Isaac Riffel. **Sr. Director, Landscaping:** Trevor Vance. **Sr. Director, Stadium**
Engineering: Todd Burrow. **Director, Ballpark Services:** Johnny Williams. **Director, Guest Services:** Travis Bryant.
Director, Event Operations: Bryan Ross.

MARKETING/BUSINESS DEVELOPMENT
VP, Marketing/Business Development: Michael Bucek. **Sr. Director, Event Presentation/Production:** Don
Costante. **Director, Event Presentation/Production:** Steven Funke. **Director, Event Presentation:** Nicole Averso. **Sr.**
Director, Digital/Social Media: Erin Sleddens. **Sr. Director, Corporate Partnerships/Broadcast Sales:** Jason Booker.
Director, Creative Services: Caitlin Wienck. **Director, Ticket Sales & Services:** Scott Wadsworth.

BASEBALL OPERATIONS

Telephone: (816) 921-8000. **Fax:** (816) 924-0347.

Dayton Moore

Sr. VP, Baseball Operations/General Manager: Dayton Moore. **Executive Asst. to the GM:** Emily Penning. **VP/Asst. GM: Major League/International Operations:** Rene Francisco. **Player Personnel:** J.J. Picollo. **Baseball Operations:** Scott Sharp. **Asst. GM: Baseball Administration:** Jin Wong. **Research & Development:** Dr. Daniel Mack. **Special Asst. to Baseball Ops/Leadership:** Blaine Boyer, Reggie Sanders, Mike Sweeney. **Sr. Directors—Leadership & Cultural Dev:** Matt Marasco. **Research & Development:** Guy Stevens. **Performance Science:** Austin Driggers. **Directors: Behavioral Science:** Dr. Ryan Maid. **Pro Development:** Jeff Diskin. **Baseball Ops:** Mitch Maier. **Asst. Directors: Behavioral Science:** Melissa Lambert. **Baseball Ops:** Malcom Culver. **Manager: Arizona Ops:** Nick Leto. **Sr. Developer:** Paul Turner. **Developers:** Joseph San Diego, Jenny Segelke. **Analysts:** Pravin Santhanam, Daniel Schoenfeld. **Assistant to Baseball Ops/Administration:** Kristin Lock.

TRAVEL/CLUBHOUSE

Sr. Directors: Clubhouse Operations/Team Travel: Jeff Davenport. **Clubhouse Operations:** Chuck Hawke. **Sr. Manager, Clubhouse Operations/Team Travel:** Nick Richie. **Managers: Equipment:** Patrick Gorman.

MAJOR LEAGUE STAFF

Manager: Mike Matheny. **Coaches: Bench**—Pedro Grifol, **Pitching**—Cal Eldred, **Hitting**—Terry Bradshaw, **First Base**—Rusty Kuntz, **Third Base**—Vance Wilson, **Bullpen**—Larry Carter. **Major League Coaches:** John Mabry. Tony Pena, Jr. **Replay/Advance Scouting Coordinator:** Bill Duplissea. **Bullpen Catchers:** Ryan Eigsti, Parker Morin. **Video:** Mark Topping. **Advanced Scouting Analyst:** Andy Ferguson.

MEDICAL/TRAINING

Team Physician: Dr. Vincent Key. **Head Athletic Trainer:** Nick Kenney. **Asst. Athletic Trainers:** Kyle Turner, Chris Delucia. **Strength & Conditioning:** Ryan Stoneberg. **Asst. Strength & Conditioning:** Luis Perez. **Physical Therapist:** Jeff Blum. **Registered Sports Dietitian:** Erika Wincheski.

PLAYER DEVELOPMENT

Directors: Hitting Performance/Player Development: Alec Zumwalt. **Pitching Performance:** Paul Gibson. **Performance Science:** John Wagle. **Managers: Minor League Ops**—Nick Relic. **Pitching Performance**—Mitch Stetter. **Special Asst. to the GM/Player Development:** Rafael Belliard, Chino Cadahia. **Field Coordinator:** Victor Baez (DSL). **Special Asst., Player Development:** John Wathan, Harry Spilman. **Special Assignment Hitting Coach:** Mike Tosar. **Coordinators:** Jason Simontacchi (Pitching), Drew Saylor (Hitting), Eddie Rodriguez (Catching), J.C. Boscan (Catching), Justin Hahn (Physical Therapy), Damon Hollins (Outfield, Bunting, Baserunning), David Iannicca (Medical), Jarret Abell (Strength/Conditioning), Rustin Sveum (Video). **Assistant Coodinators:** Keoni DeRenne (hitting), Derrick Robinson (Outfield, Bunting, Baserunning), Tony Medina (Medical/Latin America), Phil Falco (Strength/Conditioning), Jeff Suppan (Pitching Rover). **Development Coaches:** Brandon Nelson. **Support Staff:** Will Simon (Equipment), Monica Ramirez (Ed/ESL & Latin American Initiatives), Matt Sams (Performance Science Analyst)

FARM SYSTEM

Class	Club (League)	Manager	Hitting Coach	Pitching Coach
Triple-A	Omaha	Brian Poldberg	Brian Buchanan	Dane Johnson
Double-A	Northwest Arkansas	Scott Thorman	Abraham Nunez	Derrick Lewis
High-A	Quad Cities	Chris Widger	Andy LaRoche	Steve Luebber
Low-A	Columbia	Brooks Conrad	Jesus Azuaje	Carlos Martinez
Rookie	Royals (AZL)	Omar Ramirez	A. David/R. Castro	M. Davis/J. Habyan
Rookie	Royals (DSL1)	Ramon Martinez	Wilson Betemit	Rafael Feliz
Rookie	Royals (DSL2)	Sergio de Luna	Evaristo Lantigua	Jose Veras

SCOUTING

Telephone: (816) 921-8000. **Fax:** (816) 924-0347. **Assistant GM/Amateur Scouting:** Lonnie Goldberg. **Director, Pro Scouting:** Michael Cifuentes. **Assistant Director, Amateur Scouting:** Danny Ontiveros. **Coordinators: Scouting Operations:** Jack Monahan. **Amateur Video/Underclass Scout:** Tim Bavester. **Sr. Advisors:** Mike Arbuckle, Roy Clark, Gene Lamont, Art Stewart, Donnie Williams. **Special Assistants to the GM:** Tim Conroy, Jim Fregosi, Jr., Tom McNamara, Louie Medina. **Special Assignment Scouts:** Mitch Webster, Dale Sveum. **Pro Scouts:** Nate Adcock, Dennis Cardoza, Gregg Kilby, John McMichen, Mike Pazik, Jon Williams. **Part-Time Pro Scout:** Rene Lachemann. **Advance Scout:** Tony Tijerina. **Regional Supervisors: Midwest**—Gregg Miller, **Northeast**—Keith Connolly, **Southeast**—Sean Gibbs, **Southwest**— Colin Gonzales, **West**—Gary Wilson. **Pitching Assignment Scout:** Chris Reitsma. **Area Supervisors:** Joe Barbera, Tim Bittner, Cody Clark, Casey Fahy, Jim Farr, Mike Farrell, Abe Flores, Buddy Gouldsmith, Todd Guggiana, Josh Hallgren, Will Howard, Mark Leavitt, Scott Melvin, Alex Mesa, Ken Munoz, Matt Price, Joe Ross, Bobby Shore. **Underclass Scouts:** Travis Ezi, Daniel Guerrero. **Part-Time Scouts:** Eric Briggs, Rick Clendenin, Louis Collier, Jeremy Jones, Howard McCullough, Brittan Motley, Johnny Ramos, Lloyd Simmons, Adam Stern. **Asst. GM/Int'l Operations:** Albert Gonzalez. **Coordinators: Latin America:** Orlando Estevez. **Pacific Rim:** Phil Dale. **Manager, International Ops:** Fabio Herrera. **International Scouts:** Roberto Aquino (D.R.) Nicolas Bautista (D.R.), Neil Burke (Australia), Elias Despardel (D.R.), Fernando Encarnacion (D.R.), Alberto Garcia (VZ), Joelvis Gonzalez (VZ), Jose Gualdron (VZ), Djionny Joubert (Curacao), Edson Kelly (Aruba), Hyunsung Kim (S. Korea), Nathan Miller (Taiwan), Rafael Miranda (Colombia), Fausto Morel (Dominican Republic), Luis Ortiz (Texas), Hiroyuki Oya (Japan), Edis Perez (D.R), Manuel Samaniego (Mexico), Rafael Vasquez (D.R.).

LOS ANGELES ANGELS

Office Address: 2000 Gene Autry Way, Anaheim, CA 92806.
Mailing Address: 2000 Gene Autry Way, Anaheim, CA 92803.
Telephone: (714) 940-2000. **Fax:** (714) 940-2205. **Website:** www.angels.com.

OWNERSHIP

Owners: Arte & Carole Moreno. **Chairman:** Dennis Kuhl. **President:** John Carpino. **Senior Vice President, Finance/Administration:** Molly Jolly. **Executive Vice President:** Dana Wells.

BUSINESS OPERATIONS

Arte and Carole Moreno

General Counsel, Legal Affairs/Risk Management: Alex Winsberg. **Senior Director, Finance:** Doug Mylowe. **Controller:** Sue Bassett. **Assistant Controller:** Jennifer Whynott. **Financial Operations Manager:** Jennifer Jeanblanc. **Payroll Manager:** Lorelei Schlitz. **Accountants:** Kylie McManus, Matt Asato. **Accounts Payable Specialist:** Sarah Talamonte. **Senior Director, Human Resources:** Deborah Johnston. **Benefits Manager:** Cecilia Schneider. **Human Resources Manager:** Mayra Castro. **Human Resources Coordinator:** Reyna Mancilla. **Senior Director, Information Services:** Al Castro. **Senior Manager Network Infrastructure:** Neil Fariss. **Technical Services Manager:** Aron Linville. **Network Administrator:** James Sheu. **Senior Customer Support Analyst:** David Yun.

CORPORATE SALES

Senior Director, Business Development: Mike Fach. **Director, Partner Services:** Bobby Kowan. **Senior Corporate Account Executive:** Drew Zinser. **Manager, Partner Services:** Andie Mitsuda. **Account Executive:** Ashley Fleck. **Account Managers, Corporate Partnerships:** Alli Serrano, Ryan Vitelli.

ENTERTAINMENT

Director, Entertainment/Production: Peter Bull. **Manager, Video Production:** Jordan Esswein. **Production Coordinator:** Cole Dragon. **Engineer:** Zac Applegate. **Marketing and Entertainment Coordinator:** Mandi Ortiz.

MARKETING

Director, Ticket Marketing and Business Analytics: Ryan Vance. **Senior Marketing Managers:** Alex Tinyo, Vanessa Vega. **Graphic Designers:** Tricia Kami, Dominic Mitrano. **Senior Broadcast and Digital Coordinator:** Hannah Stange. **Manager, Business Analytics:** JJ Evans. **Business Analyst:** Hayden Keown.

PUBLIC/MEDIA RELATIONS/COMMUNICATIONS

Telephone: (714) 940-2014.
Director, Communications: Adam Chodzko. **Managers, Communications:** Matt Birch, Grace McNamee. **Manager, Social Media/Digital Marketing:** Danny Farris. **Team Photographer:** Blaine Ohigashi. **Photography Assistant:** Ricardo Zapata.

COMMUNITY RELATIONS

Director, Corporate & Community Partnerships: Nicole Provansal. **Manager, Foundation and Community Initiatives:** Adam Cali. **Scholarship Programs and Marketing Coordinator:** Lillea Acasio.

SALES, CLIENT SERVICES & TICKETING

Senior Director, Ticket Sales: Jim Panetta. **Director, Business Development, Premium Sales & Service:** Aaron Dragomir. **Senior Director, Ticket Operations/Service:** Tom DeTemple. **Senior Manager, Ticket Operations:** Sheila Brazelton. **Ticket Operations Manager:** Armando Reyna. **Ticket Sales Manager:** David Neumann. **Client Services Manager:** Jennifer Moran. **Senior Business Development Account Manager:** Jeff Leuenberger. **Senior Account Managers, Premium Sales:** Jared Florin, Eddie Gomez. **Premium Seating Coordinator:** Shanelle Stephens. **Account Manager, Business Development:** Lisa Saldana. **Account Executives, Business Development:** Jonathan Chodzko, Christopher Young. **Senior Account Manager, Group Sales:** Phil Gurule. **Account Manager, Group Sales:** Kristen Pepperling. **Client Services Representatives:** Taylor Nestra, Abbi Newton.

BALLPARK OPERATIONS/FACILITIES

Senior Director, Ballpark Operations: Brian Sanders. **Director, Stadium Operations:** Calvin Ching. **Director, Special Events:** Courtney Wallace. **Senior Manager, Stadium Operations:** Nathan Bautista. **Manager, Stadium Operations and Security:** Carlos Campos. **Security Manager:** Mark Macias. **Security Assistant Manager:** Jacqueline Urbanus. **Special Events and Services:** Veronica Lee. **Housekeeping Manager:** Jose Padilla. **Custodial Supervisors:** Robert Iglesias, Ray Nells. **Purchasing Manager:** Suzanne Peters. **Senior Supervisor, Stadium Facilities:** Pedro Del Castillo. **Wardrobe Supervisor:** Genaro Luna. **Housekeeping and Purchasing Supervisor:** Tyler Ogawa.

TRAVEL/CLUBHOUSE

Traveling Secretary: Tom Taylor. **Director, Equipment and Clubhouse Operations:** Guy Gallagher. **Assistant Clubhouse Manager:** Shane Demmitt. **Visiting Clubhouse Manager:** Brett Crane. **Visiting Clubhouse Assistant Manager:** Aaron Wiedeman. **Manager, Video Operations:** Adam Hunt.

BASEBALL OPERATIONS

General Manager: Perry Minasian. **Assistant GM:** Alex Tamin. **Special Assistants to the GM:** Dom Chiti, Gene Watson. **Senior Advisors:** Marcel Lachemann, Bill Stoneman. **Director, Player Personnel:** Ray Montgomery. **Director, Player Procurement:** David Haynes. **Director, Baseball Operations:** Andrew Ball. **Senior Director, R&D:** Michael Lord. **Coordinator, Baseball Administration:** Peggy Berroa-Morales. **Assistant, Baseball Operations:** Nick Spar, Andrew Zenner. **Analyst, Quantitative Analysis:** Bryce Rogan. **Assistant, Quantitative Analysis:** Matt Johnson, Connor Moffatt. **Analyst, Baseball Operations:** Jared Hughes, Jake Sauberman, Matt Spring. **Baseball Systems Developer:** Sheth Neeketh, Jonathan Jagdharry.

Perry Minasian

MAJOR LEAGUE STAFF

Manager: Joe Maddon. **Coaches: Bench** — Mike Gallego, **Pitching** — Mickey Callaway, **Hitting** — Jeremy Reed, **First Base**— Bruce Hines, **Third Base** — Brian Butterfield, **Bullpen** — Matt Wise, **Assistant Hitting** — John Mallee, **Hitting Instructor**— Paul Sorrento, **Catching** — Jose Molina. **Replay** — Ryan Garko. **Director of Equipment and Clubhouse Operations:** Guy Gallagher. **Manager, Video Operations**— Adam Hunt. **Director, Mental Conditioning** — Will Lenzner.

MEDICAL/TRAINING

Team Physician: Dr. Craig Milhouse. **Team Orthopedic Physicians:** Dr. Brian Schulz, Dr. Steve Yoon, Dr. John Itamura, Dr. Carlos Uquillas. **Assistant Director, Performance Integration:** Kenneth Smale. **Head Athletic Trainer:** Adam Nevala. **Assistant Athletic Trainer:** Eric Munson, **Athletic Training Services Coordinator:** Rick Smith. **Strength/Conditioning Coach:** Lee Fiocchi. **Assistant Strength and Conditioning:** Adam Auer. **Quality Assurance:** Tim Buss. **Massage Therapist:** Yoichi Terada. **Registered Dietician:** Rebecca Twombley.

PLAYER DEVELOPMENT

Special Assistant, Player Development: Joey Prebynski. **Coordinator, Minor League Operations:** Chris Mosch. **Assistant, Minor League Operations:** Andrea La Pointe. **Field Coordinator:** Chad Tracy. **Manager, Minor League Equipment:** Louie Raya. **Video Coordinator:** Ryan Dundee. **Roving Instructors:** Damon Mashore (Hitting), Ryan Parker (Coordinator Hitting Analysis), Buddy Carlyle (Pitching), Dylan Axelrod (Assistant Pitching), Bill Lachemann (Special Assignment, Catching Instructor), Ryan Barba (Assistant Field Coordinator), Chris Constantine (Outfield/Baserunning), Hainley Statia (Infield), Kernan Ronan (Rehab Coach), Geoff Hostetter (Medical Coordinator), Danny Escobar (Strength & Conditioning Coordinator), Humberto Miranda (Latin America Field Coordinator), Michael Noboa (Latin America Operations Coordinator), Fausto Betances (Coordinator, DR Academy Administration), and Fabio Fermin (Assistant, DR Academy Administration).

FARM SYSTEM

Class	Club	Manager	Hitting Coach	Pitching Coach
Triple-A	Salt Lake	Lou Marson	Brian Betancourth	Jairo Cuevas
Double-A	Rocket City	Jay Bell	Kenny Hook	Michael Wuertz
High A	Tri-Cities	Jack Santora	William Bradley	TBD
Low A	Inland Empire	Andy Schatzley	Ryan Sebra	TBD
Rookie	Angels (AZL)	Jack Howell	Tyler Jeske	B.Martino/B.Baumann
Rookie	Angels (DSL)	Hector De La Cruz	R. Gomez/A. De Los Santos	J.Marte/E.Gonzalez

SCOUTING

Director, Pro Scouting: Nate Horowitz. **Coordinator, Pro and International Scouting:** Nick Lampe. **Major League/Special Assignment Scout:** Ric Wilson. **Professional Scouts:** Jeff Cirillo, Nick McCoy, Jim Miller, Jayson Nix, Andrew Schmidt, Bobby Williams, Rick Williams, Ben Francisco. **Director, Amateur Scouting:** Matt Swanson. Coordinator, **Amateur Scouting:** Aidan Donovan. **National Crosscheckers:** Jeremy Schied, Jason Smith, Steffan Wilson. **Regional Supervisors:** Jason Baker, Jayson Durocher, Nick Gorneault, Brandon McArthur, Scott Richardson. **Hitting Crosschecker:** Jason Ellison. **Area Scouts:** John Burden, Ben Diggins, Drew Dominguez, Brian Gordon, Chris McAlpin, Joel Murrie. **Senior Director, International Scouting:** Brian Parker. **Director, International Scouting:** Carlos Gomez. **Asst. Director, International Scouting:** Giovanni Hernandez, Brian Cruz. **Administrator, International Scouting:** Grace Mercedes. **International Scouting Supervisor:** Marlon Urdaneta. **International Scouts:** Jochy Cabrera, Rusbell Cabrera, Joel Chicarelli, Domingo Garcia, Ender Gonzalez, Raul Gonzalez, Aneudi Mercado, Rubylin Nicasia, Francisco Tejeda.

LOS ANGELES DODGERS

Office Address: 1000 Vin Scully Ave., Los Angeles, CA 90012.
Telephone: (323) 224-1500. Fax: (323) 224-1269. **Website:** www.dodgers.com.

OWNERSHIP/EXECUTIVE OFFICE

Chairman: Mark Walter. **Partners:** Earvin 'Magic' Johnson, Peter Guber, Todd Boehly, Robert 'Bobby' Patton, Jr, Billie Jean King, Ilana Kloss, Robert L. Plummer, Alan Smolinisky. **President/CEO:** Stan Kasten.

BUSINESS OPERATIONS

Mark Walter

EMMA MCINTYRE/GETTY IMAGES

Executive Vice President/COO: Bob Wolfe. **Executive VP/Chief Marketing Officer:** Lon Rosen. **President, Dodgers Business Enterprise:** Tucker Kain. **Executive VP/General Counsel:** Sam Fernandez. **Executive VP, Planning/ Development:** Janet Marie Smith. **Senior VP, Marketing, Communications and Broadcaster:** Erik Braverman. **Senior VP, Ticket and Premium Sales & Service:** Antonio Morici. **Senior VP, Stadium Operations:** Joe Crowley. **VP, Security/ Guest Services:** Shahram Ariane.

FINANCE AND BUSINESS ANALYTICS

VP, Finance: Eric Hernandez. **Senior Director, Financial Planning/Analysis:** Gregory Buonaccorsi. **Controller:** Sara Curran. **Director, Purchasing:** Lisa McShane. **VP, Business Development & Analytics:** Royce Cohen. **Director, Business Analytics:** Michael Spetner.

GLOBAL PARTNERSHIPS

VP, Global Partnerships: Corey Norkin. **Senior Director, Global Partnership Administration & Services:** Jenny Oh. **Senior Director, Marketing Solutions:** Matt Grable. **Director, Global Partnership Services:** Corey Schimmel.

MARKETING/BROADCASTING AND COMMUNICATIONS

Senior VP, Marketing/Broadcasting Communications: Erik Braverman. **Vice President, Digital Strategy:** Caroline Morgan. **Senior Director, Public Relations:** Joe Jareck. **Executive Producer, Production:** Greg Taylor. **Senior Director, Graphic Design:** Ross Yoshida. **Senior Director, Broadcast Engineering:** Tom Darin.

HUMAN RESOURCES/LEGAL

VP, Human Resources: Marilyn Davis. **Senior Director, Human Resources:** Leonor Romero. **Associate General Counsel:** Chad Gunderson. **Associate General Counsel:** Daniel Martens.

LOS ANGELES DODGERS FOUNDATION AND COMMUNITY AFFAIRS

Chief Executive Officer, Los Angeles Dodgers Foundation: Nichol Whiteman. **VP, External Affairs/Community Relations:** Naomi Rodriguez. **COO, Los Angeles Dodgers Foundation:** Chaitali Gala Mehta.

TICKETING

Telephone: (323) 224-1471. **Fax:** (323) 224-2609.
VP, Ticket Operations: Seth Bluman. **VP, Premium Sales & Services:** Craig Sindici.

BASEBALL OPERATIONS

Telephone: (323) 224-1500. **Fax:** (323) 224-1463.
President: Andrew Friedman. **Senior Vice President:** Josh Byrnes. **Vice President &
Assistant General Manager:** Jeffrey Kingston. **Vice President & Assistant General Manager:**
Brandon Gomes. **Vice Presidents:** Dave Finley (Scouting), Galen Carr (Player Personnel), Ismael
Cruz (International Scouting), Billy Gasparino (Amateur Scouting). **Senior Directors:** Ellen
Harrigan (Baseball Administration), Scott Akasaki (Team Travel). **Directors:** Alex Slater (Baseball
Operations), Duncan Webb (Baseball Resources), Scott Powers (Quantitative Analysis), Megan
Schroeder (Performance Science), Eric Potterat (Specialized Performance Programs), John
Focht (Baseball Systems Applications), Brian McBurney (Baseball Systems Platform). **Senior
Advisors & Special Assistants:** Thomas Allison, Pat Corrales, Joel Peralta, Ron Roenicke, Chase
Utley, Jose Vizcaino.

Andrew
Friedman

MAJOR LEAGUE STAFF

Manager: Dave Roberts. **Coaches:** Bob Geren (Bench), Mark Prior (Pitching), Robert Van
Scoyoc & Brant Brown (Hitting), Clayton McCullough (First Base), Dino Ebel (Third Base), Josh Bard (Bullpen), Aaron
Bates (Assistant Hitting), Connor McGuiness (Assistant Pitching). **Coordinator, Game Planning/Communications
Coach:** Danny Lehmann. **Bullpen Catcher:** Steve Cilladi. **Director, Player Health:** Ron Porterfield. **Head Athletic
Trainer:** Neil Rampe. **Director, Player Performance:** Brandon McDaniel. **Director, Clubhouse Operations:** Alex
Torres. **Strength & Conditioning Coach:** Travis Smith. **Sports Scientist:** Kate Weiss. **Physical Therapist:** Johnathan
Erb. **Manager, Performance Nutrition:** Tyrone Hall. **Head Team Physician:** Dr. Neal ElAttrache. **Coordinator, Medical
Administrator and Billing:** Andy Otovic. **Assistant Athletic Trainers:** Yosuke Nakajima, Thomas Albert, Andrew
Hauser.

PLAYER DEVELOPMENT

Telephone: (323) 224-1500. **Fax:** (323) 224-1359.
Director, Player Development: Will Rhymes. **Assistant Director, Player Development:** Matt McGrath. **Assistant
Director, Minor League Operations:** Joe Harrington. **Manager, Minor League Administration:** Adriana Urzua.
Manager, Arizona Operations: Matt Peabody. **Field Coordinator:** Shaun Larkin. **Coordinators:** Don Alexander
(Pitching, Logistics), Gabe Ribas (Pitching, Performance), Rob Hill (Pitching, Technical Development), Brent Minta
(Pitching, Analytics), Ryan Sienko (Catching), Chris Antariksa (Hitting), Louis Iannotti (Hitting, Analytics), Bill Haselman
(Managers), Mark Kertenian (Strategy and Communication), Chris Gimenez (Game Planning), Brian Stoneberg (Strength
& Conditioning) AJ LaLonde (Strong Mind), Leo Ruiz (Strong Mind), Charles Wagner (Video), Cole Finnegan (Assistant
Video), Victor Scarpone (Medical), Brian Stoneberg (Performance), Colt Hynes (Rehab Pitching). **Special Assistants:**
Bobby Cuellar, Charlie Hough, Placido Polanco, Dontrelle Willis. **Minor League Equipment Manager:** Troy Timney.
Assistant, Minor League Equipment: Steve Morvacek. **Assistants, Player Development:** James Weilbrenner, Mac Lozer.

CAMPO LOS PALMAS

Sr. Facility Manager: Jesus Negrette. **Manager:** Marian Vasquez. **Latin American Field Coordinator:** Keyter
Collado. **Latin American Pitching Coordinator:** Luis Meza. **Latin American Defensive Coordinator:** Pedro Mega.
Latin American Medical Coordinator: Jorge Gonzalez. **Latin American S&C Coordinator:** Carl Kochan.

CAMELBACK RANCH

Manager, Arizona Operations: Matt Peabody. **Minor League Equipment Manager:** Troy Timney.

FARM SYSTEM

Class	Club (League)	Manager	Hitting Coach	Pitching Coach
Triple-A	Oklahoma City (PCL)	Travis Barbary	Manny Burriss	Jamey Wright
Double-A	Tulsa (TL)	Scott Hennessey	Brett Pill	Dave Borkowski
High A	Great Lakes (MWL)	Austin Chubb	David Popkins	Ryan Dennick
Low A	Rancho Cucamonga (CAL)	John Shoemaker	Dylan Nasiatka	S. Stroop/R. Trancoso
Rookie	Dodgers (AZL)	Danny Dorn	Beauregard/Cunningham	Cuellar/Anderson
Rookie	Dodgers (DSL)	TBA	TBA	TBA

SCOUTING

VP, Amateur/International Scouting: David Finley. **VP, Director, Amateur Scouting:** Billy Gasparino. **Assistant
Director, Amateur Scouting:** Zach Fitzpatrick. **Scouting Coordinator, Amateur Scouting:** Logan Crook. **Athleticism
Development Coordinator:** Tyler Norton. **Global Crosschecker:** John Green. **National Crosscheckers:** Brian
Stephenson, Rob St. Julien. **Pitching Consultant, Amateur Scouting:** Jack Cressend. **Advisor, Amateur Scouting:** Gary
Nickels. **Crosscheckers: Midwest**—Stephen Head, **Southwest**—Brian Kraft, **Northeast**—Jon Adkins, **Southeast**—Alan
Matthews, **West Coast**—Paul Cogan. **Area Scouts:** John Pyle, Paul Murphy, Jonah Rosenthal, Garrett Ball, Wes Sargent,
Kelvin Colon, Luis Faccio, Benny Latino, Marty Lamb, Clint Bowers, Heath Holliday, Mitch Schulewitz, Brian Compton,
Brent Mayne, Dennis Moeller, Jeff Stevens, Tom Kunis. **VP, Player Personnel:** Galen Carr. **Coordinator, Pro Scouting:**
Luke Geoghegan. **Special Assistant to Pro Scouting:** Jeff McAvoy. **Special Assignment Scouts:** Vance Lovelace, Matt
Smith. **Professional Scouts:** Tydus Meadows, Scott Groot, Peter Bergeron, Jason Lynn, Franco Frias, Lee Tackett, Phil
Stringer, Jack Murphy, Greg Golson, John Pratt. Advisor, **Pacific Rim:** Yogo Suzuki.

MIAMI MARLINS

Office Address: Marlins Park, 501 Marlins Way, Miami, FL 33125
Telephone: (305) 480-1300. **Fax:** (305) 480-3012.
Website: www.marlins.com.

OWNERSHIP
Chairman & Principal Owner: Bruce Sherman.

BUSINESS OPERATIONS
Chief Executive Officer: Derek Jeter. **General Manager:** Kim Ng. **Chief Revenue Officer:** Adam Jones. **Chief Operating Officer:** Caroline O'Connor.

ADMINISTRATIVE SERVICES
Executive Assistant to CEO: Nicolette Lawrence. **Executive Assistant, Business Operations:** Kristen Keane. **Executive Assistant:** Ivette Rosado.

FINANCE
Executive Vice President & Chief Financial Officer: Michel Bussiere. **Vice President, Accounting & Financial Planning:** Fred Koczwara. **Senior Director, Financial Panning and Accounting:** Michael Mullane. **Administrator, Payroll:** Carolina Calderon. **Assistant Payroll Administrator:** Edgar Perez. **Senior Financial Analyst:** Veronica Vega. **Senior Associate, Finance:** Claudia Avila. **Supervisor, Accounts Payable:** Anthony Paneque. **Coordinator, Finance:** Felix Anderson.

Derek Jeter

MARKETING
Director, Events/Promotions: Juan Martinez. **Manager, Digital Marketing:** Karry Pomes. **Manager, Marketing:** Mariah Monahan. **Senior Associate, Fan Programs:** Jessica Lee.

LEGAL & RISK MANAGEMENT
Vice President and General Counsel: Ashwin Krishnan. **Associate General Counsel:** Stephanie Galvin. **Director, Risk Management:** Fred Espinosa.

SALES/TICKETING
Vice President, Sales & Service: Andre Luck. **Director, Membership Sales:** Evans Adonis. **Director, Premium Sales & Service:** Ryan Sember. **Senior Premium Sales Executive:** Chema Sanchez. **Premium Sales Executives:** Brandon Grengs, Aaron Pedigo. **Membership Sales Executive:** Isaac Paladino, Christian Jablonski, Jennifer Owston. **Director, Membership Experience:** Brian Jemison. **Manager, Membership Experience:** Jason Liss. **Membership Experience Executives:** Eric Sutcliffe, Lenny Valdez, Timothy Jenkins. **Director, Group Sales & Service:** Kyle Brant. **Senior Group Sales & Service Executive:** Shoshana Baker-Bradley. **Group Sales & Service Executive:** Antonio Diz, Brad Johnson, Grant Mayfield, Ernesto Penton, Brad Johnson.

COMMUNICATIONS/MEDIA RELATIONS
VP, Communications & Broadcasting: Jason Latimer. **Assistant Director, Communications:** Jon Erik Alvarez. **Senior Associate, Social Media:** Sarah Penalver. **Player Relations & Spanish Media Liaison:** Luis Dorante. **Coordinator, Media Relations:** Daniel Kurish. **Broadcasters, Radio:** Dave Van Horne, Glenn Geffner. **Manager, Broadcasting:** Kyle Sielaff.

TRAVEL/CLUBHOUSE
Director, Team Travel: Manny Colon. **Equipment Manager:** John Silverman. **Visiting Clubhouse Manager:** Rock Hughes. **Assistant Clubhouse Manager:** Michael Diaz.

BASEBALL OPERATIONS

Telephone: (305) 480-1300. **Fax:** (305) 480-3032.

Assistant General Managers: Brian Chattin, Daniel Greenlee. **Director of Baseball Operations:** Adrian Lorenzo. **Director, Team Travel:** Max Thomas. **Assistant Director, Baseball Operations:** Joseph Nero. **Director, International Operations:** Fernando Seguignol. **Director, Amateur Scouting:** DJ Svihlik.

Kim Ng

JON SOOHOO/LA DODGERS

MAJOR LEAGUE STAFF

Manager: Don Mattingly. **Pitching Coach:** Mel Stottlemyre Jr. **Hitting Coach:** Eric Duncan. **Assistant Hitting Coach:** Robert Rodriguez. **Bench Coach:** James Rowson. **First Base Coach:** Keith Johnson. **Third Base Coach:** Trey Hillman. **Bullpen Coordinator:** Robert Flippo. **Bullpen Coach:** Wellington Cepeda. **Catching Coach:** Eddy Rodriguez. **Bullpen Catcher:** Koji Tanaka.

MEDICAL/TRAINING

Medical Director: Dr. Lee Kaplan. **Head Athletic Trainer:** Gene Basham. **Strength and Conditioning Coach:** Lee Tressel. **Equipment Manager:** John Silverman. **Visting Clubhouse Manager:** Rock Hughes. **Asssistant Home Clubhouse Manager:** Michael Diaz.

PLAYER DEVELOPMENT

Vice President, Player Development and Scouting: Gary Denbo. **Director, Amateur Scouting:** DJ Svihlik. **Director, Pro Scouting:** Hadi Raad. **Director, International Scouting:** Fernando Seguignol. **Director, Minor League Operations:** Geoffrey DeGroot. **Assistant Director, Player Development:** Hector Crespo. **Manager, Baseball Operations:** Jordan Jackson. **Manager, Pro Scouting:** Alexandria Rigoli. **Manager, International Scouting:** Jacob Jola. **Manager, Amateur Scouting:** Joshua Kapiloff. **Manager, Player Development:** Danny M. Henriquez. **Amateur Scouting Analyst:** Justin Brands. **Video Coordinators:** Julio Jauregui, Victor Martinez.

FARM SYSTEM

Class	Club (League)	Manager	Hitting Coach	Pitching Coach
Triple-A	Jacksonville	Al Pedrique	Phil Plantier	Jeremy Powell
Double-A	Pensacola	Kevin Randel	Scott Seabol	Tim Norton
High-A	Beloit	Mike Jacobs	Matt Snyder	Bruce Walton
Low-A	Jupiter	Jorge Hernandez	Ty Hawkins	Jason Erickson
Rookie	Marlins (GCL)	Luis Dorante	Jesus Merchan	Justin Pope
Rookie	Marlins (DSL)	Rigo Silverio	Esmerling De La Rosa	Nelson Prada/Emilio Linares

SCOUTING

Director, Amateur Scouting: DJ Svihlik. **Manager, Amateur Scouting:** Josh Kapiloff. **Special Assistant, Amateur Scouting:** Marti Wolever. **National Crosschecker:** Eric Valent. **Special Assignment Scout:** T.R. Lewis. **West Supervisor:** Scott Goldby. **Central Supervisor:** Ryan Wardinsky. **South Supervisor:** Carmen Carcone. **East Supervisor:** Mike Soper. **Area Scouts:** Eric Brock, Tim McDonnell, Scott Stanley, Scott Fairbanks, Joe Dunigan, Chris Joblin, Shaeffer Hall, James Vilade, Brett Bittiger, JT Zink, Blake Newsome, Hank LaRue, Alex Smith. **Director, Professional Scouting:** Hadi Raad. **Manager, Professional Scouting:** Alexandria Rigoli. **Special Assignment Scouts:** Joe Caro, Bill Masse. **Professional Scouts:** Johnny Almaraz, Jose Almonte, Jared Barnes, John Eshleman, Jim Howard, Jalal Leach, Joe Lisewski, Carlos Lugo, Alexander Noel, Adrian Puig, Alvin Rittman, Clint Robinson, Phil Rossi, Tony Russo, Brian Sikorski. **Part-Time Scouts:** Michael Kotler, Paul Ricciarini. **Director, International Scouting:** Fernando Seguignol. **Manager, International Scouting:** Jacob Jola. **Special Assignment Scout, International Operations:** Rich Arena. **Administrator, Venezuela:** Clifford Nuitter. **Scouts, Dominican Republic:** Domingo Ortega, Angel Izquierdo, Sahir Fersobe. **Scouts, Venezuela:** Tibaldo Hernandez, Nestor Moreno. **Scout, Mexico:** Andres Guzman. **Manager, Dominican Operations:** Ismael Granadillo. **Video Coordinator, Dominican Republic:** Shamir Arias.

MILWAUKEE BREWERS

Office Address: American Family Field, One Brewers Way, Milwaukee, WI 53214.
Telephone: (414) 902-4400. **Fax:** (414) 902-4053. **Website:** www.brewers.com.

OWNERSHIP

Operated By: Milwaukee Brewers Baseball Club.
Chairman/Principal Owner: Mark Attanasio.

BUSINESS OPERATIONS

President, Business Operations: Rick Schlesinger. **Senior Vice President, Communications & Affiliate Operations:** Tyler Barnes. **Senior Vice President, Stadium Operations:** Steve Ethier. **Chief Financial Officer:** Daniel Fumai. **Chief Revenue Officer:** Jason Hartlund. **Senior Vice President, Brand Experience:** Teddy Werner. **General Counsel & Senior Vice President, Administration:** Marti Wronski. **Executive Assistant, Ownership Group:** Samantha Ernest. **Executive Assistant, General Manager:** Nichole Kinateder. **Executive Assistant, Paralegal:** Kate Rock. **Executive Assistant, Revenue:** Lisa Brzeski. **Executive Assistant:** Adela Reeve. **Executive Assistant:** Kate Stempski.

FINANCE/ACCOUNTING

VP, Finance/Accounting: Jamie Norton. **Accounting Director:** Vicki Wise. **Disbursements Director:** Erica Umbach. **Senior Payroll Administrator:** Corrine Wolff. **Senior Financial Analysts:** Cory Loppnow, Mike Anheuser. **Financial Analysts:** Kristin Hahn, Pat Fennell. **Payroll Administrator:** Katie Danowski. **Senior Accounts Payable Specialist:** Taikana Bentley. **Workday Systems Analyst:** Tara Ali. **Consultant:** Bob Quinn.

HUMAN RESOURCES

VP, Human Resources: Cas Castro. **Director, Human Resources, Diversity, Equity & Inclusion:** Brenda Best. **Human Resources Business Partners:** Heather Schreiner, Kristin Rutter, Kelly Rosenquist. **Human Resources Administrator:** Genevieve Hayes.

MARKETING

VP, Marketing: Sharon McNally. **Art Director:** Jeff Harding. **Director, Digital Marketing:** Becky Imig. **Cinematographer:** Matt Gompper. **Productions Manager:** Caitlin Walter. **Manager, Content Marketing:** Ezra Siegel. **Manager, Social Media:** Bradly Ford. **Motions, Graphics Designer:** Steven Armendariz. **Graphic Designer:** Alex Pera. **Videographer:** Collin Schroeder. **Editor:** Cody Oasen. **Senior Coordinator, Marketing:** Gina Moretti. **Marketing Administrator:** Brittany Luznicky.

FAN EXPERIENCE

Executive Producer, Entertainment & Event Production: Taylor Goldman. **Director, Audio/Video Production:** Deron Anderson. **Manager, Entertainment & Event Production:** Hannah Creighton. **Coordinators, Entertainment:** Amanda Beierle, Zak Nye.

BUSINESS STRATEGY

VP, Business Analytics & Strategic Support: Sam Mahjub. **Senior Manager, Data Science:** Mike Dairyko. **Senior Coordinator, Business Intelligence Systems:** Danny Henken. **Analyst. Strategy & Analytics:** Evan Alvarez.

MEDIA RELATIONS/PUBLICATIONS

Senior Director, Media Relations: Mike Vassallo. **Director, Broadcasting & Publications:** Ken Spindler. **Director, Business Communications:** Leslie Stachowiak. **Senior Coordinator, Media Relations:** Andrew Gruman.

MILLER PARK OPERATIONS

Senior Director, Security: Randy Olewinski. **Senior Director, Event Services:** Matt Lehmann. **Senior Director, Facility Services:** Mike Brockman. **Director, Grounds:** Ryan Woodley. **Senior Manager, Event Services:** Scott Quade. **Manager, Guest Services:** Jonelle Johnson. **Manager, Grounds:** Zak Peterson. **Manager, Fields:** Tom Henke. **Manager, Warehouse:** John Weyer. **Lead, Fields:** Corey Lake, Tyler Tschetter. **Lead, Game & Event:** Josiah Spindler.

TICKET SALES

Telephone: (414) 902-4000. **Fax:** (414) 902-4056.
VP, Ticket Sales: Jim Bathey. **Sr. Director, Ticket Sales:** Billy Friess. **Sr. Director, Ticket Services & Technology:** Jess Brown. **Director, Group Sales:** Chris Kimball. **Senior Manager, Inside Sales:** Dan Winkelman. **Senior Manager, Ticket Operations:** Eric Laue. **Senior Manager, Ticket Services:** Christine Verbos. **Manager, Group Sales & Service:** Jake Mentch. **Manager, Season and Group Events:** Nicolette Finocchiaro. **Manager, Ticket Partnerships:** Connor Gorrell. **Manager, Ticket Operations:** Jerod Schultz. **Manager, Ticket Services:** Nancy Jorgensen. **Senior Account Executives, Client Services:** Hannah Bumgardner, Jason Fry, Nate Hardwick, Jeff Hibicke, Kara Kabitzke, Jason Massopust. **Senior Account Executive, Group Sales:** Zak Thomas. **Senior Account Executive, New Business Development:** Zack Nauert. **Senior Account Executive, Ticket Sales:** Bill Junker. **Account Executive, Client Services:** Steve Rosenthal. **Account Executive, Group Sales:** Ryan Blaire. **Sales Representatives, Ticket Sales:** Shannon Gibney, Emily Gutzmann, Christian Niewinski, Teddy Sibilsky, April Trewyn, Brennan Uribe. **Coordinator, Ticket Operations:** Marissa Milano. **Coordinator, Ticket Services:** Ryan Cameron. **Ticket Operations Specialists:** Tom Librizzi, John Schmid. **Ticket Services Specialist:** Adam Gruett.

Mark Attanasio

BASEBALL OPERATIONS

Telephone: (414) 902-4400. **Fax:** (414) 902-4515.

President, Baseball Operations: David Stearns. **SVP/GM:** Matt Arnold. **Special Asst., President of Baseball Operations:** Doug Melvin. **VP, Baseball Projects:** Gord Ash. **SVP, Player Personnel:** Karl Mueller. **Special Asst. to GM, Player Development:** Carlos Villanueva. **Special Asst., GM/Pro Scouting/Player Personnel:** Dick Groch. **VP, Baseball Operations:** Matt Kleine. **Director, Baseball Systems:** Will Hudgins. **Director, Baseball R&D:** Dan Turkenkopf. **Asst. Director, Baseball R&D:** Andrew Fox. **Asst., Major League Video/Spanish Translator:** Carlos Brizuela. **Special Asst., Baseball Research and Development:** Nick Davis. **Special Assignment Scout:** Scott Campbell. **Manager, Video Operations:** Matt Kerls. **Sr. Analyst, Baseball R&D:** Ethan Bein. **Analyst, Baseball R&D:** Dan Kutner. **Associate Analyst, Baseball R&D:** Kunal Singh. **Data Architect:** Matt Culhane. **Sr. Data Engineer:** Phil Hauser. **Data Engineers:** Neil Nachnani, Joshua Schaffer. **Sr. Developer, Baseball Systems:** Andy Acosta. **Developers, Baseball Systems:** DJ Michalski, Dan Yang. **Coordinator, Player Personnel:** Ben Harris. **Coordinators, Baseball Operations:** Eric Babitz, Kevin Ottsen. **Coordinator, Major League Video and Technology:** August Sandri. **Coordinator, Minor League Video Operations:** Zack Sorensen. **Development Scouts:** Davis Knapp, Kevin O'Sullivan.

David Stearns

MAJOR LEAGUE STAFF

Manager: Craig Counsell. **Coaches: Bench**—Pat Murphy, **Pitching**—Chris Hook, **Hitting**—Andy Haines, **First Base**—Quintin Berry, **Third Base**—Jason Lane, **Bullpen**—Steve Karsay. **Asst. Hitting Coach:** Jacob Cruz. **Bullpen Catchers:** Nestor Corredor, Adam Weisenburger. **Associate Pitching, Catching and Strategy Coach:** Walker McKinven. **Advisor to the Major League Coaching Staff:** Ed Sedar.

MEDICAL/TRAINING

Vice President, Medical Operations, Health and Safety: Roger Caplinger. **Head Team Physician:** Dr. William Raasch. **Team Physicians:** Dr. Mark Niedfeldt, Dr. Craig Young. **Director, Player Health:** Blair Bundy. **Director, Psychological Services:** Matt Krug. **Head Athletic Trainer:** Scott Barringer. **Asst. Athletic Trainer:** Dave Yeager. **Asst. Athletic Trainer/Physical Therapist:** Theresa Lau. **S&C Specialist:** Josh Seligman. **Asst. Strength and Conditioning Specialist/Performance Strategist:** Jason Meredith. **Rehabilitation Strength and Conditioning Specialist:** Tim Gifford. **Rehabilitation Coach:** Scott Schneider. **Asst. Director, Psychological Services:** Blake Pindyck. **Consulting Orthopedic Physician, Phoenix:** Dr. Evan Lederman. **Consulting Team Physician, Phoenix:** Dr. Carlton Richie.

PLAYER DEVELOPMENT

Vice President, Minor League Operations: Tom Flanagan. **Sr. Director, Minor League and Player Operations:** Eduardo Brizuela. **Director, Player Development Initiatives:** Jake McKinley. **Director, Player Performance:** Bryson Nakamura. **Asst. Director, Player Development Initiatives:** August Fagerstrom. **Sr. Manager, Baseball Administration:** Mark Mueller. **Minor League Clubhouse Manager:** Travis Voss. **Special Asst., Baseball Operations/Player Development:** Quinton McCracken. **Coordinator, Baseball Diversity Initiatives:** Junior Spivey. **Coordinator, Hitting Development Initiatives:** Sara Goodrum. **Field Coordinator & Catching Instructor:** Charlie Greene. **Infield Coordinator:** Bob Miscik. **Pitching Coordinator:** Cam Castro. **Asst. Hitting Coordinator, Arizona Operations:** Brenton Del Chiaro. **Asst. Pitching Coordinator:** Bryan Leslie. **Asst. Hitting Coordinator, Training Strategy:** Jordan Getzelman. **Coordinator, Minor League Medical:** Nick Jensen. **Coordinator, Minor League Medical Administration:** Frank Neville. **Analyst, Innovation/Integrative Sports Performance:** Robert Hulbert. **Asst. Innovation/Integrative Sports Performance:** Eric Crispell. **Minor League S&C Coordinator:** Ben Mendelson. **Coordinator, Education:** Adela Marquez. **Coordinator, Latin America Operations:** Manuel Vargas.

FARM SYSTEM

Class	Club (League)	Manager	Hitting Coach	Pitching Coach
Triple-A	Nashville	Rick Sweet	Al LeBoeuf	Jim Henderson
Double-A	Biloxi	Mike Guerrero	Chuckie Caufield	Nick Childs
High A	Wisconsin	Matt Erickson	Nick Stanley	Hiram Burgos
Low A	Carolina	Joe Ayrault	Bobby Spain	Fred Dabney
Rookie	Brewers Blue (AZL)	Rafael Neda	Brenton Del Chiaro	Carson Cross
Rookie	Brewers Gold (AZL)	David Tufo	TBD	TBD
Rookie	Brewers (DSL)	Victor Estevez	Luis De Los Santos	Jesus Hernandez
Rookie	Brewers/Blue Jays (DSL)	Fidel Pena	Mike Habas	TBD

SCOUTING

Vice President, Domestic Scouting: Tod Johnson. **VP, International Scouting & Player Personnel:** Mike Groopman. **Special Assignment Scout:** Scott Campbell. **Asst. Director, Domestic Scouting:** Tim McIlvaine. **Manager, Advance Scouting:** Brian Powalish. **Coordinator, Domestic and International Scouting Operations:** Oscar Garcia. **Coordinator, Scouting Operations:** Adam Hayes. **Asst. Director, Scouting:** Bryan Gale. **Asst. Director, International Scouting:** Luis Pérez. **Asst. Director, Scouting/International Player Development:** Taylor Green. **Pro Scouting Crosschecker:** Mike Berger. **Pro Scout:** Lary Aaron. **National Supervisor, Scouting:** Doug Reynolds. **Supervisor, Scout Teams/West Coast Special Assignment Scout:** Corey Rodriguez. **Regional Supervisors, Scouting:** Drew Anderson, Josh Belovsky, Dan Nellum, Mike Serbalik. **Area Scouts:** Ty Blankmeyer, Bryan Bullington, Mike Burns, Daniel Cho, Pete Orr, James Fisher, Taylor Frederick, Joe Graham, KJ Hendricks, Lazaro Llanes, Mark Muzzi, Scott Nichols, Wynn Pelzer, Jeff Simpson, Craig Smajstrla, Riley Bandelow, Steve Smith, Pete Vuckovich Jr., Shawn Whalen. **International Crosschecker/Venezuelan Operations:** Fernando Veracierto. **Supervisor:** Rodolfo Rosario. **Coordinators:** Gary Peralta, José Rodriguez. **Regional Crosschecker:** Esteban Castillo. **Scouts:** Trino Aguilar, Salvador Ayestas, José Barraza, Javier Castillo, Julio de la Cruz, Diego Flores, Kenji Galavis, Jesús Garces, Teofilo Gutierrez, Jonas Lantigua, Fabian Mendez, Mario Mendoza, Javier Meza, José Morales, Kevin Ramos, Jean Carlos Reynoso, Pedro Robles, Luis Rosario.

MINNESOTA TWINS

Office Address: Target Field, 1 Twins Way, Minneapolis, MN 55403.
Telephone: (612) 659-3400. **Fax:** 612-659-4025. **Website:** www. twinsbaseball.com.

OWNERSHIP
Operated By: The Minnesota Twins. **Executive Chair:** Jim Pohlad. **Executive Board:** Jim Pohlad, Bob Pohlad, Bill Pohlad, Dave St. Peter.

BUSINESS OPERATIONS
President/Chief Executive Officer, Minnesota Twins: Dave St. Peter. **Executive Vice President/Chief Business Officer, Business Development:** Laura Day. **Executive VP/Chief Administrative Officer/CFO:** Kip Elliott. **Senior Director, Ballpark Development/Planning:** Dan Starkey.

HUMAN RESOURCES/FINANCE/TECHNOLOGY
Sr. Vice President, Human Resources: Leticia Silva. **Sr. Director, Compensation/Benefits:** Lori Beasley. **Human Resources Generalist:** Holly Corbin. **Administrator, Payroll/HRIS:** Molly Partyka. **Specialist/Recruiter, Human Resources:** Atessa Majd. **Benefits Specialist:** Kate Rollwagen.

MARKETING
Jim Pohlad

Senior Director, Brand Experience and Innovation: Chris Iles. **Vice President, Brand Marketing:** Heather Hinkel. **Creative Director:** Kevin Hughes. **Director, Game Day Experience:** Sam Henschen. **Manager, Digital Content:** Brea Hinegardner. **Manager,Video:** Jim Diehl. **Senior Manager, Special Events/Promotions:** Mitch Retelny. **Manager, Procurement:** Beth Vail Palm.

CORPORATE PARTNERSHIPS
Senior Director, Brand Partnerships: Ryan Gorman. **Senior Managers, Corporate Partnerships:** Doug Beck, Chad Jackson. **Director, Partnership Strategy/Development**: Jordan Woodcroft. **Senior Manager, Radio Partnerships/Administration**: Amy Johnson. **Account Managers, Partnerships/Activation:** Hannah Hilbert, Joe Morin, Kevin Nelson, Alexa Torborg.

COMMUNICATIONS
Telephone: (612) 659-3471. **Fax:** (612) 659-4029.
Senior Director, Communications: Dustin Morse. **Senior Manager, Baseball Communications:** Mitch Hestad. **Senior Manager, Business Communications:** Matt Hodson. **Assistant, Communications:** Nina Zimmerman. **Senior Photographer, Baseball Content:** Brace Hemmelgarn. **Coordinator, Communications/Interpreter:** Elvis Martinez. **Team Curator:** Clyde Doepner.

COMMUNITY RELATIONS
Vice President, Community Engagement: Nancy O'Brien. **Director, Community Relations:** Kristen Rortvedt. **Executive Director, Twins Community Fund:** Stephanie Johnson. **Senior Manager, Community Engagement/Events:** Julie Vavruska. **Senior Manager, Community Relations and Youth Engagement:** Josh Ortiz. **Manager, Community Relations, Community Relations:** Sondra Ciesielski. **Senior Coordinator, Community Relations:** Chelsey Falzone. **Mascot Supervisor:** Blair Kelly. **Mascot Assistant:** Wyatt Fitzsimmons.

TICKETING/EVENTS
Telephone: 1-800-33-TWINS. **Vice President, Ticket Operations:** Paul Froehle. **Senior Director, Box Office:** Mike Stiles. **Senior Manager, Ticket Operations:** Ashley Geldert.

BALLPARK OPERATIONS
Senior Vice President, Operations: Matt Hoy. **Vice President, Ballpark Operations:** Dave Horsman. **Senior Director, Facilities:** Gary Glawe. **Senior Director, Guest Experience:** Patrick Forsland. **Senior Director, Security:** Jeff Beahen. **Director, Guest Services:** Katie Rock. **Head Groundskeeper:** Larry DiVito.

BASEBALL OPERATIONS

President, Baseball Operations: Derek Falvey. **Senior VP/General Manager:** Thad Levine. **VP, Player Personnel:** Mike Radcliff. **VP/Assistant GM:** Rob Antony. **Director, Baseball Administration:** Kate Townley. **Assistant GM:** Daniel Adler. **Assistant GM:** Jeremy Zoll. **Assistant Director, Baseball Operations:** Nick Beauchamp. **Director, Pro Player Procurement:** Brad Steil. **Special Assistants:** Michael Cuddyer, LaTroy Hawkins, Torii Hunter, Justin Morneau. **Analysts, Baseball Research:** Andrew Ettel, Sam Isenberg, Kevin Wright. **Coordinator, Amateur Scouting R&D:** Ezra Wise. **Sr. Director, Team Travel:** Mike Herman. **Senior Data Engineer, Baseball Systems:** Jerad Parish. **Developers, Baseball Systems:** Anthony Metcalfe, Hans Van Slooten, Nick Winegar. **Director, Baseball Systems:** Jeremy Raadt. **Data Quality Engineer:** John Edman. **Motion Data Analyst, Baseball Research:** Colin Robertson. **Motion Performance Coach:** Martijn Verhoeven. **Analyst, Advance Scouting:** Josh Ruffin.

Derek Falvey

MAJOR LEAGUE STAFF

Manager: Rocco Baldelli. **Coaches: Bench**—Mike Bell, **Pitching**—Wes Johnson, **Hitting**—Edgar Varela, **Hitting**—Rudy Hernandez, **Catching**—Bill Evers, **First Base**—Tommy Watkins, **Third Base**—Tony Diaz, **Bullpen Coach**—Pete Maki, **Quality Control**—Nate Dammann, **Bullpen Catchers**—Garrett Kennedy, Connor Olson. **Equipment Manager:** Rod McCormick.

MEDICAL/TRAINING

Director, Medical High Performance: Dr. Christopher Camp. **Medical Director Emeritus:** Dr. John Steubs. **Club Physicians:** Dr. Rahul Kapur, Dr. David Olson, Dr. Corey Wulf, Dr. Amy Beacom. **Head Trainer:** Michael Salazar. **Assistant Trainers:** Masamichi Abe, Matt Biancuzzo. **Physical Therapist:** Adam Diamond. **Director, Strength & Conditioning:** Ian Kadish. **Assistant Strength & Conditioning coach:** Andrea Hayden.

PLAYER DEVELOPMENT

Telephone: (612) 659-3480. **Fax:** (612) 659-4026.

Director, Player Development: Alex Hassan. **Assistant Directors, Player Development:** Drew MacPhail, Tommy Bergjans. **Senior Manager, Minor League Operations:** Brian Maloney. **Manager, Florida Operations:** Victor Gonzalez. **Assistant Manager, Florida Operations:** Jason Davila. **Director, Performance Nutrition:** Kara Lynch. **Performance Nutrition Assistant:** Megan Ryan. **Supervisor, Language and Cultural Development:** Linda Merlo. **Minor League Coordinators:** Kevin Morgan (field), Tucker Frawley (asst. field) Frankie Padulo (Run Creation), Justin Willard (pitching), Zach Bove (asst. pitching), Donegal Fergus (hitting), Billy Boyer (infield and baserunning), Mike Quade (outfield), Micheal Thomas (catching), Nat Ballenberg (special projects pitching).

FARM SYSTEM

Class	Club (League)	Manager	Hitting Coach	Pitching Coach
Triple-A	St. Paul	Toby Gardenhire	Matt Borgschulte	M. McCarthy/C. Bello
Double-A	Pensacola	Ramon Borrego	Ryan Smith	Ramirez/Vasquez
High A	Cedar Rapids	Brian Dinkelman	Bryce Berg	Salazar/Moriarty
Low A	Fort Myers	Aaron Sutton	Derek Shomon	P. Larson/C. Hernandez
Rookie	Twins (GCL)	T. Miyoshi	S. Schlecter	Gaynor/Hearn/Maduro/Urbina
Rookie	Twins (DSL)	Seth Feldman	Perez /Nanita /Rosen	K. Rodriguez/Skracic

SCOUTING

Director, Amateur Scouting: Sean Johnson. **Coordinator, Pro Scouting:** Vern Followell. **Director, Latin American Scouting & US Integration Assistant Scouting Director:** Tim O'Neil. **Senior Advisor, Scouting:** Deron Johnson. **National Crosschecker:** Billy Corrigan. **Amateur Crosschecker:** Freddie Thon. **Senior Manager, International Administration and Education:** Amanda Daley. **Coordinator, Amateur Scouting:** Brit Minder. **Scouting Supervisors: East**—Mark Quimuyog, **Mideast**—Derrick Dunbar, **Midwest**—Mike Ruth, **West**—Elliott Strankman. **Area Scouts:** Andrew Ayers, Joe Bisenius, Kyle Blackwell, Trevor Brown, Walt Burrows, Ty Dawson, J.R. DiMercurio, Brett Dowdy, John Leavitt, Mitch Morales, Jeff Pohl, Jack Powell, Michael Quesada, Nick Venuto, Matt Williams, John Wilson. **Professional Scouts:** Ken Compton, Earl Frishman, Mike Larson, John Manuel, Jose Marzan, Billy Milos, Jason Pennini, Keith Stohr, Wesley Wright, Rafael Yanez. **Coordinator, Dominican Republic Scouting:** Eduardo Soriano. **Dominican Republic:** Luis Lajara, Manuel Luciano, Eury Luis. **Coordinator, Venezuela Scouting:** Jose Leon. **Venezuela:** Marlon Nava, Oswaldo Troconis. **Pacific Rim:** David Kim. **Part-Time Scouts:** Hector Barrios (Panama), John Cortese (Italy), Koji Takahashi (Japan), Lester Victoria (Curacao) Juan Padilla, Franklin Parra (Venezuela).

NEW YORK METS

Office Address: Citi Field, 41 Seaver Way, Flushing, NY 11368.
Telephone: (718) 507-6387. **Fax:** (718) 507-6395.
Website: www.mets.com. **Twitter:** @mets.

OWNERSHIP
Owner, Chairman and CEO: Steven A. Cohen. **Owner & President, Amazin' Mets Foundation:** Alexandra M. Cohen. **Vice Chairman & Owner:** Andrew B. Cohen. **Chairman Emeritus:** Fred Wilpon.

BUSINESS OPERATIONS

Steve Cohen

President: Sandy Alderson. **Chief Financial Officer:** Steve Canna. **Chief Technology Officer:** Mark Brubaker. **Chief Revenue Officer:** Jeff Deline. **Executive Vice President & Chief Legal Officer:** David Cohen. **Executive Vice President & Chief Marketing, Content & Communications Officer:** David Newman. **Executive Vice President, Operations:** Jeffrey White. **Senior Vice President, Human Resources & Diversity:** Holly Lindvall. **Senior Vice President Foundation and Community Engagement:** Jeanne Melino. **Senior Vice President, Senior Strategy Officer:** John Ricco. **Vice President, Guest Experience & Venue Services:** Chris Brown. **Vice President, Metropolitan Hospitality:** Heather Collamore. **Vice President, Technology & Corporate Procurement:** Tom Festa. **Vice President, Alumni Public Relations & Team Historian:** Jay Horwitz. **Vice President, Strategy:** Neal Kaplan. **Vice President, Communications:** Harold Kaufman. **Vice President, Controller:** Len Labita. **Vice President, Ballpark Operations:** Sue Lucchi. **Vice President, International and Amateur Scouting:** Tommy Tanous. **Vice President, Financial Planning & Analysis:** Peter Woll.

MEDIA RELATIONS
Telephone: (718) 565-4330. **Fax:** (718) 639-3619.
Vice President, Communications: Harold Kaufman. **Senior Director, Communications:** Ethan Wilson. **Manager, Communications:** Zach Weber. **Coordinator, Communications:** Kristin Wojcik. **Bilingual Media Coordinator:** Alan Suriel. **Assistant, Communications:** Zack Becker. **Assistant, Communications:** Josh Lederman.

TRAVEL/CLUBHOUSE
Director, Team Travel: Brian Small. **Equipment Manager:** Kevin Kierst. **Visiting Clubhouse Manager:** Dave Berni. **Coordinator, Clubhouse Operations:** Jimmy Voigt.

BASEBALL OPERATIONS

Telephone: (718) 803-4013, (718) 565-4339. **Fax:** (718) 507-6391.

Acting General Manager/Senior Vice President: Zack Scott. **Vice President, Amateur & International Scouting:** Thomas Tanous. **Senior Director, Baseball Operations:** Ian Levin. **Senior Advisor, Player Development & Scouting:** Tony DeFrancesco. **Coordinator, Baseball Administration:** Brooklyn Covell. **Coordinator, Baseball Operation:** John Madsen.

MADDIE MALHOTRA/BOSTON RED SOX

Zack Scott

MAJOR LEAGUE STAFF

Manager: Luis Rojas. **Bench Coach:** David Jauss. **Hitting Coach:** Chili Davis. **Assistant Hitting Coach:** Tom Slater. **Pitching Coach:** Jeremy Hefner. **Pitching Strategist:** Jeremy Accardo. **Assistant Pitching Coach/Minor League Coaching Coordinator:** Ricky Meinhold. **First Base Coach:** Tony Tarasco. **Third Base Coach:** Gary DiSarcina. **Bullpen Coach:** Ricky Bones. **Major League Field Coordinator/Catching Coach:** Brian Schneider. **Bullpen Catcher:** Eric Langill. **Bullpen Catcher:** Dave Racaniello.

PLAYER DEVELOPMENT

Telephone: (718) 565-4302. **Fax:** (718) 205-7920.

Director, Player Development: Colin Schwarz. **Director, Hitting Development:** Hugh Quattelbaum. **Coordinator, Coaching Development and Instruction:** Dick Scott. **Field Coordinator:** Kevin Boles. **Major League Assistant Pitching Coach/Pitching Coordinator:** Ricky Meinhold. **Assistant Pitching Coordinator/Triple-A Pitching Coach:** Mike Cather. **Pitching Movement/Rehab Coach:** Kyle Driscoll. **Infield Coordinator:** Tim Teufel. **Catching Coordinator:** Bob Natal. **Outfield/Baserunning Coordinator:** Matt den Dekker. **Coordinator, Special Pitching Projects:** Brian DeLunas. **Sr. Advisor, Pitching Development:** Phil Regan. **Senior Advisors:** Guy Conti, Bobby Floyd, Ozzie Virgil.

RESEARCH AND DEVELOPMENT

Director, Baseball Analytics: Ben Zauzmer. **Manager, Baseball Analytics:** Joe Lefkowitz. **Coordinator, Pitching Analytics:** David Lang. **Analyst, Baseball Analytics:** Tatiana DeRouen. **Analyst, Baseball Analytics:** Desmond McGowan. **Analyst, Baseball Analytics Research & Development:** Jake Toffler. **Integration Analyst, Baseball Analytics:** Rosario Chiovaro. **Integration Analyst, Baseball Analytics:** Jacob Dorris. **Integration Analyst, Baseball Analytics:** Max Vogel-Freedman. **Analyst, Major League Strategy:** Jared Faust. **Analyst, Major League Strategy:** Jack Bredeson. **Manager, Video Operations:** Joe Scarola. **Senior Coordinator, Video Operations:** Sean Haggans. **Coordinator, Baseball Systems:** Matt Fleishman. **Junior Developer, Baseball Systems:** Rick Terry. **Coordinator, Minor League Information:** Colin Schwarz.

MINOR LEAGUE PERFORMANCE

Performance and Sports Science Manager: Alex Ross. **Medical Coordinator:** Matt Hunter. **Rehab and Reconditioning Coordinator:** Alanna Salituro. **Performance Coach Coordinator:** Luke Passman. **Latin America Performance Coaching Coordinator:** Alex Tavarez. **Sport Scientist:** Jackson Bertoli. **Reconditioning Specialist:** Luke Novosel. **Mental Performance Coach:** Samantha Gilmore. **Mental Performance Coach:** Cristian Guzman. **Mental Performance Coach:** Lexis Evans. **Performance Dietitian:** Geodan Stapleton.

FARM SYSTEM

Class	Club	Manager	Hitting Coach	Pitching Coach
Triple-A	Syracuse	TBA	TBA	Mike Cather
Double-A	Binghamton	Lorenzo Bundy	Bruce Fields	Jonathan Hurst
High-A	Brooklyn	TBA	TBA	TBA
Low-A	St. Lucie	TBA	TBA	TBA
Rookie	Mets (GCL)	TBA	TBA	TBA
Rookie	Mets (DSL)	TBA	TBA	TBA

SCOUTING

Telephone: (718) 565-4311. **Fax:** (718) 205-7920.

Director, Professional Scouting: Bryn Alderson. **Assistant Director, Professional Scouting:** Jeff Lebow. **Assistant, Professional Scouting:** Jason Stein. **Special Assignment Professional Scout/Manager, Pacific Rim:** Conor Brooks. **Special Assignment Scout, Professional & International Scouting:** David Keller. **Special Assignment Scout, Professional & Player Development:** Joseph Kowal. **Pro Scouts:** Jason Davis, Pat Jones, Jim Kelly, Bon Kim, Ash Lawson, Chad MacDonald, Shaun McNamara, Andy Pratt, Roy Smith, Rudy Terrasas, Ernie Young. **Director, Amateur Scouting:** Marc Tramuta. **Assistant Director, Amateur & International Scouting:** Bryan Hayes. **Assistant, Amateur & International Scouting:** Tom Fleischman. **Regional Supervisor, Midwest:** Nathan Beuster. **Underclass Supervisor:** Tom Clark. **Pitching Crosschecker:** Chris Hervey. **Special Assignment Scouts:** Jaymie Bane, Ron Hopkins. **Regional Supervisor, West:** Tyler Holmes. **East Coast Supervisor/National Crosschecker:** Mike Ledna. **National Crosschecker:** Doug Thurman. **Hitting Crosschecker:** Drew Toussaint. **Area Supervisors:** Cesar Aranguren, Gary Brown, Jet Butler Daniel Coles, Jarrett England, Chris Heidt, John Kosciak, Rusty McNamara, Marlin McPhail, Rich Morales, Claude Pelletier, Jim Reeves, Brian Reid, Harry Shelton, Scott Thomas, Jon Updike, Glenn Walker. **Director, International Scouting:** Steve Barningham. **Supervisor, Latin America:** Moises de la Mota. **Supervisor, Latin America and Puerto Rico:** Manny Batista. **Supervisor, Venezuela:** Ismael Perez. **Coordinator, Latin America:** Harold Herrera. **Coordinators, Dominican Republic:** Felix Romero, Oliver Dominguez. **Scouts, Dominican Republic:** Kelvin Dominguez, Wilson Peralta. **Scouts, Venezuela:** Robert Espejo, Carlos Perez, Andres Nunez. **Coordinator, Mexico:** Martin Arvizu. **Scout, Panama:** Elvis Rios. **Venezuelan Video Coordinator:** Manuel López. **Tryout Coach, Dominican Republic:** Alejandro Diaz. **Video Coordinator, Dominican Republic:** Jose Luis de Leon.

NEW YORK YANKEES

Office Address: Yankee Stadium, One East 161st St., Bronx, NY 10451.
Telephone: (718) 293-4300.
Website: www.yankees.com, www.yankeesbeisbol.com.
Twitter: @Yankees, @YankeesPR, @LosYankees, @LosYankeesPR.

OWNERSHIP

Managing General Partner/Co-Chairperson: Harold Z. (Hal) Steinbrenner. **General Partner/Vice Chairperson:** Jennifer Steinbrenner Swindal. **General Partner/Vice Chairperson:** Jessica Steinbrenner.

BUSINESS OPERATIONS

President: Randy Levine, Esq.
Chief Operating Officer: Lonn A. Trost, Esq.
Senior VP, Strategic Ventures: Marty Greenspun. **Senior VP, Chief Security Officer:** Sonny Hight. **Senior VP, Yankee Global Enterprises/Chief Financial Officer:** Anthony Bruno. **Chief Financial Officer/Senior VP, Financial Operations:** Scott M. Krug. **Senior VP, Corporate/ Community Relations:** Brian E. Smith. **Senior VP, Partnerships:** Michael J. Tusiani. **Senior VP, Marketing:** Deborah A. Tymon. **Senior VP, Stadium Operations:** Doug Behar. **VP/Chief Financial Officer, Accounting:** Robert B. Brown. **Senior VP & General Counsel:** Alan Chang, Esq. **Senior VP, Chief Information Officer:** Mike Lane. **Vice President, Human Resources, Employment & Labor Law:** Aryn Sobo, Esq. **Sr. Vice President, Chief Legal Officer:** Michael Mellis, Esq. **Vice President, Non-Baseball Sports Events:** Mark Holtzman. **Vice President, Events & Brand Experiences:** Emily Hamel.

Harold Z. Steinbrenner

COMMUNICATIONS/MEDIA RELATIONS

Telephone: (718) 579-4460. **Email:** media@yankees.com.
Vice President, Communications/Media Relations: Jason Zillo. **Director, Communications/Media Relations:** Michael Margolis. **Assistant Director, Baseball Information:** Lauren Moran. **Coordinator, Communications/Media Relations:** Kaitlyn Brennan. **Assistant, Communications/Media Relations:** Jon Butensky. **Assistant, Media Services:** Mark Torres. **Bilingual Media Relations Coodinator:** Marlon Abreu.

TICKET OPERATIONS

Telephone: (718) 293-6000.
VP, Ticket Sales/Service/Operations: Kevin Dart.

BASEBALL OPERATIONS

Senior VP/General Manager: Brian Cashman.
Senior VP/Assistant GM: Jean Afterman, Esq. **VP/Assistant GM:** Michael Fishman. **VP, Baseball Operations:** Tim Naehring. **Director, Team Travel & Player Services:** Ben Tuliebitz. **Director, Quantitative Analysis:** David Grabiner. **Director, Baseball Operations:** Matt Ferry. **Director, Mental Conditioning:** Chad Bohling. **Director, Baseball Systems:** Brian Nicosia.

Brian Cashman

MAJOR LEAGUE STAFF

Manager: Aaron Boone.
Coaches: Pitching—Matt Blake, **Hitting**—Marcus Thames, **Assistant Hitting**—P.J. Pilittere, **First Base**—Reggie Willits, **Third Base**—Phil Nevin, **Bench**— Carlos Mendoza, **Quality Control/Catching**— Tanner Swanson, **Bullpen**—Mike Harkey, **Bullpen Catcher**—Radley Haddad. **Coaching Assistant/Replay Coordinator**—Brett Weber.

MEDICAL/TRAINING

Head Team Physician: Dr. Christopher Ahmad. **Senior Advisor, Orthopedics:** Stuart Hershon, M.D. **Director, Player Health/Performance:** Eric Cressey. **Major League Strength & Conditioning Coach:** Brett McCabe. **Director, Medical Services:** Steve Donohue. **Director, Sports Medicine/Rehab:** Michael Schuk. **Head Athletic Trainer:** Tim Lentych. **Asst. Athletic Trainer:** Alfonso Malaguti. **Massage Therapist:** Doug Cecil.

PLAYER DEVELOPMENT

Senior Director, Player Development: Kevin Reese.
Director, Player Development: Eric Schmitt. **Assistant Director, Player Development:** Stephen Swindal Jr. **Coordinator, Player Development:** Mario Garza. **Pitching Coordinator/ Performance Science Consultant:** John Kremer. **Baseball Solutions Engineer:** Rob Owens. **Complex Coordinator/Tampa Manager:** David Adams. **Coordinator, Instruction/Outfield Coordinator:** Pat McMahon. **Hitting Coordinator:** Dillon Lawson. **Director, Pitching:** Sam Briend. **Catching Coordinator:** Aaron Gershenfeld. **Assistant Infield Coordinator/Minor League Manager:** Travis Chapman. **Baserunning Coordinator/Roving Hitting Coach:** Matt Talarico. **Minor League Hitting Coaches:** Trevor Amicone, Rachel Balkovec. **Player Development Analysts:** Brad Smith, Dan Walco. **Manager, Pitch Development:** Desi Druschel. **Manager, International Operations:** Vic Roldan. **Assistant, International Operations:** Giuliano Montanez. **Manager, Minor League Operations:** Nick Avanzato. **Assistant, Minor League Operations:** Nick Leon. **Assistant, Player Development:** Austin Zieg. **Asst. Director, Player Health & Performance:** Donovan Santas. **Coordinator, Preventative Programs:** Mike Wickland. **Assistant Head Athletic Trainer:** Greg Spratt. **Rehab Strength Coach:** Ty Hill. Physical Therapist, **Player Development:** David Colvin. **Medical Coordinator, Player Development:** Mark Littlefield. **Strength & Conditioning Coordinator:** Rigo Febles. **Minor League Nutrition Coordinator:** Sydney Boehnlein. **Minor League Dietitian:** Chandler Falcon. **Associate Director, Mental Conditioning:** Chris Passarella. **Coordinator, Cultural Development:** Héctor González. **Video Coordinator, Mental Conditioning:** David Schnabel. **Mental Conditioning Coach:** Noel Garcia. **Director, Performance Science:** David Whiteside. **Senior Biomechanist:** Gillian Weir. **Manager, Peak Performance Programs:** Joe Siara. **Sports Scientist:** Patrick Hipes. **Analyst, Performance Science:** Christina Williamson. **Video Coordinators, P.D.:** Chris Whiting, Joe Wielbruda. **Assistant Video Coordinator, P.D.:** Zach Iannarelli. **TrackMan Assistants, International P.D.:** Eliezer Beard, Javier Deyan, Kevin Valera. **Affiliate Video Managers:** Paul Henshaw, Kurt Bathelt, Mike Triller, Nick Horning, Luke Morris, Brian Sheffler. **Director, D.R. Baseball Operations:** Andrew Wright. **Director, Latin Baseball Academy:** Joel Lithgow. **Supervisor, Dominican Academy:** Josias Cabrera. **Assistants, Int'l Baseball Operations:** Manuel Castillo, J.T. Hernandez.

FARM SYSTEM

Class	Club (League)	Manager	Hitting Coach	Pitching Coach
Triple-A	Scranton/WB	TBD	TBD	TBD
Double-A	Somerset	TBD	TBD	TBD
High-A	Hudson Valley	TBD	TBD	TBD
Low-A	Tampa	TBD	TBD	TBD
Rookie	Yankees West (GCL)	TBD	TBD	TBD
Rookie	Yankees East (GCL)	TBD	TBD	TBD
Rookie	Yankees (DSL)	TBD	TBD	TBD

SCOUTING

Telephone: (813) 875-7569. **Fax:** (813) 873-2302.
VP, Domestic Amateur Scouting: Damon Oppenheimer. **Director, Professional Scouting:** Matt Daley. **Assistant Director, Professional Scouting:** Dan Giese. **Coordinator, Professional Scouting:** Adam Charnin-Aker. **Pro Scouts:** Scott Atchison, Kendall Carter, Jay Darnell, Marc DelPiano, Jonathan Diaz, Brandon Duckworth, Raul Gonzalez, Tyler Greene, Kevin Hart, Shawn Hill, Cory Melvin, Pat Murtaugh, James Stokes, JT Stotts, Alex Sunderland, Dennis Twombley, Aron Weston, Tom Wilson. **Special Assignment Scout:** Jim Hendry. **Area Scouts:** TBA. **Director, International Scouting:** Donny Rowland. **Asst. Director, International Scouting:** Brady LaRuffa. **Asst. to Director, Latin America:** Edgar Mateo. **Crosscheckers, International Scouting:** Steve Wilson, Dennis Woody, Ricardo Finol. **Crosscheckers, Latin America:** Miguel Benitez, Victor Mata, Juan Rosario, Jose Gavidia. **Coordinator, Latin America:** Raymon Sanchez. **Video Coordinator, International Scouting:** Ethan Sander. **Video Assistant, Dominican Republic:** Luis Rodriguez. **Technology/Data Analyst:** Vianco Martinez. **Technology/Data Analyst, Venezuela:** Victor Deyan. **International Scouts:** Doug Skiles, John Wadsworth, Luis Sierra, Alvaro Noriega, Esdras Abreu, Luis Brito, R. Arturo Pena, Juan Piron, Jose Ravelo, Jose Sabino, Troy Williams, Rudy Gomez, Lee Sigman, Edgard Rodriguez, Carlos Levy, Chi Lee, Peng Pu Lee, Alan Atacho, Darwin Bracho, Roney Calderon, Cesar Suarez, Jesus Taico, Luis Tinoco.

OAKLAND ATHLETICS

Office Address: 7000 Coliseum Way, Oakland, CA 94621.
Telephone: (510) 638-4900. **Fax:** (510) 562-1633. **Website:** www.athletics.com.

OWNERSHIP
Owner/Managing Partner: John Fisher. **Chairman Emeritus:** Lew Wolff. **Board Members:** Sandy Dean, Bill Gurtin, Keith Wolff.

BUSINESS OPERATIONS
President: David Kaval. **Chief of Staff:** Miguel Duarte. **VP, General Counsel, People Operations and Technology:** D'Lonra Ellis. **VP, Government Affairs:** Taj Tashombe. **Director, Special Projects:** Dash Davidson. **Senior Coordinator, Operations:** Colette Lucas-Conwell. **Executive Assistant & Board Liaison:** Curtis Wiggington. **Director, Alumni & Family Relations:** Detra Paige. **Senior Coordinator, Alumni & Family Relations:** Melissa Guzman.

David Kaval

FINANCE/ADMINISTRATION
Controller: Adam Tyhurst. **Senior Director, Finance:** Kasey Jarcik. **Director, Accounting:** John Anki. **Senior Payroll Manager:** Rose Dancil. **Senior Accountant, Accounts Payable:** Isabelle Mahaffey. **Financial Analysts:** Alex Wong, Ryan De Vera. **Senior Accountants:** Danna Mouat, Paul Basillo. **GL Accountant:** Stephen Curry. **Senior People Operations Manager:** Adam Scoggan. **People Operations Coordinator:** Mari Rodriguez. **Director, Information Technology:** Jody Johnson. **Senior Systems Administrator:** Kevin Lowe. **Senior IT Support Administrators:** Shaunna Brotherton, Dave Cramer.

MARKETING/BROADCASTING
VP, Marketing & Communications: Catherine Aker. **Director, Marketing:** Lisa Bullard. **Marketing Manager:** Alissa Persichetti. **Graphic Designer:** Garrett Lyons. **Team Photographer:** Michael Zagaris. **Senior Broadcast Producer & Host:** Chris Townsend. **Coordinating Producer, Broadcasting:** D'Aulaire Louwerse. **Broadcasting & Media Content Coordinator:** Joey Liberatore. **Multimedia Producer:** Cody Elias.

PUBLIC RELATIONS/COMMUNICATIONS
Director, Baseball Communications: Fernando Alcalá. **Director, Communications & Content:** Erica George. **Social Media Manager:** Madison Campos. **Social Media Coordinator:** Jessica Seibert. **Senior Video Producer:** Kit Karutz. **Baseball Information Manager:** Mike Selleck. **Baseball Communications Manager:** Mark Ling. **Baseball Communications Coordinator:** Olivia Hummer.

STADIUM OPERATIONS
VP, Stadium Operations: David Rinetti. **Senior Director, Stadium Operations:** Paul La Veau. **Director, Concessions & Merchandise:** Nicole Morgan. **Senior Manager, Stadium Operations Events:** Kristy Ledbetter. **Senior Manager, Stadium Services:** Randy Duran. **Senior Manager, Guest Services:** Elisabeth Aydelotte. **Senior Manager, Stadium Operations:** Matt Van Norton. **Stadium Operations Systems Manager:** Jason Silva. **HR Business Partner:** Diane Binder. **Head Groundskeeper:** Clay Wood.

TICKET SALES/OPERATIONS/SERVICES
VP, Ticket Sales & Analytics: Steve Fanelli. **Director, Ticket Operations:** David Adame. **Senior Director, Service/Retention:** Josh Ziegenbusch. **Senior Manager, Ticket Solutions:** Austin Redman. **Ticket Operations Coordinator:** Allie Guido.

TRAVEL/CLUBHOUSE
Director, Team Travel: Mickey Morabito. **Equipment Manager:** Steve Vucinich. **Visiting Clubhouse Manager:** Mike Thalblum. **Assistant Equipment Manager:** Brian Davis. **Umpire/Clubhouse Assistant:** Matt Weiss. **Arizona Senior Facility Manager:** James Gibson. **Arizona Clubhouse Manager:** Chad Yaconetti.

BASEBALL OPERATIONS
Executive VP, Baseball Operations: Billy Beane.
General Manager: David Forst. **Assistant GM, Major League & International Operations:** Dan Feinstein. **Assistant GM/Director, Player Personnel:** Billy Owens. **Sr. Director, Baseball Development & Technology:** Rob Naberhaus. **Special Assistants to GM:** Grady Fuson, Chris Pittaro. **Director, Baseball Administration:** Pamela Pitts. **Video Coordinator:** Adam Rhoden. **Special Assistant to Baseball Operations:** Scott Hatteberg. **Research Scientist:** David Jackson-Hanen. **Asst. Director, Research and Analytics:** Pike Goldschmidt. **Asst. Director, Research and Analytics:** Ben Lowry. **Analyst, Baseball Operations:** Samantha Schultz.

Billy Beane

MAJOR LEAGUE STAFF
Manager: Bob Melvin.
Coaches: Bench—Ryan Christenson. **Pitching**— Scott Emerson. **Hitting**—Darren Bush. **First Base**—Mike Aldrete. **Third Base**—Mark Kotsay. **Bullpen**—Marcus Jensen. **Assistant Hitting Coach**—Eric Martins. **Bullpen Catcher**—Phil Pohl. **Bullpen Catcher**—Dustin Hughes.

MEDICAL/TRAINING
Head Athletic Trainer: Nick Paparesta. **Assistant Athletic Trainers:** Jeff Collins, Brian Schulman. **Sport Performance Coach:** Josh Cuffe. **Asst. Sport Performance Coach:** Steve Candelaria. **Major League Massage Therapist:** Ozzie Lyles. **Team Physicians:** Dr. Allan Pont, Dr. Grant Wang. **Team Orthopedist:** Dr. Jon Dickinson. **Associate Team Orthopedist:** Dr. Will Workman. **Arizona Team Physicians:** Dr. Fred Dicke, Dr. Doug Freedberg.

PLAYER DEVELOPMENT
Telephone: (480) 387-5800. **Fax:** (480) 387-5830.
Director, Player Development: Ed Sprague. **Sr. Advisor to Player Development:** Keith Lieppman. **Advisor to Player Development:** Webster Garrison. **Director, Minor League Operations:** Zak Basch. **Manager, Minor League Operations:** Nancy Moriuchi. **Manager, Minor League Equipment:** Thomas Miller. **Latin America Field Coordinator:** Eddie Menchaca. **Minor League Infield Coordinator:** Juan Navarrete. **Minor League Outfield/Base Running Coordinator:** Steve Scarsone. **Minor League Roving Pitching Coordinator:** Gil Patterson. **Minor League Hitting Coordinator:** Jim Eppard. **Minor League Catching Coordinator:** Gabriel Ortiz. **Minor League Throwing Performance Coach:** Casey Upperman. **Minor League Medical Coordinator:** Nate Brooks. **Senior Coordinator, Medical Services:** Larry Davis. **Latin American Medical Coordinator:** Javier Alvidrez. **Minor League Sport Performance Coordinator:** J.D. Howell. **Asst. Sport Performance Coordinator:** Scott Smith. **Minor League Pitching Rehab Coordinator:** Craig Lefferts. **Minor League Rehab Coordinator:** Travis Tims. **Minor League Asst. Pitching Rehab Coordinator:** Bryan Corey. **Minor League Technology & Development Coordinator:** Ed Gitlitz. **Baseball Systems Developer:** Ben Lewis.

FARM SYSTEM

Class	Club (League)	Manager	Hitting Coach	Pitching Coach
Triple-A	Las Vegas	Fran Riordan	Tommy Everidge	Rick Rodriguez
Double-A	Midland	Bobby Crosby	Kevin Kouzmanoff	Steve Connelly
High-A	Lansing	Scott Steinmann	Javier Godard	Don Schulze
Low-A	Stockton	Rico Brogna	Francisco Santana	Chris Smith
Rookie	Athletics (AZL)	Adam Rosales	L. Turner/R. Escalera	Gabriel Ozuna
Rookie	Athletics (DSL)	Luis Baez	Rahdames Mota	David Brito

SCOUTING
Director, Scouting: Eric Kubota. **Assistant Director, Scouting:** Sean Rooney. **Assistant Director, Scouting and Baseball Operations:** Haley Alvarez. **Coordinator, Scouting and Baseball Operations:** Greg Ledford. **Master Pitching Scout:** John Hughes. **West Coast Supervisor:** Scott Kidd. **Midwest Supervisor:** Mark Adair. **Midwest Supervisor:** Armann Brown. **East Coast Supervisor:** Marc Sauer. **Pro Scouts:** Shooty Babitt, Jeff Bittiger, Grant Brittain, Dan Freed, Trevor Ryan, Will Schock, Tom Thomas, Mike Ziegler. **Area Scouts:** Steve Abney (Lawrence, KS), Anthony Aliotti (Lake Forest, CA), Anthony Aloisi (Nashville, TN), Neil Avent (Charlotte, NC), Fletcher Byrd (Dallas, TX), Jim Coffman (Portland, OR), Ruben Escalera (Carolina, PR), Tripp Faulk (Richmond, VA), Julio Franco, (Weston, FL), Matt Higginson (Grimsby, ON), Derek Lee (Frankfort, IL), Kelcey Mucker (Denham Springs, LA), Trevor Schaffer (Belleair, FL), Rich Sparks (Macomb, MI), Jemel Spearman (Cumming, GA), Dillon Tung (Los Angeles, CA), Jeff Urlaub (Phoenix, AZ), Ron Vaughn (Windsor, CT). **Special Assistant, Scouting and International Operations:** Steve Sharpe. **Director, Latin American Operations:** Raymond Abreu (Santo Domingo, D.R.). **Scouting Supervisor, Latin America:** Juan Mosquera (Panama). **International Scouts:** Javier Agelvis (Mexico), Yendri Bachelor (D.R.), Ruben Barradas (VZ), Jose Barradas (VZ), Dan Betreen (Australia), Juan Carlos De La Cruz (D.R.), Angel Eusebio (D.R.), Andri Garcia (VZ), Oswaldo Garcia (Colombia), Adam Hislop (Taiwan), Lewis Kim (South Korea), Wilfredo Magallanes (D.R.), Argenis Paez (Venezuela), Tito Quintero (Colombia), Amaurys Reyes (D.R.), Toshiyuki Tomizuka (Japan), Oswaldo Troconis (VZ).

PHILADELPHIA PHILLIES

Office Address: Citizens Bank Park, One Citizens Bank Way, Philadelphia, PA 19148.
Telephone: (215) 463-6000. **Website:** www.phillies.com.

OWNERSHIP
Operated By: The Phillies. **Managing Partner:** John Middleton. **President:** Andy MacPhail. **Chairman Emeritus:** Bill Giles.

BUSINESS OPERATIONS

David Montgomery

EXECUTIVE MANAGEMENT
Executive VP: David Buck. **Senior VP/General Counsel:** Rick Strouse. **VP, Administration:** Kathy Killian. **VP, Chief Technology Officer:** Sean Walker. **Director, Human Resources/Benefits:** JoAnn Marano. **Director, Human Resources:** Marie Hanley.

BUSINESS AFFAIRS
VP, Business Affairs: Howard Smith. **Director, Operations/Facility:** Mike DiMuzio. **Director, Operations/Security:** Sal DeAngelis. **Director, Field Operations:** Mike Boekholder.

COMMUNICATIONS
Telephone: (215) 463-6000. **Fax:** (215) 389-3050
VP, Communications: Bonnie Clark. **Director, Communications:** Greg Casterioto. **PA Announcer:** Dan Baker. **Official Scorers:** Mark Gola, Mike Maconi, Dick Shute.

FINANCE
Sr. VP/CFO: John Nickolas. **Director, Business Analytics:** Josh Barbieri. **Director, Finance:** Shannon Snellman. **Director, Payroll:** Bryan Humphreys.

BROADCAST/VIDEO SERVICES
Director, Broadcasting/Video Services: Mark DiNardo. **Director, Video Engineering:** Martin Otremsky.

MARKETING/PROMOTIONS
VP, Partnership Sales and Corporate Marketing: Jacqueline Cuddeback. **VP, Marketing Programs & Events:** Kurt Funk. **VP, Marketing & New Media:** Michael Harris. **Director, Partnership Sales & Corporate Marketing:** Rob MacPherson. **Director, Advertising Sales:** Brian Mahoney. **Director, Corporate Sales:** Scott Nickle. **Director, Marketing Events & Special Projects:** James Trout.

SALES/TICKETS
Telephone: (215) 463-1000. **Fax:** (215) 463-9878.
Sr. VP, Ticket Operations & Projects: John Weber. **Director, Ticket Technology & Development:** Chris Pohl. **Director, Sales:** Derek Schuster. **Director, Suite Sales & Business Ventures:** Kevin Beale. **Director, Group Sales:** Vanessa Mapson. **Director, Season Ticket Services:** Mike Holdren. **Director, Premium Sales & Services:** Matt Kessler. **Director, Ticket Operations:** Ken Duffy.

TRAVEL/CLUBHOUSE
Coordinator, Team Travel: Jameson Hall. **Manager, Clubhouse Services:** Phil Sheridan. **Manager, Equipment/Umpire Services:** Dan O'Rourke. **Manager, Visiting Clubhouse:** Kevin Steinhour.

BASEBALL OPERATIONS

President, Baseball Operations: David Dombrowski. **VP/General Manager:** Sam Fuld. **Assistant GM:** Bryan Minniti. **Assistant GM:** Scott Proefrock. **Assistant GM:** Ned Rice. **Assistant GM:** Jorge Velandia. **Senior Advisor:** Pat Gillick. **Senior Advisors, GM:** Larry Bowa, Charlie Manuel. **Special Assistants, GM:** Terry Ryan. **Director, Player Development:** Josh Bonifay. **Director, International Scouting:** Sal Agostinelli. **Director, Amateur Scouting:** Brian Barber. **Director, Professional Scouting:** Mike Ondo. **Director, Strategic Initiatives:** Andy Galdi. **Director, Integrative Baseball Performance:** Rob Segedin. **Director, Amateur Scouting Administration:** Rob Holiday. **Director, Minor League Operations:** Lee McDaniel. **Director, Mental Performance:** Ceci Craft.

BILLIE WEISS/BOSTON RED SOX

Dave Dombrowski

MAJOR LEAGUE STAFF

Manager: Joe Girardi. **Coaches: Bench**—Rob Thomson, **Pitching**—Caleb Cotham, **Hitting**—Joe Dillon, **First Base**—Paco Figueroa, **Third Base**—Dusty Wathan, **Infield**—Juan Castro, **Bullpen**—Dave Lundquist, **Coaching Assistant**— Bobby Meacham, **Bullpen Catcher/Catching**—Greg Brodzinski, Bob Stumpo. **Quality Assurance Coach:** Mike Calitri.

MEDICAL/TRAINING

Director, Medical Services: Dr. Michael Ciccotti. **Head Athletic Trainer:** Paul Buchheit. **Assistant Athletic Trainers:** Shawn Fcasni, Aaron Hoback. **Major League Strength & Conditioning Coach:** Paul Fournier. **Assistant Strength & Conditioning Coach:** Dong Lien. **Major League Physical Therapist:** Joe Rauch.

PLAYER DEVELOPMENT

Director, Player Development: Josh Bonifay. **Director, Minor League Operations:** Lee McDaniel. **Director, Florida Operations/GM, Clearwater Threshers:** John Timberlake. **Assistant Director, Minor League Operations/Florida:** Joe Cynar. **Assistant Director, International Operations:** Ray Robles. **Assistant Director, Player Development:** Dana Parks.

FARM SYSTEM

Class	Club (League)	Manager	Hitting Coach	Pitching Coach
Triple-A	Lehigh Valley	TBA	TBA	TBA
Double-A	Reading	TBA	TBA	TBA
High-A	Lakewood	TBA	TBA	TBA
Low-A	Clearwater	TBA	TBA	TBA
Rookie	Phillies West	TBA	TBA	TBA
Rookie	Phillies East	TBA	TBA	TBA
Rookie	Phillies 1 (DSL)	TBA	TBA	TBA
Rookie	Phillies 2 (DSL)	TBA	TBA	TBA

SCOUTING

Director, Amateur Scouting: Brian Barber. **Director, Amateur Scouting Administration:** Rob Holiday. **Assistant Director, Scouting:** Greg Schilz. **National Scouting Coordinators:** David Crowson, Darrell Conner. **Regional Supervisors:** Alex Agostino, Shane Bowers, Buddy Hernandez, Brad Holland, Brian Kohlscheen. **Performance Assistant, Amateur Scouting:** Connor Betbeze. **Special Assignment Scouts:** Dean Albany, Craig Colbert, Charley Kerfeld, Mike Koplove, Dan Wright. **Director, Professional Scouting:** Mike Ondo. **Professional Scouts:** Erick Dalton, Todd Donovan, Jon Mercurio. **Area Scouts:** Chris Duffy, Tommy Field, Zach Friedman, Ralph Garr Jr., Victor Gomez, Bryce Harman, Aaron Jersild, Tim Kissner, Kellan McKeon, Timi Moni, Justin Morgenstern, Justin Munson, Demerius Pittman, Hilton Richardson, Derrick Ross, Mike Stauffer, Jason Waugh, Jeff Zona Jr. **Director, International Scouting:** Sal Agostinelli. **International Scouting Coordinator:** Derrick Chung. **Latin America Coordinator:** Jesús Méndez. **Latin America Supervisor:** Carlos Salas. **Venezuela Supervisor:** Rafael Alvarez. **Mexico Supervisor:** Oneri Fleita. **International Crosschecker, Dominican Republic:** Andres Hiraldo. **International Crosschecker, Pacific Rim:** Howard Norsetter. **International Scouts:** Alvaro Blanco (Colombia), Jesus Blanco (Venezuela), Alex Choi (South Korea), Juan Feliciano de Castro (Dominican Republic), Elvis García (Venezuela), Luis García (Dominican Republic), Charlie Gastelum (Mexico), Gene Grimaldi (Associate Scout), Jose Guzman (Dominican Republic), Jonatan Hernandez (Venezuela), Dargello Lodowica (Curacao), William Mota (Venezuela), Bernardo Pérez (Dominican Republic), Abdiel Ramos (Panama), Philip Riccobono (Japan), Franklin Rojas (Venezuela), Claudio Scerrato (Italy), Ebert Velásquez (Venezuela), Youngster Wang (Taiwan). **Video Assiants:** Jean Montalvo (Dominican Republic), Gustavo Mogollon (Venezuela).

PITTSBURGH PIRATES

Office Address: PNC Park at North Shore, 115 Federal St., Pittsburgh, PA, 15212.
Mailing Address: PO Box 7000, Pittsburgh, PA 15212.
Telephone: (412) 323-5000. **Fax:** (412) 325-4412.
Website: www.pirates.com. **Twitter:** @Pirates.

BUSINESS OPERATIONS

Travis Williams

OWNERSHIP
Chairman of the Board: Bob Nutting.
President: Travis Williams. **Head Legal Counsel:** Frankie Garland.

COMMUNICATIONS
Senior VP, Communications/Broadcasting: Brian Warecki. **Director, Baseball Communications:** Jim Trdinich. **Director, Broadcasting:** Marc Garda. **Director, Media Relations:** Dan Hart. **Director, Business Communications/Social Media:** Terry Rodgers.

MARKETING/CORPORATE SPONSORSHIPS
Senior Director, Marketing/Advertising: Brian Chiera. **Director, Alumni Affairs/Promotions/Licensing:** Joe Billetdeaux. **Director, Special Events:** Christine Serkoch. **Director, PNC Park Events:** Ann Regan. **Manager, Advertising/Digital Marketing:** Haley Artayet. **Manager, Entertainment Media:** Paul Denillo. **Manager, Corporate Partnerships:** Chris Stevens. **Director, Corporate Partnership Activation:** Brittany Hudzik. **Senior Account Manager, Corporate Partnerships:** Dave Shinsky.

STADIUM OPERATIONS
Executive VP/General Manager, PNC Park: Dennis DaPra. **Vice President, Ballpark Operations:** Chris Hunter. **Senior VP, Florida and Dominican Operations:** Jeff Podobnik. **Director, Field Operations:** Matt Brown. **Manager, Guest Experience:** Danny Garcia. **Director, PNC Park Operations:** J.J. McGraw.

TRAVEL/CLUBHOUSE
Home Clubhouse Manager: Scott Bonnett. **Visiting Clubhouse Manager:** Kevin Conrad. **Assistant Equipment Manager:** Kiere Bulls. **Manager, Team Travel:** Ryan Denlinger.

BASEBALL OPERATIONS

Executive Vice President, General Manager: Ben Cherington.
Senior Vice President, Baseball Development: Bryan Stroh. **Assistant General Manager:** Kevan Graves. **Assistant General Manager:** Steve Sanders. **Director, Baseball Operations and Pro Scouting:** Will Lawton. **Coordinator, Baseball Operations:** Trey Rose. **Assistant, Baseball Operations:** Zach Aldrich. **Manager, Team Travel:** Ryan Denlinger.

Ben Cherington

MAJOR LEAGUE STAFF

Manager: Derek Shelton.
Bench Coach: Don Kelly. **Hitting Coach:** Rick Eckstein. **Assistant Hitting Coach:** Christian Marrero. **Major League Field Coordinator:** Mike Rabelo. **Pitching Coach:** Oscar Marin. **First Base Coach:** Tarrik Brock. **Third Base Coach:** Joey Cora. **Bullpen Coach:** Justin Meccage. **Coach:** Glenn Sherlock. **Coaching Assistant:** Heberto Andrade. **Bullpen Catcher:** Jordan Comadena.

MEDICAL/TRAINING

Director, Sports Medicine: Todd Tomczyk. **Director, Sports Performance:** A.J. Patrick.
Head Strength and Conditioning Coach: Terence Brannic. **Major League Strength & Conditioning Coach:** Adam Vish. **Head Major League Athletic Trainer:** Rafael Freitas. **Major League Assistant Athletic Trainer:** Tony Leo. **Strength and Conditioning Coach:** Glenn Nutting. **Strength and Conditioning Coach:** Nicholas Pressley. **Minor League Strength & Conditioning Coach:** Cory Cook. **Minor League Athletic Training Coordinator:** Dru Scott. **Major League Physical Therapist:** Seth Steinhauer. **Medical Director:** Dr. Patrick DeMeo. **Team Physicians:** Dr. Darren Frank, Dr. Dennis Phillips, Dr. Michael Scarpone, Dr. Robert Schilken, Dr. Edward Snell.

INFORMATICS

Senior Director, Baseball Informatics: Dan Fox. **Senior Quantitative Analyst, Baseball Informatics:** Sean Ahmed. **Senior Quantitative Analyst:** Justin Newman. **Senior Developer, Baseball Informatics:** Brian Hulick. **Data Architect, Baseball Systems:** Matthew Reiersgaard. **Developer, Baseball Informatics:** Frank Wolverton. **Software Developer, Baseball Informatics:** Nichols Siefken. **Performance Analyst:** Justin Perline. **Quantitative Analyst:** Matt Kane. **Major League Advance Coordinator:** Aaron Razum. **Assistant, Major League:** Tim McKeithan.

PLAYER DEVELOPMENT

Director, Coaching & Player Development: John Baker.
Assistant Director of Player Development, Informatics: Andrew Gibson. **Assistant Director, Minor League Operations:** Brian Selman. **Special Assistant to GM, Cultural Initiatives:** Mike Gonzalez. **Coordinator, Pitching Development:** Josh Hopper. **Coordinator, Minor League Pitching Operations:** T.J. Large. **Coordinator, Minor League Hitting Operations:** Shawn Johnston. **Coordinator, Player Development:** Michael Chernow. **Coordinator, International Operations:** Jose Cruz. **Minor League Manager:** Jonathan Johnston. **Minor League Pitching Coach:** Fernando Nieve. **Senior Advisor to Player Development & Catching Coordinator:** Brad Fischer. **Field Coordinator:** Bobby Scales. **Infield Coordinator:** Gary Green. **Latin American Field Coordinator:** Mendy Lopez. **Latin American Pitching Coordinator:** Amaury Telemaco. **Minor League Pitching Coach:** Victor Black. **Education Coordinator:** Mayu Fielding. **Director, Mental Strength:** Bernie Holliday. **Director, International Development:** Hector Morales. **Director, Sports Nutrition & Fueling:** Allison Maurer. **Coordinator, Sports Nutrition & Fueling:** Courtney Ellison. **Coordinator, Mental Strength:** Tyson Holt. **Coordinator, Mental Strength:** Andy Bass. **Coordinator, Athletic Development:** Joe Hughes. **Coordinator, Medical Services:** Carl Randolph. **Athletic Trainer, DSL:** Alexis Mena.

FARM SYSTEM

Class	Club (League)	Manager	Hitting Coach	Pitching Coach
Triple-A	Indianapolis	Brian Esposito	Jon Nunnally	Joel Hanrahan
Double-A	Altoona	Miguel Perez	David Newhan	Drew Benes
High-A	Greensboro	Kieran Mattison	Ruben Gotay	Matt Ford
Low-A	Bradenton	Jonathan Johnston	Jonny Tucker	Fernando Nieve
Rookie	Pirates (GCL)	TBA	TBA	TBA
Rookie	Pirates (DSL)	TBA	TBA	TBA

SCOUTING

Fax: (412) 325-4414.
Senior Director, Player Personnel: Steve Williams. **Special Assistant, Player Personnel:** Oz Ocampo. **Assistant Director, Player Personnel:** Max Kwan. **Assistant Director, Pro Player Valuation:** Joe Douglas. **Pro Evaluation Team Leaders:** Sean McNally, Rodney Henderson, Larry Broadway. **Pro Valuation Analyst:** Grant Jones. **Player Evaluation Analyst:** Joe Hultzen. **Senior Director, Amateur Scouting:** Joe DelliCarri. **Director, International Scouting:** Junior Vizcaino. **Assistant Director, Amateur Scouting:** Mike Mangan. **Coordinator, Amateur Scouting:** Matt Skirving. **Coordinator of International Operations:** Matt Benedict. **National Supervisors:** Jack Bowen, Jimmy Lester. **Regional Supervisors:** Jesse Flores, Trevor Haley, Sean Heffernan. **Area Supervisors:** Brett Evert, Matt Bimeal, Adam Bourassa, Eddie Charles, Jerry Jordan, Wayne Mathis, Darren Mazeroski, Cam Murphy, Nick Presto, Dan Radcliff, Mike Sansoe, Brian Tracy, Derrick Van Dusen, Anthony Wycklendt. **Major League Scouts:** Ricky Bennett, Jim Dedrick. **Special Assignment Scout:** Doug Strange. **Pro Scouts:** Matt Ruebel, Carlos Berroa, John Birkbeck, Andrew Lorraine, Everett Russell. **Scouting Assistants:** Kinza Baad, Michael Landestoy. **International Crosschecker:** Jesus Lantigua. **International Supervisors:** Saul Torres (Venezuela); Emmanuel Gomez (D.R.); Raul Lopez (Mexico); Tony Harris (International/Australia); Fu-Chun Chiang (Far East); Tom Gillespie (Europe/Africa). **International Scouts:** Esteban Alvarez, Daurys Nin, Leudy Castro, Cristino Valdez, Omelbis Corporan (D.R.); Victor Alvarez, Gregory Bolivar (Colombia), Pedro Avila, Omar Gonzalez, Jesus Morelli, Jessie Nava, Jose Partidas Dirimo Chavez (Venezuela); Roberto Saucedo (Mexico); Marcos Guimaraes (Brazil); Eugene Helder (Aruba); Mark Van Zanten (Curacao); Jose Pineda (Panama).

ST. LOUIS CARDINALS

Office Address: 700 Clark Street, St. Louis MO 63102.
Telephone: (314) 345-9600. **Fax:** (314) 345-9523. **Website:** www.cardinals.com.

OWNERSHIP

Operated By: St. Louis Cardinals, LLC. **Chairman/Chief Executive Officer:** William DeWitt, Jr. **President:** Bill DeWitt III. **Senior Administrative Assistant to Chairman:** Grace Pak. **Senior Administrative Assistant to President:** Julie Laningham. **Sr. VP & General Counsel:** Mike Whittle. **Associate Counsel:** Nick Garzia.

BUSINESS OPERATIONS

Bill DeWitt III

FINANCE

Fax: (314) 345-9520.
Senior VP/Chief Financial Officer: Brad Wood. **Director, Risk Management:** Rex Carter. **Director, Human Resources:** Ann Seeney. **VP, Event Services/Merchandising:** Vicki Bryant.

MARKETING/SALES/COMMUNITY RELATIONS

Fax: (314) 345-9529.
Senior VP, Sales & Marketing: Dan Farrell. **Administrative Assistant, VP, Sales & Marketing:** Gail Ruhling. **VP, Corporate Sales, Marketing & Stadium Entertainment:** Thane Van Breusegen.

COMMUNICATIONS

Fax: (314) 345-9530.
Director, Communications: Brian Bartow. **Manager, Baseball Communications:** Michael Whitty. **Administrator, Baseball Information & Media Services:** Chris Tunno. **Spanish Interpreter:** Antonio Mujica. **PA Announcer:** John Ulett. **Official Scorers:** Gary Muller, Jeff Durbin, Mike Smith.

STADIUM OPERATIONS

Fax: (314) 345-9535.
VP, Stadium Operations: Matt Gifford.

TICKETING

Fax: (314) 345-9522.
VP, Ticket Sales/Service: Joe Strohm. **Director, Marketing & Brand Execution:** Martin Coco. **Director, Ticket Sales & Retention:** Rob Fasoldt. **Director, Ticket Operations:** Kerry Emerson.

TRAVEL/CLUBHOUSE

Fax: (314) 345-9523.
Team Travel Director: Ernie Moore. **Equipment Manager:** Mark Walsh. **Visiting Clubhouse Manager:** Rip Rowan. **Video Coordinator:** Chad Blair.

BASEBALL OPERATIONS

President of Baseball Operations: John Mozeliak. **Vice President & General Manager:** Michael Girsch. **Senior Executive Assistant to the President of Baseball Operations:** Linda Brauer. **Assistant GM:** Moises Rodriguez. **Assistant GM & Director of Scouting:** Randy Flores. **Special Assistant to GM, Player Procurement:** Matt Slater. **Director, Baseball Administration:** John Vuch. **Director, Analytics:** Kevin Seats. **Director, Baseball Analytics & Systems:** Jeremy Cohen. **Director, Baseball Systems:** Patrick Casanta. **Project Dir./Baseball Systems:** Matt Bayer. **Manager, Player Communications:** Melody Yount. **Manager, Senior Developer:** Brian Seyfert. **Sr. Analytics Engineer:** Todd Heitmann. **Analytics Engineer:** Jack Hanley. **Baseball Operations Analyst:** Javier Duren. **Amateur Scouting Analyst:** Julia Prusaczyk. **Baseball Development Analyst:** Garrett Greenwood. **Senior Data Scientist:** Alan Kessler. **Systems Engineer II:** Isaiah Berg. **Application Developer:** Austin Lukaschewski.

John Mozeliak

MAJOR LEAGUE STAFF

Telephone: (314) 345-9600.

Manager: Mike Shildt. **Coaches: Bench**—Oliver Marmol. **Pitching**—Mike Maddux. **Hitting**—Jeff Albert. **Assistant Hitting Coach**—Jobel Jimenez. **First Base**—Richard "Stubby" Clapp. **Third Base**—Ron "Pop" Warner. **Bullpen**—Bryan Eversgerd. **Assistant Coach:** Willie McGee. **Assistant ML Hitting Coach:** Patrick Elkins. **Pitching Strategist:** Dusty Blake. **Bullpen Catchers**—Jamie Pogue, Kleininger Teran.

MEDICAL/TRAINING

Head Orthopedist Surgeon: Dr. George Paletta. **Coordinator of Medical Services & Team Physician:** Brian Mahaffey. **Director of Medical Operations:** Adam Olsen. **Director of Performance:** Robert Butler. **Assistant Athletic Trainers:** Jeremy Clipperton, Chris Conroy. **Assistant Director, Performance:** Thomas Knox. **Performance Specialist & Physical Therapist:** Jason Shutt. **Strength & Conditioning Coach:** Lance Thomason.

PLAYER DEVELOPMENT

Director, Player Development: Gary LaRocque. **Manager, Player Development:** Tony Ferreira. **Manager, Player Dev & Performance:** Emily Wiebe. **Minor League Equipment Manager:** Dave Vondarhaar. **Minor League Hitting Coordinator:** Russ Steinhorn. **Minor League Hitting Instructor/Analyst:** Daniel Nicolaisen. Tim Leveque (senior pitching). **Minor League Instructors:** Randy Niemann (pitching), Jose Oquendo (infield), Keith Joynt (medical coordinator, player development), Matt Leonard (rehab coordinator), Aaron Rhodes (strength & conditioning), DC MacLea (performance specialist), Victor Kuri (assistant rehab coordinator).

FARM SYSTEM

Class	Club (League)	Manager	Hitting Coach	Pitching Coach
Triple-A	Memphis	Ben Johnson	Brandon Allen	Dernier Orozco
Double-A	Springfield	Jose Leger	Tyger Pederson	Darwin Marrero
High-A	Peoria	Chris Swauger	Joe Hawkins	Rick Harig
Low-A	Palm Beach	Jose Leon	Daniel Nicolaisen	Dean Kiekhefer
Rookie	Cardinals (GCL)	Roberto Espinoza	Tyler Wolfe	Giovanni Carrara
Rookie	Cardinals Red (DSL)	Estuar Ruiz	Luis Cruz	Bill Villallanueva
Rookie	Cardinals Blue (DSL)	Fray Peniche	Erick Almonte	Edwin Moreno

SCOUTING

Fax: (314) 345-9519.

Assistant General Manager & Director of Scouting: Randy Flores. **Assistant Director, Scouting:** Tyler Hadzinsky. **Manager, Pro Scouting:** Jared Odom. **Special Advisor to the Scouting Director:** Jamal Strong. **Professional Scouts:** Brian Hopkins (Holly Springs, NC), Jeff Ishii (Chino, CA), Aaron Klinic (Baltimore, MD), Deric McKamey (Cincinnati, OH), Craig Richmond (Tampa, FL) Joe Rigoli (Parsippany, NJ), Kerry Robinson (Ballwin, MO). **National Crosscheckers:** Aaron Looper (Shawnee, OK), Zachary Mortimer (Pilesgrove, NJ), Jamal Strong (Surpirse, AZ). **Regional Crosscheckers:** Dominic "Ty" Boyles (Dallas, TX), Aaron Krawiec (Gilbert, AZ), Clint Brown (Braselton, GA), Sean Moran (Furlong, PA) **Area Scouts:** Jabari Barnett (Humble, TX), Nick Longmire (Cumming, GA), Jason Bryans (Tecumseh, ON), TC Calhoun (Abingdon, VA), Josh Lopez (West Palm Beach, FL), Mike Garciaparra (Manhattan Beach, CA), Dirk Kinney (Lenexa, KS), Tom Lipari (Aubrey, TX), Jim Negrych (Phoenixville, PA), Stacey Pettis (Brentwood, CA), Chris Rodriguez (Los Angeles, CA), Mauricio Rubio (Tempe, AZ), Nathan Sopena (Cary, IL). **Part-Time Scouts:** Juan C Ramos (Caguas, PR), Paul Ah Yat (Hon, HI). **Director, International Operations & Administration:** Luis Morales. **Manager, International Operations:** Joseph Quezada. **Senior International Crosschecker:** Joe Almaraz. **International & Domestic Crosschecker:** Damaso Espino. **Senior Latin American Crosschecker/DR Scouting Supervisor:** Angel Ovalles. **Latin American Crosschecker/DR Crosschecker:** Alix Martinez. **International Scouts:** Braly Guzman, Raymi Dicent, Filiberto Fernandez, Darluimis Almonte (Dominican Republic); Jhohan Acevedo, Jesus Perez, Neriel Morillo, Wilmer Castillo (Venezuela); Ramon Garcia (Mexico); Carlos Balcazar (Colombia).

SAN DIEGO PADRES

Office and Mailing Address: Petco Park, 100 Park Blvd., San Diego, CA 92101.
Telephone: (619) 795-5000.
E-mail address: comments@padres.com. **Website:** www.padres.com. **Twitter:** @padres.
Facebook: www.facebook.com/padres. **Instagram:** www.instagram.com/padres

OWNERSHIP

Operated By: Padres LP. **Owner and Chairman:** Peter Seidler. **Vice Chairman:** Ron Fowler.

BUSINESS OPERATIONS

Chief Executive Officer: Erik Greupner. **SVP, Business Administration & General Counsel:** Caroline Perry. **SVP, People & Culture:** Sara Greenspan. **VP, Information Technology:** Ray Chan. **VP, Finance:** Chris James. **VP, Sports Programs:** Bill Johnston. **VP, Special Events:** Jaclyn Lash. **VP, Hospitality:** Josh Pell. **Associate General Counsel & Baseball Operations Compliance Officer:** Stephanie Wilka.

Ron Fowler

COMMUNITY RELATIONS/MILITARY AFFAIRS

Telephone: (619) 795-5265. **Fax:** (619) 795-5266. **SVP, Community Relations & Military Affairs:** Tom Seidler. **VP, Public Affairs:** Diana Puetz.

ENTERTAINMENT/MARKETING/COMMUNICATIONS/CREATIVE SERVICES

SVP, Marketing: Chris Connolly. **VP, Broadcasting & Entertainment:** Erik Meyer. **VP, Communications:** Craig Hughner. **Sr. Director, Content:** Nicky Patriarca. **Sr. Director, Marketing:** Nicole Miller.

BALLPARK OPERATIONS/HOSPITALITY

GM, Petco Park: Mark Guglielmo. **VP, Ballpark Operations:** Ken Kawachi. **Sr. Director, Security/Transportation:** Kevin Dooley. **Sr. Director, Guest Experience:** Erin Sheehan. **Director, Field Operations:** Matt Balough. **Official Scorers:** John Maffei, David Matheson and Bill Zavestoski.

TICKETING

Telephone: (619) 795-5500. **Fax:** (619) 795-5034. **SVP, Corporate Partnerships:** Sergio Del Prado. **VP, Ticket Sales and Service:** Curt Waugh. **VP, Partnership Services:** Eddie Quinn. **VP, Business Strategy & Analytics:** Scott Robish. **Sr. Director, Membership Services:** Sindi Edelstein. **Sr. Director, Ticket Operations:** Jim Kiersnowski.

BASEBALL OPERATIONS

Telephone: (619) 795-5077. **Fax:** (619) 795-5361.

President, Baseball Operations & General Manager: A.J. Preller. **VP/Assistant GM:** Fred Uhlman Jr. **Assistant GM:** Josh Stein. **Senior Advisor, Baseball Operations:** Trevor Hoffman. **Senior Advisor/Director, Player Personnel:** Logan White. **Special Assistants to the GM:** Moises Alou, James Keller, David Post. **Special Assistant to the GM, Research & Development:** Dave Cameron. **Advisor to Baseball Operations:** Allen Craig, A.J. Ellis, Glenn Hoffman, and Ian Kinsler. **Senior Advisor, Scouting:** Ron Rizzi. **Director, Baseball Operations:** Nick Ennis. **Director, Baseball Information Services:** Matt Klotsche. **Director, Baseball Systems:** Wells Oliver. **Director, Baseball Research & Development:** Adam Esquer. **Senior Developer, Baseball Systems:** Garret Doe. **Developer, Baseball Systems:** Michael Vanger. **Manager, Baseball Administration & Special Assistant to the GM:** Michaelene Courtis. **Senior Analyst, Baseball Research & Development:** Cody Zupnick. **Manager of Amateur Analysis, Baseball R&D:** Layne Gross. **Coordinator, Baseball Operations:** Brett Becker. **Analysts, Baseball Research & Development:** Jeremy Muesing, Mario Paciuc.

A.J. Preller

MAJOR LEAGUE STAFF

Manager: Jayce Tingler. **Associate Manager:** Skip Schumaker. **Bench & Third Base Coach:** Bobby Dickerson. **Pitching Coach:** Larry Rothschild. **Hitting Coach:** Damion Easley. **First Base Coach:** Wayne Kirby. **Bullpen Coach:** Ben Fritz. **Catching & Quality Control Coach:** Rod Barajas. **Advance Scout/Development Coach:** Ryan Flaherty. **Bullpen Catchers:** Brad Flanders & Peter Summerville. **Major League Batting Practice/Hitting Instructor:** Morgan Burkhart. **Development Coordinator:** Keith Werman. **Assistant Director, Baseball Operations:** David Longley. **Coordinator, Advance Scouting:** Preston Mattingly. **Video Coordinator:** Joe McAlpin.

TRAVEL/CLUBHOUSE

Director, Player & Staff Services: TJ Lasita. **Manager, Equipment & Clubhouse:** TJ Laidlaw. **Assistant Equipment Manager/Umpire Room Attendant:** Tony Petricca. **Visiting Clubhouse Manager:** Spencer Dallin.

MEDICAL/TRAINING

Club Physician: UC San Diego Health—Dr. Catherine Robertson, Dr. Kenneth Taylor. **Director, Player Health and Performance:** Don Tricker. **Head Athletic Trainer:** Mark Rogow. **ML Physical Therapist:** Scott Hacker. **ML Assistant Athletic Trainers:** Ben Fraser, Ricky Huerta. **Director, Strength & Conditioning:** Dan Byrne. **ML Strength & Conditioning Coach:** Jay Young. **Baseball Performance Dietician:** Whitney Milano.

PLAYER DEVELOPMENT

Senior Director, Player Development: Sam Geaney. **Director, Player Development:** Ryley Westman. **Manager, Minor Leagues/Peoria Operations:** Todd Stephenson. **Special Assistant, Player Development:** Steve Finley. **Coordinators:** Steve Lyons & Eric Junge (pitching), Oscar Bernard (hitting), Kevin Hooper (infield), Brian Whatley (catching), Paul Porter (minor league ATC), JoJo Tarantino (minor league medical administration), Eric Wood & Drew Heithoff (strength & conditioning). **Physical Therapist:** Aaron Wengertsman. **Manager, Minor League Equipment & Clubhouse:** Zach Nelson. **Manager, Player Development Video Ops/Professional Scout:** Ethan Dixon. **Analyst, Player Development:** Nathan Landau. **Director, International Operations:** Cesar Rizik. **Administrator, International Operations:** Franklyn Peguero. **Director, Professional Development:** Jason Amoroso. **Coordinator, Latin American Player Development:** Vicente Cafaro. **Coordinator, Mental Skills:** Rosa Pou.

FARM SYSTEM

Class	Farm Club (League)	Manager	Hitting Coach	Pitching Coach
Triple-A	El Paso	TBA	TBA	TBA
Double-A	San Antonio	TBA	TBA	TBA
High-A	Fort Wayne	TBA	TBA	TBA
Low-A	Lake Elsinore	TBA	TBA	TBA
Rookie	Padres 1 (AZL)	TBA	TBA	TBA
Rookie	Padres 2 (AZL)	TBA	TBA	TBA
Rookie	Padres (DSL)	TBA	TBA	TBA

SCOUTING

Director, Amateur Scouting: Mark Conner. **Director, Professional Scouting:** Pete DeYoung. **Director, International Scouting/Field Coordinator:** Chris Kemp. **Director, Pacific Rim Operations:** Acey Kohrogi. **Assistant Scouting Director:** Kurt Kemp. **National Crosschecker:** Chip Lawrence. **Advisor to Amateur Scouting:** Tim Adkins. **Scouting Crosschecker:** Luke Murton. **Manager, Amateur Scouting:** Sam Ray. **Amateur Scouting Supervisors:** Yancy Ayres, Nick Brannon, Josh Emmerick, Matt Haas, Chris Kelly, Andrew Salvo. **Area & Amateur Scouts:** Stephen Baker, Justin Baughman, Carlos Fisher, Kevin Ham, Clint Harrison, Troy Hoerner, Chris Kemlo, Nick Long, Matt Maloney, John Martin, John McNamara, Stephen Moritz, James Parker, Tim Reynolds, Danny Sader, Matt Schaffner, Tyler Stubblefield. **Coordinator, Arizona Video Operations:** Max Kraust. **Special Assistant, Professional Scouting:** Spencer Graham. **Professional Scouting Crosscheckers:** Mike Juhl, Chuck LaMar, Dominic Viola. **Professional Scouts:** Keith Boeck, Patrick Coghlan, Kimball Crossley, Tim Holt, Chris Kusiolek, Mark Merila, Matt Simonetti, Tyler Tufts, Mike Venafro, Cory Wade. **International Scouting Supervisors:** Trevor Schumm, Bill McLaughlin. **Area Scout/International Crosschecker:** Jake Koenig. **Supervisor, Dominican Republic:** Alvin Duran. **Supervisor, Venezuela:** Luis Prieto. **International Scouts:** Antonio Alejos (Venezuela), Andres Cabadias (Colombia), Emenejildo Diaz (Dominican Republic), Jhonathan Feliz (Dominican Republic), Po-Hsuan Keng (Taiwan), Sherman Lacrus (Curacao), Victor Magdaleno (Venezuela), Richard Montenegro (Panama), Hoon Namgung (Korea/Taiwan), Keiji Uezono (Japan), Jose Salado (Dominican Republic), Damian Shanahan (Australia), Carlos Taveras (Dominican Republic).

SAN FRANCISCO GIANTS

Office Address: Oracle Park, 24 Willie Mays Plaza, San Francisco, CA 94107.
Telephone: (415) 972-2000. **Fax:** (415) 947-2800. **Website:** sfgiants.com, sfgigantes.com.

OWNERSHIP

Operated By: San Francisco Baseball Associates L.P.

BUSINESS OPERATIONS

President/Chief Executive Officer: Laurence M. Baer. **Executive VP:** Brian R. Sabean.
Special Assistants: Will Clark, Willie Mays. **Special Advisors:** Barry Bonds, Bruce Bochy.

Laurence M. Baer

FINANCE/LEGAL/INFORMATION TECHNOLOGY

Executive Vice President & Chief Legal Officer: Jack F. Bair. **Senior Vice President & General Counsel:** Amy Tovar. **Senior VP/Chief Financial Officer:** Lisa Pantages. **Senior VP/ CIO/Chairman, San Jose Giants:** Bill Schlough. **VP, Information Technology:** Ken Logan. **VP, Finance:** Matt Causey.

ADMINISTRATION

Executive VP, Administration: Alfonso Felder. **Senior Vice President & Chief Venue Officer, Oracle Park:** Jorge Costa. **VP, Ballpark Operations:** Gene Telucci. **VP, Security:** Tinie Roberson. **Vice President, Guest Services:** Alexis Lustbader. **Senior Vice President & Chief People Officer:** Jose Martin. **Vice President, Human Resources:** Lan Huynh Lee. **President, Giants Enterprises:** Stephen Revetria. **VP, Giants Enterprises:** Joey Nevin. **Senior VP, Event Strategy & Services:** Sara Grauf.

COMMUNICATIONS

Telephone: (415) 972-2445. **Fax:** (415) 947-2800. **Executive VP, Communications/Senior Advisor to the CEO:** Staci Slaughter. **Senior Vice President, Community Relations & Public Affairs:** Shana Daum. **Executive Director, Giants Community Fund:** Sue Petersen. **Vice President, Media Relations:** Matt Chisholm. **Senior Director, Broadcast Communications & Media Operations:** Maria Jacinto. **Senior Manager, Hispanic Communications & Marketing:** Erwin Higueros. **Media Relations Manager:** Megan Brown. **Baseball Information Manager:** Mike Passanisi.

BUSINESS OPERATIONS

Executive VP, Business Operations: Mario Alioto. **Senior Vice President & Chief Business Development Officer:** Jason Pearl. **VP, Marketing/Advertising:** Danny Dann. **Vice President,Content & Entertainment:** Paul Hodges. **Vice President, Brand Development & Digital Media:** Bryan Srabian. **PA Announcer:** Renel Brooks-Moon.

TICKETING

Telephone: (415) 972-2000. **Fax:** (415) 972-2500.
Senior VP, Ticket Sales/Services: Russ Stanley. **Vice President, Ticket & Premium Revenue:** Jeff Tucker. **VP, Business Analytics:** Rocky Koplik.

BASEBALL OPERATIONS

President of Baseball Ops.: Farhan Zaidi. **General Manager:** Scott Harris. **Senior Advisor to President of Baseball Ops:** JP Ricciardi, Dick Tidrow, John Barr. **VP/Assistant GM:** Jeremy Shelley. **VP, Baseball Resources and Development:** Yeshayah Goldfarb. **VP, Player Performance and Wellness:** Colin Cahill. **Special Assistant, Scouting:** Craig Weissmann. **Special Assistant to Baseball Ops:** Felipe Alou. **Executive Assistant to Baseball Ops/ Administration:** Karen Sweeney. **Director of Baseball Analytics:** Paul Bien. **Director of Baseball Personnel Administration:** Clara Ho. **Manager, Baseball Analytics:** Michael Schwartze. **Baseball Ops Analyst:** Rohanna Pacheco, Simon Ricci. **Data Scientist:** Brian Huey, Greg Starek. **Principal Engineer:** Caleb Whang. **Senior Engineer:** Kevin Deggelman. **Software Engineer:** Rob Bertucci, Alex Case, Jack McGeary. **Assistant, Baseball Ops:** Josh Zimmerman.

Farhan Zaidi

MAJOR LEAGUE STAFF

Manager: Gabe Kapler. **Coaches: Bench**—Kai Correa. **Director of Pitching**—Brian Bannister. **Pitching Coach**—Andrew Bailey. **Asst Pitching Coach**—J.P. Martinez. **Hitting Coach**—Donnie Ecker, Justin Viele. **Director of Hitting/ Assistant ML Hitting:** Dustin Lind. **Third Base**—Ron Wotus. **First Base**—Antoan Richardson. **Bullpen**—Craig Albernaz. **Quality Assurance Coach:** Nick Ortiz. **Assistant Coaches:** Alyssa Nakken, Mark Hallberg. **Video Coaching Analyst:** Fernando Perez. **Bullpen Catchers:** Taira Uematsu, Brant Whiting. **Manager, Baseball Video Systems:** Yo Miyamoto. **Coordinator, Baseball Video Systems:** Patrick Yount.

MEDICAL/TRAINING

Team Physicians: Dr. Anthony Saglimbeni, Dr. Ken Akizuki, Dr. Robert Murray, Dr. Chris Chung, Dr. Ben Ma. **Senior Dir. of Athletic Training:** Dave Groeschner. **Head Athletic Trainer:** Anthony Reyes. **Asst. Athletic Trainer:** LJ Petra. **Physical Therapist:** Tony Reale. **Strength & Conditioning Coach:** Brad Lawson. **Asst. Strength & Conditioning Coach/Sports Science Specialist:** Saul Martinez. **Massage Therapist:** Haro Ogawa. **Coordinator, Medical Admin.:** Chrissy Yuen. **Dir. of Mental Health & Wellness, & EAP:** Shana Alexander. **Dir. of Performance Nutrition:** Leron Sarig. **Medical Review Analyst:** Eric Ortega.

PLAYER DEVELOPMENT

Director, Player Development: Kyle Haines. **Asst. Director Player Development Administration:** Eric Flemming. **Director of Minor League Medical:** Dustin Luepker. **Minor League Field Coordinator:** Tony Diggs. **Coordinator, Minor League Pitching:** Justin Lehr. **Coordinator, Minor League Hitting:** Michael Brdar. **Coordinator of Pitching Sciences:** Matt Daniels. **Assistant Pitching Coordinator:** Clayton Rapada. **Assistant Hitting Coordinator:** Ed Lucas. **Rehab Pitching Coordinator:** Matt Yourkin. **Outfield and Baserunning Coordinator:** Tim Leiper. **Infield Coordinator:** Jason Wood. **Coordinator of Latin American Development:** Hector Borg. **Minor League Coach:** Tom Trebelhorn. **Roving Hitting Coach:** Pat Burrell. **Roving Catching Instructor:** Eli Whiteside. **Manager, Arizona Baseball Ops.:** Gabe Alvarez. **Manager, Education/Cultural Development:** Laura Nunez. **Director, Arizona Field Operations:** Josh Warstler. **Manager of Minor League Field Operations:** Jeff Winsor.

FARM SYSTEM

Class	Farm Club (League)	Manager	Hitting Coach	Pitching Coach
Triple-A	Sacramento (PCL)	Dave Brundage	Damon Minor	Garvin Alston
Double-A	Richmond (EL)	Jose Alguacil	Doug Clark	Steve Kline
High-A	Eugene (NWL)	Dennis Pelfrey	Jake Fox	Alain Quijano
Low-A	San Jose (CAL)	Lenn Sakata	Danny Santin	Paul Oseguera
Rookie	Giants Orange (AZL)	Carlos Valderrama	Travis Ishikawa	Mario Rodriguez
Rookie	Giants Black (AZL)	Lance Burkhart	Cory Elasik	Michael Couchee
Rookie	Giants 1 (DSL)	Jose Montilla	Juan Parra	Luis Pino
Rookie	Giants 2 (DSL)	Juan Ciriaco	Craig Maddox	Osiris Matos

SCOUTING

Telephone: (415) 972-2360. **Fax:** (415) 947-2929.
Director of Pro Scouting: Zack Minasian. **Director of Amateur Scouting:** Michael Holmes. **Director of International Scouting:** Joe Salermo. **Director of International Operations/Baseball Administration:** Jose Bonilla. **Coordinator of Amateur Scouting:** Mike Navolio. **Pro Scouts:** Ellis Burks, Keith Champion, Jim D'Aloia, Steve Decker, Michael Kendall, Ben McDonough, Ross Pruitt, Steve Riha, Ryan Thompson, Shane Turner, Derek Watson. **Senior Advisors to President:** JP Ricciardi, John Barr. **Special Assistant, Scouting:** Craig Weissmann. **National Crosscheckers:** Brian Bridges, John Castleberry. **National Pitching Coordinator:** Dan Murray. **Special Assignment Scout:** Bert Bradley. **Scouting Supervisors: Northeast**—Arnold Brathwaite, **Southeast**—Jim Buckley, **Midwest** —Andrew Jefferson, **West**—Matt Woodward. **Area Scouts:** Jose Alou, Ray Callari, Brad Cameron, Larry Casian, Todd Coryell, John DiCarlo, Chuck Fick, Jim Gabella, Chuck Hensley Jr., DJ Jauss, James Mouton, Mark O'Sullivan, Jared Schlehuber, Keith Snider, Jeff Wood, Paul Faulk. **International Crosscheckers:** Jose Alou, Michael Silvestri, Charlie Sullivan. **Director, Dominican Republic Operations:** Pablo Peguero. **Asst. Director, DR Operations/International Crosschecker:** Felix Peguero. **Director of Venezuela Operations:** Ciro Villalobos. **Venezuela Crosschecker:** Edgar Fernandez. **Dominican Republic Crosschecker:** Jesus Stephens. **International Scouts (Dominican Republic):** Abner Abreu, Jonathan Bautista, Gabriel Elias, Luis Polonia Jr. **International Scouts (Venezuela):** Jonathan Arraiz, Jose Beyronti, Carlos Leon, Juan Marquez, Oscar Montero, Robert Moron, Ciro Villalobos Jr. **International Scouts:** Daniel Mavarez (Colombia), Sandy Moreno (Nicaragua), Rogelio Castillo (Panamá), Evan Hsueh (Pacific Rim).

SEATTLE MARINERS

Office Address: 1250 First Ave. South, Seattle, WA 98134.
Mailing Address: PO Box 4100, Seattle, WA 98194.
Telephone: (206) 346-4000. **Fax:** (206) 346-4400. **Website:** www.mariners.com.

OWNERSHIP

Board of Directors: John Stanton (Chairman), John Ellis, Howard Lincoln. **Chairman Emeriti:** Chris Larson, Jeff Raikes, Buck Ferguson, Betsy Pepper Larson. **Senior VP/Special Advisor to the Chairman and CEO:** Randy Adamack.

BUSINESS OPERATIONS

John Stanton

FINANCE

Executive Vice President and CFO: Tim Kornegay. **VP, Finance:** Greg Massey. **Director, Internal Audit Operations:** Connie McKay. **Senior VP, People and Culture:** Lisa Winsby.

LEGAL & GOVERNMENTAL AFFAIRS/ COMMUNITY RELATIONS

Executive Vice President and General Counsel: Fred Rivera. **VP, Deputy General Counsel:** Melissa Robertson.

SALES

Senior VP, Sales: Frances Traisman. **Senior Director, Partnerships, Strategy/Activation:** Ingrid Russell-Narcisse. **VP, Ticket Sales & Service:** Cory Carbary.

MARKETING/COMMUNICATIONS

Telephone: (206) 346-4000. **Fax:** (206) 346-4400.
Senior VP, Marketing/Communications: Kevin Martinez. **VP, Communications:** Tim Hevly. **VP, Marketing:** Gregg Greene. **Senior Director, Public Information:** Rebecca Hale. **Senior Manager, Baseball Information:** Kelly Munro. **Coordinators, Baseball Information:** Adam Gresch, Alex Mayer. **Senior Director, Mariners Productions:** Ben Mertens. **Director, Marketing:** Mandy Lincoln. **Director, Graphic Design:** Carl Morton.

TICKETING

Telephone: (206) 346-4001. **Fax:** (206) 346-4100.
VP, Ticket Operations and Event Services: Malcolm Rogel. **Senior Director, Ticket Services:** Jennifer Sweigert.

STADIUM OPERATIONS

Senior VP, Ballpark Events & Operations: Trevor Gooby. **Senior Director, Event Sales:** Alisia Anderson. **Director, Ballpark Services:** Juan Rodriguez. **Director, Security:** Jessica Reid-Bateman. **Director, Facilities:** Dave Wilke. **Director, Information Systems:** Oliver Roy. **Director, Database/Applications:** Justin Stolmeier.
Senior Director, Procurement: Norma Cantu. **Head Groundskeeper:** Tim Wilson. **PA Announcer:** Tom Hutyler.

MERCHANDISING

Sr. Director, Retail Operations: Julie McGillivray. **Director, Retail Merchandising:** Renee Steyh. **Director, Retail Stores:** Mary Beeman.

TRAVEL/CLUBHOUSE

Director, Major League Operations: Jack Mosimann. **Clubhouse Manager:** Ryan Stiles. **Visiting Clubhouse Manager:** Jeff Bopp. **Video Coordinator:** Patrick Hafner.

BASEBALL OPERATIONS

Executive VP/General Manager: Jerry Dipoto.
Assistant GM: Justin Hollander **Director, Major League Operations:** Jack Mosimann.
Director, Baseball Operations: Tim Stanton. **Asst. Director, Baseball Projects:** David
Hesslink. **Coordinator, Advance Scouting:** Sam Reinertsen. **Manager, Data Strategy:**
Skylar Shibayama. **Senior Director, Analytics:** Jesse Smith. **Director, Analytics:** Joel Firman.
Manager, Analytics: John Choiniere.

MAJOR LEAGUE STAFF

Manager: Scott Servais. **Bench**—Jared Sandberg. **Pitching**—Pete Woodworth. **Hitting**—
Tim Laker. **Asst. Hitting:** Jarret DeHart. **First Base**—Perry Hill. **Third Base**—Manny Acta.
Bullpen—Trent Blank. **Bullpen Catcher**—Fleming Baez. **Field Coordinator**—Carson Vitale.
Video Coordinator: Patrick Hafner. **Video Assistant:** Dan Kaplan.

Jerry Dipoto

MEDICAL/TRAINING

Head Orthopedist: Dr. Jason King. **Head Athletic Trainer:** Kyle Torgerson. **Asst. Athletic Trainer:** Taylor Bennett,
Kevin Orloski. **Physical Therapist:** Ryan Bitzel. **Director, Performance Training:** James Clifford. **Asst. Performance
Specialist:** Derek Cantieni.

PLAYER DEVELOPMENT

Telephone: (206) 346-4316. **Fax:** (206) 346-4300.
Director, Player Development: Andy McKay. **Asst. Director, Player Development:** Emanuel Sifuentes
Coordinator, Player Development: Mat Snider. **Special Assistants, Player Development:** Alvin Davis, Dan Wilson,
Mike Cameron, Franklin Gutiérrez. **Coordinator, Medical/Athletic Training:** John Walker. **Director, Pitching Strategy:**
Trent Blank. **Hitting Strategist:** Edward Paparella. **Field Coordinator:** Tony Arnerich. **Hitting Coordinator:** Connor
Dawson. **Pitching Coordinator:** Max Weiner. **Coordinator, Minor League Rehab:** Michael Feliciano. **Latin American
Development Coordinator:** Cesar Nicolas. **Performance Specialist Coordinator:** Aaron Reis.

FARM SYSTEM

Class	Club (League)	Manager	Hitting Coach	Pitching Coach
Triple-A	Tacoma	Kristopher Negron	Roy Howell	Rob Marcello
Double-A	Arkansas	Collin Cowgill	Joe Thurston	Alon Leichman
High-A	Everett	Louis Boyd	Shawn O'Malley	Sean McGrath
Low-A	Modesto	Eric Farris	Rob Benjamin	Nathan Bannister
Rookie	Peoria (AZL)	Austin Knight	Michael Fransoso	Zac Livingston
Rookie	Mariners (DSL)	Luis Caballero	Brett Schneider	Jose Amancio

SCOUTING

Director, Amateur Scouting: Scott Hunter. **Asst. Director, Amateur Scouting:** Frankie Piliere. **Director, Player
Personnel:** Brendan Domaracki. **Crosscheckers:** Ben Collman (German Valley, IL), Jesse Kapellusch (Cooper City,
FL), Mark Lummus (Godley, TX), Devitt Moore (Bryn Mawr, PA), Chris Pelekoudas (Mesa, AZ). **Regional Scouts:** Ty
Bowman (Phoenix, AZ), Preston Higbe (Clear Lake, IA), Dan Holcomb (Nashville, TN), Ryan Holmes (Thousand Oaks,
CA), Tyler Holub (Durham, NC), Chris Hom (Benicia, CA), Bobby Korecky (Estero, FL), Jackson Laumann (Florence, KY),
Derek Miller (Sugar Land, TX), Rob Mummau (Palm Harbor, FL), Patrick O'Grady (Dallas, TX), David Pepe (Boonton, NJ),
John Wiedenbauer (Jacksonville, FL). **Scouting Analysts:** Matt Doughty, Tyler Warmoth, Austin Yamada. **Director,
International Amateur Scouting:** Frankie Thon (Doral, FL). **Asst. Director, International Scouting:** Andrew Herrera.
International Crosschecker: Kevin Fox (Roseville, CA). **Supervisor, Dominican Republic:** Audo Vicente (Santo
Domingo, DR). **Latin America Supervisor:** David Brito (Baranquilla, CO). **Venezuela Supervisor:** Federico Hernandez
(Caracas, VZ). **International Scouts:** Felipe Burin (Brazil), Alfredo Celestin (D.R.), Rodrigo Cortez (Venezuela) Franklin
Diaz (D.R.) Luis Fuenmayor (Venezuela), Sam Kao (Taiwan), Luis Martinez (Venezuela), Rafael Mateo (D.R.), Manabu Noto
(Japan), Rigoberto Rangel (Panama), Ismael Rosado (Dominican Republic), Illich Salazar (Venezuela).

TAMPA BAY RAYS

Office Address: Tropicana Field, One Tropicana Drive, St. Petersburg, FL 33705.
Telephone: (727) 825-3137. **Fax:** (727) 825-3111.

OWNERSHIP
Principal Owner: Stuart Sternberg.

BUSINESS OPERATIONS

Stuart Sternberg

DOUG BENC/GETTY IMAGES

Presidents: Brian Auld, Matt Silverman
Chief Development Officer: Melanie Lenz. **Senior Vice President, Administration/ General Counsel:** John Higgins. **Senior Vice President, Baseball Operations/General Manager:** Erik Neander. **VP, Public Affairs & Corporate Communications:** Rafaela A. Amador. **VP, Baseball Development:** Peter Bendix. **VP/Chief Financial Officer:** Rob Gagliardi. **VP, Communications:** Dave Haller. **VP, Business Operations & Analytics:** Barry Newell. **VP, Information Technology:** Juan Ramirez. **VP, Corporate Partnerships:** Brian Richeson. **VP, Player Development & International Scouting:** Carlos Rodriguez. **VP, Ticket Sales and Service:** Jeff Tanzer. **VP, Human Resources and Organizational Engagement:** Jennifer Lyn Tran. **VP, Strategy & Development:** Bill Walsh. **VP, Marketing & Creative Services:** Eric Weisberg. **VP, Employee & Community Development:** Bill Wiener, Jr.

FINANCE
Senior Director, Controller: Patrick Smith. **Director, Financial Planning and Analysis:** Jason Gray.

MARKETING/COMMUNITY RELATIONS
Director, Creative: Warren Hypes. **Director, Marketing & Creative Services:** Emily Miller. **Executive Director, Rays Baseball Foundation:** Stephen Thomas. **Director, Community Relations:** David Egles.

GAME OPERATIONS
Director, Game Presentation & Production: Mike Weinman. **Director, Guest Services:** Scott Wilson. **Director, Promotions:** Stephon Thomas.

COMMUNICATIONS/BROADCASTING
Senior Director, Broadcasting: Larry McCabe. **Director, Communications:** Ryan Sheets.

STADIUM OPERATIONS
Senior Director, Building Operations: George Dowling. **Senior Director, Partner and VIP Relations:** Cass Halpin. **Senior Director, Security & Stadium Operations:** Jim Previtera. **Director, Building Operations:** Chris Raineri. **Director, Security:** Steve Estep. **Director, Stadium Operations:** Mike Ferrario. **Head Groundskeeper & Director of Operations, Charlotte Sports Park:** Dan Moeller. **Director, Team Travel & Logistics:** Chris Westmoreland. **Manager, Home Clubhouse & Equipment:** Tyler Wall. **Manager, Visitor Clubhouse:** Brandon "Tank" Richesin. **Video Coordinator:** Chris Fernandez.

BASEBALL OPERATIONS

Senior VP Baseball Operations/GM: Erik Neander. **VP, Baseball Development:** Peter Bendix. **VP, Player Development/International Operations:** Carlos Rodriguez. **Special Assistant to the GM:** Bobby Heck. **Special Assistant, Baseball Operations:** Denard Span. **Senior Director, Baseball Systems:** Brian Plexico. **Director, Baseball Operations:** Hamilton Marx. **Director, Development Strategy:** Sandy Sternberg. **Director, Staff Development and Recruiting:** Chanda Lawdermilk. **Director, Team Travel and Logistics:** Chris Westmoreland. **Director, Baseball Performance Science:** Joe Myers. **Director, Baseball R&D:** Will Cousins. **Assistant Director, Baseball R&D:** Anirudh Kilambi. **Analyst, Baseball Development:** Jeff Sullivan. **Assistants, Baseball Development:** Brad Ballew, Danielle Dockx, Mark Watson. **Manager, Baseball Administration:** Samantha Bireley. **Manager, Major League Operations:** Jeremy Sowers. **Manager, Baseball Performance Science:** Ryan Pennell. **Assistants, Performance Science:** Allison DeKuiper, Mike Lambiaso, Vishnu Sarpeshkar. **Video Coordinator:** Brett Ebers. **Lead Sports Dietician:** Ryan Harmon. **Head of Mental Performance:** Justin Su'a. **Biomechanist:** Mike McNally.

SKIP MILOS

Erik Neander

MAJOR LEAGUE STAFF

Manager: Kevin Cash. **Coaches: Bench**—Matt Quatraro, **Pitching**—Kyle Snyder, **Hitting**—Chad Mottola, **First Base**—Ozzie Timmons, **Third Base**—Rodney Linares, **Bullpen**—Stan Boroski, **Field Coordinator**—Paul Hoover. **Process/Analytics Coach**—Jonathan Erlichman.

MEDICAL/TRAINING

Medical Director: Dr. James Andrews. **Orthopedic Team Physician:** Dr. Koco Eaton. **Team Chiropractor:** Christopher Williams. **Massage Therapist:** Ray Allen. **ML Medical Coordinator:** Paul Harker. **Head Trainer:** Joe Benge.

PLAYER DEVELOPMENT

Telephone: (727) 825-3267. **Fax:** (727) 825-3493.

Director, Minor League Operations: Jeff McLerran. **Senior Advisor, Player Development and Baseball Operations:** Mitch Lukevics. **Assistant Director, Minor League Operations:** George Pappas. **Assistant Director, Minor League Operations/Baseball Development:** Simon Rosenbaum. **Sr. Administrator, International/Minor League Operations:** Giovanna Rodriguez. **Director, Pitching Development:** Dewey Robinson. **Assistant Director, Pitching Development:** Winston Doom. **Assistant Director, Hitting Development:** Cole Figueroa. **Assistant, Minor League Operations:** Wilson Made. **Assistant, Minor League Operations:** Isha Rahman. **Minor League Equipment Manager:** Tim McKechney. **Assistant Minor League Equipment Manager:** Shane Rossetti. **Education Coordinator:** Lenore Sutton. **Field Coordinators:** Alejandro Freire, Michael Johns. **Minor League Coordinators: Pitching:** Jorge Moncada, Rolando Garza. **Hitting:** Greg Brown, Dan Dement, Steve Livesey. **Catching:** Tomas Francisco. **Infield:** Ivan Ochoa. **OF/Baserunning:** Christian Prieto. **Medical:** Aaron Scott. **Rehab:** Joel Smith. **Latin America Medical:** Chris Tomashoff. **Latin America Cultural:** Jairo De La Rosa. **S&C:** Patrick Trainor. **Mental Skills:** Josh Kozuch, Kris Goodman, Jenny Ferriter, Carla Hodel.

FARM SYSTEM

Class	Club (League)	Manager	Hitting Coach	Pitching Coach
Triple-A	Durham	Brady Williams	Kyle Wilson	Rick Knapp
Double-A	Montgomery	Morgan Ensberg	Jamie Nelson	Brian Reith
High-A	Bowling Green	Jeff Smith	Brady North	Steve Watson
Low-A	Charleston	Blake Butera	W. Rincones	Jim Paduch
Rookie	Rays (GCL)	R. Valenzuela	M.Castillo/F. Maldonado	A.Bastardo/J.Gonzalez
Rookie	Rays 1(DSL)	Julio Zorrilla	Omar Luna	L. Urena/Y. Almonte
Rookie	Rays 2 (DSL)	Esteban Gonzalez	Alejandro Segovia	L. Romero/J. Sanchez

SCOUTING

Sr. Director, Pro Personnel & Pro Scouting: Kevin Ibach. **Assistant Director, Pro Personnel & Pro Scouting:** Ryan Bristow. **Analyst, Pro Personnel & Pro Scouting:** Tyler Chamberlain-Simon. **Sr. Director, Amateur Scouting:** Rob Metzler. **Senior Advisor, Scouting/Baseball Operations:** R.J. Harrison. **National Crosschecker:** Chuck Ricci **Coordinator, Amateur Scouting:** Jeff Johnson. **Administrator, Amateur Scouting:** Sydney Malone. **Special Assignment Scout:** Fred Repke. **Pro Personnel Specialists:** Mike Brown, Jason Cole, Jason Grey, Mike Langill. **Pro Scouts:** Ken Califano, Max Cohen, JD Elliby, Jose Gomez, Carlos Herazo, Nate Howard, Ken Kravec, Dave Myers, Jaylon Pimentel, Jeff Stewart. **Pro Scouting Consultants:** Tyler Stohr, Wood Myers. **Midwest Regional Supervisor:** Jeff Cornell. **Northeastern Regional Supervisor:** Brian Hickman. **Southeastern Regional Supervisor:** Kevin Elfering. **Western Regional Supervisor:** Jake Wilson. **Pitching Crosschecker:** Ryan Henderson. **Scout Supervisors:** Matt Alison, Steve Ames, James Bonnici, Zach Clark, Tom Couston, Rickey Drexler, Brett Foley, Tim Fortugno, Luke Harrigan, Landon Lassiter, David Hamlett, Joe Hastings, Milt Hill, Jaime Jones, Paul Kirsch, Reggie Lawson, Pat Murphy, Greg Whitworth. **Part-Time Area Scouts:** Josh Jackson, Jose Hernandez, Dave Jorn, Gil Martinez, Casey Onaga, Jack Sharp, Marcos Tovar, Lou Wieben. **International Crosschecker/South Florida Supervisor:** Victor Rodriguez. **Director, International Scouting:** Steve Miller. **Director, International Operations:** Patrick Walters. **Assistant Director, International Operations:** Ronnie Blanco. **International Crosschecker:** Brad Budzinski. **Consultant, International Operations:** John Gilmore. **Scouting Supervisor, Colombia:** Angel Contreras. **Scouting Supervisor, Dominican Republic:** Danny Santana. **Venezuela Crosschecker:** William Bergolla. **Regional Crosschecker, Dominican Republic:** Rigo De Los Santos. **International Scouts:** Miguel De La Cruz, Felix Fermin, Remmy Hernandez, Jorge Perez (Dominican Republic), Marlon Roche, Juan Francisco Castillo, Carlos Leon, Frank Tineo (Venezuela), Tiago Campos (Brazil), Karla Espinoza, Jesus Valdez (Mexico), Keith Hsu (Taiwan), Chairon Isenia (Curacao), Joe Park (Korea), Tateki Uchibori (Japan), Gustavo Zapata (Panama).

TEXAS RANGERS

Office Address: 734 Stadium Drive, Arlington, TX 76011.
Telephone: (817) 273-5222. **Website:** www.texasrangers.com. **Twitter:** @Rangers.

OWNERSHIP
Chairman/Managing Partner: Ray C. Davis. **Chairman, Executive Committee:** Bob R. Simpson. **Chief Operating Officer:** Neil Leibman.

BUSINESS OPERATIONS
Executive VP, Business Operations: Rob Matwick. **Executive VP, Chief Marketing & Revenue Officer:** Joe Januszewski. **Executive VP/CFO:** Kellie Fischer. **Executive VP/General Counsel:** Katie Pothier. **Executive VP, Communications:** John Blake. **Executive VP, Ballpark Entertainment/Productions:** Chuck Morgan. **Executive VP, Sports and Entertainment:** Sean Decker. **Sr. VP/Finance:** Starr Gulledge.

Ray Davis

HUMAN RESOURCES/LEGAL/INFORMATION TECHNOLOGY
VP, Human Resources: Jeff Miller. **Sr. Corporate Counsel:** Erin Kearney. **Director, Human Resources:** Mercedes Riley. **Managers, Human Resources:** Shannon Abbott, Chandler Conley, Eri Cuevas. **Senior Paralegal:** Joanna Landon. **Administrative Assistant:** Emily Caruso. **VP, Info Technology:** Mike Bullock.

PROJECT DEVELOPMENT
Senior VP, Project Development: Jack Hill. **Project Accountant:** Kelley Walker.

COMMUNICATIONS/COMMUNITY RELATIONS
VP, Broadcasting/Communications: Angie Swint. **Asst. VP, Player/Alumni Relations:** Taunee Paur Taylor. **Sr. Director, Communications:** Rich Rice. **Director, Photography:** Kelly Gavin. **Manager, Baseball Information:** Matt Mallian. **Coordinator, Communications:** Tyler Strachan. **Coordinator, Player Relations:** Ashley Quintilone. **Senior Vice President, Community Impact & Executive Director, Foundation:** Karin Morris. **Director, Youth Baseball and Youth Academy Programs:** Juan Leonel Garciga. **Manager, Development:** Justin Henry. **Manager, Foundation & Community Impact:** Reynaldo Casas.

FACILITIES/RETAIL/EVENTS
Sr. VP, Ballpark Venue Operations & Guest Experience: Mike Healy. **VP, Security & Parking:** Blake Miller. **Sr. Director, Parking & Security:** Mike Smith. **Sr. Director, Maintenance:** Mike Call. **Director, Major League Grounds:** Dennis Klein. **Director, Complex Grounds:** Steve Ballard. **Director, Security Special Projects & Events:** John Marsh. **Director, Parking Services:** Dana Jons. **Senior Director, Events Marketing & PR:** Lindsey Hopper. **Vice President, Events:** Jared Schrom. **Director, Event Operations:** Pedro Soto, Jr.

TICKET AND SPONSORSHIP SALES
Senior Vice President, Ticket Retention & Premium Services: Paige Farragut. **Sr. VP, Partnerships & Client Services:** Jim Cochrane. **Vice President, Ticket Sales:** Dan Hessling. **Vice President, Ticket Retention & New Business Development:** Nick Richardson. **Director, Group Sales:** Jamie Roberts. **Director, Suites & Premium Services:** Delia Willms. **Director Ticket Operations:** Mike Lentz. **Vice President, Business Analytics & Ticket Strategy:** Katie Morgan. **Director, Business Partnerships:** Chad Wynn. **Director, Corporate Partnerships:** Sean Ferretti.

MARKETING/GAME PRESENTATION
VP, Marketing: Travis Dillon. **Director, Marketing & Advertising:** Kyle Bartlett. **Creative Director:** Scott Biggers. **Senior Director, Game Entertainment/Productions:** Chris DeRuyscher. **Director, Digital & Social Media:** Kyle Smith.

BASEBALL OPERATIONS

Telephone: (817) 273-5222. **Fax:** (817) 273-5285.

President, Baseball Operations: Jon Daniels. **Executive Assistant to President, Baseball Operations/GM:** Joda Parent. **Assistant General Managers:** Josh Boyd, Mike Daly, Shiraz Rehman. **Special Assistants to the GM:** Colby Lewis, Brandon McCarthy, Darren Oliver, Ivan Rodriguez, Michael Young. **Senior Director, Baseball Systems:** Todd Slavinsky. **Director, Pitching Analysis:** Todd Walther. **Director, Baseball Analytics:** Ryan Murray. **Assistant Director, Baseball Systems:** Ben Baroody. **Assistant Director, Baseball Operations:** Ethan Faggett. **Senior Developers, Baseball Systems:** Bradley Ankrom, Kim Eskew. **Senior Analyst:** Alexander Booth. **Analysts, Baseball Operations:** Bobby Bandelow, Brett Mele, Randall Puffer, R.J. Walsh.

Jon Daniels

MAJOR LEAGUE STAFF

Manager: Chris Woodward.

Coaches: Bench—Don Wakamatsu. **Pitching**—Doug Mathis, Brendan Sagara. **Hitting**—Luis Ortiz. **First Base**—Corey Ragsdale. **Third Base**—Tony Beasley. **Catching**—Bobby Wilson. **Assistant Hitting Coach**—Callix Crabbe.

MEDICAL/TRAINING

Medical Director: Jamie Reed. **Team Physician:** Dr. Keith Meister. **Head Trainer:** Matt Lucero. **Trainer:** Jacob Newburn. **Physical Therapist:** Regan Wong. **Strength/Conditioning Coach:** José Vázquez.

PLAYER DEVELOPMENT

Telephone: (817) 436-5999. **Fax:** (817) 273-5285.

Director, Minor League Operations: Paul Kruger. **Coordinators:** Danny Clark (pitching), Jono Armold (pitching), Cody Atkinson (hitting), Greg Hibbard (roving pitching), Geno Petralli (roving coach), Turtle Thomas (roving catching coach), Brett Hayes/Alex Burg (run prevention), Keith Comstock (rehab). **Performance Coach:** Napoleon Pichardo. **Medical/Rehab Coordinators:** Sean Fields, Chris Olson. **Minor League Strength Coordinator:** Logan Frandsen. **Director, Arizona Operations:** Stosh Hoover.

FARM SYSTEM

Class	Club (League)	Manager	Hitting Coach	Pitching Coach
Triple-A	Round Rock	Kenny Holmberg	Chase Lambin	Bill Simas
Double-A	Frisco	Jared Goedert	Josue Perez	Jeff Andrews
High-A	Hickory	Josh Johnson	Chad Comer	Steve Mintz
Low-A	Down East	Carlos Cardoza	Eric Dorton	Jordan Tiegs
Rookie	Rangers (AZL)	Jay Sullenger	S. Adriana/R. Tuntland	J. Delgado/J. Jaimes
Rookie	Rangers (DSL)	Carlos Maldonado	E. Gonzalez/T. Coolbaugh	P. Blanco/R. Valencia/J. Valdez

SCOUTING

Senior Director, Pro/International Scouting: Ross Fenstermaker. **Assistant, Pro Scouting:** Mike Parnell. **Special Assistants:** Mike Anderson, Scot Engler, Scott Littlefield, Greg Smith. **Pro Scouts:** Russ Ardolina, Elliott Blair, Jay Eddings, Jonathan George, Mike Grouse, Donzell McDonald, Mitchell Webb. **Special Assignment Scout:** Curtis Jung. **Senior Director, Amateur Scouting:** Kip Fagg. **Assistant Director, Amateur Scouting:** Adam Lewkowicz. **National Crosscheckers: Eastern Crosschecker:** Ryan Coe. **Special Assignment Crosschecker:** Bobby Crook. **West Coast Crosschecker:** Casey Harvie. **National Crosschecker:** Jake Krug. **Midwest Crosschecker:** Demond Smith. **Southeast Crosschecker:** Brian Williams. **Area Scouts:** Brett Campbell, Chris Collias, Tommy Duenas, Steve Flores, Jay Heafner, Levi Lacey, Brian Matthews, Gary McGraw, Michael Medici, Brian Morrison, Patrick Perry, Takeshi Sakurayama, Gabe Sandy, Josh Simpson, Dustin Smith, Randy Taylor, Derrick Tucker, Tyler Carroll. **Director, International Scouting:** Rafic Saab. **Assistant Director, International Scouting:** Hamilton Wise. **Asst. International Scouting:** Jonny Clum. **Supervisor, Dominican Republic:** Willy Espinal. **International Scouts:** Jhonny Gomez (Crosschecker, Venezuela). Chu Halabi (Latin America Crosschecker). Jose Fernandez (International Scout). Yfrain Linares (Latin America Crosschecker), Jhonny Gomez (Crosschecker, Venezuela), Maikol Rojas (D.R.Video Scout), JC Alvarez (D.R. Crosschecker), Christian Cabral (D.R., Nelson Muniz (D.R.), Carlos Plaza (Venezuela), Jose Gabriel Rodriguez (Venezuela), Juan Salazar (Venezuela), Rafael Cedeno (Panama), Hamilton Sarabia (Colombia), Efrain Lara (Mexico). **Senior Advisor, Major League Scouting (Hokkaido):** Randy Smith. **Director, International Scouting (Hokkaido):** Al Hargesheimer. **Director, Pacific Rim Operations:** Joe Furukawa (Japan). **Manager, Pacific Rim:** Hajime Watabe (Japan). **International Scout:** Daniel Chang (Taiwan).

TORONTO BLUE JAYS

Office/Mailing Address: 1 Blue Jays Way, Suite 3200, Toronto, Ontario M5V 1J1.
Telephone: (416) 341-1000. **Fax:** (416) 341-1245. **Website:** www.bluejays.com.

OWNERSHIP

Operated by: Toronto Blue Jays Baseball Club. **Principal Owner:** Rogers Communications Inc. **Chairman, Toronto Blue Jays:** Edward Rogers. **Vice Chairman, Rogers Communications Inc.:** Phil Lind. **President and CEO, Rogers Communication:** Joe Natale. **Chief Financial Officer, Rogers Communication:** Tony Staffieri.

BUSINESS OPERATIONS

Mark Shapiro

President and CEO: Mark A. Shapiro. **President Emeritus:** Paul Beeston. **Executive Vice President, Baseball Operations/General Manager:** Ross Atkins. **Executive Vice President, Marketing and Business Operations:** Marnie Starkman. **Senior Vice Presidents, Business Operations:** Anuk Karunaratne. **Executive Assistant to the President/CEO:** Gail Ricci.

FINANCE/ADMINISTRATION

Director, Finance: Janet Chant. **Senior Manager, Blue Jays US Payroll & Benefits:** Sharon Dykstra. **Senior Managers, Finance:** Josh Hoffman, Derek Nicholson. **Manager, Finance:** Leslie Galant-Gardiner. **Manager, Treasury & Vault Operations:** Garrett Mercer. **Senior Payroll Analyst:** Joy Baybayan. **Payroll Analyst:** Joyce Chan. **Senior Financial Analysts:** Troy Mercuri, Melissa Patterson.

MARKETING/COMMUNITY RELATIONS

Director, Creative Services & Marketing Management: Sherry Oosterhuis. **Senior Manager, Game Entertainment & Producer:** Stefanie Wright. **Senior Manager, Player Relations & Community Marketing:** Shannon Curley. **Manager, Social Media:** Simone Gervais. **Program Manager, Amateur Baseball:** T.J. Burton. **Manager, Creative Services:** Maureen Kinghorn. **Marketing Department Manager & Alumni Relations:** Maria Cresswell. **Senior Motion Graphics Designer:** Michael Campbell. **Senior Graphics Designer:** Corey McDonald. **Motion Graphics Designer:** Ben Simpson. **Graphic Designer:** Meghan Koebel. **Social Community Manager:** Alykhan Ravjiani. **Social Content Specialist:** Nico Canavo. **Program Specialist, Amateur Baseball:** Jeff Holloway. **Digital Marketing Specialist:** Shirley Chan. **Specialist, Game Entertainment & Production:** MaryBeth Holba. **Authentics Specialist:** Mike Ferguson. **Program Assistant, Amateur Baseball:** Lucas McKernan. **Coordinator, Community Marketing:** Erinn White.

BASEBALL MEDIA

Communications Advisor & Liaison: Richard Griffin. **Director, Communications:** Jessica Beard. **Manager, Communications:** Madeleine Davidson. **Coordinators, Communications:** Adam Felton, Rodney Hiemstra.

TRAVEL/CLUBHOUSE

Director, Team Travel/Clubhouse Operations: Mike Shaw. **Senior Manger, Visiting Clubhouse:** Kevin Malloy. **Senior Manager, Clubhouse Operations:** Scott Blinn. **Manager, Home Clubhouse Operations:** Mustafa Hassan.

BASEBALL OPERATIONS

Senior Vice President, Player Personnel: Tony Lacava. **Vice President, International Scouting:** Andrew Tinnish. **Assistant General Manager:** Joe Sheehan. **Director, Baseball Operations:** Michael Murov. **Director, Team Travel & Clubhouse Operations:** Michael Shaw. **Assistant Director, Research & Development:** Sanjay Choudhury. **Assistant Director, Baseball Operations:** Jeremy Reesor. **Assistant Director and Technical Lead, Baseball Systems:** Peter Saunders. **Coordinator, Baseball Research:** Adam Yudelman. **Assistant, Baseball Research:** Cal Aldred. **Coordinator, Baseball Research:** Graydon Carruthers. **Assistant, Baseball Research:** Liam Stevenson. **Player Personnel Analyst:** John Babocsi. **Assistant, Pro Scouting & Baseball Operations:** Megan Evans. **Baseball Operations Fellow:** Ginger Poulson. **Baseball Systems Developer:** Shanna Shi. **Baseball Systems Developer:** Spencer Estey. **Bullpen Catcher:** Alex Andreopoulos. **Bullpen Catcher:** Nevin Ashley. **Major League Video Coordinator:** Eric Slotter. **Video Advisor:** Robert Baumander. **Executive Assistant to the General Manager:** Anna Coppola. **Bilingual Player Interpreter:** Hector Lebron. **Analytics Developer:** John Meloche. **Analyst, Advanced Scouting:** Theron Simpson.

Ross Atkins

MAJOR LEAGUE STAFF

Manager: Charlie Montoyo. **Coaches: Bench**—Dave Hudgens, **Pitching**—Pete Walker, **Hitting**—Guillermo Martinez, **First Base**—Mark Budzinski, **Third Base**—Luis Rivera, **Bullpen**—Matt Buschmann. **Major League Coach** — John Schneider. **Bullpen Catchers:** Alex Andreopoulos, Nevin Ashley.

HIGH PERFORMANCE/MEDICAL STAFF

VP, High Performance: Angus Mugford. **Assistant Director, High Performance Operations:** Dehra Harris. **Head Athletic Trainer:** Jose Ministral. **Major League Assistant Athletic Trainer:** Voon Chong. **Medical Research Coordinator:** Scott Peters. **Head Strength & Conditioning Coach:** Scott Weberg. **Medical Coordinator:** Pat Chasse. **Major League Assistant & Athletic Training Coordinator:** Drew MacDonald.

PLAYER DEVELOPMENT

Telephone: (727) 734-8007. **Fax:** (727) 734-8162.
Director, Player Development: Gil Kim. **Director, Minor League Operations:** Charlie Wilson. **Director, Latin America Operations:** Sandy Rosario. **Business Manager, Minor League Operations:** Michelle Rodgers. **Assistant Director, Player Development:** Joe Sclafani. **Assistant, Player Development:** Michael Rivera. **Field Coordinator:** Casey Candaele. **Hitting Coordinator:** Hunter Mense. **Infield Coordinator:** Danny Solano. **Special Assistant to Player Development:** Tim Raines. **Pitching Programs Coordinator & GCL Pitching Coach:** Corey Popham. **Pitching Analysis Coordinator & GCL Assistant Pitching Coach:** Matt Tracy. **Swing Consultant & Affiliate Hitting Coach:** Matt Hague. **Minor League Hitting Analyst:** Reed Kienle. **Player Development Analyst:** Evan Short. **Equipment Coordinator:** Billy Wardlow. **Technology Operations Coordinator:** Matt von Roemer. **Minor League Assistant Coach & Batting Practice Pitcher:** Zach Stewart. **Education Coordinator:** Sonia De La Cruz. **Player Development & HP Operations Assistant:** Will Habib.

FARM SYSTEM

Class	Club (League)	Manager	Hitting Coach	Pitching Coach	Position Coach
Triple-A	Buffalo	TBD	TBD	TBD	TBD
Double-A	New Hampshire	TBD	TBD	TBD	TBD
High-A	Vancouver	TBD	TBD	TBD	TBD
Low-A	Dunedin	TBD	TBD	TBD	TBD
Rookie	Blue Jays (GCL)	TBD	TBD	TBD	TBD
Rookie	Blue Jays (DSL)	TBD	TBD	TBD	TBD

SCOUTING

Director, Pro Scouting: Ryan Mittleman. **Pro Scouting Analyst:** Tommy Farah. **Assistant, Pro Scouting & Baseball Operations:** Megan Evans. **Special Assignment Scout:** Russ Bove. **Special Assignment Scout:** Dean Decillis. **Major League Scouts:** Sal Butera, Jim Skaalen. **Professional Scouts:** Matt Anderson, Kevin Briand, Blake Bentley, Justin Coleman, David May Jr., Marc Lippman, Mitch Leeds, Tim Rooney. **Pacific Rim Scout:** Hideaki Sato. **Player Personnel Coordinators:** Carson Cistulli, Jon Lalonde, Nick Manno, Brent Urcheck. **Player Personnel Analyst:** John Babocsi. **Pro Scouting Fellow:** Stephen Yoo.
Director, Amateur Scouting: Shane Farrell. **Manager, Amateur & International Scouting:** Harry Einbinder. **Manager, Amateur Scouting:** Kory Lafreniere. **National Supervisor:** Blake Crosby. **Regional Crosscheckers:** Matt Bishoff, CJ Ebarb, Jamie Lehman, Michael Youngberg. **Crosscheckers:** Brian Johnston, Paul Tinnell. **Area Scouts:** Adam Arnold, Joey Aversa, Coulson Barbiche, Brandon Bishoff, Tom Burns, Chris Curtis, Ryan Fox, Pete Holmes, Matt Huck, Randy Kramer, Jim Lentine, Nate Murrie, Don Norris, Matt O'Brien, Manny Padron, Wes Penick, Max Semler, Bud Smith, Mike Tidick. **Scouts:** Roberto Santana, Gerald Turner. **Amateur Scouting Video Coordinator:** Chirag Nanavati. **Scouting Video Associates:** Tony Cho, Adam McInturff. **Canadian Scouting:** Patrick Griffin, Jay Lapp, Jasmin Roy, Rene Tosoni.
Director, Latin American Operations: Sandy Rosario. **Scouting Supervisors:** Aaron Acosta (MX), Jose Contreras (VZ) Lorenzo Perez (DR). **Scouting Coordinator, South America:** Francisco Plasencia. **Assistant, International Scouting:** Julio Ramirez. **Assistant, International Operations:** Tyler Baldwin. **International Scouting:** Franklin Briceno (VZ), Alexis de la Cruz (DR), Luciano del Rosario (DR), Oscar Delgado (VZ), Enrique Falcon (COL), Jhoan Gomez (DR), Miguel Leal (VZ), Alirio Ledezma (VZ), Jose Natera (DR), Luis Natera (DR), Eric Ramirez (DR), Daniel Sotelo (NIC), Alex Zapata (PAN).

WASHINGTON NATIONALS

Office Address: 1500 South Capitol Street SE, Washington, DC 20003.
Telephone: (202) 640-7000. **Fax:** (202) 547-0025.
Website: www.nationals.com.

OWNERSHIP

Managing Principal Owner: Mark D. Lerner. **Founding Principal Owner:** Theodore N. Lerner.
Principal Owners: Annette M. Lerner, Marla Lerner Tanenbaum, Debra Lerner Cohen, Robert K. Tanenbaum, Edward L. Cohen, Judy Lenkin Lerner.

BUSINESS OPERATIONS

Chief Operating Officer, Lerner Sports: Alan H. Gottlieb. **Chief Financial Officer:** Lori Creasy. **Senior Vice President:** Elise Holman.

Mark Lerner

BALLPARK ENTERPRISES

Vice President, Corporate Strategy: Emily Dunham.

LEGAL

Vice President & General Counsel: Betsy Philpott. **Associate Counsel:** Nicolette Miranda.

HUMAN RESOURCES

Senior Vice President & Chief People Officer: Bob Frost. **Senior Director, Human Resources:** Kelvin Scott. **Director, Benefits:** Stephanie Giroux.

COMMUNICATIONS

Vice President, Communications: Jennifer Giglio. **Director, Communications:** Kyle Brostowitz. **Manager, Communications:** Melissa Strozza. **Manager, Communications:** Christopher Browne. **Coordinator, Communications:** Devon Bridges.

COMMUNITY RELATIONS

Senior Vice President, Community Engagement: Gregory McCarthy. **Executive Director, Player & Community Relations:** Shawn Bertani. **Director, Community Relations:** Nicole Murray.

BROADCASTING/GAME PRESENTATION

Senior Vice President, Marketing, Broadcasting & Game Presentation: Jacqueline Coleman. **Director, Promotions & Events:** Lindsey Norris. **Vice President, Production & Broadcasting:** Dave Lundin. **Director, Game Production:** Michael Masino. **Director, Video & Broadcast Engineering:** Benjamin Smith.

TICKETING/SALES

Vice President, Ticket Sales & Service: Ryan Bringger.

BALLPARK OPERATIONS

Senior Vice President, Ballpark Operations: Frank Gambino.

EXPERIENCE AND HOSPITALITY

Vice President, Experience and Hospitality: Jonathan Stahl.

REVENUE AND MARKETING

Executive Vice President, Business Operations: Jake Burns.

CORPORATE PARTNERSHIPS

Senior Vice President, Business Development: Vito Iaia. **Vice President, Corporate Partnerships:** Matt Lemire.

BASEBALL OPERATIONS

President of Baseball Operations and General Manager: Mike Rizzo. **Assistant General Manager & Vice President, Player Personnel:** Doug Harris. **Assistant General Manager & Vice President, Scouting Operations:** Kris Kline. **Assistant General Manager & Vice President, Finance:** Ted Towne. **Assistant General Manager & Vice President, International Operations:** Johnny DiPuglia. **Assistant General Manager, Baseball Operations:** Michael DeBartolo. **Assistant General Manager, Baseball Research & Development:** Sam Mondry-Cohen. **Assistant General Manager, Player Development:** Mark Scialabba. **Senior Advisor to the General Manager:** Jack McKeon. **Special Assistant, Major League Administration:** Harolyn Cardozo. **Assistant, Major League Administration:** Jordan Missal. **Senior Analyst, Baseball Operations:** James Badas. **Coordinator, Baseball Operations:** John Wulf. **Manager, Advance Scouting:** Jonathan Tosches. **Coordinator, Advance Scouting:** Greg Ferguson. **Assistant, Major League Video/Technology:** Kenny Diaz.

Mike Rizzo

BASEBALL RESEARCH AND DEVELOPMENT

Director, Baseball Research: Lee Mendelowitz. **Director, Software Development:** Isaac Gerhart-Hines. **Senior Analyst, Baseball R&D:** Max Ehrman, Scott Van Lenten. **Analysts, Baseball R&D:** Saul Forman, David Gagnon, David Higgins, Jordan Rassman. **Data Engineer, Baseball R&D:** Chris Jordan. **Senior Developer, Baseball R&D:** Jay Liu.

MAJOR LEAGUE OPERATIONS

Vice President, Clubhouse Operations & Team Travel: Rob McDonald. **Clubhouse & Equipment Manager:** Mike Wallace. **Visiting Clubhouse Manager:** Matt Rosenthal. **Equipment Manager:** Dan Wallin. **Assistant, Clubhouse & Team Travel:** Ryan Wiebe. **Clubhouse Assistants:** Mike Gordon, Andrew Melnick, Gregory Melnick.

MAJOR LEAGUE STAFF

Manager: Dave Martinez. **Coaches: Bench**— Tim Bogar. **Pitching**—Jim Hickey. **Hitting**—Kevin Long. **First Base**— Randy Knorr. **Third Base**— Bob Henley. **Bullpen**—Henry Blanco. **Assistant Hitting Coach:** Pat Roessler.

MEDICAL/TRAINING

Executive Director, Medical Services: Harvey Sharman. **Lead Team Physician:** Dr. Robin West. **Director, Mental Conditioning:** Mark Campbell. **Director, Athletic Training:** Paul Lessard. **Head Athletic Trainer:** Dale Gilbert.

PLAYER DEVELOPMENT

Vice President, Senior Advisor to the General Manager: Bob Boone. **Director, Minor League Operations:** Ryan Thomas. **Senior Advisor, Player Development:** Spin Williams. **Co-Field Coordinator/Infield Coordinator, Extended Spring Training Manager:** Jeff Garber. **Co-Field Coordinator, Wilmington Blue Rocks Manager:** Tommy Shields. **Pitching Coordinator:** Brad Holman. **Hitting Coordinator:** Troy Gingrich. **Outfield/Base running Coordinator:** Gary Thurman. **Catching Coordinator:** Michael Barrett. **Rehab Pitching Coordinator:** Mark Grater. **Medical/Rehab Coordinator:** Jon Kotredes. **Assistant Medical Coordinator:** Jeff Allred. **Strength and Conditioning Coordinator:** Tony Rogowski. **Minor League Clubhouse/Equipment Coordinator:** Carlos Felix. **Minor League Clubhouse Operations:** Scott Paquin.

FARM SYSTEM

Class	Club	Manager	Hitting Coach	Pitching Coach
Triple-A	Rochester	Matt LeCroy	Brian Daubach	Michael Tejera
Double-A	Harrisburg	Tripp Keister	Brian Rupp	Sam Narron
High-A	Wilmington	Tommy Shields	Luis Ordaz	Justin Lord
Low-A	Fredericksburg	Mario Lisson	Jorge Mejia	Pat Rice
Rookie	Nationals (GCL)	Jake Lowery	Mark Harris	F. Bravo/L. Pardo
Rookie	Nationals (DSL)	Sandy Martinez	Freddy Guzman	Edwin Hurtado

SCOUTING

Director, Scouting Operations: Eddie Longosz. **Director, Player Procurement:** Kasey McKeon. **Director, Pitching Evaluation & Special Asst. to the President of Baseball Ops & GM:** Jeff Zona. **Assistant Director, Amateur Scouting:** Mark Baca. **Special Assistants to the President of Baseball Operations & GM:** Steve Arnieri, Chuck Cottier, Mike Cubbage, Mike Daughtry, Dan Jennings, Jay Robertson, Bob Schaefer, Pete Vuckovich, De Jon Watson. **East Crosschecker:** Alan Marr. **Midwest Crosschecker:** Jimmy Gonzales. **West Crosschecker:** Fred Costello. **Southeast Crosschecker and Area Supervisor:** Alex Morales. **Area Supervisors:** Bryan Byrne, Brian Cleary, Ben Gallo, Jerad Head, Tommy Jackson, Brandon Larson, Steve Leavitt, John Malzone, Bobby Myrick, Scott Ramsay, Eric Robinson, Mitch Sokol, Cody Staab. **Director, International Operations:** Mike Cadahia. **Director, Latin American Scouting:** Fausto Severino. **Assistant, International Scouting:** Taisuke Sato. **Crosscheckers:** Tony Arias, Alex Rodriguez, Modesto Ulloa, Riki Vasquez. **Coordinator, Venezuela:** German Robles. **Colombia:** Eduardo Cabrera. **Curacao and Aruba:** David Leer. **Dominican Republic Supervisor:** Pablo Arias. **Dominican Republic:** Virgilio De Leon, Bolivar Pelletier, Carlos Ulloa. **Panama:** Miguel Ruiz. **Venezuela:** Oscar Alvarado, Salvador Donadelli, Juan Indriago, Ronald Morillo, Juan Munoz.

MEDIA
INFORMATION

LOCAL MEDIA INFORMATION

AMERICAN LEAGUE

BALTIMORE ORIOLES
Radio Announcers: Kevin Brown, Geoff Arnold, Melanie Newman, Brett Hollander. **Flagship Station:** WJZ-FM 105.7 The Fan.

TV Announcers: Geoff Arnold, Kevin Brown, Scott Garceau, Ben McDonald, Melanie Newman, Jim Palmer. **Flagship Station:** Mid-Atlantic Sports Network.

BOSTON RED SOX
Radio Announcers: Joe Castiglione, Will Flamming, Sean McDonough, Lou Merloni. **Flagship Station:** WEEI (93.7 FM).

TV Announcers: Dave O'Brien, Jerry Remy, Dennis Eckersley, Mike Monaco. **Flagship Station:** New England Sports Network (regional cable).

CHICAGO WHITE SOX
Radio Announcers: Len Kasper, Darrin Jackson. **Flagship Station:** WLS-AM 720.

TV Announcers: Steve Stone, Jason Benetti. **Flagship Stations:** WGN TV-9, WPWR-TV, NBC Sports Chicago (regional cable).

CLEVELAND INDIANS
Radio Announcers: Tom Hamilton, Jim Rosenhaus. **Flagship Station:** WTAM 1000-AM.

TV Announcers: Rick Manning, Matt Underwood, Andre Knott. **Flagship Station:** FOX Sports Ohio.

DETROIT TIGERS
Radio Announcers: Dan Dickerson, Jim Price. **Flagship Station:** WXYT 97.1 FM and AM 1270.

TV Announcers: Jack Morris, Kirk Gibson, Matt Shepherd, Craig Monroe, John Keating. **Flagship Station:** FOX Sports Detroit (regional cable).

HOUSTON ASTROS
Radio Announcers: Steve Sparks, Robert Ford. **Spanish:** Alex Trevino, Francisco Romero. **Flagship Stations:** KBME 790-AM, KLAT 1010-AM (Spanish).

TV Announcers: Todd Kalas, Geoff Blum, Julia Morales. **Flagship Station:** AT&T Sports Net Southwest.

KANSAS CITY ROYALS
Radio Announcers: Denny Matthews, Steve Physioc, Steve Stewart. **Kansas City Affiliate:** KCSP 610-AM.

TV Announcers: Ryan Lefebvre, Rex Hudler, Joel Goldberg, Steve Physioc, Jeff Montgomery (pre-game). **Flagship Station:** FOX Sports Kansas City.

LOS ANGELES ANGELS
Radio Announcers: Terry Smith, Mark Langston, Jose Tolentino (Spanish). **Flagship Station:** AM 830, 1330 KWKW (Spanish).

TV Announcers: Mark Gubicza, Jose Mota. **Flagship TV Station:** Fox Sports West (regional cable).

MINNESOTA TWINS
Radio Announcers: Cory Provus, Dan Gladden. **Radio Network Studio Host:** Kris Atteberry. **Spanish Radio:** Alfonso Fernandez, Tony Oliva. **Flagship Station:** WCCO-AM 830. **TV Announcers:** Bert Blyleven, Dick Bremer, Roy Smalley, Jack Morris, LaTroy Hawkins, Justin Morneau. **Flagship Station:** Fox Sports North.

NEW YORK YANKEES
Radio Announcers: John Sterling, Suzyn Waldman. **Flagship Station:** WFAN 660-AM, WADO 1280-AM. **Spanish Radio Announcers:** Francisco Rivera, Rickie Ricardo.

TV Announcers: David Cone, Jack Curry, John Flaherty, Michael Kay, Ryan Ruocco, Meredith Marakovits, Paul O'Neill, Ken Singleton. **Flagship Station:** YES Network (Yankees Entertainment & Sports).

OAKLAND ATHLETICS
Radio Announcers: Vince Cotroneo, Ken Korach, Ray Fosse. **Flagship Station:** KTRB 860 AM.

TV Announcers: Ray Fosse, Glen Kuiper, Dallas Braden. **Flagship Stations:** NBC Sports California.

SEATTLE MARINERS
Radio Announcers: Rick Rizzs, Aaron Goldsmith. **Flagship Station:** 710 ESPN Seattle (KIRO-AM 710).

TV Announcers: Mike Blowers, Dave Sims, Aaron Goldsmith, Alex Rivera. **Flagship Station:** ROOT Sports Northwest.

TAMPA BAY RAYS
Radio Announcers: Andy Freed, Dave Wills. **Flagship Station:** WDAE 620 AM/95.3 FM Tampa/St. Petersburg **TV Announcers:** Brian Anderson, Dewayne Staats, Tricia Whitaker. **Flagship Station:** FOX Sports Sun.

TEXAS RANGERS
Radio Announcers: Eric Nadel, Matt Hicks. **Spanish:** Eleno Ornelas, Jose Guzman. **Flagship Station:** 105.3 The FAN FM, KFLC 1270 AM (Spanish).

TV Announcers: Dave Raymond, Tom Grieve, C.J. Nitkowski, David Murphy, Emily Jones. **Flagship Station:** FOX Sports Southwest (regional cable).

TORONTO BLUE JAYS
Radio Announcers: Ben Wagner. **Flagship Station:** SportsNet Radio Fan 590-AM.

TV Announcers: Buck Martinez, Dan Shulman, Hazel Mae. **Flagship Station:** Rogers Sportsnet.

NATIONAL LEAGUE

ARIZONA DIAMONDBACKS
Radio Announcers: Greg Schulte, Tom Candiotti, Mike Ferrin, Rodrigo Lopez (Spanish), Oscar Soria (Spanish), Richard Saenz (Spanish). **Flagship Stations:** Arizona Sports 98.7 FM, TUDN 105.1 (Spanish).
TV Announcers: Steve Berthiaume, Bob Brenly. **Flagship Stations:** FOX Sports Arizona (regional cable).

ATLANTA BRAVES
Radio Announcers: Jim Powell, Ben Ingram. **Flagship Stations:** WCNN-AM 680 The Fan.
TV Announcers: Chip Caray, Joe Simpson, Tom Glavine, Jeff Francoeur. **Flagship Stations:** FOX Sports South/Southeast (regional cable).

CHICAGO CUBS
Radio Announcers: Pat Hughes, Ron Coomer. **Flagship Station:** WSCR-670 The Score.
TV Announcers: Len Kasper, Jim Deshaies. **Flagship Stations:** Marquee Sports Network.

CINCINNATI REDS
Radio Announcers: Jeff Brantley, Doug Flynn, Tommy Thrall. **Flagship Station:** WLW 700-AM.
TV Announcers: Chris Walsh, Jeff Brantley, John Sadak, Barry Larkin, Jim Day. **Flagship Station:** Fox Sports Ohio.

COLORADO ROCKIES
Radio Announcers: Jack Corrigan, Mike Rice, Salvador Hernandez (Spanish), Carlos Valdaz (Spanish). **Flagship Station:** KOA 850-AM & 94.1 FM, Rockies Spanish Radio 1150 AM.
TV Announcers: Drew Goodman, Jeff Huson, Ryan Spilborghs. **Flagship Station:** AT&T SportsNet.

LOS ANGELES DODGERS
Radio Announcers: Rick Monday, Charley Steiner, Tim Neverett. **Spanish:** Jaime Jarrín, Jorge Jarrin. **Flagship Stations:** AM570 Fox Sports LA, KTNQ 1020-AM (Spanish).
TV Announcers: Joe Davis, Orel Hershiser, Nomar Garciaparra, Alanna Rizzo, Tim Neverett. **Spanish:** Pepe Yniguez, Fernando Valenzuela. **Flagship Stations:** SportsNet LA (regional cable).

MIAMI MARLINS
Radio Announcers: Dave Van Horne, Glenn Geffner. **Flagship Stations:** WINZ 940-AM.
TV Announcers: Paul Severino, Todd Hollandsworth. **Flagship Stations:** FSN Florida (regional cable).

MILWAUKEE BREWERS
Radio Announcers: Bob Uecker, Jeff Levering, Lane Grindle. **Flagship Station:** WTMJ 620-AM.
TV Announcers: Brian Anderson, Bill Schroeder, Matt Lepay, Sophia Minnaert. **Flagship Station:** Fox Sports Wisconsin.

NEW YORK METS
Radio Announcers: Howie Rose, Ed Coleman and Wayne Randazzo. **Flagship Station:** WCBS 880-AM.
TV Announcers: Gary Cohen, Keith Hernandez, Ron Darling, Steve Gelbs, Todd Zeile. **Flagship Stations:** Sports Net New York (regional cable), PIX11-TV.

PHILADELPHIA PHILLIES
Radio Announcers: Scott Franzke, Larry Andersen, Jim Jackson, Bill Kulik (Spanish Radio). **Flagship Station:** SportsRadio 94WIP (94.1 FM).
TV Announcers: Tom McCarthy, Ben Davis, Kevin Frandsen, Jimmy Rollins, John Kruk, Gregg Murphy, Mike Schmidt. **Flagship Stations:** NBC 10 (regional cable).

PITTSBURGH PIRATES
Radio Announcers: Joe Block, Matt Capps, Kevin Young, Michael McKenry, Greg Brown, Bob Walk, John Wehner. **Flagship Station:** Sports Radio 93.7 FM The Fan.
TV Announcers: Joe Block, Matt Capps, Kevin Young, Michael McKenry, Greg Brown, Bob Walk, John Wehner. **Flagship Station:** AT&T SportsNet Pittsburgh (regional cable).

ST. LOUIS CARDINALS
Radio Announcers: Mike Shannon, John Rooney, Ricky Horton, Mike Claiborne. **Flagship Station:** KMOX 1120 AM. **Spanish Radio Announcers:** Polo Ascencio, Bengie Molina. **Flagship Station:** WJIR 880
TV Announcers: Dan McLaughlin, Ricky Horton, Al Hrabosky, Brad Thompson, Jim Edmonds, Tim McCarver, Jim Hayes, Erica Weston, Scott Warmann. **Flagship Station:** Fox Sports Midwest.

SAN DIEGO PADRES
Radio Announcers: Ted Leitner, Jesse Agler, Tony Gwynn Jr. **Flagship Stations:** 97.3 The Fan.
TV Announcers: Don Orsillo, Mark Grant. **Flagship Station:** Fox Sports San Diego. **Spanish Announcers:** Eduardo Ortega, Carlos Hernandez on XEMO-860-AM.

SAN FRANCISCO GIANTS
Radio Announcers: Mike Krukow, Duane Kuiper, Jon Miller, Dave Flemming.
Spanish: Tito Fuentes, Edwin Higueros. **Flagship Station:** KNBR 680-AM (English); ESPN Deportes-860AM (Spanish).
TV Announcers: Mike Krukow, Duane Kuiper, Jon Miller, Dave Flemming. **Flagship Stations:** KNTV-NBC 11, CSN Bay Area (regional cable).

WASHINGTON NATIONALS
Radio Announcers: Charlie Slowes, Dave Jageler. **Flagship Station:** WJFK 106.7 FM.
TV Announcers: Bob Carpenter, FP Santangelo, Alex Chappell. **Flagship Station:** Mid-Atlantic Sports Network.

NATIONAL MEDIA INFORMATION

BASEBALL STATISTICS

ELIAS SPORTS BUREAU INC. NATIONAL MEDIA BASEBALL STATISTICS
Official Major League Statistician Mailing Address: 500 Fifth Ave., Suite 2140, New York, NY 10110.
Telephone: (212) 869-1530. **Fax:** (212) 354-0980. **Website:** esb.com.
President: Joe Gilston.
Vice President: Chris Thorn. **Email Address:** Chris.Thorn@ESB.com
Manager, Baseball Operations: John Labombarda. **Email Address:** John.Labombarda@ESB.com

MLB ADVANCED MEDIA
Official Minor League Statistician Mailing Address: 1271 Avenue of the Americas, New York, NY, 10020.
Telephone: (212) 485-3444. **Fax:** (212) 485-3456.
Director, Stats: Chris Lentine. **Senior Manager, Stats:** Shawn Geraghty.
Senior Stats Supervisors: Jason Rigatti, Ian Schwartz. **Stats Supervisors:** Lawrence Fischer, Jake Fox, Dominic French, Kelvin Lee.

MILB.COM OFFICIAL WEBSITE OF MINOR LEAGUE BASEBALL
Mailing Address: 1271 Avenue of the Americas, New York, NY, 10020.
Telephone: (212) 485-3444. **Fax:** (212) 485-3456. **Website:** MiLB.com.
Director, Minor League Club Initiatives: Nathan Blackmon. **Sr. Producer, MiLB.com:** Dan Marinis.

STATS PERFORM
Mailing Address: 203 N. LaSalle St. Chicago, IL, 60601.
Telephone: (847) 583-2100. **Fax:** (847) 470-9140. **Website:** statsperform.com.
Email: sales@stats.com. **Twitter:** @STATSBiznews; @STATS_MLB. **CEO:** Carl Mergale. **Chief Operating Officer:** Mike Perez. **Chief Revenue Officer:** Steve Xeller. **Chief Financial Officer:** Ashley Milton. **Chief Technology Officer:** Dr. Helen Sun. **Advanced Analytics Coordinatior:** Micah Parshall.

GENERAL INFORMATION

SCOUTING

SCOUT OF THE YEAR FOUNDATION
Mailing Address: P.O. Box 211585, West Palm Beach, FL 33421.
Telephone: (561) 798-5897, (561) 818-4329. **E-mail Address:** bertmazur@aol.com.
President: Roberta Mazur. **Vice President:** Tracy Ringolsby. **Treasurer:** Ron Mazur II. **Board of Advisers:** Pat Gillick, Roland Hemond. **Scout of the Year Program Advisory Board:** Grady Fuson, Roland Hemond, Dan Jennings, Linda Pereira, Gene Watson.

MUSEUMS

NATIONAL BASEBALL HALL OF FAME AND MUSEUM
Address: 25 Main St., Cooperstown, NY 13326.
Telephone: (888) 425-5633, (607) 547-7200. **Fax:** (607) 547-2044. **E-mail Address:** info@baseballhall.org. **Website:** www.baseballhall.org.
Year Founded: 1939.
Chairman: Jane Forbes Clark. **President:** Tim Mead.
Museum Hours: Open daily, year-round, closed only Thanksgiving, Christmas and New Year's Day. 9 a.m.-5 p.m. Summer hours, 9 a.m.-9 p.m. (Memorial Day weekend through the day before Labor Day.)
2021 Hall of Fame Induction Weekend: Canceled due to Covid-19 concerns.

NEGRO LEAGUES BASEBALL MUSEUM
Mailing Address: 1616 E. 18th St., Kansas City, MO 64108.
Telephone: (816) 221-1920. **Fax:** (816) 221-8424.
E-mail Address: bkendrick@nlbm.com. **Website:** www.nlbm.com.
Year Founded: 1990.
President: Bob Kendrick.
Museum Hours: Tues.-Sat. 9 a.m.-6 p.m.; Sun. noon-6 p.m.

RESEARCH

SOCIETY FOR AMERICAN BASEBALL RESEARCH
Mailing Address: Cronkite School at ASU, 555 N Central Ave., #416 , Phoenix, AZ 85004.
Website: www.sabr.org.
Year Founded: 1971.
President: Mark Armour. **Executive Vice President:** Scott Carter. **Vice President:** Leslie Heaphy. **Secretary:** Todd

Lebowitz. **Treasurer:** F.X. Flinn. **Directors:** Bill Nowlin, Daniel Levitt, Allison Levin, Tyrone Brooks. **CEO:** Scott Bush. **Director of Editorial Content:** Jacob Pomrenke. **Community Engagement Manager:** Chanel Zapata.

ALUMNI ASSOCIATIONS

MAJOR LEAGUE BASEBALL PLAYERS ALUMNI ASSOCIATION
Mailing Address: 1631 Mesa Ave., Copper Building, Suite D, Colorado Springs, CO 80906.
Telephone: (719) 477-1870. **Fax:** (719) 477-1875.
E-mail Address: postoffice@mlbpaa.com. **Website:** www.baseballalumni.com.
Facebook: facebook.com/majorleaguebaseballplayersalumniassociation. **Twitter:** @MLBPAA.
Chief Executive Officer: Dan Foster (dan@mlbpaa.com). **Chief Operating Officer:** Geoffrey Hixson (geoff@mlbpaa.com). **Vice President, Operations:** Mike Groll (mikeg@mlbpaa.com). **Director, Communications:** Nikki Warner (nikki@mlbpaa.com). **Vice President, Membership/Content:** Kate Tyo (Kate@mlbpaa.com). **Director, Memorabilia Operations:** Greg Thomas (greg@mlbpaa.com). **Database Manager:** Chris Burkeen (cburkeen@mlbpaa.com).

BASEBALL ASSISTANCE TEAM (B.A.T.)
Mailing Address: 1271 Avenue of the Americas, New York, NY 10020
Telephone: (212) 931-7822, **Fax:** (212) 949-5433.
Website: www.baseballassistanceteam.com.

MINISTRY

BASEBALL CHAPEL
Mailing Address: P.O. Box 10102, Largo FL 33773.
Telephone: (610) 999-3600.
E-mail Address: office@baseballchapel.org. **Website:** www.baseballchapel.org.
Year Founded: 1973.
President: Vince Nauss. **Hispanic Ministry:** Cali Magallanes, Gio Llerena. **Ministry Operations:** Rob Crose, Steve Sisco. **Board of Directors:** Don Christensen, Greg Groh, Dave Howard, Vince Nauss, Walt Wiley.

CATHOLIC ATHLETES FOR CHRIST
Mailing Address: 3703 Cameron Mills Road, Alexandria, VA 22305.
Telephone: (703) 239-3070.
E-mail Address: info@catholicathletesforchrist.org. **Website:** www.catholicathletesforchrist.org.
Year Founded: 2006.
President: Ray McKenna. **MLB Ministry Coordinator:** Kevin O'Malley. **MLB Athlete Advisory Board Members:** Mike Sweeney (Chairman), Jeff Suppan (Vice Chairman), Sal Bando, Lauren Bauer, David Eckstein, Terry Kennedy, Jack McKeon, Darrell Miller, Mike Piazza, Vinny Rottino, Craig Stammen.

TRADE/EMPLOYMENT

BASEBALL WINTER MEETINGS
E-Mail Address: BaseballWinterMeetings@milb.com. **Website:** www.baseballwintermeetings.com.
2021 Convention: Dec. 6-9, Orlando

BASEBALL TRADE SHOW
E-Mail Address: TradeShow@MiLB.com. **Website:** www.BaseballTradeShow.com.
Contact: Noreen Brantner, Sr. Asst. Director, Exhibition Services & Sponsorships.
2021 Convention: Dec. 6-9, Orlando

PROFESSIONAL BASEBALL EMPLOYMENT OPPORTUNITIES
Mailing Address: P.O. Box A, St. Petersburg, FL 33731-1950.
Telephone: 866-WE-R-PBEO. **Fax:** 727-821-5819.
Email: info@PBEO.com. **Website:** www.PBEO.com.

REVIVING BASEBALL IN INNER CITIES

Mailing Address: 1271 Avenue of the Americas, New York, NY 10020
Telephone: (212) 931-7800. **Fax:** (212) 949-5695
Year Founded: 1989
Executive Vice President, Baseball & Softball Development: Tony Reagins (Tony.Reagins@mlb.com). **Vice President, Baseball & Softball Development:** David James (David.James@mlb.com). **E-mail:** rbi@mlb.com. **Website:** www.mlb.com/rbi

MLB YOUTH ACADEMIES

CINCINNATI REDS YOUTH ACADEMY
Director: Jerome Wright
Asst. Director: Jeremy Hamilton
Mailing Address: 2026 E. Seymour Avenue. Cincinnati, OH 45327
Phone Number: 513-765-5000

COMPTON YOUTH ACADEMY
Vice President: Darrell Miller
Mailing Address: 901 East Artesia Blvd. Compton, CA

HOUSTON ASTROS YOUTH ACADEMY
Director: Daryl Wade
Mailing Address: 2801 South Victory Drive. Houston, TX 77088.
Email: uya@astros.com

KANSAS CITY ROYALS URBAN YOUTH ACADEMY
Executive Director: Darwin Pennye
Email: Darwin.Pennye@royals.com

NEW ORLEANS YOUTH ACADEMY
Director: Eddie Anthony Davis III
Mailing Address: 6403 Press Drive. New Orleans, LA 70126
Phone Number: 504-282-0443

PHILADELPHIA PHILLIES YOUTH ACADEMY
Director: Jon Joaquin
Phone Number: 215-218-5634
Director: Rob Holiday
Phone Number: 215-218-5204

PUERTO RICO BASEBALL ACADEMY AND HIGH SCHOOL
Phone Number: 787-712-0700
Lucy Batista: Headmaster
Phone Number: 787-531-1768

TEXAS RANGERS YOUTH ACADEMY
Director: Juan Leonel Garciga
Mailing Address: 1000 Ballpark Way, Arlington, TX 76011
Phone Number: 817-273-5297

WASHINGTON NATIONALS YOUTH ACADEMY
Executive Director: Tal Alter
Mailing Address: 3675 Ely Place SE. Washington, DC 20019
Phone Number: 202-827-8960

SPRING TRAINING

CACTUS LEAGUE

ARIZONA DIAMONDBACKS

MAJOR LEAGUE

Complex Address: Salt River Fields at Talking Stick, 7555 North Pima Road, Scottsdale, AZ 85256. **Telephone:** (480) 270-5000. **Seating Capacity:** 11,000 (7,000 fixed seats, 4,000 lawn seats). **Location:** From Loop-101, use exit 44 (Indian Bend Road) and proceed west for approximately one-half mile; turn right at Pima Road to travel north and proceed one-quarter mile; three entrances to Salt River Fields will be available on the right-hand side.

MINOR LEAGUE

Complex Address: Same as major league club.

CHICAGO CUBS

MAJOR LEAGUE

Complex Address: Sloan Park, 2330 West Rio Salado Parkway, Mesa, AZ 85201. **Telephone:** (480) 668-0500. **Seating Capacity:** 15,000. **Location:** on the land of the former Riverview Golf Course, bordered by the 101 and 202 interchange in Mesa.

MINOR LEAGUE

Complex Address: 2510 W. Rio Salado Parkway, Mesa, AZ 85201. **Telephone:** (480) 668-0500

CHICAGO WHITE SOX

MAJOR LEAGUE

Complex Address: Camelback Ranch-Glendale, 10710 West Camelback Road, Phoenix, AZ 85037. **Telephone:** (623) 302-5000. **Seating Capacity:** 13,000. **Hotel Address:** Residence Inn Phoenix Glendale Sports and Entertainment District, 7350 N Zanjero Blvd, Glendale, AZ 85305, **Telephone:** (623) 772-8900. **Hotel Address:** Renaissance Glendale Hotel & Spa, 9495 W Coyotes Blvd, Glendale, AZ 85305. **Telephone:** 629-937-3700.

MINOR LEAGUE

Complex/Hotel Address: Same as major league club.

CINCINNATI REDS

MAJOR LEAGUE

Complex Address: Cincinnati Reds Player Development Complex, 3125 S Wood Blvd, Goodyear, AZ 85338. **Telephone:** (623) 932-6590. **Ballpark Address:** Goodyear Ballpark, 1933 S Ballpark Way, Goodyear, AZ 85338. **Telephone:** (623) 882-3120. **Hotel Address:** Marriott Residence Inn, 7350 N Zanjero Blvd, Glendale, AZ 85305. **Telephone:** (623) 772-8900. **Fax:** (623) 772-8905.

MINOR LEAGUE

Complex/Hotel Address: Same as major league club.

CLEVELAND INDIANS

MAJOR LEAGUE

Complex Address: Cleveland Indians Player Development Complex 2601 S Wood Blvd, Goodyear, AZ 85338; Goodyear Ballpark 1933 S Ballpark Way, Goodyear, AZ 85338. **Telephone:** (623) 882-3120. **Location: From Downtown Phoenix/East Valley:** West on I-10 to Exit 127, Bullard Avenue and proceed south (left off exit), Bullard Avenue turns into West Lower Buckeye Road. Turn left onto Wood Blvd. **Hotel Address:** (Media) Hampton Inn and Suites, 2000 N Litchfield Rd, Goodyear, AZ 85395. **Telephone:** (623) 536-1313. **Hotel Address:** Holiday Inn Express, 1313 N Litchfield Rd, Goodyear, AZ 85395. **Telephone:** (623) 535-1313. **Hotel Address:** TownePlace Suites, 13971 West Celebrate Life Way, Goodyear, AZ 85338. **Telephone:** (623) 535-5009. **Hotel Address:** Residence Inn by Marriott, 2020 N Litchfield Rd, Goodyear, AZ 85395. **Telephone:** (623) 866-1313.

MINOR LEAGUE

Complex Address: Same as major league club.

COLORADO ROCKIES

MAJOR LEAGUE

Complex Address: Salt River Fields at Talking Stick, 7555 North Pima Rd, Scottsdale, AZ 85258. **Telephone:** (480) 270-5800. **Seating Capacity:** 11,000 (7,000 fixed seats, 4,000 lawn seats). **Location:** From Loop-101, use exit 44 (Indian Bend Road Talking Stick Way) and proceed west for approximately one-half mile; turn right at Pima Road to travel north and proceed one-quarter mile; three entrances to Salt River Fields will be available on the right-hand side. **Visiting Team Hotel:** The Scottsdale Plaza Resort, 7200 North Scottsdale Road, Scottsdale, AZ 85253. **Telephone:** (480) 948-5000. **Fax:** (480) 951-5100.

MINOR LEAGUE

Complex/Hotel Address: Same as major league club.

KANSAS CITY ROYALS

MAJOR LEAGUE

Complex Address: Surprise Stadium, 15850 North Bullard Ave, Surprise, AZ 85374. **Telephone:** (623) 222-2000. **Seating Capacity:** 10,700. **Location:** I-10 West to Route 101 North, 101 North to Bell Road, left on Bell for five miles, stadium on left. **Hotel Address:** Wigwam Resort, 300 East Wigwam Blvd, Litchfield Park, Arizona 85340. **Telephone:** (623) 935-3811.

MINOR LEAGUE

Complex Address: Same as major league club. **Hotel Address:** Comfort Hotel and Suites, 13337 W Grand Ave, Surprise, AZ 85374. **Telephone:** (623) 583-3500.

LOS ANGELES ANGELS

MAJOR LEAGUE

Complex Address: Tempe Diablo Stadium, 2200 West Alameda Drive, Tempe, AZ 85282. **Telephone:** (480) 858-7500. **Seating Capacity:** 9,558. **Location:** I-10 to exit 153B (48th Street), south one mile on 48th Street to Alameda Drive, left on Alameda.

MINOR LEAGUE

Complex Address: Tempe Diablo Minor League Complex, 2225 W Westcourt Way, Tempe, AZ 85282. **Telephone:** (480) 858-7558.

LOS ANGELES DODGERS

MAJOR LEAGUE
   Complex Address: Camelback Ranch, 10710 West Camelback Rd, Phoenix, AZ 85037. **Seating Capacity:** 13,000, plus standing room. **Location:** I-10 or I-17 to Loop 101 West or North, Take Exit 5, Camelback Road West to ballpark. **Telephone:** (623) 302-5000. **Hotel:** Unavailable.

MINOR LEAGUE
   Complex/Hotel Address: Same as major league club.

MILWAUKEE BREWERS

MAJOR LEAGUE
   Complex Address: Maryvale Baseball Park, 3600 N 51st Ave, Phoenix, AZ 85031. **Telephone:** (623) 245-5555. **Seating Capacity:** 9,000. **Location:** I-10 to 51st Ave, north on 51st Ave. **Hotel Address:** Unavailable.

MINOR LEAGUE
   Complex Address: Maryvale Baseball Complex, 3805 N 53rd Ave, Phoenix, AZ 85031. **Telephone:** (623) 245-5600. **Hotel Address:** Unavailable.

OAKLAND ATHLETICS

MAJOR LEAGUE
   Complex Address: Hohokam Stadium, 1235 North Center Street, Mesa, AZ 85201. **Telephone:** 480-907-5489. **Seating Capacity:** 10,000.

MINOR LEAGUE
   Complex Address: Fitch Park, 160 East 6th Place, Mesa, AZ 85201. **Telephone:** 480-387-5800. **Hotel Address:** Unavailable.

SAN DIEGO PADRES

MAJOR LEAGUE
   Complex Address: Peoria Sports Complex, 8131 West Paradise Lane, Peoria, AZ 85382. **Telephone:** (619) 795-5720. **Fax:** (623) 486-7154. **Seating Capacity:** 12,000. **Location:** I-17 to Bell Road exit, west on Bell to 83rd Ave. **Hotel Address:** La Quinta Inn & Suites (623) 487-1900, 16321 N 83rd Avenue, Peoria, AZ 85382.

MINOR LEAGUE
   Complex/Hotel: Country Inn and Suites (623) 879-9000, 20221 N 29th Avenue, Phoenix, AZ 85027.

SAN FRANCISCO GIANTS

MAJOR LEAGUE
   Complex Address: Scottsdale Stadium, 7408 East Osborn Rd, Scottsdale, AZ 85251. **Telephone:** (480) 990-7972. **Fax:** (480) 990-2643. **Seating Capacity:** 11,500. **Location:** Scottsdale Road to Osborne Road, east on Osborne for a 1/2 mile. **Hotel Address:** Hilton Garden Inn Scottsdale Old Town, 7324 East Indian School Rd, Scottsdale, AZ 85251. **Telephone:** (480) 481-0400.

MINOR LEAGUE
   Complex Address: Giants Minor League Complex 8045 E Camelback Road, Scottsdale, AZ 85251. **Telephone:** (480) 990-0052. **Fax:** (480) 990-2349.

SEATTLE MARINERS

MAJOR LEAGUE
   Complex Address: Seattle Mariners, 15707 North 83rd Street, Peoria, AZ 85382. **Telephone:** (623) 776-4800. **Fax:** (623) 776-4829. **Seating Capacity:** 12,339. **Location:** Hwy 101 to Bell Road exit, east on Bell to 83rd Ave, south on 83rd Ave. **Hotel Address:** La Quinta Inn & Suites, 16321 N 83rd Ave, Peoria, AZ 85382. **Telephone:** (623) 487-1900.

MINOR LEAGUE
   Complex Address: Peoria Sports Complex (1993), 15707 N 83rd Ave, Peoria, AZ 85382. **Telephone:** (623) 776-4800. **Fax:** (623) 776-4828. **Hotel Address:** Hampton Inn, 8408 W Paradise Lane, Peoria, AZ 85382. **Telephone:** (623) 486-9918.

TEXAS RANGERS

MAJOR LEAGUE
   Complex Address: Surprise Stadium, 15754 North Bullard Ave, Surprise, AZ 85374. **Telephone:** (623) 266-8100. **Seating Capacity:** 10,714. **Location:** I-10 West to Route 101 North, 101 North to Bell Road, left at Bell for seven miles, stadium on left. **Hotel Address:** Residence Inn Surprise, 16418 N Bullard Ave, Surprise, AZ 85374. **Telephone:** (623) 249-6333.

MINOR LEAGUE
   Complex Address: Same as major league club. **Hotel Address:** Holiday Inn Express and Suites Surprise, 16549 North Bullard Ave, Surprise AZ 85374. **Telephone:** (800) 939-4249.

GRAPEFRUIT LEAGUE

ATLANTA BRAVES

MAJOR LEAGUE
Complex Address: Cool Today Park, 18800 South West Villages Pkwy Venice, FL 34293. **Telephone:** (941) 413-5000. **Seating Capacity:** 8,000. **Location:** From I-75S: Take Exit 191 (River Rd Englewood/North Port). Keep Right onto River Road for 3.9 miles. Turn Right onto US 41/Tamiami Trail. In 1.5 miles take a left onto W. Villages Pkwy. Continue on W. Villages Pkwy for .75 miles.
From I-75N: Take Exit 191 (River Rd Englewood/North Port). Turn left onto River Road. Continue for 3.9 miles. Turn Right onto US 41/Tamiami Trail. In 1.5 miles take a left onto W. Villages Pkwy. Continue on W. Villages Pkwy for .75 miles.
Hotel Address: Unavailable.

MINOR LEAGUE
Complex Address: Same as major league club. **Telephone:** (407) 939-2232. **Fax:** (407) 939-2225. **Hotel Address:** Marriot Village at Lake Buena Vista, 8623 Vineland Ave, Orlando, FL 32821. **Telephone:** (407) 938-9001.

BALTIMORE ORIOLES

MAJOR LEAGUE
Complex Address: Ed Smith Stadium, 2700 12th Street, Sarasota, FL 34237. **Telephone:** (941) 893-6300. **Fax:** (941) 893-6377. **Seating Capacity:** 7,500. **Location:** I-75 to exit 210, West on Fruitville Road, right on Tuttle Avenue.

MINOR LEAGUE
Complex Address: Buck O'Neil Baseball Complex at Twin Lakes Park, 6700 Clark Rd, Sarasota, FL 34241. **Telephone:** (941) 923-1996.

BOSTON RED SOX

MAJOR LEAGUE
Complex Address: JetBlue Park at Fenway South, 11500 Fenway South Drive, Fort Myers, FL 33913. **Telephone:** (239) 334-4700. **Directions: From the North:** Take I-75 South to Exit 131 (Daniels Parkway); Make a left off the exit and go east for approximately two miles; JetBlue Park will be on your left. **From the South:** Take I-75 North to Exit 131 (Daniels Parkway); Make a right off exit and go east for approximately two miles; JetBlue Park will be on your left.

MINOR LEAGUE
Complex/Hotel Address: Fenway South, 11500 Fenway South Drive, Fort Myers, FL 33913.

DETROIT TIGERS

MAJOR LEAGUE
Complex Address: Joker Marchant Stadium, 2301 Lakeland Hills Blvd, Lakeland, FL 33805. **Telephone:** (863) 686-8075. **Seating Capacity:** 9,568. **Location:** I-4 to exit 33 (Lakeland Hills Boulevard).

MINOR LEAGUE
Complex Address: Tigertown, 2125 N Lake Ave, Lakeland, FL 33805. **Telephone:** (863) 686-8075.

HOUSTON ASTROS

MAJOR LEAGUE
Complex Address: The Ballpark of the Palm Beaches, 5444 Haverhill Road, West Palm Beach, FL 33407. **Telephone:** (844) 676-2017. **Seating Capacity:** 7,838. **Location:** Exit Florida's Turnpike onto Okeechobee Blvd. Proceed east to Haverhill Road turning left onto Haverhill Road. On game days, all vehicles may park in one of two grass parking areas. Proceed toward the stadium for disabled parking or drop-off. The North entrance on Haverhill Road will be right-out only. **Hotel Address:** Unavailable.

MINOR LEAGUE
Complex Information: Same as major league club. **Hotel Address:** Unavailable.

MIAMI MARLINS

MAJOR LEAGUE
Complex Address: Roger Dean Stadium, 4751 Main Street, Jupiter, FL 33458. **Telephone:** (561) 775-1818. **Telephone:** (561) 799-1346. **Seating Capacity:** 7,000. **Location:** I-95 to exit 83, east on Donald Ross Road for one mile to Central Blvd, left at light, follow Central Boulevard to circle and take Main Street to Roger Dean Stadium. **Hotel Address:** Palm Beach Gardens Marriott, 4000 RCA Boulevard, Palm Beach Gardens, FL 33410. **Telephone:** (561) 622-8888. **Fax:** (561) 622-0052.

MINOR LEAGUE
Complex/Hotel Address: Same as major league club.

MINNESOTA TWINS

MAJOR LEAGUE
Complex Address: Centurylink Sports Complex/Hammond Stadium, 14100 Six Mile Cypress Parkway, Fort Myers, FL 33912. **Telephone:** (239) 533-7610. **Seating Capacity:** 8,100. **Location:** Exit 21 off I-75, west on Daniels Parkway, left on Six Mile Cypress Parkway. **Hotel Address:** Four Points by Sheraton, 13600 Treeline Avenue South, Ft. Myers, FL 33913. **Telephone:** (800) 338-9467.

MINOR LEAGUE
Complex/Hotel Address: Same as major league club.

NEW YORK METS

MAJOR LEAGUE
Complex Address: Tradition Field, 525 NW Peacock Blvd, Port St. Lucie, FL 34986. **Telephone:** (772) 871-2100. **Seating Capacity:** 7,000. **Location:** Exit 121C (St Lucie West Blvd) off I-95, east 1/4 mile, left onto NW Peacock. **Hotel Address:** Hilton Hotel, 8542 Commerce Centre Drive, Port St. Lucie, FL 34986. **Telephone:** (772) 871-6850.

MINOR LEAGUE
Complex Address: Same as major league club. **Hotel Address:** Main Stay Suites, 8501 Champions Way, Port St. Lucie, FL 34986. **Telephone:** (772) 460-8882.

NEW YORK YANKEES

MAJOR LEAGUE
Complex Address: George M. Steinbrenner Field, One Steinbrenner Drive, Tampa, FL 33614. **Telephone:** (813) 875-7753. **Hotel:** Unavailable.

MINOR LEAGUE
Complex Address: Yankees Player Development/ Scouting Complex, 3102 N Himes Ave, Tampa, FL 33607. **Telephone:** (813) 875-7569. **Hotel:** Unavailable.

PHILADELPHIA PHILLIES

MAJOR LEAGUE
Complex Address: BayCare Ballpark, 601 N Old Coachman Road, Clearwater, FL 33765. **Telephone:** (727) 467-4457. **Fax:** (727) 712-4498. **Seating Capacity:** 8,500. **Location:** Route 60 West, right on Old Coachman Road, ballpark on right after Drew Street. **Hotel Address:** Holiday Inn Express, 2580 Gulf to Bay Blvd, Clearwater, FL 33765. **Telephone:** (727) 797-6300. **Hotel Address:** La Quinta Inn, 21338 US 19 North, Clearwater, FL 33765. **Telephone:** (727) 799-1565.

MINOR LEAGUE
Complex Address: Carpenter Complex, 651 N Old Coachman Rd, Clearwater, FL 33765. **Telephone:** (727) 799-0503. **Fax:** (727) 726-1793. **Hotel Addresses:** Hampton Inn, 21030 US Highway 19 North, Clearwater, FL 34625. **Telephone:** (727) 797-8173. **Hotel Address:** Econolodge, 21252 US Hwy 19, Clearwater, FL 34625. **Telephone:** (727) 799-1569.

PITTSBURGH PIRATES

MAJOR LEAGUE
Stadium Address: 17th Ave West and Ninth Street West, Bradenton, FL 34205. **Seating Capacity:** 8,500. **Location:** US 41 to 17th Ave, west to 9th Street. **Telephone:** (941) 747-3031. **Fax:** (941) 747-9549.

MINOR LEAGUE
Complex: Pirate City, 1701 27th St E, Bradenton, FL 34208.

ST. LOUIS CARDINALS

MAJOR LEAGUE
Complex Address: Roger Dean Stadium, 4751 Main Street, Jupiter, FL 33458. **Telephone:** (561) 775-1818. **Fax:** (561) 799-1380. **Seating Capacity:** 7,000. **Location:** I-95 to exit 58, east on Donald Ross Road for 1/4 mile. **Hotel Address:** Embassy Suites, 4350 PGA Blvd, Palm Beach Gardens, FL 33410. **Telephone:** (561) 622-1000.

MINOR LEAGUE
Complex: Same as major league club. **Hotel:** Double Tree Palm Beach Gardens. **Telephone:** (561) 622-2260.

TAMPA BAY RAYS

MAJOR LEAGUE
Stadium Address: Charlotte Sports Park, 2300 El Jobean Road, Port Charlotte, FL 33948. **Telephone:** (941) 206-4487. **Seating Capacity:** 6,823 (5,028 fixed seats). **Location:** I-75 to US-17 to US-41, turn left onto El Jobean Rd. **Hotel Address:** None.

MINOR LEAGUE
Complex: Same as major league club.

TORONTO BLUE JAYS

MAJOR LEAGUE
Stadium Address: Florida Auto Exchange Stadium, 373 Douglas Ave, Dunedin, FL 34698. **Telephone:** (727) 733-9302. **Seating Capacity:** 5,509. **Location:** US 19 North to Sunset Point; west on Sunset Point to Douglas Avenue; north on Douglas to Stadium; ballpark is on the southeast corner of Douglas and Beltrees.

MINOR LEAGUE
Complex Address: Bobby Mattick Training Center at Englebert Complex, 1700 Solon Ave, Dunedin, FL 34698. **Telephone:** (727) 734-8007. **Hotel Address:** Clarion Inn & Suites, 20967 US Highway 19 North Clearwater, FL 33765. **Telephone:** (727) 799-1181.

WASHINGTON NATIONALS

MAJOR LEAGUE
Stadium Address: The Ballpark of the Palm Beaches, 5444 N. Haverhill Road, West Palm Beach, FL 33407. **Telephone:** (844) 676-2017.

MINOR LEAGUE
Complex: Same as major league club.

MINOR
LEAGUES

TRIPLE-A EAST

STADIUM INFORMATION

| Club | Stadium | Opened | Dimensions | | | Capacity | 2019 Att. |
			LF	CF	RF		
Buffalo	Sahlen Field	1988	325	404	325	18,025	518,741
Charlotte	BB&T Ballpark	2015	325	400	315	10,002	581,006
Columbus	Huntington Park	2009	325	400	318	10,100	590,504
Durham	Durham Bulls Athletic Park	1995	305	400	327	10,000	529,105
Gwinnett	Coolray Field	2009	335	400	335	10,427	212,342
Indianapolis	Victory Field	1996	320	402	320	14,500	586,860
Iowa	Principal Park	1992	335	400	335	11,000	489,173
Jacksonville	Baseball Grounds of Jacksonville	2003	321	420	317	11,000	327,388
Lehigh Valley	Coca-Cola Park	2008	336	400	325	10,000	585,110
Louisville	Louisville Slugger Field	2000	325	400	340	13,131	485,356
Memphis	AutoZone Park	2000	319	400	322	10,000	327,753
Nashville	First Tennessee Park	2015	330	405	310	10,000	578,291
Norfolk	Harbor Park	1993	333	400	318	12,067	350,086
Omaha	Werner Park	2011	310	402	315	9,023	328,307
Rochester	Frontier Field	1997	335	402	325	10,840	451,853
St. Paul	CHS Field	2015	330	396	320	7,140	394,970
Scranton/WB	PNC Field	2013	330	408	330	10,000	414,891
Syracuse	NBT Bank Stadium	1997	330	400	330	11,671	327,478
Toledo	Fifth Third Field	2002	320	408	315	10,300	481,496
Worcester	Polar Park	2021	330	403	320	9,508	—

BUFFALO BISONS

Address: Sahlen Field, One James D. Griffin Plaza, Buffalo, NY 14203.
Telephone: (716) 846-2000. **Fax:** (716) 852-6530.
E-Mail Address: info@bisons.com. **Website:** www.bisons.com.
Affiliation (first year): Toronto Blue Jays (2013). **Years in League:** 2021-

OWNERSHIP/MANAGEMENT

Operated By: Rich Products Corp. **Principal Owner/President:** Robert Rich Jr. **President, Rich Entertainment Group:** Melinda Rich. **Vice President/Chief Operating Officer, Rich Entertainment Group:** Joseph Segarra. **President, Rich Baseball Operations:** Mike Buczkowski. **VP/Secretary:** William Gisel. **Corporate Counsel:** Jill Bond, William Grieshober. **VP/Operations & Finance:** Kevin Parkinson. **VP/Food Service Operations:** Robert Free. **General Manager:** Anthony Sprague. **Assistant General Manager/Marketing & PR:** Brad Bisbing. **Director, Stadium Operations:** Brian Phillips. **Senior Accountants:** Chas Fiscella. **Accountants:** Amy Delaney, Tori Dwyer. **Director, Ticket Operations:** Mike Poreda. **Graphic Design:** Michele Cicatello. **Director, Corporate Sales:** Jim Harrington. **Director, Sales:** Geoff Lundquist. **Entertainment/Promotions Manager:** Mike Simoncelli. **Sales Coordinators:** Rachelle Szymanski. **Account Executives:** Nick Iacona, Kim Milleville, Shaun O'Lay. **Manager, Merchandise:** Theresa Cerabone. **Executive Assistant:** Tina Lesher. **Community Relations:** Gail Hodges. **Director, Food & Beverage Operations:** Sean Regan. **Food Service Operations Supervisor:** Curt Anderson. **Chief Engineer:** Gerald Hamilton. **Home Clubhouse/Baseball Operations Coordinator:** Scott Lesher. **Visiting Clubhouse Manager:** Steve Morris.

FIELD STAFF

Manager: TBA. **Pitching Coach:** TBA. **Hitting Coach:** TBA. **Defensive Coach:** TBA. **Athletic Trainer:** TBA. **Strength/Conditioning Coach:** TBA.

GAME INFORMATION

Radio Announcers: Pat Malacaro, Duke McGuire. **No. of Games Broadcast:** 142. **Flagship Station:** ESPN 1520.
PA Announcer: Jerry Reo, Tom Burns. **Official Scorers:** Kevin Lester, Jon Dare.
Stadium Name: Sahlen Field. **Location:** From north, take I-190 to Elm Street exit, left onto Swan Street; From east, take I-190 West to exit 51 (Route 33) to end, exit at Oak Street, right onto Swan Street; From west, take I-190 East, exit 53 to I-90 North, exit at Elm Street, left onto Swan Street. **Standard Game Times:** 7:05 pm, Sun. 1:05. **Ticket Price Range:** TBA.

CHARLOTTE KNIGHTS

Address: BB&T Ballpark, 324 S. Mint St., Charlotte, NC 28202.
Telephone: (704) 274-8300. **Fax:** 704-274-8330.
E-Mail Address: knights@charlotteknights.com. **Website:** www.charlotteknights.com.
Affiliation (first year): Chicago White Sox (1999). **Years in League:** 2021-

OWNERSHIP/MANAGEMENT

Operated by: Knights Baseball, LLC. **Principal Owners:** Don Beaver, Bill Allen. **Chief Operating Officer:** Dan Rajkowski. **General Manager:** Rob Egan. **Director, Special Projects:** Julie Clark. **Finance/HR Manager:** Sara Maple. **VP, Communications:** Tommy Viola. **VP, Sponsorship Sales:** Marty Steele. **VP, Marketing:** Matt DuBois. **VP, Stadium Operations:** Tom Gorter. **Executive Director of Entertainment & Creative Services:** Thomas Delves. **Director, Field Operations:** Matt Parrott. **Director, Broadcasting/Team Travel:** Matt Swierad. **Director, Community Relations:** Megan Smithers. **Director, Stadium Operations:** Nick Braun. **Director, Ticket Sales:** Yogi Brewington. **Director, Ticket Operations:** Jonathan English. **Director, Special Events:** Grace Eng. **Business Development Executives:** Corey Bass, Josh Otterline. **Client Services Manager:** Taylor Fike. **Senior Account Executive:** Carter Buffkin. **Senior Ticket Sales Account Executive:** Alex Michel. **Merchandise Director:** Elijah Saint Blanchard. **Creative/IT Director:** Bill Walker. **Digital Media and Graphic Design Manager:** Jason Furst. **Entertainment Coordinator:** Nick Farmer.

FIELD STAFF

Manager: Wes Helms. **Pitching Coach:** Matt Zaleski. **Hitting Coach:** Chris Johnson. **Trainer:** Cory Barton. **Performance Coach:** Shawn Powell.

GAME INFORMATION

Radio Announcers: Matt Swierad, Mike Pacheco. **No. of Games Broadcast:** 142. **Flagship Station:** 730 The Game ESPN Charlotte. **PA Announcer:** Ken Conrad. **Official Scorers:** Dave Friedman, Jim Morrison, Richard Walker. **Stadium Name:** Truist Field. **Location:** Exit 10 off Interstate 77. **Ticket Price Range:** $10-$23. **Visiting Club Hotel:** DoubleTree by Hilton Charlotte, 895 W. Trade St., Charlotte, NC 28202.

COLUMBUS CLIPPERS

Address: 330 Huntington Park Lane, Columbus, OH 43215.
Telephone: (614) 462-5250. **Fax:** (614) 462-3271. **Tickets:** (614) 462-2757.
E-Mail Address: info@clippersbaseball.com. **Website:** www.clippersbaseball.com.
Affiliation (first year): Cleveland Indians (2009). **Years in League:** 2021-

OWNERSHIP/MANAGEMENT

President/General Manager: Ken Schnacke. **Vice-President:** Mark Warren. **Assistant General Manager:** Mark Galuska. **Director, Ticket Operations:** Scott Ziegler Director, **Merchandising:** Krista Oberlander. **Director, Communications/Media:** Joe Santry. **Director, Finance/Administration:** Ashley Ramirez. **Director, Multimedia/ Telecast:** Larry Mitchell. **Director, Marketing/In-Game Entertainment:** Steve Kuilder. **Director, Game Operations/ Creative Services:** Yoshi Ando. **Assistant Director, Ticket Operations:** Eddie Langhenry. **Assistant Director, Media Relations/Statistics:** Anthony Slosser. **Ballpark Operations:** Tom Rinto & Spencer Harrison. **Assistant Directors of Ticket Sales:** Kevin Daniels & Matthew Harrison. **Assistant Director, Sales, Special Events/Birthday Parties:** Travis Allard. **Ballpark Superintendent:** Gary Delozier. **Director, Corporate Sales:** Jason Hillyer. **Assistant Director, Marketing/School Programs/Kids Club:** Emily Poynter. **Assistant Director, Marketing:** Austin Smith. **Assistant Directors of Group Sales:** Jacob Fleming & Cedric Hatton.

Executive Assistant to the President/GM: Ashley Held. **Maintenance Supervisor:** Curt Marcum. **Director, Sponsorship Relations:** Joyce Martin. **Director, Event Planning:** Micki Shier. **Assistant Director, Multimedia/ Telecast:** Pat Welch. **Assistant Director, Business Operations:** Shelby White. **Assistant Director, Group Sales:** Chase Green. **Assistant Director, Merchandising:** Schuyler Wright. **Director, Broadcasting:** Ryan Mitchell. **Assistant Director, Broadcasting:** Scott Leo. **Director, Social Media/Website:** Matt Leininger. **Assistant Director Social Media/ Website:** Aaliyah Phounsavath. **Director, Field Operations:** Wes Ganobcik. **Manager, Field Operations:** Connor Smith. **GM, Levy Food/Beverage:** Jeff Roberts. **Home Clubhouse Manager:** Colin Shaub. **Support Services:** Marvin Dill.

FIELD STAFF

Field Manager: Andy Tracy. **Pitching Coach:** Rigo Beltran. **Hitting Coach:** Jason Esposito. **Assistant Coach:** J.T. Maguire. **Trainer:** Jeremy Heller. **Strength/Conditioning Coach:** Travis Roberson.

GAME INFORMATION

Stadium Name: Huntington Park. **No. of Games Broadcast:** 142. **Location: From North:** South on I-71 to I-670 west, exit at Neil Avenue, turn left at intersection onto Neil Avenue. **From South:** North on I-71, exit at Front Street (#100A); turn left at intersection onto Front Street, turn left onto Nationwide Blvd. **From East:** West on I-70, exit at Fourth Street, continue on Fulton Street to Front Street, turn right onto Front Street, turn left onto Nationwide Blvd. **From West:** East on I-70, exit at Fourth Street, continue on Fulton Street to Front Street, turn right onto Front Street, turn left onto Nationwide Blvd. **Ticket Price Range:** $5-21. **Visiting Club Hotel:** Sonesta Columbus Downtown (formerly Crowne Plaza), 33 East Nationwide Blvd, Columbus, OH 43215. **Telephone:** (614) 461-4100. **Visiting Club Hotel:** Drury Hotels Columbus Convention Center, 88 East Nationwide Blvd, Columbus, OH 43215. **Telephone:** (614) 221-7008. **Visiting Club Hotel:** Hyatt Regency Downtown, 350 North High Street, Columbus, OH 43215. **Telephone:** (614) 463-

1234. **Visiting Club Hotel:** Red Roof Inn, 111 East Nationwide Blvd., Columbus Ohio 43215. **Telephone:** 614-224-6539.

DURHAM BULLS

Office Address: 409 Blackwell St., Durham, NC 27701. **Mailing Address:** PO Box 507, Durham, NC 27702
Telephone: (919) 687-6500. **Fax:** (919) 687-6560
Website: durhambulls.com. **Twitter:** @DurhamBulls
Affiliation (first year): Tampa Bay Rays (1998). **Years in League:** 2021-

OWNERSHIP/MANAGEMENT
Operated by: Capitol Broadcasting Company, Inc. **President/COO:** Jimmy Goodmon. **Vice President of Baseball Operations:** Mike Birling. **Assistant General Manager, Sales:** Chip Allen. **Assistant General Manager, Operations:** Scott Strickland. **Assistant Business Manager:** Theresa Stocking. **Senior Accountant:** Jordan Tucker. **Director of Corporate Partnerships:** Nick Bavin. **Senior Sponsorship Account Executive:** Andrew Ferrier. **Sponsorship Account Executive:** Kathleen Dwulet. **Head Groundskeeper:** Cameron Brendle. **Head Groundskeeper, Durham Athletic Park:** Joe Stumpo. **Director, Special Events:** LaTosha Smith. **Promotions Director:** Emily Almond. **Video & Digital Production Manager:** Patrick Norwood. **Digital & Social Content Manager:** Andrew Green. **Production Designer:** Paxton Rembis. **Season Membership Services Manager:** Izzy Piedmonte. **Group Ticket Sales Manager:** Cassie Fowler. **Group Sales Account Executive:** Fulton Beasley. **Director of Merchandising and Team Travel:** Bryan Wilson. **Assistant Director of Merchandise, E-Commerce:** Ashley Larson. **Director of Food and Beverage:** Dave Levey. **Assistant Director of Food and Beverage:** Todd Feneley. **Concessions Manager:** Andrew Houston. **Executive Chef:** Jason Boone.

FIELD STAFF
Manager: Brady Williams. **Pitching Coach:** Rick Knapp. **Hitting Coach:** Kyle Wilson. **Coach:** Reinaldo Ruiz. **Bullpen Coaches:** Alberto Bastardo (1st half)/Jose Gonzalez (2nd half). **Athletic Trainers:** Scott Thurston/Kris Williams. **Strength Coach:** Bryan King.

GAME INFORMATION
Broadcasters: Patrick Kinas, Scott Pose. **No. of Games Broadcast:** 142. **Flagship Station:** 96.5 FM and 99.3 FM. **PA Announcer:** Tony Riggsbee. **Official Scorer:** Brent Belvin. **Stadium Name:** Durham Bulls Athletic Park. **Location:** From Raleigh, I-40 West to Highway 147 North, exit 12B to Willard, two blocks on Willard to stadium; From I-85, Gregson Street exit to downtown, left on Chapel Hill Street, right on Mangum Street. **Standard Game Times:** 7:05 pm, Sat. 6:35 pm, Sun. 5:05 pm. **Ticket Price Range:** $7-14.
Visiting Club Hotel: TBA. **Telephone:** TBA.

GWINNETT STRIPERS

Office Address: 2500 Buford Drive, Lawrenceville, GA 30043.
Mailing Address: P.O. Box 490310, Lawrenceville, GA 30049.
Telephone: (678) 277-0300. **Fax:** (678) 277-0338.
E-Mail Address: stripersinfo@braves.com. **Website:** www.gostripers.com.
Affiliation (first year): Atlanta Braves (1966). **Years in League:** 2021-

OWNERSHIP/MANAGEMENT
Vice President & General Manager: Adam English. **Assistant General Manager:** Erin O'Donnell. **Office Manager:** Tyra Williams. **Manager of Corporate Partnerships:** Ryan Kees. **Corporate Partnership Account Executive:** Robbie Burnstein. **Partnership Services Coordinator:** Hannah Craig. **Account Executives:** Jordan Bradford, Zach Mandelblatt, Carlos Ortiz, Dylan Powers, Taylor Roach. **Ticket Operations Coordinator:** Jimmy Pembroke. **Media Relations Manager & Broadcaster:** Dave Lezotte. **Director of Fun:** Nino Dandan. **Promotions Coordinator:** Kyle Kamerbeek. **Creative Services Coordinator:** Nick Gosen. **Merchandise Coordinator:** Taryn Taylor. **Director, Stadium Operations:** Ryan Stoltenberg. **Stadium Operations Coordinator:** Rick Fultz. **Facilities Engineer:** Gary Hoopaugh. **Sports Turf Manager:** McClain Murphy. **Home Clubhouse Manager:** Nick Dixon. **Director of Operations, Professional Sports Catering:** Chiara Perkins.

FIELD STAFF
Manager: Matt Tuiasosopo. **Pitching Coach:** Mike Maroth. **Hitting Coach:** Carlos Mendez. **Coach:** Wigberto Nevarez. **Athletic Trainer:** TJ Saunders. **Strength/Conditioning Coach:** TBA.

GAME INFORMATION
Radio Announcer: Dave Lezotte. **No. of Games Broadcast:** 142. **Flagship Station:** TBA. **PA Announcer:** Kevin Kraus **Official Scorers:** TBA. **Stadium Name:** Coolray Field.
Location: I-85 (at Exit 115, State Road 20 West) and I-985 (at Exit 4); follow signs to park. **Ticket Price Range:** $8-45.
Visiting Club Hotels: Courtyard by Marriott Buford/Mall of Georgia, 1405 Mall of Georgia Boulevard, Buford, GA 30519. **Telephone:** (678) 745-3380. Fairfield Inn & Suites Atlanta Buford/Mall of Georgia, 1355 Mall of Georgia Boulevard, Buford, GA 30519. **Telephone:** (678) 714-0248.

INDIANAPOLIS INDIANS

Address: 501 W. Maryland Street, Indianapolis, IN 46225.
Telephone: (317) 269-3542. **Fax:** (317) 269-3541.
E-Mail Address: Indians@IndyIndians.com. **Website:** www.indyindians.com.
Affiliation (first year): Pittsburgh Pirates (2005). **Years in League:** 2021-

OWNERSHIP/MANAGEMENT

Chairman of the Board & Chief Executive Officer: Bruce Schumacher. **President & General Manager:** Randy Lewandowski. **Chairman Emeritus:** Max Schumacher. **Assistant General Manager, Corporate Sales & Marketing:** Joel Zawacki. **Assistant General Manager, Tickets & Operations:** Matt Guay. **Director, Business Systems & Talent:** Bryan Spisak. **Business Intelligence Analyst:** Bill Fulton. **Business Operations Manager:** Sarah Haynes. **Guest Relations Coordinator:** Michelle Trevino. **Director, Communications:** Cheyne Reiter. **Baseball Communications Coordinator:** Anna Kayser. **Voice of the Indians:** Howard Kellman. **Broadcaster:** Andrew Kappes. **Director, Corporate Sales:** Christina Toler. **Senior Director, Facilities:** Tim Hughes. **Senior Facilities Manager:** Allan Danehy. **Facilities Maintenance Tech:** Kyle Winters. **Director, Field Operations:** Joey Stevenson. **Field Operations Manager:** Adam Basinger. **Community Outreach Manager:** Jo Garcia. **Director, Marketing & Promotions:** Kim Stoebick. **Game Presentation & Promotions Manager:** Hayden Barnack. **Digital Marketing Manager:** Shayla Smith. **Telecast & Production Coordinator:** Alex Leachman. **Social Media Coordinator:** Casey McGaw. **Graphic Designers:** Jessica Davis, Matthew Lipke. **Director, Merchandise:** Mark Schumacher. **Merchandise Manager:** Patrick Westrick. **Partnership Activation Manager:** Kylie Kinder. **Operations Support:** Ki Hubbard, Sandra Reaves. **Home Clubhouse Manager & Operations Support:** Bobby Martin. **Visiting Clubhouse Manager:** Jeremy Martin. **Director, Ticket Sales:** Chad Bohm. **Director of Tickets, Premium Services & Events:** Kerry Vick. **Stadium Events Manager:** Paige McClung. **Premium & Ticket Services Manager:** Kathryn Bobel. **Ticket Services Coordinator:** Cara Carrion. **Senior Ticket Sales Account Executives:** Ryan Barrett, Jonathan Howard, Garrett Rosh. **Ticket Sales Account Executives:** Ty Eaton, Matt Marencik, Nathan Watson. **ARAMARK General Manager:** Chris Scherrer. **Concession Manager:** Jamie Nicholson.

FIELD STAFF

Manager: Brian Esposito. **Pitching Coach:** Joel Hanrahan. **Hitting Coach:** Jon Nunnally. **Coach:** Gustavo Omana. **Athletic Trainer:** Justin Ahrens. **Strength & Conditioning Coach:** Alan Burr.

GAME INFORMATION

Radio Announcers: Howard Kellman. **Flagship Station:** Fox Sports 1260 AM.
PA Announcer: David Pygman. **Official Scorers:** Ed Holdaway, Bill McAfee, Kim Rogers, Geoff Sherman, Jeff Williams. **Stadium Name:** Victory Field. **Location:** I-70 to West Street exit, north on West Street to ballpark; I-65 to Martin Luther King and West Street exit, south on West Street to ballpark. **Standard Game Times:** 7:05 pm; 1:35 (Wed/Sun.); 7:15 (Fri.). **Ticket Price Range:** $11-17. **Visiting Club Hotel:** Holiday Inn Indy Downtown, 515 S. West Street, Indianapolis, IN 46225. **Telephone:** (317) 631-9000.

IOWA CUBS

Address: One Line Drive, Des Moines IA 50309.
Telephone: (515) 243-6111. **Fax:** (515) 243-5152.
Website: www.iowacubs.com.
Affiliation (first year): Chicago Cubs (1981). **Years in League:** 2021-

OWNERSHIP/MANAGEMENT

Chairman/Principal Owner: Michael Gartner. **Corporate Secretary:** Michael Giudicessi. **President/General Manager:** Sam Bernabe. **Vice Chairman/Shareholder:** Mike C. Gartner. **Shareholder:** Dr. Doug Dorner. **VP/Assistant GM:** Randy Wehofer. **VP/CFO:** Sue Tollefson. **Director, Media Relations:** Shelby Cravens. **Director, Video and Multimedia Arts:** Justin Walters. **Director, Ticket Operations:** Clayton Grandquist. **Director, Broadcasting:** Alex Cohen. **Director, Group Outings:** Jason Gellis. **VP/Director, Luxury Suites:** Brent Conkel. **VP/Stadium Operations:** Jeff Tilley. **Manager, Stadium Operations:** Andrew Quillin, Dustin Halderson. **Supervisor, Stadium Operations:** Josh Stephens. **Account Executive:** John Roggs, Nick Long. **Group Sales:** Beth Kneeskern. **VP/Head Groundskeeper:** Chris Schlosser. **Assistant Groundskeeper:** Chase Manning. **Director, Merchandise:** Lisa Hufford. **Accounting:** Lori Auten. **Chief Technology Officer:** Ryan Clutter. **Manager, Digital Media:** Matt Evers. **Director of Stuff:** Scott Sailor. **Landscape Coordinator:** Shari Kramer.

FIELD STAFF

Manager: Marty Pevey. **Hitting Coaches:** Desi Wilson, Will Remillard. **Pitching Coach:** Ron Villone. **Athletic Trainers:** Ed Halbur, Toby Williams. **Strength/Conditioning:** Keegan Knoll.

GAME INFORMATION

Radio Announcers: Alex Cohen, Deene Ehlis. **No. of Games Broadcast:** 140. **Flagship Station:** AM 940 KPSZ. **PA Announcers:** Mark Pierce, Corey Coon, Rick Stageman, Joe Hammen. **Official Scorers:** Michael Pecina, James Hilchen, Steve Mohr. **Stadium Name:** Principal Park. **Location:** I-80 or I-35 to I-235, to Third Street exit, south on Third Street, left on Line Drive. **Standard Game Times:** 12:08/7:08 pm, Sun. 1:08. **Ticket Price Range:** $5-35. **Visiting Hotel:** Hampton Inn and Suites Downtown, 120 SW Water Street, Des Moines IA 50309. **Telephone:** (515) 244-1650.

JACKSONVILLE JUMBO SHRIMP

Office Address: 301 A. Philip Randolph Blvd, Jacksonville, FL 32202.
Telephone: (904) 358-2846. **Fax:** (904) 358-2845.
E-Mail Address: info@jaxshrimp.com. **Website:** www.jaxshrimp.com.
Affiliation (first year): Miami Marlins (2009). **Years In League:** 2021-

OWNERSHIP/MANAGEMENT

Operated by: Jacksonville Baseball LLC.
Owner & Chief Executive Officer: Ken Babby. **Executive Assistant to Ken Babby:** Jill Popov. **President, Fast Forward Sports Group:** Jim Pfander. **Chief Human Resources Office:** Leatrice Buck. **Chief Financial Officer:** Shawn Carlson. **Executive Vice President/General Manager:** Harold Craw. **Assistant General Manager:** Noel Blaha. **Vice President, Sales & Marketing:** Linda McNabb. **Director, Field Operations:** Christian Galen. **Director, Food & Beverage:** Ernest Hopkins. **Director, Community Relations:** Andrea Williams. **Director, Promotions & Special Events:** David Ratz. **Assistant Director, Ticket Operations:** Peter Ercey. **Assistant Director, Food & Beverage, Suites & Catering:** Chris Harper. **Stadium Operations Manager:** Tom Snyder. **Creative Services Manager:** Brian DeLettre. **Merchandise Manager:** Brennan Earley. **Media/Public Relations Manager, Broadcaster:** Scott Kornberg. **Business Manager:** Teresa Lively-Hall. **Food & Beverage Manager:** Jordan Burroughs. **Box Office Manager:** Cody Davis. **Partner Services Coordinator:** Holden Hitchcock. **Account Executives:** Damon Aultman, Stephen Sawayda, Jenna Smith, Devin Walker. **Accounting Assistant:** Jacob Yurdakul. **Stadium Operations Assistant:** Matthew Maynard. **Office Manager:** Christine Collins.

FIELD STAFF

Manager: Al Pedrique. **Pitching Coach:** Jeremy Powell. **Hitting Coach:** Phil Plantier. **Defensive Coach:** Danny Black. **Athletic Trainer:** Greg Harrl. **Strength/Conditioning Coach:** Jon Cioffi.

GAME INFORMATION

Radio Announcers: Scott Kornberg. **No. of Games Broadcast:** 140. **Flagship Station:** TBA.
PA Announcer: John Leard. **Official Scorer:** Jason Eliopulos. **Stadium Name:** 121 Financial Ballpark. **Location:** I-95 South to Martin Luther King Parkway exit, follow Gator Bowl Blvd around TIAA Bank Field; I-95 North to Exit 347 (Emerson Street), go right to Hart Bridge Expressway, take Sports Complex exit, left at light to stop sign, take left and follow around TIAA Bank Field; From Mathews Bridge, take A Philip Randolph exit, right on A Philip Randolph, straight to ballpark. **Standard Game Times:** 7:05 pm, Sat. 6:05 pm, Sun. 3:05 pm. **Ticket Price Range:** TBA. **Visiting Club Hotel:** Doubletree by Hilton Hotel Jacksonville Riverfront, 1201 Riverplace Blvd., Jacksonville, FL 32207. **Telephone:** (904) 398-8800.

LEHIGH VALLEY IRONPIGS

Address: 1050 IronPigs Way, Allentown, PA 18109.
Telephone: (610) 841-7447. **Fax:** (610) 841-1509.
E-Mail Address: info@ironpigsbaseball.com. **Website:** www.ironpigsbaseball.com.
Affiliation (first year): Philadelphia Phillies (2008). **Years in League:** 2021-

OWNERSHIP/MANAGEMENT

Ownership: LV Baseball LP. **President & General Manager:** Kurt Landes. **Senior Vice President:** Brian DeAngelis. **Vice President, Marketing:** Tricia Matsko. **Manager, Media Relations:** Mike Ventola. **Director, Digital Media & Communications:** Natalie Krajsa. **Director, Multimedia Design:** Kevin Whitehead. **Manager, Multimedia Design:** Alfred Greenbaum. **Director, Promotions/Entertainment:** Kelly Scott. **Manager, Promotions:** Jessica Morgan. **Director, IronPigs Charities:** Emily Bettys. **Vice President, Food & Beverage:** Alex Rivera. **Director, Food & Beverage:** Brock Hartranft. **Director, Special Events:** Allison Valentine. **Manager, Catering & Hospitality:** Jared Takacs. **Executive Chef:** Heather Williams. **Director, Corporate Partnerships:** Tom Bendetti. **Director, Sponsorship Services:** Maria Valentyn. **Manager, Sponsorship Services:** Nick Wilder. **Administrative Assistant:** Pat Golden. **Director, Field Operations:** Ryan Hills. **Vice President, Stadium Operations:** Jason Kiesel. **Managers, Stadium Operations:** Mike Moneta, Tyler Woscek. **Vice President, Administration:** Michelle Perl. **Director, Finance:** Stephen Doll. **Senior Manager, Corporate Partnerships:** Zach Betkowski. **Manager, Corporate Partnerships:** Ray Bleam. **Director, Guest Experience:** Brad Ludwig. **Director, Group Sales:** Ryan Hines. **Managers, Group Sales:** Josh Mullin, Daniel Sterenberg. **Director, Memberships:** Erik Hoffman. **Managers, Memberships:** Cody Hallman. **Director, Ticket Operations:** Brittany Balonis. **Manager, Ticket Operations & Analytics:** Collin DeJong. **Managers, Ticket Coordinator:** Nick DiChristofaro, Erik Kerns. **Manager, Corporate Ticket Sales:** Tanner Case. **Director, Merchandise:** Mike Luciano.

FIELD STAFF

Manager: TBA. **Pitching Coach:** TBA. **Hitting Coach:** TBA. **Defensive Coach:** TBA. **Athletic Trainer:** TBA. **Strength/Conditioning Coach:** TBA.

GAME INFORMATION

Radio Announcers: Pat McCarthy and Mike Ventola. **No. of Games Broadcast:** 140. **Flagship Radio Station:** FOX Sports Radio 1230/1320 AM & 94.7 FM. **Television Station:** TV2. **Television Announcers:** Mike Zambelli, Steve Degler, Doug Heater. **No. of Games Televised:** 72 (all home games). **PA Announcer:** Chris Roman. **Official Scorers:** Mike Falk, Jack Logic, David Sheriff, Dick Shute. **Stadium Name:** Coca-Cola Park. **Location:** Take US 22 to exit for Airport Road South, head south, make right on American Parkway, left into stadium. **Standard Game Times:** 7:05 pm, Sat. 6:35, Sun. 1:35.

LOUISVILLE BATS

Address: 401 E Main St, Louisville, KY 40202.
Telephone: (502) 212-2287. **Fax:** (502) 515-2255.
E-Mail Address: info@batsbaseball.com. **Website:** www.batsbaseball.com.
Affiliation (first year): Cincinnati Reds (2000). **Years in League:** 2021-

OWNERSHIP/MANAGEMENT

Chairman: Stuart and Jerry Katzoff (MC Sports).
Board of Directors: Dan Ulmer Jr., Edward Glasscock, Gary Ulmer, Kenny Huber, Steve Trager, Michael Brown.
President: Vic Gregovits. **Senior Vice President:** Greg Galiette. **Vice President, Stadium Operations/Technology:** Scott Shoemaker. **Controller:** Michele Anderson. **Director, Director of Marketing:** Tony Brown. **Manager Ticket Sales & Service:** David Barry. **Box Office Manager:** Brett Jones. **Director of Business Development:** Jillian Waitkus. **Head Clubhouse Manager:** Derrick Jewell. **Club Physicians:** Walter Badenhausen, M.D.; John A. Lach, Jr., M.D. **Club Dentist:** Pat Carroll, D.M.D. **Chaplains:** Bob Bailey, Jose Castillo.

FIELD STAFF

Manager: Pat Kelly. **Pitching Coach:** Seth Etherton. **Hitting Coach:** Alex Pelaez. **Bench Coach:** Kevin Mahar. **Trainer:** Steve Gober. **Strength/Conditioning Coach:** Justin Bucko.

GAME INFORMATION

Radio Announcers: TBA. **No. of Games Broadcast:** 140. **Flagship Station:** WKRD 790-AM.
PA Announcer: Charles Gazaway. **Official Scorer:** Nick Evans, Neil Rohrer. **Organist:** Bob Ramsey.
Stadium Name: Louisville Slugger Field. **Location:** I-64 and I-71 to I-65 South/North to Brook Street exit, right on Market Street, left on Jackson Street; stadium on Main Street between Jackson and Preston. **Ticket Price Range:** $9-55.
Visiting Club Hotel: Omni Hotel, 400 South 2nd Street, Louisville, KY 40202. **Telephone:** (502) 313-6664.

MEMPHIS REDBIRDS

Office Address: 198 Union, Memphis, TN 38103.
Stadium Address: 198 Union Ave, Memphis, TN 38103.
Telephone: (901) 721-6000. **Fax:** (901) 328-1102. **Website:** www.memphisredbirds. com.
Affiliation (first year): St. Louis Cardinals (1998). **Years in League:** 2021-

OWNERSHIP/MANAGEMENT

Ownership: Peter B. Freund.
President/General Manager: Craig Unger. **Vice President, Marketing and Sales:** Andy Steavens. **Vice President, Stadium and Baseball Operations:** Mike Voutsinas. **Director of Ticket Sales & Service:** Aaron Johnson. **Director, Field Operations:** Eric Taylor. **Manager, Ticket Operations:** Nate Deavers. **Manager, Corporate Sales:** Tyler Gilles. **Coordinator, Marketing:** Kayla Hezel. **Stadium Entertainment, Manager:** Paul Mullin. **Motion Graphics & Video Production:** Nicholas Mejia. **Manager, Guest Services and Baseball Operations:** Marissa Zvolanek. **Accounting Manager:** Cindy Neal. **Facilities Manager:** Spencer Shields.

FIELD STAFF

Manager: Ben Johnson. **Hitting Coach:** Brandon Allen. **Pitching Coach:** Dernier Orozco. **Trainer:** Dan Martin. **Strength & Conditioning:** Frank Witkowski.

GAME INFORMATION

Radio Announcer: TBA **No. of Games Broadcast:** 140. **Flagship Station:** online. **PA Announcer:** Greg Ratliff. **Official Scorers:** TBA. **Stadium Name:** AutoZone Park. **Location:** North on I-240, exit at Union Avenue West, one and half miles to park. **Standard Game Times:** Mon-Wed. 6:45, Thu-Fri. 7:10, Sat. 6:**35, Sun 2:**05. **Ticket Price Range:** $9-24. **Visiting Club Hotel:** TBA.

NASHVILLE SOUNDS

Address: 19 Junior Gilliam Way, Nashville, TN 37219.
Telephone: (615) 690-HITS. **Fax:** (615) 256-5684.
E-Mail address: info@nashvillesounds.com. **Website:** www.nashvillesounds.com.
Affiliation (first year): Milwaukee Brewers (2021). **Years in League:** 2021-

OWNERSHIP/MANAGEMENT

Operated By: MFP Baseball. **Owners:** Frank Ward, Masahiro Honzawa.
GM/Chief Operating Officer: Adam Nuse. **VP, Operations:** Doug Scopel. **VP, Sales:** Bryan Mayhood. **Director, Finance:** Barb Walker. **Director, Sales:** Taylor Fisher. **Director, Corporate Partnerships:** Danielle Gaw. **Director, Media Relations:** Chad Seely. **Director, Marketing:** Alex Wassel. **Director, Entertainment:** Mary Hegley. **Director, Retail:** Katie Ward. **Director, Broadcasting:** Jeff Hem. **Director, Stadium Operations:** Jeremy Wells. **Video and Production**

Manager: Neil Rosan. **Manager, Digital Marketing:** Abby Holman. **Manager, Fan Services:** Travis Williams. **Manager, Business Development:** Sierra Seigel. **Business Development, Corporate Partnerships:** Jon Brownfield. **Merchandise Manager:** Wade Becker. **Ticket Operations Manager:** Kyle Hargrove. **Stadium Operations Manager:** Caleb Yorks. **Account Executive:** Kelsen Adeni, Kevin Kurowski. **Ticket Operations Coordinator:** Ben Whalin. **Mascot Coordinator:** Buddy Yelton. **Production Event Coordinator:** Stephen Hart. **Groundskeeper:** Thomas Trotter. **Assistant Groundskeeper:** Shay Adams. **Clubhouse & Equipment Manager:** Matt Gallant. **Visiting Clubhouse Manager:** Patrick King. **Team Photographer:** Casey Gower.

FIELD STAFF

Manager: Rick Sweet. **Hitting Coach:** Al LeBoeuf. **Pitching Coach:** Jim Henderson. **Coach:** Ned Yost IV. **Athletic Trainer:** Lanning Tucker. **Strength & Conditioning Specialist:** Andrew Emmick.

GAME INFORMATION

Radio Announcer: Jeff Hem. **No. of Games Broadcast:** 140. **Flagship Station:** TBD. **Official Scorers:** Eric Jones, Cody Bush, Eric Moyer. **Stadium Name:** First Horizon Park. **Location:** I-65 to exit 85 (Rosa L Parks Blvd) and head south; Turn left on Jefferson St, then turn right onto 5th Ave North, then turn left on Jackson St. **Standard Game Times:** 7:05, 6:35, 6:15, 2:05. **Ticket Price Range:** $10-35. **Visiting Club Hotel:** Millennium Maxwell House, 2025 Rosa L Parks Blvd, Nashville, TN, 37228.

NORFOLK TIDES

Address: 150 Park Ave, Norfolk, VA 23510.
Telephone: (757) 622-2222. **Fax:** (757) 624-9090.
E-Mail Address: receptionist@norfolktides.com. **Website:** www.norfolktides.com.
Affiliation (first year): Baltimore Orioles (2007). **Years in League:** 2021-

OWNERSHIP/MANAGEMENT

Operated By: Tides Baseball Club Inc.
President: Ken Young. **General Manager:** Joe Gregory.
Director, Sales and Fan Experience: Mike Watkins. **Director, Operations:** Mike Zeman. **Director, Ticket Operations:** Sze Fong. **Director, Ticket Sales:** John Muszkewycz. **Business Manager:** Dawn Coutts. **Head Groundskeeper:** Kenny Magner. **Home Clubhouse Manager:** Adam Sehlmeyer. **Visiting Clubhouse Manager:** Jack Brenner.

FIELD STAFF

Manager: Gary Kendall. **Pitching Coach:** Kennie Steenstra. **Hitting Coach:** Tim Gibbons. **Fundamentals Coach:** Ramon Sambo. **Development Coach:** Malcolm Holland. **Strength Coach:** Trey Wiedman. **Trainer:** Chris Poole.

GAME INFORMATION

Radio Announcers: Pete Michaud. **No. of Games Broadcast:** 140. **Flagship Station:** ESPN 94.1 FM. **PA Announcer:** Jack Ankerson. **Official Scorers:** Mike Holtzclaw, Jim Hodges. **Stadium Name:** Harbor Park. **Location:** Exit 9, 11A or 11B off I-264, adjacent to the Elizabeth River in downtown Norfolk. **Standard Game Times:** 6:35 pm during weekdays in April & May, 7:05 pm, Sun 1:05 pm (first half of season); 4:05 pm (second half of season). **Ticket Price Range:** $10-15. **Visiting Club Hotel:** Sheraton Waterside, 777 Waterside Dr, Norfolk, VA 23510. **Telephone:** (757) 622-6664.

OMAHA STORM CHASERS

Address: Werner Park, 12356 Ballpark Way, Papillion, NE 68046.
Administrative Office Phone: (402) 734-2550. **Ticket Office Phone:** (402) 738-5100. **Fax:** (402) 734-7166.
E-mail Address: info@omahastormchasers.com. **Website:** www.omahastormchasers.com.
Affiliation (first year): Kansas City Royals (1969). **Years in League:** 2021-

OWNERSHIP/MANAGEMENT

Operated By: Alliance Baseball Managing Partners. **Owners:** Gary Green, Larry Botel, Brian Callaghan, Eric Foss, Stephen Alepa, Peter Huff, Evan Friend.
CEO: Gary Green. **President:** Martie Cordaro. **Vice President/General Manager:** Laurie Schlender. **Assistant GM, Events/Sales:** Andrea Bedore. **Human Resources Manager:** Aniya Tate. **Senior Corporate Sales Executive:** Mark Nasser. **Director/Operations:** Steve Farrens. **Head Groundskeeper:** Derek York. **Broadcaster:** Jake Eisenberg. **Promotions/Game Operations Manager:** Rachel Rea. **Client Services Manager:** Mackenzie Parker. **Media/Public Relations Manager:** Tony Boone. **Video/Multimedia Coordinator:** Scott Popp. **Director/Ticket Operations:** Anna Corbett. **Group Sales Manager:** Zach Ziler. **Corporate Sales Executive:** Blake Paris. **Retail Operations Manager:** Mitch Cunningham. **Bookkeepers:** Rachael Sefren and Pennie Martindale. **Grounds Manager:** Tom Walter. **Home Clubhouse Manager:** Mike Brown. **Front Office Assistants:** Donna Kostal, Michelle VanBemmelen.

FIELD STAFF

Manager: Brian Poldberg. **Hitting Coach:** Brian Buchanan. **Pitching Coach:** Dane Johnson. **Athletic Trainer:** James Stone. **Strength Coach:** Yannick Plante.

GAME INFORMATION

Radio Announcers: Jake Eisenberg. **No. of Games Broadcast:** 140. **Flagship Station:** KZOT-AM 1180. **PA Announcer:** Craig Evans. **Official Scorers:** Frank Adkisson, Gary Sharp & Ryan White. **Stadium Name:** Werner Park. **Location:** Highway 370, just east of I-80 (exit 439). **Standard Game Times:** 6:35 pm (April-May), 7:05 (June-Sept), Fri./Sat. 7:05, Sun. 2:05. **Visiting Club Hotel:** Courtyard Omaha La Vista, 12560 Westport Parkway, La Vista, NE 68128. **Telephone:** (402) 339-4900. **Fax:** (402) 339-4901.

ROCHESTER RED WINGS

Address: One Morrie Silver Way, Rochester, NY 14608.
Telephone: (585) 454-1001. **Fax:** (585) 454-1056.
E-Mail: info@redwingsbaseball.com. **Website:** RedWingsBaseball.com.
Affiliation (first year): Washington Nationals (2021). **Years in League:** 2021-

OWNERSHIP/MANAGEMENT

Operated by: Rochester Community Baseball, Inc.
President/CEO/COO: Naomi Silver.
Chairman: Gary Larder. **General Manager:** Dan Mason. **Assistant GM:** Will Rumbold. **Controller:** Michelle Schiefer. **Director, Human Resources:** Paula LoVerde. Ticket Office Mgr. & **Business Coordinator:** Dave Welker. **Director, Communications:** Nate Rowan. **Director, Corporate Development:** Nick Sciarratta. Manager, **Social Media & Promotions:** Tim Doohan. **Director, Group Sales:** Bob Craig. **Group Sales & Tickets Reps:** Kevin Lute & Mike Ewing. **Senior Director, Sales:** Matt Cipro. **Director, Ticket Operations:** Rob Dermody. **Director, Video Production:** John Blotzer. **Director, Merchandising:** Nicole Boyle. **Merchandising Assistant:** Kathy Bills. **Head Groundskeeper:** Gene Buonomo. **Assistant Groundskeeper:** Geno Buonomo. **Office Manager:** Amber Johnson. **GM, Food/Beverage:** Jeff Desantis. **Business Manager, Food/Beverage:** Dave Bills. **Manager, Concessions:** Jeff Savidge. Director, **Catering & Hospitality:** Steve Gonzalez. Ryan Donalty. **Sous Chef:** Nick Johnson.

FIELD STAFF

Manager: Matt LeCroy. **Hitting Coach:** Brian Daubach. **Pitching Coach:** Michael Tejera. **Athletic Trainer:** Eric Montague. **Strength Coach:** Mike Warren.

GAME INFORMATION

Radio Announcer: Josh Whetzel. **No. of Games Broadcast:** 140. **Flagship Stations:** WHTK 1280-AM. **PA Announcers:** Kevin Spears, Rocky Perrotta. **Official Scorers:** Warren Kozireski, Brendan Harrington, Craig Bodensteiner. **Stadium Name:** Frontier Field. **Location:** I-490 East to exit 12 (Brown/Broad Street) and follow signs; I-490 West to exit 14 (Plymouth Ave) and follow signs. **Standard Game Times:** 7:05 pm, Sun 1:05. **Ticket Price Range:** $9-14. **Visiting Club Hotel:** Holiday Inn Rochester Downtown, 70 State St, Rochester, NY 14608. **Telephone:** (585) 546-3450..

ST. PAUL SAINTS

Office Address: 360 Broadway Street, St. Paul, MN 55101.
Telephone: (651) 644-3517. **Fax:** (651) 644-1627.
Email Address: funisgood@saintsbaseball.com.
Website: saintsbaseball.com.
Affiliation: Minnesota Twins (2021). **Years in League:** 2021-

OWNERSHIP/MANAGEMENT

Chairman of the Board: Marvin Goldklang. **President:** Mike Veeck. **Executive VP/General Manager:** Derek Sharrer. **Executive VP/Business Development:** Tom Whaley. **Senior Vice President, Assistant GM:** Chris Schwab. **Vice President, Director of Media Relations/Broadcasting:** Sean Aronson. **Director, Sales and Corporate Partnerships:** Zane Heinselman. **Director, Marketing & Promotions:** Sierra Bailey. **Director, Ticket Operations:** Aaron Boettger. **Manager, Marketing and Creative Services:** Rob Thompson. **Director, Digital Media and Video Production:** Jordan Lynn. **Multi-Media Content Producer:** Zach Neubauer. **Digital Media Specialist:** Aly May. **Account Executive/Ticket Sales & Corporate Partnerships:** Will Harris. **Account Executive/Ticket Sales:** Michael Villafana. **Director, Community Partnerships and Fan Services:** Eddie Coblentz. **Manager, Special Events:** Anna Gutknecht. **Business Manager/Community Relations:** Krista Schnelle. **Office Manager:** Gina Kray. **Director, Ballpark Operations:** Curtis Nachtsheim. **Head Groundskeeper, Sports Turf Manager:** Marcus Campbell. **Vice President of Operations, Professional Sports Catering:** Justin Grandstaff. **Director of Operations, Professional Sports Catering:** Gregg Kraly.

FIELD STAFF

Manager: Toby Gardenhire. **Pitching Coaches:** Cibney Bello and Mike McCarthy. **Hitting Coach:** Matt Borgschulte. **Infield Coach:** Tyler Smarslok. **Athletic Trainer:** Jason Kirkman. **Strength/Conditioning Coach:** Jacob Dean.

GAME INFORMATION

Radio Announcer: Sean Aronson. **Games Broadcast:** 140. **Flagship Station:** KFAN+ 96.7 FM. **Webcast Address:** www.saintsbaseball.com. **Stadium Name:** CHS Field. **Location:** From the west take I-94 to the 7th St. Exit and head south to 5th & Broadway. From the east take I-94 to the Mounds Blvd/US-61N exit. Turn left on Kellogg and a right on Broadway until you reach 5th St. **Standard Game Times:** Mon.-Sat., 7:05 pm, Sun., 5:05 pm.

SCRANTON/WILKES-BARRE
RAILRIDERS

Address: 235 Montage Mountain Rd., Moosic, PA 18507.
Telephone: (570) 969-2255. **Fax:** (570) 963-6564.
E-Mail Address: info@swbrailriders.com.
Website: www.swbrailriders.com.
Affiliation (first year): New York Yankees (2007). **Years in League:** 2021-

OWNERSHIP/MANAGEMENT

President: John Adams. **General Manager:** Katie Beekman. **Corporate Services & Design:** Kristina Knight. **Director, Communications/Broadcaster:** Adam Marco. **Director, Community Relations:** Jordan Maydole. **Corporate Sales Manager:** Jordan Perrine. **Director of Ticket Operations:** Felicia Adamus. Director, **Season Ticket Sales & Service:** Kelly Cusick. **Season Ticket & Client Services:** Tyler Movsessian. **Premium Sales Manager:** Tim Duggan. **Premium Sales Executive:** Mike Phipps. **Group Sales Manager:** Mike Harvey. Director, **Youth Baseball & Sports Sales:** Robby Judge. **Group Sales Executives:** Sean Allison, Michael Didato. **Senior Accountant:** Patrick Cawley. **Field Operations:** Steve Horne. **Assistant Groundskeeper:** Dustin Spiegel. **Director, Facility Operations:** Ryan Long. **Stadium Operations Manager:** Nick Bolka.

FIELD STAFF

Manager: TBA. **Pitching Coach:** TBA. **Hitting Coach:** TBA. **Defensive Coach:** TBA. **Athletic Trainer:** TBA. **Strength/Conditioning Coach:** TBA.

GAME INFORMATION

Radio Announcer: Adam Marco. **No. of Games Broadcast:** 140. **Flagship Stations:** 1340 WYCK-AM, 1400 WICK-AM, 1440 WCDL-AM. **Television Announcer:** Adam Marco. No. **of Games Broadcast:** TBA. **Flagship Station:** TBA. **PA Announcers:** Unavailable. **Official Scorers:** Dean Corwin, Dick Devans, Mark Ligi &Armand Rosamilia. **Stadium Name:** PNC Field. **Location:** Exit 182 off Interstate 81; stadium is on Montage Mountain Road. **Standard Game Times:** 6:35 pm (April/May) 7:05 pm (June-August); Sun. 1:05 pm. **Ticket Price Range:** $10-$16. **Visiting Club Hotel:** Hilton Scranton & Conference Center. **Telephone:** (570) 343-3000.

SYRACUSE METS

Address: One Tex Simone Drive, Syracuse NY, 13208
Telephone: 315-474-7833. **Fax:** 315-474-2658.
E-Mail Address: baseball@syracusemets.com. **website:** syracusemets.com
Affiliation (First year): New York Mets (2019). **Years in league:** 2021

OWNERSHIP/MANAGEMENT

Operated by: NY Mets. **General Manager:** Jason Smorol. **Assistant GM, Sales:** Clint Cure. **Assistant GM, Business Development:** Katie Berger. **Assistant GM, Stadium/Business Ops:** Brian Paupeck. **Director, Sales/Marketing:** Kathleen McCormick. **Senior Staff Accountant:** Patrick Taylor. **Staff Accountant:** Frank Santoro. **Director, Broadcasting/Media Relations:** Michael Tricarico. **Director, Ticket Operations:** Will Commisso. **Director, Multimedia Production:** Anthony Cianchetta. **Senior Corporate Sales Executive:** Julie Cardinali. **Manager, Suites/Hospitality:** Bill Ryan. **Manager, Social Media/Graphics:** Danny Tripodi. **Manager, Equipment/Clubhouse Operations:** Jody Pucello. **Head Groundskeeper/Director, Turf Management:** John Stewart.

FIELD STAFF

Manager: TBD. **Pitching Coach:** TBD. **Hitting Coach:** Joel Chimelis. **Bench Coach:** TBD.

GAME INFORMATION

Radio Announcer: Michael Tricarico. **No. of Games Broadcast:** 140. **Flagship Station:** The Score 1260 AM. **PA Announcers:** Nick Aversa. **Official Scorer:** Dom Leo. **Stadium Name:** NBT Bank Stadium. **Location:** New York State Thruway to exit 36 (I-81 South); to 7th North Street exit, left on 7th North, right on Hiawatha Boulevard. **Standard Game Times:** 6:35 pm, Sun. 1:05 pm. **Ticket Price Range:** $10-18. **Visiting Club Hotel:** Embassy Suites @ Destiny USA.

TOLEDO MUD HENS

Address: 406 Washington St., Toledo, OH 43604.
Telephone: (419) 725-4367. **Fax:** (419) 725-4368.
E-Mail Address: mudhens@mudhens.com. **Website:** www.mudhens.com.
Affiliation (first year): Detroit Tigers (1987). **Years in League:** 2021-

OWNERSHIP/MANAGEMENT

Operated By: Toledo Mud Hens Baseball Club, Inc. **Chairman of the Board:** Michael Miller. **Vice President:** David Huey. **Secretary/Treasurer:** Charles Bracken. **President/CEO:** Joseph Napoli. **GM/Executive Vice President:** Erik Ibsen. **President, CFO:** Brian Leverenz. **Assistant Controller:** Tom Mitchell. **Director, Strategic Planning and Projects:** Michael Keedy. **Director, Communications/Media:** Andi Roman. **Social Media Coordinator:** Amanda Jerzykowski. **Director Corporate Partnerships:** Ed Sintic. **Director Ticket Sales :** Kyle Moll. **Game Plan Consultants:** John Dotson, Becky Fitts, Adam Haman, Rita Natter.   **Manager, Ticket Service Team:** Troy Hammersmith. **Manager, Box Office Sales:** Jennifer Hill. **Game Day Coordinator:** Tyler Clark. Director, **Merchandise & Licensing:** Craig Katz. Manager, Swamp Shop. **Turf Manager:** Kyle Leppelmeier. **Clubhouse Manager:** Joe Sarkisian.

FIELD STAFF

Manager: Tom Prince. **Hitting:** Mike Hessman. **Pitching Coach:** Doug Bochtler. **Developmental:** CJ Wamsley. **Trainer:** Jason Schwartzman. **Strength and Conditioning:** Dan Morrison.

GAME INFORMATION

Radio Announcer: Jim Weber. **No. of Games Broadcast:** 140. **Flagship Station:** WCWA 1230-AM. **TV Announcers:** Jim Weber, Matt Melzak. No. **of Games Broadcast:** 70 (all home games). **TV Flagship:** Buckeye Cable Sports Network (BCSN). **PA Announcer:** Mason. **Official Scorers:** Jeff Businger, Ron Kleinfelter, John Malkoski Jr., Jack Malkoski., Lee Schuh. **Stadium Name:** Fifth Third Field. **Location:** From Ohio Turnpike 80/90, exit 54 (4A) to I-75 North, follow I-75 North to exit 201-B, left onto Erie Street, right onto Washington Street; From Detroit, I-75 South to exit 202-A, right onto Washington Street; From Dayton, I-75 North to exit 201-B, left onto Erie Street, right on Washington Street; From Ann Arbor, Route 23 South to I-475 East, I-475 east to I-75 South, I-75 South to exit 202-A, right onto Washington Street. **Ticket Price Range:** $12. **Visiting Club Hotel:** Park Inn, 101 North Summit, Toledo, OH 43604. **Telephone:** (419) 241-3000.

WORCESTER RED SOX

Office Address: Polar Park, 100 Madison St., Worcester, MA 01610.
Mailing Address: PO Box 3180, Worcester, MA 01613.
Telephone: (508) 500-8888. **Fax:** TBA
E-Mail Address: info@woosox.com. **Website:** www.woosox.com.
Affiliation (first year): Boston Red Sox (2021). **Years in League:** 2021-

OWNERSHIP/MANAGEMENT

Principal Owner & Chairman: Larry Lucchino. **Vice Chairman:** Mike Tamburro. **President:** Dr. Charles Steinberg. **Executive Vice President/Real Estate Development & Business Affairs:** Dan Rea III. **Treasurer:** Jeff White. **Executive Vice President/General Counsel:** Kim Miner. **Senior Vice President/Communications:** Bill Wanless. **Senior Vice President/Corporate Partnerships:** Michael Gwynn. **Senior Vice President/Sales & Marketing:** Rob Crain. **Senior Vice President/Chief Financial & Technology Officer:** Matt Levin. **Vice President/Corporate Partnerships:** Jack Verducci. **Vice President/Marketing:** Brooke Cooper. **Vice President/Baseball Operations & Community Relations:** Joe Bradlee. **Vice President/Ticket Sales:** Matt Harper. **Executive Assistant to the Chairman:** Fay Scheer. **Special Assistant to the Chairman & Director of Ballpark Planning:** Bart Harvey. **Special Assistant to the President & Intern Coordinator:** Jackie Wilkes. **Senior Director of Ticket Operations:** Samantha Saccoia-Beggs. **Senior Director of Fan Services:** Rick Medeiros. **Director of Client Services:** Bernadette Provost. **Director of Production:** Joe Jacobs. **Director of Special Events:** Hannah Butler. **Office Manager:** Carol Krushnowski. **Corporate & Community Partnerships:** Mike Lyons. **Director of Ticket Sales & Strategy:** Anthony Cahill. **Corporate Event Manager:** Jim Cain. **Group Event Manager:** Ryan Meagher. **Staff Accountant:** Dan Fontaine. **Director of Worcester Operations:** Steve Oliveira. **Director of Warehouse Operations:** Jeff Caster. **Facilities Maintenance Manager:** Dave Crowley. **Executive Chef:** Tom Whalen. **Manager of Merchandising:** Kat Burns. **Community Relations Assistant:** Alex Richardson. **Operations Coordinator, WooSox Foundation:** Sabriya Chaudhry. **Manager of Productions:** Tim Quitadamo. **Client Services Manager:** Dan Diggins. **Ballpark Design Coordinator:** Ben Weingarten. **Field Superintendent:** Matt McKinnon. **Assistant Groundskeeper:** Alex Tedesco. **Clubhouse Managers:** Josh Liebenow & Mario Oliveira. **Radio/TV Broadcasters:** Josh Maurer, Jim Cain, Mike Antonellis, Jay Burnham.

FIELD STAFF

Field Manager: Billy McMillon. **Hitting Coach:** Rich Gedman. **Pitching Coach:** Paul Abbott. **Coaches:** Bruce Crabbe & Michael Montville. **Trainer:** David Herrera. **Strength & Conditioning Coach:** Ben Chadwick.

GAME INFORMATION

Radio Announcers: Josh Maurer, Jim Cain. **No. of Games Broadcast:** 140. **Flagship Station:** NASH Icon 98.9-FM. **PA Announcers:** Ben DeCastro. **Official Scorer:** Bruce Guindon. **Stadium Name:** Polar Park. **Location:** Canal District Worcester, MA Standard Game Times: 6:35 pm, Sat. 4:**05**, Sun 1:**05**. **Ticket Price Range:** $8-21. **Visiting Club Hotel:** TBA.

TRIPLE-A WEST

STADIUM INFORMATION

Club	Stadium	Opened	LF	CF	RF	Capacity	2019 Att.
Albuquerque	Isotopes Park	2003	340	400	340	13,500	542,832
El Paso	Southwest University Park	2014	322	406	322	8,018	522,894
Las Vegas	Cashman Field	1983	328	433	328	11,500	650,934
Oklahoma City	Chickasaw Bricktown Ballpark	1998	325	400	325	9,000	444,131
Reno	Aces Ballpark	2009	339	410	340	9,100	336,215
Round Rock	Dell Diamond	2000	330	405	325	8,722	597,928
Sacramento	Raley Field	2000	330	403	325	14,014	549,440
Salt Lake	Smith's Ballpark	1994	345	420	315	14,511	433,596
Sugar Land	Constellation Field	2012	348	405	325	7,500	304,753
Tacoma	Cheney Stadium	1960	325	425	325	6,500	347,378

ALBUQUERQUE ISOTOPES

Address: 1601 Avenida Cesar Chavez SE, Albuquerque, NM 87106
Telephone: (505) 924-2255. **Fax:** (505) 242-8899.
E-Mail Address: info@abqisotopes.com. **Website:** www.abqisotopes.com.
Affiliation (first year): Colorado Rockies (2015). **Years in League:** 2021-

OWNERSHIP/MANAGEMENT

President: Ken Young. **Vice President/Secretary/Treasurer:** Emmett Hammond. **VP/GM:** John Traub. **Assistant GM, Business Operations:** Chrissy Baines. **Assistant GM, Sales/Marketing:** Adam Beggs. **Director, Public Relations:** TBD. **Director, Retail Operations:** Michael Malgieri. **Director, Stadium Operations:** Bobby Atencio. **Director, Accounting/Human Resources:** Cynthia DiFrancesco. **Box Office/Administration Manager:** Mark Otero. **Director, Community Relations:** Michelle Montoya. **Marketing/Promotions Manager:** Dylan Storm. **Director of Game Production:** Kris Shepard. **Suite Relations Manager:** TBD. **Travel Coordinator/Home Clubhouse Manager:** Ryan Maxwell. **Ticket Sales Executives:** Terry Clark, Aaron Robinson. **Graphic Designer:** Rebecca Zook. **Event Operations Coordinator:** Summer Noelle. **Head Groundskeeper:** Clint Belau. **Assistant Groundskeeper:** TBD. **GM, Spectra:** Boris Revilla. **Executive Chef, Spectra:** Ryan Kagimoto.

FIELD STAFF

Manager: Warren Schaeffer. **Hitting Coach:** Tim Doherty. **Pitching Coach:** Blaine Beatty. **Athletic Trainer:** Heath Townsend. **Physical Performance Coach:** Phil Bailey.

GAME INFORMATION

Radio Announcer: TBD. **No. of Games Broadcast:** 140. **Flagship Station:** KNML 95.9-FM & 610-AM. **PA Announcer:** Francina Walker. **Official Scorers:** Gary Herron, Brent Carey, John Miller, Frank Mercogliano. **Stadium Name:** Isotopes Park. **Location:** From 1-25, exit east on Avenida Cesar Chavez SE to University Boulevard; From I-40, exit south on UniversityBoulevard SE to Avenida Cesar Chavez. **Standard Game Times:** 6:35 pm / 7:05 pm. **Sun 1:35/6:**05 pm. **Ticket Price Range:** $8-$27. **Visiting Club Hotel:** Sheraton Albuquerque Airport Hotel, 2910 Yale Blvd SE, Albuquerque, NM 87106. **Telephone:** (505) 843-7000.

EL PASO CHIHUAHUAS

Address: 1 Ballpark Plaza, El Paso, TX 79901.
Telephone: (915) 533-2273. **Fax:** (915) 242-2031.
E-Mail Address: info@epchihuahuas.com. **Website:** www.epchihuahuas.com.
Affiliation (first year): San Diego Padres (2014). **Years in League:** 2021-

OWNERSHIP/MANAGEMENT

Owner/Chairman of the Board: Paul Foster. **Owner/CEO/Vice Chairman:** Josh Hunt. **Owners:** Alejandra de la Vega Foster, Woody Hunt. **President:** Alan Ledford. **Senior Vice President/General Manager:** Brad Taylor. **Senior Director, Finance & Administration:** Pamela De La O. **Senior Accounting Manager:** Heather Hagerty. **Accounts Payable/Accounts Receivable Supervisor and Payroll Coordinator:** Pamela Nieto. **Staff Accountant:** Antonio Mendoza. **Director, Corporate Partnerships & Suites:** Judge Scott. **Account Executive, Corporate Partnership & Activation:** Adrian Arvizo. **Account Executive, Corporate Partnerships:** Javier Delgado. **Senior Director, Ticket Sales & Service:** Nick Seckerson. **Manager, Season Seat Sales:** Primo Martinez. **Director, Business Development Analytics & Ticket Operations:** Ross Rotwein. **Manager, Group Sales:** Brittany Morgan. **Supervisor, Group Ticket Services:** Killian Vallieu. **Senior Account Executives, Ticket Sales:** Matt Heiligenberg, Jay Morris. **Account Executive, Ticket Sales:** Ethan Andersen. **Senior Account Executives, Group Sales:** Corey Cerrone, Janine Quiroz, Austin Weber. **Account Executives, Group Sales:** Korey Dunn, Alex Rodriguez. **Manager, Ticket Operations:** Ruben Armendariz. **Ticketing Specialists:** Sorrel Hoover, Hector Marquez. **Senior Director, Marketing & Communications:** Angela Olivas. **Senior**

Manager, Video & Digital Production: Juan Gutierrez. **Senior Manager, Broadcast & Media Relations:** Tim Hagerty. **Director, Promotions & Community Relations:** Andy Imfeld. **Manager, Fan Engagement & Community Programs:** Grant Gorham. **Production & Social Media Coordinator:** Gage Freeman. **Community Relations & Promotions Coordinator:** Kate Lewis. **Creative Services & Digital Marketing Coordinator:** Ilene Serna. **Assistant, Promotions & Community Relations:** Kate Starr. **Senior Director, Guest Services & Baseball Operations:** Lizette Espinosa. **Director, Grounds & Building Operations:** Travis Howard. **Assistant Groundskeeper:** Andrew Faust. **Assistant Groundskeeper:** Tony Tafoya. **Manager, Facilities:** Michael Raymundo. **Manager, Baseball Operations & Guest Services:** Latoya Wright. **Manager, Retail & Merchandise Operations:** Leslie Holt. **Director, Special Events:** Gina Roe-Davis.

FIELD STAFF
Manager: TBA. **Hitting Coach:** TBA. **Pitching Coach:** TBA. **Coach:** TBA. **Trainers:** TBA.

GAME INFORMATION
Broadcaster: Tim Hagerty. **No. of Games Broadcast:** 140. **Flagship Station:** ESPN 600 AM El Paso. **PA Announcer:** Larry Berg. **Official Scorer:** Bernie Ricono. **Stadium Name:** Southwest University Park. **Standard Game Times:** 7:05, **Sun 1:05 or 6:**05. **Ticket Price Range:** $5-10.50. **Visiting Club Hotel:** Hilton Garden Inn.

LAS VEGAS AVIATORS

Address: 1650 S. Pavilion Center Drive, Las Vegas, NV 89135.
Telephone: (702) 939-7200. **Fax:** (702) 943-7214.
E-Mail Address: info@aviatorslv.com. **Website:** www.aviatorslv.com.
Affiliation (first year): Oakland Athletics (2019). **Years in League:** 2021-

OWNERSHIP/MANAGEMENT
Operated By: Summerlin Las Vegas Baseball Club LLC.
President/COO: Don Logan. General Manager/**Vice President, Sales/Marketing:** Chuck Johnson. **Vice President, Ticket Sales:** Erik Eisenberg. **Vice President/Accounting:** Scott Montes. **Vice President/Ballpark Support:** Nick Fitzenreider. **Vice President/Retail & Ballpark Operations:** Jason Weber. **Vice President/Public Safety:** Bill Corder. **Director, Ticket Operations:** Siobhan Steiermann. **Director, Ticket Sales:** TJ Thedinga. **Director, Sponsorships:** James Jensen. **Director, Broadcasting:** Russ Langer. **Director, Ballpark Operations:** Johnathan Jensen. **Director, Business Development:** Larry Brown. **Media Relations Director:** Jim Gemma. **Director/Game Entertainment:** Gary Arlitz. **Director, Retail Operations:** Edward Dorville. **Director/Team Operations:** Steve Dwyer.
Senior Account Executive: Bryan Frey. **Account Executives, Ticket Sales:** Nathan Erbach, Ariel Greenberg, David Moses, Kyle Nakama. **Senior Staff Accountant:** Brian Winslow. **Staff Accountant:** Danniel Recinos. **Ballpark Operations Manager:** Deonte Hawkins. **Ballpark Support Manager:** Chip Vespe. **Special Events Manager:** Jenna Potter. **Box Office Manager:** Annette Evans. **Ticket Operations Supervisor:** Michelle Taggart. **Executive Assistant:** Jan Dillard. **Ticket Services & Community Relations Coordinators:** Katie Greener, Hayley Smith. **Administrative Support Specialist:** Kirsten Sheff. **Retail Operations Manager:** Mariz Arellano. **Retail Sales Associates:** Thomas Brazile, Andrew Lockhart. **Chief Engineer:** Ronnie Cabrera.

FIELD STAFF
Manager: Fran Riordan. **Hitting Coach:** Tommy Everidge. **Pitching Coach:** Rick Rodriguez. **Assistant Hitting Coach:** Brian McArn. **Head Athletic Trainer:** Justin Whitehouse. **Sport Performance Coach:** Omar Hamed.

GAME INFORMATION
Radio Announcer: Russ Langer. **No. of Games Broadcast:** 140. **Flagship Station:** KRLV 920 AM
PA Announcer: Dan Bickmore. **Official Scorer:** Peter Legner. **Stadium Name:** Las Vegas Ballpark. **Location:** I 215 North Beltway to Sahara Avenue (exit east), left on Pavilion Center Drive; 1 215 South Beltway to Charleston Blvd. (exit east), right on Pavilion Center Drive. **Standard Game Time:** 7:05 pm. **Ticket Price Range:** $12-60. **Visiting Club Hotel:** Red Rock Casino Resort & Spa, 11011 W. Charleston Blvd. Las Vegas, NV 89135. **Telephone:** (702) 797-7777.

OKLAHOMA CITY DODGERS

Address: 2 S Mickey Mantle Dr., Oklahoma City, OK 73104.
Telephone: (405) 218-1000. **Fax:** (405) 218-1001.
E-Mail Address: info@okcdodgers.com. **Website:** www.okcdodgers.com.
Affiliation (first year): Los Angeles Dodgers (2015). **Years in League:** 2021-

OWNERSHIP/MANAGEMENT
Operated By: MB OKC LLC. **Principal Owner:** Mandalay Baseball
President/General Manager: Michael Byrnes. **Senior Vice President:** Jenna Byrnes. **Vice President, Ticket Sales:** Kyle Daugherty. **Director, Finance/Accounting:** John MacDonald. **Senior Director, Operations:** Mitch Stubenhofer. **Senior Director, Marketing/Communications:** Ben Beecken. **Director, Business Intelligence:** Kyle Logan. **Director, Corporate Partnerships:** Ryan Vanlow. **Director, Ticket Operations:** Bethany Staub. **Director, Partner Services:** Katy White. **Director, Communications/Broadcasting:** Alex Freedman. **Director, Food Service Operations:** Lindsay Robb. **Executive Director, OKC Dodgers Baseball Foundation:** Carol Herrick. **Communications Coordinator:** Lisa

Johnson. **Baseball Operations Coordinator:** Billy Maloney. **Merchandise Manager:** Jasmine Buchanan. **Special Events Manager:** Shelby Kirkes. **Game Presentation Manager:** A.J. Navarro. **Office Manager:** Travis Hunter. **Head Groundskeeper:** Jeff Jackson. **Clubhouse Manager:** T.J. Leonard.

FIELD STAFF
Manager: Travis Barbary. **Hitting Coach:** Emmanuel Burriss. **Pitching Coach:** Jamey Wright. **Bench Coach:** Bill Haselman. **Bullpen Coach:** Justin DeFratus. **Athletic Trainers:** Shawn McDermott and Chelsea Willette. **Performance Coach:** Jeff Taylor.

GAME INFORMATION
Radio Announcer: Alex Freedman. **No. of Games Broadcast:** 140. **Station:** KGHM-AM 1340 (www.1340thegame.com). **PA Announcer:** Jared Gallagher. **Official Scorers:** Jim Byers, Mark Heusman, Rich Tortorelli. **Stadium Name:** Chickasaw Bricktown Ballpark. **Location:** Bricktown area in downtown Oklahoma City, near interchange of I-235 and I-40, off I-235 take Sheridan exit to Bricktown; off I-40 take Shields exit, north to Bricktown. **Standard Game Times:** 7:05 pm, Sun 2:05 (April-June), 6:05 (July-Aug). **Ticket Price Range:** $9-28. **Visiting Club Hotel:** Courtyard Oklahoma City Downtown, 2 West Reno Ave., Oklahoma City, OK 73102. **Telephone:** (405) 232-2290.

RENO ACES

Address: 250 Evans Ave, Reno, NV 89501.
Telephone: (775) 334-4700. **Fax:** (775) 334-4701.
Website: www.renoaces.com.
Affiliation (first year): Arizona Diamondbacks (2009). **Years in League:** 2021-

OWNERSHIP/MANAGEMENT
President: Eric Edelstein.
General Manager: Emily Jaenson. **Chief Operations Officer:** Doug Raftery. **Chief Revenue Officer:** Samantha Hicks. **Chief Financial Officer:** Stacey Bowman. **VP of Business Development:** Brian Moss. **Director of Ticket Operations:** Sarah Bliss. **Accounting Director:** Adam Hyde. **Staff Accountant:** Jose Mata. **Marketing Director:** Vince Ruffino. **Social Media Coordinator:** AJ Grimm. **Group Sales Director:** Alex Strathearn. **Entertainment Manager:** Devin Levan-Galang. **Ticket Operations Manager:** Kristina Solis. **Facilities Manager:** Miguel Paredes. **Creative Manager:** Blake O'Brien. **Corporate Partnerships Director:** Max Margulies. **Public Relations and Communications Manager:** Kevin Bass. **Corporate Partnerships Services Account Manager:** Courtney Baker. **Member Services Director:** Laura Raymond. **Stadium Operations Assistant:** Myles Fresquez. **Senior Account Executive:** Henry Fassinger. **Head Groundskeeper:** Leah Withrow. **Visiting Clubhouse Manager:** TBA.

FIELD STAFF
Manager: Blake Lalli. **Hitting Coach:** Rick Short. **Pitching Coach:** Jeff Bajenaru. **Coach:** Jorge Cortes. **Trainer:** Michael Powell. **Strength Coordinator:** Derek Somerville.

GAME INFORMATION
Radio Announcer: Zack Bayrouty. **PA Announcers:** Cory Smith, Chris Payne. **Official Scorers:** Alan Means, Greg Erny, Gregg Zive. **Stadium Name:** Greater Nevada Field. **Location: From north, south and east:** I-80 West, Exit 14 (Wells Ave.), left on Wells, right at Kuenzil St., field on right; From West, I-80 East to Exit 13 (Virginia St.), right on Virginia, left on Second, field on left. **Standard Game Times:** 7:05 p.m., 6:35 p.m., 1:05 p.m. **Ticket Price Range:** $8-35.

ROUND ROCK EXPRESS

Address: 3400 East Palm Valley Blvd, Round Rock, TX 78665.
Telephone: (512) 255-2255. **Fax:** (512) 255-1558.
E-Mail Address: info@rrexpress.com. **Website:** www.RRExpress.com.
Affiliation (first year): Texas Rangers (2011). **Year in League:** 2021-

OWNERSHIP/MANAGEMENT
Operated By: Ryan Sanders Sports & Entertainment. **Principal Owners:** Nolan Ryan, Don Sanders. **Owners:** Reid Ryan, Reese Ryan, Bret Sanders, Brad Sanders, Eddie Maloney. **Chief Executive Officer, Ryan Sanders Sports & Entertainment:** Reid Ryan. **Chief Operating Officer, Ryan Sanders Sports & Entertainment:** JJ Gottsch. **Chief Financial Officer, Ryan Sanders Sports & Entertainment:** Jonathan Germer. **Executive Assistant, Ryan Sanders Sports & Entertainment:** Debbie Bowman. **Administrative Assistant, Ryan Sanders Sports & Entertainment:** Jacqueline Bowman. **President:** Chris Almendarez. **General Manager:** Tim Jackson. **Executive Advisor to President & General Manager:** Dave Fendrick. **Senior Vice President, Marketing:** Laura Fragoso. **Vice President, Administration & Accounting:** Debbie Coughlin. **Assistant General Manager, Sales:** Stuart Scally. **Senior Director, Stadium Operations & Security:** Gene Kropff. **Senior Director, United Heritage Conference Center:** Scott Allen. **Director, Ballpark Entertainment:** Steve Richards. **Director, Broadcasting:** Mike Capps. **Director, Community Relations:** Elisa Fogle. **Director, Express Select:** Chris Godwin. **Director, Information Technology:** Mark Ramos. **Director, Retail Operations:** Joe Belger. **Director, Stadium Maintenance:** Aurelio Martinez. **Manager, Baseball Operations:** Chase Almendarez. **Manager, Clubhouse Operations:** Kenny Bufton. **Manager, Development & Programs, Nolan Ryan Foundation:** Peyton Chapman. **Manager, Group Sales:** Alyssa Coggins. **Manager, Office:** Wendy Abrahamsen. **Manager, Post-Event Cleaning:** Mark Maloney. **Manager, PR & Communications:** Andrew Felts. **Manager,**

Promotional Events: Casey Wright. **Manager, Season Memberships & Service:** Oscar Rodriguez. **Manager, Ticket Operations:** Aschley Carvalho. **Manager, Venue Operations:** Alex Blair. **Specialist, Digital Content:** Taylor Shipp. **Account Executive:** Connor Truitt. **Assistant, Brand Marketing:** Karlie Dyer. **Head Groundskeeper:** Nick Rozdilski. **Field Crew:** Ben Hartman, Tyler Midkiff. **Housekeeping Staff:** Ofelia Gonzalez. **Electrician/HVAC Maintenance Staff:** Leslie Hitt. **Consultant, Human Resources:** Missy Martin.

FIELD STAFF

Manager: Kenny Holmberg. **Hitting Coach:** Chase Lambin. **Pitching Coach:** Bill Simas. **Athletic Trainer:** Carlos Olivas. **Strength and Conditioning Coach:** Wade Lamont.

GAME INFORMATION

Radio Announcer: Mike Capps. **No. of Games Broadcast:** 140. **Flagship Station:** AM 1300 The Zone. **PA Announcer:** Glen Norman. **Official Scorer:** David Boyd.

Stadium Name: Dell Diamond. **Location:** US Highway 79, 3.5 miles east of Interstate 35 (exit 253) or 1.5 miles west of Texas Tollway 130. **Standard Game Times:** 7:05 pm, 6:05, 1:05, 11:35. **Ticket Price Range:** $7-$30.

Visiting Club Hotel: LaQuinta Inn & Suites by Wyndham Round Rock East, 3900 East Palm Valley Blvd., Round Rock, TX 78665. **Telephone:** (737) 300-6008.

SACRAMENTO RIVER CATS

Address: Sutter Health Park - 400 Ballpark Drive, West Sacramento, CA 95691
Telephone: (916) 376-4700. **Fax:** (916) 376-4710.
E-Mail Address: reception@rivercats.com. **Website:** www.rivercats.com
Affiliation (first year): San Francisco Giants (2015). **Years in League:** 2021-

OWNERSHIP/MANAGEMENT

Majority Owner/CEO: Susan Savage. **President:** Jeff Savage. **General Manager:** Chip Maxson. **Director, Human Resources:** Isabella Guedes. **Coordinator, Human Resources:** Vanessa Villanueva. **Vice President, Finance:** Maddie Strika. **Accounting Coordinator:** N/A **Executive Assistant:** N/A **Front Desk Administrator:** N/A. **Vice President, Partner Services:** Greg Coletti. **Director, Corporate Partnerships:** N/A. **Manager, Key Accounts:** N/A. **Coordinator, Partnership Activation:** Krystal Jones. **Coordinator, Partnership Activation:** N/A. **Senior Manager, Communications and Baseball Operations:** N/A. **Coordinator, Media and Baseball:** Conner Penfold. **Radio Broadcaster:** Johnny Doskow. **Multimedia Designer:** Mike Villarreal. **Graphic Design Coordinator:** N/A. **Manager, Marketing:** Melissa Adams. **Marketing Coordinator:** N/A. **Promotions Manager:** N/A **Director, Ticket Operations:** Joe Carlucci. **Director, Ticket Sales:** Justice Hoyt. **Senior Manager, Group Sales:** N/A. **Manager, Membership Sales:** N/A. **Manager, Business Development:** Jack Barbour. **Manager, Corporate Sales:** John Watts. **Senior Membership Experience Specialist:** Kyle Strom N/A. **Account Executives, Corporate Sales:** Cole Scieszinski. **Account Executives, Group Sales:** Mohammed Halabi. **Account Executives, Inside Sales:** N/A. **Manager, Merchandise:** N/A. **Manager, Merchandise Marketing & Online Sales:** Erin Kilby. **Coordinator, Website/Research:** Brent Savage. **Vice President, Ballpark Experience:** Corey Brandt. **Director, Events/Entertainment:** Brittney Nizuk. **Senior Coordinator, Events/Entertainment:** N/A. **Coordinator, Events/Entertainment:** Lauren Baldwin. **Director, Field Operations:** Chris Shastid. **Facility Supervisor:** Anthony Hernandez. **Manager, Security:** Rich Bentley. **Stadium Operations Supervisor:** Mike Correa. **Stadium Operations:** N/A. **Coordinator, Field Operations:** Marcello Clamar. **Landscaper:** N/A. **Manager, Concessions:** Sean Gerkensmeyer. **Manager, Suites & Premium Hospitality:** N/A. **Food & Beverage HR Coordinator:** N/A.

FIELD STAFF

Manager: Dave Brundage. **Hitting Coach:** Damon Minor. **Pitching Coach:** Garvin Alston. **Fundamentals Coach:** Jolbert Cabrera. **Bullpen Coach:** TBD. **Athletic Trainers:** David Getsoff, Hiro Sato. **Strength & Conditioning Coach:** TBD.

GAME INFORMATION

Radio Broadcaster: Johnny Doskow. **No. of Games Broadcast:** 142. **PA Announcer:** TBD. **Official Scorers:** TBD. **Stadium Name:** Sutter Health Park. **Location:** I-5 to Business-80 West, exit at Jefferson Boulevard. **Standard Game Time:** 7:05 p.m. **Ticket Price Range:** $10-$70. **Visiting Club Hotel:** Holiday Inn Sacramento Downtown - Arena.

SALT LAKE BEES

Address: 77 W 1300 South, Salt Lake City, UT 84115.
Telephone: (801) 325-2337. **Fax:** (801) 485-6818.
E-Mail Address: info@slbees.com. **Website:** www.slbees.com.
Affiliation (first year): Los Angeles Angels (2001). **Years in League:** 2021-.

OWNERSHIP/MANAGEMENT

Principal Owner: Gail Miller. **President/General Manager:** Marc Amicone. **President, Smith Entertainment Group & Utah Jazz:** Jim Olson. **Chief Revenue Officer:** Chris Barney. **Chief Financial Officer:** John Larson. **Chief Communications Officer:** Frank Zang. **Chief Marketing Officer:** Bart Sharp. **Vice President, People & Culture:** Amber Robinson. **General Counsel:** Sam Harkness. **Assistant GM:** Bryan Kinneberg. **Director, Broadcasting:** Steve Klauke. **VP Ticket Sales:** Trevor Haws. **Director, Ticket Sales:** Brad Jacoway. **Sr. Director, Corporate Partnership Activation:**

Kim Brown. **Director, Corporate Partnerships:** Jackson Brown. **Director, Marketing:** Brady Brown. **Director, Ticket Operations:** Derrek DeGraaff. **Box Office Manager:** Duane Sartori **Communications Manager:** Kraig Williams. **Youth Programs Coordinator:** Nate Martinez. **Home Clubhouse Manager:** Cole Filosa. **Visiting Clubhouse Manager:** Chris Simonsen. **Head Groundskeeper:** Brian Soukup. **Asst. Head Groundskeeper:** Paul Sheffield.

FIELD STAFF

Manager: TBA. **Pitching Coach:** TBA. **Hitting Coach:** TBA. **Defensive Coach:** TBA. **Athletic Trainer:** TBA. **Strength/Conditioning Coach:** TBA.

GAME INFORMATION

Radio Announcer: Steve Klauke. **No. of Games Broadcast:** 140. **Flagship Station:** 1280 AM.
PA Announcer: Jeff Reeves. **Official Scorers:** Jeff Cluff, Brooke Frederickson.
Stadium Name: Smith's Ballpark. **Location:** I-15 North/South to 1300 South exit, east to ballpark at West Temple. **Standard Game Times:** 6:35 (Night games), 1:05 Sunday day games, 12:05 (weekday day games). **Ticket Price Range:** $10-24.

SUGAR LAND SKEETERS

Office Address: 1 Stadium Drive, Sugar Land, Texas, 77498.
Telephone: (281) 240-4487.
Affiliation (first year): Houston Astros (2021). **Years in League:** 2021-

OWNERSHIP/MANAGEMENT

Owners: Bob, Kevin and Marcie Zlotnik. **President:** Christopher Hill. **Special Advisor:** Deacon Jones. **General Manager:** Tyler Stamm. **Senior Vice President, Sales and Marketing:** Bob Merril. **Vice President, Community:** Kyle Dawson. **Office Administrator:** Ashley Richter. **Director of Finance:** Greg Hodges. **Executive Advisor:** Larry Lobue. **Director, Ticket Sales:** Jennifer Schwarz. **Box Office Manager:** Kaitlin Nieberding. **Head Groundskeeper:** Brad Detmore. **Assistant Groundskeeper:** Austin Baudler.

Vice President, Events: Matt Thompson. **Special Events Manager:** Eddy Juarez. **Event Operations Manager:** Russell Wohldmann. **Stadium and Event Operations:** Douglas Failing, Andrew Wagar. **Senior Business Development Manager:** Sunny Okpon. **Business Development Managers:** Dolores Townley, Cassie Turzillo, Kimberly Munroy. **Vice President, Sponsorship Sales:** Chris Parsons. **Director of Special Projects:** Teneisha Richardson. **Marketing/Digital Media Coordinator:** Megan Murnane. **Marketing Coordinator:** Erin Keir. **Media Relations Director/Broadcaster:** Ryan Posner. **Community Relations Manager:** Sallie Weir. **Video Production Coordinator:** Troy Young. **Graphics Coordinator:** Shay Villarreal. **Mascot Coordinator:** Megan Brown. **Legends General Manager:** Greg Hernandez. **Legends Events Manager:** Jay Lero. **Legends Accountant:** Andrea Jennings. **Legends Operations Manager:** Ginavieve Strickland. **Executive Chef:** Eric Robison.

FIELD STAFF

Manager: TBA. **Pitching Coach:** TBA. **Hitting Coach:** TBA. **Defensive Coach:** TBA. **Athletic Trainer:** TBA. **Strength/Conditioning Coach:** TBA.

GAME INFORMATION

Radio Announcer: Ryan Posner. **No. of Games Broadcast:** 140. **Flagship Streaming Station:** YouTube. **Standard Game Times:** Mon.-Fri., 7:05 pm, Sat., 6:05 pm, Sun., 2:05 pm. **Visiting Club Hotel:** Sugar Land Marriott Town Square. **Telephone:** (281) 275-8400.

TACOMA RAINIERS

Address: 2502 South Tyler St, Tacoma, WA 98405.
Telephone: (253) 752-7707. **Fax:** (253) 752-7135.
Website: www.tacomarainiers.com
Affiliation (first year): Seattle Mariners (1995). **Years in League:** 2021-

OWNERSHIP/MANAGEMENT

Owners: The Baseball Club of Tacoma. **President:** Aaron Artman. **CFO:** Brian Coombe. **Assistant General Manager:** Nick Cherniske. **Vice President, Sales:** Shane Santman. **Director of Administration and Assistant to the President:** Patti Stacy. **Senior Director, Ticket Sales:** Tim O'Hollaren. **Director, Business Development:** Ben Nelson. **Manager, Corporate Sales:** Kevin Drugge. **Director, Group Sales and Event Marketing:** Caitlin Calnan. **Manager, Group Sales:** Chris Aubertin. **Premium Experience and Events Manager:** Hannah Hall. **Vice President, Marketing:** Megan Mead. **Director, Creative:** Casey Catherwood. **Director, Media Relations and Content Development:** AJ Garcia. **Graphic Designer:** Delaney Saul. **Graphic Designer:** Erin Fogerty. **Director, Technical:** Anthony Phinney. **Specialist, Multimedia:** Adam Wygle. **Broadcaster:** Mike Curto. **Director, Partner Services:** Yvette Yzaguirre. **Director, Baseball Ops and Merchandise:** Ashley Schutt. **Manager, Team Store:** Kyle McGilvray. **Staff Accountant:** Amy Tucci. **Head Groundskeeper:** Michael Kerns. **Assistant Groundskeeper:** Josh Wonsley.

FIELD STAFF

Manager: Kristopher Negrón. **Hitting Coach:** Roy Howell. **Pitching Coach:** Rob Marcello Jr. **Coach:** Eric Young Jr. **Trainers:** TBA. **Performance Specialist:** TBA.

GAME INFORMATION

Radio Broadcaster: Mike Curto. **No. of Games Broadcast:** 140. **Flagship Station:** KHHO 850-AM. **PA Announcer:** Randy McNair. **Official Scorers:** Kevin Kalal, Gary Brooks, Michael Jessee, Jon Gilbert. **Stadium Name:** Cheney Stadium. **Location:** From I-5, take exit 132 (Highway 16 West) for 1.2 miles to 19th Street East exit, merge right onto 19th Street, right onto Clay Huntington Way and follow into parking lot of ballpark. **Standard Game Times:** 7:05, Sun. 1:35. (Monday–Wednesday games start at 6:05pm in April–June). **Ticket Price Range:** $7.50-$25.50. **Visiting Club Hotel:** Hotel Murano, 1320 Broadway Plaza, Tacoma, WA 98402. **Telephone:** (253) 238-8000.

DOUBLE-A NORTHEAST

STADIUM INFORMATION

Club	Stadium	Opened	Dimensions			Capacity	2019 Att.
			LF	CF	RF		
Akron	Canal Park	1997	331	400	337	7,630	340,187
Altoona	Peoples Natural Gas Field	1999	325	405	325	7,210	308,464
Binghamton	NYSEG Stadium	1992	330	400	330	6,012	182,990
Bowie	Prince George's Stadium	1994	309	405	309	10,000	224,686
Erie	UPMC Park	1995	317	400	328	6,000	215,444
Harrisburg	Metro Bank Park	1987	325	400	325	6,300	258,909
Hartford	Dunkin' Donuts Park	2018	325	400	325	6,146	414,946
New Hampshire	Northeast Delta Dental Stadium	2005	326	400	306	6,500	306,511
Portland	Hadlock Field	1994	315	400	330	7,368	357,647
Reading	FirstEnergy Stadium	1951	330	400	330	9,000	398,314
Richmond	The Diamond	1985	330	402	330	9,560	400,321
Somerset	TD Bank Ballpark	1999	317	402	315	6,100	344,641

AKRON RUBBERDUCKS

Address: 300 S Main St, Akron, OH 44308.
Telephone: (330) 253-5151. (855) 97-QUACK. **Fax:** (330) 253-3300.
E-Mail Address: information@akronrubberducks.com.
Website: www.akronrubberducks.com.
Affiliation (first year): Cleveland Indians (1989). **Years in League:** 2021-

OWNERSHIP/MANAGEMENT

Operated By: Fast Forward Sports Group/Akron Baseball, LLC. **Principal Owner/CEO:** Ken Babby.
President: Jim Pfander. **CFO:** Shawn Carlson. **General Manager/COO:** Jim Pfander. **Assistant GM/Vice President, Operations:** Scott Riley. **Vice President, Sales:** Dave Burke. **Controller:** Leslie Wenzlawsh. **Assistant, Finance:** Bryson Lenderman. **Manager, Promotions:** Kyle Hixenbaugh. **Coordinator, Media Relations:** Pat McGuire. **Lead Broadcaster:** Marco LaNave. **Coordinator, Merchandise:** Jamie Vanaman. **Coordinator, Creative Services:** Gabe Wasylko. **Director, Stadium Operations:** Adam Horner. **Head Groundskeeper:** Chris Walsh. **Assistant Groundskeeper:** Colt Boxler. **Assistant Director, Ballpark Operations:** James Parsons. **Director, Food/Beverage:** Brian Manning. **Assistant Director, Food/Beverage:** Chad Nock. **Director, Premium Experience:** Sam Dankoff. **Manager, Culinary Operations:** Louis Willmon-Holland. **Office Manager:** Missy Dies. **Coordinator, Community Relations:** Austin Stephens. **Manager, Season Ticket Sales & Service:** Mitch Cromes. **Senior Manager, Amateur Baseball Development/Group Sales & Service:** Roy Jacobs. **Box Office Manager:** Ian Wilkinson. **Ticket Sales Executives:** Trevor McGuire. **Manager, Corporate Partnerships:** Anthony Chadwick. **Coordinator, Corporate Partnerships:** Brian Lobban. **Art Director:** Scott Watkins. **Director, Player Facilities:** Shad Gross.

FIELD STAFF

Manager: Rouglas Odor. **Hitting Coach:** Junior Betances. **Pitching Coach:** Owen Dew. **Bench Coach:** Mike Mergenthaler. **Trainer:** Jake Legan. **Strength Coach:** Scott Nealon.

GAME INFORMATION

Radio Announcers: Marco LaNave, Jim Clark. **No. of Games Broadcast:** 120. **Flagship Station:** Fox Sports Radio 1350-AM. **PA Announcer:** DJ Nivens. **Official Scorer:** Chuck Murr. **Stadium Name:** Canal Park. **Location:** From I-76 East or I-77 South, exit onto Route 59 East, exit at Exchange/Cedar, right onto Cedar, left at Main Street; From I-76 West or I-77 North, exit at Main Street/Downtown, follow exit onto Broadway Street, left onto Exchange Street, right at Main Street. **Standard Game Time:** 6:35 (non-fireworks game); 7:05 pm (fireworks games), Sun 2:05. **Ticket Price Range:** $5-11. **Visiting Club Hotel:** Fairfield Inn & Suites by Marriott Akron Fairlawn. **Telephone:** (330) 665-0641.

ALTOONA CURVE

Address: Peoples Natural Gas Field, 1000 Park Avenue, Altoona, PA 16602
Telephone: (814) 943-5400. **Fax:** (814) 942-9132
E-Mail Address: frontoffice@altoonacurve.com. **Website:** www.altoonacurve.com
Affiliation (first year): Pittsburgh Pirates (1999). **Years in League:** 2021-

OWNERSHIP/MANAGEMENT

Operated By: Lozinak Professional Baseball.
Managing Members: Bob and Joan Lozinak. **COO:** David Lozinak. **CFO:** Mike Lozinak. **General Manager:** Derek Martin. **Senior Advisor:** Sal Baglieri. **Assistant General Manager:** Nathan Bowen. **Director of Finance:** Mary Lamb. **Assistant Director of Finance:** TBD. **Administrative Assistant:** Michelle Anna. **Director of Communications & Broadcasting:** TBD. **Communications & Broadcasting Assistant:** TBD. **Director of Ticketing:** Jess Knott. **Box Office**

Manager: TBD. **Senior Ticket Account Manager:** TBD. **Ticket Sales Manager:** TBD. **Ticket Sales Manager:** TBD. **Ticket Sales Manager:** Corbin Padgett. **Manager of Partnership Services:** TBD. **Director of Community Relations & Social Media:** Annie Choiniere. **Director of Ballpark Operations:** Doug Mattern. **Head Groundskeeper:** James Petrella. **Director of Concessions:** Glenn McComas. **Assistant Director of Concessions:** Ashley Daley. **Director of Entertainment and Branding:** Isaiah Arpino. **Director of Creative Services:** Braeden Appleman. **Creative Services Assistant:** Megan Corcoran. **Director of Marketing, Promotions & Special Events:** Mike Kessling. **Director of Merchandise:** Michelle Gravert.

FIELD STAFF
Manager: Miguel Perez. **Hitting Coach:** David Newhan. **Pitching Coach:** Drew Benes. **Coach:** Gary Green. **Trainer:** Tyler Brooks.

GAME INFORMATION
Radio Announcers: TBD. **No. of Games Broadcast:** 120. **Flagship Station:** WRTA 98.5 FM and 1240 AM. **PA Announcer:** Rich DeLeo. **Official Scorers:** Ted Beam, Dick Wagner. **Stadium Name:** Peoples Natural Gas Field. **Location:** Located just off the Frankstown Road Exit off I-99. **Standard Game Times:** TBD. (Weekdays, April-May); TBD. (Weekdays, June-August); Fri TBD.; Sat. TBD. and TBD.; Sun TBD and TBD. **Ticket Price Range:** $8-17. **Visiting Club Hotel:** Microtel Inn & Suites Altoona.

BINGHAMTON RUMBLE PONIES

Office Address: 211 Henry St., Binghamton, NY 13901.
Mailing Address: PO Box 598, Binghamton, NY 13902.
Telephone: (607) 722-3866. **Fax:** (607) 723-7779.
E-Mail Address: info@bingrp.com. **Website:** www.bingrp.com.
Affiliation (first year): New York Mets (1992). **Years in League:** 2021-

OWNERSHIP/MANAGEMENT
President: John Hughes. **Managing Director:** John Bayne. **Director of Business Operations:** Kelly Hust. **Director of Broadcasting & Media Relations:** Jacob Wilkins. **Director of Video Production:** Mark Perley. **Director of Stadium Operations:** Dan Rose. **Scholastic Programs Coordinator:** Lou Ferraro.

FIELD STAFF
Manager: Lorenzo Bundy. **Hitting Coach:** Bruce Fields. **Pitching Coach:** Jonathan Hurst. **Bench Coach:** Joe Raccuia.

GAME INFORMATION
Radio Announcer: Jacob Wilkins. **No. of Games Broadcast:** 120.. **PA Announcer:** Frank Perney. **Official Scorer:** Matt Ferraro. **Stadium Name:** RumbleTown Stadium. **Location:** I-81 to exit 4S (Binghamton), Route 11 exit to Henry Street. **Standard Game Times:** 6:35, 7:05 (Fri), 1:05 (Day Games). **Ticket Price Range:** $8 - $14. **Visiting Club Hotel:** Holiday Inn Downtown.

BOWIE BAYSOX

Address: Prince George's Stadium, 4101 NE Crain Hwy, Bowie, MD 20716.
Telephone: (301) 805-6000. **Fax:** (301) 464-4911.
E-Mail Address: info@baysox.com. **Website:** www.baysox.com.
Affiliation (first year): Baltimore Orioles (1993). **Years in League:** 2021-

OWNERSHIP/MANAGEMENT
Owned By: Maryland Baseball Holding LLC. **President:** Ken Young. **General Manager:** Brian Shallcross. **Assistant GM:** Phil Wrye. **Business Manager:** Landon Ferrell. **Director, Ticket Operations:** Charlene Fewer. **Director, Sponsorships:** Matt McLaughlin. **Promotions Manager:** TBD. **Communications Manager:** TBD. **Director of Broadcasting:** Adam Pohl. **Assistant Director of Ticket Operations:** TBD. **Assistant Director of Ticket Operations:** TBD. **Box Office Manager:** TBD.
Director, Video Production: TBD. **Head Groundskeeper:** Richard Douglas. **Stadium Operations Manager:** Tim Lillis. **Director. Gameday Personnel:** Darlene Mingioli. **Clubhouse Manager:** Dallas Darling.

FIELD STAFF
Manager: Buck Britton. **Hitting Coach:** Tim Gibbons. **Pitching Coach:** Justin Ramsey. **Fundamentals Coach:** TBD. **Athletic Trainer:** TBD. **Development Coach:** Grant Anders.

GAME INFORMATION
Radio Announcer: Adam Pohl. **No. of Games Broadcast:** 120. **Flagship Station:** www.1430wnav.com. **PA Announcer:** Adrienne Roberson. **Official Scorers:** Dan Gretz, Patrick Stevens. **Stadium Name:** Prince George's Stadium. **Location:** 1/4 mile south of US 50/Route 301 Interchange in Bowie. **Standard Game Times:** Mon-Thu, Sat. 6:35 pm, Fri 7:05 pm, Sun 1:35 pm. **Ticket Price Range:** $8-$18. **Visiting Club Hotel:** Crowne Plaza Annapolis, 173 Jennifer Rd, Annapolis, MD 21401; **Telephone:** (410) 266-3131.

ERIE SEAWOLVES

Address: 831 French St, Erie, PA 16501.
Telephone: (814) 456-1300.
E-Mail Address: seawolves@seawolves.com. **Website:** www.seawolves.com.
Affiliation (first year): Detroit Tigers (2001). **Years in League:** 2021-

OWNERSHIP/MANAGEMENT

Principal Owners: At Bat Group, LLC.
CEO: Fernando Aguirre. **President:** Greg Coleman. **Assistant GM, Communications:** Greg Gania. **Assistant GM, Sales:** Mark Pirrello. **Director, Accounting/Finance:** Amy McArdle. **Director, Operations:** Mike Lockhart. **Director, Entertainment:** David Micik. **Community Engagement Manager:** Christopher McDonald. **Director, Merchandise:** Christy Buchar. **Director, Food/Beverage:** Jeff Burgess. **Director of Ticket Sales:** Tom Barnes.

FIELD STAFF

Manager: Arnie Beyeler. **Hitting Coach:** Adam Melhuse. **Pitching Coach:** Mark Johnson. **Developmental Coach:** Tony Smith. **Trainer:** Chris Vick. **Strength/Conditioning Coach:** Phil Hartt.

GAME INFORMATION

Radio Announcer: Greg Gania. **No. of Games Broadcast:** 120. **Flagship Station:** Fox Sports Radio WFNN 1330-AM. **PA Announcer:** TBA. **Official Scorer:** Bob Shreve. **Stadium Name:** UPMC Park. **Location:** US 79 North to East 12th Street exit, left on State Street, right on 10th Street. **Standard Game Times:** 6:05 p.m. (May), 7:05 p.m. (June-Sept), **Sun 1:**35 p.m. **Ticket Price Range:** TBA. **Visiting Club Hotel:** Baymont Inn & Suites, 8170 Perry Hwy., Erie, PA 16509. **Telephone:** (814) 866-8808.

HARRISBURG SENATORS

Office Address: FNB Field, City Island, Harrisburg, PA 17101.
Mailing Address: PO Box 15757, Harrisburg, PA 17105.
Telephone: (717) 231-4444. **Fax:** (717) 231-4445.
E-Mail address: information@senatorsbaseball.com. **Website:** www.senatorsbaseball.com.
Affiliation (first year): Washington Nationals (2005). **Years in League:** 2021-

OWNERSHIP/MANAGEMENT

President: Kevin Kulp. **Vice President/General Manager:** Randy Whitaker. **Accounting Manager:** Donna Demczak. **Senior Corporate Sales Executive:** Todd Matthews. **Corporate Sales Executive:** Nathan Rovenolt. **Assistant General Manager, Group Sales:** Jessica Moyer. **Director, Ticket Operations:** Matt McGrady. **Account Executive:** Max Hrip. **Assistant General Manager, Marketing:** Ashley Grotte. **Radio Broadcaster & Media Relations:** Terry Byrom. **Communications Manager:** Steph Pagliaro. **Director, Merchandise:** Ann Marie Naumes. **Director, Game Entertainment:** Jess Knaster. **Director, Community Relations:** JK McKay. **Vice President of Stadium Operations:** Tim Foreman. **Head Groundskeeper:** Brandon Forsburg.

FIELD STAFF

Manager: Tripp Keister. **Coach:** Brian Rupp. **Pitching Coach:** Sam Narron. **Trainer:** T.D. Swinford. **Strength Coach:** R.J. Guyer.

GAME INFORMATION

Radio Announcers: Terry Byrom. **No. of Games Broadcast:** 120. **Flagship Station:** CBS Sports Radio Harrisburg. **PA Announcer:** TBD. **Official Scorers:** Andy Linker and Mick Reinhard. **Stadium Name:** FNB Field. **Location:** I-83, exit 23 (Second Street) to Market Street, bridge to City Island. **Ticket Price Range:** $9-35. **Visiting Club Hotel:** Comfort Inn and Suites Harrisburg Airport, 1589 W. Harrisburg Pike, Middletown, PA 17057. **Telephone:** (717) 857-8776. **Visiting Team Workout Facility:** TBD.

HARTFORD YARD GOATS

Address: Dunkin' Donuts Park, 1214 Main Street, Hartford CT 06103
Telephone: (860) 246-4628. **Fax:** (860) 247-4628
E-Mail Address: info@yardgoatsbaseball.com. **Website:** www.YardGoatsBaseball.com
Affiliation (first year): Colorado Rockies (2015). **Years in League:** 2021-

OWNERSHIP/MANAGEMENT

President: Tim Restall. **General Manager:** Mike Abramson.
Assistant General Manager, Sales: Josh Montinieri. **Assistant General Manager, Operations:** Dean Zappalorti. **Director, Broadcasting & Media Relations:** Jeff Dooley. **Executive Director of Business Development:** Steve Given. **Events Manager:** Jess Gorman. **Stadium Operations Manager:** Andrew Girard. **Executive Director, Yard Goats Foundation:** Tiffany Young. **Fundraising and Community Engagement Manager:** Tom Baxter. **Controller:** Jim Bonfiglio. **Promotions & Marketing Manager:** Danielle Chylinski. **Game Production Manager:** Mike Delgado.

Box Office Manager: Matt DiBona. Director of Ticket Sales: Steve Mekkelsen. Ticket Sales Account Executive: Shawn Perry. Ticket Sales Account Executive: Jacob Michney. Sports Turf Manager: Kyle Calhoon. Administrative Assistant: Shania Myers. Professional Sports Catering, Regional Vice President: Scott Gustafson. Director of Operations: Jenny Nelson. Concessions Manager: Andrew Labov. Executive Chef: Joe Bartlett.

FIELD STAFF

Manager: Chris Denorfia. Hitting Coach: Tom Sutaris. Pitching Coach: Frank Gonzalez. Trainer: Hoshito Mizutani. Physical Performance Coach: Mason Rook.

GAME INFORMATION

Radio Announcers: Jeff Dooley, Dan Lovallo. No. of Games Broadcast: 120. Flagship Station: News Radio 1410*FM 100.9 Spanish Danny Rodriguez, Derik Rodriguez. PA Announcer: Jared Doyon. Official Scorer: Jim Keener. Stadium Name: Dunkin' Donuts Park. Directions: From the West: Take 84 East to Exit 50 (Main Street). Take Exit 50 toward Main St. Use the left lane to merge onto Chapel St S. Turn left onto Trumbull St. Use the middle lane to turn left onto Main St. From the East: Take 84 West to Exit 50 (US-44 W/Morgan Street). Follow I-91 S/Main St. Take a slight right onto Main St. From the North: Take 91 South to Exit 32A - 32B (Trumbull St). Turn left onto Market St. Turn right onto Morgan St. Take a slight right onto Main St. From the South: Take 91 North to Exit 32A - 32B (Market St). Use the left lane to take Exit 32A-32B for Trumbull St. Use the middle lane to turn left onto Market St. Turn right onto Morgan St. Take a slight right onto Main St. Ticket Price Range: $6-22. Visiting Club Hotel: Holiday Inn Express, 2553 Berlin Turnpike, Newington, CT 06111. (860) 372-4000.

NEW HAMPSHIRE
FISHER CATS

Address: 1 Line Dr, Manchester, NH 03101.
Telephone: (603) 641-2005. Fax: (603) 641-2055.
E-Mail Address: info@nhfishercats.com. Website: www.nhfishercats.com.
Affiliation (first year): Toronto Blue Jays (2004). Years in League: 2021-

OWNERSHIP/MANAGEMENT

Operated By: DSF Sports. Managing Partner: Art Solomon. Partner: Rick Brenner. Partner: Tom Silvia.
President: Mike Ramshaw. Senior VP, Sales: Jeff Tagliaferro. VP, Stadium Operations: Tim Hough. VP, Business Development: Erik Lesniak. Director, Hospitality and Special Events: Stephanie Fournier. Senior Account Executive: Nate Newcombe. Box Office Manager: Tara Leeth. Marketing and Promotions Manager: Sarah Lenau. Broadcasting and Media Relations Manager: Tyler Murray. Facility Operations Manager: D.J. Peer. Turf Manager: Greg Nigrello. Corporate Sales and Promotions Coordinator: Andrew Marais. Ticket Sales Account Executive: Andrew Larson. Professional Sports Catering, Director, Food & Beverage: Jesse DaSilva.

FIELD STAFF

TBA.

GAME INFORMATION

Radio Announcers: Tyler Murray, Bob Lipman.
No. of Games Broadcast: 120. Flagship Station: WGIR 610-AM. PA Announcer: Ben Altsher. Official Scorers: Chick Smith, Lenny Parker. Stadium Name: Northeast Delta Dental Stadium. Location: From I-93 North, take I-293 North to exit 5 (Granite Street), right on Granite Street, right on South Commercial Street, right on Line Drive. Ticket Price Range: $12. Visiting Club Hotel: Country Inn & Suites, 250 South River Rd., Bedford, N.H. 03110. Telephone: (603) 666-4600.

PORTLAND SEA DOGS

Office Address: 271 Park Ave, Portland, ME 04102.
Mailing Address: PO Box 636, Portland, ME 04104.
Telephone: (207) 874-9300. Fax: (207) 780-0317.
E-Mail address: seadogs@seadogs.com. Website: www.seadogs.com.
Affiliation (first year): Boston Red Sox (2003). Years in League: 2021-

OWNERSHIP/MANAGEMENT

Operated By: Portland, Maine Baseball, Inc.
Chairman: Bill Burke. Treasurer: Sally McNamara. President/General Manager: Geoff Iacuessa. Senior VP: John Kameisha. VP/Financial Affairs & Game Operations: Jim Heffley. VP/Communications & Fan Experience: Chris Cameron. Assistant General Manager/Sales: Dennis Meehan. Director, Corporate Sales: Justin Phillips. Ticket Office Manager: Bryan Pahigian. Assistant Ticket Office Manager: Allison Casiles. Director, Creative Services: Ted Seavey. Mascot Coordinator: Tim Jorn. Director, Media Relations & Broadcasting: Emma Tiedemann. Director, Food Services: Mike Scorza. Assistant Director, Food Services: Greg Moyes. Ticket Office Coordinator: Alan Barker. Account Executive: Melissa Mayhew. Senior Advisor: Charlie Eshbach. Clubhouse Manager: Mike Coziahr. Head Groundskeeper: Jason Cooke. Assistant Groundskeeper: Andy Cashman.

FIELD STAFF

Manager: Corey Wimberly. **Hitting Coach:** Lance Zawadzki. **Pitching Coach:** Lance Carter. **Coach:** Ako Thomas. **Athletic Trainer:** Scott Gallon. **Strength & Conditioning Coach:** Jeff Dolan.

GAME INFORMATION

Radio Announcer: Emma Tiedemann. **No. of Games Broadcast:** 120. **Flagship Station:** WPEI 95.9 FM. **PA Announcer:** Paul Coughlin. **Official Scorer:** Thom Hinton. **Stadium Name:** Hadlock Field. **Location:** From South, I-295 to exit 5, merge onto Congress Street, left at St John Street, merge right onto Park Ave; From North, I-295 to exit 6A, right onto Park Ave. **Ticket Price Range:** $6-11. **Visiting Club Hotel:** Fireside Inn & Suites, 81 Riverside St., Portland, ME 04103. **Telephone:** (207) 774-5601.

READING FIGHTIN PHILS

Office Address: Route 61 South/1900 Centre Ave, Reading, PA 19605. **Mailing Address:** PO Box 15050, Reading, PA 19612.
Telephone: (610) 370-2255. **Fax:** (610) 373-5868.
E-Mail Address: info@fightins.com. **Website:** www.fightins.com.
Affiliation (first year): Philadelphia Phillies (1967). **Years in League:** 2021-

OWNERSHIP/MANAGEMENT

Operated By: E&J Baseball Club, Inc. **Principal Owner:** Reading Baseball LP. **Managing Partner:** Craig Stein. **General Manager:** Scott Hunsicker. **Assistant General Manager:** Matt Hoffmaster. **Exec. Director, Sales:** Joe Bialek. **Exec. Director, Baseball Operations:** Kevin Sklenarik. **Exec. Director, Tickets & Groups:** Mike Becker. **Exec. Director, Community & Fan Development:** Mike Robinson. **Exec. Director, Business Development:** Anthony Pignetti. **Controller:** Kris Haver. **Head Groundskeeper:** Dan Douglas. **Chief Director, Promotions:** Todd Hunsicker. **Director, Marketing & Exec. Director, Baseballtown Charities:** Tonya Petrunak. **Video Director:** Andy Kauffman. **Director, Food & Beverage:** Travis Hart. **Office Manager:** Deneen Giesen. **Director, Groups:** Jon Nally. **Director, Client Fulfillment/Clubhouse Operations:** Andrew Nelson. **Director, Graphic Arts/Merchandise:** Ryan Springborn. **Account Executive:** Nick Helber. **Account Executive:** Mara Fulmer. **Extra Events/Baseballtown Charities Manager:** Jenna Lawville. **Stadium Operations Manager:** Heath Skimski. **Media Relations/Broadcasting Manager:** Emily Messina.

FIELD STAFF

TBA.

GAME INFORMATION

Radio Announcer: Emily Messina. **No. of Games Broadcast:** 60. **Flagship Station:** TBD. **Official Scorers:** Kyle Matschke, Brian Kopetsky, Josh Leiboff, Dick Shute. **Stadium Name:** FirstEnergy Stadium. **Location:** From east, take Pennsylvania Turnpike West to Morgantown exit, to 176 North, to 422 West, to Route 12 East, to Route 61 South exit; From west, take 422 East to Route 12 East, to Route 61 South exit; From north, take 222 South to Route 12 exit, to Route 61 South exit; From south, take 222 North to 422 West, to Route 12 East exit at Route 61 South. **Standard Game Times:** 7:10 pm, 6:45, **Sundays 2:15 or 5:**15. **Ticket Price Range:** $7-13. **Visiting Club Hotel:** Crowne Plaza Reading Hotel 1741 Papermill Road, Wyomissing, PA 19610. **Telephone:** (610) 376-3811.

RICHMOND FLYING SQUIRRELS

Address: 3001 N Boulevard, Richmond, VA 23230.
Telephone: (804) 359-3866. **Fax:** (804) 359-1373.
E-Mail Address: info@squirrelsbaseball.com. **Website:** www.squirrelsbaseball.com.
Affiliation: San Francisco Giants (2010). **Years in League:** 2021-

OWNERSHIP/MANAGEMENT

Operated By: Navigators Baseball LP. **President/Managing Partner:** Lou DiBella. **CEO:** Todd "Parney" Parnell. **Vice President/General Manager:** Ben Rothrock. **Controller:** Faith Casey-Harriss. **Executive Director, Corporate Sales:** Ben Terry. **Director of Group Hospitality:** Sam Mireles. **Director of Group Sales:** Garrett Erwin. **Executive Director, Marketing & Promotions:** Anthony Oppermann. **Director of Communications & Broadcasting:** Trey Wilson. **Special Events Manager:** Hannah DeFrank. **Social Media Manager:** Caroline Phipps. **Creative Services & Production Manager:** Nick Elder. **Manager of Field Operations:** Kyle Nichols. **Director of Food & Beverage:** Josh Barban.

FIELD STAFF

Manager: Jose Alguacil. **Hitting Coach:** Doug Clark. **Pitching Coach:** Steve Kline. **Fundamentals Coach:** Lipso Nava. **Bullpen Catcher:** Victor Cairo. **Athletic Trainer:** Garrett Havig. **Strength Coach:** Mark Spadavecchia.

GAME INFORMATION

Radio Announcer: Trey Wilson. **No. of Games Broadcast:** 120. **Flagship Station:** Sports Radio 910 The Fan WRNL. **PA Announcer:** Anthony Opperman. **Official Scorer:** Bob Flynn. **Stadium Name:** The Diamond. **Location:** Right off I-64 at the Boulevard exit. **Standard Game Times:** 6:35 pm, Fri., 7:05, Sat. 6:05, Sun. 1:05. **Ticket Price Range:** $8-12. **Visiting Club Hotel:** Fairfield Inn & Suites by Marriott Richmond Short Pump/1-64. **Telephone:** (804) 545-4200.

SOMERSET PATRIOTS

Office Address: One Patriots Park, Bridgewater, NJ 08807.
Telephone: (908) 252-0700. **Fax:** (908) 252-0776.
Website: somersetpatriots.com.
Affiliation: New York Yankees (2021). **Years in League:** 2021-

OWNERSHIP/MANAGEMENT

Operated by: Somerset Baseball Partners, LLC. **Principal Owners:** Steve Kalafer, Josh Kalafer, Jonathan Kalafer. **Chairman Emeritus:** Steve Kalafer. **Chairmen:** Josh Kalafer and Jonathan Kalafer. **President/GM:** Patrick McVerry. **Senior VP, Marketing:** Dave Marek. **VP, Public Relations:** Marc Russinoff. **VP, Operations:** Bryan Iwicki. **VP, Ticket Operations:** Matt Kopas.

Senior Director, Merchandise: Rob Crossman. **Director, Tickets:** Nick Cherrillo. **Director, Broadcasting & Media Relations:** Marc Schwartz. **Director, Marketing:** Hal Hansen.

Director, Operations: Zach Keller. **Corporate Sales Manager:** Ken Smith. **Ticket Office Manager:** Ken Woolley. **Controller:** Suzanne Colon. **Accountant:** Stephanie DePass. **Head Groundskeeper:** Dan Purner. **Broadcast and Media Relations Assistant:** Brandon Pelter. **Homeplate Catering and Hospitality VP/General Manager:** Mike McDermott. **Assistant General Manager of Homeplate Catering and Hospitality:** Jimmy Search.

FIELD STAFF

TBA.

GAME INFORMATION

Radio Announcer: Marc Schwartz. **No. of Games Broadcast:** 120. **Flagship Station:** WCTC 1450-AM. **Video Streams:** SPN.tv. **Ballpark Name:** TD Bank Ballpark. **Standard Game Times:** Mon.- Thurs. 6:35 pm/ 7:05 pm, Fri & Sat., 7:05 pm, Sun., 1:05 pm/ 5:05 pm.

DOUBLE-A SOUTH

STADIUM INFORMATION

Club	Stadium	Opened	Dimensions LF	CF	RF	Capacity	2019 Att.
Biloxi	MGM Park	2015	335	400	335	6,000	146,845
Birmingham	Regions Field	2013	320	400	325	8,500	379,707
Chattanooga	AT&T Field	2000	325	400	330	6,362	228,662
Mississippi	Trustmark Park	2005	335	402	332	7,416	163,841
Montgomery	Riverwalk Stadium	2004	314	380	332	7,000	216,839
Pensacola	Blue Wahoos Stadium	2012	325	400	335	6,000	296,095
Rocket City	Toyota Field	2021	326	400	326	7,500	—
Tennessee	Smokies Stadium	2000	330	400	330	6,000	287,708

BILOXI SHUCKERS

Address: 105 Caillavet Street, Biloxi, MS 39530
Telephone: (228) 233-3465.
E-Mail Address: info@biloxishuckers.com. **Website:** www.biloxishuckers.com.
Affiliation (first year): Milwaukee Brewers (2015). **Years in League:** 2021-.

OWNERSHIP/MANAGEMENT

Operated By: Biloxi Baseball LLC.
President: Ken Young. **General Manager:** Hunter Reed. **Assistant General Manager:** Trevor Matifes. **Group Sales Coordinator:** Layton Markwood. **Corporate Partnerships Coordinator:** Stephanie Chapman. **Sales & Marketing Coordinator:** Dustin Fishman. **Creative Services Manager:** Stephanie Carr. **Human Resources & Accounting Manager:** Lisa Turner.

FIELD STAFF

Manager: Mike Guerrero. **Hitting Coach:** Chuckie Caufield. **Pitching Coach:** Nick Childs. **Athletic Trainer:** Jeff Paxson. **Strength/Conditioning Coach:** Jason Morriss.

GAME INFORMATION

PA Announcer: Kyle Curley. **Official Scorer:** Scotty Berkowitz. **No. of Games Broadcast:** 120. **Stadium Name:** MGM Park. **Location:** I-10 to I-110 South toward beach, take Ocean Springs exit onto US 90 (Beach Blvd), travel east one block, turn left on Caillavet Street, stadium is on the left. **Ticket Price Range:** $7-$24. **Visiting Club Hotel:** DoubleTree by Hilton Biloxi on Beach Blvd.

BIRMINGHAM BARONS

Office Address: 1401 1st Ave South, Birmingham, AL, 35233. **Mailing Address:** PO Box 877, Birmingham, AL, 35201.
Telephone: (205) 988-3200. **Fax:** (205) 988-9698.
E-Mail Address: barons@barons.com. **Website:** www.barons.com.
Affiliation (first year): Chicago White Sox (1986). **Years in League:** 2021-

OWNERSHIP/MANAGEMENT

Principal Owners: Don Logan, Jeff Logan, Stan Logan.
President/General Manager: Jonathan Nelson. **Vice President of Business Development & Entertainment:** John Cook. **CFO:** Randy Prince. **Director of Group Sales Operations:** Tyler Gore. **Director of Group Sales & Sponsorship Sales Coordinator:** Cole Buck. **Group Sales Manager:** John Hudson. **Corporate Sales Manager:** Rich Smyth. **Corporate Sales Manager:** Richard Coats. **Marketing & Promotions Manager:** Samantha Beck. **Marketing & Promotions Coordinator:** Hannah Echols. **Ticket Sales Manager:** Jordan Smith. **Assistant Ticket Sales Manager:** Josh Freund. **Senior Director of Hospitality & Events:** Jennifer McGee. **Special Events Manager:** Amanda Callahan. **Director, Broadcasting:** Curt Bloom. **Merchandise Manager:** David Lindsey. **Receptionist:** Ashlee Bryant. **Director, Stadium Operations:** Mike Craven. **Director, Customer Service:** George Chavous. **Head Groundskeeper:** Zach Van Voorhees. **Director of Food and Beverage:** Gus Stoudemire. **Director of Concessions:** Andy Jackson. **Catering Manager:** Joie Tucker. **Inventory Control Accountant:** Jonathan Judge. **Executive Chef:** Nick Tittle. **Sous Chef:** Vic Arnold.

FIELD STAFF

Manager: Justin Jirschele. **Hitting Coach:** Cameron Seitzer. **Pitching Coach:** Richard Dotson. **Head Athletic Trainer:** Hyeon Kim. **Performance Coach:** George Timke.

GAME INFORMATION
Radio Announcer: Curt Bloom. **No of Games Broadcast:** 120. **Flagship Station:** JOX 94.5-WJOX-FM. **PA Announcers:** Derek Scudder, Andy Parish. **Official Scorers:** Jeff Allison, David Tompkins. **Stadium Name:** Regions Field. **Location:** I-65 (exit 259B) in Birmingham. **Standard Game Times:** 7:05 pm, Sat. 6:30, Sun 4:00. **Ticket Price Range:** $8-15. **Visiting Club Hotel:** Hyatt Regency Birmingham-The Wynfrey Hotel, 1000 Riverchase Galleria, Birmingham, AL 35244. **Telephone:** (205) 705-1234.

CHATTANOOGA LOOKOUTS

Office Address: 201 Power Alley, Chattanooga, TN 37402.
Mailing Address: PO Box 11002, Chattanooga, TN 37401.
Telephone: (423) 267-2208. **Fax:** (423) 267-4258.
E-Mail Address: lookouts@lookouts.com. **Website:** www.lookouts.com.
Affiliation (first year): Cincinnati Reds (2019). **Years in League:** 2021-

OWNERSHIP/MANAGEMENT
Operated By: Chattanooga Lookouts, LLC
Principal Owner: Hardball Capital. **Managing Partner:** Jason Freier. **President:** Rich Mozingo. **Public/Media Relations Manager:** Dan Kopf. **Head Groundskeeper:** N/A. **Marketing & Promotions Manager:** Alex Tainsh. **Director of Broadcasting:** Larry Ward. **Operations Manager:** Michael Matheson. **Vice President:** Andrew Zito. **Ticket Partnership Manager:** Jennifer Crum. **Ticket Partnership Manager:** Nolan Turner. **Ticket Partnership Manager:** Jarrah Vella-Wright. **Ticket Operations Manager:** Graham Hartman. **Concessions Manager:** William Marr.

FIELD STAFF
Manager: Ricky Gutierrez. **Hitting Coach:** Todd Takayoshi. **Pitching Coach:** Rob Wooten. **Coach:** Lenny Harris.

GAME INFORMATION
Radio Announcers: Larry Ward. **No. of Games Broadcast:** 120. **Flagship Station:** 98.1 The LAKE. **PA Announcer:** Ron Hall. **Official Scorers:** Howard Runyon, Andy Paul, David Jenkins. **Stadium Name:** AT&T Field. **Location:** From I-24, take US 27 North to exit 1C (4th Street), first left onto Chestnut Street, left onto Third Street. **Ticket Price Range:** TBD. **Visiting Club Hotel:** Holiday Inn, 2232 Center Street, Chattanooga, TN 37421. **Telephone:** (423) 485-1185.

MISSISSIPPI BRAVES

Office Address: Trustmark Park, 1 Braves Way, Pearl, MS 39208.
Mailing Address: PO Box 97389, Pearl, MS 39288.
Telephone: (601) 932-8788. **Fax:** (601) 936-3567.
E-Mail Address: mississippibraves@braves.com. **Web site:** www.mississippibraves.com.
Affiliation (first year): Atlanta Braves (2005). **Years in League:** 2021-

OWNERSHIP/MANAGEMENT
Operated By: Atlanta National League Baseball Club Inc.
Vice President & General Manager: Pete Laven. **Assistant General Manager/Director of Sales:** Tim Mueller. **Office Manager:** Christy Shaw. **Ticket Manager:** Jeff Olson. **Account Executive:** Darius Green. **Head Groundskeeper:** Will Earnhart. **Director of Group Sales:** David Kerr. **Director of Stadium Operations:** Zach Evans. **Director of Communications, Media & Broadcasting:** Chris Harris. **Promotions & Entertainment Manager:** Ali Nerini. **Merchandise Manager:** TBD. **Food & Beverage Director:** Felicia Thompson.

FIELD STAFF
TBA.

GAME INFORMATION
Radio Announcer: Chris Harris. **No. of Games Broadcast:** 120. **Flagship Station:** TBA
PA Announcer: Greg Flynn. **Official Scorer:** Mark Beason.
Stadium Name: Trustmark Park. **Location:** I-20 to exit 48/Pearl (Pearson Road). **Ticket Price Range:** $6-$25.
Visiting Club Hotel: Hilton Garden Inn Jackson Flowood, 118 Laurel Park Cove, Flowood, MS 39232. **Telephone:** (601) 487-0800.

MONTGOMERY BISCUITS

Address: 200 Coosa St., Montgomery, AL 36104.
Telephone: (334) 323-2255. **Fax:** (334) 323-2225.
E-Mail address: info@biscuitsbaseball.com. **Website:** www.biscuitsbaseball.com.
Affiliation (first year): Tampa Bay Rays (2004). **Years in League:** 2021-

OWNERSHIP/MANAGEMENT
Operated By: Biscuits Baseball LLC. **Managing Owner:** Lou DiBella

President: Todd "Parney" Parnell. **Chief Operating Officer:** Brendon Porter. **General Manager:** Michael Murphy. **Executive Consultant:** Greg Rauch. **Corporate & Military Partnerships:** Jay Jones. **Director of Group Sales:** Chris Walker. **Group Sales Executive:** Daniel Jones. **Community Engagement Coordinator:** Kenny Flores. **Box Office Manager, Season Ticket Coordinator:** Justin Ross. **Marketing & Multimedia:** Jared McCarthy. **Broadcaster, Media Relations:** Chris Adams-Wall. **Retail Manager:** Ashley Williams. **Director, Food & Beverage:** Risa Juliano. **Assistant Director of Food & Beverage:** Michael Parham. **Director, Stadium Operations:** Steve Blackwell. **Stadium Operations Assistant:** Thomas Constant. **Head Groundskeeper:** Alex English. **Business Manager:** Tracy Mims. **Financial Specialist:** Joan Burden. **Executive Administrator:** Jeannie Burke.

FIELD STAFF
Manager: Morgan Ensberg. **Pitching Coach:** Brian Reith. **Coach:** Gary Redus. **Coach:** Jamie Nelson. **Athletic Trainer:** James Ramsdell. **Conditioning Coach:** Carlos Gonzalez

GAME INFORMATION
Radio Announcer: Chris Adams-Wall. **No of Games Broadcast:** 120. **Flagship Station:** WMSP 740-AM. **PA Announcer:** Rick Hendrick. **Official Scorer:** Brian Wilson. **Stadium Name:** Montgomery Riverwalk Stadium. **Location:** I-65 to exit 172, east on Herron Street, left on Coosa Street. **Ticket Price Range:** $8-16. **Visiting Club Hotel:** TBA.

PENSACOLA BLUE WAHOOS

Telephone: (850) 934-8444. **Fax:** (850) 791-6256.
E-Mail Address: info@bluewahoos.com. **Website:** www.bluewahoos.com
Affiliation (first year): Miami Marlins (2021). **Years in League:** 2021-

OWNERSHIP/MANAGEMENT
Operated by: Northwest Florida Professional Baseball LLC. **Principal Owners:** Quint Studer, Rishy Studer. **Minority Owners:** Bubba Watson, Derrick Brooks, Randall Wells, John List, Dana Suskind. **President:** Jonathan Griffith. **Vice President of Operations:** Donna Kirby. **Vice President of Sales:** Alex Sides. **Receptionist:** Dawn Williams. **Facilities Manager:** Mike Crenshaw. **Head Groundskeeper:** Dustin Hannah. **Director, Human Relations:** Candice Miller. **Director of Communications:** Daniel Venn. **Senior Writer:** Bill Vilona. **Communications Coordinator:** Katie Florio **Broadcaster:** Chris Garagiola. **Creative Services Manager:** Adam Waldron. **Creative Services Assistant Manager:** Derek Diamond. **Merchandise and Community Relations Manager:** Anna Striano. **Ticket Operations Manager:** Kyle Williamson. **Box Office Assistant Manager:** Danny Do. **Group Sales Executives:** Greg Liebbe, Jordan Newman. **Corporate Sales Executive:** Steven Unser. **Season Ticket Concierge:** JP Stanzell. **Hospitality & Sales Coordinator:** Jordan Morrow. **CFO:** Brad Oldham. **Finance Manager:** Sally Jewell. **Accounts Payable:** Pam Handlin.

FIELD STAFF
Manager: Kevin Randel. **Pitching Coach:** Tim Norton. **Hitting Coach:** Scott Seabol. **Defensive Coach:** Jose Ceballos. **Trainer:** Jason Roberts. **Hitting Coach:** Amanda Sartoris.

GAME INFORMATION
Radio Announcer: Chris Garagiola. **No. of Games Broadcast:** 120. **Flagship Station:** ESPN Pensacola. **PA Announcer:** Josh Gay, Kevin Peterson, Chris James. **Official Scorer:** Craig Cooper, Don Burns. **Stadium Name:** Blue Wahoos Stadium. **Standard Game Times:** 6:35 pm, Sat. 6:05, Sun. 4:05. **Ticket Price Range:** $5-$19.

ROCKET CITY TRASH PANDAS

Address: 1 Trash Pandas Way. Madison, AL 35758.
Telephone: (256) 325-1403.
E-Mail Address: Info@trashpandasbaseball.com. **Website:** www.trashpandasbaseball.com.
Affiliation (first year): Los Angeles Angels (2017). **Years in League:** 2021.

OWNERSHIP/MANAGEMENT
Owned and Operated by: BallCorps, LLC. **Managing Partner, President and CEO:** Ralph Nelson. **Executive Vice President and General Manager:** Garrett Fahrmann. **Vice President, Marketing, Promotions and Entertainment:** Lindsey Knupp. **Special Advisor to the President and CEO:** Elizabeth Nelson. **Senior Director, Finance:** Jill Webb. **Senior Director, Operations:** Ken Clary. **Director, Food and Beverage Operations:** Ryan Curry. **Groundskeeper:** Charlie Weaver.

FIELD STAFF
Manager: Jay Bell. **Hitting Coach:** Kenny Hook. **Pitching Coach:** Michael Wuertz. **Defensive Coach:** Derek Florko. **Team Trainer:** Matt Morrell. **Strength and Conditioning Coach:** Jon Hill.

GAME INFORMATION
Director, Broadcasting and Baseball Information: Josh Caray. **No. of Games Broadcast:** 120. **Radio:** WUMP-FM 103.9. **Website:** www.umpsports.com. **PA Announcer:** Antonio MacBeath. **Stadium Name:** Toyota Field. **Location:** I-565 to Toyota Field Exit. **Standard Game Times:** 6:35 pm (Monday-Saturday) 2:35 pm (Sundays, April-June, Sept.), 6:35 pm (Sundays, July-Aug). **Ticket Price Range:** $8-22. **Visiting Club Hotel:** AVID Hotel 125 Graphics Dr, Madison, AL 35758 (256) 325-1800.

TENNESSEE SMOKIES

Address: 3540 Line Drive, Kodak, TN 37764.
Telephone: (865) 286-2300. **Fax:** (865) 523-9913.
E-Mail Address: info@smokiesbaseball.com. **Website:** www.smokiesbaseball.com.
Affiliation (first year): Chicago Cubs (2007-). **Years in League:** 2021-

OWNERSHIP/MANAGEMENT

Owners: Randy and Jenny Boyd.
CEO: Doug Kirchhofer. **President/COO:** Chris Allen. **Vice President:** Jeremy Boler. **General Manager:** Tim Volk. **Assistant General Manager, Stadium Operations:** Bryan Webster. **Director of Broadcasting:** Mick Gillispie. **Director of Marketing & Entertainment:** Aris M Theofanopoulos. **Media Relations & Merchandising Manager:** Leslie Soffa. **Administrative Assistant:** Tolena Trout. **Partnership Activation Manager:** Baylor Love. **Business Manager:** Suzanne French. **Admin/Finance Assistant:** Michelle Conway. **Director of Food & Beverage:** Chris Franklin. **Hospitality Manager:** Morgan Messick. **Concessions Coordinator:** Tyler Kennedy. **Concessions Coordinator:** Caleb Miles. **Director of Ticket Sales:** Brett Adams. **Account Executive:** Stephen Haselton. **Account Executive:** Emily White.

FIELD STAFF

Manager: Mark Johnson. **Hitting Coach:** Chad Allen. **Pitching Coach:** Terry Clark. **Coach:** Ben Carhart. **Strength Coach:** Jason Morriss. **Athletic Trainer:** Toby Williams.

GAME INFORMATION

Radio Announcer: Mick Gillispie. **No. of Games Broadcast:** 120. **Flagship Station:** WNML 99.1-FM/990-AM.
PA Announcer: George Yardley. **Official Scorer:** Wade Mitchell. **Stadium Name:** Smokies Stadium. **Location:** I-40 to exit 407, Highway 66 North. **Standard Game Times:** 7:00 pm, Sat. 7:00 pm, Sun. 2:00 pm. **Ticket Price Range:** $10-$14.
Visiting Club Hotel: Hampton Inn & Suites Sevierville, 105 Stadium Drive, Kodak, TN 37764. **Telephone:** (865) 465-0590.

DOUBLE-A CENTRAL

STADIUM INFORMATION

Club	Stadium	Opened	Dimensions			Capacity	2019 Att.
			LF	CF	RF		
Amarillo	Hodgetown	2019	325	405	325	7,300	427,791
Arkansas	Dickey-Stephens Park	2007	332	413	330	5,842	311,021
Corpus Christi	Whataburger Field	2005	325	400	315	5,362	323,688
Frisco	Dr Pepper Ballpark	2003	335	409	335	10,216	455,765
Midland	Security Bank Ballpark	2002	330	410	322	4,669	285,368
NW Arkansas	Arvest Ballpark	2008	325	400	325	6,500	284,829
San Antonio	Wolff Stadium	1994	310	402	340	9,200	337.485
Springfield	John Q. Hammons Field	2003	315	400	330	6,750	328,217
Tulsa	ONEOK Field	2010	330	400	307	7,833	374,501
Wichita	Riverfront Stadium	2021	340	400	325	10,000	—

AMARILLO SOD POODLES

Ballpark Address: 715 S. Buchanan Street, Amarillo, TX 79101
Mailing Address: P.O. Box 9880, Amarillo, TX 79105
Main Phone: (806) 803-7762
Stadium Name: Hodgetown. **Estimated Capacity:** 7,300
Affiliation: Arizona Diamondbacks (2021). **Years in League:** 2021-

OWNERSHIP/MANAGEMENT

Owners: Elmore Sports Group.
President & General Manager: Tony Ensor. **Assistant General Manager, Director of Ticket Sales and Service:** Jeff Turner. **Director of Finance:** Ben Knowles. **Merchandise Director:** Lynn Ensor. **Director of Public Relations and Baseball Operations:** Shane Philipps. **Director of Broadcasting:** Sam Levitt. **Video Production Manager:** Joe Corbisiero. **Director of Marketing:** Tess Bloom. **Director of Partnerships:** Matt Hamilton. **Promotions Manager:** Sierra Todd. **Director of Group Sales:** Dustin True. **Ticket Operations Manager:** Nick Yardley. **Partnerships Account Executive:** Jacob Helmus. **Account Executive:** Matt Sutherland. **Group Account Executive:** Zak McGrath. **Account Executive:** Michael Little. **Head Groundskeeper:** Zach Severns. **Director of Food and Beverage:** Mike Lindal.

FIELD STAFF

Manager: Shawn Roof. **Hitting Coach:** Travis Denker. **Pitching Coach:** Doug Drabek. **Fielding Coach:** Carlos Mesa. **Strength & Conditioning Coach:** Derek Clovis. **Athletic Trainers:** Joe Rosauer.

GAME INFORMATION

Radio Announcer: Sam Levitt. **No. of Games Broadcast:** 120. **Flagship Station:** KIXZ 940 AM (Townsquare Media Amarillo). **PA Announcer:** N/A. **Official Scorer:** N/A. **Stadium Name:** HODGETOWN. **Standard Game Times:** 1:05 p.m., 6:05 p.m., 7:05 p.m. CT. **Ticket Price Range:** $6-18. **Visiting Club Hotel:** Home2 Suites by Hilton. **Telephone:** 806-803-7762.

ARKANSAS TRAVELERS

Office Address: Dickey-Stephens Park, 400 West Broadway, North Little Rock, AR 72114.
Mailing Address: PO Box 3177, Little Rock, AR 72203.
Telephone: (501) 664-1555. **Fax:** (501) 664-1834.
E-Mail address: travs@travs.com. **Website:** www.travs.com.
Affiliation (first year): Seattle Mariners (2017). **Years in League:** 2021-

OWNERSHIP/MANAGEMENT

Ownership: Arkansas Travelers Baseball Club, Inc.
President: Russ Meeks.
Executive Vice President/Chief Executive Officer: Rusty Meeks. **General Manager:** Paul Allen. **Assistant General Manager/Marketing:** Sophie Ozier. **Assistant General Manager/Sales:** Lance Restum. **Broadcaster:** Steven Davis. **Chief Financial Officer:** Brad Eagle. **Assistant Corporate Secretary:** Patti Clark. **Director, In-Game Entertainment:** Tommy Adam. **Park Superintendent:** Greg Johnston. **Assistant Park Superintendent:** Reggie Temple. **Director, Assistant Grounds Manager:** Taylor Woelfel. **Director, Tickets:** John Sjobeck. **Director of Merchandise/Marketing Assistant:** Lindsey Chaplin. **Corporate Event Planners:** Cameron Jefferson, Montag Genser. **Director of Luxury Suites:** Mike Johnson. **Receptionist:** Jean Belken. **Director of Food and Beverage:** Ben Hornbrook. **Assistant Director of Food and Beverage:** Hunter Johnston.

FIELD STAFF

Manager: Collin Cowgill. **Hitting Coach:** Joe Thurston. **Pitching Coach:** Alon Leichman. **Performance Coach:** Ryan McLaughlin.

GAME INFORMATION

Radio Announcer: Steven Davis. **No. of Games Broadcast:** 120. **Flagship Station:** KARN 920 AM.
PA Announcer: Russ McKinney. **Official Scorer:** Tim Cooper. **Stadium Name:** Dickey-Stephens Park. **Location:** I-30 to Broadway exit, proceed west to ballpark, located at Broadway Avenue and the Broadway Bridge. **Standard Game Time:** 7:10 pm. **Ticket Price Range:** $3-13. **Visiting Club Hotel:** Crowne Plaza, 201 S. Shackleford Rd, Little Rock, AR 72211. **Telephone:** (501) 223-3000.

CORPUS CHRISTI HOOKS

Address: 734 East Port Ave, Corpus Christi, TX 78401.
Telephone: (361) 561-4665. **Fax:** (361) 561-4666.
E-Mail Address: info@cchooks.com. **Website:** www.cchooks.com.
Affiliation (first year): Houston Astros (2005). **Years in League:** 2021-

OWNERSHIP/MANAGEMENT

Owned/Operated By: Houston Astros. **General Manager:** Brady Ballard. **Director, Business Development:** Maggie Freeborn. **Account Executive, Corporate Partnerships:** Kaleb Womack. **Manager, Sales:** Kaley O'Brien. **Account Executive:** Gabi Cerise. **Coordinator, Ticket Operations:** Paul Perez. **Director, Media Relations/Broadcasting:** Michael Coffin. **Manager, Ballpark Entertainment:** Amy Johnson. **Manager, Creative Services:** Courtney Merritt. **Manager, Marketing & Communications:** Dan Reiner. **Senior Manager, Operations:** Brett Howsley. **Manager, Home Clubhouse:** Marcus Tramp. **Coordinator, Special Events/Operations:** Jorden Klaevemann. **Stadium Operations:** Mike Shedd. **Stadium Operations:** Mike Hoffman. **Maintenance Assistant:** Jay Conerly. **Head Groundskeeper:** Quince Landry. **Assistant Groundskeeper:** Anthony Hernandez. **Manager, Accounting:** Jessica Fearn. **Accounting Analyst:** Crystal Stanislav. **Online Retail Manager/Store Supervisor:** Eric Suniga. **Receptionist:** Denise Perez. **Receptionist:** Trisha Torres.

FIELD STAFF

Manager: TBA. **Hitting Coach:** TBA. **Pitching Coach:** TBA. **Trainer:** TBA.

GAME INFORMATION

Radio Announcers: Michael Coffin, Gene Kasprzyk. **No. of Games Broadcast:** 120. **Flagship Station:** KKTX-AM 1360. **PA Announcer:** Amy Montez Frye. **Stadium Name:** Whataburger Field. **Location:** 734 E. Port Ave: I-37 to end of interstate, left at Chaparral, left at Hirsh Ave. **Ticket Price Range:** $6-20. **Visiting Club Hotel:** Best Western Corpus Christi; 300 N Shoreline Blvd, Corpus Christi, TX 78401; (361) 883-5111.

FRISCO ROUGHRIDERS

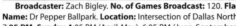

Address: 7300 RoughRiders Trail, Frisco, TX 75034.
Telephone: (972) 731-9200. **Fax:** (972) 731-5355.
E-Mail Address: info@ridersbaseball.com. **Website:** www.ridersbaseball.com.
Affiliation (first year): Texas Rangers (2003). **Years in League:** 2021-

OWNERSHIP/MANAGEMENT

Operated by: Frisco RoughRiders LP
Chairman/CEO/General Partner: Chuck Greenberg. **President & General Manager:** Victor Rojas. **Chief Operating Officer:** Scott Burchett. **Chief Business Development Officer:** Erik Haag. **Vice President, Ticket Sales:** Skip Wallace. **Director of Marketing & Communications:** Lauren Callender. **Director, Partner Services:** David Kosydar. **Customer Service Agents:** Claudia Kipp, Vicki Sohn. **Vice President, Sales:** Ross Lanford. **Director of Ticket Operations:** Jesse Evans. **Ticket Sales:** Monica Man, Tom Baker, Alex Sandborn & Sydney Peterson. **VP, Community Development:** Breon Dennis, Jr. **Broadcaster:** Zach Bigley. **Director, Professional Sports Catering:** Tim Arseneau. Senior Director, **Sports Turf & Grounds Manager:** David Bicknell. **Clubhouse Manager:** Mitch Brasher. **Maintenance Director:** Alfonso Bailon. **Team Dog:** Brooks

FIELD STAFF

Manager: Jared Goedert. **Hitting Coach:** Josue Perez. **Pitching Coach:** Jeff Andrews. **Bench Coach:** Hector Ortiz. **Athletic Trainer:** Alex Rodriguez. **Strength & Conditioning Coach:** Adam Noel.

GAME INFORMATION

Broadcaster: Zach Bigley. **No. of Games Broadcast:** 120. **Flagship Station:** www.RidersBaseball.com. **Stadium Name:** Dr Pepper Ballpark. **Location:** Intersection of Dallas North Tollway & State Highway 121. **Standard Game Times:** 7:05 PM, Sunday 4:05 PM (April-May), 6:05 PM (June-September). **Visiting Club Hotel:** Comfort Suites at Frisco Square, 9700 Dallas Parkway, Frisco, TX 75033. **Visiting Club Hotel Phone:** (972) 668-9700. **Visiting Club Hotel Fax:** (972) 668-9701.

MIDLAND ROCKHOUNDS

Address: Momentum Bank Ballpark, 5514 Champions Drive, Midland, TX 79706.
Telephone: (432) 520-2255. **Fax:** (432) 520-8326.
Website: www.midlandrockhounds.org.
Affiliation (first year): Oakland Athletics (1999). **Years in League:** 2021-

OWNERSHIP/MANAGEMENT

Operated By: Midland Sports, Inc. **Principal Owners:** Miles Prentice, Bob Richmond.
President: Miles Prentice. **Executive Vice President:** Bob Richmond. **General Manager:** Monty Hoppel.
Assistant GM: Jeff VonHolle. **Assistant GM, Marketing/Tickets:** Jamie Richardson. **Assistant GM, Operations:**
Ray Fieldhouse. **Director, Broadcasting/Publications:** Bob Hards. **Director, Business Operations:** Eloisa Galvan.
Director, Ticketing/Office Manager: Ryan Artzer. **Director, Client Services/ Marketing:** Shelly Haenggi. **Director,
Community and Media Relations:** Rachael DiLeonardo. **Manager, Operations:** Dan Knapinski. **Assistant Box Office
Manager/Sales Executive:** Joshua Selaya. **Office Intern:** Chloe Killebrew. **Head Groundskeeper:** TBA. **Director, Game
Entertainment/Video Board:** Peyton Wilkins. **Operations Assistant:** Mitch Riddle. **Assistant Concessions Manager:**
Al Melville. **Home Clubhouse Manager:** TBA. **Visiting Clubhouse Manager:** TBA.

FIELD STAFF

Manager: Bobby Crosby. **Hitting Coach:** Kevin Kouzmanoff. **Pitching Coach:** Steve Connelly. **Coach:** Juan Dilone.
Athletic Trainer: Shane Zdebiak. **Strength/Conditioning Coach:** Matt Mosiman.

GAME INFORMATION

Radio Announcer: Bob Hards. **No. of Games Broadcast:** 120. **Flagship Station:** KCRS 550 AM. **PA Announcer:**
Wes Coles. **Official Scorer:** Steve Marcum. **Stadium Name:** Momentum Bank Ballpark. **Location:** From I-20, exit Loop
250 North to Highway 191 intersection. **Standard Game Times: Sunday:** 2:00 pm, **Monday-Wednesday:** 6:30 pm,
Thursday-Saturday: 7:00 pm. **Ticket Price Range:** $8-16. **Visiting Club Hotel:** Sleep Inn& Suites, 5612 Deauville Blvd,
Midland, TX 79706. **Telephone:** (432) 694-4200.

NORTHWEST ARKANSAS
NATURALS

Address: 3000 Gene George Blvd, Springdale, AR 72762.
Telephone: (479) 927-4900. **Fax:** (479) 756-8088.
E-Mail Address: tickets@nwanaturals.com. **Website:** www.nwanaturals.com.
Affiliation (first year): Kansas City Royals (1995). **Years in League:** 2021-

OWNERSHIP/MANAGEMENT

Principal Owner: Rich Products Corp. **Owner/President:** Robert Rich Jr. **President, Rich Entertainment Group:**
Melinda Rich. **Chief Operating Officer, Rich Entertainment Group:** Joseph Segarra. **President, Rich Baseball
Operations:** Mike Buczkowski. **Vice President/General Manager:** Justin Cole. **Director, Sales:** Mark Zaiger. **Director,
Business:** Morgan Helmer. **Director, Marketing/PR:** Dustin Dethlefs. **Director, Ballpark Operations:** Jeff Windle.
Head Groundskeeper: Brock White. **Ticket Office Manager:** Matt Fanning. **Creative Services Coordinator:** Adam
Annaratone. **Clubhouse Manager:** Danny Helmer.

FIELD STAFF

Manager: Scott Thorman. **Hitting Coach:** Abraham Nunez. **Pitching Coach:** Doug Henry.

GAME INFORMATION

Radio Announcer: TBA. **No. of Games Broadcast:** 120. **Flagship Station:** TBA. **PA Announcer:** TBA. **Official
Scorers:** Kyle Stiles, Walter Woodie & Paul Boyd. **Stadium Name:** Arvest Ballpark. **Location:** I-49 to US 412 West (Sunset
Ave), Left on Gene George Blvd. **Standard Game Times:** 7:05 pm, 6:05 pm (Saturday), 2:05 pm (Sunday). **Visiting Club
Hotel:** Holiday Inn Springdale, 1500 S 48th St, Springdale, AR 72762. **Telephone:** (479) 751-8300.

SAN ANTONIO MISSIONS

Address: 5757 Highway 90 West, San Antonio, TX 78227.
Telephone: (210) 675-7275. **Fax:** (210) 670-0001.
E-Mail Address: sainfo@samissions.com. **Website:** www.samissions.com.
Affiliation (first year): San Diego Padres (2021). **Years in League:** 2021-

OWNERSHIP/MANAGEMENT

Operated by: Elmore Sports Group. **Principal Owner:** David Elmore.
President: Burl Yarbrough. **General Manager:** Dave Gasaway. **Assistant GMs:** Mickey Holt, Jeff Long, Bill Gerlt.
GM, Diamond Concessions: Deanna Mierzwa. **Controller:** Eric Olivarez. **Office Manager:** Delia Rodriguez. **Director,**

Ticketing: JJ Jimenez.

FIELD STAFF
TBA.

GAME INFORMATION
No. of Games Broadcast: 120. **Flagship Station:** 93.3 FM. **PA Announcer:** Roland Ruiz. **Official Scorer:** David Humphrey. **Stadium Name:** Nelson Wolff Stadium. **Location:** From I-10, I-35 or I-37, take US Hwy 90 West to Callaghan Road exit. **Standard Game Times:** 7:05 pm, Sun 2:05pm/6:05pm. **Visiting Club Hotel:** Holiday Inn Northwest/Sea World. **Telephone:** (210) 520-2508.

SPRINGFIELD CARDINALS

Address: 955 East Trafficway, Springfield, MO 65802.
Telephone: (417) 863-0395. **Fax:** (417) 832-3004.
E-Mail Address: springfield@cardinals.com. **Website:** springfieldcardinals.com.
Affiliation (first year): St. Louis Cardinals (2005). **Years in League:** 2021-

OWNERSHIP/MANAGEMENT
Operated By: St. Louis Cardinals.
Vice President/General Manager: Dan Reiter. **VP, Baseball/Business Operations:** Scott Smulczenski. **Director, Market Development:** Brad Beattie. **Director, Ticket Operations:** Angela Deke. **Manager, Public Relations/Broadcaster:** Andrew Buchbinder. **Public Relations/Digital Media Specialist:** Matt Turer. **Marketing/Event Coordinator:** Regina Norris. **Manager, Production:** Kent Shelton. **Graphic Designer:** T.J. Patton. **Manager, Premium Sales/Marketing:** Zack Pemberton. **Manager, Ticket Sales:** Eric Tomb. **Director, Stadium Operations:** Aaron Lowrey. **Director, Field Operations:** Brock Phipps. **Manager, Field & Stadium Operations:** Derek Edwards.

FIELD STAFF
Manager: Jose Leger. **Hitting Coach:** Tyger Pederson. **Pitching Coach:** Darwin Marrero. **Trainer:** Chris Whitman.

GAME INFORMATION
Radio Announcer: Andrew Buchbinder. **No. of Games Broadcast:** 120. **Flagship Station:** TBA. **PA Announcer:** Eric Tomb. **Official Scorers:** Mark Stillwell, Phillip Dowden. **Stadium Name:** Hammons Field. **Location:** Highway 65 to Chestnut Expressway exit, west to National, south on National, west on Trafficway. **Standard Game Time:** 7:10 pm. **Ticket Price Range:** $7-28. **Visiting Club Hotel:** University Plaza Hotel, 333 John Q Hammons Parkway, Springfield, MO 65806. **Telephone:** (417) 864-7333.

TULSA DRILLERS

Address: 201 N. Elgin Ave, Tulsa, OK 74120.
Telephone: (918) 744-5998. **Fax:** (918) 747-3267.
E-Mail Address: mail@tulsadrillers.com. **Website:** www.tulsadrillers.com.
Affiliation (first year): Los Angeles Dodgers (2015). **Years in League:** 2021-

OWNERSHIP/MANAGEMENT
Operated By: Tulsa Baseball Inc.
Co-Chairman: Dale Hubbard. **Co-Chairman:** Jeff Hubbard. **President/GM:** Mike Melega. **Executive VP/Assistant GM:** Jason George. **Vice President, Operations:** Mark Hilliard. **Vice President, Media & Public Relations:** Brian Carroll. **Vice President, Marketing:** Justin Gorski. **Vice President, Food Service:** Robert Founds. **Director, Ticket Sales:** Andrew Aldenderfer. **Director, Operations:** Marshall Schellhardt. **Director, Business Strategy:** Mike Storozyszyn. **Manager, Ticket Sales:** Joanna Hubbard. **Executive, Corporate Partnerships:** Cameron Gordon. **Account Executive:** Justin Perkins. **Manager, Graphic Design:** Allasyn Lieneck. **Manager, Community Relations:** Taylor Levacy. **Manager, Promotions & Merchandise:** Alex Kossakoski. **Accountant:** Jenna Savill. **Ticket Operations Assistant:** Lana Mark. **Ticket Sales Assistants:** Tommy Boldt, Joey Parks, Brianna Root. **Accountant Assistant:** Terry Jenner. **Media & Public Relations Assistant:** Brandon Hawkins. **Video Production Assistants:** Sam Cohen, Will Leggett. **Assistant Accountant:** Katie Martin. **Receptionist & Events Coordinator:** Kelsi Tulk. **Head Groundskeeper:** Gary Shepherd. **Facilities Manager:** Micah Wade. **Mascot Coordinator:** Chris Carozza. **Director, Culinary Operations:** Chris Bullis. **Director, Hospitality:** Amanda Coe. **Team Photographers:** Rich Crimi, Tim Campbell.

FIELD STAFF
Manager: Scott Hennessey. **Hitting Coach:** Brett Pill. **Pitching Coach:** Dave Borkowski. **Coach:** Chris Gutierrez. **Performance Coach:** Noah Huff. **Athletic Trainer:** Yuya Mukaihara. **Video Associate:** Danny-David Linihan.

GAME INFORMATION
Radio Announcer: Dennis Higgins. **No. of Games Broadcast:** 120. **Flagship Station:** KTBZ 1430-AM. **PA Announcer:** Kirk McAnany. **Official Scorers:** Bruce Howard, Duane DaPron, Larry Lewis, Barry Lewis, Greg Stanzak. **Stadium Name:** ONEOK Field. **Location:** I-244 to Cincinnati/Detroit Exit (6A), north on Detroit Ave, right onto John Hope Franklin Blvd, right on Elgin Ave. **Standard Game Times:** 7:00 pm, Sun. 1:00 (April-June), 7:00 (July-Aug). **Visiting Club Hotel:** Marriott Tulsa Hotel Southern Hills, 1902 E 71st Street, Tulsa, OK 74136. **Telephone:** (918) 493-7000.

WICHITA WIND SURGE

Address: 300 S. Sycamore Street, Wichita KS 67213
Telephone: (316) 221-8000. **Fax:** TBD
E-Mail Address: info@windsurge.com. **Website:** www.windsurge.com
Affiliation (first year): Minnesota Twins (2021). **Years in League:** 2021-

OWNERSHIP/MANAGEMENT

General Partner: Jane Schwechheimer. **Partner/CEO:** Jordan Kobritz. **Chief Operating Officer/Chief Financial Officer:** Matt White. **SVP/General Manager:** Jared Forma. **Assistant General Manager:** Bob Moullette. **Director of Finance:** Lori Engleman. **Director of Sales:** Brian Turner. **Director of Broadcasting & Team Travel:** Tim Grubbs. **Stadium Operations Manager:** Andrew Crawford. **Sales Associate:** Adam Mettler. **Sales Associate:** Jessi Holman. **Marketing Associate:** Jenn Schwechheimer. **Sales Associate:** Nick Bernabe. **Director of Food & Beverage:** Randy Robinson.

FIELD STAFF

Manager: Ramon Borrego. **Hitting Coach:** Ryan Smith. **Pitching Coach:** Luis Ramirez. **Pitching Coach:** Virgil Vasquez. **Catching Coach:** Joe Mangiameli. **Athletic Trainer:** Chris McNeely. **Strength Coach:** Travis Koon

GAME INFORMATION

Radio Announcers: Tim Grubbs. **No. of Games Broadcast:** 120. **Flagship Station:** KGSO 1410 AM and 93.9 FM.
PA Announcer: TBD **Official Scorer:** TBD. **Stadium Name:** Riverfront Stadium. **Location: From Airport:** US-400 E/US-54 E from Eisenhower Airport Pkwy, Take the Seneca St exit from US-400 E/US-54 E, Continue on S Sycamore St to your destination. **Standard Game Times:** TBD. **Ticket Price Range:** $8-15. **Visiting Club Hotel:** Hyatt Regency Wichita, 400 W Waterman Street, Wichita, KS 67202. **Telephone:** (316) 293-1234.

HIGH-A CENTRAL

STADIUM INFORMATION

Club	Stadium	Opened	Dimensions LF	CF	RF	Capacity	2019 Att.
Beloit	ABC Supply Stadium	2021	345	400	325	3,850	73,200
Cedar Rapids	Veterans Memorial Stadium	2002	315	400	325	5,300	150,278
Dayton	Fifth Third Field	2000	338	402	338	6,830	545,108
Fort Wayne	Parkview Field	2009	336	400	318	8,100	371,259
Great Lakes	Dow Diamond	2007	332	400	325	5,200	195,904
Lake County	Classic Park	2003	320	400	320	6,157	200,756
Lansing	Cooley Law School Stadium	1996	305	412	305	11,000	311,028
Peoria	Dozer Park	2002	310	400	310	7,000	198,545
Quad Cities	Modern Woodmen Park	1931	343	400	318	7,140	150,905
South Bend	Four Winds Fields	1987	336	405	336	5,000	319,616
West Michigan	Fifth Third Ballpark	1994	317	402	327	9,281	360,295
Wisconsin	Neuroscience Group Field	1995	325	400	325	5,170	218,037

BELOIT SNAPPERS

Office Addresses: 2301 Skyline Drive, Beloit, WI 53511 (Pohlman Field). 217 Shirland Ave., Beloit, WI 53511 (ABC Supply Stadium—late summer 2021)
Mailing Address: P.O. Box 855, Beloit, WI 53512. **Telephone:** (608) 362-2272.
E-Mail: snappy@snappersbaseball.com. **Website:** www.snappersbaseball.com.
Affiliation (first year): Miami Marlins (2021). **Years in League:** 2021-

OWNERSHIP/MANAGEMENT
President: Jeff Jurgella. **VP, Sales/Marketing:** TBD. **VP, Operations:** Riley Gostisha. **Box Office Manager:** Phil Masterson. **Merchandise Manager:** Bob Villarreal. **Media & Public Relations Manager:** Brent Bartels. **Head Groundskeeper:** TBD.

FIELD STAFF
Manager: Mike Jacobs. **Pitching Coach:** Bruce Walton. **Hitting Coach:** Matt Snyder. **Defensive Coach:** Chris Briones. **Trainer:** Melissa Hampton. **Strength Coach:** Gregory Bourn.

GAME INFORMATION
Radio Announcer: TBD. **No. of Games Broadcast:** TBD. **Flagship Station:** TBD. **Stadium Name:** Pohlman Field. ABC Supply Stadium opening late summer 2021. **Standard Game Times:** Mon.-Sat. 6:35pm, Sun 2:05pm. **Ticket Price Range:** $8-22. **Visiting Club Hotel:** Home2 Suites by Hilton. 2750 Cranston Road. Beloit, WI 53511. **Telephone:** (608) 467-5500.

CEDAR RAPIDS KERNELS

Office Address: 950 Rockford Road SW, Cedar Rapids, IA 52404.
Mailing Address: PO Box 2001, Cedar Rapids, IA 52406.
Telephone: (319) 363-3887. **Fax:** (319) 363-5631.
E-Mail: kernels@kernels.com. **Website:** www.kernels.com.
Affiliation (first year): Minnesota Twins (2013). **Years in League:** 1962-

OWNERSHIP/MANAGEMENT
President: Greg Churchill. **Chief Executive Officer:** Doug Nelson. **General Manager:** Scott Wilson. **Senior Director of Ticket/Group Sales:** Andrea Brommelkamp. **Senior Director of Corporate Sales & Marketing:** Jessica Fergesen. **Senior Director of Food and Beverage:** Nathan Varner. **Controller/Human Relations:** Cindy Oldfather. **Community Relations Manager:** Aron Brecht. **Director of Food & Beverage:** Brett Heikkila. **Sales & Marketing Coordinator:** Lakin Goodman. **Group Sales Coordinator:** Morgan Johnson. **Food & Beverage Staffing Manager:** Jazmyne Truesdale. **Stadium Operations Manager:** Patrick Kelly. **Office Manager/Donations Coordinator:** Sherry Downey. **Sports Turf Manager:** Jesse Roeder. **Radio Broadcaster:** Chris Kleinhans-Schulz. **Clubhouse Manager:** Nate Sinnott.

FIELD STAFF
Field Manager: Brian Dinkelman. **Hitting Coach:** Bryce Berg. **Pitching Coach:** Richard Salazar. **Pitching Coach:** Mark Moriarty. **Coach:** Jairo Rodriguez. **Trainer:** Tyler Blair. **Strength Coach:** Colin Feikles.

GAME INFORMATION
Radio Announcer: Chris Kleinhans-Schulz. **No. of Games Broadcast:** 120. Streaming Internet Only. **PA Announcer:** David Schulte. **Official Scorers:** TBD. **Stadium Name:** Perfect Game Field at Veterans Memorial Stadium. **Directions to Stadium:** From I-380 North, take the Wilson Ave exit, turn left on Wilson Ave, after the railroad tracks, turn right

on Rockford Road, proceed .8 miles, stadium is on left; from I-380 South, exit at First Avenue West (exit 19b), Go west to 15th street and turn left. Turn left onto 8th Ave, then right onto Kurt Warner Way (tennis courts). **Standard Game Times:** Mon.-Sat., 6:35 pm, Sun. 2:05 pm. **Ticket Price Range:** $9-13 in advance, $10-14 day of game. **Visiting Club Hotel:** Comfort Inn & Suites, 2025 Werner Ave NE, Cedar Rapids, IA 52402. **Telephone:** (319) 378-8888.

DAYTON DRAGONS

Office Address: Day Air Ballpark, 220 N. Patterson Blvd., Dayton, OH 45402.
Mailing Address: PO Box 2107, Dayton, OH 45401.
Telephone: (937) 228-2287. **Fax:** (937) 228-2284.
E-Mail Address: dragons@daytondragons.com. **Website:** www.daytondragons.com.
Affiliation (first year): Cincinnati Reds (2000). **Years in League:** 2021-

OWNERSHIP/MANAGEMENT

Operated By: Palisades Arcadia Baseball LLC.
President & General Manager: Robert Murphy. **Executive Vice President:** Eric Deutsch. **VP, Assistant General Manager:** Brandy Guinaugh. **VP, Accounting/Finance:** Mark Schlein. **VP, Corporate Partnerships:** Brad Eaton, Trafton Eutsler. **Director, Media Relations & Broadcasting:** Tom Nichols. **Senior Director, Operations:** John Wallace. **Director, Facility Operations:** Jason Fleenor. **Senior Director, Entertainment:** Kaitlin Rohrer. **Director, Entertainment:** Katrina Gibbs. **Director, Ticket Operations:** Stefanie Mitchell. **Director, Ticket Sales:** Andrew Hayes. **Director, Group Sales:** Carl Hertzberg. **Senior Inside Sales Manager:** Mandy Roselli. **Business Development Manager:** Andrew Zellers. **Corporate Partnerships Managers:** Megan Norkunas, Brittany Snyder, Alex Wilker. **Sports Turf Manager:** Taylor Balhoff. **Manager of Retail Operations:** Kyle Dunlap. **Media Relations Assistant:** Jack Kizer. **Motion Graphics Designer & Production Manager:** David Luehring. **Staff Accountant:** Dawn Reed.

FIELD STAFF

Manager: Jose Moreno. **Hitting Coach:** Daryle Ward. **Pitching Coach:** Brian Garman. **Development Coach:** Darren Bragg. **Trainer:** Ryan Ross. **Strength/Conditioning:** Dan Donahue.

GAME INFORMATION

Radio Announcers: Tom Nichols and Jack Kizer. **No. of Games Broadcast:** 120. **Flagship Station:** WONE 980 AM. **Television Announcer:** Tom Nichols and Jack Pohl. No. **of Games Broadcast:** Home-25. **Flagship Station:** WBDT Channel 26. **PA Announcer:** Ben Oburn. **Official Scorers:** Matt Lindsay, Mike Lucas. **Stadium Name:** Day Air Ballpark. **Location:** I-75 South to downtown Dayton, left at First Street; I-75 North, right at First Street exit. **Ticket Price Range:** $9-$19. **Visiting Club Hotel:** Courtyard by Marriott, 100 Prestige Place, Miamisburg, OH 45342. **Telephone:** 937-433-3131. **Fax:** 937-433-0285.

FORT WAYNE TINCAPS

Address: 1301 Ewing St., Fort Wayne, IN 46802.
Telephone: (260) 482-6400. **Fax:** (260) 471-4678.
E-Mail Address: info@tincaps.com. **Website:** www.tincaps.com.
Affiliation (first year): San Diego Padres (1999). **Years in League:** 2021-

OWNERSHIP/MANAGEMENT

Operated By: Hardball Capital. **Owner:** Jason Freier.
President: Mike Nutter. **Vice President, Corporate Partnerships:** David Lorenz. **VP, Finance:** Brian Schackow. VP, **Marketing & Promotions:** Michael Limmer. **Creative Director:** Tony DesPlaines. **Director of Video Production:** Melissa Darby. **Assistant Video Production Manager:** Tim Bajema. **Broadcasting/Media Relations Manager:** John Nolan. **Assistant Director of Marketing & Promotions:** Morgan Olson. **Community & Fan Engagement Manager:** Brenda Feasby. **Group Sales Assistant Director:** Brent Harring. **Senior Ticket Account Manager:** Austin Allen. **Ticket Account Manager:** Dalton McGill. **Ticket & Corporate Account Manager:** Jenn Sylvester. **Ticketing Director:** Paige Watson. **Reading Program Director/Assistant Director of Ticketing:** Kade Zvokel. **Special Events Coordinator:** Holly Raney. **Banquet Event Manager:** Alexis Strabala. **Food/Beverage Director:** Bill Lehn. **Executive Chef/Culinary Director:** Pisarn Amornarthakij. **VIP Services Manager:** Rebekah Carr. **Commissary Manager:** Michael Shidler. **Head Groundskeeper:** Keith Winter. **Facilities Director:** Tim Burkhart. **Accounting Manager/Facilities Manager:** Erik Lose. **Groundskeeping/Ballpark Operations Assistant:** Jake Sperry. **Groundskeeping Assistant:** Jackson Boyce. **Merchandise Manager:** Emma Reese. **Ballpark Cleaning Supervisor:** Dakota Steele. **Human Resources/Office Manager:** Cathy Tinney.

FIELD STAFF

TBD

GAME INFORMATION

Radio Announcers: John Nolan, Mike Maahs, Jack McMullen. **No. of Games Broadcast:** 120. **Flagship Station:** WKJG 1380-AM/100.9-FM. **TV Announcers:** John Nolan, Brett Rump, Tracy Coffman. No. **of TV Games Broadcast:** Home–60. **Flagship Station:** Comcast Network 81. **PA Announcer:** Jared Parcell. **Official Scorers:** Rich Tavierne, Bill Scott, Dan Watson. **Stadium Name:** Parkview Field. **Location:** 1301 Ewing St., Fort Wayne, IN, 46802. **Ticket Price Range:** $6-$14.

GREAT LAKES LOONS

Address: 825 East Main St., Midland, MI 48640.
Telephone: (989) 837-2255. **Fax:** (989) 837-8780.
E-MailAddress: info@loons.com. **Website:** www.loons.com.
Affiliation (first year): Los Angeles Dodgers (2007). **Years in League:** 2021-

OWNERSHIP/MANAGEMENT

Stadium Ownership: Michigan Baseball Foundation. **Founder, CEO:** William Stavropoulos. **Interim President, GM:** Mike Hayes. **Vice President, CFO:** Jana Chotivkova. **Vice President, Business Development:** Chris Mundhenk. **Director, ESPN100.9-FM Sales:** Jay Arons. **Director, Marketing & Promotions:** Cameron Bloch. **Coordinator, ESPN 100.9-FM Radio Traffic:** Andrew Booms. **General Manager, Dow Diamond Events:** Dave Gomola. **Associate, Ticket Sales: Director, Corporate Partnerships:** Tyler Kring. **Executive Chef:** Andrea Noonan. **Director, ESPN 100.9-FM Production & Operations:** Jerry O'Donnell. **Director, Ticket Sales:** Sam PeLong. **Vice President, Business Applications & Ticket Sales:** Eric Ramseyer. **Head Groundskeeper:** Kelly Rensel. **Director, Accounting:** Jamie Start. **Assistant GM, Facility Operations:** Dan Straley. **Manager, Manager, ESPN 100.9-FM Programming & Play-by-Play Broadcaster:** Brad Tunney. **CorporateAccount Executive:** Joe Volk. **Vice President, Baseball Operations & Gameday Experience:** Tiffany Wardynski. **Executive Administrative Assistant:** Jessica Gillespie.

FIELD STAFF

Manager: Austin Chubb. **Hitting Coach:** David Popkins. **Pitching Coach:** Ryan Dennick. **Bench Coach:** Elian Herrera. **Assistant Pitching Coach:** Durin O'Linger

GAME INFORMATION

Play-by-Play Broadcaster: Brad Tunney. **No.ofGames Broadcast:** 120. **Flagship Station:** WLUN, ESPN 100.9-FM (ESPN1009.com). **PA Announcer:** Jerry O'Donnell. **Official Scorers:** Steve Robb, Jason Wirtz. **Stadium Name:** Dow Diamond. **Location:** I-75 to US-10 W, Take the M-20/US-10 Business exit on the left toward downtown Midland, Merge onto US-10 W/MI-20 W (also known as Indian Street), Turn left onto State Street, the entrance to the stadium is at the intersection of Ellsworth and State Streets. **Standard Game Times:** Mon.-Sat., 6:05 pm (April), 7:05 pm (May-Sept), Sun. 2:05 pm. **Ticket Price Range:** $7-13. **Visiting Club Hotel:** Holiday Inn, 810 Cinema Drive, Midland, MI 48642. **Telephone:** (989) 794-8500.

LAKE COUNTY CAPTAINS

Address: 35300 Vine St., Eastlake, OH 44095-3142.
Telephone: (440) 975-8085. **Fax:** (440) 975-8958.
E-Mail Address: jyorko@captainsbaseball.com
Website: www.captainsbaseball.com.
Affiliation (first year): Cleveland Indians (2003). **Years in League:** 2021-

OWNERSHIP/MANAGEMENT

Operated By: Cascia LLC. **Owners:** Peter and Rita Carfagna, Ray and Katie Murphy.
Chairman/Secretary/Treasurer: Peter Carfagna. **Vice Chairman:** Rita Carfagna. **Vice President:** Ray Murphy. **General Manager:** Jen Yorko. **Assistant General Manager:** Kate Roth. **Director, Turf Operations:** Drew Maskey. **Director, Finance:** Nicole Owens. **Manager of Broadcasting, Media Relations & Social Media:** Andrew Luftglass.

FIELD STAFF

Field Manager: Greg DiCenzo. **Hitting Coach:** Grant Fink. **Pitching Coach:** Kevin Erminio. **Bench Coach:** Jordan Smith. **Athletic Trainer:** Matt Beauregard. **Strength & Conditioning Coach:** Trent Kaltenbach.

GAME INFORMATION

Radio Announcer: Andrew Luftglass. **No. of Games Broadcast:** 120. **PA Announcer:** Jasen Sokol. **Official Scorers: Location:** From Ohio State Route 2 East, exit at Ohio 91, go left and the stadium is 1/4 mile north on your right; From Ohio State Route 90 East, exit at Ohio 91, go right and the stadium is approximately five miles north on your right. **Standard Game Times:** Mon.-Sat., 6:30 pm, Sun. 1:30 pm. **Visiting Club Hotel:** Red Roof Inn 4166 State Route 306, Willoughby, Ohio 44094. **Telephone:** (440)-946-9872.

LANSING LUGNUTS

Address: 505 E. Michigan Ave., Lansing, MI 48912.
Telephone: (517) 485-4500. **Fax:** (517) 485-4518.
E-Mail Address: info@lansinglugnuts.com. **Website:** www.lansinglugnuts.com.
Affiliation (first year): Oakland Athletics (2021). **Years in League:** 2021-

OWNERSHIP/MANAGEMENT

Operated By: Take Me Out to the Ballgame LLC. **Principal Owners:** Tom Dickson, Sherrie Myers.

General Manager: Tyler Parsons. **Director of Human Resource and Business Operations:** Angela Sees. **Director of Finance:** Brianna Pfeil. **Group Sales Manager: Kyle England, Corporate Sales Manager:** Dylan Meyer. **Director of Retail:** Matt Hicks. **Director of Events:** Greg Kigar. **Stadium Operations & Events Manager:** Jake Beczkiewicz. **Food/Beverage Director:** Anthony Hilla. **Executive Chef:** Kirk Hansen. **Production Manager:** Terry Alapert. **Corporate Partnerships Manager:** Ashley Loudan. **Head Groundskeeper:** Paul Kuhna.

FIELD STAFF

Manager: Scott Steinmann. **Hitting Coach:** Javier Godard. **Pitching Coach:** Don Schulze. **Assistant Hitting Coach:** Anthony Phillips. **Athletic Trainer:** Brian "Doc" Thorson. **Strength & Conditioning Coach:.** Connor Hughes.

GAME INFORMATION

Radio Announcer: Jesse Goldberg-Strassler. **No. of Games Broadcast:** 120. **Flagship Station:** The Game 730am. **PA Announcer:** Unavailable. **Official Scorer:** Timothy Zeko. **Stadium Name:** Jackson Field. **Location:** I-96 East/West to US 496, exit at Larch Street, north of Larch, stadium on left. **Ticket Price Range:** $8-$36. **Visiting Club Hotel:** Radisson Hotel.

PEORIA CHIEFS

Address: 730 SW Jefferson, Peoria, IL 61605.
Telephone: (309) 680-4000. **Fax:** (309) 680-4080.
E-Mail Address: feedback@chiefsnet.com. **Website:** www.peoriachiefs.com.
Affiliation (first year): St. Louis Cardinals (2013). **Years in League:** 2021-

OWNERSHIP/MANAGEMENT

Operated By: Peoria Chiefs Community Baseball Club LLC.

General Manager: Jason Mott. **Chief Revenue Officer:** Ben Garrod. **Digital Marketing Manager:** Trevor Travis. **Box Office Manager:** Kenton Smith. **Stadium Maintenance Manager:** Brandon Cook. **Head Groundskeeper:** Mike Reno.

FIELD STAFF

Manager: Chris Swauger. **Hitting Coach:** Joe Hawkins. **Pitching Coach:** Rick Harig. **Trainer:** Alex Wolfinger. **Strength Coach:** Jacqueline Gover.

GAME INFORMATION

Radio Announcer: Nathan Baliva. **No. of Games Broadcast:** 120. **Flagship Station:** www.peoriachiefs.com, Tune-In Radio. **4PA Announcer:** Dustin Fitzpatrick, Rodney Knuppel. **Official Scorers:** Nathan Baliva & TBA. **Stadium Name:** Dozer Park. **Location:** From South/East, I-74 to exit 93 (Jefferson St), continue one mile, stadium is one block on left; From North/West, I-74 to Glen Oak Exit, turn right on Glendale, which turns into Kumpf Blvd, turn right on Jefferson, stadium on left. **Standard Game Times:** Mon.-Sat., 6:35 p.m. Sun., 1:35 pm. **Ticket Price Range:** $9-15. **Visiting Club Hotel:** Quality Inn & Suites, 4112 Brandywine Dr, Peoria, IL, 61614. **Telephone:** (309) 685-2556.

QUAD CITIES RIVER BANDITS

Address: 209 S. Gaines St., Davenport, IA 52802.
Telephone: (563) 324-3000. **Fax:** (563) 324-3109.
E-Mail Address: bandit@riverbandits.com. **Website:** www.riverbandits.com.
Affiliation (first year): Houston Astros (2013). **Years in League:** 2021-

OWNERSHIP/MANAGEMENT

Operated by: Main Street Iowa LLC, Dave Heller, Roby Smith and Ken Croken.

General Manager: Joe Kubly. **VP, Sales:** Shawn Brown.**Executive Director, Special Events:** Taylor Satterly. **Assistant GM, Ballpark Operations:** Seth Reeve. **Assistant GM, Baseball Operations:** Paul Kleinhans-Schulz. **Assistant GM, Amusements:** Mike Clark. **Assistant GM, Marketing:** Josh Michalsen. **Director, Finance and HR:** Julie James. **Director, Sales and Ticketing:** Julia McNeil. **Director, Marketing:** Allie Bettenhausen. **Director, Media Relations:** TBD. **Director, Creative Services and Production:** TBD. **Director, Sports Turf:** TBD. **Director: Ballpark Operations:** TBD. **Director, Food/Beverage:** TBD. **Executive Chef:** TBD.

FIELD STAFF

Manager: Chris Widger. **Hitting Coach:** Andy LaRoche. **Pitching Coach:** Steve Luebber. **Coach:** Mike Jirschele.

GAME INFORMATION

Radio Announcer: TBD. **No. of Games Broadcast:** TBD. **Flagship Station:** TBD. **PA Announcer:** TBD. **Official Scorer:** TBD. **Stadium Name:** Modern Woodmen Park. **Location:** From I-74, take Grant Street exit left, west onto River Drive, left on South Gaines Street; from I-80, take Brady Street exit south, right on River Drive, left on S. Gaines Street. **Standard Game Times:** TBD. **Ticket Price Range:** $5-$20. **Visiting Club Hotel:** TBD. **Telephone:** TBD.

SOUTH BEND CUBS

Office Address: 501 W. South St., South Bend, IN 46601.
Mailing Address: PO Box 4218, South Bend, IN 46634.
Telephone: (574) 235-9988. **Fax:** (574) 235-9950.
E-Mail Address: cubs@southbendcubs.com. **Website:** www.southbendcubs.com
Affiliation (first year): Chicago Cubs (2015). **Years in League:** 2021-

OWNERSHIP/MANAGEMENT
Owner: Andrew Berlin. **President:** Joe Hart. **Vice President/General Manager, Business Development:** Nick Brown. **Assistant GM, Tickets:** Andy Beuster. **Director, Ticket Operations and Customer Service:** McKaila Hutchinson. **Senior Account Executive:** Logan Lee. **Account Executives:** Ryan Coleman. **Account Manager, Human Resources:** Melissa Christlieb. **Director, Food/Beverage:** Nick Barkley. **Catering/Business Manager:** Kelly Kalsch. **Executive Chief:** Josh Farmer. **Concession Manager:** Kyle Hoffmann. **Asst. Director, Media/Promotions:** Chris Hagstrom-Jones. **Promotions Assistant & Office Manager:** TBD. **Merchandise Manager:** Mary-Lou Pallo. **Assistant GM, Operations:** Peter Argueta. **Executive Chef:** Josh Farmer. **Stadium Operations Assistant:** Josh Stephens. **Head Groundskeeper:** Jairo Rubio.

FIELD STAFF
Manager: Buddy Bailey. **Hitting Coach:** Dan Puente. **Pitching Coach:** Clayton Mortensen. **Bench Coach:** George Thanopoulos. **Athletic Trainer:** German Suncin. **Strength & Conditioning Coach:** Austin Smith.

GAME INFORMATION
Radio Announcer: Darin Pritchett. **Flagship Station:** 96.1 FM WSBT. **PA Announcer:** Gregg Sims, Jon Thompson. **Official Scorer:** Peter Yarbro. **Stadium Name:** Four Winds Field. **Location:** I-80/90 toll road to exit 77, take US 31/33 south to South Bend to downtown (Main Street), to Western Ave., right on Western, left on Taylor. **Standard Game Times:** Mon.-Sat., 7:05 pm, Sun. 2:05 pm. **Ticket Price Range:** Advance $11-13, Day of Game $12-14. **Visiting Club Hotel:** Aloft South Bend. **Hotel Telephone:** (574) 288-8000.

WEST MICHIGAN WHITECAPS

Office Address: 4500 West River Dr., Comstock Park, MI 49321.
Mailing Address: PO Box 428, Comstock Park, MI 49321.
Telephone: (616) 784-4131. **Fax:** (616) 784-4911.
E-Mail Address: playball@whitecapsbaseball.com.
Website: www.whitecapsbaseball.com.
Affiliation (first year): Detroit Tigers (1997). **Years in League:** 2021-

OWNERSHIP/MANAGEMENT
Chairmen and Founders: Lew Chamberlin / Denny Baxter. **CEO:** Joe Chamberlin. **President:** Steve McCarthy. **Vice President/General Manager:** Jim Jarecki. **Vice President, Sales:** Dan Morrison. **Director of Marketing and Media Relations:** Steve Van Wagoner. **Director of Ticket Sales:** Chad Sayen. **Director of Food and Beverage:** Matt Timon. **Creative and Digital Design Manager:** Elaine Boonenberg. **MultiMedia Specialist:** Jack Powers. **Promotions and Fan Entertainment Manager:** Ben Love. **Social Media and Digital Marketing Coordinator:** Alex Brodsky. **Assistant Director of Ticket Sales:** Drew Willard. **Ticket Sales Manager:** Shaun Pynnonen. **Ticket Operations Coordinator:** Emily Milne. **Account Executive:** Dean Exoo. **Account Executive:** JD Triemstra. **Partnership Coordinator:** Leah Austin. **Community Relations Manager:** Jenny Garone. **Merchandising Manager:** Lori Ashcroft. **Hospitality Manager:** Amanda Stephan. **Food and Beverage Operations Manager:** Danielle O'Connor. **Food and Beverage Assistant:** Ashley Mesman. **Event Chef:** Matt Schumaker. **Operations Manager:** Brett Frieze. **Facility Maintenance Manager:** Kipp Jelinski. **Facility Maintenance Assistant:** Scott Feenstra. **Head Groundskeeper:** Mitch Hooten. **Facility Events Manager:** Mike Klint. **Corporate Events Sales Manager:** Alanna Klomp, CMP,CMM. **Human Resources:** Courtney Lutz. **Controller:** Dave Rozema. **Accounts Receivable Coordinator:** Zack Harvey. **IT Administrator:** Scott Lutz. **IT Assistant:** Kyle Willacker. **Administrative Assistants:** Martha Beals, Lisa Gutting, Chris Parsons. **Radio Play-by-Play:** Dan Hasty

FIELD STAFF
Manager: Brayan Pena. **Hitting Coach:** Bill Springman. **Pitching Coach:** Willie Blair. **Developmental Coach:** Kevin Guthrie. **Athletic Trainer:** Cody Derby, ATC. **Strength Coach:** Ryan Maedel. **Clubhouse Manager:** Sam Reatini. **Clubhouse Assistant:** Jeff Baar.

GAME INFORMATION
Radio Announcers: Dan Hasty/Mike Coleman. **No. of Games Broadcast:** 114. **Flagship Station:** The TICKET 106.1FM Grand Rapids. **PA Announcers:** Mike Newell, Bob Wells. **Official Scorers:** Don Thomas, Joey Sutherlin. **Stadium Name:** LMCU Ballpark. **Location:** US 131 North from Grand Rapids to exit 91 (West River Drive). **Ticket Price Range:** $9-18. **Visiting Club Hotel:** Hampton Inn, 500 Center Dr NW, Grand Rapids, MI 49544 . **Telephone:** (616) 647-1000.

WISCONSIN TIMBER RATTLERS

Office Address: 2400 N. Casaloma Dr., Appleton, WI 54913.
Mailing Address: PO Box 7464, Appleton, WI 54912.
Telephone: (920) 733-4152. **Fax:** (920) 733-8032.
E-Mail Address: info@timberrattlers.com. **Website:** www.timberrattlers.com.
Affiliation (first year): Milwaukee Brewers (2009). **Years in League:** 2021-

OWNERSHIP/MANAGEMENT

Owned by: Third Base Ventures, LLC
Principal Owner: Craig Dickman. **President/General Manager:** Rob Zerjav. **Vice President/Assistant GM:** Aaron Hahn. **Vice President, Tickets:** Ryan Moede. **Vice President, Marketing/ Assistant GM:** Hilary Bauer. **Director, Food/ Beverage:** Ryan Grossman. **Director, Security:** Scott Hoelzel. **Director, Community Relations:** Dayna Baitinger. **Director, Corporate Partnerships:** Ryan Cunniff. **Director of Grounds:** Kyle Slaton. **Director, Merchandise:** Jay Grusznski. **Director, Media Relations:** Chris Mehring. **Senior Manager, Ticket Sales & Service:** Kyle Fargen. **Ticket Account Executives:** Jon Bellis, Noah Feinstein. **Corporate Marketing Manager:** Seth Merrill. **Box Office Manager:** Tyler Van Rossum. **Controller:** Eric Dresang. **Director of Catering & Events:** Kim Chonos. **Wedding Sales & Events Manager:** Alycia Stephan. **Executive Chef:** Charles Behrmann. **Executive Sous Chef:** Chris Prentice. **Assistant, Food/ Beverage Director:** Megan Andrews. **Director, Stadium Operations:** Justin Peterson. **Creative Director:** Ann Lindeman. **Entertainment Coordinator:** Jacob Jirschele. **Graphic Designer:** Nick Guenther. **Accounting/Human Resources Manager:** Brooke Brefczynski. **Production Manager:** Cam Leung. **Clubhouse Manager:** TBA. **Office Manager:** Mary Robinson.

FIELD STAFF

Manager: Matt Erickson. **Hitting Coach:** Nick Stanley. **Pitching Coach:** Hiram Burgos. **Athletic Trainer:** Benny Arroyo.

GAME INFORMATION

Radio Announcer: Chris Mehring. **No. of Games Broadcast:** All. **Flagship Station:** WNAM 1280-AM. **Television Announcer:** Chris Mehring (Radio Simulcast). **Television Affiliates:** TBA. No. **of Games Broadcast:** TBA. **PA Announcer:** Joey D. **Official Scorer:** Jay Gruzsnski. **Stadium Name:** Neuroscience Group Field at Fox Cities Stadium. **Location:** Highway 41 to Highway 15 (00) exit, west to Casaloma Drive, left to stadium. **Standard Game Times:** Mon.-Fri., 6:35 pm (April-May), 7:05 pm (June-Sept.), Sat., 6:35 pm, Sun., 1:05 pm. **Ticket Price Range:** $8-31. **Visiting Club Hotel:** AmericInn by Wyndham 132 N. Mall Drive, Appleton, WI 54913

HIGH-A EAST

STADIUM INFORMATION

Club	Stadium	Opened	Dimensions LF	CF	RF	Capacity	2019 Att.
Aberdeen	Ripken Stadium	2002	310	400	310	6,000	118,357
Asheville	McCormick Field	1992	326	373	297	4,000	187,718
Bowling Green	Bowling Green Ballpark	2009	318	400	326	4,559	190,877
Brooklyn	MCU Park	2001	315	412	325	7,500	174,522
Greensboro	First National Bank Field	2005	322	400	320	7,599	306,136
Greenville	Fluor Field at the West End	2006	310	400	302	5,000	329,733
Hudson Valley	Dutchess Stadium	1994	325	400	325	4,494	148,158
Hickory	L.P. Frans Stadium	1993	330	401	330	5,062	137,546
Jersey Shore	FirstEnergy Park	2001	325	400	325	6,588	308,318
Rome	State Mutual Stadium	2003	335	400	330	5,100	152,874
Wilmington	Frawley Stadium	1993	325	400	325	6,532	231,325
Winston-Salem	BB&T Ballpark	2010	315	399	323	5,500	264,879

ABERDEEN IRONBIRDS

Address: 873 Long Drive, Aberdeen, MD 21001
Telephone: (410) 297-9292. **Fax:** (210) 297-6653
E-Mail Address: Info@ironbirdsbaseball.com. **Website:** ironbirdsbaseball.com
Affiliation (first year): Baltimore Orioles (2002). **Years in league:** 2021-

OWNERSHIP/MANAGEMENT
Operated By: Ripken Professional Baseball LLC. **Principal Owner:** Cal Ripken Jr. **Co-Owner/Executive Vice President:** Bill Ripken. **General Manager:** Jack Graham. **Director, Ticketing:** Justin Gentilcore. **Director, Creative Services:** Kevin Jimenez. **Manager, Event Operations:** Jessie Rushing. **Director, Corporate Partnerships:** Ryan Christy. **Director, Finance & Administration:** Wayne Leonard. **Manager, Community Relations and Retail:** Amelia Adams. **Sports Turf Superintendent:** Todd Bradley. **Manager, Facilities:** Larry Gluch. **Facilities Assistant:** David Dawson. **Sr. Marketing Manager:** Tyler Weigandt. **Coordinator, Memberships Services & Retention:** Micki Quartucci. **Account Executive:** Brian O'Shaughnessy.

FIELD STAFF
Manager: Kyle Moore. **Hitting Coach:** Tom Eller. **Pitching Coach:** Josh Conway. **Fundamentals Coach:** Tim DeJohn. **Development Coach:** Ryan Goll. **Athletic Trainer:** Adam Sparks. **Strength & Conditioning:** TBA.

GAME INFORMATION
Radio Announcer: Michael Lehr. **No. of Games Broadcast:** 76. **Flagship Station:** WAMD 970 AM. **PA Announcer:** Ray Atkinson. **Official Scorer:** Joe Stetka. **Stadium Name:** Leidos Field at Ripken Stadium. **Location:** I-95 to exit 85 (route 22), west on 22, right onto long drive. **Ticket Price Range:** $5-$39. **Visiting Club Hotel:** Comfort Inn-Aberdeen.

ASHEVILLE TOURISTS

Address: McCormick Field, 30 Buchanan Place, Asheville, NC 28801.
Telephone: (828) 258-0428. **E-Mail Address:** info@theashevilletourists.com.
Website: www.theashevilletourists.com.
Affiliation (first year): Houston Astros 1982-1993, 2021-. **Years in League:** 2021-

OWNERSHIP/MANAGEMENT
Operated By: DeWine Seeds-Silver Dollar Baseball, LLC. **President:** Brian DeWine. **General Manager:** Larry Hawkins. **Assistant General Manager:** Sam Fischer. **Senior Sales Executive:** Chris Smith. **Director of Broadcasting/Media Relations:** Doug Maurer. **Stadium Operations Director:** Michael Mueller. **Director of Food & Beverage:** Tyler Holt. **Director of Ticket Operations:** Hannah Martin. **Merchandise Manager:** Kali DeWine. **Publications:** Bill Ballew.

FIELD STAFF
TBA

GAME INFORMATION
Radio Announcer: Doug Maurer. **No. of Games Broadcast:** TBD. **Flagship Station:** Asheville Tourists Online Radio Network. **PA Announcer:** Tim Lolley. **Official Scorer:** Steven Grady, Bob Rose. **Stadium Name:** McCormick Field. **Location:** I-240 to Charlotte Street South exit, south one mile on Charlotte, left on McCormick Place. **Ticket Price Range:** $6.50-13.50.

BOWLING GREEN HOT RODS

Address: Bowling Green Ballpark, 300 8th Avenue, Bowling Green, KY 42101.
Telephone: (270) 901-2121. **Fax:** (270) 901-2165.
E-Mail Address: fun@bghotrods.com. **Website:** www.bghotrods.com.
Affiliation (first year): Tampa Bay Rays (2009). **Years in League:** 2021-

OWNERSHIP/MANAGEMENT

Operated By: BG SKY, LLC.
President/Managing Partner: Jack Blackstock. **General Manager/COO:** Eric C. Leach. **Assistant General Manager:** Kyle Wolz. **Manager, Ticket Sales:** Taylor Dunn. **Manager, Stadium Operations:** David Heimerdinger. **Assistant, Stadium Operations:** Austin Doherty. **Director, Creative Services:** Holli Hawkins. **Head Groundskeeper:** Joseph Golding. **Manager, Broadcasting & Media Relations:** Shawn Murnin. **Assistant, Marketing & Promotions:** Leslie Martin. **Manager, Corporate Marketing:** Ashlee Wilson. **Account Executive & Retail Store Manager:** Jessica Pollitt. **Assistant, Graphic Design:** Christian Aguiar. **Manager, Video Production:** Blake Forshee. **Bookkeeper:** Kim Myers.

FIELD STAFF

Manager: Jeff Smith. **Pitching Coach:** Jim Paduch. **Hitting Coach:** Brady North. **Assistant Coach:** Skeeter Barnes. **Athletic Trainer:** Brian Newman. **Strength & Conditioning Coach:** Jordan Brown.

GAME INFORMATION

Radio Announcer: Shawn Murnin. **No. of Games Broadcast:** 120. **Flagship Station:** WBGN 94.1 FM.
PA Announcer: Unavailable. **Official Scorer:** Unavailable. **Stadium Name:** Bowling Green Ballpark. **Location:** From I-65, take Exit 26 (KY-234/Cemetery Road) into Bowling Green for 3 miles, left onto College Street for .2 miles, right onto 8th Avenue. **Standard Game Times:** Mon.-Sat., 6:35 pm, Sun., 2:05/5:05 pm. **Ticket Price Range:** $10-24. **Visiting Club Hotel:** Tru by Hilton. **Telephone:** (270) 904-2260.

BROOKLYN CYCLONES

Address: 1904 Surf Ave, Brooklyn, NY 11224.
Telephone: (718) 372-5596. **Fax:** (718) 449-6368.
E-Mail Address: info@brooklyncyclones.com. **Website:** www.brooklyncyclones.com.
Affiliation (first year): New York Mets (2001) **Years in League:** 2021-

OWNERSHIP/MANAGEMENT

Owner, Chairman & CEO: Steven A. Cohen. **Owner & President, Amazin Mets Foundation:** Alexandra M. Cohen. **Vice Chariman & Owner:** Andrew B. Cohen. **Chairman Emeritus:** Fred Wilpon.
Vice President: Steve Cohen. **General Manager:** Kevin Mahoney. **Assistant GM:** Gary Perone. **Director, Marketing & Communications:** Billy Harner. **Operations Manager:** Vladimir Lipsman. **Box Office Manager:** Nick Monteleone. **Marketing Manager:** Alyssa Morel. **Director, Community Relations:** Christina Moore. **Account Executives:** Tommy Cardona, Mordechai Twersky, Bryan Wynne, Keith Raad, Miraya Ramirez, Jeremy Allen, Anthony Genna, Ricky Viola. **Senior Accountant:** Tatiana Isdith. **Administrative Assistant, Community Relations:** Sharon Lundy. **Clubhouse Manager & Head Groundskeeper:** Max Colten.

FIELD STAFF

Manager: Ed Blankmeyer. **Hitting Coach:** Nic Jackson. **Pitching Coach:** Royce Ring. **Bench Coach:** Mariano Duncan. **Athletic Trainer:** Vanessa Weisbach. **Performance Coach:** Ryan Orr.

GAME INFORMATION

Radio Announcer: Keith Raad. **No. of Games Broadcast:** 120. **Flagship Station:** Web Streaming Only. **PA Announcer:** Mark Fratto. **Official Scorer:** Howard Kaplan, Patrick McCormack.
Stadium Name: TBD. **Location:** Belt Parkway to Cropsey Ave South, continue on Cropsey until it becomes West 17th St, continue to Surf Ave, stadium on south side of Surf Ave; By subway, west/south to Stillwell Ave./Coney Island station. **Ticket Price Range:** $10-22. **Visiting Club Hotel:** Unavailable.

GREENSBORO GRASSHOPPERS

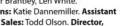

Address: 408 Bellemeade St, Greensboro, NC 27401.
Telephone: (336) 268-2255. **Fax:** (336) 273-7350.
E-Mail Address: info@gsohoppers.com. **Website:** www.gsohoppers.com.
Affiliation (first year): Pittsburgh Pirates (2019) **Years in League:** 2021-

OWNERSHIP/MANAGEMENT

Operated By: Greensboro Baseball LLC. **Principal Owners:** Wes Elingburg, Cooper Brantley, Len White. **President/General Manager:** Donald Moore. **Vice President, Baseball Operations:** Katie Dannemiller. **Assistant General Manager:** Tim Vangel. **Chief Financial Officer:** Brad Falkiewicz. **Director of Sales:** Todd Olson. **Director,**

Ticket Sales/Services: Erich Dietz. **Director, Creative Services:** Amanda Williams. **Manager, Promotions/Community Relations:** Stephen Johnson. **Manager, Video Production:** Jak Kerley. **Concessions Manager:** Kevin Miller, **Stadium Operations:** Cody Grube, **Groundskeeper:** Anthony Alejo.

FIELD STAFF
Manager: Kieran Mattison. **Hitting Coach:** Ruben Gotay. **Pitching Coach:** Matt Ford. **Developmental Coach:** Blake Butler. **Athletic Trainer:** Victor Silva. **Strength & Conditioning Coach:** TBD.

GAME INFORMATION
Announcer: Stuart Barefoot. **Official Scorer:** TBD. **Stadium Name:** First National Bank Field. **Location:** From I-85, take Highway 220 South (exit 36) to Coliseum Blvd, continue on Edgeworth Street, ballpark at corner of Edgeworth and Bellemeade Streets. **Standard Game Times:** TBD **Ticket Price Range:** $7-11. **Visiting Club Hotel:** LaQuinta Inn @ **Greensboro Airport**—7905 Triad Center Drive, Greensboro, NC 27409. **Telephone:** (336) 840.1550.

GREENVILLE DRIVE

Mailing Address: 935 South Main St, Suite 202, Greenville, SC 29601.
Stadium Address: 945 South Main St. Greenville, SC 29601.
Telephone: (864) 240-4500. **E-Mail Address:** info@greenvilledrive.com.
Website: www.greenvilledrive.com. **Affiliation (first year):** Boston Red Sox (2005).
Years in League: 2021-

OWNERSHIP/MANAGEMENT
Owner/President: Craig Brown. **General Manager:** Eric Jarinko. **VP, Marketing:** Jeff Brown.
VP, Finance/Administration: Jordan Smith. **VP, Ticketing:** Phil Bargardi. **VP, Grounds/Operations:** Greg Burgess.
Director, Game Entertainment: Alex Guest. **Director, West End Events at Fluor Field:** Beth Rusch. **Director, Media/Creative Services:** Davis Simpson. **Director, Merchandise:** Jenny Burgdorfer. **Director, Sponsorships/Community Engagement:** Katie Batista. **Director, Video Production:** Lance Fowler. **Director, Facility Operations:** Timmy Hinds. **Director, Food & Beverage:** TBD. **Director, Ticket Operations:** TBD. **Senior Ticket Account Executive:** Houghton Flanagan. **Executive Chef:** Wilbert Sauceda. **Business/Team Operations Manager:** Amanda Medlin. **Office Manager:** Allison Roedell. **Premium Hospitality Services Manager:** Elise Parish. **Assistant Groundskeeper:** Zack Pagans. **Clubhouse Manager:** Brady Andrews. **West End Events at Fluor Field Manager:** Kristin Kipper.

FIELD STAFF
Manager: Iggy Suarez. **Hitting Coach:** Nate Spears. **Pitching Coach:** Bob Kipper. **Bench Coach:** John Shelby III. **Athletic Trainer:** Nick Kuchwara. **Strength & Conditioning Coach:** Joe Hudson.

GAME INFORMATION
Radio Announcer: Dan Scott & Tom Van Hoy. **Flagship Station:** GreenvilleDrive.com. **PA Announcer:** Chuck Hussion, William Qualkinbush. **Official Scorer:** Jordan Caskey. Chandler Simpson. **Stadium Name:** Fluor Field at the West End. **Location:** I-385 into Downtown Greenville; Left onto Church Street; Right onto University Ridge; Right onto Augusta Street; **Left onto Field Street Standard Game Times:** Mon.-Sat., 7:05 p.m., Sun. 3:05 p.m. **Ticket Price Range:** Advance $8-$12, Day of Game $9-13. **Visiting Club Hotel:** Wingate by Wyndham. **Hotel Telephone:** (864) 281-1281.

HUDSON VALLEY RENEGADES

Office Address: Dutchess Stadium, 1500 Route 9D, Wappingers Falls, NY 12590.
Mailing Address: PO Box 661, Fishkill, NY 12524.
Telephone: (845) 838-0094. **Fax:** (845) 838-0014.
E-Mail Address: info@hvrenegades.com. **Website:** www.hvrenegades.com.
Affiliation (first year): New York Yankees (2021). **Years in League:** 2021-

OWNERSHIP/MANAGEMENT
Operated by: Keystone Professional Baseball Club Inc. **Principal Owner:** Marvin Goldklang.
President/General Manager: Steve Gliner. **Vice President/Assistant General Manager:** Tyson Jeffers. **Vice President:** Rick Zolzer. **Vice President of Community Partnerships:** Kristen Huss. **Director, Baseball Operations:** Joe Ausanio. **Director of Stadium Operations/Head Groundskeeper:** Tom Hubmaster.

FIELD STAFF
TBD

GAME INFORMATION
Radio Announcer: Rob Adams **No. of Games Broadcast:** All home games broadcast at hvrenegades.com. **PA Announcer:** Rick Zolzer. **Official Scorer:** Mike Ferraro. **Stadium Name:** Dutchess Stadium. **Location:** I-84 to exit 41 (Route 9D North), north one mile to stadium. **Standard Game Times:** Mon.-Fri., 7:05 pm, Sat, 6:05 pm, Sun., 4:35 pm. **Visiting Club Hotel:** Courtyard By Marriott Fishkill, 17 Westage Drive, Fishkill, NY, 12524. **Telephone:** (845) 897-2400.

HICKORY CRAWDADS

Office Address: 2500 Clement Blvd. NW, Hickory, NC 28601.
Mailing Address: 2500 Clement Blvd. NW, Hickory, NC 28601.
Telephone: (828) 322-3000.
E-Mail Address: crawdad@hickorycrawdads.com.
Website: www.hickorycrawdads.com.
Affiliation (first year): Texas Rangers (2009). **Years in League:** 2021-

OWNERSHIP/MANAGEMENT

Operated by: Hickory Baseball Inc. **Principal Owners:** Texas Rangers.
President: Neil Leibman. **General Manager:** Douglas Locascio. **Business Manager:** Donna White. **Director of Marketing, Communications & Merchandise:** Ashley Salinas. **Director of Sales:** Robby Willis. **Director of Operations & Special Events:** Daniel Barkley. **Director of Ticket Operations:** Kristen Buynar. **Head Groundskeeper:** Caleb Bryan. **Director of Promotions and Community Relations:** Amanda Height. **Group Sales Executives:** Samantha Baldini, Joey Norris, Emily Weidman. **General Manager of Food and Beverage:** Ryan Spangler.

FIELD STAFF

Manager: Joshua Johnson. **Hitting Coach:** Chad Comer. **Pitching Coach:** Steve Mintz. **Bench Coach:** Hiram Bocachica. **Athletic Trainer:** Yuichi Takizawa. **Strength and Conditioning Coach:** Jon Nazarko.

GAME INFORMATION

PA Announcers: Jason Savage, Rob Eastwood. **Official Scorers:** Mark Parker. **Stadium Name:** LP Frans Stadium. **Location:** I-40 to exit 123 (Lenoir North), 321 North to Clement Blvd, left for 1/2 mile. **Standard Game Times:** Mon.-Sat., 7 pm, Sun., 5 pm. **Visiting Club Hotel:** Crowne Plaza, 1385 Lenior-Rhyne Boulevard SE, Hickory, NC 28602. **Telephone:** (828) 323-1000.

JERSEY SHORE BLUECLAWS

Address: 2 Stadium Way, Lakewood, NJ 08701.
Telephone: (732) 901-7000. **Fax:** (732) 901-3967.
E-Mail Address: info@blueclaws.com. **Website:** www.blueclaws.com
Affiliation (first year): Philadelphia Phillies (2001). **Years in League:** 2021-

OWNERSHIP/MANAGEMENT

Managing Partner/Shore Town Baseball: Art Matin. **President/General Manager:** Joe Ricciutti. **Assistant General Manager:** Kevin Fenstermacher. **Sr. VP, Ticket Sales:** Bob McLane. **Sr. VP, Corporate Partnerships:** Clint Wulfekotte, **VP, Ticket Sales:** Jim McNamara. **VP, Promotions & Entertainment:** Jamie Bertram, **VP, Retail Operations:** Ben Cecil. **VP, Finance:** Don Rodgers. **Sr. Director, Sponsorship:** Rob Vota. **Director of Communications:** Greg Giombarrese. **Director, Ticket Operations:** Garrett Herr. **Director, Events & Operations:** Kayla Reilly, **Director, Partnership Services:** Zack Nicol. **Director, Season Tickets:** Rob McGillick. **Senior Sales Executive:** Craig Ebinger. **Ticket Memberships Manager:** Joel Podos, Jamie Wagner. **Group Sales Executive:** Adam Polsky. **Digital Marketing & Design Manager:** Jess Szewczyk, **Ticket & Fan Services Coordinator:** Brendan Earls, **Food & Beverage Manager:** Kathryn Raso. **Partnership Services Manager:** Ben Wilson. **Heads Groundskeeper:** Mike Morvay.

FIELD STAFF

Manager: TBA. **Hitting Coach:** TBA. **Pitching Coach:** TBA. **Coach:** TBA. **Trainer:** TBA. **Strength & Conditioning Coach:** TBA.

GAME INFORMATION

Radio Announcers: Greg Giombarrese. **No. of Games Broadcast:** 70. **Flagship Station:** BlueClaws.com. **PA Announcers:** Jeff Fromm. **Official Scorers:** Joe Bellina. **Stadium Name:** FirstEnergy Park. **Location:** Route 70 to New Hampshire Avenue, North on New Hampshire for 2.5 miles to ballpark. **Standard Game Times:** 7:05 pm, 6:35 pm (April-May); Sun 1:05. **Ticket Price Range:** $9-18. **Visiting Team Hotel:** Days Hotel, Toms River...290 NJ-37, Toms River, NJ 08753...732-244-4000.

ROME BRAVES

Office Address: State Mutual Stadium, 755 Braves Blvd, Rome, GA 30161.
Mailing Address: PO Box 1915, Rome, GA 30162-1915.
Telephone: (706) 378-5100. **Fax:** (706) 368-6525.
E-Mail Address: romebraves@braves.com. **Website:** www.romebraves.com.
Affiliation (first year): Atlanta Braves (2003). **Years in League:** 2021-

OWNERSHIP MANAGEMENT

Operated By: Atlanta National League Baseball Club LLC. **VP and General Manager:** David Cross. **Director, Business Operations:** Bob Askin. **Director, Stadium Operations:** Morgan McPherson. **Director, Sales:** Scott Casten.

Ticket Manager: Jalaam Robinson. **Manager, Suites, Catering & Special Events:** Anna Winstead. **Graphic Design Manager:** Drew Gibby. **Marketing Manager:** Stephen Brunson. **Account Representative:** Katie Aspin. **Account Representative:** Hashim Cole. **Field Turf Manager:** Joseph Brooks. **Retail Manager:** Starla Roden. **Food and Beverage Director:** Jonathan Jackson. **Culinary Director:** Owen Reppert.

FIELD STAFF
Manager: Kanekoa Texeira. **Hitting Coach:** Danny Santiesteban. **Pitching Coach:** Bo Henning. **Coach:** Angel Flores. **Athletic Trainer:** TBD. **Strength Coach:** TBD.

GAME INFORMATION
Radio Announcer: Kevin Karel. **No. of Games Broadcast:** TBD. **Flagship Station:** TBD, RomeBraves.com (home games). **PA Announcer:** Anthony McIntosh, Sr. **Official Scorers:** Jim O'Hara, Lyndon Huckaby. **Stadium Name:** State Mutual Stadium. **Location:** I-75 North to exit 190 (Rome/Canton), left off exit and follow Highway 411/Highway 20 to Rome, right at intersection on Highway 411 and Highway 1 (Veterans Memorial Highway), stadium is at intersection of Veterans Memorial Highway and Riverside Parkway. **Ticket Price Range:** $6-15. (purchased in advance). **Visiting Club Hotel:** Days Inn, 840 Turner McCall Blvd, Rome, GA 30161. **Telephone:** (706) 295-0400.

WILMINGTON BLUE ROCKS

Address: 801 Shipyard Drive, Wilmington, DE 19801.
Telephone: (302) 888-2015. **Fax:** (302) 888-2032.
E-Mail Address: info@bluerocks.com. **Website:** www.bluerocks.com.
Affiliation (first year): Washington Nationals (2021). **Years in League:** 2021-

OWNERSHIP/MANAGEMENT
Operated by: Wilmington Blue Rocks LP. **Honorary President:** Matt Minker. **Club President:** Clark Minker. **Owners:** Main Street Baseball. **Managing Partner/League Director & CEO, Main Street Baseball:** Dave Heller. **General Manager:** VInce Bulik. **Director of Web and Creative Services:** Mike Diodati. **VP, Corporate Sales:** Robert Ford. **Director of Ticket Operations:** Nathanial Giblin. **Director, Managing/Fulfillment:** Liz Welch.

FIELD STAFF
Manager: Tommy Shields. **Hitting Coach:** Luis Ordaz. **Pitching Coach:** Justin Lord. **Athletic Trainer:** Don Neidig. **Strength Coach:** Shane Hill.

GAME INFORMATION
Radio Announcer: TBD. **No. of Games Broadcast:** 132. **Flagship Station:** TBD. **PA Announcer:** TBD. **Official Scorer:** Dick Shute. **Stadium Name:** Judy Johnson Field at Daniel S. Frawley Stadium. **Location:** I-95 North to Maryland Ave (exit 6), right on Maryland Ave, and through traffic light on Martin Luther King Blvd, right at traffic light on Justison St, follow to Shipyard Dr; I-95 South to Maryland Ave (exit 6), left at fourth light on Martin Luther King Blvd, right at fourth light on Justison St, follow to Shipyard Dr. **Standard Game Times:** 6:35 pm, (Mon-Thur) 7:05 (Fri) 6:05 (Sat) Sun. 1:35 p.m. **Ticket Price Range:** $6-$15. **Visiting Club Hotel:** TBD.

WINSTON-SALEM DASH

Office Address: 926 Brookstown Ave, Winston-Salem, NC 27101.
Stadium Address: 951 Ballpark Way, Winston-Salem, NC 27101.
Telephone: (336) 714-2287. **Fax:** (336) 714-2288.
E-Mail Address: info@wsdash.com. **Website:** www.wsdash.com.
Affiliation (first year): Chicago White Sox (1997). **Years in League:** 2021-

OWNERSHIP/MANAGEMENT
Operated by: W-S Dash. **Principal Owner:** Billy Prim.
President: CJ Johnson. **VP, Chief Financial Officer:** Kurt Gehsmann. **VP:** Corey Bugno. **VP, Baseball Operations:** Ryan Manuel. **Director of Ballpark Experience and Branding:** Jessica Aveyard. **Director of Corporate Partnership Services:** Ayla Acosta. **Director of Facility Management:** Jeff Kelly. **Head Groundskeeper:** Corey Church. **Accounting Manager:** Amanda Elbert. **Coordinator of Fun:** Rosanna Stewart. **Director Food and Beverage:** Kit Edwards. **Catering Manager:** Beverly Becker. **Concessions Manager:** Zachary Mounce.

FIELD STAFF
Manager: Ryan Newman. **Hitting Coach:** Mike Daniel. **Pitching Coach:** Danny Farquhar. **Trainer:** Carson Wooten. **Strength Coach:** Tim Rodmaker.

GAME INFORMATION
Radio Announcer: TBA. **No. of Games Broadcast:** TBA. **Flagship Station:** The Triad Sports Hub - 101.5 FM & 600 AM (Thursdays) or wsdash.com (all games). **PA Announcer:** Jeffrey Griffin. **Official Scorer:** TBA. **Stadium Name:** Truist Stadium. **Location:** Salem Parkway to Peters Creek Parkway exit. **Standard Game Times:** M-F 7 p.m., Sat. 6 p.m., Sun. 2 p.m. **Visiting Club Hotel:** Best Western Plus- University Inn.

HIGH-A WEST

STADIUM INFORMATION

| Club | Stadium | Opened | Dimensions | | | Capacity | 2019 Att. |
			LF	CF	RF		
Eugene	PK Park	2010	335	400	325	4,000	131,467
Everett	Everett Memorial Stadium	1984	324	380	330	3,682	116,630
Hillsboro	Hillsboro Ballpark	2013	325	400	325	4,500	133,605
Spokane	Avista Stadium	1958	335	398	335	7,162	200,273
Tri-City	Dust Devils Stadium	1995	335	400	335	3,700	87,021
Vancouver	Nat Bailey Stadium	1951	335	395	335	6,500	235,980

EUGENE EMERALDS

Office Address: 2760 Martin Luther King Jr. Blvd, Eugene, OR 97401.
Mailing Address: PO Box 10911, Eugene, OR 97440.
Telephone: (541) 342-5367. **Fax:** (541) 342-6089.
E-Mail Address: info@emeraldsbaseball.com. **Website:** www.emeraldsbaseball.com.
Affiliation (first year): San Francisco Giants (2021). **Years in League:** 2021-

OWNERSHIP/MANAGEMENT
Operated By: Elmore Sports Group Ltd. **Principal Owner:** David Elmore.
General Manager: Allan Benavides. **Assistant GM:** Matt Dompe. **Director, Food/Beverage:** Turner Elmore.
Director, Tickets: Kennedy Schull. **Event Manager:** Chris Bowers. **Graphic Designer:** Danny Cowley. **Director, Community Affairs:** Anne Culhane. **Sponsorship Sales:** Matt Dompe. **Home Radio:** Matt Dompe. **Away Radio:** Alex Stimson.

FIELD STAFF
Manager: Dennis Pelfrey. **Hitting Coach:** Jake Fox. **Pitching Coach:** Alain Quijano. **Fundamentals Coach:** Lipso Nava. **Athletic Trainer:** Tim Vigue. **Strength Coach:** Matt Jordan.

GAME INFORMATION
Radio Announcer: Matt Dompe. **No. of Games Broadcast:** 120. **Flagship Station:** 95.3-FM The Score. **PA Announcer:** Ted Welker. **Official Scorer:** George McPherson. **Stadium Name:** PK Park. **Standard Game Time:** Mon.-Sat., TBD, Sun., TBD. **Ticket Price Range:** TBD. **Visiting Club Hotel:** Holiday Inn, Eugene Springfield.

EVERETT AQUASOX

Mailing Address: 3802 Broadway, Everett, WA 98201.
Telephone: (425) 258-3673. **Fax:** (425) 258-3675.
E-Mail Address: info@aquasox.com. **Website:** www.aquasox.com.
Affiliation (first year): Seattle Mariners (1995). **Years in League:** 2021-

OWNERSHIP/MANAGEMENT
Operated by: 7th Inning Stretch, LLC.
Directors: Chad Volpe, Pat Filippone. **General Manager:** Danny Tetzlaff. **Assistant GM:** Rick Maddox. **Director, Corporate Partnerships/Broadcasting:** Pat Dillon. **Director, Tickets:** Bryan Martin. **Corporate Partnership Manager:** Kieran McMahon. **Director of Community Relations & Merchandise:** TBD. **Marketing & Social Media Manager:** Sarah Newgarde. **Account Executives:** Scott Brownlee, Conner Grant.

FIELD STAFF
Manager: Louis Boyd. **Hitting Coach:** Shawn O'Malley. **Pitching Coach:** Sean McGrath. **Coach:** Jose Umbria.

GAME INFORMATION
Radio Announcer: Pat Dillon. **No. of Games Broadcast:** TBD. **Flagship Station:** KRKO 1380-AM, 95.3-FM. **PA Announcer:** Tom Lafferty. **Official Scorer:** Patrick Lafferty. **Stadium Name:** Everett Memorial Stadium. **Location:** I-5, exit 192. **Standard Game Times:** Mon.-Sat., 7:05 pm, Sun., 4:05 pm. **Ticket Price Range:** $8-18. **Visiting Club Hotel:** Best Western Cascadia Inn, 2800 Pacific Ave, Everett, WA 98201. **Telephone:** (425) 258-4141.

HILLSBORO HOPS

Address: 4460 NE Century Blvd., Hillsboro, OR, 97124. **Telephone:** (503) 640-0887.
E-Mail Address: info@hillsborohops.com. **Website:** www.hillsborohops.com.
Affiliation (first year): Arizona Diamondbacks (2001). **Years in League:** 2021-

OWNERSHIP/MANAGEMENT
Operated by: Short Season LLC. **Managing Partners:** Mike McMurray, Josh Weinman, Myron Levin.
Chairman and CEO: Mike McMurray. **President and General Manager:** K.L. Wombacher. **Chief Financial Officer:**
Laura McMurray. **Vice President Corporate Partnerships:** Matt Kolasinski, **Vice President, Tickets:** Jason Gavigan.
Manager, Merchandise: Hannah August. **Manager, Marketing and Communications:** Casey Sawyer. **Director,**
Broadcasting: Rich Burk.

FIELD STAFF
Manager: Vince Harrison. **Hitting Coach:** K.C Judge. **Pitching Coach:** Shane Loux. **Coach:** Juan Francia. **Coach:** Ben
Petrick.

GAME INFORMATION
PA Announcer: Jason Swygard. **Official Scorer:** Blair Cash. **Stadium Name:** Ron Tonkin Field. **Location:** 4460 NE
Century Blvd., Hillsboro, OR. 97124. **Standard Game Times:** Mon.-Sat., 7:05 pm, Sun., 4:05 pm. **Ticket Price Range:**
$7-$20. **Visiting Club Hotel:** Aloft by Marriott, Hillsboro, OR. **Telephone:** (503) 277-1900.

SPOKANE INDIANS

Office Address: Avista Stadium, 602 N Havana, Spokane, WA 99202.
Mailing Address: PO Box 4758, Spokane, WA 99220.
Telephone: (509) 535-2922. **Fax:** (509) 534-5368.
E-Mail Address: mail@spokaneindians.com. **Website:** www.spokaneindians.com.
Affiliation (first year): Colorado Rockies (2021). **Years in League:** 2021-

OWNERSHIP/MANAGEMENT
Operated By: Longball Inc. **Principal Owner:** Bobby Brett. **Co-Owner/Senior Advisor:** Andrew Billig.
President: Chris Duff. **Senior Vice President:** Otto Klein. **VP, Concessions & Hospitality:** Josh Roys. **VP, Business
Operations:** Lesley DeHart. **General Manager:** Kyle Day. **Assistant General Manager:** Sean Bozigian. **Assistant GM,
Tickets:** Nick Gaebe. Director, **Concessions & Hospitality:** Darby Moore. **Business Operations Manager:** MacKenzie
White. **Partner Services Coordinator:** Gina Giesseman. **Director of Public Relations:** John Collett. **Communications
Consultant:** Bud Bareither. **Account Executive:** James Lange. **Director of Group Sales:** Sean Dorsey. **Group Sales
Coordinator:** Jamie Isaacson. **Personal Account Manager:** Ryan Songey. **Chief Financial Officer:** Greg Sloan.
Controller: Tim Gittel. **Director of Facilities & Grounds:** Tony Lee. **Assistant Director, Stadium Operations:** Larry
Blumer.

FIELD STAFF
Supervisor of Development: Pedro Lopez. **Manager:** Scott Little. **Pitching Coach:** Ryan Kibler. **Hitting Coach:** Zach
Osborne. **Trainer:** Kelsey Branstetter.

GAME INFORMATION
Radio Announcer: Mike Boyle. **Flagship Station:** 1510 AM/103.5 FM. **PA Announcer:** Unavailable. **Official Scorer:**
Todd Gilkey. **Stadium Name:** Avista Stadium. **Location:** From west, I-90 to exit 283B (Thor/Freya), east on Third Avenue,
left onto Havana; From east, I-90 to Broadway exit, right onto Broadway, left onto Havana. **Standard Game Time:** Mon.-
Sat., 6:30 pm, Sun., 5:09 pm. **Ticket Price Range:** $5-24. **Visiting Club Hotel:** Mirabeau Park Hotel & Convention Center,
1100 N. Sullivan Rd, Spokane, WA 99037. **Telephone:** (509) 924-9000.

TRI-CITY DUST DEVILS

Address: 6200 Burden Blvd, Pasco, WA 99301.
Telephone: (509) 544-8789. **Fax:** (509) 547-9570.
E-Mail Address: info@dustdevilsbaseball.com.
Website: dustdevilsbaseball.com.
Affiliation (first year): Los Angeles Angels (2021). **Years in League:** 2021-

OWNERSHIP/MANAGEMENT
Operated by: Northwest Baseball Ventures. **Principal Owners:** George Brett, Yoshi Okamoto, Brent Miles.
President: Brent Miles. **Vice President/General Manager:** Derrel Ebert. **Assistant General Manager, Business
Operations:** Trevor Shively. **Assistant General Manager, Sponsorships:** Ann Shively. **Assistant General Manager,
Tickets:** Riley Shintaffer. **Sponsorship Operations Manager:** Brennan McIntire. **Head Groundskeeper:** Michael Angel.

FIELD STAFF
Manager: Andy Schatzley. **Hitting Coach:** William Bradley. **Pitching Coach:** TBD. **Defensive Coach:** Jack Santora.

Trainer: Yusuke Takahashi. **Strength Coach:** Andrea Nunez.

GAME INFORMATION
Radio Announcer: Chris King. **No. of Games Broadcast:** 120. **Flagship Station:** 870-AM KFLD. **PA Announcer:** Patrick Harvey. **Official Scorers:** Tony Wise, Scott Tylinski. **Stadium Name:** Gesa Stadium. **Location:** I-182 to exit 9 (Road 68), north to Burden Blvd, right to stadium. **Standard Game Time:** Varies. **Ticket Price Range:** $9-15. **Visiting Club Hotel:** Hampton Inn & Suites Pasco/Tri-Cities, 6826 Burden Blvd., Pasco, WA 99301. **Telephone:** (509) 792-1660.

VANCOUVER CANADIANS

Address: Scotiabank Field at Nat Bailey Stadium, 4601 Ontario St, Vancouver, B.C. V5V 3H4.
Telephone: (604) 872-5232. **Fax:** (604) 872-1714.
E-Mail Address: staff@canadiansbaseball.com.
Website: www.canadiansbaseball.com.
Affiliation (first year): Toronto Blue Jays (2011). **Years in League:** 2021-

OWNERSHIP/MANAGEMENT
Operated by: Vancouver Canadians Professional Baseball LLP.
Managing General Partner: Jake Kerr. **Co-Owner:** Jeff Mooney. **President:** Andy Dunn. **General Manager:** Allan Bailey. **Assistant General Manager:** Stephani Ellis. **Financial Controller:** Brenda Chmiliar. **Senior Advisor, Business Development:** Walter Cosman. **Manager, Ticket Operations:** Stephen Maisey. **Coordinator, Sales & Marketing:** Jonah Morris. **Assistant Financial Controller:** Charlene Shamku. **Head Groundskeeper:** Ross Baron. **Manager, Ballpark Operations/Home Clubhouse Attendant:** TBD. **Concessions:** Iain Graham (Aramark).

FIELD STAFF
TBD

GAME INFORMATION
Radio/TV Announcer: TBD. **No. of Games Broadcast:** 120. **Flagship Station:** Sportsnet650 AM. **PA Announcer:** Niall O'Donohoe. **Official Scorer:** Mike Hanafin. **Stadium Name:** Nat Bailey Stadium. **Location:** From downtown, take Cambie Street Bridge, left on East 29th Ave., left on Ontario St. to stadium; From south, take Highway 99 to Oak Street, right on 41st Ave, left on Cambie St. right on East 29th Ave., left on Ontario St to stadium. **Standard Game Times:** Mon.-Sat., 7:05 pm, Sun., 1:05 pm. **Ticket Price Range:** $20-32. **Visiting Club Hotel:** Sandman Hotel Vancouver Airport, 3233 St. Edwards Dr., Richmond, B.C., V6X 1N4. **Telephone:** (604) 303-8888.

LOW-A WEST

STADIUM INFORMATION

			Dimensions				
Club	Stadium	Opened	LF	CF	RF	Capacity	2019 Att.
Fresno	Chukchansi Park	2002	324	400	335	12,500	380,090
Inland Empire	San Manuel Stadium	1996	330	410	330	5,000	181,253
Lake Elsinore	The Diamond	1994	330	400	310	7,866	172,280
Modesto	John Thurman Field	1952	312	400	319	4,000	139,762
Rancho Cucamo.	LoanMart Field	1993	335	400	335	6,615	162,085
San Jose	Municipal Stadium	1942	320	390	320	5,208	155,253
Stockton	Banner Island Ballpark	2005	300	399	326	5,200	179,465
Visalia	Recreation Ballpark	1946	320	405	320	2,468	129,118

FRESNO GRIZZLIES

Address: 1800 Tulare St, Fresno, CA 93721.
Telephone: (559) 320-4487. **Fax:** (559) 264-0795.
E-Mail Address: info@fresnogrizzlies.com. **Website:** www.FresnoGrizzlies.com.
Affiliation (first year): Colorado Rockies (2021). **Years in League:** 2021-

OWNERSHIP/MANAGEMENT

Operated By: Fresno Sports & Events.

Managing Partner: Michael Baker. **Chief Financial Officer:** Michael Moran. **President:** Derek Franks. **Assistant General Manager:** Andrew Milios. **Vice President of Operations:** Shaun O'Brien. **Director, Stadium Operations:** Harvey Kawasaki. **Head Groundskeeper:** David Jacinto. **Vice President, Sales:** Jason Hannold. **Manager, Ticket Office:** Eric Moreno. **Controller:** Allison Ferrell. **Manager, Marketing:** Jonathan Bravo.

FIELD STAFF

Development Supervisor: Steve Soliz. **Manager:** Robinson Cancel. **Hitting Coach:** Zach Osborne. **Pitching Coach:** Ryan Kibler. **Trainer:** Kelsey Branstetter.

GAME INFORMATION

No. of Games Broadcast: 120. **Stadium Name:** Chukchansi Park. **Location:** 1800 Tulare St, Fresno, CA 93721. **Directions:** From 99 North, take Fresno Street exit, left on Fresno Street, left on Inyo or Tulare to stadium. From 99 South, take Fresno Street exit, left on Fresno Street, right on Broadway to H Street. From 41 North, take Van Ness exit toward Fresno, left on Van Ness, left on Inyo or Tulare, stadium is straight ahead. From 41 South, take Tulare exit, stadium is located at Tulare and H Streets, or take Van Ness exit, right on Van Ness, left on Inyo or Tulare, stadium is straight ahead. **Ticket Price Range:** $10-19.

INLAND EMPIRE 66ERS

Address: 280 South E St., San Bernardino, CA 92401.
Telephone: (909) 888-9922. **Fax:** (909) 888-5251. **Website:** www.66ers.com.
Affiliation (first year): Los Angeles Angels (2011). **Years in League:** 2021-

OWNERSHIP/MANAGEMENT

Operated by: Inland Empire 66ers Baseball Club of San Bernardino. **Principal Owners:** David Elmore, Donna Tuttle. **President:** David Elmore. **Chairman:** Donna Tuttle. **General Manager:** Joe Hudson. **Assistant GM:** Daniel Vazquez. **Director, Broadcasting:** Steve Wendt. **Director, Community Relations:** Stephanie O'Quinn. **Director, Group Sales:** Hollee Haines. **Director, Ticket Operations/Sales:** Sean Peterson. **Manager, Creative Services:** Dusty Ferguson. **Manager, Promotions:** Mary Grinnan. **Account Executives:** Jarrett Stark, **Manager, Facility:** Richard Morales. **Head Groundskeeper:** Dominick Guerrero. **Accountant:** Karly Strahl. **Director, Food & Beverage (Diamond Creations):** Ryan Liptrot.

FIELD STAFF

Manager: Jack Howell. **Hitting Coach:** Ryan Sebra. **Pitching Coach:** TBD. **Defensive Coach:** Trevor Nyp. **Athletic Trainer:** Nicholas Faciana. **Strength and Conditioning Coach:** Omar Porras.

GAME INFORMATION

Radio Announcer: Steve Wendt. **Flagship Station:** 66ers Radio on TuneIn. **PA Announcer:** Renaldo Gonzales. **Official Scorer:** Bill Maury-Holmes. **Stadium Name:** San Manuel Stadium. **Location:** From south, I-215 to 2nd Street exit, east on 2nd, right on G Street; from north, I-215 to 3rd Street exit, left on Rialto, right on G Street. **Standard Game Times:** Mon.-Sat. 7:05 pm; Sun. 2:05 pm (1st Half) 5:35 pm (2nd Half). **Ticket Price Range:** TBD. **Visiting Club Hotel:** TBD. **Telephone:** (909) 796-1000.

LAKE ELSINORE STORM

Address: 500 Diamond Drive, Lake Elsinore, CA 92530
Telephone: (951) 245-4487. **Fax:** (951) 245-0305.
E-Mail Address: info@stormbaseball.com. **Website:** www.stormbaseball.com.
Affiliation (first year): San Diego Padres (2001). **Years in League:** 2021-

OWNERSHIP/MANAGEMENT
Owners: Gary Jacobs, Len Simon. **CEO/Co-General Manager:** Shaun Brock. **CFO/Co-General Manager:** Christine Kavic. **General Manager of Game Presentation and Events:** Mark Beskid. **Assistant General Manager of Baseball:** Terrance Tucker. **Assistant CFO:** Andres Pagan. **Senior Manager of Ticket operations:** Eric Theiss. **Box Office Manager:** Krista Williams. **Fulfillment and Processing:** Natalie Gates. **Emcee and Manager of Entertainment:** Kaz Egan. **Production Manager:** Jon Gripe. **Head Groundskeeper:** Anthony Anaya. **Operations and Facilities Manager:** Jason Natale. **Director of Food and Beverage:** Jason Wozniak. **Executive Chef:** Luciano Mulito. **Corporate Sales Executive:** Janelle Metzger. **HR Generalist:** Katherine Strehlow

FIELD STAFF
TBD

GAME INFORMATION
Radio Announcer: TBD. **No. of Games Broadcast:** 0. **Flagship Station:** TBD. **PA Announcer:** Dave McCrory. **Official Scorer:** Lloyd Nixon. **Stadium Name:** The Lake Elsinore Diamond Stadium. **Location:** From I-15, exit at Diamond Drive, west one mile to stadium. **Standard Game Times:** TBD. **Ticket Price Range:** $7-$30. **Visiting Club Hotel:** TBD

MODESTO NUTS

Office Address: 601 Neece Dr, Modesto, CA 95351. **Mailing Address:** PO Box 883, Modesto, CA 95353.
Telephone: (209) 572-4487. **Fax:** (209) 572-4490
E-Mail Address: fun@modestonuts.com. **Website:** www.modestonuts.com.
Affiliation (first year): Seattle Mariners (2017). **Years in League:** 2021-

OWNERSHIP/MANAGEMENT
Operated by: Seattle Mariners.
General Manager: Zach Brockman. **Director of Marketing & Promotions:** Veronica Hernandez. **Head Groundskeeper:** Alan Jones. **Director of Ticket Sales:** Chris Fleischmann. **Ticket Sales Manager:** Steven Webster. **Office Manager:** Kate Mendoza. **Food and Beverage Manager:** Robert Provencio.

FIELD STAFF
Manager: Eric Farris. **Pitching Coach:** Nathan Bannister. **Hitting Coach:** Rob Benjamin. **Bench Coach:** Geoff Jimenez. **Trainer:** TBD.

GAME INFORMATION
Radio Announcer: TBD. **PA Announcer:** Unavailable. **Official Scorer:** Unavailable. **Stadium Name:** John Thurman Field. **Location:** Highway 99 in southwest Modesto to Tuolumne Boulevard exit, west on Tuolumne for one block to Neece Drive, left for 1/4 mile to stadium. **Standard Game Times:** 7:05 pm, Sun. 2:05pm/6:05 pm. **Ticket Price Range:** $8-14. **Visiting Club Hotel:** DoubleTree Modesto.

RANCHO CUCAMONGA
QUAKES

Office Address: 8408 Rochester Ave., Rancho Cucamonga, CA 91730.
Mailing Address: P.O. Box 4139, Rancho Cucamonga, CA 91729.
Telephone: (909) 481-5000. **Fax:** (909) 481-5005.
E-Mail Address: info@rcquakes.com. **Website:** www.rcquakes.com.
Affiliation (first year): Los Angeles Dodgers (2011). **Years in League:** 2021-

OWNERSHIP/MANAGEMENT
Operated By: Bobby Brett. **Principal Owner:** Bobby Brett.
President: Brent Miles. **Vice President/General Manager:** Grant Riddle. **Vice President/Tickets:** Monica Ortega. **Vice President/Groups:** Linda Rathfon. **Vice President/Sponsorships:** Chris Pope. **Director of Sponsorships:** David Fields. **Director, Fan Engagement:** Bobbi Salcido. **Director, Group Sales:** Kyle Burleson. **Director, Season Tickets/ Operations:** Eric Jensen. **Accounting:** Amara McCellan. **Director, Public Relations/Voice of the Quakes:** Mike Lindskog. **Office Manager:** Shelley Scebbi. **Director, Food/Beverage:** TBD.

FIELD STAFF

Manager: John Shoemaker. **Hitting Coach:** Dylan Nasiatka. **Pitching Coaches:** Stephanos Stroop/Ramon Trancoso.

GAME INFORMATION

Radio Announcer: Mike Lindskog. **No. of Games Broadcast:** All. **Flagship Station:** Fox Sports AM 1350 KPWK. **PA Announcer:** Chris Albaugh. **Official Scorer:** Steve Wishek/Curt Christiansen. **Stadium Name:** LoanMart Field. **Location:** I-10 to I-15 North, exit at Foothill Boulevard, left on Foothill, left on Rochester to Stadium. **Standard Game Times:** 7:05 pm; **First Half Sundays at 2:**05 pm (May through June); **Second Half Sundays 5:**05 pm (July through Sept). **Visiting Club Hotel:** Best Western Heritage Inn, 8179 Spruce Ave, Rancho Cucamonga, CA 91730. **Telephone:** (909) 466-1111.

SAN JOSE GIANTS

Office Address: 588 E Alma Ave, San Jose, CA 95112.
Mailing Address: PO Box 21727, San Jose, CA 95151.
Telephone: (408) 297-1435. **Fax:** (408) 297-1453.
E-Mail Address: info@sjgiants.com. **Website:** www.sjgiants.com.
Affiliation (first year): San Francisco Giants (1988). **Years in League:** 2021-

OWNERSHIP/MANAGEMENT

Operated by: Progress Sports Management. **Principal Owners:** San Francisco Giants, Heidi Stamas, Richard Beahrs. **President/CEO:** Daniel Orum. **Chief Operating Officer:** Ben Taylor. **VP, Sales:** Jeff Di Giorgio. **VP, Marketing:** Matt Alongi. **VP, Game Day Operations and Human Resources:** Tara Tallman. **Director, Player Personnel:** Linda Pereira. **Director, Broadcasting:** Joe Ritzo. **Manager, Finance:** Joshua Chang. **Manager, Ticketing:** Ryan Anthony. **Manager, Retail/Merchandise:** Sierra Hanley. **Manager, Food and Beverage:** Ramiro Mijares. **Coordinator, Marketing and Community Relations:** David Baez. **Digital Media Assistant:** Sam Barasch. **Groundskeeper:** Roman Ornelas. **Assistant Groundskeeper:** Kevin Tallman.

FIELD STAFF

Manager: Lenn Sakata. **Hitting Coach:** Danny Santin. **Pitching Coach:** Paul Oseguera. **Fundamentals Coach:** Eliezer Zambrano. **Athletic Trainer:** Vitto Maffei. **Strength & Conditioning Coach:** Jesse White.

GAME INFORMATION

Radio Announcers: Joe Ritzo, Justin Allegri. **No. of Games Broadcast:** TBD.
Flagship: sjgiants.com. **Television Announcers:** Joe Ritzo, All home games on MiLB.TV. **PA Announcer:** Russ Call. **Official Scorer:** Mike Hohler. **Stadium Name:** Excite Ballpark. **Location:** South on I-280: Take 10th/11th Street Exit, turn right on 10th Street, turn left on Alma Ave. North on **I-280:** Take the 10th/11th Street Exit, Turn left on 10th Street, turn left on Alma Ave. **Standard Game Times:** 7 p.m., 6:30 p.m, Sat. 6 p.m., Sun 1 p.m. (5 p.m. after June 1). **Ticket Price Range:** $8-24.

STOCKTON PORTS

Address: 404 W Fremont St, Stockton, CA 95203.
Telephone: (209) 644-1900. **Fax:** (209) 644-1931.
E-Mail Address: info@stocktonports.com. **Website:** www.stocktonports.com.
Affiliation (first year): Oakland Athletics (2005). **Years in League:** 2021-

OWNERSHIP/MANAGEMENT

Operated By: 7th Inning Stretch LLC. **Chairman/CEO:** Tom Volpe.
President: Pat Filippone. **Assistant General Manager:** Luke Johnson. **Assistant General Manager:** Gary Olson. **Director of Ticket Operations:** Christine Bowling. **Community Relations Manager:** Jordy Feneck. **Group Sales Manager:** Doren Weil. **Director of Entertainment:** Vince Zielen. **Ticket Sales and Merchandise Executive:** Owen Hopkins. **Front Office Manager:** Christa Leri. **Bookkeeper:** Lyla Jacobson.

FIELD STAFF

Manager: Rico Brogna. **Hitting Coach:** Francisco Santana. **Pitching Coach:** Chris Smith. **Assistant Hitting Coach:** Craig Conklin. **Athletic Trainer:** Nick Voelker. **Sport Performance Coach:** Kevin Guild. **Club House Manager:** Vic Zapien.

GAME INFORMATION

Radio Announcer: Alex Jensen. **No of Games Broadcast:** 132. **Flagship Station:** TuneIn App. **PA Announcer:** Gary Ellenbolt. **Official Scorer:** Paul Muyskens. **Stadium Name:** Banner Island Ballpark. **Location:** From I-5/99, take Crosstown Freeway (Highway 4) exit El Dorado Street, north on El Dorado to Fremont Street, left on Fremont. **Standard Game Times:** 7:05 pm. **Ticket Price Range:** $10-$20. **Visiting Club Hotel:** Best Western, 111 E March Lane, Stockton, CA 95207. **Telephone:** 209-474-3301.

VISALIA RAWHIDE

Address: 300 N Giddings St, Visalia, CA 93291.
Telephone: (559) 732-4433. **Fax:** (559) 739-7732.
E-Mail Address: info@rawhidebaseball.com.
Website: www.rawhidebaseball.com.
Affiliation (first year): Arizona Diamondbacks (2007). **Years in League:** 2021-

OWNERSHIP/MANAGEMENT

Ownership: First Pitch Entertainment, Team President: Sam Sigal. **Co-General Managers:** Mike Candela and Julian Rifkind. **Assistant General Manager:** Brady Hochhalter. **Director of Ticketing:** Markus Hagglund. **Director of Broadcasting & Media Relations:** Jill Gearin. **Director of Facilities & Grounds:** James Templeton. **Community Partnership Manager:** Joe Ross. **Ballpark Operations Assistant:** Ryan O'Hara.

FIELD STAFF

Manager: Javier Colina. **Hitting Coach:** Micah Franklin. **Pitching Coach:** Barry Enright. **Coach:** Darrin Garner. **Trainer:** Daniel Fifer, **Strength & Conditioning Coach:** Logan Jones.

GAME INFORMATION

Radio Announcers: Jill Gearin. **No. of Games Broadcast:** 120. **Flagship Station:** MiLB.com.

PA Announcer: Brian Anthony. **Official Scorer:** Harry Kargenian and Mark "Scooter" Cossentine. **Stadium Name:** Rawhide Ballpark. **Location:** From Highway 99, take 198 East to Mooney Boulevard exit, left at second signal on Giddings; four blocks to ballpark. **Standard Game Times:** 6 pm, Sun. **1pm Ticket Price Range:** $13-30. **Visiting Club Hotel:** Quality Inn, 1010 E Prosperity Ave, Tulare, CA 93274.

LOW-A EAST

STADIUM INFORMATION

| Club | Stadium | Opened | Dimensions | | | Capacity | 2019 Att. |
			LF	CF	RF		
Augusta	SRP Park	2018	330	395	318	4,782	266,569
Carolina	Five County Stadium	1991	330	400	309	6,500	193,568
Charleston	Joseph P. Riley, Jr. Ballpark	1997	306	386	336	5,800	301,320
Columbia	Segra Park	2016	319	400	330	7,501	245,522
Delmarva	Arthur W. Perdue Stadium	1996	309	402	309	5,200	218,794
Down East	Grainger Stadium	1949	335	390	335	4,100	110,619
Fayetteville	SEGRA Stadium	2019	319	400	330	4,786	246,961
Fredericksburg	Fredericksburg Ballpark	2020	326	402	327	7,000	———
Kannapolis	Atrium Health Ballpark	2020	325	400	315	4,930	———
Lynchburg	City Stadium	1939	325	390	325	4,000	117,029
Myrtle Beach	TicketReturn.com Field	1999	308	400	328	5,200	226,247
Salem	Salem Memorial Stadium	1995	325	401	325	6,415	171,866

AUGUSTA GREENJACKETS

Office Address: 187 Railroad Ave. North Augusta, SC 29841.
Mailing Address: 187 Railroad Ave. North Augusta, SC 29841.
Telephone: (803) 349-9467. **Fax:** (803) 349-9434.
E-Mail Address: info@greenjacketsbaseball.com. **Website:** www.greenjacketsbaseball.com.
Affiliation (first year): Atlanta Braves (2021). **Years in League:** 2021-

OWNERSHIP/MANAGEMENT
Ownership Group: AGON Sports & Entertainment. **Owner:** Chris Schoen.
President: Jeff Eiseman. **HR & Business Operations:** Missy Martin. **Vice President:** Tom Denlinger. **General Manager:** Brandon Greene. **Director of Ticket Sales:** Troy Pakusch. **Accounting:** Debbie Brown. **Director of Stadium Operations:** Billy Nowak. **Director of Marketing & Community Relations:** Catie Jagodzinski. **Director of Corporate Partnerships:** Greg Dietz. **Director of Group Sales:** Yari Natal. **Senior Group Sales Executive:** James Mullins. **Ticket & Events Sales Executive:** Jamie Martin **Sales & Event Services Coordinator:** Marquisha Grovner. **Senior Membership Account Specialist:** Austin Lowndes. **Multimedia Video & Creative Services Specialist:** Alexis Ludovici. **Stadium Operations Coordinator:** Adam Pinckard. **Ticket Operations Manager:** Tyler Henderson. **Director of Retail & Merchandise Sales:** Chelsea Galbraith. **Director of Food & Beverage Director:** John Schow. **Food & Beverage Manager:** David Hutto. **Groundskeeper:** Darrell Lemmer.

FIELD STAFF
TBD

GAME INFORMATION
PA Announcer: Scott Skaden. **Stadium Name:** SRP Park. **Standard Game Times:** Mon.-Fri., 7:05 pm, Sat., 6:05 pm, Sun., 2:05 pm through All Star Break, Sun., 5:05 pm after All Star Break. **Ticket Price Range:** $9-$28. **Visiting Club Hotel:** Comfort Suites, 2911 Riverwest Dr, Augusta, GA. **Telephone:** (706) 434-2540.

CAROLINA MUDCATS

Office Address: 1501 NC Hwy 39, Zebulon, NC 27597.
Mailing Address: PO Drawer 1218, Zebulon, NC 27597.
Telephone: (919) 269-2287. **Fax:** (919) 269-4910.
E-Mail Address: muddy@carolinamudcats.com.
Website: www.carolinamudcats.com.
Affiliation (first year): Milwaukee Brewers (2017-). **Years in League:** 2021-

OWNERSHIP/MANAGEMENT
Ownership: Milwaukee Brewers Baseball Club
Operated by: Milwaukee Brewers Baseball Club
General Manager, Baseball & Stadium Operations: Eric Gardner. **General Manager, Business Development & Brand Marketing:** David Lawrence. **Manager, Tickets & Business Development:** Mitchell Lister. **Associate, Business Development:** Brandon Diorio. **Director, Marketing & Broadcast Media:** Greg Young. **Manager, Multimedia:** Evan Moesta. **Coordinator, Social Media/Marketing/Graphics:** Aaron Bayles. **Manager, Merchandise & Office Operations:** Amy Peterson. **Coordinator, Stadium Operations:** Michael Lincoln. **Director, Food and Beverage:** Dwayne Lucas. **Manager, Grounds:** John Packer.

FIELD STAFF

Manager: Joe Ayrault. **Pitching Coach:** Fred Dabney. **Hitting Coach:** Bobby Spain. **Coach:** Liu Rodriguez. **Athletic Trainer:** Matt Deal. **Strength Coach:** Jonah Mergen.

GAME INFORMATION

Radio Announcer: Greg Young. **No. of Games Broadcast:** 60. **Flagship Station:** TuneIn Radio. **PA Announcer:** Hayes Permar. **Official Scorer:** Bill Woodward. **Stadium Name:** Five County Stadium.

Location: From Raleigh, US 64 East to 264 East, exit at Highway 39 in Zebulon. **Standard Game Times:** 7:00 pm(Mon-Fri), 5:00 pm (Sat), 1:00 PM (Sun). **Ticket Price Range:** $10-15. **Visiting Club Hotel:** Doubletree by Hilton Midtown, 2805 Highwoods Blvd, Raleigh, NC, 27604.

CHARLESTON RIVERDOGS

Office Address: 360 Fishburne St, Charleston, SC 29403.
Mailing Address: PO Box 20849, Charleston, SC 29403.
Telephone: (843) 723-7241. **Fax:** (843) 723-2641.
E-Mail Address: admin@riverdogs.com. **Website:** www.riverdogs.com.
Affiliation (first year): Tampa Bay Rays (2021). **Years in League:** 2021-

OWNERSHIP/MANAGEMENT

Operated by: The Goldklang Group/South Carolina Baseball Club LP.

Chairman: Marv Goldklang. **President:** Jeff Goldklang. **Club President/General Manager:** Dave Echols. **President Emeritus:** Mike Veeck. **Director, Fun:** Bill Murray. **Co-Owners:** Peter Freund, Gene Budig, Al Phillips. **VP, Corporate Sales:** Andy Lange. **Assistant GM:** Ben Abzug. **Director, Promotions:** Nate Kurant. **VP, Food/Beverage:** Josh Shea. **Director, Ticket Sales:** Garret Randle. **Director Community Outreach:** Chris Singleton. **Director, Operations:** Brandon Dunnam. **Director, Video Production:** Ryan Perry. **Business Manager:** Dale Stickney. **Head Groundskeeper:** Kevin Coyne.

FIELD STAFF

Manager: Blake Butera. **Hitting Coach:** Wuarnner Rincones. **Pitching Coach:** Doc Watson. **Coach:** Sean Smedley.

GAME INFORMATION

Radio Announcer: TBD. **No. of Games Broadcast:** TBD. **Flagship Station:** WTMA 1250-AM. **PA Announcer:** TBD. **Official Scorer:** Mike Hoffman. **Stadium Name:** Joseph P. Riley, Jr. **Location:** 360 Fishburne St, Charleston, SC 29403, From US 17, take Lockwood Dr. North, right on Fishburne St. **Standard Game Times:** Mon.-Fri., 7:05pm, Sat. 6:05 pm, Sun. 5:05 pm. **Ticket Price Range:** $8-20. **Visiting Club Hotel:** Aloft Charleston Airport.

COLUMBIA FIREFLIES

Office Address: 1640 Freed Street, Columbia, SC 29201.
Mailing Address: 1640 Freed Street, Columbia, SC 29201.
Telephone: (803) 726-4487.
E-Mail Address: info@columbiafireflies.com. **Website:** www.columbiafireflies.com.
Affiliation (first year): Kansas City Royals (2021). **Years in League:** 2021-

OWNERSHIP/MANAGEMENT

Operated By: Columbia Fireflies Baseball, LLC.

President: John Katz. **Executive Vice President:** Brad Shank. **Senior Vice President/Food & Beverage:** Scott Burton. **Vice President of Corporate Partnerships:** Blake Buchanan. **Director, Accounting & Baseball Operations:** Jonathan Mercier. **Director, Marketing:** Ashlie DeCarlo. **Office Manager:** Katie Maroney. **Director, Ticketing:** Joe Shepard. **Director, Group Sales:** Juan Encarnacion. **Senior Corporate Account Manager:** Jeff Berger, Scott Rhodes. **Ticket Account Manager:** Nick Spano, Derrick Bradford, Ty Jamieson. **Graphics Manager:** Casey Vecchio. **Promotions Manager:** Brooke Buckley. **Digital Content Manager:** Brendan McDowell. **Community Engagement Manager:** McKenzie Brown. **Merchandise Manager:** Mallory Turnbull. **Executive Chef:** Bobby Hunter. **Food & Beverage Manager:** Michael Bolt. **Director of Stadium Operations:** Anthony Altamura. **Assistant Director of Stadium Operations:** Matt Lundquist. **Stadium Operations Manager:** Tyler Restrepo. **Head Groundskeeper:** Drew Tice. **Assistant Groundskeeper:** Joe Golding. **Corporate Partnerships Account Executive:** Jason Haller. **Director of Special Events:** Allison Abercrombie.

FIELD STAFF

Manager: Brooks Conrad. **Hitting Coach:** Jesus Azuaje. **Pitching Coach:** Carlos Martinez. **Coach:** Glenn Hubbard.

GAME INFORMATION

Radio Announcer: John Kocsis. **No. of Games Broadcast:** 70. **Flagship Station:** Unavailable. **PA Announcer:** Bryan Vacchio. **Official Scorer:** Unavailable. **Stadium Name:** Segra Park. **Location:** 1640 Freed Street, Columbia, SC 29201. **Standard Game Times:** Mon.-Fri., 7:05pm, Sat. 6:05pm, Sun. TBD. **Ticket Price Range:** $5-$10. **Visiting Club Hotel:** Hyatt Place Columbia/Harbison, 1130 Kinley Road, Irmo, SC 29063.

DELMARVA SHOREBIRDS

Office Address: 6400 Hobbs Rd, Salisbury, MD 21804.
Mailing Address: PO Box 1557, Salisbury, MD 21802.
Telephone: (410) 219-3112. **Fax:** (410) 219-9164.
E-Mail Address: info@theshorebirds.com. **Website:** www.theshorebirds.com.
Affiliation: Baltimore Orioles (1997). **Years in League:** 2021-

OWNERSHIP/MANAGEMENT
Operated By: 7th Inning Stretch, LP. **Owner:** Tom Volpe. **President:** Pat Filippone. **General Manager:** Chris Bitters. **Assistant GM:** Jimmy Sweet. **Director of Marketing:** Ben Vigliarolo. **Director of Broadcasting & Communications:** TBD. **Community Relations Manager:** Chip Woytowitz. **Director of Tickets:** Brandon Harms. **Director of Ticket & Merchandise Operations:** Benjamin Posner. **Ticket Sales Account Executive:** Joe DeLucia. **Director of Stadium Operations:** Billy Blackwell. **Head Groundskeeper:** Caroline Beauchamp. **Accounting Manager:** Matt Figard.

FIELD STAFF
Manager: Dave Anderson. **Pitching Coach:** Robbie Aviles. **Hitting Coach:** Patrick Jones. **Fundamentals Coach:** Matt Packer. **Development Coach:** Dave Barry. **Athletic Trainer:** Gary Smith.

GAME INFORMATION
Radio: TBD. **No. of Games Broadcast:** TBD. **Flagship Station:** TBD. **Stadium Name:** Arthur W. Perdue Stadium. **Location:** From US 50 East, right on Hobbs Rd; From US 50 West, left on Hobbs Road. **Standard Game Time:** 7:05 pm. **Ticket Price Range:** $10-$15. **Visiting Club Hotel:** TBD.

DOWN EAST WOOD DUCKS

Address: 400 East Grainger Avenue, Kinston, NC 28502
Telephone: (252) 686-5165
E-Mail Address: jbullock@wooducksbaseball.com. **Website:** wooducksbaseball.com
Affiliation (first year): Texas Rangers (2017). **Years in League:** 2021-

OWNERSHIP/MANAGEMENT
Operated By: Texas Rangers, LLC.
Chief Operating Officer & Chairman, Ownership Committee: Neil Leibman. **Executive Vice President, Sports & Entertainment:** Sean Decker. **Vice President:** Wade Howell. **Assistant GM of Operations:** Janell Bullock. **Assistant GM Of Sales:** Jon Clemmons. **Creative Services Director:** Matthew Edwards. **Director of Marketing:** Alexa Kay. **Director of Broadcasting:** TBD. **Group Sales Executive:** Jackson Cook. **Group Sales Executive:** John McCormick. **Head Groundskeeper:** Stephen Watson.

FIELD STAFF
Manager: Carlos Cardoza. **Hitting Coach:** Eric Dorton. **Pitching Coach:** Jordan Tiegs. **Coach:** Kevin Torres. **Trainer:** Derrick Decker. **Strength & Conditioning Coach:** Luke Earp.

GAME INFORMATION
Radio Announcer: TBD. **PA Announcer:** Bryan Hanks. **Stadium Name:** Grainger Stadium. **Standard Game Times:** 7:00 (weekdays), 6:00 (Saturdays), 2:00 (Sundays). **Ticket Price Range:** $7-11. **Visiting Club Hotel:** Mother Earth Motor Lodge, 501 N Herritage St., Kinston, NC 28501.

FAYETTEVILLE WOODPECKERS

Address: 460 Hay St., Fayetteville, NC 28301
Telephone: 910-339-1989.
E-Mail Address: Woodpeckers@astros.com. **Website:** fayettevillewoodpeckers.com.
Affiliation (first year): Houston Astros (2019). **Years in League:** 2021-

OWNERSHIP/MANAGEMENT
Principal Owner: Houston Astros.
Director, Finance: Jennifer Carpenter. **Director, Sales:** Chaz Dawson. **Director, Marketing:** Pete Subsara. **Director, Stadium Operations:** Chris Cominse. **Director, Field Operations:** Alpha Jones. **Manager, Retail:** Brittany Tschida. **Manager, Corporate Partnerships:** Sarah Suggs. **Manager, Baseball Operations:** Mike Montesino. **Manager, Ticket Operations:** Gabriel Evans. **Manager, Events:** Rachel Smith. **Manager, Creative Services:** Ryan LeFevre. Manager, **Community Relations & Media Relations:** Victoria Huggins. **Account Executive, Ticketing:** Elizabeth Adams. **Account Executive, Sponsorships:** Kevin Hughes. **Account Executive, Ticketing:** Travis Gortman.

FIELD STAFF
Manager: Nate Shaver. **Hitting Coach:** Rafael Peña. **Pitching Coach:** Thomas Whitsett.

GAME INFORMATION

Radio Announcer: Matt Dean. **No. of Games Broadcast:** 120. **Flagship Station:** N/A.
PA Announcer: Ray Thomas. **Official Scorer:** Eddy Southard. **Stadium Name:** Segra Stadium. **Standard Game Times:** M-F 6:30pm, Sat. 5pm, Sun. 2pm. **Visiting Club Hotel:** Fairfield Inn. **Telephone:** 910-223-7867.

FREDERICKSBURG NATIONALS

Office Address: 42 Jackie Robinson Way, Fredericksburg, VA 22401
Mailing Address: 42 Jackie Robinson Way, Fredericksburg, VA 22401
Telephone: (540) 858-4242. **E-Mail Address:** info@frednats.com.
Website: www.frednats.com.
Affiliation (first year): Washington Nationals (2005). **Years in League:** 2021-

OWNERSHIP/MANAGEMENT

Operated By: SAJ Baseball LLC. **Principal Owner:** Art Silber.
President: Lani Silber Weiss. **Executive VP/General Manager:** Nick Hall. **Director of Partnerships:** Tory Goodman. **Manager of Partnership Fulfillment:** Gibson Stoffer. **Director of Ticket Operations:** Derrick Mangerum. **Director of Ticket & Hospitality Sales:** David Woodard. **Ticket Sales Account Executive:** Jimmy Burns. **Ticket Sales Account Executive:** Ally Chism. **Director of Operations:** Eliot Williams. **Manager of Stadium Operations:** Zak Kerns. **Director of Merchandise:** McKenzie Goodman. **Head Groundskeeper:** Jake Mays. **VP of Creative Services:** Robert Perry. **Director of Design:** Alexis Deegan. **Marketing Coordinator:** Paige Honaker.

FIELD STAFF

Manager: Mario Lisson. **Hitting Coach:** Jorge Mejia. **Pitching Coach:** Pat Rice. **Athletic Trainer:** Kirby Craft. **Strength & Conditioning Coach:** Ryan Grose.

GAME INFORMATION

Radio Announcer: Erik Bremer. **No. of Games Broadcast:** 120. **Flagship:** www.frednats.com. **PA Announcer:** TBD. **Official Scorer:** TBD. **Stadium Name:** TBD. **Location:** From I-95, take exit 130B onto VA-3W/Plank Road for 0.7 miles. Turn right onto Carl D. Silver Pkwy. Stay straight for 1.8 miles until you reach stadium parking lot. **Standard Game Times:** 7:05pm. **Ticket Price Range:** $10-$16. **Visiting Club Hotel:** Country Inn and Suites.

KANNAPOLIS CANNON BALLERS

Office Address: 216 West Ave. Kannapolis, NC 28081
Mailing Address: 216 West Ave. Kannapolis, NC 28081
Telephone: (704) 932-3267
Email Address: info@kcballers.com. **Website:** kcballers.com
Affiliation (first year): Chicago White Sox (2001). **Years in League:** 2021-

OWNERSHIP/MANAGEMENT

Operated by: Temerity Baseball Club, LLC. **Operating Partner:** Scotty Brown. **General Manager:** Matt Millward. **Assistant GM:** Vince Marcucci. **Account Executive:** Walker Brooke. **Broadcasting & Baseball Operations Manager:** Trevor Wilt. **Director of Retail Operations:** Tayler Gainer. **Director of Ticket Operations:** Jake "The Ticket Leprechaun" Brewer. **Director of Special Events:** Rachel Kilinski. **Director of Stadium Operations:** Michael Wolf. **Director of Entertainment:** Blair Jewell. **Digital Media & Creative Designer:** Caitlyn Gardner. **Head Groundskeeper:** Billy Ball. **Director of Video Production:** Melissa Clark. **Director of Food & Beverage Operations:** Chris Beasley.

FIELD STAFF

Manager: Guillermo Quiroz. **Pitching Coach:** John Ely. **Hitting Coach:** Charlie Romero. **Coach:** Patrick Leyland.

GAME INFORMATION

Radio Announcer: Trevor Wilt. **No. of Games Broadcast:** TBD. **Flagship Station:** kcballers.com/TuneIn Radio App. **PA Announcer:** Jordan Connell. **Official Scorer:** Jimmy Lewis. **Stadium Name:** Atrium Health Ballpark. **Location:** Exit 58 on I-85, turn west on to South Cannon Blvd., continue straight until left turn on Dale Earnhardt Blvd., take right on Vance, then left on West Ave. **Standard Game Times:** Mon-Sat: 7:00p.m./Sun: 1:30p.m. **Ticket Price Range:** $9-$15. **Visiting Club Hotel:** TBA.

LYNCHBURG HILLCATS

Address: Lynchburg City Stadium, 3180 Fort Ave, Lynchburg, VA 24501.
Telephone: (434) 528-1144. **Fax:** (434) 846-0768.
E-Mail Address: info@lynchburg-hillcats.com. **Website:** www.Lynchburg-hillcats.com.
Affiliation (first year): Cleveland Indians (2015). **Years in League:** 2021-

OWNERSHIP/MANAGEMENT

Operated By: Elmore Sports Group.

President and General Manager: Chris Jones. **Assistant General Manager:** Peter Billups. **Director of Field Operations:** Collin Tyzinski. **General Manager of Food and Beverage:** Matt Ramstead. **Director of Broadcasting and Media Relations:** Maura Sheridan. **Operations/Clubhouse Manager:** Ryan Henson.

FIELD STAFF

Manager: Dennis Malavé. **Hitting Coach:** Chris Smith. **Pitching Coach:** Tony Arnold. **Bench Coach:** Juan De Le Cruz. **Strength & Conditioning Coach:** Juan Acevedo. **Athletic Trainer:** Patrick Reynolds.

GAME INFORMATION

Radio Announcer: Maura Sheridan. **No. of Games Broadcast:** 120. **Official Scorers:** Dan Fallen. **Stadium Name:** Bank of the James Stadium. **Location:** US 29 Business South to Bank of the James Stadium (exit 6); US 29 Business North to Bank of the James Stadium (exit 4). **Ticket Price Range:** $8-16. **Visiting Club Hotel:** TBD.

MYRTLE BEACH PELICANS

Mailing Address: 1251 21st Avenue N. Myrtle Beach, SC 29577.
Telephone: (843) 918-6000. **Fax:** (843) 918-6001.
E-Mail Address: info@myrtlebeachpelicans.com.
Website: www.myrtlebeachpelicans.com.
Affiliation: (first year): Chicago Cubs (2015). **Years in League:** 2021-

OWNERSHIP/MANAGEMENT

Owners, Greenberg Sports Group: Chuck Greenberg. **President:** Ryan Moore. **General Manager:** Ryan Moore. **Associate General Manager:** Kristin Call. **Sr. Director, Finance:** Anne Frost. **Administrative Assistant:** Beth Freitas. **Director of Sales:** Ryan Cannella. **Sports & Tourism Sales Manager:** Todd Chapman. **Corporate Sales Representative:** Robert Buchanan. **Box Office Manager:** Shannon Barbee. **Sponsorship Execution Coordinator:** Samantha Parnell. **Fan Engagement:** Hunter Horenstein. **Director of Operations:** TBD. **Merchandise Manager/ Pro Shop:** Dan Bailey. **Director, Food & Beverage:** TBD. **Sports Turf Manager:** Jordan Barr. **Director of Video Productions:** Ryan Nicholson. **Media Relations:** Noah Cloonan.

FIELD STAFF

Manager: Buddy Bailey. **Pitching Coach:** Clayton Mortensen. **Hitting Coach:** Dan Puente. **Development Coach:** George Thanapoulos. **Athletic Trainer:** German Suncin. **Strength Coach:** Austin Smith.

GAME INFORMATION

PA Announcer: TBA. **Official Scorer:** TBA. **Stadium Name:** Ticketreturn.com Field at Pelicans Ballpark. **Location:** US Highway 17 Bypass to 21st Ave. North, half mile to stadium. **Standard Game Times:** 7:05 p.m. **Ticket Pirce Range:** $9-$15. **Visiting Club Hotel:** Doubletree Resorts, 3200 South Ocean Blvd., Myrtle Beach, S.C., 29577. **Telephone:** (843) 315-7100.

SALEM RED SOX

Office Address: 1004 Texas St., Salem, VA 24153.
Mailing Address: PO Box 842, Salem, VA 24153.
Telephone: (540) 389-3333. **Fax:** (540) 389-9710.
E-Mail Address: info@salemsox.com. **Website:** www.salemsox.com.
Affiliation (first year): Boston Red Sox (2009). **Years in League:** 2021-

OWNERSHIP/MANAGEMENT

Operated By: Carolina Baseball LLC/Fenway Sports Group.
Managing Director: Dave Beeston. **General Manager:** Allen Lawrence. **VP of Tickets:** Blair Hoke. **VP of Corporate Partnerships:** Steven Elovich. **Facilities Manager/Head Groundskeeper:** Joey Elmore. **Director of Ticket Sales:** Charlie Umland. **Ticket Operations Manager:** Lior Bittan. **Director of Food/Beverage:** Mike Ferrero. **Bookkeeper:** Barry Stephens. **Video Production Manager:** Cameron Moist. **Merchandise & Special Events Manager:** Kayla Keegan. **Ticket Sales & Client Service AE:** Payton Powell. **Clubhouse Manager:** Tom Wagner.

FIELD STAFF

Manager: Luke Montz. **Hitting Coach:** Nelson Paulino. **Pitching Coach:** Nick Green. **Coach:** Frankie Rios. **Trainer:** Bobby Stachura. **Strength & Conditioning Coach:** Michael Hernandez.

GAME INFORMATION

Radio Announcer: TBD. **No. of Games Broadcast:** 120. **Flagship Station:** TBD. **PA Announcer:** TBD. **Official Scorer:** Billy Wells. **Stadium Name:** Salem Memorial Ballpark. **Location:** I-81 to exit 141 (Route 419), follow signs to Salem Civic Center Complex. **Standard Game Times:** 7:05 pm, Sat./Sun. 6:**05/4:**05. **Ticket Price Range:** $7-15. **Visiting Club Hotel:** Comfort Suites Ridgewood Farms, 2898 Keagy Rd., Salem, VA 24153. **Telephone:** (540) 375-4800.

LOW-A SOUTHEAST

STADIUM INFORMATION

Club	Stadium	Opened	Dimensions			Capacity	2019 Att.
			LF	CF	RF		
Bradenton	McKechnie Field	1923	335	400	335	8,654	71,284
Clearwater	Spectrum Field	2004	330	400	330	8,500	180,069
Daytona	Jackie Robinson Ballpark	1930	317	400	325	4,200	143,189
Dunedin	Florida Auto Exchange Stadium	1977	335	400	327	5,509	11,757
Fort Myers	Hammond Stadium	1991	330	405	330	7,900	108,800
Jupiter	Roger Dean Chevrolet Stadium	1998	330	400	325	6,871	62,684
Lakeland	Publix Field at Joker Marchant Stadium	1966	340	420	340	7,961	50,770
Palm Beach	Roger Dean Chevrolet Stadium	1998	330	400	325	6,871	57,418
St. Lucie	First Data Field	1988	338	410	338	7,000	82,581
Tampa	Steinbrenner Field	1996	318	408	314	10,270	61,290

BRADENTON MARAUDERS

Address: 1701 27th Street East, Bradenton, FL 34208.
Telephone: (941) 747-3031. **Fax:** (941) 747-9442.
E-Mail Address: MaraudersInfo@pirates.com
Website: bradentonmarauders.com
Affiliation (first year): Pittsburgh Pirates (2010). **Years in League:** 2021-.

OWNERSHIP/MANAGEMENT
Operated By: Pittsburgh Associates of Florida
VP, **Florida & Dominican Operations:** Jeff Podobnik. **General Manager/Director of Sales & Marketing:** Craig Warzecha. **Director, Florida Operations:** Ray Morris. **Director, Concessions & Retail:** Chuck Knapp. **Assistant General Manager/Manager, Ticket Sales:** Jackie Riggleman. **Manager, Game Presentation:** Rebekah Rivette. **Head Groundskeeper:** Joseph Knight.

FIELD STAFF
Manager: Jonathan Johnston. **Pitching Coach:** Fernando Nieve. **Hitting Coach:** Jonny Tucker. **Bench Coach:** Jim Horner. **Trainer:** Matt McNamee. **Strength Coach:** Nick Pressley.

GAME INFORMATION
PA Announcer: Jeff Phillips. **Official Scorer:** Dave Taylor. **Stadium Name:** LECOM Park. **Location:** I-75 to exit 220 (220B from I-75N) to SR 64 West/Manatee Ave, Left onto 9th St West, LECOM PARK on the left. **Standard Game Times:** 6:30 pm, Sun. 1:00 pm. **Ticket Price Range:** $6-10. **Visiting Club Hotel:** Holiday Inn Express West, 4450 47th St W, Bradenton, FL 34210. **Telephone:** (941) 747-3031.

CLEARWATER THRESHERS

Address: 601 N Old Coachman Road, Clearwater, FL 33765.
Telephone: (727) 712-4300. **Fax:** (727) 712-4498.
Website: www.threshersbaseball.com.
Affiliation (first year): Philadelphia Phillies (1985). **Years in League:** 2021-

OWNERSHIP/MANAGEMENT
Operated by: Philadelphia Phillies.
Director of Florida Operations: John Timberlake. **General Manager of Clearwater Threshers:** Jason Adams. **Senior Manager of Corporate Partnerships:** Dan McDonough. **Business Manager:** Dianne Gonzalez. **General Manager, BayCare Ballpark:** Doug Kemp. **Assistant GM, Clearwater Threshers:** Dan Madden. **Community Engagement/Media Manager:** Robert Stretch. **Food and Beverage Manager:** Justin Gunsaulus. **Assistant Food and Beverage Manager:** Justin Stone. **Corporate Sales Associate:** Cory Sipe. **Clubhouse Manager:** Mark Meschede. **Manager, Ticket Operations:** Pat Prevelige. **Facility and Operations Coordinator:** Sean McCarthy. **Manager, Promotions and Game Entertainment:** Dominic Repper. **Merchandise Assistant:** Shan Isett. **Group Sales Assistant:** Victoria Phipps. **Fun Team Coordinator:** Lindsey Settlemire. **Operations Assistant:** Will Priest. **Field Supervisor:** Ray Sayre.

FIELD STAFF
Manager: TBA. **Hitting Coach:** TBA. **Pitching Coach:** TBA.

GAME INFORMATION
PA Announcer: Don Guckian. **Official Scorer:** Larry Wiederecht. **Stadium Name:** BayCare Ballpark. **Location:** US 19 North and Drew Street in Clearwater. **Standard Game Times:** Mon.-Thu. 7 pm, Fri.-Sat. 6:30 pm, Sun. 1 p.m., most

Wednesdays are day games. **Ticket Price Range:** $6-10. **Visiting Club Hotel:** La Quinta Inn, 21338 US Highway 19 N, Clearwater, FL 33765. **Telephone:** (727) 799-1565.

DAYTONA TORTUGAS

Address: 110 E Orange Ave, Daytona Beach, FL 32114.
Telephone: (386) 257-3172. **Fax:** (386) 523-9490.
E-Mail Address: info@daytonatortugas.com. **Website:** www.daytonatortugas.co┆
Affiliation (first year): Cincinnati Reds (2015). **Years in League:** 2021-

OWNERSHIP/MANAGEMENT
Operated By: Tortugas Baseball Club LLC. **Principal Owner/President:** Reese Smith III. **Co-Owners:** Bob Fregolle, Rick French. **General Manager:** Jim Jaworski. **Director of Ticket Operations:** Paul Krenzer. **Community Relations Manager:** Josh McCann. **Broadcaster and Media Relations Manager:** Justin Rocke. **Stadium Operations and Grounds Manager:** Cole Underwood.

FIELD STAFF
Manager: Gookie Dawkins. **Pitching Coach:** Forrest Hermann. **Hitting Coach:** Darryl Brinkley. **Development Coach:** Dick Schofield. **Development Coach:** Reggie Williams. **Athletic Trainer:** Wade Hebrink. **Strength & Conditioning Coach:** Kyle Laughlin.

GAME INFORMATION
Radio Announcer: Justin Rocke. **No. of Games Broadcast:** 120. **Flagship Station:** TuneIn only. **PA Announcer:** Tim Lecras. **Official Scorer:** Don Roberts. **Stadium Name:** Jackie Robinson Ballpark. **Location:** I-95 to International Speedway Blvd Exit, east to Beach Street, south to Magnolia Ave east to ballpark; A1A North/South to Orange Ave west to ballpark. **Standard Game Time:** 7:05 p.m. (Mon-Sat); 5:35 p.m. (Sun). **Ticket Price Range:** $8-15.00. **Visiting Club Hotel:** Holiday Inn Resort Daytona Beach Oceanfront, 1615 S. Atlantic Ave Daytona Beach, FL 32118. **Telephone:** (386) 255-0921.

DUNEDIN BLUE JAYS

Address: 373 Douglas Ave Dunedin, FL 34698.
Telephone: (727) 733-9302. **Fax:** (727) 734-7661.
E-Mail Address: dunedin@bluejays.com. **Website:** dunedinbluejays.com.
Affiliation (first year): Toronto Blue Jays (1987). **Years in League:** 2021-

OWNERSHIP/MANAGEMENT
Director Florida Operations: Shelby Nelson. **Senior Manager of TD Ballpark Operations:** Zac Phelps. **Senior Manager of TD Ballpark Business Operations:** Kathi Beckman. **Accounting Manager:** Gayle Gentry. **Supervisor, Ticket and Box Office Operations:** Craig Ball. **Administrative Assistant/Receptionist:** Dea Jones. **Head Superintendent:** Patrick Skunda.

FIELD STAFF
Manager: TBA. **Hitting Coach:** TBA. **Pitching Coach:** TBA. **Position Coach:** TBA. **Strength & Conditioning Coach:** TBA. **Athletic Trainer:** TBA.

GAME INFORMATION
PA Announcer: Nate Kurant. **Official Scorer:** Steven Boychuk. **Stadium Name:** TD Ballpark. **Location:** From I-275, north on Highway 19, exit on Drew Street, right on North Keene Road, left onto Union Street. Right onto Douglas Avenue and stadium is on the right. **Standard Game Times:** 6:30 pm, Sun. 1:00 pm. **Ticket Price Range:** TBD. **Visiting Club Hotel:** La Quinta, 21338 US Highway 19 North, Clearwater, FL. **Telephone:** (727) 799-1565.

FORT MYERS MIGHTY MUSSELS

Address: 14400 Six Mile Cypress Pkwy, Fort Myers, FL 33912.
Telephone: (239) 768-4210. **Fax:** (239) 768-4211.
E-Mail Address: frontdesk@mightymussels.com.
Website: www.mightymussels.com.
Affiliation (first year): Minnesota Twins (1992). **Years in League:** 2021-

OWNERSHIP/MANAGEMENT
Operated By: Kaufy Baseball, LLC. **Owner:** Andrew Kaufmann. **Partner:** Jason Hochberg
President: Chris Peters. **General Manager, Director of Operations:** Judd Loveland. **Director of Business Operations:** Diana Burch. **Assistant GM:** Andy Wood. **Broadcast & Media Relations Manager:** John Vittas. **Marketing Manager:** Shannon Rankin. **Operations Coordinator/Sales Associate:** Rachel Raymer. **Director of Food & Beverage:** Loren Merrigan. **Merchandise Manager:** Lynn Izzo.

FIELD STAFF

Manager: Aaron Sutton. **Hitting Coach:** Brian Meyer. **Hitting Coach:** Brian Meyer. **Pitching Coach:** Peter Larson. **Pitching Coach:** Carlos Hernandez. **Athletic Trainer:** Ben Myers. **Strength & Conditioning Coach:** Chuck Bradway.

GAME INFORMATION

Radio Announcer: John Vittas. **No. of Games Broadcast:** 120. **Internet Broadcast:** www.mightymussels.com. **PA Announcer:** Allen Woodard. **Official Scorer:** Scott Pedersen. **Stadium Name:** William H. Hammond Stadium at the CenturyLink Sports Complex. **Location:** Exit 131 off I-75, west on Daniels Parkway, left on Six Mile Cypress Parkway. **Standard Game Times:** Mon-Fri 6:30 or 7:00 pm, Sat. 6:00 or 7:00; Sun. 12:00. **Ticket Price Range:** $10-$15. **Visiting Club Hotel:** Fairfield Inn & Suites Fort Myers Cape Coral, 7090 Cypress Terrace, Fort Myers, FL 33907.

JUPITER HAMMERHEADS

Address: 4751 Main Street, Jupiter, FL 33458.
Telephone: (561) 775-1818. **Fax:** (561) 691-6886.
E-Mail Address: PalmBeachCardinals@rogerdeanchevroletstadium.com.
Affiliation (first year): Miami Marlins (1998). **Years in League:** 2021-

OWNERSHIP/MANAGEMENT

Owned By: Miami Marlins, Jupiter Stadium, LTD.
General Manager, Jupiter Stadium, LTD: Mike Bauer. **General Manager:** Andrew Seymour. **Executive Assistant:** Lynn Besaw. **Media Relations Coordinator:** Andrew Miller. **Media Relations Assistant:** Ryer Gardenswartz. **Director of Accounting:** Pam Satory. **Ticket Operations Manager:** Alexa Harshbarger. **Director of Corporate Partnerships:** Jamie Toole. **Marketing & Promotions Manager:** Sarah Campbell. **Building Manager:** Walter Herrera. **Director, Grounds & Facilities:** Jordan Treadway. **Assistant Director, Grounds & Facilities:** Mitchell Moenster. **Merchandise Manager:** Kali Gumprecht.

FIELD STAFF

Manager: TBA. **Pitching Coach:** TBA. **Hitting Coach:** TBA. **Strength & Conditioning Coach:** TBA. **Athletic Trainer:** TBA. **Defensive Coach:** TBA.

GAME INFORMATION

PA Announcers: John Frost, Jay Zeager. **Official Scorer:** Brennan McDonald. **Stadium Name:** Roger Dean Chevrolet Stadium. **Location:** I-95 to exit 83, east on Donald Ross Road for 1/4 mile, left on Parkside Dr. **Standard Game Times:** 6:30 pm, Sat. 5:30pm, Sun. 1:00pm. **Ticket Price Range:** $7- $10. **Visiting Club Hotel:** Fairfield Inn by Marriott, 6748 Indiantown Road, Jupiter, FL 33458. **Telephone:** (561) 748-5252.

LAKELAND FLYING TIGERS

Address: 2301 Lakeland Hills Blvd., Lakeland, FL 33805.
Telephone: (863) 686-8075. **Fax:** (863) 687-4127.
Website: www.lakelandflyingtigers.com.
Affiliation (first year): Detroit Tigers (1967). **Years in League:** 2021-

OWNERSHIP/MANAGEMENT

Owned By: Detroit Tigers, Inc.
President and CEO, Ilitch Holdings, Inc. and Chairman and CEO, Detroit Tigers: Christopher Ilitch. **Director, Florida Operations:** Ron Myers. **General Manager:** Zach Burek. **Manager, Administration/Operations Manager:** Shannon Follett. **Ticket Manager:** Ryan Eason. **Assistant General Manager:** Dan Lauer.

FIELD STAFF

Manager: Andrew Graham. **Hitting Coach:** John Murrian. **Pitching Coach:** Carlos Bohorquez. **Developmental Coach:** Ollie Kadey. **Athletic Trainer:** Sean McFarland. **Strength & Conditioning Coach:** Dax Fiore. **Clubhouse Manager:** Pete Mancuso.

GAME INFORMATION

PA Announcer: Unavailable. **Official Scorer:** Joe Falatek. **Stadium Name:** Publix Field at Joker Marchant Stadium. **Location:** Exit 33 on I-4 to 33 South (Lakeland Hills Blvd.), 1.5 miles on left. **Standard Game Times:** TBD. **Ticket Price Range:** $5-10. **Visiting Club Hotel:** TBD. **Telephone:** TBD.

PALM BEACH CARDINALS

Address: 4751 Main Street, Jupiter, FL 33458.
Telephone: (561) 775-1818. **Fax:** (561) 691-6886.
E-Mail Address: PalmBeachCardinals@rogerdeanchevroletstadium.com.
Affiliation (first year): St. Louis Cardinals (2003). **Years in League:** 2021-

OWNERSHIP/MANAGEMENT

Owned By: St. Louis Cardinals, Jupiter Stadium, LTD.

General Manager, Jupiter Stadium, LTD: Mike Bauer. **General Manager:** Andrew Seymour. **Executive Assistant:** Lynn Besaw. **Media Relations Coordinator:** Andrew Miller. **Media Relations Assistant:** Ryer Gardenswartz. **Director of Accounting:** Pam Satory. **Ticket Operations Manager:** Alexa Harshbarger. **Director of Corporate Partnerships:** Jamie Toole. **Marketing & Promotions Manager:** Sarah Campbell. **Building Manager:** Walter Herrera. **Director, Grounds & Facilities:** Jordan Treadway. **Assistant Director, Grounds & Facilities:** Mitchell Moenster. **Merchandise Manager:** Kali Gumprecht.

FIELD STAFF

Manager: Jose Leon **Pitching Coach:** Dean Kiekhefer. **Hitting Coach:** Daniel Nicolaisen. **Strength & Conditioning Coach:** Ross Hasegawa. **Certified Athletic Trainer:** Chris Walsh.

GAME INFORMATION

PA Announcers: John Frost, Jay Zeager. **Official Scorer:** Lou Villano. **Stadium Name:** Roger Dean Chevrolet Stadium. **Location:** I-95 to exit 83, east on Donald Ross Road for 1/4 mile, left on Parkside Dr. **Standard Game Times:** TBA. **Ticket Price Range:** TBA. **Visiting Club Hotel:** Fairfield Inn by Marriott, 6748 Indiantown Road, Jupiter, FL 33458. **Telephone:** (561) 748-5252.

ST. LUCIE METS

Address: 31 Piazza Drive, Port St Lucie, FL 34986.
Telephone: (772) 871-2100. **Fax:** (772) 878-9802.
Website: www.stluciemets.com.
Affiliation (first year): New York Mets (1988). **Years in League:** 2021-

OWNERSHIP/MANAGEMENT

Owner/Chairman/CEO: Steven A. Cohen. **Owner & President of Mets Foundation:** Alexandra M. Cohen. **Vice Chairman:** Andrew B. Cohen. **President:** Sandy Alderson. **Executive Director, Minor League Facilities:** Paul Taglieri. **General Manager:** Traer Van Allen. **Executive Assistant:** Mary O'Brien. **Coordinator, Group Sales:** Josh Sexton. **Staff Accountant:** Shannon Murray. **Director, Sales/Corporate Partnerships:** Lauren DeAcetis. **Assistant General Manager, Team Operations, Ticketing & Merchandise:** Kyle Gleockler. **Manager, Media/Broadcast Relations:** Adam MacDonald. **Assistant General Manager, Game Operations, Community Relations & Group Sales:** Kasey Blair. **Coordinator, Social Media and Graphic Design:** Marissa Kappus. **Maintenance:** Jeff Montpetit.

FIELD STAFF

TBD

GAME INFORMATION

PA Announcer: Evan Nine. **Official Scorer:** Bill Whitehead. **Stadium Name:** Clover Park. **Location:** Exit 121 (St Lucie West Blvd) off I-95, east 1/2 mile, left on NW Peacock Blvd. **Standard Game Times:** N/A. **Ticket Price Range:** $6-$10. **Visiting Club Hotel:** SpringHill Suites by Marriott, 2000 NW Courtyard Circle, Port St Lucie, FL 34986. **Telephone:** (772) 871-2929.

TAMPA TARPONS

Address: One Steinbrenner Drive, Tampa, FL 33614.
Telephone: (813) 875-7753. **Fax:** (813) 673-3186
E-Mail Address: vsmith@yankees.com. **Website:** tarponsbaseball.com
Affiliation (first year): New York Yankees (1994). **Years in League:** 2021-

OWNERSHIP/MANAGEMENT

Operated by: Florida Bomber Baseball LLC. **VP Business Operations:** Vance Smith. **General Manager:** TBD. **Assistant GM:** Jeremy Ventura. **Premium Ticket Services:** Jennifer Magliocchetti. **Digital/Social Media Coordinator:** TBD. **Manager, Stadium Operations:** Ralph Caputo. **Director, Grounds:** Ritchie Anderson. **Stadium Supervisor:** Ron Kaufman. **Head Groundskeeper:** Jeff Eckert.

FIELD STAFF

TBD

GAME INFORMATION

Radio: TBD. **PA Announcer:** TBD. **Official Scorer:** Unavailable. **Stadium Name:** George M. Steinbrenner Field. **Location:** I-275 to Dale Mabry Hwy, North on Dale Mabry Hwy (Facility is at corner of West Martin Luther King Blvd/Dale Mabry Hwy). **Standard Game Times:** Mon-Sat. 6:30pm, Sun 1:00 pm. **Ticket Price Range:** $5-8. **Visiting Club Hotel:** TBD.

INDEPENDENT/ PARTNER LEAGUES

AMERICAN ASSOCIATION

Mailing and Street Address: PO Box 995, Moorhead, MN 56561-0995.
Telephone: (218) 512-0380.
Email: info@aabaseball.com
Websites: aabaseball.com, aabaseball.tv
Year Founded: 2005.
Commissioner: Joshua E. Schaub. **Deputy Commissioner:** Josh Buchholz. **Director of Umpires:** Ronnie Teague.
Director of Digital Media: Jake Kranz.
Directors: Jim Abel, Mark Brandmeyer, Daryn Eudaly, Dr. Bob Froehlich, Shawn Hunter, Sam Katz, Mark Ogren, John Roost, Patrick Salvi, Bruce Thom and Mike Zimmerman.
Opening Date: May 18. **Closing Date:** September 6.
Regular Season: 100 games.
Division Structure: North—Chicago Dogs, Gary SouthShore RailCats, Fargo-Moorhead RedHawks, Kane County Cougars, Milwaukee Milkmen, Winnipeg Goldeyes. **South**—Cleburne Railroaders, Houston Apollos (travel team), Kansas City Monarchs, Lincoln Saltdogs, Sioux City Explorers, Sioux Falls Canaries.
Playoff Format: Top two teams in each division play in best-of-five series. Winners play in best-of-five American Association Finals. **Roster Limit:** 23.
Player Eligibility Rule: Minimum of five first-year players; maximum of five veterans (at least six or more years of professional service).
Brand of Baseball: Rawlings.
Statistician: Pointstreak.com, Stack Sports, 5360 Legacy Dr #150, Plano, TX 75024.

STADIUM INFORMATION

Club	Stadium	Opened	LF	CF	RF	Capacity	2019 Att.
Chicago	Impact Field	2018	313	389	294	6,300	166,672
Cleburne	The Depot at Cleburne Station	2017	335	400	320	3,750	78,624
Fargo-Moorhead	Newman Outdoor Field	1996	314	408	318	4,172	161,857
Gary SouthShore	U.S. Steel Yard	2002	320	400	335	6,139	167,887
Kane County	Northwestern Medicine Field	1991	335	400	335	10,923	350,305
Kansas City	Legends Field	2003	300	396	328	6,270	156,058
Lincoln	Haymarket Park	2001	335	403	325	4,500	168,394
Milwaukee	Franklin Field	2019	330	407	330	4,000	59,459
Sioux City	Mercy Field at Lewis and Clark Park	1993	330	400	330	3,800	51,618
Sioux Falls	Sioux Falls Stadium	1964	313	410	312	4,462	114,452
Winnipeg	Shaw Park	1999	325	400	325	7,481	195,787

CHICAGO DOGS

Office Address: 9800 Balmoral Avenue, Rosemont, IL, 60018
Telephone: 847.636.5450.
E-mail: info@thechicagodogs.com. **Website:** thechicagodogs.com.
Owners: Shawn Hunter, Steven Gluckstern.
Chief Operating Officer & Baseball Operations: Trish Zuro. **Corporate Sponsorships:** Chris Lennon. **Corporate Sales Manager:** Scott Foley. **Sales and Event Manager:** Evan Gersonde. **Senior Account Executive:** Jon Ryan, Mackenzie Thomas. **Account Executive:** Genny Bernardoni. **Game Entertainment and Social Media Manager:** Pat Hunt. **Media Relations:** Alexandra Jakubiak. **Community Relations:** Daniela Barrios. **Broadcast and Media Relations Manager:** Sam Brief. **Website Design/Photographer:** Matt Zuro. **Assistant Director, Operations:** Kyle Lindquist. **Executive Chef:** Mike Blase.
Field Manager: Butch Hobson. **Pitching Coach:** Stu Cliburn. **Clubhouse Manager:** Daniel Langston.

GAME INFORMATION

Stadium Name: Impact Field, 9850 Balmoral Avenue, Rosemont, IL 60018.
Standard Game Times: Mon., Tues., Weds., Sat., 7:05 pm, Thur., 6:05pm, Sun., 3:05 pm

CLEBURNE RAILROADERS

Address: 1906 Brazzle Boulevard, Cleburne, TX 76033.
Telephone: (817) 945-8705.
Email address: info@railroaderbaseball.com. **Website:** railroaderbaseball.com.
Co-Owner/General Manager: John Junker. **Co-Owner:** Daryn Eudaly.
Director, Baseball Operations: Josh Robertson. **Director, Business Operations:** Bill Adams. **Director, Sales:** David Kirk. **Ticket Office Manager:** Hollie Bunn. **Broadcasting and Media Relations Manager:** Denning Gerig. **Press Box Manager:** Justin Terry.

Field Manager: Mike Jeffcoat.

GAME INFORMATION

Broadcasters: Brad Allred and Denning Gerig. **Games Broadcast:** 100. **Webcast Address:** www.953khits.com. **Stadium Name:** The Depot at Cleburne Station. **Directions:** From Chisholm Trail Parkway (toll road) continue south across US HWY 67, turn left onto Cleburne Station Boulevard. From US HWY 67 South, exit Nolan River Road, turn left onto Nolan River Road, turn left onto Cleburne Station Boulevard. From US HWY 67 North, exit Nolan River Road, turn right onto Nolan River Road, turn left onto Cleburne Station Boulevard. **Standard Game Times:** Mon.-Sat., 7:06 pm, Sun., 6:00 pm

FARGO-MOORHEAD REDHAWKS

Address: 1515 15th Ave N Fargo, ND 58102
Telephone: (701) 235-6161. **Fax:** (701) 297-9247.
Email Addresses: redhawks@fmredhawks.com media@fmredhawks.com.
Website: fmredhawks.com
Operated by: Fargo Baseball LLC. **Chairman of the Board:** N. Bruce Thom. **President & CEO:** Brad Thom.
General Manager: Matt Rau. **Vice President, Finance:** Rick Larson. **Assistant General Manager:** Karl Hoium. **Director of Communications:** Chad Ekren. **Group Sales Manager:** Cole Milberger. **Community Relations and Merchandise Manager:** Ashley McCoy. **Stadium Superintendent/Head Groundskeeper:** Tom Drietz.
Field Manager: Chris Coste. **Hitting Coach:** Anthony Renz. **Bullpen Coach:** Robbie Lopez. **Clubhouse Manager:** TBA. **Player Personnel Consultant:** Jeff Bittiger.

GAME INFORMATION

Radio Announcers: Jack Michaels & Chase Miller. **Games Broadcast:** 100. **Flagship Station:** 740 THE FAN (KNFL-740AM, K297BW 107.3FM). **Stadium Name:** Newman Outdoor Field (1996). **Location:** I-29 North to exit 67, east on 19th Ave North, right on Albrecht Boulevard. **Standard Game Times:** M-F. 7:02 pm Sat.: 6:00 pm, Sun.: 1:00 pm.

GARY SOUTHSHORE RAILCATS

Address: One Stadium Plaza, Gary, IN 46402.
Telephone: (219) 882-2255. **Fax:** (219) 882-2259.
Email Address: info@railcatsbaseball.com. **Website:** railcatsbaseball.com.
Operated by: Salvi Sports Enterprises.
Owner/CEO: Pat Salvi. **Owner:** Lindy Salvi.
President, Salvi Sports Enterprises: Brian Lyter. **General Manager:** Brian Flenner. **Assistant Director, Business Development:** Matt Marquez. **Marketing Consultant:** Renee Connelly. **Senior Director, Hospitality and Special Events:** Yvonne Lopez. **Senior Director, Operations & Head Groundskeeper:** Noah Simmons. **Manager, Marketing and Promotions:** Ashley Nylen. **Manager, Food & Beverage:** Rod MacKenzie. **Account Executive & Box Office Coordinator:** Matt Murphy. **Broadcasting Coordinator.** Max Kelton.
Field Manager: Greg Tagert.

GAME INFORMATION

Games Broadcast: 100. **Flagship Station:** WEFM 95.9-FM. **Broadcaster:** Max Kelton. **Stadium Name:** Steel Yard. **Location:** Take I-65 North to end of highway at U.S. 12/20 (Dunes Highway). Turn left on U.S. 12/20 heading west for 1.5 miles (three stop lights). Stadium is on left side. **Standard Game Times:** Mon.-Fri., 7:10 pm, Sat., 4:10 pm, Sun., 2:10 pm.

KANE COUNTY COUGARS

Address: 34W002 Cherry Lane, Geneva, IL 60134.
Telephone: (630) 232-8811. **Fax:** (630) 232-8815.
Website: www.kccougars.com.
Operated By: Cougars Baseball Partnership/American Sports Enterprises, Inc. **Chairman/Chief Executive Officer/President:** Dr. Bob Froehlich. **Owners:** Dr. Bob Froehlich, Cheryl Froehlich. **Board of Directors:** Dr. Bob Froehlich, Cheryl Froehlich, Stephanie Froehlich, Chris Neidhart, Marianne Neidhart.
Vice President/General Manager: Curtis Haug. **Senior Director, Finance/Administration:** Douglas Czurylo. **Accounting:** Sally Sullivan. **Director, Sales:** R. Michael Patterson. **Director, Ticket Services/Community Relations:** Amy Mason. **Ticket Operations:** Jeff Weaver. **Director, Security:** Dan Klinkhamer. **Promotions Director/Communications Coordinator:** Claire Jacobi. **Design/Graphics:** Emmet Broderick. **Media Placement Coordinator:** Bill Baker. **Office Manager:** Sherri Johnson. **Video Director:** Andy Cozzi. **Director, Food/Beverage:** TBD. **Director,Sales/Facilities:** Mike Klafehn. **Stadium Operations Manager:** Scott Anderson. **Director, Maintenance:** Jeff Snyder. **Head Groundskeeper:** Sean Ehlert.
Field Manager: TBD. **Hitting Coach:** TBD. **Pitching Coach:** TBD. **Bench Coach:** TBD. **Athletic Trainer:** TBD. **Strength & Conditioning Coach:** TBD. **Clubhouse Manager:** TBD.

GAME INFORMATION

Radio Announcer: Joe Brand. **No. of Games Broadcast:** 100. **Flagship Station:** TBD. **Official Scorer:** Mike Haase. **Stadium Name:** Northwestern Medicine Field. **Location:** From east or west, I-88 Ronald Reagan Memorial Tollway) to Farnsworth Ave. North exit, north five miles to Cherry Lane, left into stadium complex. From northwest, I-90 (Jane Addams Memorial Tollway) to Randall Rd. South exit, south 15 miles to Fabyan Parkway, east to Kirk Rd., north to Cherry Lane, left into stadium complex. **Standard Game Times:** Mon.-Sat., 6:30 pm, Sun., 1:00 pm.

KANSAS CITY MONARCHS

Office Address: 1800 Village West Parkway, Kansas City, KS 66111.
Telephone: 913-328-5618.
Email: info@monarchsbaseball.com. **Web:** monarchsbaseball.com.
Operated by: Max Fun Entertainment, LLC.
Principal Owner: Mark Brandmeyer. **Partner/Chief Commercial Officer:** Mark McKee.
President & General Manager: Jay S. Hinrichs. **Vice President, Hospitality:** Jim Cundiff. **Vice President, Stadium Operations:** Paul Wagner. **Vice President, Sales:** Jeff Foster. **Chief Financial Officer:** Tom Ross. **Manager, Special Events & Community Engagement:** Suzi Hallas. **Manager, Diversity & Civic Engagement:** Jesse Pedraza. **Manager, Group Sales:** Nick Restivo. **Manager, Production & Digital Assets:** Morgan Kolenda.
Field Manager: Joe Calfapietra. **Coaches:** Frank White, Bill Sobbe, Mike Henneman. **Equipment Manager:** John West.

GAME INFORMATION

Radio Announcer: Dan Vaughan. **Games broadcast:** 100. **Site:** www.monarchsbaseball.com. **Stadium Name:** Legends Field. **Location:** State Avenue West off I-435 and State Ave. **Standard Game Times:** Mon-Sat., 7:00 pm, Sun., 1:00 pm.

LINCOLN SALTDOGS

Office Address: 403 Line Drive Circle, Suite A, Lincoln, NE 68508.
Telephone: (402) 474-2255. **Fax:** (402) 474-2254.
Email Address: info@saltdogs.com. **Website:** saltdogs.com.
Chairman: Jim Abel. **President/GM:** Charlie Meyer.
Director, Broadcasting/Communications: Michael Dixon. **Director, Stadium Operations:** Dave Aschwege.
Director, Video Production: Ty Schweer. **Assistant Director, Stadium Operations:** Dan Busch. **Manager, Ticket Sales:** Colter Clarke. **Group Sales Executive:** Daniel Thomas. **Athletic Turf Manager:** Kyle Trewhitt. **Office Manager:** Kaydra Brodine. **Director of Operations for Concessions:** Steve Deriese. **Director of Kitchen Operations:** Katie Wilkinson.
Field Manager: James Frisbie. **Coach:** Tommy Gregg.

GAME INFORMATION

Public Address Announcer: Heath Kramer. **Broadcast Team:** Jeff Briden. **No. of Games Broadcast:** 100. **Flagship Station:** KLMS 1480AM & ESPN101.5 FM. **Stadium Name:** Haymarket Park. **Location:** I-80 to Cornhusker Highway West, left on First Street, right on Sun Valley Boulevard, left on Line Drive. **Standard Game Times:** Mon.-Sat., 7:05 pm, Sun., 1:35 pm.

MILWAUKEE MILKMEN

Office Address: 7044 S. Ballpark Drive, Ste 300, Franklin WI 53132
Telephone: (414) 224-9823
Email: Website: www.milwaukeemilkmen.com.
Owner: Michael Zimmerman. **COO/General Manager:** Dan Kuenzi.
Director, Corporate Partnership & Ticket Sales: Joe Zimmerman. **Director, Entertainment & Events:** Scot Johnson. **Director, Finance:** Tom Johns. **Medical Staff:** Midwest Orthopedic Speciality Hospital.
Field Manager: Anthony Barone. **Coach:** Matt Passarelle.

GAME INFORMATION

Stadium Name: Franklin Field. **Location:** 7035 S. Ballpark Drive, Franklin, WI 53132. **Standard Game Times:** Mon.-Fri., 7:05 pm. Sat., 6:05 pm. Sun., 1:05 pm.

SIOUX CITY EXPLORERS

Office Address: 3400 Line Drive, Sioux City, IA 51106.
Telephone: (712) 277-9467. **Fax:** (712) 277-9406.
Email Address: promotions@xsbaseball.com. **Website:** www.xsbaseball.com.
President: Matt Adamski.
Director, Stadium Operations & Baseball Operations: Boyd Pitkin. **Director, Sales:** Melissa Harbeck. **Director, Media Relations/Radio Broadcaster:** Connor Ryan.
Field Manager: Steve Montgomery. **Coaches:** Bobby Post, Derek Wolfe. **Athletic Trainer:** Bruce Fischbach.
Clubhouse Manager: Robby Loraditch.

GAME INFORMATION

Radio Announcer: Connor Ryan. **No. of Games Broadcast:** 100. **Flagship Station:** KSCJ 1360-AM. **Webcast Address:** www.xsbaseball.com. **Stadium Name:** Mercy Field at Lewis and Clark Park. **Location:** I-29 to Singing Hills Blvd, North, right on Line Drive. **Standard Game Times:** Mon.-Fri., 7:05 pm, Sat., 6:05 pm, Sun., 4:05 pm.

SIOUX FALLS CANARIES

Office Address: 1001 N West Ave, Sioux Falls, SD 57104.
Telephone: (605) 336-6060.
Email Address: info@sfcanaries.com. **Website:** www.sfcanaries.com.
Operated by: Canaries Baseball, LLC. **CEO/Managing Partner:** Tom Garrity.
General Manager: Duell Higbe. **Sales:** Andrew Candela.
Field Manager: Mike Meyer.

GAME INFORMATION

Radio Announcer: Joey Zanaboni. **No. of Games Broadcast:** 100. **Flagship Station:** MixLR.com/canaries-radio-network . **Webcast Address:** www.kwsn.com. **Stadium Name:** Sioux Falls Stadium. **Location:** I-29 to Russell Street, east one mile, south on West Avenue. **Standard Game Times:** Mon.-Fri., 7:05 pm, Sat., 6:05 pm, Sun., 1:05 pm.

WINNIPEG GOLDEYES

Office Address: One Portage Ave E, Winnipeg, Manitoba R3B 3N3.
Telephone: (204) 982-2273. **Fax:** (204) 982-2274.
Email Address: goldeyes@goldeyes.com. **Website:** www.goldeyes.com.
Operated by: Winnipeg Goldeyes Baseball Club, Inc.
Principal Owner/President: Sam Katz. **General Manager:** Andrew Collier. **Vice President & COO:** Regan Katz. **CFO:** Jason McRae-King. **Director, Sales/Marketing:** Dan Chase. **Manager, Box Office:** Paul Duque. **Coordinator, Food/Beverage:** Melissa Schlichting. **Account Executives:** Steve Schuster, Will Sutton, Bill Hibbard. **Suite Manager/Sales & Marketing:** Angela Sanche. **Media Coordinator:** Jason Young. **Manager, Retail:** Kendra Gibson. **Controller:** Kim Saito. **Facility Manager:** Don Ferguson.
Field Manager/Director, Player Procurement: Rick Forney. **Coach:** Kash Beauchamp. **Clubhouse Manager:** Jamie Samson. **Athletic Therapist:** Evan Fehr.

GAME INFORMATION

Radio Announcer: Steve Schuster. **No. of Games Broadcast:** 100. **Flagship Station:** CJNU 93.7 FM. **Stadium Name:** Shaw Park. **Location:** North on Pembina Highway to Broadway, East on Broadway to Main Street, North on Main Street to Water Avenue, East on Water Avenue to Westbrook Street, North on Westbrook Street to Lombard Avenue, East on Lombard Avenue to Mill Street, South on Mill Street to ballpark. **Standard Game Times:** Mon.-Fri., 7:00 pm, Sat., 6:00 pm, Sun., 1:00 pm.

ATLANTIC LEAGUE

Mailing Address: PO Box 5190, Lancaster, Pa., 17606.
Telephone: (303) 915-8414 or (978) 790-5421.
Email Address: suggestions@atlanticleague.com. **Website:** atlanticleague.com.
Year Founded: 1998.
Founder/Chairman: Frank Boulton.
Board of Directors: Brandon Bellamy, Frank Boulton, Jack Lavoie, Bill Shipley, Coy O. Willard, Jr., Bob Zuckerman.
President: Rick White. **League Administrator:** Emily Merrill.
Division Structure: Freedom—Lancaster, Long Island, Southern Maryland, York. **Liberty**—Gastonia, High Point, Lexington, West Virginia.
Regular Season: 120 games (split-schedule).
2021 Opening Date: May 27. **Closing Date:** Oct. 10.
Playoff Format: First-half division winners meet second-half winners in best-of-five series; Winners meet in best-of-five final for league championship.
Roster Limit: 25. **Eligibility Rule:** No restrictions; MLB and MiLB suspensions honored.
Brand of Baseball: Rawlings. **Statistical Service:** Major League Baseball.

STADIUM INFORMATION

Club	Stadium		Opened	LF	CF	RF	Capacity	2019 Att.
					Dimensions			
Gastonia	FUSE Stadium		2021	306	400	326	5,000	N/A
High Point Rockers	BB&T Point		2019	336	400	339	4,024	144,486
Lancaster	Clipper Magazine Stadium		2005	372	400	300	6,000	285,441
Lexington	Whitaker Bank Ballpark		2001	320	401	318	6,033	270,224
Long Island	Bethpage Ballpark		2000	325	400	325	6,002	328,194
So. Maryland	Regency Furniture Stadium		2008	305	400	320	6,000	200,889
West Virginia	Appalachian Power Park		2005	330	400	320	4,300	118,446
York	PeoplesBank Park		2007	300	400	325	5,000	199,045

GASTONIA HONEY HUNTERS

Address: 800 West Franklin Blvd., Gastonia, NC 28254. **Email:** info@gohoney-hunters.com. **Website:** www.gohoneyhunters.com.
Owner: Brandon Bellamy. **COO/GM:** David Martin.
Box Office Mgr.: Lauren Teer. **Operations Mgr.:** Brian Fisher. **Director of Food & Beverage:** Marcus Williams. **Account Executives:** Blair Minton, Nancy Rosemond, David Traylor, Floyd Louallen
Manager & Player Procurement: Mauro "Goose" Gozzo. **Hitting Coach:** Chuck Stewart. **Pitching Coach:** Reggie Harris.

GAME INFORMATION
Stadium Name: FUSE Stadium. **Game Times:** Mon-Sat–6:50 p.m., Sun–4:50 p.m.

HIGH POINT ROCKERS

Office Address: 301 N. Elm Street, High Point, NC 27262.
Telephone: (336) 888-1000.
E-Mail Address: info@highpointrockers.com. **Website:** highpointrockers.com
Owner: High Point Baseball, Inc.
Chairman, Board of Directors: Coy Williard. **President:** Pete Fisch. **General Manager:** Christian Heimall. **Director of Ticket Sales:** Susan Ormond. **Ticket Operations Manager:** Leighton Foster. **Facilities Operations Manager:** Shane Poling. **Sales Executive:** Caroline Cooling.
Promotions/Merchandise Manager: Mackenzie Barnes. **Director of Corporate Sales:** Caroline Keating. **Controller:** Matthew McCree. **Media Consultant:** Steve Shutt.
Field Manager: Jamie Keefe.

GAME INFORMATION
Games Broadcast: 120. **Flagship Station:** highpointrockers.com. **Stadium Name:** Truist Point. **Location:** 301 N. Elm Street, High Point, NC 27262. **Standard Game Times:** TBD

LEXINGTON LEGENDS

Address: 207 Legends Lane, Lexington, KY 40505. **Telephone:** (859) 252-4487. **Fax:** (859) 252-0747. **E-Mail Address:** community@lexingtonlegends.com. **Website:** www.lexingtonlegends.com.

Operated By: STANDS LLC. **Principal:** Susan Martinelli. **President/CEO:** Andy Shea. **Chief Operating Officer:** Jesse Scaglion.

Chief Brand Officer: Kara Shepherd. **Director of Ticket Sales & Service:** Colin Dodd. **Director of Fan Engagement:** Michael Allison.

Ticket Sales Manager: Ashley Grigsby. **Baseball Operations Manager:** Michael Koltak. **Retail Manager:** Sidney Laughlin. **Senior Corporate Sales Account Executive:** Ron Borkowski. **Corporate Sales Account Executive:** Adam Vrzal.

Field Manager: PJ Phillips. **Team Doctor:** Dr. Ben Kibler

GAME INFORMATION

Radio Announcer: TBD. **PA Announcer:** Bill Salee. **Official Scorer:** Joseph Hardiman.

Stadium Name: Whitaker Bank Ballpark. **Location:** From I-64/75, take exit 113, right onto North Broadway toward downtown Lexington for 1.2 miles, past New Circle Road (Highway 4), right into stadium, located adjacent to Northland Shopping Center. **Standard Game Times:** Tues., Thurs., Fri., 7:05 pm, Wed., 12:35 pm, Sat., 6:35 pm. Sun., 2:05 pm. **Ticket Price Range:** $5-$25.

LONG ISLAND DUCKS

Mailing Address: Fairfield Properties Ballpark, 3 Court House Dr, Central Islip, NY 11722.

Telephone: (631) 940-3825. **Fax:** (631) 940-3800.

Email Address: info@liducks.com. **Website:** liducks.com.

Operated by: Long Island Ducks Professional Baseball Club, LLC.

Founder/CEO: Frank Boulton. **Owner/Chairman:** Seth Waugh. **Owner:** Bud Harrelson. **President/General Manager:** Michael Pfaff. **Assistant GM/Senior VP, Sales:** Doug Cohen. **Senior Director, Administration:** Gerry Anderson. **VP, Sales/Operations:** John Wolff. **Director, Season Sales:** Brad Kallman.

Director, Media Relations/Broadcasting: Michael Polak. **Staff Accountant:** Annmarie DeMasi. **Manager, Group Sales:** Sean Smith. **Manager, Merchandise/Client Services:** Katelyn Paquette. **Head Groundskeeper:** Andrew Wright. **Coordinator, Administration:** Michelle Jensen. **Account Executives:** Anthony Fiorelli, Jack Fagan. **GM, Food & Beverage, Great South Bay Hospitality, LLC:** Alan Goodman.

Field Manager: Wally Backman. **Hitting Coach:** Lew Ford. **Pitching Coach:** TBD. **Coordinator, Medical Services:** Tony Amin. **Head Trainer:** Deanna Reynolds.

SOUTHERN MARYLAND BLUE CRABS

Office Address: 11765 St. Linus Drive, Waldorf, Maryland 20602.

Telephone: (301) 638-9788.

Principal Owners: Crabs On Deck LLC.

General Manager: Courtney Knichel. **Marketing Manager:** Sam Rubin. **Director, Communications:** Andrew Bandstra. **Operations Manager: Sheila Wilkerson Groundskeeper:** Ben Baker.

Field Manager: Stan Cliburn. **Bench Coach:** Joe Walsh. **Pitching Coach:** Daryl Thompson

GAME INFORMATION

Radio Announcer: Andrew Bandstra. **Stadium Name:** Regency Furniture Stadium.

Standard Game Times: Mon.-Sat., 6:35 pm; Sun. 2:05 pm.

WEST VIRGINIA POWER

Address: 601 Morris St., Suite 201, Charleston, WV 25301.

Telephone: (304) 344-2287.

E-Mail Address: info@wvpower.com. **Website:** www.wvpower.com.

Years in League: 2021.

OWNERSHIP/MANAGEMENT

Operatedn By: West Virginia Baseball, LLC. **Managing Partner/CEO:** Andy Shea. **Chief Operating Officer:** Jesse Scaglion.

General Manager: Jeremy Taylor. **Assistant General Manager/Director of Food & Beverage:** Aaron Simmons. **Accountant:** Darren Holstein. **Box Office Manager:** Zach Kurdin. **Director of Sales:** George Levandoski. **Game

Entertainment/Production Manager: Jenna Hruska. **Community Outreach Manager:** Lindsey Webb.
Manager: TBD.

GAME INFORMATION

Radio Announcer: David Kahn. **Stadium Name:** Appalachian Power Park. **Location:** I-77 South to Capitol Street exit, left on Lee Street, left on Brooks Street.

YORK REVOLUTION

Office Address: 5 Brooks Robinson Way, York, PA 17401.
Telephone: (717) 801-4487. **Fax:** (717) 801-4499.
Email Address: info@yorkrevolution.com. **Website:** yorkrevolution.com.
Operated by: York Professional Baseball Club, LLC.
Principal Owners: York Professional Baseball Club, LLC.
President: Eric Menzer. **General Manager/Vice President, Operations:** John Gibson. **VP, Business Development:** Nate Tile. **Finance Coordinator:** Jen Martin. **Director of Ticket and Retail Operations:** Cindy Brown. **Director, Marketing/Communications:** Doug Eppler. **Creative Director:** Cody Bannon. **Creative Services Manager:** Will Young. **Marketing Manager:** Sarah Dailey. **Director of Group Sales:** Brandon Tesluk. **Account Executive:** Devin Kolodziej. **Director, Client Services:** Tylor Toll. **Director, Operations:** David Dicce. **Revolution Hospitality GM:** Rob Wilson. **Revolution Hospitality Chef:** Tiffany Livering. **Revolution Hospitality Concessions Manager:** Amanda Shusko. **Director of Grounds and Field Operations:** Chris Carbaugh.
Field Manager: Mark Mason. **Bench/Third Base Coach:** Enohel Polanco.

GAME INFORMATION

WOYK GM/Broadcaster: Darrell Henry. **No. of Games Broadcast:** 120. **Flagship Station:** WOYK 1350 AM. **Official Scorer:** Brian Wisler. **Stadium Name:** PeoplesBank Park. **Standard Game Times:** Mon.-Sat., 6:30 pm, Sun., 2:00 pm. **Visiting Club Hotel:** Wyndham Garden York, 2000 Loucks Road, York, PA 17408. **Telephone:** (717) 846-9500.

FRONTIER LEAGUE

Office Address: 2041 Goose Lake Rd Suite 2A, Sauget, IL 62206.
Telephone: (618) 215-4134. **Fax:** (708) 286-6481
Email Address:office@frontierleague.com. **Website:** www.frontierleague.com.
Year Founded: 1993.
Commissioner Emeritus: Bill Lee.
Deputy Commissioners: Kevin Winn, Steve Tahsler. **Umpire Supervisor:** Deron Brown
President: John Stanley (Evansville) **Vice Presidents:** Brian Lyter (Schaumburg), Al Dorso (Sussex County), Tom Kramig (Lake Erie).
Board of Directors: David DelBello (Florence), Rich Sauget Jr. (Gateway), Nick Semaca (Joliet), Greg Lockard (New Jersey), Shawn Reilly (New York), Sam Katz (Ottawa), Michel Laplante (Quebec), Mike Pinto (Southern Illinois), Rick Murphy (Tri-City), Rene Martin (Trois-Rivieres), Stu Williams (Washington), Mike VerSchave (Windy City).
Division Structure – **Can-Am Conference:** Atlantic – New York, Quebec, Tri-City, Trois-Rivieres. Northeast – New Jersey, Ottawa, Sussex County, Washington.
Midwestern Conference: Central – Joliet, Lake Erie, Schaumburg, Windy City. West – Evansville, Gateway, Florence, Southern Illinois.
Regular Season: 96 games. **2021 Opening Date:** May 27. **Closing Date:** Sept 12.
Playoff Format: Division winners best-of-five series for conference championship. Conference champions in best-of-five championship series.
Roster Limit: 24. **Eligibility Rule:** Minimum of ten Rookie 1/Rookie 2 players. Maximum of three players born before October 1, 1992. **Brand of Baseball:** Rawlings.
Statistician: Pointstreak/Stack Sports, 5360 Legacy Drive, Suite #150, Plano, TX 75024.

STADIUM INFORMATION

Club	Stadium	Opened	LF	CF	RF	Capacity	2019 Att.
Evansville	Bosse Field	1915	315	415	315	5,110	100,051
Florence	UC Health Stadium	2004	325	395	325	4,200	99,308
Gateway	GCS Ballpark	2002	318	395	325	5,500	112,252
Joliet	DuPage Medical Group Field	2002	330	400	327	6,229	121,730
Lake Erie	Mercy Health Stadium	2009	325	400	325	5,000	100,915
New Jersey	Yogi Berra Stadium	1998	308	398	308	3,784	76,658
New York	Provident Bank Park	2011	323	403	313	4,750	123,999
Ottawa	RCGT Park	1993	325	404	325	n/a	
Quebec	Stade Canac de Québec	1938	315	385	315	4,500	119,060
Schaumburg	Schaumburg Stadium	1999	355	400	353	8,107	156,383
So. Illinois	Rent One Park	2007	325	400	330	4,500	101,441
Sussex County	Skylands Stadium	1994	330	392	330	4,200	72,594
Tri-City	Joseph L. Bruno Stadium	2002	325	400	325	4,500	131,529
Trois-Rivieres	Stade Quillorama	1938	342	372	342	4,500	85,506
Washington	Wild Things Park	2002	325	400	325	3,200	90,638
Windy City	Ozinga Field	1999	335	390	335	2,598	79,171

EVANSVILLE OTTERS

Mailing Address: 23 Don Mattingly Way, Evansville, IN 47711.
Telephone: (812) 435-8686.
Website: www.evansvilleotters.com.
Facebook—Evansville Otters, **Twitter**—@EvilleOtters, **Instagram**—@evansvilleotters
Operated by: Evansville Baseball, LLC.
Owner: Bussing family. **President:** John Stanley. **Vice President, Sales:** Joel Padfield. **General Manager:** Travis Painter. **Director of Communications:** Preston Leinenbach. **Account Executive:** Keith Millikan. **Director of Marketing/Community Relations:** Brittany Skinner. **PA Announcer:** Zane Clodfelter. **Field Manager:** Andy McCauley.

GAME INFORMATION

No. of Games Broadcast: Home-48, Away-48. **Radio/Video Stream:** evansvilleotters.com (Otters Digital Network). **Stadium Name:** Bosse Field (Opened in 1915). **Directions:** US 41 to Lloyd Expressway West (IN-62), Main St Exit, Right on Main St, ahead 1 mile to Bosse Field. **Standard Game Times:** Mon.-Sat., 6:35pm, Sun., 12:35pm, - 5:05pm.
Doubleheaders: 5:35 p.m. **Visiting Club Hotel:** The Comfort Inn & Suites, 3901 Highway 41 North, Evansville, IN 47711. Phone 812-423-5818.

GATEWAY GRIZZLIES

Telephone: (618) 337-3000. Email Address: info@gatewaygrizzlies.com.
Website: www.gatewaygrizzlies.com.
Owner: Rich Sauget.
General Manager: Steve Gomric. Assistant General Manager: Kurt Ringkamp. Assistant General Manager: James Caldwell. Director of Group Sales and Business Development: Brady Huber. Director of Promotions and Fan Engagement: Jennifer Wunder.
Manager: Phil Warren. Pitching Coach: Cam Roth. Hitting Coach: Darin Kinsolving. Director of Player Personnel: Bobby Brown. Bench Coach: Scott Brown.

GAME INFORMATION

No. of Games Broadcast: Home-48, Away-48. PA Announcer: Tom Calhoun. Stadium Name: GCS Credit Union Ballpark. Location: I-255 at exit 15 (Mousette Lane). Standard Game Times: Mon.-Sat., 7:05 pm, Sun., 6:05 pm.

JOLIET SLAMMERS

Office Address: 1 Mayor Art Schultz Dr, Joliet, IL 60432
Telephone: (815) 722-2287
E-Mail Address: info@jolietslammers.com. Website: www.jolietslammers.com.
Owner: Joliet Community Baseball & Entertainment, LLC.
General Manager: Heather Mills. Vice President, Sales & Marketing: John Wilson. Director of Food & Beverage: Tom Fremarek. Director of Community Relations: Ken Miller. Director of Sales: Lauren Rhodes. Team Photographer: Adam Jomant.
Field Manager/Director, Baseball Operations: Aaron Nieckula

GAME INFORMATION

No. of Games Broadcast: 96. Flagship Station: www.jolietslammers.com. Stadium Name: DuPage Medical Group Field. Location: 1 Mayor Art Schultz Drive, Joliet, IL 60432. Standard Game Times: Mon.-Fri., 7:05 pm, Sat., 6:05 pm., Sun., 1:05 pm.

LAKE ERIE CRUSHERS

Address: 2009 Baseball Boulevard. Avon, Ohio 44011.
Telephone: 440-934-3636. Website: www.lakeeriecrushers.com.
Operated by: Blue Dog Baseball, LLC. Managing Officer: Tom Kramig. Sr. Vice President: Matt Moos.
Director of Stadium Operations: Wayne Loeblein. Controller: DJ Saylor. Director, Concessions/Catering: Greg Kobunski. Digital Marketing Manager: Eric Davies. Promotions Manager: Allison Albers. Sr. Ticketing Manager: Kyle Wagoner. Account Executives: Katelyn Caniford, Justin Peck. Box Office Manager: Patrick Crumb. Director, Broadcasting: Andy Barch.
Field Manager: Dan Rohn.

GAME INFORMATION

Stadium Name: Mercy Health Stadium. Location: Intersection of I-90 and Colorado Ave in Avon, OH. Standard Game Times: Mon-Fri., 7:05 pm, Sat., 6:05 pm, Sun., 2:05 pm.

NEW JERSEY JACKALS

Office Address: 8 Yogi Berra Drive, Little Falls, NJ 07424. Telephone: (973) 746-7434.
Email Address: contact@jackals.com. Website: www.jackals.com.
Owner/President: Al Dorso. President, Baseball Operations: Gregory Lockard.
Sr. Vice President, Operations: Al Dorso Jr. Vice President, Marketing: Mike Dorso. General Manager: Gil Addeo. Director, Creative Services: William Romano. Public Relations: Chris Faust
Field Manager: Brooks Carey.

GAME INFORMATION

No. of Games Broadcast: 96. Webcast Address: www.jackals.com. Stadium Name: Yogi Berra Stadium. Location: On the campus of Montclair State University; Route 80 or Garden State Parkway to Route 46, take Valley Road exit to Montclair State University. Standard Game Times: Mon.-Fri., 7:05 pm, Sat., 6:05 pm., Sun., 2:05 pm.

NEW YORK BOULDERS

Team President/GM/Managing Partner: Shawn Reilly. **EVP:** Rob Janetschek. **Assistant GM, Box Office & Digital Media:** Megan Ciampo. **VP of Business Development:** Seth Cantor. **Director of Finance:** Michele Almash. **Director of Brand Marketing:** Julie Trainor. **Ticket Sales Manager:** Karen McCombs. **Assistant Ticket Sales Manager:** Courtney Vardi. **Media Relations:** Ken Kostik. **Facilities and Operations Coordinator:** Bobby Nodelman. **Educational Director:** Gail Gultz. **PR & Media Coordinator:** Steve Balsan. **Spectacor Office Manager:** Tara Culwell. **Field Manager:** TJ Stanton. **Player Procurement/Scouting:** Kevin Tuve.

GAME INFORMATION

Stadium Name: Palisades Credit Union Park. **Location:** 1 Palisades Credit Union Park Drive. **Standard Game Times:** Mon.-Fri. 7pm, Sat. 6:30pm. Sun. May/June. 1:30pm. July/August. 5pm

OTTAWA TITANS

Address: 300 Coventry Road, Ottawa, Ontario, K1K 4P5. **Telephone:** 343-633-2273. **Operated by:** Ottawa Titans Baseball Inc. **Principal Owner/President:** Sam Katz. **Co-Owners:** Ottawa Sports & Entertainment Group, Jacques J.M. Shore. **Vice President:** Regan Katz. **Assistant GM:** Sebastien Boucher. **Vice President, Sales & Operations:** Davyd Balloch. **Media Manager/Broadcaster:** Davide Disipio. **Clubhouse Manager:** Marc Leduc. **Field Manager:** Steve Brook.

GAME INFORMATION

Stadium Name: Raymond Chabot Grant Thornton Park (RCGT Park). **Location:** 300 Coventry Road, Ottawa, Ontario.

QUEBEC CAPITALES

Owners: Jean Tremblay, Pierre Tremblay, Michel Laplante **President:** Michel Laplante. **General Manager:** Charles Demers. **Director of Baseball Operations and Media Relations:** Jean Grignon-Francke. **Accounting:** Frederique Plamondon. **Ticketing Coordinator:** Philippe Turmel. **Promotions and Community Coordinator. Fondation of Capitales:** Janel Laplante. **Administrative assistant:** Francine Gendron. **Victoria Baseball Complex:** Alexandre Harvey. **Graphic consultant:** Frédéric Gariépy. **Gift Shop Manager:** Jean-Philippe Otis. **Field Manager:** Patrick Scalabrini.

GAME INFORMATION

Stadium Name: Stade Canac de Québec. **Location:** Highway 40 to Highway 173 (Centre-Ville) exit 2 to Parc Victoria. **Standard Game Times:** Mon.-Fri., 7:05 pm, Sat., 6:05 pm, Sun., 1:05 pm.

SOUTHERN ILLINOIS MINERS

Office Address: Rent One Park, 1000 Miners Drive, Marion, IL 62959. **Telephone:** (618) 998-8499. **Fax:** (618) 969-8550. **Email Address:** info@southernillinoisminers.com. **Website:** southernillinoisminers.com. **Operated by:** Southern Illinois Baseball Group. **Owner:** Jayne Simmons. **Chief Operating Officer:** Mike Pinto. **General Manager:** Cathy Perry. **Assistant General Manager:** Will Niermann. **Stadium Operations:** Nick Nelson. **Director, Video Production/Creative Services:** Jon Weaver. **Director, Promotions:** Jake Varney. **Director, Radio Broadcasting/Media Relations:** Jason Guerette. **Account Executives:** Cole Landon, Austin Elkin. **Field Manager:** Mike Pinto. **Hitting Coach:** TBA. **Instructor:** Ralph Santana. **Strength & Conditioning Coordinator:** Chris Stone.

GAME INFORMATION

Games Broadcast: www.103.5espn.com. **Stadium Name:** Rent One Park. **Location:** US 57 to Route 13 East, right at Halfway Road to Fairmont Drive. **Standard Game Times:** Mon-Fri., 7:05 pm, Sat., 6:05 pm, Sun., 5:05 pm. **Visiting Club Hotel:** Best Western, 400 Comfort Drive, Marion, IL 62959. **Phone:** 618-998-1220.

SCHAUMBURG BOOMERS

Office Address: 1999 Springinsguth Road, Schaumburg, IL 60193
Email Address: info@boomersbaseball.com. **Website:** www.boomersbaseball.com.
Owned by: Pat and Lindy Salvi.
Vice President & General Manager: Michael Larson. **Assistant GM:** Anthony Giammanco.
Director of Facilities: Mike Tlusty. **Director Food/Beverage:** Devin Maney. **Broadcaster:** Tim Calderwood.
Box Office Manager: Alec Marovitz. **Director of Promotions:** Lexi Fiolka. **Director of Community Relations:** Peter Long.
Account Executive: Hanna Olson. **Corporate Sales Executive:** Pete Thompson.
Field Manager: Jamie Bennett.

GAME INFORMATION

Broadcaster: Tim Calderwood. **No. of Games Broadcast:** Home-48, Away-48. **Flagship Station:** WRMN 1410 AM Elgin.
Stadium: Wintrust Field. **Location:** I-290 to Thorndale Ave Exit, head West on Elgin-O'Hare Expressway until Springinsguth
Road Exit, second left at Springinsguth Road (shared parking lot with Schaumburg Metra Station). **Visiting Club Hotel:**
SpringHill Suites 1550 McConnor Pkwy, Schaumburg, IL 60173

SUSSEX COUNTY MINERS

Owner, President: Al Dorso Sr. **Vice President, Operations:** Al Dorso Jr.
Vice President, Marketing: Mike Dorso. **General Manager:** Justin Ferrarella.
Director, Broadcasting and Media Relations: Bret Leuthner. **Manager, Corporate
Sales:** Joann Ciancitto. **Youth Programs Coordinator:** Adrienne Lina. **Senior Graphic
Design:** Will Romano. **Broadcasting, PXP, & Media Relations:** Sean Bretherick. **Social Media Coordinator:** Carolyn Clites.
Manager, Facilities: Shane White. **Group Sales Manager:** Alex Kashmann.
Field Manager/Director of Baseball Operations: Bobby Jones. **President, Baseball Operations:** Greg Lockard.

GAME INFORMATION

Broadcaster: Bret Leuthner. **No. of Games Broadcast:** 100. **Webcast Address:** www.scminers.com. **Stadium Name:**
Skylands Stadium. **Location:** In New Jersey, I-80 to exit 34B (Route 15 North) to Route 565 North; From Pennsylvania, I-84
to Route 6 (Matamoras) to Route 206 North to Route 565 North. **Standard Game Times:** Mon.-Fri., 7:05 pm, Sat., 6:05 pm,
Sun., 2:05 pm

TRI-CITY VALLEYCATS

Office Address: Joseph L Bruno Stadium, 80 Vandenburg Ave, Troy, NY 12180.
Mailing Address: PO Box 694, Troy, NY 12181.
Telephone: (518) 629-2287. **Fax:** (518) 629-2299.
E-Mail Address: info@tcvalleycats.com. **Website:** www.tcvalleycats.com

OWNERSHIP/MANAGEMENT

Operated By: Tri-City ValleyCats Inc. **Principal Owners:** Martin Barr, John Burton, Doug Gladstone, Rick Murphy, Alfred
Roberts, Stephen Siegel. **President:** Rick Murphy. **General Manager:** Matt Callahan. **Assistant GM:** Michelle Skinner.
Ticket Office and Operations Manager: Jessica Guido. **Food & Beverage Manager:** Missy Henry. **Stadium Operations
Manager:** Derek Norberg.

FIELD STAFF

Manager: Pete Incaviglia. **Hitting Coach:** TBD. **Pitching Coach:** TBD.
Radio Announcer: TBD. **No. of Games Broadcast:** 48. **Flagship Station:** TBD. **PA Announcer:** Anthony Pettograsso.
Official Scorer: TBD. **Stadium Name:** Joseph Bruno Stadium. **Location:** From north, I-87 to exit 7 (Route 7), go east 1
1/2 miles to I-787 South, to Route 378 East, go over bridge to Route 4, right to Route 4 South, one mile to Hudson Valley
Community College campus on left; From south, I-87 to exit 23 (I-787), I-787 north six miles to exit for Route 378 east, over
bridge to Route 4, right to Route 4 South, one mile to campus on left; From east, Massachusetts Turnpike to exit B-1 (I-90),
nine miles to Exit 8 (Defreestville), left off ramp to Route 4 North, five miles to campus on right; From west, I-90 to exit 24
(I-90 East), I-90 East for six miles to I-787 North (Troy), 2.2 miles to exit for Route 378 East, over bridge to Route 4, right to
Route 4 south for one mile to campus on left. **Standard Game Times:** 7pm, Sun. 5 pm. **Ticket Price Range:** $5.50-$12.50.
Visiting Club Hotel: The Desmond Hotel Albany, 660 Albany-Shaker Road, Albany, NY 12211. **Telephone:** (518) 869-8100.

TROIS-RIVIÈRES AIGLES

Office Address: 1760 Avenue Gilles-Villeneuve, Trois-Rivières, QC G9A 5K8.
Telephone: (819) 379-0404. **Email Address:** info@lesaiglestr.com.
Website: www.lesaiglestr.com
Owners: Côté-Reco Group and Vertdure Group
President: René Martin. **General Manager:** Simon Laliberté.
Director, Marketing: Zoé Newbury. **Operations Director:** Frédérik Bélanger.
Advisor, Partnerships And Events: Étienne Rivard. **Ticketing Coordinator:** Sylvie Dubé.
Field Manager: Matt Rusch. **Coaches:** Kyle Lafrenz, Luis Alen.

GAME INFORMATION

No. of Games Broadcast: 48. **Webcast Address:** www.cfou.ca/direct.php.
Stadium Name: Stade Quillorama. **Location:** Take Hwy 40 West, exit Boul. des Forges/Centre-ville, keep right, turn right at light, turn right at stop sign.

WASHINGTON WILD THINGS

Office Address: One Washington Federal Way, Washington, PA 15301.
Telephone: (724) 250-9555. **Fax:** (724) 250-2333.
Email Address: info@washingtonwildthings.com. **Website:** washingtonwildthings.com.
Owned by: Sports Facility, LLC. **Operated by:** Washington Frontier League Baseball, LLC.
Managing Partner: Francine W. Williams. **Executive Director:** Steve Zavacky.
President/General Manager: Tony Buccilli. **Vice President of Corporate Partnerships:** Christine Blaine. **Ticket Sales and Community Relations Manager:** Hanna Luckenbach. **Broadcaster and Ticket Manager:** Kyle Dawson. **Vice President, Finance:** JJ Heider. **Creative Services:** Craig Lion.
Field Manager: Tom Vaeth.

GAME INFORMATION

Stadium Name: Wild Things Park. **Location:** I-70 to exit 15 (Chestnut Street), right on Chestnut Street to Washington Crown Center Mall, right at mall entrance, right on to Mall Drive to stadium. **Standard Game Times:** Mon.-Sat., 7:05 pm, Sun., 5:35 pm. **Visiting Club Hotel:** Red Roof Inn.

WINDY CITY THUNDERBOLTS

Office Address: 14011 South Kenton Avenue, Crestwood, IL 60418
Telephone: (708) 489-2255. **Fax:** (708) 489-2999.
Email Address: info@wcthunderbolts.com. **Website:** www.wcthunderbolts.com.
Owned by: Franchise Sports, LLC.
General Manager: Mike VerSchave. **Assistant GM:** Bill Waliewski. **Director, Community Relations:** Johnny Sole, **Director, Not-For-Profit Events:** Karen Engel.
Field Manager: Brian Smith.

GAME INFORMATION

Director of Media Relations: Terry Bonadonna. **No. of Games Broadcast:** 96. **Flagship Station:** WXAV, 88.3 FM. **Official Scorer:** Chris Gbur. **Stadium Name:** Ozinga Field. **Location:** I-294 to South Cicero Ave, exit (Route 50), south for 1 1/2 miles, left at Midlothian Turnpike, right on Kenton Ave; I-57 to 147th Street, west on 147th to Cicero, north on Cicero, right on Midlothian Turnpike, right on Kenton. **Standard Game Times:** Mon.-Fri., 7:05 pm, Sat., 6:05 pm, Sun., 2:05 pm. **Visiting Club Hotel:** Georgio's Quality Inn & Suites, 8800 W 159th St, Orland Park, IL 60462. **Telephone:** (708) 403-1100.

PIONEER BASEBALL LEAGUE

Office Address: 812 W. 30th Avenue, Spokane, WA 99203.
Telephone: (509) 456-7615. **Fax:** (509) 456-0136.
E-Mail Address: fanmail@pioneerleague.com.
Website: www.pioneerleague.com.
Years League Active: 1939-42, 1946-
President: Mike Shapiro. **Comissioner:** Jim McCurdy.
Directors: Dave Baggott (Ogden), Peter C. Davis (Missoula), Chris Phillips (Rocky Mountain), Kevin Greene (Idaho Falls), Hal Roth (Grand Junction), Vinny Purpura (Great Falls), Dave Heller (Billings), Jeff Eiseman (Boise) and Jeff Katofsky (Windsor).
Regular Season: 96 games (split schedule). **2021 Opening Date:** May 22. **Closing Date:** Sept. 10.
Playoff Format: Single-game playoff. Winners meet in best-of-three series for league championship. **Roster Limit:** 25 active, minimum of 22 dressed for each game. **Player Eligibility Rule:** TBA. **Brand of Baseball:** Rawlings.

STADIUM INFORMATION

Club	Stadium	Opened	Dimensions LF	CF	RF	Capacity	2019 Att.
Billings	Dehler Park	2008	329	410	350	3,071	96,594
Boise	Memorial Stadium	1989	335	400	335	3,426	129,805
Grand Junction	Sam Suplizio Field	1949	302	400	333	7,014	102,015
Great Falls	Centene Stadium at Legion Park	1956	335	414	335	3,800	83,826
Idaho Falls	Melaleuca Field	1976	340	400	350	3,400	81,870
Missoula	Ogren Park at Allegiance Field	2004	309	398	287	3,500	87,981
Ogden	Lindquist Field	1997	335	396	334	5,000	88,751
Rocky Mountain	Security Service Field	1988	350	410	350	8,500	88,112

BILLINGS MUSTANGS

Office Address: Dehler Park, 2611 9th Avenue North, Billings, MT 59101.
Mailing Address: PO Box 1553, Billings, MT 59103-1553.
Telephone: (406) 252-1241. **Fax:** (406) 252-2968.
E-Mail Address: mustangs@billingsmustangs.com. **Website:** billingsmustangs.com.
Years in League: 1948-63, 1969-
Operated By: Mustangs Baseball LLC.
President/CEO: Dave Heller. **General Manager:** Gary Roller. **Director, Stadium Operations:** Matt Schoonover. **Director, Broadcasting/Media Relations:** TBA. **Director, Food and Beverage Services:** Curt Prchal. **Director, Field Operations:** Sam Sheets.

FIELD STAFF

Manager: TBA. **Hitting Coach:** TBA. **Pitching Coach:** TBA. **Bench Coach:** TBA. **Athletic Trainer:** TBA. **Strength & Conditioning Coach:** TBA.
Game information
Radio Broadcaster: TBA. **No. of Games Broadcast:** 96. **Flagship Station:** ESPN 910-AM KBLG. **PA Announcer:** Sarah Spangle. **Official Scorer:** Evan O'Kelly. **Stadium Name:** Dehler Park. **Location:** I-90 to Exit 450, north on 27th Street North to 9th Avenue North. **Standard Game Times:** Mon.–Sat., 6:35 pm, Sun., 1:05 pm. **Ticket Price Range:** $6-$12.

BOISE HAWKS

Address: 5600 N. Glenwood St. Boise, ID 83714.
Telephone: (208) 322-5000. **Fax:** (208) 322-6846.
Website: www.boisehawks.com
Years in League: 1975-76, 1978, 1987-Present.
Operated by: Boise Professional Baseball LLC. **President:** Jeff Eiseman. **HR & Operations:** Missy Martin. **Vice President:** Bob Flannery. **General Manager:** Mike Van Hise. **Director, Stadium Ops/Food & Beverage:** Jake Lusk. **Manager, Accounting/Office:** Judy Peterson. **Ticket Sales Manager:** Matt Osbon. **Group Event Executive:** Colton Hampson. **Account Executive:** Kristi Croteau, Andrew Lee. **Assistant Director, Stadium Operations:** Christian Lomeli. **Media Relations/Marketing Manager:** Paige Plotzke. **Head Groundskeeper:** John Gides.

FIELD STAFF

Manager: Gary Van Tol. **Hitting Coach:** Travis Buck. **Pitching Coach:** Michiel van Kampen.

GAME INFORMATION

Radio Announcer: Leonard Barry. **No. of Games Broadcast:** 96. **Flagship Station:** TBD. **PA Announcer:** Jeremy Peterson. **Official Scorer:** Curtis Haines. **Stadium Name:** Memorial Stadium. **Location:** I-84 to Cole Rd., north to Western Idaho Fairgrounds at 5600 North Glenwood St. **Standard Game Time:** 7:15 pm. **Ticket Price Range:** $8-35. **Visiting Club Hotel:** Simple Suites.

GRAND JUNCTION ROCKIES

Address: 1315 North Ave., Grand Junction, CO, 81501
Telephone: (970) 255-7625. **Fax:** (970) 241-2374
Email: mritter@gjrockies.com. **Website:** www.gjrockies.com
Years in League: 2001–
Principal Owners/Operated by: GJR, LLC. **President:** Mick Ritter. **Assistant GM:** Matt Allen. **Director of Broadcasting and Sales:** Kyle Kercheval.

FIELD STAFF
Manager: TBA. **Hitting Coach:** TBA. **Pitching Coach:** TBA. **Supervisor:** TBA.

GAME INFORMATION
Radio Announcer: Kyle Kercheval. **No. of Games Broadcast:** 98. **Flagship Station:** TBA, gjrockies.com. **Television Announcer:** Kyle Kercheval. No. **of Games Televised:** 48. **Flagship:** KGJT, My Network, Dish Network. **Produced by:** Colorado Mesa University. **PA Announcer:** Tim Ray. **Official Scorers:** Unknown. **Stadium Name:** Suplizio Field. **Location:** 1315 North Ave. Grand Junction, CO 81501. **Standard Game Times:** 6:40 pm. **Ticket Price Range:** $7-$12.

GREAT FALLS VOYAGERS

Address: 1015 25th St N, Great Falls, MT 59401.
Telephone: (406) 452-5311. **Fax:** (406) 454-0811.
E-Mail Address: voyagers@gfvoyagers.com. **Website:** www.gfvoyagers.com.
Years in League: 1948-1963, 1969-

OWNERSHIP/MANAGEMENT
Operated By: Great Falls Baseball Club.
CEO: Vinny Purpura. **President:** Scott Reasoner. **General Manager:** Scott Lettre.

FIELD STAFF
Manager: Tommy Thompson. **Hitting Coach:** TBD. **Pitching Coach:** TBD.

GAME INFORMATION
Radio Announcer: Shawn Tiemann. **No. of Games Broadcast:** 96. **Flagship Station:** KXGF-1400 AM. **PA Announcer:** Chris Evans. **Official Scorer:** Mike Lewis. **Stadium Name:** Centene Stadium. **Location:** From I-15 to exit 281 (10th Ave S), left on 26th, left on Eighth Ave North, right on 25th, ballpark on right, past railroad tracks. **Ticket Price Range:** $8-15. **Visiting Club Hotel:** Days Inn, 101 14th Ave NW, Great Falls, MT 59404. **Telephone:** (406) 727-6565

IDAHO FALLS CHUKARS

Office Address: 900 Jim Garchow Way, Idaho Falls, ID 83402.
Mailing Address: PO 2183, Idaho, ID 83403.
Telephone: (208) 522-8363. **Fax:** (208) 522-9858.
E-Mail Address: chukarsbaseball@gmail.com. **Website:** www.ifchukars.com.
Years in League: 1940-42, 1946-

OWNERSHIP/MANAGEMENT
Operated By: The Elmore Sports Group. **Principal Owner:** David Elmore.
President/General Manager: Kevin Greene. **Vice President:** Paul Henderson. **Assistant GM:** Chris Hall. **Clubhouse Manager:** TBA. **Head Groundskeeper:** Tony McCarty.

FIELD STAFF
Manager: TBA. **Hitting Coach:** TBA. **Pitching Coach:** TBA.

GAME INFORMATION
Radio Announcer: John Balginy. **No. of Games Broadcast:** 96. **Flagship Station:** ESPN 980-AM & 94.5 and 105.1FM. **PA Announcer:** Javier Hernandez. **Official Scorer:** John Balginy. **Stadium Name:** Melaleuca Field. **Location:** I-15 to West Broadway exit, left onto Memorial Drive, right on Mound Avenue, 1/4 mile to the stadium. **Standard Game Times:** Mon.-Sat., 7:15 pm, Sun., 4:00 pm. **Ticket Price Range:** $10-14. **Visiting Club Hotel:** Shilo Inn, 780 Lindsay Blvd, Idaho Falls, ID 83402. **Telephone:** (208) 523-0088.

MISSOULA PADDLEHEADS

Address: 140 N Higgins, Suite 201, Missoula, MT 59802. Telephone: (406) 543-3300. E-Mail Address: mellis@gopaddleheads.com. Website: www.gopaddleheads.com.
Years in League: 1956-60, 1999-
Operated By: Big Sky Professional Baseball LLC. Co-Chairs: Peter & Susan Crampton Davis.
Vice President: Matt Ellis. Director of Sales: Kim Klages Johns. Director of Marketing & PR: Taylor Rush. Director of Entertainment and Promotions: Sam Boyd. Retail Manager: Dawna Kulaski. Stadium Operations Manager: Brett Shure. Director of Sales: Kim Klages Johns Office Manager: Jeanie Leidholt. Accounting Manager: Judy Powell. Ticket Sales & Box Office Specialist: Halle Nurse.

FIELD STAFF
Manager: TBA. Hitting Coach: TBA. Pitching Coach: TBA. Bench Coach: TBA. Athletic Trainer: TBA. Strength & Conditioning Coach: TBA.

GAME INFORMATION
Radio Announcer: TBA. No. of Games Broadcast: 98. Flagship Station: ESPN 102.9 FM. PA Announcer: TBA. Official Scorer: TBA. Stadium Name: Ogren Park Allegiance Field. Location: 700 Cregg Lane, Missoula MT 59801
Directions: Take Orange Street to Cregg Lane, west on Cregg Lane, stadium west of McCormick Park past railroad trestle. Standard Game Times: Mon.-Sat., 7:05 pm, Sun., 5:05 pm. Ticket Price Range: $9-$17.

OGDEN RAPTORS

Address: 2330 Lincoln Ave, Ogden, UT 84401. Telephone: (801) 393-2400. Fax: (801) 393-2473.
E-Mail Address: homerun@ogden-raptors.com. Website: www.ogden-raptors.com.
Years in League: 1939-42, 1946-55, 1966-74, 1994-Present
Operated By: Ogden Professional Baseball, Inc. Principal Owners: Dave Baggott, John Lindquist.
President/General Manager: Dave Baggott. Director, Media Relations/Broadcaster: Andrew Haynes. Assistant General Manager: Trever Wilson. Assistant Director of Game Day Operations: Richard Armstrong. Director, Social Media: Kevin Johnson. Director, Information Technology: Chris Greene. Public Relations: Pete Diamond. Groundskeeper: Kenny Kopinski. Assistant Groundskeeper: Bob Richardson.

FIELD STAFF
Manager: TBD. Hitting Coach: TBD. Pitching Coach: TBD. Clubhouse Manager: Dave "MacGyver" Ackerman.

GAME INFORMATION
Radio Announcer: Andrew Haynes. No. of Games Broadcast: 96. Flagship Station: ogden-raptors.com. PA Announcer: Pete Diamond. Official Scorer: Dennis Kunimura. Stadium Name: Lindquist Field. Location: I-15 North to 21th Street exit, east to Lincoln Avenue, south three blocks to park. Standard Game Times: Mon.-Sat., 7 pm, Sun., 4pm. Ticket Price Range: $6-12. Visiting Club Hotel: Unavailable.

ROCKY MOUNTAIN VIBES

Address: 4385 Tutt Blvd., Colorado Springs, CO 80922.
Telephone: (719) 597-1449. Fax: (719) 597-2491.
E-Mail address: info@vibesbaseball.com. Website: www.vibesbaseball.com.
Years in League: 2019-
Operated By: Rocky Mountain Vibes. Principal Owner: Dave Elmore. President/General Manager: Chris Phillips. Assistant GM: Keith Hodges.
Ticketing/Merchandise Manager: Aaron Griffith. Director Promotions: Cliff Cage. Director, Marketing: Kyle Fritzke. VP, Field Operations: Steve DeLeon. Group Sales Manager: Jake Hathaway. Event Manager: Brien Smith. Clubhouse Manager: David Ortiz

FIELD STAFF
Manager: Dave Hajek. Pitching Coach: Mark Lee

GAME INFORMATION
No. of Games Broadcast: 96. Flagship Station: TuneIn. PA Announcer: TBD. Official Scorer: TBD. Stadium Name: UCHealth Park. Location: I-25 South to Woodmen Road exit, east on Woodmen to Powers Blvd., right on Powers to Barnes Road. Standard Game Times: Mon.-Fri., 6:40 pm, Sat., 6:00 pm, Sun., 1:30 pm. Ticket Price Range: $5-15.

INDEPENDENT LEAGUES

PECOS LEAGUE

Website: www.PecosLeague.com.
Address: PO Box 271489, Houston, TX 77277.
Telephone: (575) 680-2212.
E-mail: info@pecosleague.com.
Commissioner: Andrew Dunn.
Pacific All-Star Game: Monterey July 5
Mountain All-Star Game: (site TBA) July 12
Mountain Division—Almogordo, N.M.; Alpine Cowboys, Alpine, Texas; Colorado Springs Snow Sox, Colorado Springs, Colo.; Garden City Wind, Garden City, Kan.; Roswell Invaders, Roswell, N.M.; Salina Stockade, Salina, Kan.; Santa Fe Fuego, Santa Fe, N.M.; Trinidad Triggers, Trinidad, Colo.; Tucson Saguaros, Tucson, Ariz.
Pacific Division—Bakersfield Train Robbers, Bakersfield, Calif.; California City Whiptails, California City, Calif.; High Desert Yardbirds, High Desert, Calif.; Martinez Sturgeon, Martinez, Calif.; Monterey Amberjacks, Monterey, Calif.; San Rafael Pacifics, San Rafael, Calif.; Santa Cruz Seaweed, Santa Cruz, Calif.; Wasco Reserves, Wasco Calif.
Year Founded: 2010.
Regular Season: 64 games. **Start Date:** June 2. **Finish Date:** Aug. 5.
Eligibility Rules: 25 and under.
Brand of Baseball: Rawlings.

UNITED SHORE PROFESSIONAL BASEBALL LEAGUE

Location: Jimmy Johns Field. 7171 Auburn Rd, Utica, MI. 48317
Telephone: (248) 601-2400
Email: baseballoperations@uspbl.com. **Website:**www.uspbl.com
Ownership Group: General Sports & Entertainment. **CEO:** Andrew D. Appelby. **COO:** Dana L. Schmitt.
Director of Premium Sales and Services: Jonathon Hebel. **VP of Groups Sales & Events:** Theresa Doan. **VP of Client Services:** Jeremiah Hergott. **Director of Ballpark Operations:** Dillon Dubois. **Senior Director of Marketing & PR:** Katie Page. **Director of Food & Beverage:** Nathan Liska.
Director of Baseball Operations: Justin Orenduff. **Director of Baseball Administration:** Mike Zielinski. **Fielding Coordinator:** Paul Niggebrugge.
Teams: Birmingham-Bloomfield Beavers, Eastside Diamond Hoppers, Utica Unicorns, Westside Woolly Mammoths.
Managers: Birmingham-Von Joshua; Eastside-Paul Noce; Utica-Jim Essian; Westside-Paul Niggebrugge.
DVS Pitching: Shane McCatty. **DVS Performance:** Alan Oaks. **Scouting Consultant:** Ryan Pothakos. **Development Coaches:** Pat Biondi, John Dombrowski, Daniel Jipping. **Scouting Advisor:** Ray Ortega.
Roster Limit: 20. **Eligibility Rules:** Players must be between 18 and 26 years old.
2021 Start Date: May 28th. **End Date:** Sept. 4. **All-Star Game:** July 10. **Playoffs:** Sept. 10-12. **Season length:** 50 games per team. **Playoff Format:** Single-game elimination.

INTERNATIONAL

AMERICAS

MEXICO
MEXICAN LEAGUE

NOTE: The Mexican League is a member of the National Association of Professional Baseball Leagues and has a Triple-A classification. However, its member clubs operate largely independent of the 30 major league teams, and for that reason the league is listed in the international section.

Address: Avenida Insurgentes Sur #797 Interior 3 y 4. Col. Nápoles. C.P. 03810, Benito Juárez, Ciudad de México.. **Telephone:** 52-5557-1007. **E-Mail Address:** oficina@lmb.com.mx. **Website:** lmb.com.mx.

Years League Active: 1955-.

President: Horacio De la Vega Flores. **Director, Administration:** Oscar Neri Rojas Salazar.

Division Structure: North—Aguascalientes, Dos Laredos, Durango, Laguna, Monclova, Monterrey, Saltillo, Tijuana. **South**—Campeche, Leon, Mexico City, Oaxaca, Puebla, Quintana Roo, Tabasco, Yucatan.

Regular Season: 114 games (split-schedule). **2021 Opening Date:** May 20. **Closing Date:** Aug. 6.

Playoff Format: Five teams from each division qualify for a four-round playoff. Championship round is best-of-seven series.

Roster Limit: 28. **Roster Limit, Imports:** 7.

AGUASCALIENTES RIELEROS
Office Address: Andador Manuel Madrigal 102 Héroes 20190 Aguascalientes. **Telephone:** 01 449 915 15 96 y 97. **E-Mail Address:** rieleros.2020redes@rielerosags.com. **Website:** rielerosags.com
Manager: Luis Rivera.

CAMPECHE PIRATAS
Office Address: Calle Filiberto Qui Farfan No. 2, Col. Camino Real, CP 24020, Campeche, Campeche. **Telephone:** (52) 981-827-4759. **E-Mail Address:** piratas@prodigy.net.mx. **Website:** piratasdecampeche.mx.
President: Jorge Carlos hurtado Montero. **General Manager:** Gabriel Lozano Berron.
Manager: Francisco Campos.

DOS LAREDOS TECOLOTES
Office Address: Reforma 4310, Col. México, Nuevo Laredo, Tamps. **Telephone:** (52) 1 867 279 8519. **E-Mail Address:** contacto@tecolotes2laredos.com. **Website:** tecolotes2laredos.com.
President: Jose Antonio Mansur. **General Manager:** Chara Mansur Beltran.
Manager: Pablo Ortega.

DURANGO GENERALES
Office Address: De Los Deportes, Unidad Deportiva, 98065_00 Zacatecas, ZAC. **Telephone:**(52) 667-788-9900. **E-Mail Address:** info@generales.mx. **Website:** generales.mx.
President: Virgilio Ruiz Isassi.
Manager: Felix Fermin.

LAGUNA ALGODONEROS
Office Address: Algodoneros Unión Laguna Juan Gutemberg s/n C.P. 27000 Torreón, Coah. Estadio Revolución. **Telephone:** (52) 871-718-5515. **E-Mail Address:** info@unionlaguna.mx. **Website:** unionlaguna.mx.
President: Francisco Orozco Marín. **General Manager:** Jorge Luis Lechuga Torres.
Manager: Omar Malave.

LEON BRAVES
Office Address: Estadio Domingo Santana Boulevard Congreso de Chilpancingo 803, Unidad Deportiva. León Guanajuato, México. CP 37237. **Telephone:** (52) 477-272-8675. **E-Mail Address:** contacto@bravosdeleon.mx. **Website:** bravosdeleon.com.
President: Arturo Blanco Díaz. **General Manager:** Daniel Espino.
Manager: Tim Johnson.

MEXICO CITY DIABLOS ROJOS
Office Address: Av río Churubusco #1001, Colonia ex-ejidos de la Magdalena Mixhuca, Alcaldía Iztacalco, C.P. 08010 CDMX. **Telephone:** (56) 91-28-72-92. **E-Mail Address:** contacto@diablos-rojos.com. **Website:** diablos.com.mx.
President: Alfredo Harp Helu. **General Manager:** Juan Osvaldo Barón Flores.
Manager: Miguel Ojeda.

MONCLOVA ACEREROS
Office Address: Cuauhtemoc #299, Col Ciudad Deportiva, CP 25750, Monclova, Coahuila. **Telephone:** (52) 866-636-2650. **E-Mail Address:** contacto@acereros.com.mx. **Website:** acereros.com.mx.
President: Gerardo Benavides Pape. **General Manager:** Miguel Valentin Gamez Mendoza.
Manager: Pat Listach.

MONTERREY SULTANES
Office Address: Estadio de Béisbol Monterrey, en Av. Manuel L. Barragán S/N, Col. Regina, CP. 64290 Monterrey, N.L. **Telephone:** (52) 81-2270-2000. **E-Mail Address:** sultanes@sultanes.com.mx. **Website:** sultanes.com.mx.
President: José Maiz Garcia. **General Manager:** Miguel Flores.
Manager: Homar Rojas.

OAXACA GUERREROS
Office Address: Calz. Héroes de Chapultepec S.N. esq calle de los Derechos Humanos Col. Centro, Oaxaca de Juárez. **Telephone:** (52) 951-515-5522. **E-Mail Address:** contacto@guerreros.mx. **Website:** guerreros.mx.
President: Lorenzo Peón Escalante. **General Manager:** Jaime Brena Núñez.
Manager: Erick Rodriguez.

PUEBLA PERICOS
Office Address: Calz. Ignacio Zaragoza 666, Maravillas. 72220 Puebla, Mexico. **E-Mail Address:** contacto@pericosdepuebla.com. **Website:** pericosdepuebla.com.
President: Jose Miguel Bejos. **General Manager:** Mario Valenzuela.
Manager: Carlos Alberto Gastelum.

QUINTANA ROO TIGRES
Office Address: SM 21, 21, 77500 Cancún, Quintana Roo. **Telephone:** (52) 998-887-3108. **E-Mail Address:** medios@tigresqroo.com. **Website:** tigresqroo.com.
President: Fernando Valenzuela Burgos. **General Manager:** Francisco Minjarez Garcia.
Manager: Adan Munoz.

SALTILLO SARAPEROS
Office Address: Blvd. Jesús Valdéz Sánchez y Nazario Ortíz, Cd. Deportiva, Saltillo, Mexico 25280. **Telephone:** (52) 844-416-9455. **Website:** saraperos.com.mx.
President: Alvaro Ley Lopez. **General Manager:** Eduardo Valenzuela Guajardo.

Manager: Roberto Vizcarra.

TABASCO OLMECAS
Office Address: Avenida Velodromo de la Ciudad Deportiva S/N, Atasta, 86100 Villahermosa, Tabasco. **Telephone:** (52) 993-352-2787. **E-Mail Address:** hola@olmecastasco.mx. **Website:** olmecastabasco.mx.
President: Ángel Solis Carballo. **General Manager:** Felix Zulueta García.
Manager: Pedro Mere.

TIJUANA TOROS
Office Address: Mision de Santo Tomas Rio Eufrates con, Col. Infonavit Capistrano, 22223 Tijuana, B.C., Mexico. **Telephone:** (52) 664-635-5600. **E-Mail Address:** contacto@torosdetijuana.com. **Website:** torosdetijuana.com.
Presidente: Alberto Ignacio Uribe Maytorena.
Manager: Omar Vizquel.

YUCATAN LEONES
Office Address: Calle 6 Nº315 x 35, Col. Morelos Oriente, Mérida, Yucatán. C.P. 97174. **Telephone:** (52) 999-432-0655. **E-Mail Address:** contacto@leones.mx. **Website:** leones.mx.
President: Erick Ernesto Arellano Hernández. **General Manager:** Alejandro Orozco Garcia.
Manager: Geronimo Gil.

MEXICAN ACADEMY

Rookie Classification
Mailing Address: Ubicación: Av. El Fundador #100, Col. San Miguel, El Carmen N.L., C.P. 66550. **Telephone:** (81) 8158-7900. **Fax:** (52) 555-395-2454. **E-Mail Address:** pgarza@academia-lmb.com. **Website:** academia-lmb.com.
President: C.P. Plinio Escalante Bolio. **Director General:** Salvador Viera Higuera. **Communications:** Pablo Garza Garcia.
Regular Season: 50 games. **Opening Date:** Not available. **Closing Date:** Not available.

DOMINICAN REPUBLIC
DOMINICAN SUMMER LEAGUE

Member, National Association
Rookie Classification
Mailing Address: Calle Segunda No 64, Reparto Antilla, Santo Domingo, Dominican Republic. **Telephone:** (809) 532-3619. **Website:** dominicansummerleague.com. **E-Mail Address:** ligadeverano@codetel.net.do.
Years League Active: 1985-.
President: Orlando Diaz.
Member Clubs/Division Structure: North—Cubs 1, Dodgers Shoemaker, Indians, Blue Jays/Brewers, Pirates 1, Rangers 1, Rays2, Red Sox 2. **South**—Angels, Cardinals Blue, Mets 1, Nationals, Orioles 2, Phillies Red, Rockies, Twins, Yankees. **Northwest**—Astros, Athletics, Braves, Dodgers Bautista, Marlins, Rays 1, Red Sox 1, Royals 1. **Baseball City**—Blue Jays, D-backs 1, Orioles 1, Padres, Reds, White Sox. **San Pedro de Macoris**—Brewers, Cardinals Red, Cubs 2, D-backs 2, Mets 2, Phillies White, Rangers 2, Tigers 1. **Northeast**—Colorado, Giants, Mariners, Pirates 2, Royals 2, Tigers 2.
Regular Season: 72 games. **Opening Date:** Unavailable. **Closing Date:** Unavailable.
Playoff Format: Six teams qualify for playoffs, including four division winners and two wild-card teams. Teams with two best records receive a bye to the semifinals; four other playoff teams play best-of-three series. Winners advance to best-of-three semifinals. Winners advance to best-of-five championship series.
Roster Limit: 35 active. **Player Eligibility Rule:** No player may have four or more years of prior minor league service. No draft-eligible player from the U.S. or Canada (not including players from Puerto Rico) may participate in the DSL. No age limits apply.

JAPAN
Mailing Address: Mita Bellju Building, 11th Floor, 5-36-7 Shiba, Minato-ku, Tokyo 108-0014. **Telephone:** 03-6400-1189. **Fax:** 03-6400-1190.
Website: npb.or.jp, npb.or.jp/eng
Commissioner: Atsushi Saito.
Secretary General: Atsushi Ihara. **Executive Director, Baseball Operations:** Minoru Hata. **Executive Director, NPB Rules & Labor:** Nobuhisa "Nobby" Ito.
Executive Director, Central League Operations: Kazuhide Kinefuchi. **Executive Director, Pacific League Operations:** Kazuo Nakano.
Nippon Series: Best-of-seven series between Central and Pacific League champions, begins Nov. 13.
All-Star Series: July 16 at Metlife Dome; July 17 at Rajyteb Seimei Park Miyagi.
Roster Limit: 70 per organization (one major league club, one minor league club). Major league club is permitted to register 28 players at a time, though just 25 may be available for each game.
Roster Limit, Imports: Four in majors (no more than three position players or pitchers); unlimited in minors.

CENTRAL LEAGUE
Regular Season: 143 games.
2021 Opening Date: March 26. **Closing Date:** Oct. 17.

Playoff Format: Second-place team meets third-place team in best-of-three series. Winner meets first-place team in best-of-seven series to determine representative in Japan Series (first-place team has one-game advantage to begin series).

CHUNICHI DRAGONS
Mailing Address: Chunichi Bldg 6F, 4-1-1 Sakae, Naka-ku, Nagoya 460-0008. **Telephone:** 052-261-8811.
Field Manager: Tsuyoshi Yoda.

HANSHIN TIGERS
Mailing Address: 2-33 Koshien-cho, Nishinomiya-shi, Hyogo-ken 663-8152. **Telephone:** 0798-46-1515.
Field Manager: Akihiro Yano.

HIROSHIMA TOYO CARP
Mailing Address: 2-3-1 Minami Kaniya, Minami-ku, Hiroshima 732-8501. **Telephone:** 082-554-1000.
Field Manager: Shinji Sasaoka.

TOKYO YAKULT SWALLOWS
Mailing Address: Seizan Bldg, 4F, 2-12-28 Kita Aoyama, Minato-ku, Tokyo 107-0061. **Telephone:** 03-3405-8960.
Field Manager: Shingo Takatsu.

YOKOHAMA DENA BAYSTARS
Mailing Address: Kannai Arai Bldg, 7F, 1-8 Onoe-cho,

Naka-ku, Yokohama 231-0015. **Telephone:** 045-681-0811.
 Field Manager: Daisuke Miura.

YOMIURI GIANTS

Mailing Address: Yomiuri Shimbun Bldg, 26F, 1-7-1
Otemachi, Chiyoda-ku, Tokyo 100-8151. **Telephone:**
03-3246-7733. **Fax:** 03-3246-2726.
 Manager: Tatsunori Hara.

PACIFIC LEAGUE

Regular Season: 143 games.
 2021 Opening Date: March 26. **Closing Date:** Oct. 21.
 Playoff Format: Second-place team meets third-place
team in best-of-three series. Winner meets first-place
team in best-of-seven series to determine league's representative in Japan Series (first-place team has one-game
advantage to begin series).

CHIBA LOTTE MARINES

Mailing Address: 1 Mihama, Mihama-ku, Chiba-shi,
Chiba-ken 261-8587. **Telephone:** 03-5682-6341.
 Field Manager: Tadahito Iguchi.

FUKUOKA SOFTBANK HAWKS

Mailing Address: Fukuoka Yahuoku Japan Dome,
Hawks Town, 2-2-2 Jigyohama, Chuo-ku, Fukuoka 810-
0065. **Telephone:** 092-847-1006. **Owner:** Masayoshi Son.
 Field Manager: Kimiyasu Kudo.

HOKKAIDO NIPPON HAM FIGHTERS

Mailing Address: 1 Hitsujigaoka, Toyohira-ku,
Sapporo 062-8655. **Telephone:** 011-857-3939.
 Field Manager: Hideki Kuriyama.

ORIX BUFFALOES

Mailing Address: 3-Kita-2-30 Chiyozaki, Nishi-ku,
Osaka 550-0023. **Telephone:** 06-6586-0221. **Fax:**
06-6586-0240.
 Field Manager: Satoshi Nakajima.

SAITAMA SEIBU LIONS

Mailing Address: 2135 Kami-Yamaguchi, Tokorozawa-
shi, Saitama-ken 359-1189. **Telephone:** 04-2924-1155.
Fax: 04-2928-1919.
 Field Manager: Hatsuhiko Tsuji.

TOHOKU RAKUTEN GOLDEN EAGLES

Mailing Address: 2-11-6 Miyagino, Miyagino-ku,
Sendai-shi, Miyagi-ken 983-0045. **Telephone:** 022-298-
5300. **Fax:** 022-298-5360.
 Field Manager: Kazuhisa Ishii.

KOREA

KOREA BASEBALL ORGANIZATION

Mailing Address: 946-16 Dokokdong, Kangnam-gu,
Seoul, Korea. **Telephone:** (02) 3460-4600. **Fax:** (02) 3460-
4639.
 Years League Active: 1982-.
 Website: koreabaseball.com.
 Commissioner: Ji-Taek Ji. **Secretary General:** Yang
Hae-Young.
 Member Clubs: Doosan Bears, Hanwha Eagles, Kia
Tigers, KT Wiz, LG Twins, Lotte Giants, NC Dinos, Kiwoom
Heroes, Samsung Lions, SK Wyverns.
 Regular Season: 144 games. **2021 Opening Date:**
March 20.
 Playoffs: Third- and fourth-place teams meet in best-
of-three series; winner advances to meet second-place
team in best-of-five series; winner meets first-place team
in best-of-seven Korean Series for league championship.
 Roster Limit: 26 active through Sept 1, when rosters
expand to 31. **Imports:** Two active.

TAIWAN

CHINESE PROFESSIONAL BASEBALL LEAGUE

Mailing Address: 2F, No 32, Pateh Road, Sec 3, Taipei,
Taiwan 10559. **Telephone:** 886-2-2577-6992. **Fax:** 886-2-
2577-2606. **Website:** cpbl.com.tw.
 Years League Active: 1990-.
 Commissioner: Chi-Chang Tsai.
 Member Clubs: EDA Rhinos, Chinatrust Brothers,
Lamigo Monkeys, Uni-President 7-Eleven Lions, Weichuan
Dragons.
 Regular Season: 120 games. Each team plays 60
games in the first and second halves of the season.
 Player Limits: 25 active players. Three foreign players
and no more than two foreign players on the field per
team at any time.
 2021 Opening Date: March 13. **Playoffs:** Half-season
winners are eligible for the postseason. If a non-half-
season winner team possesses a higher overall winning
percentage than any other half-season winner, then this
team gains a wild card and will play a best-of-five series
against the half-season winner with the lower winning
percentage. The winner of the playoff series advances to
Taiwan Series (best-of-seven). If the same team clinches
both first- and second-half seasons, then that team is
awarded one win to start the Taiwan Series.

EUROPE

NETHERLANDS
DUTCH MAJOR LEAGUE CLUBS

Mailing Address: Koninklijke Nederlandse Baseball en Softball Bond (Royal Dutch Baseball and Softball Association), Postbus 2650, 3430 GB Nieuwegein, Holland.Telephone: 31-30-202-0100. **Website:** www. knbsb.

AMERSFOORT
Mailing Address: Postbus 780, 3800 AT Amersfoort. **Telephone:** +31 (0) 33-461-1914. **Website:** www.bsc-quick.nl

AMSTERDAM PIRATES
Mailing Address: Herman Bonpad 5, 1067 SN Amsterdam. **Telephone:** +31 (0) 20-616-2151. **Website:** www.amsterdampirates.nl

DSS
Mailing Address: Rijksstraatweg 206, 2022 DH Haarlem. **Telephone:** +31 (0) 23-527-2678. **Website:** www.dss-honksoftbal.nl

HAGUE STORKS
Mailing Address: Postbus 53016, 2505 AA 'S-Gravenhage. **Telephone:** +31 (0) 70-323-4151. **Website:** www.storks.nl

HCAW
Mailing Address: Zanderijweg 4-6, 1403 XV Bussum. **Telephone:** +31 (0) 35-693-1430. **Website:** www.hcaw.nl

HOOFDDORP PIONIERS
Mailing Address: Postbus 475, 2130 AL Hoofddorp. **Telephone:** +31 (0) 23-561-3557. **Website:** www.hoofd-dorp-pioniers.nl

NEPTUNUS
Mailing Address: Kastanjesingel 25, 3053 HG Rotterdam. **Telephone:** +31 (0) 10-437-5369. **Website:** www.neptunussport.com

OOSTERHOUT TWINS
Mailing Address: Postbus 4085, 4900 CB Oosterhout NB. **Telephone:** +31 (0) 162-433-760. **Website:** www. twins-sc.com

ITALY
ITALIAN BASEBALL LEAGUE CLUBS

Mailing Address: Federazione Italiana Baseball Softball, Viale Tiziano 74, 00196 Roma, Italy. **Telephone:** 39-06-32297201. **FAX:** 39-06-01902684. **Website:** www.fibs.it
President: Andrea Marcon.

BOLOGNA
Mailing Address: Stadio Gianni Falchi, Piazzale Atleti Azzurri d'Italia, Bologna. **Telephone:** 39-051-479618.
E-Mail Address: info@fortitudobaseball.it .
Website: www.fortitudobaseball.it.
President: Pierluigi Bissa. **Manager:** Daniele Frignani.

COLLECCHIO
Mailing Address: Via Maria Montessori 5/A, Collecchio (PR) 43044. **Telephone:**39-0521-800943.
E-Mail Address: ufficiostampa@collecchio-bs.it
Website: www.collecchio-bs.it
President: Carlo Levati. **Manager:** Marcello Saccardi.

GODO
Mailing Address: Viale Rivalona 5, Godo di Russi 48010. **Telephone:** 39-0544-414352.
E-Mail Address: uffstampa.baseballgodo@gmail.com
Website: www.baseball-godo.com
President: Carlo Naldoni. **Manager:** Marco Bortolotti.

MACERATA
Mailing Address: Via Cioci 5, 62100 Macerata. **Telephone:** 39-0348-280-5345.
E-Mail Address: info@macerataangels.it.
Website: http://www.macerataangels.it.
President: Andrea Graziani. **Manager:** David Daniels.

PARMA
Mailing Address: Via Teresa Confalonieri Casati 22, 43125 Parma. **Telephone:** 39-0521-152-3413.
E-Mail Address: info@parmabaseball.it.
Website: www.parmabaseball.it.
President: Paolo Zbogar. **Manager:** Gianguido Poma.

SAN MARINO
Mailing Address: Via Costa del Bello 2,Serravalle, Repubblica di San Marino. **Telephone:** 39-0549-961217.
E-Mail Address: info@sanmarinobaseball.com
Website: www.sanmarinobaseball.com.
President: Mauro Fiorini. **Manager:** Mario Chiarini.

WINTER BASEBALL

CARIBBEAN BASEBALL CONFEDERATION
Mailing Address: Frank Feliz Miranda No 1 Naco, Santo Domingo, Dominican Republic. **Telephone:** (809) 381-2643. **Fax:** (809) 565-4654.
Commissioner: Juan Francisco Puello. **Secretary:** Benny Agosto.
Member Countries: Cuba, Colombia, Dominican Republic, Mexico, Nicaragua, Panama, Puerto Rico, Venezuela.
2021 Caribbean Series: Dominican Republic, February.

DOMINICAN LEAGUE

Office Address: Ave. Tiradentes, Ensanche La Fé, Estadio Quisqueya, Santo Domingo, Dominican Republic. **Telephone:** (809) 567-6371. **Fax:** (809) 567-5720. **E-Mail Address:** ligadom@hotmail.com. **Website:** lidom.com.
Years League Active: 1951-.
President: Vitelio Mejía Ortiz. **Vice President:** Winston Llenas Davila.
Member Clubs: Aguilas Cibaenas, Estrellas de Oriente, Gigantes del Cibao, Leones del Escogido, Tigres del Licey, Toros del Este.

Regular Season: 50 games.

Playoff Format: Top four teams meet in 18-game round-robin. Top two teams advance to best-of-nine series for league championship. Winner advances to Caribbean Series.

Roster Limit: 30. **Imports:** 7.

MEXICAN PACIFIC LEAGUE

Mailing Address: Ave. Américas No. 1905, 5to. Piso, Col. Colomos Providencia, Guadalajara, Jalisco. **Telephone:** (52) 662-310-9714. **E-Mail Address:** medios@lmp.mx. **Website:** lmp.mx.

Years League Active: 1958-.

President: Omar Canizales Soto. **General Manager:** Christian Veliz Valencia.

Member Clubs: Culiacan Tomateros, Guasave Algodoneros, Hermosillo Naranjeros, Jalisco Charros, Los Mochis Cañeros, Mazatlan Venados, Mexicali Aguilas, Monterrey Sultanes, Navojoa Mayos, Obregon Yaquis.

Regular Season: 68 games.

Playoff Format: Six teams advance to best-of-seven quarterfinals. Three winners and losing team with best record advance to best-of-seven semifinals. Winners meet in best-of-seven series for league championship. Winner advances to Caribbean Series.

Roster Limit: 30. **Imports:** 5.

PUERTO RICAN LEAGUE

Office Address: Avenida Munoz Rivera 1056, Edificio First Federal, Suite 501, Rio Piedras, PR 00925. **Mailing Address:** PO Box 191852 San Juan, PR 00919-1852. **Telephone:** (786) 244-1146. **Website:** ligapr.com. **E-mail address:** info@ligapr.com

Years League Active: 1938-2007; 2008-

President: Juan Flores Galarza. **Operations Director:** Carlos J. Berroa Puertas. **Press Director:** Edna Garcia.

Member Clubs: Caguas Criollos, Carolina Gigantes, Mayaguez Indios, Manati Atenienses, RA12, Santurce Cangrejeros.

Regular Season: 40 games.

Playoff Format: Top four teams meet in round robin series, with top two teams advancing to best-of-seven final. Winner advances to Caribbean Series.

Roster Limit: 30. **Imports:** 5.

VENEZUELAN LEAGUE

Mailing Address: Avenida Casanova, Centro Comercial "El Recreo," Torre Sur, Piso 3, Oficinas 6 y 7, Sabana Grande, Caracas, Venezuela. **Telephone:** (58) 212-761-6408. **Website:** lvbp.com.

Years League Active: 1946-.

President: Giuseppe Palmisano. **Vice Presidents:** Humberto Oropeza, Antonio Jose Herrera. **General Manager:** Domingo Alvarez.

Member Clubs: Anzoategui Caribes, Aragua Tigres, Caracas Leones, La Guaira Tiburones, Lara Cardenales, Magallanes Navegantes, Margarita Bravos, Zulia Aguilas.

Regular Season: 64 games.

Playoff Format: Top two teams in each division, plus a wild-card team, meet in 16-game round-robin series. Top two finishers meet in best-of-seven series for league championship. Winner advances to Caribbean Series.

Roster Limit: 26. **Imports:** 7.

COLOMBIAN LEAGUE

Office/Mailing Address: Hotel Eslait Cra 53 No. 72-27 2do piso, Barranquilla. **Telephone:** (57) 368-6561. **E-mail Address:** r.mendoza@diprobeisbol.com. **Website:** lpbcol.com.

President: Pedro Salzedo Salom. **Director, Operations:** Abdala Villa Eljach. **Director, Communications:** Ricardo Mendoza Puccini.

Member Clubs: Barranquilla Caimanes, Barranquilla Gigantes, Cartagena Tigres, Monteria Vaqueros, Santa Maria Leones, Sincelejo Toros.

Regular season: 42 games.

Playoff Format: Top three teams play 10-game round robin. Top two teams meet in best-of-seven finals for league championship.

AUSTRALIA

AUSTRALIAN BASEBALL LEAGUE

Address: Suite 3.03 (Level 3) 88 Albert Road South Melbourne, VIC 3205. **Telephone:** (61) 3 9915 9900. **E-Mail Address:** playbaseball@baseball.com.au. **Website:** theabl.com.au.

CEO: Cam Vale. **General Manager:** Shane Tonkin, Andrew Reynolds.

Teams: Adelaide Giants, Brisbane Bandits, Canberra Cavalry, Melbourne Aces, Perth Heat, Sydney Blue Sox.

Opening Date: Unavailable. Play usually opens in November with playoffs in February.

Playoff Format: The teams with the best four records qualify for the playoffs. Teams are seeded 1-4, with the top two seeds hosting all three games of the best-of-three semifinal series. Winners advance to a best-of-three championship series.

DOMESTIC LEAGUE

ARIZONA FALL LEAGUE

Mailing Address: Arizona Fall League C/O Salt River Fields - Centerfield Office 7555 North Pima Road Scottsdale, AZ 85258. **Telephone:** (480)-990-1005. **E-Mail Address:** afl@mlb.com. **Website:** mlb.com/arizona-fall-league. **Years League Active:** 1992-.

Operated by: Major League Baseball.

Executive Director: Bill Bavasi. **Administrative Supervisor:** Darlene Emert. **Communications:** Paul Jensen.

Teams: Glendale Desert Dogs, Mesa Solar Sox, Peoria Javelinas, Salt River Rafters, Scottsdale Scorpions, Surprise Saguaros.

Regular season: 32 games. **Opening Date:** Unavailable. Play usually opens in mid-September.

Playoff Format: Division champions meet in one-game championship.

Roster Limit: 35 players per team plus a "taxi squad" of reserve players. Each major-league organization is required to provide seven players. Triple-A and Double-A players are eligible provided they are on Double-A or Triple-A rosters no later than August 15. Each organization is permitted to send two high Class A level players and two players below high Class A. No players with more than one year active or two years total of credited major-league service as of August 31 (including major league disabled list time) are eligible. Each team is allotted 20 pitchers but only 15 are designated "active" each game day.

COLLEGES

COLLEGE ORGANIZATIONS

NATIONAL COLLEGIATE ATHLETIC ASSOCIATION

Mailing Address: 700 W. Washington Street, PO Box 6222, Indianapolis, IN 46206. **Telephone:** (317) 917-6222. **Fax:** (317) 917-6826 (championships), (317) 917-6710 (baseball).

E-mail Addresses: Division I Championship: aholman@ncaa.org (Anthony Holman), rlburhr@ncaa.org (Randy Buhr), ctolliver@ncaa.org (Chad Tolliver), thalpin@ncaa.org (Ty Halpin), jhamilton@ncaa.org (JD Hamilton), kgiles@ncaa.org (Kim Giles). **Division II Championship:** ebreece@ncaa.org (Eric Breece). **Division III:** jpwilliams@ncaa.org (J.P. Williams).

Websites: www.ncaa.org, www.ncaa.com.
President: Dr. Mark Emmert. **Managing director, Division I Championships/Alliances:** Anthony Holman. **Director, Division I Championships/Alliances:** Randy Buhr. **Associate Director, Championships/Alliances:** Chad Tolliver. **Division II Assistant Director, Championships/Alliances:** Eric Breece. **Division III Assistant Director, Championships/Alliances:** J.P. Williams. **Media Contact, Division I Championships, Alliances/College World Series:** TBD. **Playing Rules Contact:** Ty Halpin. **Statistics Contacts:** Jeff Williams (Division I and RPI); Mark Bedics (Division II); Sean Straziscar (Division III).

Chairman, Division I Baseball Committee: Jeff Altier (Director of Athletics, Stetson).

Division I Baseball Committee: Mike Buddie (Director of Athletics, Army); Jennifer Cohen (Director of Athletics, Washington); John Cohen (Director of Athletics, Mississippi State); James Cole (Director of Athletics, Mercer); Kirby Hocutt (Director of Athletics, Texas Tech); Matthew Hogue (Director of Athletics, Coastal Carolina); Bob Moosburger (Director of Athletics, Bowling Green State); Desiree Reed-Francois (Director of Athletics, UNLV); Marianne Vydra (Deputy Athletics Director, Oregon State); Gregory Walter (Associate Commissioner, Missouri Valley Conference).

Chairman, Division II Baseball Committee: Todd Resser (Director of Athletics, Columbus State). **Chairman, Division III Baseball Committee:** Paul F. Murphy (Associate Director of Athletics, Gwynedd Mercy, Pa.).

2022 National Convention: Jan. 19-22 at Indianapolis.

2021 CHAMPIONSHIP TOURNAMENTS

NCAA DIVISION I
College World Series: Omaha, June 19-29/30
Super Regionals (8): Campus sites, June 11-14
Regionals (16): Campus sites, June 4-7

NCAA DIVISION II
World Series: USA Baseball National Training Complex, Cary, N.C. June 5-12.

NCAA DIVISION III
World Series: Veterans Memorial Stadium, Cedar Rapids, Iowa, June 3-9

NATIONAL JUNIOR COLLEGE ATHLETIC ASSOCIATION

Mailing Address: 8801 JM Keynes Drive, Suite 450, Charlotte, NC 28262. **Telephone:** (719) 590-9788. **Fax:** (719) 590-7324. **E-Mail Address:** mgarrison@njcaa.org. **Website:** www.njcaa.org.

Executive Director: Christopher Parker. **Director, Division I Baseball Tournament:** Rod Lovett. **Director, Division II Baseball Tournament:** Angelo Maltese. **Director, Division III Baseball Tournament:** Antonio Cannavaro. **Director, Media Relations:** McKenzie Garrison.

2021 CHAMPIONSHIP TOURNAMENTS

DIVISION I
World Series: Grand Junction, CO, May 29-June 4/5.

DIVISION II
World Series: Enid, OK, May 29-June 4/5.

DIVISION III
World Series: Greeneville, TN, May 29-June 4/5.

CALIFORNIA COMMUNITY COLLEGE ATHLETIC ASSOCIATION

Mailing Address: 2017 O St., Sacramento, CA 95811. **Telephone:** (916) 444-1600. **Fax:** (916) 444-2616. **E-Mail Addresses:** ccarter@cccaasports.org, jboggs@cccaasports.org. **Website:** www.cccaasports.org.
Executive Director: Jennifer Cardone, Interim. **Director, Championships:** George Mategakis. **Administrative Assistant:** Rima Trotter, rtrotter@cccaasports.org.

2021 CHAMPIONSHIP TOURNAMENT

State Championship: TBD.

NORTHWEST ATHLETIC CONFERENCE

Mailing Address: Clark College TGB 121, 1933 Fort Vancouver Way, Vancouver, WA 98663. **Telephone:** (360) 992-2833. **Fax:** (360) 696-6210. **E-Mail Address:** nwaacc@clark.edu. **Website:** www.nwacsports.org.
Executive Director: Marco Azurdia. **Executive Assistant:** Donna Hays. **Sports Information Director:** Tracy Swisher. **Director, Operations:** Alli Young.

2021 CHAMPIONSHIP TOURNAMENT

NWAC Championship: TBD.

AMERICAN BASEBALL COACHES ASSOCIATION

Office Address: 4101 Piedmont Parkway, Suite C, Greensboro, NC 27410. **Telephone:** (336) 821-3140. **Fax:** (336) 886-0000. **E-Mail Address:** abca@abca.org. **Website:** www.abca.org.
Executive Director: Craig Keilitz. **Deputy Executive Director:** Jon Litchfield. **Asst. Executive Director, Trade Show:** Juahn Clark. **Asst. Executive Director, Convention/Marketing:** Zach Haile. **Asst. Executive Director, Coaching Outreach:** Ryan Brownlee.
Chairman: Keith Madison. **President:** Dan McDonnell (Louisville).
2022 National Convention: Jan. 6-9 in Chicago.

NCAA DIVISION I CONFERENCES

AMERICA EAST CONFERENCE

Mailing Address: 451 D Street, Suite 702, Boston, MA 02127. **Telephone:** (617) 695-6369. **Fax:** (617) 695-6380. **Website:** www.americaeast.com. **Baseball Members (First Year):** Albany (2002), Binghamton (2002), Hartford (1990), Maine (1990), Maryland-Baltimore County (2004), Massachusetts-Lowell (2014), New Jersey Tech (2021), Stony Brook (2002). **2021 Tournament:** Four teams, double-elimination, May 27-30, hosted by No. 1 seed.

AMERICAN ATHLETIC CONFERENCE

Mailing Address: 545 E. John Carpenter Freeway, Third Floor, Irving, TX 75062. **Telephone:** (469) 284-5167. **E-Mail Address:** csullivan@theamerican.org. **Website:** www.theamerican.org. **Baseball Members:** (First Year): Central Florida (2014), Cincinnati (2014), East Carolina (2015), Houston (2014), Memphis (2014), South Florida (2014), Tulane (2015), Wichita State (2018). **Director, Communications:** Chuck Sullivan. **2021 Tournament:** Eight teams, double-elimination, May 25-30 at Spectrum Field, Clearwater, Fla.

ATLANTIC COAST CONFERENCE

Mailing Address: 4512 Weybridge Ln., Greensboro, NC 27407. **Telephone:** (336) 851-6062. **Fax:** (336) 854-8797. **E-Mail Address:** sphillips@theacc.org. **Website:** www.theacc.com. **Baseball Members (First Year):** Boston College (2006), Clemson (1954), Duke (1954), Florida State (1992), Georgia Tech (1980), Miami (2005), North Carolina (1954), North Carolina State (1954), Notre Dame (2014), Louisville (2015), Pittsburgh (2014), Virginia (1955), Virginia Tech (2005), Wake Forest (1954). **Associate Director, Communications:** Steve Phillips. **2021 Tournament:** 12 teams, group play followed by single-elimination semifinals and finals. May 25-30 at TBD.

ATLANTIC SUN CONFERENCE

Mailing Address: 3301 Windy Ridge Parkway SE, Suite 350, Atlanta, GA 30339. **E-Mail Address:** greg.mette@asunsports.org. **Website:** www.asunsports.org. **Baseball Members:** (First Year): Bellarmine (2021), Florida Gulf Coast (2008), Jacksonville (1999), Kennesaw State (2006), Liberty (2019), Lipscomb (2004), North Alabama (2019), North Florida (2006), Stetson (1986). **Director, Sports Information:** Greg Mette. **2021 Tournament:** Eight teams, four three-game series first round, double-elimination four-team tournament follows. First round May 21-23 at Swanson Stadium, Fort Myers, Fla., second round May 27-29 at Sessions Stadium, Jacksonville.

ATLANTIC 10 CONFERENCE

Mailing Address: 11827 Canon Blvd., Suite 200, Newport News, VA 23606. **Telephone:** (757) 706-3059. **Fax:** (757) 706-3042. **E-Mail Address:** ddickerson@atlantic10.org. **Website:** www.atlantic10.com. **Baseball Members:** (First Year): Davidson (2015), Dayton (1996), Fordham (1996), George Mason (2014), George Washington (1977), La Salle (1996), Massachusetts (1977), Rhode Island (1981), Richmond (2002), St. Bonaventure (1980), Saint Joseph's (1983), Saint Louis (2006), Virginia Commonwealth (2013). **Commissioner:** Bernadette V. McGlade. **Director, Communications:** Drew Dickerson. **2021 Tournament:** Four teams, double elimination. May 27-29, hosted by No. 1 seed.

BIG EAST CONFERENCE

Mailing Address: BIG EAST Conference, 655 3rd Avenue, 7th Floor, New York, NY 10017. **Telephone:** (212) 969-3181. **Fax:** (212) 969-2900. **E-Mail Address:** kquinn@bigeast.com. **Website:** www.bigeast.com. **Baseball Members:** (First Year): Butler (2014), Connecticut (1979-2013, 2021), Creighton (2014), Georgetown (1985), St. John's (1985), Seton Hall (1985), Villanova (1985), Xavier (2014). **Assistant Commissioner, Olympic Sports/Marketing Communications:** Kristin Quinn. **2021 Tournament:** Four teams, modified double-elimination. May 27-30 at Prasco Park, Mason, Ohio.

BIG SOUTH CONFERENCE

Mailing Address: 7233 Pineville-Matthews Rd., Suite 100, Charlotte, NC 28226. **Telephone:** (704) 341-7990. **Fax:** (704) 341-7991. **E-Mail Address:** brandonm@bigsouth.org. **Website:** www.bigsouthsports.com. **Baseball Members (First Year):** Campbell (2012), Charleston Southern (1983), Gardner-Webb (2009), High Point (1999), Longwood (2013), UNC Asheville (1985), Presbyterian (2009), Radford (1983), South Carolina-Upstate (2019), Winthrop (1983). **Assistant Director, Public Relations/Baseball Contact:** Brandon McGinnis. **2021 Tournament:** Four teams, double-elimination. May 27-29, at SEGRA Stadium, Fayetteville, N.C.

BIG TEN CONFERENCE

Mailing Address: 5440 Park Place, Rosemont, IL 60018. **Telephone:** (847) 696-1010. **Fax:** (847) 696-1110. **E-Mail Addresses:** kkane@bigten.org. **Website:** www.bigten.org. **Baseball Members (First Year):** Illinois (1896), Indiana (1906), Iowa (1906), Maryland (2015), Michigan (1896), Michigan State (1950), Minnesota (1906), Nebraska (2012), Northwestern (1898), Ohio State (1913), Penn State (1992), Purdue (1906), Rutgers (2015). **2021 Tournament:** None.

BIG 12 CONFERENCE

Mailing Address: 400 E. John Carpenter Freeway, Irving, TX 75062. **Telephone:** (469) 524-1009. **E-Mail Address:** russell@big12sports.com. **Website:** www.big12sports.com. **Baseball Members (First Year):** Baylor (1997), Kansas (1997), Kansas State (1997), Oklahoma (1997), Oklahoma State (1997), Texas Christian (2013), Texas (1997), Texas Tech (1997), West Virginia (2013). **Assistant Director, Media Relations:** Russell Luna. **2021 Tournament:** Eight teams, double-elimination. May 26-30 at Chickasaw Bricktown Ballpark, Oklahoma City.

BIG WEST CONFERENCE

Mailing Address: 2 Corporate Park, Suite 206, Irvine, CA 92606. **Telephone:** (949) 261-2525. **Fax:** (949) 261-2528. **E-Mail Address:** jstcyr@bigwest.org. **Website:** www.bigwest.org. **Baseball Members (First Year):** Cal Poly (1997), UC Davis (2008), UC Irvine (2002), UC Riverside (2002), UC San Diego (2021), UC Santa Barbara (1970), Cal State Bakersfield (2021), Cal State Fullerton (1975), Cal State Northridge (2001), Hawaii (2013), Long Beach State (1970). **Director, Communications:** Julie St. Cyr. **2021 Tournament:** None.

COLONIAL ATHLETIC ASSOCIATION

Mailing Address: 8625 Patterson Ave., Richmond, VA 23229. **Telephone:** (804) 754-1616. **Fax:** (804) 754-1973. **E-Mail Address:** rwashburn@caasports.com. **Website:**

www.caasports.com. **Baseball Members (First Year):** College of Charleston (2014), Delaware (2002), Elon (2015), Hofstra (2002), James Madison (1986), UNC Wilmington (1986), Northeastern (2006), Towson (2002), William & Mary (1986). **Associate Commissioner/Communications:** Rob Washburn. **2021 Tournament:** Six teams, double-elimination. May 26-30 at Brooks Field, Wilmington, NC.

CONFERENCE USA

Mailing Address: 5201 N. O'Connor Blvd., Suite 300, Irving, TX 75039. **Telephone:** (214) 774-1300. **Fax:** (214) 496-0055. **E-Mail Address:** rdanderson@c-usa.org. **Website:** www.conferenceusa.com. **Baseball Members (First Year):** Alabama-Birmingham (1996), Charlotte (2014), Florida Atlantic (2014), Florida International (2014), Louisiana Tech (2014), Marshall (2006), Middle Tennessee State (2014), Old Dominion (2014), Rice (2006), Southern Mississippi (1996), Texas-San Antonio (2014), Western Kentucky (2015). **Assistant Commissioner, Baseball Operations:** Russell Anderson. **2020 Tournament:** Eight teams, double-elimination. May 26-30 at Love Field, Ruston, La.

HORIZON LEAGUE

Mailing Address: 129 E. Market Street, Suite 900, Indianapolis, IN 46204. **Telephone:** (317) 237-5622. **Fax:** (317) 237-5620. **E-Mail Address:** dgliot@horizonleague.org. **Website:** www.horizonleague.org. **Baseball Members (First Year):** Illinois-Chicago (1994), Northern Kentucky (2016), Oakland (2014), Purdue-Fort Wayne (2021), Wright State (1994), Wisconsin-Milwaukee (1994), Youngstown State (2002). **Director, Communications and Digital Media Strategy:** Dan Gliot. **2021 Tournament:** Six teams, modified double-elimination. May 28-29, hosted by No. 1 seed.

IVY LEAGUE

Mailing Address: 228 Alexander Rd., Second Floor, Princeton, NJ 08544. **Telephone:** (609) 258-6426. **Fax:** (609) 258-1690. **E-Mail Address:** trevor@ivyleaguesports. com. **Website:** www.ivyleaguesports.com. **Baseball Members (First Year):** Rolfe—Brown (1948), Dartmouth (1930), Harvard (1948), Yale (1930). Gehrig—Columbia (1930), Cornell (1930), Pennsylvania (1930), Princeton (1930). **Assistant Executive Director, Communications/Championships:** Trevor Rutledge-Leverenz. **2021 Tournament:** None.

METRO ATLANTIC ATHLETIC CONFERENCE

Mailing Address: 712 Amboy Ave., Edison, NJ 08837. **Telephone:** (732) 738-5455. **E-Mail Address:** taylor.oconnor@maac.org. **Website:** www.maacsports.com. **Baseball Members (First Year):** Canisius (1990), Fairfield (1982), Iona (1982), Manhattan (1982), Marist (1998), Monmouth (2014), Niagara (1990), Quinnipiac (2014), Rider (1998), Saint Peter's (1982), Siena (1990). **Director, New Media:** Taylor O'Connor. **2021 Tournament:** Four teams, double elimination at TBD.

MID-AMERICAN CONFERENCE

Mailing Address: 24 Public Square, 15th Floor, Cleveland, OH 44113. **Telephone:** (216) 566-4622. **Fax:** (216) 858-9622. **E-Mail Address:** jguy@mac-sports. com. **Website:** www.getmesomeaction.com. **Baseball Members (First Year):** Akron (2020), Ball State (1973), Bowling Green State (1952), Central Michigan (1971), Eastern Michigan (1971), Kent State (1951), Miami (1947),

Northern Illinois (1997), Ohio (1946), Toledo (1950), Western Michigan (1947). **Assistant Commissioner, Communications and Social Media:** Jeremy Guy. **2021 Tournament:** None.

MID-EASTERN ATHLETIC CONFERENCE

Mailing Address: 2730 Ellsmere Ave., Norfolk, VA 23513. **Telephone:** (757) 951-2055. **Fax:** (757) 951-2077. **E-Mail Address:** cunninghamj@themeac.com; porterp@themeac.com. **Website:** www.meacsports. com. **Baseball Members (First Year):** Bethune-Cookman (1979), Coppin State (1985), Delaware State (1970), Florida A&M (1979), Maryland-Eastern Shore (1970), Norfolk State (1998), North Carolina A&T (1970), North Carolina Central (2012). **Assistant Director, Media Relations:** Jeff Cunningham. **2021 Tournament:** Four teams, double-elimination. May 20-22 at Miller Field, Norfolk, Va.

MISSOURI VALLEY CONFERENCE

Mailing Address: 1818 Chouteau Ave., St. Louis, MO 63103. **Telephone:** (314) 444-4300. **Fax:** (314) 444-4333. **E-Mail Address:** davis@mvc.org. **Website:** www. mvc-sports.com. **Baseball Members (First Year):** Bradley (1955), Dallas Baptist (2014), Evansville (1994), Illinois State (1980), Indiana State (1976), Missouri State (1990), Southern Illinois (1974), Valparaiso (2019). **Assistant Commissioner, Communications:** Ryan Davis. **2021 Tournament:** Six teams, double-elimination. May 26-29 at Richard "Itchy" Jones Stadium, Carbondale, Ill.

MOUNTAIN WEST CONFERENCE

Mailing Address: 10807 New Allegiance Dr., Suite 250, Colorado Springs, CO 80921. **Telephone:** (719) 488-4052. **Fax:** (719) 487-7241. **E-Mail Address:** sbuchanan@ themw.com. **Website:** www.themw.com. **Baseball Members (First Year):** Air Force (2000), Fresno State (2013), Nevada (2013), Nevada-Las Vegas (2000), New Mexico (2000), San Diego State (2000), San Jose State (2014). **Director, Strategic Communication:** Stuart Buchanan. **2021 Tournament:** None.

NORTHEAST CONFERENCE

Mailing Address: 200 Cottontail Lane, Vantage Court South, Somerset, NJ 08873. **Telephone:** (732) 469-0440. **Fax:** (732) 469-0744. **E-Mail Address:** rventre@northeast conference.org. **Website:** www.northeastconference.org. **Baseball Members (First Year):** Bryant (2010), Central Connecticut State (1999), Fairleigh Dickinson (1981), Long Island (1981), Merrimack (2020), Mount St. Mary's (1989), Sacred Heart (2000), Wagner (1981). **Director, Communications/Social Media:** Ralph Ventre. **2021 Tournament:** Four teams, double-elimination. May 27-30 at TBD.

OHIO VALLEY CONFERENCE

Mailing Address: 215 Centerview Dr., Suite 115, Brentwood, TN 37027. **Telephone:** (615) 371-1698. **Fax:** (615) 891-1682. **E-Mail Address:** kschwartz@ovc.org. **Website:** www.ovcsports.com. **Baseball Members (First Year):** Austin Peay State (1962), Belmont (2013), Eastern Illinois (1996), Eastern Kentucky (1948), Jacksonville State (2003), Morehead State (1948), Murray State (1948), Southeast Missouri State (1991), Southern Illinois-Edwardsville (2012), Tennessee-Martin (1992), Tennessee Tech (1949). **Assistant Commissioner:** Kyle Schwartz. **2021 Tournament:** Eight teams, double-elimination, May 27-29 at TBD.

PACIFIC-12 CONFERENCE

Mailing Address: Pac-12 Conference 360 3rd Street, 3rd Floor San Francisco, CA 94107. **Telephone:** (415) 580-4200. **Fax:** (415)549-2828. **E-Mail Address:** jolivero@pac-12.org. **Website:** www.pac-12.com. **Baseball Members (First Year):** Arizona (1979), Arizona State (1979), California (1916), UCLA (1928), Oregon (2009) Oregon State (1916), Southern California (1923), Stanford (1918), Utah (2012), Washington (1916), Washington State (1919). **Public Relations Contact:** Jon Olivero. **2021 Tournament:** None.

PATRIOT LEAGUE

Mailing Address: 3773 Corporate Pkwy., Suite 190, Center Valley, PA 18034. **Telephone:** (610) 289-1950. **Fax:** (610) 289-1951. **E-Mail Address:** rsakamoto@patriotleague.com. **Website:** www.patriotleague.org. **Baseball Members (First Year):** Army (1993), Bucknell (1991), Holy Cross (1991), Lafayette (1991), Lehigh (1991), Navy (1993). **Assistant Commissioner, Communications:** Ryan Sakamoto. **2021 Tournament:** four teams, two rounds of best-of-three series, hosted at campus sites.

SOUTHEASTERN CONFERENCE

Mailing Address: 2201 Richard Arrington Blvd. N., Birmingham, AL 35203. **Telephone:** (205) 458-3000. **Fax:** (205) 458-3030. **E-Mail Address:** scartell@sec.org. **Website:** www.secsports.com. **Baseball Members (First Year): East Division**—Florida (1933), Georgia (1933), Kentucky (1933), Missouri (2013), South Carolina (1992), Tennessee (1933), Vanderbilt (1933). **West Division**—Alabama (1933), Arkansas (1992), Auburn (1933), Louisiana State (1933), Mississippi (1933), Mississippi State (1933), Texas A&M (2013). **Director, Communications:** Chuck Dunlap. **2021 Tournament:** 12 teams, modified single/double-elimination. May 25-30 at Hoover Metropolitan Stadium, Hoover, Ala.

SOUTHERN CONFERENCE

Mailing Address: 702 N. Pine St., Spartanburg, SC 29303. **Telephone:** (864) 591-5100. **Fax:** (864) 591-3448. **E-Mail Address:** jwashington@socon.org. **Website:** www.soconsports.com. **Baseball Members (First Year):** The Citadel (1937), East Tennessee State (1979-2005, 2015), Furman (1937), Mercer (2015), UNC Greensboro (1998), Samford (2009), VMI (1925-2003, 2015), Western Carolina (1977), Wofford (1998). **Media Relations Assistant:** Jasmine Washington. **2021 Tournament:** Four teams, double-elimination, May 27-29 at Fluor Field, Greenville, S.C.

SOUTHLAND CONFERENCE

Mailing Address: 2600 Network Blvd, Suite 150, Frisco, Texas 75034. **Telephone:** (972) 422-9500. **Fax:** (972) 422-9225. **E-Mail Address:** jyonis@southland.org **Website:** southland.org. **Baseball Members (First Year):** Abilene Christian (2014), Central Arkansas (2007), Houston Baptist (2014), Incarnate Word (2014), Lamar (1999), McNeese State (1973), New Orleans (2014), Nicholls State (1992), Northwestern State (1988), Sam Houston State (1988), Southeastern Louisiana (1991), Stephen F. Austin State (2006), Tarleton State (2021), Texas A&M-Corpus Christi (2007). **Assistant Communications Director:** Josh Yonis. **2021 Tournament:** Eight teams, double-elimination. May 26-29 at Kenelly Diamond, Hammond, La.

SOUTHWESTERN ATHLETIC CONFERENCE

Mailing Address: 1101 22nd Street South, Birmingham, AL 35205. **Telephone:** (205) 251-7573. **Fax:** (205) 297-9820. **E-Mail Address:** a.roberts@swac.org. **Website:** www.swac.org. **Baseball Members (First Year): East Division**—Alabama A&M (2000), Alabama State (1982), Alcorn State (1962), Jackson State (1958), Mississippi Valley State (1968). **West Division**—Arkansas-Pine Bluff (1999), Grambling State (1958), Prairie View A&M (1920), Southern (1934), Texas Southern (1954). **Assistant Commissioner, Communications:** Andrew Roberts. **2021 Tournament:** Eight teams, double-elimination. May 19-23 at Smith Wills Stadium, Jackson, Miss.

SUMMIT LEAGUE

Mailing Address: 340 W. Butterfield Rd., Suite 3D, Elmhurst, IL 60126. **Telephone:** (630) 516-0661. **Fax:** (630) 516-0673. **E-Mail Address:** powell@thesummitleague.org. **Website:** www.thesummitleague.org. **Baseball Members (First Year):** Nebraska-Omaha (2013), North Dakota State (2008), Oral Roberts (1998), South Dakota State (2008), Western Illinois (1984). **Associate Commissioner, Communications:** Ryan Powell. **2021 Tournament:** Four teams, double-elimination. May 27-29 at Omaha.

SUN BELT CONFERENCE

Mailing Address: 1500 Sugar Bowl Dr., New Orleans, LA 70112. **Telephone:** (504) 556-0884. **Fax:** (504) 299-9068. **E-Mail Address:** nunez@sunbeltsports.org. **Website:** www.sunbeltsports.org. **Baseball Members (First Year): East Division**—Appalachian State (2015), Coastal Carolina (2017), Georgia Southern (2015), Georgia State (2014), South Alabama (1976), Troy (2006). **West Division**—Arkansas-Little Rock (1991), Arkansas State (1991), Louisiana-Lafayette (1991), Louisiana-Monroe (2007), Texas-Arlington (2014), Texas State (2014). **Assistant Commissioner, Digital & Creative Services:** Keith Nunez. **2021 Tournament:** Eight teams, double-elimination. May 25-30 at Riverwalk Stadium, Montgomery, Ala.

WESTERN ATHLETIC CONFERENCE

Mailing Address: 9250 East Costilla Ave., Suite 300, Englewood, CO 80112. **Telephone:** (303) 799-9221. **Fax:** (303) 799-3888. **E-Mail Address:** cthompson@wac.org. **Website:** www.wacsports.com. **Baseball Members (First Year):** California Baptist (2019), Grand Canyon (2014), Dixie State (2021), New Mexico State (2006), Northern Colorado (2014), Sacramento State (2006), Seattle (2013), Texas-Rio Grande Valley (2014), Utah Valley (2014). **Director, Media Relations:** Chris Thompson. **2021 Tournament:** Six teams, double-elimination, May 26-29/30 at Hohokam Stadium, Mesa, Ariz.

WEST COAST CONFERENCE

Mailing Address: 951 Mariners Island Blvd., Third Floor, San Mateo, CA 94404. **Telephone:** (650) 873-8622. **Fax:** (650) 873-7846. **E-Mail Addresses:** rmccrary@westcoast.org. **Website:** www.wccsports.com. **Baseball Members (First Year):** Brigham Young (2012), Gonzaga (1996), Loyola Marymount (1968), Pacific (2014), Pepperdine (1968), Portland (1996), Saint Mary's (1968), San Diego (1979), San Francisco (1968), Santa Clara (1968). **Assistant Commissioner, Communications:** Ryan McCrary. **2021 Tournament:** None.

NCAA DIVISION I TEAMS

* Denotes recruiting coordinator

ABILENE CHRISTIAN WILDCATS

Conference: Southland.
Mailing Address: ACU Box 27916, Abilene, TX 79699-7916. **Website:** www.acusports.com.
Head Coach: Rick McCarty. **Telephone:** 325-674-2325. **Baseball SID:** Zach Carlyle. **Telephone:** 325-674-6171.
Assistant Coaches: Craig Parry, Blaze Lambert, Marc Mumper. **Telephone:** 325-674-2817.
Home Field: Crutcher Scott Field. **Seating Capacity:** 4,000. **Outfield Dimensions:** LF--334, CF--400, RF--334.

AIR FORCE FALCONS

Conference: Mountain West.
Mailing Address: 2169 Field House Drive, U.S. Air Force Academy, CO 80840-9500. **Website:** www.goair-forcefalcons.com.
Head Coach: Mike Kazlausky. **Telephone:** 719-333-0835. **Baseball SID:** Dan Whitaker. **Telephone:** 719-333-3950.
Assistant Coaches: Ryan Forrest, Jimmy Roesinger, Steve Serratore. **Telephone:** 719-333-7539.
Home Field: Falcon Field. **Seating Capacity:** 500. **Outfield Dimensions:** LF--349, CF--400, RF--316.

AKRON ZIPS

Conference: Mid-American.
Mailing Address: The University of Akron Department of Intercollegiate Athletics James A. Rhodes Arena, Suite 83, Akron, OH 44325. **Website:** www.gozips.com.
Head Coach: Chris Sabo. **Telephone:** (330) 972-5131. **Baseball SID:** Brian Dennison. **Telephone:** (330) 972-6292.
Assistant Coaches: Connor Faix, *Cory Mee. **Telephone:** (330) 972-5131.
Home Field: Skeeles Field at Lee R. Jackson Complex. **Seating Capacity:** 1500. **Outfield Dimensions:** LF--320, CF--390, RF--305.

ALABAMA CRIMSON TIDE

Conference: SEC.
Mailing Address: 1201 Coliseum Drive, Coleman Coliseum, Tuscaloosa, AL 35401. **Website:** www.RollTide.com.
Head Coach: Brad Bohannon. **Telephone:** (205) 348-4029. **Baseball SID:** Alex Thompson. **Telephone:** (205) 348-6084.
Assistant Coaches: Jason Jackson, *Jerry Zulli. **Telephone:** (205) 348-4029.
Home Field: Sewell-Thomas Stadium. **Seating Capacity:** 5,867. **Outfield Dimensions:** LF--320, CF--390, RF--320.

ALABAMA A&M BULLDOGS

Conference: Southwestern Athletic.
Mailing Address: 4900 Meridian Street, North Normal, Alabama 35762. **Website:** www.aamusports.com.
Head Coach: Elliot Jones. **Telephone:** 256-372-7213. **Baseball SID:** Joshua J. Darling. **Telephone:** 256-372-4550.
Assistant Coaches: Corben Green. **Telephone:** 256-372-7213.
Home Field: Bulldog Field. **Seating Capacity:** 500. **Outfield Dimensions:** LF--330, CF--400, RF--318.

ALABAMA STATE HORNETS

Conference: Southwestern Athletic.
Mailing Address: 915 S Jackson St. Montgomery AL 36014. **Website:** bamastatesports.com.
Head Coach: Jose Vazquez. **Telephone:** (334) 229-5600. **Baseball SID:** Travis Jarome. **Telephone:** (334) 229-2601.
Assistant Coaches: *Drew Clark, Matt Crane. **Telephone:** (334) 229-5601.
Home Field: Wheeler Watkins Complex. **Seating Capacity:** 550. **Outfield Dimensions:** LF--330, CF--400, RF--330.

ALABAMA-BIRMINGHAM BLAZERS

Conference: Conference USA.
Mailing Address: 617 13th St S Birmingham, AL 35294. **Website:** uabsports.com.
Head Coach: Perry Roth. **Telephone:** 205-934-5184. **Baseball SID:** Hailee Roe. **Telephone:** (205) 934-0722.
Assistant Coaches: Daniel Furuto, Adam Revelette. **Telephone:** 205-934-5182.
Home Field: Young Memorial Field. **Seating Capacity:** 1000. **Outfield Dimensions:** LF--330, CF--400, RF--330.

ALBANY GREAT DANES

Conference: America East.
Mailing Address: 1400 Washington Avenue Albany, NY 12222. **Website:** Ualbanysports.com.
Head Coach: Jon Mueller. **Telephone:** 518-442-3014. **Baseball SID:** John Reilly. **Telephone:** 518-442-5733.
Assistant Coaches: Jason Falcon, *Jeff Kaier. **Telephone:** (518) 442-3337.
Home Field: Varsity Field. **Outfield Dimensions:** LF--346, CF--388, RF--323.

ALCORN STATE BRAVES

Conference: Southwestern Athletic.
Mailing Address: 1000 ASU Drive, Lorman MS 39096. **Website:** www.alcornsports.com.
Head Coach: Bretton Richardson. **Telephone:** 601-877-4090. **Baseball SID:** Morganne Lander.
Assistant Coaches: Ryan Fuentes.
Home Field: Willie E. "Rat" McGowan Stadium.

APPALACHIAN STATE MOUNTAINEERS

Conference: Sun Belt.
Mailing Address: App State Strategic Communications 425 Jack Branch Drive Boone, NC 28608. **Website:** appstatesports.com.
Head Coach: Kermit Smith. **Telephone:** (828) 262-6097. **Baseball SID:** Bret Strelow. **Telephone:** (828) 963-3069.
Assistant Coaches: Justin Aspegren, *Britt Johnson. **Telephone:** (828) 262-8664.
Home Field: Beaver Field at Smith Stadium. **Seating Capacity:** 827. **Outfield Dimensions:** LF--335, CF--405, RF--330.

ARIZONA WILDCATS

Conference: Pac-12.
Mailing Address: 1 National Championship Drive. **Website:** ArizonaWildcats.com.
Head Coach: Jay Johnson. **Telephone:** (520) 621-4102. **Baseball SID:** Brett Gleason. **Telephone:** (520) 621-0917.
Assistant Coaches: *Dave Lawn, Nate Yeskie.

Telephone: (520) 621-4714.
Home Field: Hi Corbett Field. **Seating Capacity:** 9000.
Outfield Dimensions: LF--366, CF--392, RF--349.

ARIZONA STATE SUN DEVILS

Conference: Pac-12.
Mailing Address: 5999 E Van Buren Phoenix AZ.
Website: thesundevils.com.
Head Coach: Tracy Smith. **Baseball SID:** Jeremy
Hawkes. **Telephone:** 480-965-9544.
Assistant Coaches: Ben Greenspan, Jason Kelly.
Telephone: 480-965-1904.
Home Field: Phoenix Municipal Stadium. **Seating
Capacity:** 8775. **Outfield Dimensions:** LF--345, CF--410,
RF--345.

ARKANSAS RAZORBACKS

Conference: SEC.
Mailing Address: 350 N Razorback Road Fayetteville,
AR 72701. **Website:** arkansasrazorbacks.com.
Head Coach: Dave Van Horn. **Telephone:** 479-575-
3655. **Baseball SID:** Kyle Parkinson. **Telephone:** 479-
575-2752.
Assistant Coaches: Matt Hobbs, Nate Thompson.
Telephone: 479-575-8626.
Home Field: Baum-Walker Stadium. **Seating
Capacity:** 10737. **Outfield Dimensions:** LF--320, CF--400,
RF--312.

ARKANSAS STATE RED WOLVES

Conference: Sun Belt.
Mailing Address: 217 Olympic Drive, Jonesboro, AR
72401. **Website:** www.astateredwolves.com.
Head Coach: Tommy Raffo. **Telephone:** (870) 972-
2700. **Baseball SID:** Miya Garrett. **Telephone:** (870)
972-2541.
Assistant Coaches: *Rick Guarno, Rowdy Hardy.
Telephone: (501) 352-5005.
Home Field: Tomlinson Stadium/Kell Field. **Seating
Capacity:** 1200. **Outfield Dimensions:** LF--330, CF--400,
RF--330.

ARKANSAS-LITTLE ROCK TROJANS

Conference: Sun Belt.
Mailing Address: 2801 South University Ave. Little
Rock, AR 72204. **Website:** www.lrtrojans.com.
Head Coach: Chris Curry. **Telephone:** 501-519-2452.
Baseball SID: Rand Champion. **Telephone:** 501-569-
3167.
Assistant Coaches: *Noah Sanders, R.D. Spiehs.
Telephone: 501-351-5264.
Home Field: Gary Hogan Field. **Seating Capacity:**
1200. **Outfield Dimensions:** LF--335, CF--390, RF--305.

ARKANSAS-PINE BLUFF GOLDEN LIONS

Conference: Southwestern.
Mailing Address: 1200 North University Dr., Mail Slot
4891, Pine Bluff, AR 71601. **Website:** www.uapblionsroar.
com.
Head Coach: Carlos James. **Telephone:** 870-575-8995.
Baseball SID: Duane Lewis. **Telephone:** 870-575-7949.
Assistant Coaches: Roger Mallison, Ryan Gaynor.
Telephone: 870-575-8995.
Home Field: Torii Hunter Baseball Complex. **Seating
Capacity:** 1000. **Outfield Dimensions:** LF--331, CF--401,
RF--331.

ARMY BLACK KNIGHTS

Conference: Patriot.
Mailing Address: 639 Howard Rd.. **Website:**
GoArmyWestPoint.com.
Head Coach: Jim Foster. **Telephone:** (845) 938-4938.
Baseball SID: Nick Lovera. **Telephone:** (845) 938-2351.
Assistant Coaches: Logan Parker, Brock Keener.
Telephone: 845-938-4929.
Home Field: Doubleday Field. **Seating Capacity:** 880.
Outfield Dimensions: LF--327, CF--400, RF--375.

AUBURN TIGERS

Conference: SEC.
Mailing Address: 392 S Donahue Drive, Auburn, AL
36849. **Website:** auburntigers.com.
Head Coach: Butch Thompson. **Telephone:** 334-
844-4990. **Baseball SID:** George Nunnelley. **Telephone:**
502-609-9982.
Assistant Coaches: Gabe Gross, Karl Nonemaker.
Home Field: Plainsman Park. **Seating Capacity:** 4096.
Outfield Dimensions: LF--315, CF--385, RF--331.

AUSTIN PEAY GOVERNORS

Conference: Ohio Valley.
Mailing Address: Box 4515, 601 College St.,
Clarksville, TN 37044. **Website:** www.letsgopeay.com.
Head Coach: Travis Janssen. **Telephone:** 931-221-
6266. **Baseball SID:** Cody Bush. **Telephone:** 931-221-
7561.
Assistant Coaches: Trevor Fitts, David Weber, Elliott
McCummings. **Telephone:** 931-221-7324.
Home Field: Raymond C. Hand Park. **Seating
Capacity:** 777. **Outfield Dimensions:** LF--319, CF--392,
RF--327.

BALL STATE CARDINALS

Conference: Mid-American.
Mailing Address: HP266 Ball State University Muncie,
IN 47603. **Website:** ballstatesports.com.
Head Coach: Rich Maloney. **Telephone:** 765-285-
1425. **Baseball SID:** Josh Rattray. **Telephone:** 765-285-
7841.
Assistant Coaches: *Blake Beemer, Larry Scully.
Telephone: .765-2858226
Home Field: Ball Diamond at First Merchants Ballpark.
Seating Capacity: 1600. **Outfield Dimensions:** LF--325,
CF--400, RF--325.

BAYLOR BEARS

Conference: Big 12.
Mailing Address: 1311 S. 5th Street, Waco, TX 76706.
Website: www.baylorbears.com.
Head Coach: Steve Rodriguez. **Telephone:** (254)
710-3029. **Baseball SID:** Zach Rhodes. **Telephone:** (254)
710-3784.
Assistant Coaches: Jon Strauss, *Mike Taylor.
Telephone: (254) 710-3041.
Home Field: Baylor Ballpark. **Seating Capacity:** 5000.
Outfield Dimensions: LF--330, CF--400, RF--330.

BELLARMINE KNIGHTS

Conference: Atlantic Sun.
Mailing Address: 2001 Newburg Rd., Louisville, KY.
Website: www.athletics.bellarmine.edu.
Head Coach: Larry Owens. **Telephone:** 502-272-8278.
Baseball SID: Adam Pruiett. **Telephone:** 502-272-8079.

Assistant Coaches: Nick Eversole, Austin Upshaw, Ross Spurgeon. **Telephone:** 502-272-8278.
Home Field: Knights Field. **Outfield Dimensions:** LF--355, CF--380, RF--335.

BELMONT BRUINS

Conference: Ohio Valley.
Mailing Address: 1900 Belmont Boulevard, Nashville Tn, 37143. **Website:** www.belmontbruins.com.
Head Coach: Dave Jarvis. **Telephone:** (615) 460-6166.
Baseball SID: Grant Cohen. **Telephone:** (416) 460-6698.
Assistant Coaches: Caleb Longshore, *Aaron Smith. **Telephone:** (615) 460-6165.
Home Field: E.S. Rose Park. **Seating Capacity:** 500.
Outfield Dimensions: LF--330, CF--400, RF--330.

BETHUNE-COOKMAN WILDCATS

Conference: Mid-Eastern.
Mailing Address: 640 Dr. Mary McLeod Bethune Blvd., Daytona Beach, FL 32114. **Website:** www.bcuathletics.com.
Head Coach: Jonathan Hernandez. **Telephone:** 386-481-2224.
Assistant Coaches: Jose Carballo.
Home Field: Jackie Robinson Ballpark. **Seating Capacity:** 4200. **Outfield Dimensions:** LF--317, CF--400, RF--325.

BINGHAMTON BEARCATS

Conference: America East.
Mailing Address: 440 Vestal Parkway East, Binghamton, NY, 13902. **Website:** https://bubearcats.com/sports/baseball.
Head Coach: Tim Sinicki. **Telephone:** (607) 777-2525.
Baseball SID: John Hartrick. **Telephone:** (607) 777-6800.
Assistant Coaches: Mike Folli, *Ryan Hurba. **Telephone:** (607) 777-5808.
Home Field: Bearcat Sports Complex. **Seating Capacity:** 464. **Outfield Dimensions:** LF--325, CF--390, RF--325.

BOSTON COLLEGE EAGLES

Conference: ACC.
Mailing Address: 140 Comm. Ave., Chestnut Hill, MA 02467. **Website:** bceagles.com.
Head Coach: Mike Gambino. **Telephone:** 617-552-2674. **Baseball SID:** Brendan Flynn. **Telephone:** 617-552-2004.
Assistant Coaches: *John Murphy, Alex Trezza. **Telephone:** 617-552-1131.
Home Field: Harrington Athletics Village. **Seating Capacity:** 1000. **Outfield Dimensions:** LF--330, CF--403, RF--330.

BOWLING GREEN STATE FALCONS

Conference: Mid-American.
Mailing Address: 1600 Stadium Drive; Bowling Green, OH 43403. **Website:** https://bgsufalcons.com/sports/baseball/.
Head Coach: Kyle Hallock. **Telephone:** 419-372-7095.
Baseball SID: James Nahikian. **Telephone:** (419) 372-7105.
Assistant Coaches: N/A , *Ryan Shay. **Telephone:** 419-372-7641.
Home Field: Steller Field. **Seating Capacity:** 1100.
Outfield Dimensions: LF--345, CF--400, RF--345.

BRADLEY BRAVES

Conference: Missouri Valley.
Mailing Address: 1501 W. Bradley Ave., Peoria, IL 61625. **Website:** bradleybraves.com.
Head Coach: Elvis Dominguez. **Telephone:** 309-677-2684. **Baseball SID:** Bobby Parker. **Telephone:** 309-677-2624.
Assistant Coaches: Kyle Trewyn, Andrew Werner, Kody Larson. **Telephone:** 309-677-4583.
Home Field: Dozer Park. **Seating Capacity:** 7500.
Outfield Dimensions: LF--310, CF--400, RF--310.

BRIGHAM YOUNG COUGARS

Conference: West Coast.
Mailing Address: 111 Miller Park, Provo UT 84602. **Website:** www.byucougars.com.
Head Coach: Mike Littlewood. **Telephone:** (801) 422-5049. **Baseball SID:** N/A. **Telephone:** N/A.
Assistant Coaches: *Brent Haring, Trent Pratt. **Telephone:** (801) 422-5048.
Home Field: Miller Park. **Seating Capacity:** 2220.
Outfield Dimensions: LF--330, CF--400, RF--330.

BROWN BEARS

Conference: Ivy League.
Mailing Address: 235 Hope St., Box 1932, Providence, R.I. 02912. **Website:** www.brownbears.com.
Head Coach: Grant Achilles. **Telephone:** 401-863-3090. **Baseball SID:** Nick Dow. **Telephone:** 401-863-6069.
Assistant Coaches: Mike McCormack. **Telephone:** 401-863-2032.
Home Field: Attanasio Family Field at Murray Stadium. **Seating Capacity:** 1000.

BRYANT BULLDOGS

Conference: Northeast.
Mailing Address: 1150 Douglas Pike Smithfield, RI 02917. **Website:** bryantbulldogs.com.
Head Coach: Ryan Klosterman. **Telephone:** (401) 232-6397. **Baseball SID:** Tristan Hobbes. **Telephone:** 401-232-6558 x1.
Assistant Coaches: Ted Hurvul, *Eric Pelletier. **Telephone:** (401) 232-6967 ext. 2.
Home Field: Conaty Park. **Seating Capacity:** 500.
Outfield Dimensions: LF--330, CF--400, RF--330.

BUCKNELL BISON

Conference: Patriot League.
Mailing Address: One Dent Drive, Lewisburg, PA 17837. **Website:** www.bucknellbison.com.
Head Coach: Scott Heather. **Telephone:** 570-577-3593. **Baseball SID:** Cole Cloonan. **Telephone:** 570-577-1227.
Assistant Coaches: Jason Neitz, Connor Bechtel. **Telephone:** 570-577-1059.
Home Field: Depew Field. **Seating Capacity:** 1000.
Outfield Dimensions: LF--330, CF--400, RF--330.

BUTLER BULLDOGS

Conference: Big East.
Mailing Address: 555 W 52nd St., Indianapolis, IN 46268. **Website:** https://butlersports.com.
Head Coach: Dave Schrage. **Telephone:** (317) 940-6536. **Baseball SID:** Kit Stetzel. **Telephone:** (317) 940-9994.
Assistant Coaches: Matt Kennedy, *Ben Norton.

Telephone: (317) 940-6536.
  Home Field: Bulldog Park. **Seating Capacity:** 800.
Outfield Dimensions: LF--325, CF--400, RF--320.

CAL BAPTIST LANCERS

Conference: Western Athletic.
Mailing Address: 8432 Magnolia Avenue Riverside,
CA 92504. **Website:** www.cbulancers.com.
  Head Coach: Gary Adcock. **Telephone:** (951) 343-
4382. **Baseball SID:** Andrew Shortall. **Telephone:** (951)
343-4779.
  Assistant Coaches: *Tyler Hancock, Jesse Zepeda.
Telephone: (951) 343-4581.
  Home Field: James W. Totman Stadium. **Seating
Capacity:** 800. **Outfield Dimensions:** LF--331, CF--406,
RF--317.

CAL POLY MUSTANGS

Conference: Big West.
Mailing Address: 1 Grand Avenue, San Luis Obispo,
CA 93407. **Website:** www.GoPoly.com.
  Head Coach: Larry Lee. **Telephone:** (805) 756-6367.
Baseball SID: Eric Burdick. **Telephone:** (805) 756-6550.
  Assistant Coaches: Jake Silverman, *Teddy Warrecker.
Telephone: (805) 756-2462.
  Home Field: Baggett Stadium. **Seating Capacity:**
3138. **Outfield Dimensions:** LF--335, CF--405, RF--335.

CAL STATE BAKERSFIELD ROADRUNNERS

Conference: Big West.
Mailing Address: 9001 Stockdale Hwy Gym,
Bakersfield, CA 93311. **Website:** www.gorunners.com.
  Head Coach: Jeremy Beard. **Telephone:** (661) 654-
2678. **Baseball SID:** Daniel Sperl. **Telephone:** 661-654-
6071.
  Assistant Coaches: *Ryan Cisterna, Quinn
Hawksworth. **Telephone:** 661.654.2678.
  Home Field: Hardt Field. **Seating Capacity:** 1500.
Outfield Dimensions: LF--325/375, CF--390, RF--325/
375.

CAL STATE FULLERTON TITANS

Conference: Big West.
Mailing Address: TH-100 800 State College Blvd
Fullerton, CA 92831. **Website:** www.fullertontitans.com
  Head Coach: Rick Vanderhook. **Telephone:** (657) 278-
3789. **Baseball SID:** TBD.
  Assistant Coaches: *Sergio Brown, Daniel Ricabal.
Telephone: (657) 278-8449.
  Home Field: Goodwin Field. **Seating Capacity:** 3500.
Outfield Dimensions: LF--330, CF--385, RF--330.

CAL STATE NORTHRIDGE MATADORS

Conference: Big West.
Mailing Address: 18111 Nordhoff St., Northridge, CA,
91330. **Website:** gomatadors.com.
  Head Coach: Dave Serrano. **Telephone:** (818) 677-
7055. **Baseball SID:** Nick Bocanegra. **Telephone:** (818)
677-7188.
  Assistant Coaches: *Eddie Cornejo, Neil Walton.
Telephone: (818) 677-3218.
  Home Field: Matador Field. **Seating Capacity:** 1000.
Outfield Dimensions: LF--325, CF--390, RF--325.

CALIFORNIA GOLDEN BEARS

Conference: Pac-12.
Mailing Address: Haas Pavilion #4422 Berkeley, CA
94720-4422. **Website:** www.calbears.com.
  Head Coach: Mike Neu. **Telephone:** (510) 643-6006.
Baseball SID: Gerrit Van Genderen. **Telephone:** (510)
642-5363.
  Assistant Coaches: Matt Flemer, *Noah Jackson.
Telephone: (510) 643-6006.
  Home Field: Evans Diamond. **Seating Capacity:** 2500.
Outfield Dimensions: LF--320, CF--395, RF--320.

CAMPBELL FIGHTING CAMELS

Conference: Big South.
Mailing Address: 76 Upchurch Ln, Buies Creek, NC
27506. **Website:** gocamels.com.
  Head Coach: Justin Haire. **Telephone:** (910) 893-1338.
Baseball SID: Jason Williams. **Telephone:** (910) 814-4367.
  Assistant Coaches: Tyler Robinson, *Tyler Shewmaker.
Telephone: (910) 814-5510.
  Home Field: Jim Perry Stadium. **Seating Capacity:**
1000. **Outfield Dimensions:** LF--337, CF--395, RF--328.

CANISIUS GOLDEN GRIFFINS

Conference: Metro Atlantic.
Mailing Address: 2001 Main Street, Buffalo, N.Y.,
14208. **Website:** gogriffs.com.
  Head Coach: Matt Mazurek. **Telephone:** (716) 888-
8479. **Baseball SID:** Marshall Haim. **Telephone:** (716)
888-8266.
  Assistant Coaches: Brandon Bielecki, Garrett
Cortright. **Telephone:** (716) 888-.
  Home Field: Demske Sports Complex. **Seating
Capacity:** 1200.

CENTRAL ARKANSAS BEARS

Conference: Southland.
Mailing Address: PO Box 5004, Conway, AR 72035.
Website: www.ucasports.com.
  Head Coach: Allen Gum. **Telephone:** 501-499-1707.
Baseball SID: Steve East. **Telephone:** 501-450-5743.
  Assistant Coaches: Nick Harlan, Justin Cunningham,
Jared Gates. **Telephone:** 402-366-5948.
  Home Field: Bear Stadium. **Seating Capacity:** 1000.

CENTRAL CONNECTICUT STATE BLUE DEVILS

Conference: Northeast.
Mailing Address: 1615 Stanley Street, New Britain, CT
06050. **Website:** www.CCSUBlueDevils.com.
  Head Coach: Charlie Hickey. **Telephone:** (860)
832-3074. **Baseball SID:** Jeff Mead. **Telephone:** (860)
832-3057.
  Assistant Coaches: Rob Bono, *Pat Hall. **Telephone:**
(860) 832-3579.
  Home Field: CCSU Baseball Field. **Outfield
Dimensions:** LF--330, CF--400, RF--310.

CENTRAL FLORIDA KNIGHTS

Conference: American Athletic.
Mailing Address: 4422 Knights Victory Way, Orlando,
FL 32816. **Website:** ucfknights.com.
  Head Coach: Greg Lovelady. **Baseball SID:** Collin
Yeager. **Telephone:** (407) 823-5395.
  Assistant Coaches: Nick Otte, *Ted Tom. **Telephone:**
(689) 208-9294.
  Home Field: John Euliano Park. **Seating Capacity:**

3841. **Outfield Dimensions:** LF--320, CF--390, RF--320.

CENTRAL MICHIGAN CHIPPEWAS

Conference: Mid-American.
Mailing Address: 100 Rose Center, Mount Pleasant MI, 48859. **Website:** www.cmuchippewas.com
Head Coach: Jordan Bischel. **Telephone:** (989) 774-4392. **Baseball SID:** Cullen Maksimowski. **Telephone:** (989) 774-3277.
Assistant Coaches: Tony Jandron, *Kyle Schroeder. **Telephone:** (989) 774-1484.
Home Field: Theunissen Stadium. **Seating Capacity:** 2046. **Outfield Dimensions:** LF--330, CF--400, RF--339.

CHARLESTON SOUTHERN BUCCANEERS

Conference: Big South.
Mailing Address: 9200 University Blvd. Charleston, SC 29406. **Website:** csusports.com.
Head Coach: Marc MacMillan. **Telephone:** (843) 863-7832. **Baseball SID:** Harrison Huntley. **Telephone:** (843) 863-7289.
Assistant Coaches: *Anthony Izzio, Matt den. **Telephone:** (843) 863-7832.
Home Field: Nielsen Field at CSU Ballpark. **Seating Capacity:** 1000. **Outfield Dimensions:** LF--330, CF--400, RF--330.

CHARLOTTE 49ERS

Conference: Conference USA.
Mailing Address: 9201 University City Blvd.. **Website:** Charlotte49ers.com.
Head Coach: Robert Woodard. **Telephone:** (704) 687-0726. **Baseball SID:** Sean Fox. **Telephone:** (704) 687-1023.
Assistant Coaches: *Toby Bicknell, Bo Robinson. **Telephone:** (704) 687-0727.
Home Field: Hayes Stadium. **Seating Capacity:** 3200. **Outfield Dimensions:** LF--335, CF--390, RF--315.

CINCINNATI BEARCATS

Conference: American Athletic.
Mailing Address: Richard E. Lindner Center, 2751 O'Varsity Way Cincinnati, Ohio 45221-0021. **Website:** www.gobearcats.com.
Head Coach: Scott Googins. **Telephone:** 556-0566. **Baseball SID:** Andre Foushee. **Telephone:** (513) 556-5182.
Assistant Coaches: *JD Heilmann, Kyle Sprague. **Telephone:** (513) 556-0565.
Home Field: Bearcats Stadium. **Seating Capacity:** 3085. **Outfield Dimensions:** LF--325, CF--400, RF--325.

CITADEL BULLDOGS

Conference: SoCon.
Mailing Address: 171 Moultrie Street, Charleston, SC, 29409. **Website:** https://citadelsports.com/sports/baseball.
Head Coach: Tony Skole. **Telephone:** (843) 901-7199. **Baseball SID:** John Brush. **Telephone:** (843) 953-6795.
Assistant Coaches: Blake Cooper, *Zach Lucas. **Telephone:** (502) 759-5710.
Home Field: Joeseph P. Riley Park. **Seating Capacity:** 7500. **Outfield Dimensions:** LF--305, CF--399, RF--337.

CLEMSON TIGERS

Conference: ACC.
Mailing Address: 100 Perimeter Road; Clemson, SC 29633. **Website:** ClemsonTigers.com.
Head Coach: Monte Lee. **Telephone:** (864) 656-1947. **Baseball SID:** Brian Hennessy. **Telephone:** (864) 656-1921.
Assistant Coaches: *Bradley LeCroy, Andrew See. **Telephone:** (864) 656-1950.
Home Field: Doug Kingsmore Stadium. **Seating Capacity:** 6272. **Outfield Dimensions:** LF--310, CF--390, RF--320.

COASTAL CAROLINA CHANTICLEERS

Conference: Sun Belt.
Mailing Address: 965 One Landon Loop, Conway, SC 29526. **Website:** www.goccusports.com/sports/baseball.
Head Coach: Gary Gilmore. **Telephone:** (843) 349-2524. **Baseball SID:** Kevin Davis. **Telephone:** (843) 349-2822.
Assistant Coaches: *Kevin Schnall, Drew Thomas. **Telephone:** (843) 234-3460.
Home Field: Springs Brooks Stadium. **Seating Capacity:** 5400. **Outfield Dimensions:** LF--320, CF--390, RF--320.

COLLEGE OF CHARLESTON COUGARS

Conference: Colonial.
Mailing Address: 66 George St. Charleston, SC 29424. **Website:** cofcsports.com.
Head Coach: Chad Holbrook. **Telephone:** (843) 953-5961. **Baseball SID:** Whitney Noble. **Telephone:** (843) 953-3683.
Assistant Coaches: Will Dorton, *Kevin Nichols. **Telephone:** (843) 953-7013.
Home Field: Patriots Point. **Seating Capacity:** 3000. **Outfield Dimensions:** LF--310, CF--408, RF--330.

COLUMBIA LIONS

Conference: Ivy League.
Mailing Address: 505 W 218th Street, New York, NY 10034. **Website:** gocolumbialions.com.
Head Coach: Brett Boretti. **Telephone:** (212) 854-8448. **Baseball SID:** Mike Kowalsky. **Telephone:** (212) 854-7064.
Assistant Coaches: Erik Supplee, *Dan Tischler. **Telephone:** (212) 851-0105.
Home Field: Robertson Field at Satow Stadium. **Seating Capacity:** 1500.

CONNECTICUT HUSKIES

Conference: Big East.
Mailing Address: 2095 Hillside Road, U-1173 | Storrs, CT 06269-1173. **Website:** UCONNHUSKIES.COM.
Head Coach: Jim Penders. **Telephone:** (860) 208-9140. **Baseball SID:** Chris Jones. **Telephone:** (860) 486-3531.
Assistant Coaches: Jeff Hourigan, *Joshua MacDonald. **Telephone:** (860) 486-4089.
Home Field: Elliot Ballpark. **Seating Capacity:** 1500. **Outfield Dimensions:** LF--330, CF--400, RF--320.

COPPIN STATE EAGLES

Conference: Mid-Eastern.
Mailing Address: 2500 West North Avenue Baltimore, MD 21216. **Website:** coppinstatesports.com.
Head Coach: Sherman Reed, Sr.. **Telephone:** (410)

951-3723. **Baseball SID:** Steve Kramer. **Telephone:** (410) 951-3729.

Assistant Coaches: *Matthew Greely, Jovanny Zarzabal. **Telephone:** (410) 951-6764.

Home Field: Joe Cannon Stadium. **Seating Capacity:** 1500. **Outfield Dimensions:** LF--325, CF--410, RF--325.

CORNELL BIG RED

Conference: Ivy League.

Mailing Address: Teagle Hall, Campus Drive, Ithaca, N.Y. 14853. **Website:** www.cornellbigred.com.

Head Coach: Dan Pepicelli. **Baseball SID:** Brandon Thomas. **Telephone:** 607-255-5627.

Assistant Coaches: Tom Ford, Frank Hager. **Telephone:** 607-255-6604.

Home Field: Hoy Field. **Seating Capacity:** 1000. **Outfield Dimensions:** LF--315, CF--405, RF--325.

CREIGHTON BLUEJAYS

Conference: Big East.

Mailing Address: 2500 California Ave., Omaha, NE, 68178. **Website:** gocreighton.com.

Head Coach: Ed Servais. **Telephone:** (402) 280-2483. **Baseball SID:** Glen Sisk. **Telephone:** (402) 280-2433.

Assistant Coaches: *Connor Gandossy, Eric Wordekemper.

Home Field: TD Ameritrade Park Omaha. **Seating Capacity:** 24500. **Outfield Dimensions:** LF--335, CF--408, RF--335.

DALLAS BAPTIST PATRIOTS

Conference: Missouri Valley.

Mailing Address: 3000 Mountain Creek Pkwy Dallas, TX 75211. **Website:** www.dbupatriots.com.

Head Coach: Dan Heefner. **Telephone:** (214) 333-5324. **Baseball SID:** Reagan Ratcliff. **Telephone:** (214) 333-5942.

Assistant Coaches: *Dan Fitzgerald, Micah Posey, Noah Shackles. **Telephone:** (214) 333-6987.

Home Field: Horner Ballpark. **Seating Capacity:** 200. **Outfield Dimensions:** LF--330, CF--390, RF--330.

DARTMOUTH BIG GREEN

Conference: Ivy League.

Mailing Address: 6083 Alumni Gym, Hanover, NH 03755. **Website:** https://dartmouthsports.com.

Head Coach: Bob Whalen. **Telephone:** (603) 646-2477. **Baseball SID:** Rick Bender. **Telephone:** (603) 646-1030.

Assistant Coaches: *Conor Burke, Blake McFadden. **Telephone:** (603) 646-2765.

Home Field: Red Rolfe Field at Biondi Park. **Seating Capacity:** 2000. **Outfield Dimensions:** LF--325, CF--403, RF--340.

DAVIDSON WILDCATS

Conference: Atlantic 10.

Mailing Address: Box 7158, Davidson, NC 28035. **Website:** davidsonwildcats.com.

Head Coach: Rucker Taylor. **Telephone:** (704) 892-2772. **Baseball SID:** Justin Parker. **Telephone:** (704) 894-2931.

Assistant Coaches: Parker Bangs, *Ryan Munger. **Telephone:** (704) 892-2002.

Home Field: Wilson Field. **Seating Capacity:** 700. **Outfield Dimensions:** LF--320, CF--385, RF--330.

DAYTON FLYERS

Conference: Atlantic 10.

Mailing Address: University of Dayton, 300 College Park, Dayton, OH 45469. **Website:** www.daytonflyers. com.

Head Coach: Jayson King. **Telephone:** (603) 381-1279. **Baseball SID:** Eric Robinson. **Telephone:** (815) 325-0986.

Assistant Coaches: Kyle Decker, *Travis Ferrick. **Telephone:** (540) 903-4967.

Home Field: Woerner Field at DP&L Stadium. **Seating Capacity:** 2000. **Outfield Dimensions:** LF--330, CF--400, RF--330.

DELAWARE BLUE HENS

Conference: Colonial.

Mailing Address: 631 S College Ave., Newark, DE 19716. **Website:** BlueHens.com.

Head Coach: Jim Sherman. **Telephone:** (302) 831-8596. **Baseball SID:** Erik Oakley. **Telephone:** (302) 530-0537.

Assistant Coaches: Dan Hammer, *Jad Prachniak. **Telephone:** (302) 831-2723.

Home Field: Bob Hannah Stadium. **Seating Capacity:** 1300. **Outfield Dimensions:** LF--320, CF--410, RF--330.

DELAWARE STATE HORNETS

Conference: Mid-Eastern.

Mailing Address: 1200 N. Dupont Hwy., Dover, DE 19901. **Website:** www.dsuhornets.com.

Head Coach: J.P. Blandin. **Telephone:** 302-857-6035. **Baseball SID:** Dennis Jones. **Telephone:** 302-857-6068.

Assistant Coaches: Geoff Kimmel, Matt Domian, Cameron Jiminez. **Telephone:** 302-857-7809.

Home Field: Soldier Field. **Seating Capacity:** 500.

DIXIE STATE TRAILBLAZERS

Conference: Western Athletic.

Mailing Address: 225 S. 700 E., St. George, UT 84770. **Website:** www.dixieathletics.com.

Head Coach: Chris Pfatenahuer. **Telephone:** (435) 652-7530. **Baseball SID:** Steve Johnson. **Telephone:** (435) 652-7524.

Assistant Coaches: *Bobby Rinard, Zach Wilkins. **Telephone:** (435) 652-7530.

Home Field: Bruce Hurst Field. **Seating Capacity:** 2500. **Outfield Dimensions:** LF--325, CF--380, RF--335.

DUKE BLUE DEVILS

Conference: ACC.

Mailing Address: Scott Family Performance Center Duke Baseball Box 90005 Durham NC 27708. **Website:** https://goduke.com/sports/baseball.

Head Coach: Chris Pollard. **Telephone:** (919) 384-6172. **Baseball SID:** Kat Castner. **Telephone:** (919) 684-8708.

Assistant Coaches: *Josh Jordan, Jason Stein. **Telephone:** (919) 698-0932.

Home Field: DBAP. **Seating Capacity:** 10000. **Outfield Dimensions:** LF--318, CF--405, RF--330.

EAST CAROLINA PIRATES

Conference: American Athletic.

Mailing Address: 102 Clark-LeClair Stadium Greenville, NC 27858. **Website:** www.ecupirates.com.

Head Coach: Cliff Godwin. **Telephone:** (252) 737-1985. **Baseball SID:** Malcolm Gray. **Telephone:** (252)

737-4523.
Assistant Coaches: Jason Dietrich, *Jeff Palumbo.
Telephone: (252) 737-1984.
Home Field: Clark-Leclair Stadium. **Seating Capacity:** 5800. **Outfield Dimensions:** LF--330, CF--390, RF--330.

EAST TENNESSEE STATE BUCCANEERS

Conference: Southern.
Mailing Address: PO Box 70707, Johnson City, TN 37614. **Website:** www.etsubucs.com.
Head Coach: Joe Pennucci. **Telephone:** 423-439-4496.
Baseball SID: David Czarlinsky. **Telephone:** 423-439-8212.
Assistant Coaches: Ross Oeder, Jamie Pinzino, Daniel Sweeney. **Telephone:** 423-439-4485.
Home Field: Thomas Stadium. **Seating Capacity:** 1000. **Outfield Dimensions:** LF--325, CF--400, RF--325.

EASTERN ILLINOIS PANTHERS

Conference: Ohio Valley.
Mailing Address: 600 Lincoln Ave. **Website:** eiupanthers.com.
Head Coach: Jason Anderson. **Baseball SID:** Rich Moser. **Telephone:** (217) 581-7480.
Assistant Coaches: Tim Brown, Ryan Cooper, Derek Francis.
Home Field: Coaches Stadium. **Seating Capacity:** 500. **Outfield Dimensions:** LF--340, CF--380, RF--340.

EASTERN KENTUCKY COLONELS

Conference: Ohio Valley.
Mailing Address: 115 Alumni Coliseum, 521 Lancaster Ave. Richmond, KY 40475. **Website:** ekusports.com.
Head Coach: Chris Prothro. **Telephone:** (859) 622-2128. **Baseball SID:** Kevin Britton. **Telephone:** (859) 622-2006.
Assistant Coaches: *Walt Jones, Cody Wofford. **Telephone:** (859) 622-8295.
Home Field: Turkey Hughes Field at Earle Combs Stadium. **Seating Capacity:** 1000. **Outfield Dimensions:** LF--340, CF--410, RF--330.

EASTERN MICHIGAN EAGLES

Conference: Mid-American.
Mailing Address: 799 N Hewitt Rd Ypsilanti, MI.
Website: emueagles.com.
Head Coach: Eric Roof. **Telephone:** (734) 487-1985.
Baseball SID: Alex Jewell. **Telephone:** (734) 487-0317.
Assistant Coaches: *AJ Achter, Jonathan Roof. **Telephone:** (734) 487-0315.
Home Field: Oestrike Stadium. **Seating Capacity:** 2500.

ELON PHOENIX

Conference: Colonial.
Mailing Address: 100 Campus Drive, Elon, NC 27244. **Website:** elonphoenix.com.
Head Coach: Mike Kennedy. **Telephone:** (336) 278-6741. **Baseball SID:** Pierce Yarberry. **Telephone:** (336) 278-6712.
Assistant Coaches: *Robbie Huffstetler, Jerry Oakes. **Telephone:** (336) 278-6794.
Home Field: Walter C. Latham Park. **Seating Capacity:** 2000. **Outfield Dimensions:** LF--317, CF--385, RF--327.

EVANSVILLE PURPLE ACES

Conference: Missouri Valley.
Mailing Address: 1800 Lincoln Ave., Evansville, IN 47722. **Website:** www.gopurpleaces.com.
Head Coach: Wes Carroll. **Telephone:** 812-488-2059.
Baseball SID: Michael Robertson. **Telephone:** 812-488-2238.
Assistant Coaches: A.J. Gaura, Keirce Kimbel, Jared Morton. **Telephone:** 812-488-1027.
Home Field: German American Bank Field at Charles H. Braun Stadium. **Seating Capacity:** 1200. **Outfield Dimensions:** LF--330, CF--400, RF--330.

FAIRFIELD STAGS

Conference: Metro Atlantic.
Mailing Address: 1073 N Benson Rd, Fairfield, CT 06824. **Website:** fairfieldstags.com.
Head Coach: Bill Currier. **Telephone:** (203) 254-4000 (ext. 2605). **Baseball SID:** Ivey Speight. **Telephone:** (203) 254-4000 (ext. 2878).
Assistant Coaches: *Brian Fay, Jordan Tabakman. **Telephone:** (203)-254-4000 (ext. 3178).
Home Field: Alumni Diamond. **Seating Capacity:** 350. **Outfield Dimensions:** LF--330, CF--400, RF--330.

FAIRLEIGH DICKINSON KNIGHTS

Conference: Northeast.
Mailing Address: 1130 River Rd. Teaneck, NJ 07666.
Website: www.fduknights.com.
Head Coach: Rob DiToma. **Telephone:** (201) 692-2245. **Baseball SID:** Bryan Jackson. **Telephone:** (201) 692-2149.
Assistant Coaches: *Stephen Adkins, Ethan Newton. **Telephone:** (201) 692-2245.
Home Field: Naimoli Family Baseball Complex. **Seating Capacity:** 500. **Outfield Dimensions:** LF--321, CF--370, RF--321.

FLORIDA GATORS

Conference: SEC.
Mailing Address: University of Florida. **Website:** FloridaGators.com.
Head Coach: Kevin O'Sullivan. **Telephone:** (352) 375-4683 (ext. 4457). **Baseball SID:** Zach Dirlam. **Telephone:** (352) 375-4683 (ext. 6175).
Assistant Coaches: Craig Bell, Chuck Jeroloman, Lars Davis. **Telephone:** (352) 375-4683 (ext. 4421).
Home Field: Florida Ballpark. **Seating Capacity:** 7000. **Outfield Dimensions:** LF--330, CF--400, RF--330.

FLORIDA A&M FAMU

Conference: Mid-Eastern.
Mailing Address: 1800 Whanish Way. **Website:** www. FAMUAthletics.com.
Head Coach: Jamey Shouppe. **Telephone:** (850) 599-3202. **Baseball SID:** Curtis Ford. **Telephone:** (850) 599-3849.
Assistant Coaches: Bryan Henry, *Jamey Shouppe. **Telephone:** (850) 599-7391.
Home Field: Moore-Kittles Field. **Seating Capacity:** 500. **Outfield Dimensions:** LF--330, CF--410, RF--330.

FLORIDA ATLANTIC OWLS

Conference: Conference USA.
Mailing Address: 777 Glades Road, Boca Raton, FL 33431. **Website:** www.fausports.com.

Head Coach: John McCormack. **Telephone:** (561) 297-1055. **Baseball SID:** Jonathan Fraysure. **Telephone:** (561) 430-7148.

Assistant Coaches: David Kopp, *Greg Mamula. **Telephone:** (561) 297-3956.

Home Field: FAU Baseball Stadium. **Seating Capacity:** 1718. **Outfield Dimensions:** LF--330, CF--400, RF--330.

FLORIDA GULF COAST EAGLES

Conference: Atlantic Sun.
Mailing Address: 10501 FGCU Boulevard South | Fort Myers, Fla. 33965. **Website:** FGCUAthletics.com.
Head Coach: Dave Tollett. **Telephone:** (239) 590-7051. **Baseball SID:** Meg Ellis. **Telephone:** N/A.
Assistant Coaches: *Brandon Romans, Brandon Romans. **Telephone:** (239) 590-7058.
Home Field: Swanson Stadium. **Seating Capacity:** 1500. **Outfield Dimensions:** LF--325, CF--400, RF--375.

FLORIDA INTERNATIONAL PANTHERS

Conference: Conference USA.
Mailing Address: University Park 11200 S.W. 8th St Miami, Fl 33199. **Website:** fiuathletics.com.
Head Coach: Mervyl Melendez. **Telephone:** (305) 348-3166. **Baseball SID:** Tyler Brian. **Telephone:** (305) 348-2084.
Assistant Coaches: Willie Collazo, *Dax Norris.
Home Field: FIU Baseball Stadium. **Seating Capacity:** 2000. **Outfield Dimensions:** LF--325, CF--400, RF--325.

FLORIDA STATE SEMINOLES

Conference: ACC.
Mailing Address: 403 W. Stadium Drive Tallahassee, FL 32304. **Website:** www.seminoles.com.
Head Coach: Mike Martin, Jr.. **Telephone:** (850) 644-9129. **Baseball SID:** Steven McCartney. **Telephone:** --.
Assistant Coaches: Jimmy Belanger, *Mike Metcalf. **Telephone:** (850) 644-1075.
Home Field: Mike Martin Field at Dick Howser Stadium. **Seating Capacity:** 6700. **Outfield Dimensions:** LF--340, CF--400, RF--320.

FORDHAM RAMS

Conference: Atlantic 10.
Mailing Address: 441 E. Fordham Rd, Bronx, NY 10458. **Website:** www.fordhamsports.com.
Head Coach: Kevin Leighton. **Telephone:** 718-817-4292. **Baseball SID:** Scott Kwiatkowski. **Telephone:** 718-817-4219.
Assistant Coaches: Elliot Glynn, Pat Porter, Jared Franklin. **Telephone:** 718-817-4295.
Home Field: Houlihan Park. **Seating Capacity:** 1000. **Outfield Dimensions:** LF--338, CF--400, RF--338.

FRESNO STATE BULLDOGS

Conference: Mountain West.
Mailing Address: 1620 East Bulldog Lane OF 87 Fresno, CA 93740. **Website:** www.gobulldogs.com.
Head Coach: Mike Batesole. **Telephone:** (559) 278-2178. **Baseball SID:** Travis Blanshan. **Telephone:** (559) 278-4647.
Assistant Coaches: Greg Gonzalez, *Ryan Overland. **Telephone:** (559) 278-2178.
Home Field: Pete Beiden Field at Bob Bennett Stadium. **Seating Capacity:** 3575. **Outfield Dimensions:** LF--330, CF--400, RF--330.

GARDNER-WEBB BULLDOGS

Conference: Big South.
Mailing Address: 110 S. Main St., Boiling Springs, N.C. 28017. **Website:** www.gwusports.com.
Head Coach: Jim Chester. **Telephone:** 704-406-4421. **Baseball SID:** Ryan Bridges. **Telephone:** 704-406-3523.
Assistant Coaches: Conner Scarborough, Anthony Marks, Jake Marinelli. **Telephone:** 704-406-3557.
Home Field: Bill Masters Field at John Henry Moss Stadium. **Seating Capacity:** 550.

GEORGE MASON PATRIOTS

Conference: Atlantic 10.
Mailing Address: 5501 University Drive, Fairfax, Va. 22030. **Website:** GoMason.com.
Head Coach: Bill Brown. **Telephone:** (703) 993-3282. **Baseball SID:** Steve Kolbe. **Telephone:** (703) 993-3268.
Assistant Coaches: Shawn Camp, *Brian Pugh. **Telephone:** (703) 993-3328.
Home Field: Spuhler Field. **Seating Capacity:** 1000. **Outfield Dimensions:** LF--320, CF--400, RF--320.

GEORGE WASHINGTON COLONIALS

Conference: Atlantic 10.
Mailing Address: 600 22nd St. NW, Washington, DC 20052. **Website:** GWsports.com.
Head Coach: Gregg Ritchie. **Telephone:** (202) 994-7399. **Baseball SID:** Kevin Burke. **Telephone:** (202) 994-5666.
Assistant Coaches: Chad Marshall, *Rick Oliveri. **Telephone:** (202) 994-5933.
Home Field: Tucker Field at Barcroft Park. **Seating Capacity:** 500. **Outfield Dimensions:** LF--330, CF--380, RF--330.

GEORGETOWN HOYAS

Conference: Big East.
Mailing Address: 3700 O St. NW, Washington, D.C. 20057. **Website:** www.GUHoyas.com.
Head Coach: Edwin Thompson. **Telephone:** (202) 687-2462. **Baseball SID:** Brendan Thomas. **Telephone:** (202) 687-6783.
Assistant Coaches: N/A.
Home Field: Shirley Povich Field. **Seating Capacity:** 1500. **Outfield Dimensions:** LF--330, CF--375, RF--330.

GEORGIA BULLDOGS

Conference: SEC.
Mailing Address: P.O. Box 1472, Athens, Ga. 30603. **Website:** georgiadogs.com.
Head Coach: Scott Stricklin. **Telephone:** (706) 542-8041. **Baseball SID:** Christopher Lakos. **Telephone:** (706) 542-7994.
Assistant Coaches: *Scott Daeley, Sean Kenny. **Telephone:** (706) 542-0400.
Home Field: Foley Field. **Seating Capacity:** 2760. **Outfield Dimensions:** LF--350, CF--404, RF--314.

GEORGIA SOUTHERN EAGLES

Conference: Sun Belt.
Mailing Address: 651 Fair Road, Statesboro, Ga. 30458. **Website:** gseagles.com.
Head Coach: Rodney Hennon. **Telephone:** (912) 478-7360. **Baseball SID:** Aaron Socha.
Assistant Coaches: *Alan Beck, BJ Green. **Telephone:** (912) 478-1331.

Home Field: J.I. Clements Stadium. **Seating Capacity:** 3000. **Outfield Dimensions:** LF--335, CF--390, RF--329.

GEORGIA STATE PANTHERS

Conference: Sun Belt.
Mailing Address: 755 Hank Aaron Drive, Atlanta, GA 30315. **Website:** GeorgiaStateSports.com.
Head Coach: Brad Stromdahl. **Telephone:** (404) 290-1743. **Baseball SID:** Allison George. **Telephone:** (404) 413-4032.
Assistant Coaches: Dalton Martinez, *Matt Taylor. **Telephone:** (404) 374-7477.
Home Field: GSU Baseball Complex. **Seating Capacity:** 1000. **Outfield Dimensions:** LF--334, CF--385, RF--338.

GEORGIA TECH YELLOW JACKETS

Conference: ACC.
Mailing Address: 255 Ferst Drive Atlanta, GA 30308. **Website:** ramblinwreck.com.
Head Coach: Danny Hall. **Telephone:** (404) 894-5471. **Baseball SID:** Andrew Clausen. **Telephone:** (404) 894-5445.
Assistant Coaches: Danny Borrell, *James Ramsey, Zeke Pinkham. **Telephone:** (404) 894-2261.
Home Field: Russ Chandler Stadium. **Seating Capacity:** 4157. **Outfield Dimensions:** LF--328, CF--400, RF--334.

GONZAGA BULLDOGS

Conference: West Coast.
Mailing Address: 502 E. Boone, Spokane, WA. **Website:** GoZags.com.
Head Coach: Mark Machtolf. **Telephone:** (509) 313-4209. **Baseball SID:** Jenna Larson. **Telephone:** (509) 313-4227.
Assistant Coaches: *Danny Evans, Brandon Harmon. **Telephone:** (509) 313-4078.
Home Field: Patterson Ballpark and Steve Hertz Field. **Seating Capacity:** 2500. **Outfield Dimensions:** LF--326, CF--405, RF--326.

GRAMBLING STATE TIGERS

Conference: Southwestern.
Mailing Address: 100 N. Stadium Drive, Grambling, LA 71245. **Website:** www.gsutigers.com.
Head Coach: James Cooper. **Telephone:** 318-274-6566. **Baseball SID:** Habtom Keleta. **Telephone:** 318-243-9996.
Assistant Coaches: Davin Pierre, B.J. Johnson. **Telephone:** 318-274-2416.
Home Field: Wilbert Ellis Field at Ralph Waldo Emerson Jones Park. **Seating Capacity:** 1100. **Outfield Dimensions:** LF--315, CF--400, RF--350.

GRAND CANYON LOPES

Conference: Western Athletic.
Mailing Address: 3300 W Camelback Rd, Phoenix, AZ 85017. **Website:** gculopes.com.
Head Coach: Andy Stankiewicz. **Telephone:** (602) 639-6042. **Baseball SID:** Josh Hauser. **Telephone:** (602) 639-8328.
Assistant Coaches: *Gregg Wallis, Jon Wente. **Telephone:** (602) 639-7676.
Home Field: Brazell Field at GCU Ballpark. **Seating Capacity:** 4000. **Outfield Dimensions:** LF--320, CF--375, RF--330.

HARTFORD HAWKS

Conference: America East.
Mailing Address: 200 Bloomfield Ave, West Hartford, CT 06117. **Website:** https://www.hartfordhawks.com/index.aspx?path=baseball.
Head Coach: Justin Blood. **Telephone:** (860) 768-5760. **Baseball SID:** Tyrell Walden-Martin. **Telephone:** (860) 768-4501.
Assistant Coaches: Steve Malinowski, *Trey Stover. **Telephone:** (570) 502-1405.
Home Field: Fiondella Field. **Seating Capacity:** 1000. **Outfield Dimensions:** LF--325, CF--400, RF--325.

HARVARD CRIMSON

Conference: Ivy League.
Mailing Address: 65 N. Harvard St., Boston, MA 02163. **Website:** www.gocrimson.com.
Head Coach: Bill Decker. **Telephone:** 617-495-2629. **Baseball SID:** Devan Horahan. **Telephone:** 617-495-2206.
Assistant Coaches: Bryan Stark, Brady Kirkpatrick, Kyle Decker. **Telephone:** 617-496-1435.
Home Field: O'Donnell Field. **Seating Capacity:** 1600. **Outfield Dimensions:** LF--335, CF--415, RF--335.

HAWAII RAINBOW WARRIORS

Conference: Big West.
Mailing Address: 1337 Lower Campus Rd., Honolulu, HI 96822. **Website:** hawaiiathleticds.com.
Head Coach: Mike Trapasso. **Telephone:** 808 956-6247. **Baseball SID:** Fletcher Like. **Telephone:** (808) 956-4480.
Assistant Coaches: *Mike Brown, Carl Fraticelli, Kila Ka'aihue. **Telephone:** (808) 400-5303.
Home Field: Les Murakami Stadium. **Seating Capacity:** 4312. **Outfield Dimensions:** LF--325, CF--385, RF--325.

HIGH POINT PANTHERS

Conference: Big South.
Mailing Address: 1 University Pkwy, High Point, NC, 28267. **Website:** https://highpointpanthers.com/.
Head Coach: Craig Cozart. **Telephone:** (336) 841-9190. **Baseball SID:** Joe Templin. **Telephone:** (336) 841-4638.
Assistant Coaches: Jason Laws, *Rick Marlin. **Telephone:** (336) 841-4614.
Home Field: Williard Stadium. **Seating Capacity:** 550. **Outfield Dimensions:** LF--325, CF--400, RF--330.

HOFSTRA PRIDE

Conference: Colonial.
Mailing Address: 230 Hofstra University, PEC 232, Hempstead, NY 11549. **Website:** http://www.GoHofstra.com.
Head Coach: John Russo. **Telephone:** (516) 463-3759. **Baseball SID:** Len Skoros. **Telephone:** (516) 463-4602.
Assistant Coaches: Blake Nation, *Matt Wessinger. **Telephone:** (516) 463-5065.
Home Field: University Field. **Seating Capacity:** 400. **Outfield Dimensions:** LF--322, CF--382, RF--337.

HOLY CROSS CRUSADERS

Conference: Patriot.
Mailing Address: 1 College St, Worcester, MA 01610. **Website:** goholycross.com.
Head Coach: Ed Kahovec. **Telephone:** (508) 793-2753.

Baseball SID: Sarah Kirkpatrick. **Telephone:** (508) 793-2780.

Assistant Coaches: Sam Tinkham, Zach Hubbard, Ryan O'Rourke.

Home Field: Hanover Insurance Park at Fitton Field. **Seating Capacity:** 3000. **Outfield Dimensions:** LF--332, CF--385, RF--313.

HOUSTON COUGARS

Conference: American Athletic.
Mailing Address: 3204 Cullen Blvd. Houston, TX 77004. **Website:** UHCougars.com.
Head Coach: Todd Whitting. **Baseball SID:** Andrew Pate.
Assistant Coaches: Sammy Esposito, *Terry Rooney.
Home Field: Don Sanders Field at Darryl & Lori Schroeder Park. **Seating Capacity:** 3500. **Outfield Dimensions:** LF--330, CF--390, RF--330.

HOUSTON BAPTIST HUSKIES

Conference: Southland.
Mailing Address: 7502 Fondren Rd., Houston, TX 77074. **Website:** www.hbuhuskies.com.
Head Coach: Jared Moon. **Telephone:** 281-649-3332. **Baseball SID:** Russ Reneau. **Telephone:** 281-649-3098.
Assistant Coaches: Xavier Hernandez, Russell Stockton, Jared LaRocque. **Telephone:** 281-649-3262.
Home Field: Husky Field. **Seating Capacity:** 500. **Outfield Dimensions:** LF--330, CF--406, RF--330.

ILLINOIS FIGHTING ILLINI

Conference: Big Ten.
Mailing Address: Bielfeldt Athletics Administration Building 1700 S. Fourth Street Champaign, IL 61820 217-333-3631. **Website:** FightingIllini.com.
Head Coach: Dan Hartleb. **Telephone:** (217) 244-8144. **Baseball SID:** Brett Moore. **Telephone:** (217) 244-2092.
Assistant Coaches: Mark Allen, *Adam Christ. **Telephone:** (217) 300-2220.
Home Field: Illinois Field. **Seating Capacity:** 3000. **Outfield Dimensions:** LF--330, CF--400, RF--330.

ILLINOIS STATE REDBIRDS

Conference: Missouri Valley.
Mailing Address: 700 Gregory St Normal IL 61761. **Website:** https://goredbirds.com/sports/baseball.
Head Coach: Steve Holm. **Telephone:** (309) 438-4458. **Baseball SID:** Scott Beaton.
Assistant Coaches: TJ Bennett, *Wally Crancer, Ross Learnard. **Telephone:** (309) 438-5151.
Home Field: Duffy Bass Field. **Seating Capacity:** 1200. **Outfield Dimensions:** LF--330, CF--400, RF--330.

ILLINOIS-CHICAGO FLAMES

Conference: Horizon.
Mailing Address: 839 West Roosevelt Rd, Chicago, IL 60608. **Website:** uicflames.com.
Head Coach: Mike Dee. **Telephone:** (312) 996-8645. **Baseball SID:** Dan Wallace. **Telephone:** (312) 355-3139.
Assistant Coaches: *John Flood, Sean McDermott. **Telephone:** (312) 355-2973.
Home Field: Curtis Granderson Stadium. **Seating Capacity:** 1800. **Outfield Dimensions:** LF--325, CF--400, RF--325.

INCARNATE WORD CARDINALS

Conference: Southland.
Mailing Address: 4301 Broadway, San Antonio, TX 78209. **Website:** uiwcardinals.com.
Head Coach: Ryan Shotzberger. **Baseball SID:** Cari Gold. **Telephone:** (210) 829-6041.
Assistant Coaches: *Greg Evans, Kyle Winkler, Jake Arledge.
Home Field: Sullivan Field. **Seating Capacity:** 500. **Outfield Dimensions:** LF--326, CF--396, RF--326.

INDIANA HOOSIERS

Conference: Big Ten.
Mailing Address: 1001 E. 17th Street, Bloomington, IN 47408. **Website:** iuhoosiers.com.
Head Coach: Jeff Mercer. **Telephone:** (812) 855-9155. **Baseball SID:** Scott Burns. **Telephone:** (812) 856-2939.
Assistant Coaches: *Dan Held, Justin Parker. **Telephone:** (812) 855-9155.
Home Field: Bart Kaufman Field. **Seating Capacity:** 4000. **Outfield Dimensions:** LF--330, CF--400, RF--340.

INDIANA STATE SYCAMORES

Conference: Missouri Valley.
Mailing Address: 401 N. 4th Street Arena Suite Terre Haute, IN 47809. **Website:** GoSycamores.com.
Head Coach: Mitch Hannahs. **Telephone:** (812) 237-4051. **Baseball SID:** Tim McCaughan. **Telephone:** (812) 237-4161.
Assistant Coaches: *Brian Smiley, Brad Vanderglas. **Telephone:** (812) 237-4630.
Home Field: Bob Warn Field. **Seating Capacity:** 2000. **Outfield Dimensions:** LF--335, CF--400, RF--335.

IONA GAELS

Conference: Metro Atlantic.
Mailing Address: Hynes Center, 715 North Avenue, New Rochelle, N.Y. 10801. **Website:** www.icgaels.com.
Head Coach: Paul Panik. **Telephone:** 914-633-2319. **Baseball SID:** Brian Beyrer. **Telephone:** 914-637-2726.
Assistant Coaches: J.T. Genovese, Ryan Moretti, Anthony Fava. **Telephone:** 914-633-2319.
Home Field: City Park. **Outfield Dimensions:** LF--355, CF--385, RF--335.

IOWA HAWKEYES

Conference: Big Ten.
Mailing Address: S300 CHA, Iowa City, IA 52242. **Website:** hawkeyesports.com.
Head Coach: Rick Heller. **Telephone:** (319) 335-9390. **Baseball SID:** James Allan. **Telephone:** (319) 335-6439.
Assistant Coaches: Robin Lund, *Marty Sutherland. **Telephone:** (319) 335-9329.
Home Field: Duane Banks Field. **Seating Capacity:** 3000. **Outfield Dimensions:** LF--329, CF--395, RF--329.

JACKSON STATE TIGERS

Conference: Southwestern.
Mailing Address: 1400 John R. Lynch St., Jackson, MS 39217. **Website:** www.gojsutigers.com.
Head Coach: Omar Johnson. **Telephone:** 601-979-3930. **Baseball SID:** Dennis Driscoll. **Telephone:** 601-979-0857.
Assistant Coaches: Chadwick Hall, Kevin Whiteside. **Telephone:** 601-979-3928.
Home Field: Braddy Field. **Seating Capacity:** 800.

Outfield Dimensions: LF--325, CF--400, RF--325.

JACKSONVILLE DOLPHINS

Conference: Atlantic Sun.
Mailing Address: 2800 University Blvd., Jacksonville, FL, 32211. **Website:** judolphins.com.
Head Coach: Chris Hayes. **Telephone:** (904) 256-7476. **Baseball SID:** Scott Manze. **Telephone:** (904) 256-7402.
Assistant Coaches: Jerry Edwards, *Brad Wilkerson. **Telephone:** (904) 256-7429.
Home Field: John Sessions Stadium. **Seating Capacity:** 1750. **Outfield Dimensions:** LF--340, CF--405, RF--340.

JACKSONVILLE STATE GAMECOCKS

Conference: Ohio Valley.
Mailing Address: 700 Pelham Road North, Jacksonville, AL 36265. **Website:** www.jsugamecock-sports.com.
Head Coach: Jim Case. **Telephone:** (256) 782-5367. **Baseball SID:** Tony Schmidt. **Telephone:** (256) 782-5377.
Assistant Coaches: *Evan Bush, Mike Murphree. **Telephone:** (256) 782-5358.
Home Field: Jim Case Stadium. **Seating Capacity:** 1600. **Outfield Dimensions:** LF--330, CF--403, RF--335.

JAMES MADISON DUKES

Conference: Colonial.
Mailing Address: 800 S Main St, Harrisonburg, VA 22807. **Website:** www.jmusports.com.
Head Coach: Marlin Ikenberry. **Telephone:** (540) 568-3932. **Baseball SID:** Christian Howe. **Telephone:** (540) 568-7910.
Assistant Coaches: Alex Guerra. **Telephone:** (540) 568-3630.
Home Field: Eagle Field at Veterans Memorial Park. **Seating Capacity:** 1200. **Outfield Dimensions:** LF--340, CF--400, RF--320.

KANSAS JAYHAWKS

Conference: Big 12.
Mailing Address: 1651 Naismith Drive, Lawrence, Kansas. **Website:** KUAthletics.com.
Head Coach: Ritch Price. **Telephone:** -. **Baseball SID:** Brent Beerends. **Telephone:** -.
Assistant Coaches: Ryan Graves, *Ritchie Price. **Telephone:** -.
Home Field: Hoglund Ballpark. **Seating Capacity:** 2500. **Outfield Dimensions:** LF--330, CF--400, RF--330.

KANSAS STATE WILDCATS

Conference: Big 12.
Mailing Address: 1800 College Ave, Manhattan, KS 66502. **Website:** kstatesports.com.
Head Coach: Pete Hughes. **Baseball SID:** Christopher Brown. **Telephone:** (785) 532-7976.
Assistant Coaches: *Ryan Connolly, Buck Taylor. **Telephone:** ((785) 473-8158.
Home Field: Tointon Family Stadium. **Seating Capacity:** 2344. **Outfield Dimensions:** LF--325, CF--390, RF--320.

KENNESAW STATE OWLS

Conference: Atlantic Sun.
Mailing Address: 590 Cobb Avenue MD O201 Kennesaw, Ga. || 1000 Chastain Rd Kennesaw GA 30144. **Website:** ksuowls.com.

Head Coach: Mike Sansing. **Telephone:** (470) 578-6264. **Baseball SID:** Matteen Zibanejadrad || Nathan Bryant. **Telephone:** (470) 578-7792.
Assistant Coaches: *Trey Fowler, Travis McClanahan. **Telephone:** (470) 578-2098.
Home Field: Stillwell Stadium. **Seating Capacity:** 900. **Outfield Dimensions:** LF--330, CF--400, RF--330.

KENT STATE GOLDEN FLASHES

Conference: Mid-American.
Mailing Address: 1025 Risman Dr. Kent Ohio 44242. **Website:** KentStateSports.com.
Head Coach: Jeff Duncan. **Telephone:** (330) 672-8468. **Baseball SID:** Dan Griffinb. **Telephone:** (330) 672-8468.
Assistant Coaches: Mike Birkbeck, *Barrett Serrato. **Telephone:** (330) 672-8468.
Home Field: Schoonover Stadium. **Seating Capacity:** 1000. **Outfield Dimensions:** LF--335, CF--395, RF--335.

KENTUCKY WILDCATS

Conference: SEC.
Mailing Address: 510 Wildcat Ct., Lexington, KY, 40506. **Website:** www.ukathletics.com.
Head Coach: Nick Mingione. **Telephone:** (859) 257-8052. **Baseball SID:** Matt May. **Telephone:** (859) 257-8504.
Assistant Coaches: *Will Coggin, Dan Roszel. **Telephone:** (859) 257-8052.
Home Field: Kentucky Proud Park. **Seating Capacity:** 5000. **Outfield Dimensions:** LF--335, CF--400, RF--320.

LA SALLE EXPLORERS

Conference: Atlantic 10.
Mailing Address: 1900 W. Olney Ave., Philadelphia, PA 19141. **Website:** goexplorers.com.
Head Coach: David Miller. **Telephone:** (215) 951-5157. **Baseball SID:** Nick Lantz. **Telephone:** (215) 991-2886.
Assistant Coaches: *Andrew Amaro, Rob Varvaro. **Telephone:** (267) 760-3204.
Home Field: Hank DeVincent Field. **Seating Capacity:** 1000.

LAFAYETTE LEOPARDS

Conference: Patriot.
Mailing Address: 730 High St, Easton, PA 18042. **Website:** goleopards.com.
Head Coach: Tim Reilly. **Telephone:** 610-330-5945. **Baseball SID:** Hannah Simmons. **Telephone:** 610-330-5518.
Assistant Coaches: John Lyons-Harrison, Ryan Ricci, Garrett Siemek. **Telephone:** (610) 330-3257.
Home Field: Hilton Rahn '51 Field at Kamine Stadium. **Seating Capacity:** 500. **Outfield Dimensions:** LF--332, CF--403, RF--335.

LAMAR CARDINALS

Conference: Southland.
Mailing Address: 4400 South Martin Luther King Blvd. Beaumont, TX 77705. **Website:** lamarcardinals.com.
Head Coach: Will Davis. **Baseball SID:** James Dixon. **Telephone:** (409) 880-8329.
Assistant Coaches: *Scott Hatten, Sean Snedeker, Hunter Doucet. **Telephone:** (409) 880-8135.
Home Field: Vincent-Beck Stadium. **Seating Capacity:** 3500. **Outfield Dimensions:** LF--325, CF--380, RF--325.

LEHIGH MOUNTAIN HAWKS

Conference: Patriot.
Mailing Address: 27 Memorial Dr W, Bethlehem, PA 18015. **Website:** lehighsports.com.
Head Coach: Sean Leary. **Telephone:** (610) 758-4315. **Baseball SID:** Josh Liddick. **Telephone:** (610) 758-5043.
Assistant Coaches: Sean Buchanan, *AJ Miller. **Telephone:** (610) 758-4315.
Home Field: J. David Walker Field at Legacy Park. **Seating Capacity:** 370. **Outfield Dimensions:** LF--320, CF--400, RF--320.

LIBERTY FLAMES

Conference: Atlantic Sun.
Mailing Address: 1971 University Blvd Lynchburg, VA 24515. **Website:** https://www.liberty.edu/flames/?PID=36964&teamID=1.
Head Coach: Scott Jackson. **Telephone:** (434) 582-2103. **Baseball SID:** Ryan Bomberger. **Telephone:** (434) 582-2292.
Assistant Coaches: *Tyler Cannon/Matt, Matt Williams.
Home Field: Liberty Baseball Stadium. **Seating Capacity:** 4500. **Outfield Dimensions:** LF--325, CF--395, RF--325.

LIPSCOMB BISONS

Conference: Atlantic Sun.
Mailing Address: 3901 Granny White Pike Nashville, TN 37204-3951. **Website:** lipscombsports.com.
Head Coach: Jeff Forehand. **Telephone:** (615) 966-5716. **Baseball SID:** Jack Bluhm. **Telephone:** (952) 687-1307.
Assistant Coaches: Grayson Crawford, *Brian Ryman, Will Hawks. **Telephone:** (615) 966-5879.
Home Field: Dugan Field. **Seating Capacity:** 750. **Outfield Dimensions:** LF--330, CF--400, RF--330.

LONG BEACH STATE DIRTBAGS

Conference: Big West.
Mailing Address: 1250 Bellflower Blvd, Long Beach, CA 90840. **Website:** https://longbeachstate.com/sports/baseball.
Head Coach: Eric Valenzuela. **Telephone:** (562) 985-8215. **Baseball SID:** Roger Kirk. **Telephone:** (562) 985-7565.
Assistant Coaches: *Daniel Costanza, Bryan Peters, Ryan Day. **Telephone:** (562) 985-4661.
Home Field: Blair Field. **Seating Capacity:** 7000. **Outfield Dimensions:** LF--335, CF--395, RF--330.

LONG ISLAND SHARKS

Conference: Northeast.
Mailing Address: 720 Northern Blvd., Brookville, N.Y. 11548. **Website:** www.liuathletics.com.
Head Coach: Dan Pirillo. **Telephone:** 516-299-2939. **Baseball SID:** Casey Snedecor. **Telephone:** 718-488-1307.
Assistant Coaches: Mike Gaffney, Tom Carty. **Telephone:** 516-299-2287.
Home Field: LIU Baseball Stadium. **Outfield Dimensions:** LF--330, CF--400, RF--330.

LONGWOOD LANCERS

Conference: Big South.
Mailing Address: 201 High St., Tabb Building, Farmville, VA 23909. **Website:** www.longwoodlancers.com.
Head Coach: Ryan Mau. **Telephone:** 434-395-2843. **Baseball SID:** Sam Hovan. **Telephone:** 434-395-2345.
Assistant Coaches: Daniel Wood, C.J. Rhodes, Blake Urquhart. **Telephone:** 434-395-2757.
Home Field: Buddy Bolding Stadium. **Seating Capacity:** 500. **Outfield Dimensions:** LF--335, CF--394, RF--335.

LOUISIANA STATE TIGERS

Conference: SEC.
Mailing Address: Nicholson Dr. @ N. Stadium Dr. Baton Rouge, LA 70803. **Website:** www.lsusports.net.
Head Coach: Paul Mainieri. **Telephone:** (225) 578-4148. **Baseball SID:** Bill Franques. **Telephone:** (225) 578-8226.
Assistant Coaches: *Nolan Cain, Alan Dunn. **Telephone:** (225) 578-4148.
Home Field: Alex Box Stadium. **Seating Capacity:** 10326. **Outfield Dimensions:** LF--330, CF--405, RF--330.

LOUISIANA TECH BULLDOGS

Conference: Conference USA.
Mailing Address: Ruston, LA 71270. **Website:** https://latechsports.com/sports/baseball.
Head Coach: Lane Burroughs. **Baseball SID:** Tyler Hotz. **Telephone:** (318) 257-5305.
Assistant Coaches: *Mitch Gaspard, Mike Silva, Matt Miller.
Home Field: J.C. Love at Pat Patterson Park. **Seating Capacity:** 2000. **Outfield Dimensions:** LF--315, CF--387, RF--325.

LOUISIANA-LAFAYETTE RAGIN' CAJUNS

Conference: Sun Belt.
Mailing Address: 201 Reinhardt Dr. Lafayette, LA 70506. **Website:** ragincajuns.com.
Head Coach: Matt Deggs. **Telephone:** (337) 482-5191. **Baseball SID:** Tim Wiemann.
Assistant Coaches: Jeremy Talbot, *Jake Wells. **Telephone:** (337) 482-5189.
Home Field: M.L. 'Tigue' Moore Field at Russo Park. **Seating Capacity:** 6015. **Outfield Dimensions:** LF--330, CF--400, RF--330.

LOUISIANA-MONROE WARHAWKS

Conference: Sun Belt.
Mailing Address: 308 Warhawk Way, Monroe, LA 71203. **Website:** ulmwarhawks.com.
Head Coach: Michael Federico. **Telephone:** (318) 342-3591. **Baseball SID:** Mike Hammett. **Telephone:** (318) 342-7925.
Assistant Coaches: *Jacob Carlson, Matt Collins. **Telephone:** (318) 342-5396.
Home Field: Warhawk Field. **Seating Capacity:** 1800. **Outfield Dimensions:** LF--330, CF--400, RF--330.

LOUISVILLE CARDINALS

Conference: ACC.
Mailing Address: 215 Central Avenue, Louisville, KY 40292. **Website:** www.gocards.com.
Head Coach: Dan McDonnell. **Telephone:** (502) 852-

0103. **Baseball SID:** Stephen Williams. **Telephone:** (502) 852-4857.

Assistant Coaches: *Eric Snider, Roger Williams. **Telephone:** (502) 852-8145.

Home Field: Jim Patterson Stadium. **Seating Capacity:** 4000. **Outfield Dimensions:** LF--330, CF--402, RF--330.

LOYOLA MARYMOUNT LIONS

Conference: West Coast.
Mailing Address: 1 Loyola Marymount University Drive., Los Angeles, CA 90045. **Website:** lmulions.com.
Head Coach: Nathan Choate. **Telephone:** (310) 338-4533. **Baseball SID:** Steven Esparza. **Telephone:** (310) 338-7638.

Assistant Coaches: *Tony Asaro, Matt Curtis. **Telephone:** (310) 338-4533.

Home Field: George C. Page Stadium. **Seating Capacity:** 600. **Outfield Dimensions:** LF--326, CF--406, RF--321.

MAINE BLACK BEARS

Conference: America East.
Mailing Address: 5745 Mahaney Clubhouse, Orono ME 04469. **Website:** goblackbears.com.
Head Coach: Nicholas Derba. **Telephone:** (207) 581-1090. **Baseball SID:** Tyler Neville. **Telephone:** (207) 581-4849.

Assistant Coaches: *Scott Heath, Josh Kieffer.
Home Field: Mahaney Diamond. **Seating Capacity:** 4400. **Outfield Dimensions:** LF--330, CF--400, RF--330.

MANHATTAN JASPERS

Conference: Metro Atlantic.
Mailing Address: 4513 Manhattan College Parkway; Riverdale, NY 10471. **Website:** www.gojaspers.com.
Head Coach: Mike Cole. **Telephone:** (718) 862-7821. **Baseball SID:** Kevin Ross. **Telephone:** (716) 969-6126.

Assistant Coaches: Chris Cody, *Mike Cole.
Telephone: (718) 862-7821.

Home Field: VCP. **Seating Capacity:** Unlimited. **Outfield Dimensions:** LF--325, CF--395, RF--325.

MARIST RED FOXES

Conference: Metro Atlantic.
Mailing Address: McCann Center, 3399 North Road, Poughkeepsie, N.Y. 12601. **Website:** www.goredfoxes.com.
Head Coach: Chris Tracz. **Telephone:** 845-575-3000 ext. 2570. **Baseball SID:** Steve Speedling. **Telephone:** 845-575-3000 ext. 2441.

Assistant Coaches: Mike Coss, Andrew Pezzuto.
Home Field: McCann Baseball Field. **Outfield Dimensions:** LF--320, CF--390, RF--320.

MARSHALL THUNDERING HERD

Conference: Conference USA.
Mailing Address: 1 John Marshall Dr. Huntington, WV 25703. **Website:** www.herdzone.com.
Head Coach: Jeff Waggoner. **Telephone:** (304) 696-6454. **Baseball SID:** Cody Linn. **Telephone:** (304) 696-2418.

Assistant Coaches: Brian Karlet, *Joe Renner. **Telephone:** (304) 696-7146.

Home Field: The Kennedy Center. **Seating Capacity:** 100. **Outfield Dimensions:** LF--310, CF--405, RF--310.

MARYLAND TERRAPINS

Conference: Big Ten.
Mailing Address: 8500 Paint Branch Drive, College Park MD 20742. **Website:** umterps.com.
Head Coach: Rob Vaughn. **Telephone:** (301) 314-7003. **Baseball SID:** Hunter Dortenzo. **Telephone:** N/A.

Assistant Coaches: Corey Muscara, *Matt Swope. **Telephone:** (301) 314-7003.

Home Field: Bob "Turtle"" Smith Stadium". **Seating Capacity:** 2500. **Outfield Dimensions:** LF--320, CF--385, RF--325.

MARYLAND-BALTIMORE COUNTY RETRIEVERS

Conference: America East.
Mailing Address: 1000 Hilltop Circle Catonsville MD 21250. **Website:** https://umbcretrievers.com/sports/bsb/index.
Head Coach: Liam Bowen. **Baseball SID:** Dave Castellanos. **Telephone:** (410) 455-2639.

Assistant Coaches: Matt Marsh, *Ryan Terrill.
Home Field: Alumni Field. **Seating Capacity:** 1000. **Outfield Dimensions:** LF--330, CF--360, RF--330.

MARYLAND-EASTERN SHORE HAWKS

Conference: Mid-Eastern.
Mailing Address: 1 Backbone Rd. Princess Anne, MD. 21853. **Website:** https://easternshorehawks.com/sports/baseball.
Head Coach: Brian Hollamon. **Telephone:** (410) 651-7864. **Baseball SID:** Shawn Yonker. **Telephone:** (410) 651-6289.

Assistant Coaches: Chris Bengel, *Ben Kirk. **Telephone:** (410) 651-7041.

Home Field: Shorebird Stadium. **Seating Capacity:** 5200. **Outfield Dimensions:** LF--309, CF--400, RF--309.

MASSACHUSETTS MINUTEMEN

Conference: Atlantic 10.
Mailing Address: 131 Commonwealth Ave. Amherst, MA 01003. **Website:** https://umassathletics.com/sports/baseball.
Head Coach: Matt Reynolds. **Telephone:** (413) 545-3120. **Baseball SID:** Ryan Gallant. **Telephone:** (413) 687-3793.

Assistant Coaches: *Nate Cole, Mark Royer. **Telephone:** (774) 210-0311.

Home Field: Earl Lorden Field. **Seating Capacity:** 1000. **Outfield Dimensions:** LF--330, CF--400, RF--330.

MASSACHUSETTS-LOWELL RIVER HAWKS

Conference: America East.
Mailing Address: 1 University Ave Lowell, MA 01854 || 220 Pawtucket St, Lowell, MA 01854. **Website:** www.goriverhawks.com.
Head Coach: Ken Harring. **Telephone:** (978) 934-2344. **Baseball SID:** Jordyn Rochon. **Telephone:** (978) 934-6685.

Assistant Coaches: Joe Consolmagno, *Brad Cook. **Telephone:** (978) 934-2138.

Home Field: LeLacheur Park. **Seating Capacity:** 4800. **Outfield Dimensions:** LF--335, CF--400, RF--305.

MCNEESE STATE COWBOYS

Conference: Southland.
Mailing Address: 700 E. McNeese Street - Lake Charles, LA 70609. **Website:** mcneesesports.com.

Head Coach: Justin Hill. **Telephone:** N/A. **Baseball SID:** Matt Bonnette. **Telephone:** (337) 475-5207.
Assistant Coaches: Jimmy Rcklefsen, *Nick Zaleski. **Telephone:** N/A.
Home Field: Joe Miller Ballpark. **Seating Capacity:** 1500. **Outfield Dimensions:** LF--330, CF--400, RF--330.

MEMPHIS TIGERS

Conference: American Athletic.
Mailing Address: 570 Norma; St, Memphis TN 38152.
Website: gotigersgo.com.
Head Coach: Daron Schoenrock. **Baseball SID:** John Galatas. **Telephone:** (901) 678-2337.
Assistant Coaches: *Clay Greene, Russ Mcnickle. **Telephone:** (423) 737-8532.
Home Field: Fed Ex Park. **Seating Capacity:** 2500. **Outfield Dimensions:** LF--320, CF--380, RF--320.

MERCER BEARS

Conference: SoCon.
Mailing Address: 1501 Mercer University Drive, Macon, Ga. 31207. **Website:** www.MercerBears.com.
Head Coach: Craig Gibson. **Telephone:** (478) 301-2396. **Baseball SID:** Travis Rae. **Telephone:** (478) 301-5219.
Assistant Coaches: *Brent Shade, Willie Stewart. **Telephone:** (478) 301-5210.
Home Field: OrthoGeorga Park. **Seating Capacity:** 1500. **Outfield Dimensions:** LF--330, CF--400, RF--320.

MERRIMACK WARRIORS

Conference: Northeast.
Mailing Address: 315 Turnpike Street North Andover, MA 01845. **Website:** www.merrimackathletics.com.
Head Coach: Nick Barese. **Telephone:** (978) 837-5230. **Baseball SID:** Mike Sullivan. **Telephone:** (978) 837-5036.
Assistant Coaches: *Cody Kauffman, Cody Kauffman.
Home Field: Warrior Baseball Diamond. **Outfield Dimensions:** LF--335, CF--390, RF--335.

MIAMI HURRICANES

Conference: ACC.
Mailing Address: 6201 San Amaro Drive Coral Gables, FL 33146. **Website:** www.miamihurricanes.com.
Head Coach: Gino DiMare. **Telephone:** (305) 284-4171. **Baseball SID:** David Villavicencio. **Telephone:** (305) 284-3244.
Assistant Coaches: J.D. Arteaga, *Norberto Lopez. **Telephone:** (305) 284-4171.
Home Field: Alex Rodriguez Park at Mark Light Field. **Seating Capacity:** TBD. **Outfield Dimensions:** LF--330, CF--400, RF--330.

MIAMI (OHIO) REDHAWKS

Conference: Mid-American.
Mailing Address: 230 Millett Hall, Oxford, OH 45056. **Website:** www.miamiredhawks.com.
Head Coach: Danny Hayden. **Telephone:** 513-529-6631. **Baseball SID:** Dave Meyer. **Telephone:** 513-529-0402.
Assistant Coaches: Justin Dedman, Matthew Passauer, Dusty Hess.
Home Field: McKie Field at Hayden Park. **Seating Capacity:** 600.

MICHIGAN WOLVERINES

Conference: Big Ten.
Mailing Address: 1000 South State Street, Ann Arbor, MI 48109. **Website:** mgoblue.com.
Head Coach: Erik Bakich. **Baseball SID:** Kurt Svoboda. **Telephone:** (734) 615-0331.
Assistant Coaches: *Nick Schnabel, Nick Schnabel.
Home Field: Ray Fisher Stadium. **Seating Capacity:** 4000. **Outfield Dimensions:** LF--312, CF--395, RF--320.

MICHIGAN STATE SPARTANS

Conference: Big Ten.
Mailing Address: Baseball office: RM. 304 Jenison Field House, 223 Kalamazoo St., East Lansing, Mi 48824-1025. **Website:** MSUSpartans.com.
Head Coach: Jake Boss Jr.. **Telephone:** (517) 355-4486. **Baseball SID:** Zach Fisher. **Telephone:** (517) 355-2271.
Assistant Coaches: *Graham Sikes, Mark Van. **Telephone:** (517) 355-0259.
Home Field: McLane Baseball Stadium at Kobs Field. **Seating Capacity:** 2500. **Outfield Dimensions:** LF--340, CF--400, RF--302.

MIDDLE TENNESSEE STATE BLUE RAIDERS

Conference: Conference USA.
Mailing Address: 1301 E Main St, Murfreesboro, TN 37132. **Website:** goblueraiders.com.
Head Coach: Jim Toman. **Telephone:** 898-2961. **Baseball SID:** Brady McBride. **Telephone:** 904-8209.
Assistant Coaches: Kyle Bunn, *Blake Hunt. **Telephone:** 494-8796.
Home Field: Reese Smith Jr. Field. **Seating Capacity:** 2600. **Outfield Dimensions:** LF--330, CF--390, RF--330.

MINNESOTA GOPHERS

Conference: Big Ten.
Mailing Address: Baseball Gibson-Nagurski Complex 600 15th Avenue SE Minneapolis, MN 55455. **Website:** GopherSports.com.
Head Coach: John Anderson. **Telephone:** (612) 625-1060. **Baseball SID:** Sullivan Bortner.
Assistant Coaches: *Packy Casey, Ty McDevitt. **Telephone:** (612) 625-3568.
Home Field: Siebert Field. **Seating Capacity:** 1420. **Outfield Dimensions:** LF--330, CF--390, RF--330.

MISSISSIPPI REBELS

Conference: SEC.
Mailing Address: 908 All-American Drive, University, MS, 38677. **Website:** olemisssports.com.
Head Coach: Mike Bianco. **Telephone:** (662) 915-6643. **Baseball SID:** Alex Sims. **Telephone:** (662) 915-1083.
Assistant Coaches: Mike Clement, *Carl Lafferty. **Telephone:** (662) 915-6643.
Home Field: Swayze Field. **Seating Capacity:** 11477. **Outfield Dimensions:** LF--330, CF--390, RF--330.

MISSISSIPPI STATE BULLDOGS

Conference: SEC.
Mailing Address: 110 Coliseum Circle; Mississippi State, MS 39762. **Website:** hailstate.com/sports/baseball.
Head Coach: Chris Lemonis. **Telephone:** (662) 325-3597. **Baseball SID:** Greg Campbell. **Telephone:** --.
Assistant Coaches: Scott Foxhall, *Jake Gautreau. **Telephone:** (662) 325-3597.
Home Field: Dudy Noble Field. **Seating Capacity:**

15,000. **Outfield Dimensions:** LF--330, CF--400, RF--305.

MISSISSIPPI VALLEY STATE DELTA DEVILS

Conference: Southwestern.
Mailing Address: 14000 Highway 82 West, Itta Bena, MS 38941. **Website:** www.mvsusports.com.
Head Coach: Aaron Stevens. **Telephone:** 662-254-3834. **Baseball SID:** Demetrius Howse. **Telephone:** 682-220-8165.
Home Field: Magnolia Field. **Seating Capacity:** 200.

MISSOURI TIGERS

Conference: SEC.
Mailing Address: 1 Champions Drive, Suite 200, Columbia, MO 65211. **Website:** MUTigers.com.
Head Coach: Steve Bieser. **Telephone:** (573) 884-6428. **Baseball SID:** Ben Ramirez.
Assistant Coaches: *Fred Corral, Jason Hagerty. **Telephone:** (573) 884-4783.
Home Field: Taylor Stadium. **Seating Capacity:** 3031. **Outfield Dimensions:** LF--340, CF--400, RF--340.

MISSOURI STATE BEARS

Conference: Missouri Valley.
Mailing Address: 901 S National, Springfield, MO 65897. **Website:** www.missouristatebears.com.
Head Coach: Keith Guttin. **Telephone:** (417) 836-4497. **Baseball SID:** Ben Adamson. **Telephone:** (417) 836-4584.
Assistant Coaches: *Paul Evans, Matt Lawson. **Telephone:** (417) 836-4496.
Home Field: Hammons Field. **Seating Capacity:** 8000. **Outfield Dimensions:** LF--315, CF--400, RF--330.

MONMOUTH HAWKS

Conference: Metro Atlantic.
Mailing Address: 400 Cedar Ave West Long Branch, NJ 07764. **Website:** www.monmouth.edu.
Head Coach: Dean Ehehalt. **Telephone:** (732) 263-5186. **Baseball SID:** Gary Kowal. **Telephone:** (732) 263-5557.
Assistant Coaches: *Chris Collazo, Josh Epstein. **Telephone:** (732) 263-5347.
Home Field: MU Baseball Field. **Outfield Dimensions:** LF--325, CF--395, RF--325.

MOREHEAD STATE EAGLES

Conference: Ohio Valley.
Mailing Address: 195 AAC Playforth Place, Morehead, KY 40351. **Website:** https://msueagles.com/sports/baseball.
Head Coach: Mik Aoki. **Telephone:** (606) 783-2881. **Baseball SID:** Matt Schabert. **Telephone:** (606) 783-2556.
Assistant Coaches: *Shane Conlon, Brady Ward. **Telephone:** (606) 783-2881.
Home Field: Allen Field. **Seating Capacity:** 1200. **Outfield Dimensions:** LF--318, CF--333, RF--320.

MOUNT ST MARY'S MOUNTAINEERS

Conference: Northeast.
Mailing Address: 16300 Old Emmitsburg Road, Emmitsburg, MD 21727. **Website:** mountathletics.com.
Head Coach: Scott Thomson. **Telephone:** (301) 447-3806. **Baseball SID:** Matt McCann. **Telephone:** (301) 447-5384.
Assistant Coaches: *Jeff Gergic, Dan Gerjets. **Telephone:** (301) **447-3806.Home Field:** E.T. Straw

Family Stadium.

MURRAY STATE RACERS

Conference: Ohio Valley.
Mailing Address: 102 Curris Center, Murray, KY 42071. **Website:** goracers.com.
Head Coach: Dan Skirka. **Telephone:** (270) 809-4892. **Baseball SID:** Justine Ertl. **Telephone:** (270) 809-7044.
Assistant Coaches: Tanner Gordon, Charles Bradley. **Telephone:** (270) 809-3475.
Home Field: Reagan Field. **Seating Capacity:** 800. **Outfield Dimensions:** LF--330, CF--400, RF--330.

NAVY MIDSHIPMEN

Conference: Patriot.
Mailing Address: 566 Brownson Road, Annapolis, Md. 21402. **Website:** navysports.com.
Head Coach: David Gerhart. **Telephone:** (410) 293-5571. **Baseball SID:** David Gerhart. **Telephone:** (410) 293-8787.
Assistant Coaches: Bobby Applegate, *Jeff Kane. **Telephone:** (410) 293-5428.
Home Field: Terwilliger Brothers Field at Max Bishop Stadium. **Seating Capacity:** 1500. **Outfield Dimensions:** LF--318, CF--390, RF--300.

NEBRASKA CORN HUSKERS

Conference: Big Ten.
Mailing Address: 403 Line Drive Circle, Lincoln, Nebraska 68508. **Website:** https://huskers.com/sports/baseball.
Head Coach: Will Bolt. **Telephone:** (402) 472-2269. **Baseball SID:** Jeremy Foote. **Telephone:** (402) 472-7778.
Assistant Coaches: Jeff Christy, *Lance Harvell.
Home Field: Haymarket Park. **Seating Capacity:** 8757. **Outfield Dimensions:** LF--335, CF--395, RF--330.

NEBRASKA-OMAHA MAVERICKS

Conference: Summit.
Mailing Address: 6001 Dodge Street Attention Sapp Fieldhouse Omaha Nebraska 68182. **Website:** https://omavs.com/.
Head Coach: Evan Porter. **Telephone:** (402) 250-4459. **Baseball SID:** Jared Meister. **Telephone:** (402) 380-5291.
Assistant Coaches: Brian Strawn, Payton Kinney. **Telephone:** (402) 554-2141.
Home Field: Tal Anderson Field. **Seating Capacity:** 1500. **Outfield Dimensions:** LF--325, CF--400, RF--325.

NEVADA WOLF PACK

Conference: Mountain West.
Mailing Address: 1664 N. Virginia St. Reno, NV 89557. **Website:** www.nevadawolfpack.com.
Head Coach: T.J. Bruce. **Telephone:** (775) 682-6978. **Baseball SID:** Katie Rihn. **Telephone:** (775) 682-6963.
Assistant Coaches: Abe Alvarez, *Troy Buckley.
Home Field: Don Weir Field at Peccole Park. **Seating Capacity:** 3000. **Outfield Dimensions:** LF--330, CF--400, RF--330.

NEVADA-LAS VEGAS REBELS

Conference: Mountain West.
Mailing Address: 4505 S. Maryland Parkway, Las Vegas, NV 89154. **Website:** unlvrebels.com.
Head Coach: Stan Stolte. **Telephone:** (702) 895-3499. **Baseball SID:** Jeffrey Seals. **Telephone:** (702) 895-3134.
Assistant Coaches: Kevin Higgins, *Cory Vanderhook.

Telephone: (702) 895-3835.
Home Field: Earl E. Wilson Stadium. **Seating Capacity:** 3000. **Outfield Dimensions:** LF--335, CF--400, RF--335.

NEW MEXICO LOBOS

Conference: Mountain West.
Mailing Address: 1414 University Drive, Albuquerque, N.M. 87106. **Website:** www.golobos.com.
Head Coach: Ray Birmingham. **Telephone:** 505-925-5720. **Baseball SID:** Sofia Lucero. **Telephone:** (505) 795-3876.
Assistant Coaches: Brandon Higelin, Jon Coyne, Nate Causey. **Telephone:** 505-925-5720.
Home Field: Santa Ana Star Field. **Seating Capacity:** 1000. **Outfield Dimensions:** LF--344, CF--408, RF--336.

NEW MEXICO STATE AGGIES

Conference: Western Athletic.
Mailing Address: 1815 Wells Street Las Cruces, NM 88003-8001. **Website:** NMStateSports.com.
Head Coach: Mike Kirby. **Telephone:** (575) 646-7693. **Baseball SID:** Oliver Grigg. **Telephone:** (575) 646-3269.
Assistant Coaches: Mike Pritchard, *Keith Zuniga. **Telephone:** (575) 646-5813.
Home Field: Presley Askew Field. **Seating Capacity:** 1000. **Outfield Dimensions:** LF--345, CF--400, RF--385.

NEW ORLEANS PRIVATEERS

Conference: Southland.
Mailing Address: 2000 Lakeshore Dr. New Orleans, LA 70148. **Website:** www.UNOPrivateers.com.
Head Coach: Blake Dean. **Telephone:** (504) 280-3879. **Baseball SID:** Emmanuel Pepis. **Telephone:** (504) 280-6284.
Assistant Coaches: AJ Battisto, *Brett Stewart. **Telephone:** (504) 280-7021.
Home Field: Maestri Field. **Seating Capacity:** 3000. **Outfield Dimensions:** LF--330, CF--405, RF--330.

NIAGARA PURPLE EAGLES

Conference: Metro Atlantic.
Mailing Address: Upper Level Gallagher Center, PO Box 2009, Niagara University, N.Y. 14109. **Website:** www.purpleeagles.com.
Head Coach: Rob McCoy. **Telephone:** 716-286-7361. **Baseball SID:** Breanna Jacobs. **Telephone:** 716-286-8586.
Assistant Coaches: Matt Spatafora. **Telephone:** 716-286-8624.
Home Field: Bobo Field. **Outfield Dimensions:** LF--327, CF--394, RF--315.

NICHOLLS STATE COLONELS

Conference: Southland.
Mailing Address: PO Box 2032, Thibodaux, LA 70310. **Website:** www.geauxcolonels.com.
Head Coach: Seth Thibodeaux. **Telephone:** 985-449-7149. **Baseball SID:** Jay Sullivan. **Telephone:** 985-448-4282.
Assistant Coaches: Tyler Cook, Ford Pemberton, Lee Clark. **Telephone:** 985-448-4807.
Home Field: Ben Meyer Diamond at Ray E. Didier Field. **Seating Capacity:** 3200. **Outfield Dimensions:** LF--331, CF--400, RF--331.

NJIT HIGHLANDERS

Conference: America East.
Mailing Address: University Heights, Newark, N.J. 07102-1982. **Website:** www.njithighlanders.com.
Head Coach: Robbie McClellan. **Telephone:** 973-596-8396. **Baseball SID:** Myles Rudnick. **Telephone:** 973-596-8261.
Assistant Coaches: Giuseppe Papaccio, Anthony Deleo, Kyle Norman. **Telephone:** 973-596-5827.
Home Field: Riverfront Stadium. **Seating Capacity:** 6200. **Outfield Dimensions:** LF--302, CF--394, RF--320.

NORFOLK STATE SPARTANS

Conference: Mid-Eastern.
Mailing Address: 700 Park Ave., Norfolk, VA 23504. **Website:** www.nsuspartans.com.
Head Coach: Keith Shumate. **Telephone:** 757-823-8196. **Baseball SID:** Matt Michalec. **Telephone:** 757-823-2628.
Assistant Coaches: Matt Mitchell.
Home Field: Marty L. Miller Field. **Seating Capacity:** 1500. **Outfield Dimensions:** LF--330, CF--402, RF--318.

NORTH ALABAMA LIONS

Conference: Atlantic Sun.
Mailing Address: UNA Box 5071, Florence, AL 35632. **Website:** www.roarlions.com.
Head Coach: Mike Keehn. **Telephone:** 256-756-4635. **Baseball SID:** Jeff Hodges. **Telephone:** 256-756-4595.
Assistant Coaches: Anthony DeCicco, Nick McGregor. **Telephone:** 256-756-5065.
Home Field: Mike D. Lane Field. **Outfield Dimensions:** LF--330, CF--385, RF--320.

NORTH CAROLINA TAR HEELS

Conference: ACC.
Mailing Address: 101 Ridge Road. **Website:** goheels.com.
Head Coach: Scott Forbes. **Telephone:** (919) 962-2351. **Baseball SID:** Aury St. Germain. **Telephone:** (919) 962-2123.
Assistant Coaches: *Bryant Gaines, Jesse Wierzbicki. **Telephone:** (919) 962-2351.
Home Field: Bryson Field at Boshamer Stadium. **Seating Capacity:** 4100. **Outfield Dimensions:** LF--335, CF--400, RF--355.

NORTH CAROLINA A&T AGGIES

Conference: Mid-Eastern.
Mailing Address: 1601 E. Market St., Greensboro, N.C. 27411. **Website:** www.ncataggies.com.
Head Coach: Ben Hall. **Telephone:** 336-285-4272. **Baseball SID:** Brian Holloway. **Telephone:** (336) 285-3608.
Assistant Coaches: Jamie Serber, Stefan Jordan, Marquis Riley. **Telephone:** 336-285-2434.
Home Field: World War Memorial Stadium. **Seating Capacity:** 7500. **Outfield Dimensions:** LF--327, CF--401, RF--327.

NORTH CAROLINA CENTRAL EAGLES

Conference: Mid-Eastern.
Mailing Address: 1801 Fayetteville st. Durham, NC 27707. **Website:** NCCUeaglepride.com.
Head Coach: Jim Koerner. **Telephone:** (919) 530-6723. **Baseball SID:** Kyle Serba. **Telephone:** (919) 530-7054.

Assistant Coaches: Brad Mincey, *Tyler Rost. **Telephone:** (919) 530-5439.
Home Field: Durham Athletic Park. **Seating Capacity:** 5000. **Outfield Dimensions:** LF--330, CF--405, RF--290.

NORTH CAROLINA STATE WOLFPACK

Conference: ACC.
Mailing Address: 1050 Varsity Drive Raleigh, NC 27695. **Website:** www.gopack.com.
Head Coach: Elliott Avent. **Telephone:** (919) 515-3613. **Baseball SID:** Lizzie Hattrich. **Telephone:** N/A.
Assistant Coaches: Clint Chrysler, *Chris Hart. **Telephone:** (919) 513-0093.
Home Field: Doak Field at Dail Park. **Seating Capacity:** 3048. **Outfield Dimensions:** LF--325, CF--400, RF--330.

NORTH DAKOTA STATE BISON

Conference: Summit.
Mailing Address: 1600 University Dr. N. Fargo, ND 58102. **Website:** www.gobison.com.
Head Coach: Tod Brown. **Telephone:** (701) 231-8853. **Baseball SID:** Ryan Workman. **Telephone:** (701) 231-5591.
Assistant Coaches: *Tyler Oakes, David Pearson. **Telephone:** (701) 231-7817.
Home Field: Newman Outdoor Field. **Seating Capacity:** 4419. **Outfield Dimensions:** LF--318, CF--408, RF--314.

NORTH FLORIDA OSPREYS

Conference: Atlantic Sun.
Mailing Address: University of North Florida | 1 UNF Drive Jacksonville, FL 32224. **Website:** www.unfospreys.com.
Head Coach: Tim Parenton. **Telephone:** (904) 620-1556. **Baseball SID:** Brock Borgeson. **Telephone:** (904) 420-2596.
Assistant Coaches: *Tommy Boss, Andrew Hannon. **Telephone:** (904) 620-2586.
Home Field: Harmon Stadium. **Seating Capacity:** 1000. **Outfield Dimensions:** LF--335, CF--400, RF--335.

NORTHEASTERN HUSKIES

Conference: Colonial.
Mailing Address: 360 huntington ave, 219 cabot center, boston ma 02115. **Website:** nuhuskies.com.
Head Coach: Mike Glavine. **Telephone:** (617) 373-3657. **Baseball SID:** Sky Kerstein. **Telephone:** (703) 597-4950.
Assistant Coaches: *Kevin Cobb, Nick Puccio. **Telephone:** (617) 373-5256.
Home Field: Friedman Diamond. **Seating Capacity:** 2400. **Outfield Dimensions:** LF--326, CF--400, RF--342.

NORTHERN COLORADO BEARS

Conference: Western Athletic.
Mailing Address: 270D Butler-Hancock Athletic Center, Greeley, CO 80639. **Website:** www.uncbears.com.
Head Coach: Carl Iwasaki. **Telephone:** 970-351-1714. **Baseball SID:** Thomas Hoffman. **Telephone:** 970-351-1065.
Assistant Coaches: Pat Jolley, Dan Martony, Joe Kraus. **Telephone:** 970-351-1203.
Home Field: Jackson Field. **Seating Capacity:** 1500. **Outfield Dimensions:** LF--349, CF--416, RF--356.

NORTHERN ILLINOIS HUSKIES

Conference: Mid-American.
Mailing Address: 1525 W. Lincoln Highway DeKalb, IL 60115. **Website:** www.niuhuskies.com.
Head Coach: Mike Kunigonis. **Telephone:** (815) 753-0147. **Baseball SID:** Mike Haase. **Telephone:** (815) 753-9538.
Assistant Coaches: *Andrew Maki, Luke Stewart.
Home Field: Ralph McKinzie Field. **Seating Capacity:** 1500. **Outfield Dimensions:** LF--312, CF--395, RF--322.

NORTHERN KENTUCKY NORSE

Conference: Horizon.
Mailing Address: 100 Nunn Drive Highland Heights, KY 41076. **Website:** www.nku.edu.
Head Coach: Todd Asalon. **Telephone:** (859) 572-6474. **Baseball SID:** Robby Johnson. **Telephone:** (859) 572-5100.
Assistant Coaches: Pat Hyde, *Dizzy Peyton. **Telephone:** (859) 572-5940.
Home Field: Bill Aker Baseball Complex. **Seating Capacity:** 500. **Outfield Dimensions:** LF--320, CF--365, RF--320.

NORTHWESTERN STATE DEMONS

Conference: Southland.
Mailing Address: 468 Capsari Drive, Natchitoches, LA 71497. **Website:** www.NSUDemons.com.
Head Coach: Bobby Barbier. **Telephone:** (318) 357-4139. **Baseball SID:** Jason Pugh. **Telephone:** (318) 357-6468.
Assistant Coaches: *Chris Bertrand, Spencer Goodwin. **Telephone:** (318) 357-4176.
Home Field: Brown-Stroud Field. **Seating Capacity:** 1200. **Outfield Dimensions:** LF--320, CF--400, RF--320.

NORTHWESTERN WILDCATS

Conference: Big Ten.
Mailing Address: 1501 Central st Evanston, IL. **Website:** nusports.com.
Head Coach: Spencer Allen. **Baseball SID:** Amit Mallik. **Telephone:** (267) 218-6205.
Assistant Coaches: Dusty Napoleon, *Josh Reynolds.
Home Field: Rocky & Berenice Miller Park. **Seating Capacity:** 2500. **Outfield Dimensions:** LF--326, CF--402, RF--315.

NOTRE DAME FIGHTING IRISH

Conference: ACC.
Mailing Address: Notre Dame, IN 46556. **Website:** und.com.
Head Coach: Link Jarrett. **Telephone:** (574) 631-4840. **Baseball SID:** Matt Paras. **Telephone:** (401) 215-5656.
Assistant Coaches: Chuck Ristano, *Rich Wallace.
Home Field: Frank Eck Stadium. **Seating Capacity:** 2500. **Outfield Dimensions:** LF--330, CF--405, RF--330.

OAKLAND GOLDEN GRIZZLIES

Conference: Horizon.
Mailing Address: 569 Pioneer Drive Rochester, MI 48309. **Website:** www.goldengrizzlies.com.
Head Coach: Jordon Banfield. **Telephone:** (248) 370-4228. **Baseball SID:** Meyke Phelps. **Telephone:** (248) 370-2933.
Assistant Coaches: *Dan McKinney, Brian Nelson. **Telephone:** (248) 370-4228.

Home Field: Oakland Baseball Field. **Seating Capacity:** 500. **Outfield Dimensions:** LF--333, CF--380, RF--320.

OHIO BOBCATS

Conference: Mid-American.
Mailing Address: 95 Richland Ave, Athens, Ohio, 45701. **Website:** OhioBobcats.com.
Head Coach: Craig Moore. **Telephone:** (740) 593-1954. **Baseball SID:** Michael Scholze. **Telephone:** (740) 593-1298.
Assistant Coaches: *Mitch Mormann, Nick Bredeson.
Home Field: Bob Wren Stadium. **Seating Capacity:** 3000. **Outfield Dimensions:** LF--340, CF--405, RF--340.

OHIO STATE BUCKEYES

Conference: Big Ten.
Mailing Address: 650 Borror Dr. Columbus, OH 43210. **Website:** ohiostatebuckeyes.com.
Head Coach: Greg Beals. **Telephone:** (614) 292-1075. **Baseball SID:** Gary Petit. **Telephone:** (614) 292-3270.
Assistant Coaches: *Matt Angle, Dan DeLucia.
Home Field: Nick Swisher Field at Bill Davis Stadium. **Seating Capacity:** 4500. **Outfield Dimensions:** LF--330, CF--400, RF--330.

OKLAHOMA SOONERS

Conference: Big 12.
Mailing Address: 401 Imhoff Rd, Norman, OK 73072. **Website:** SoonerSports.com.
Head Coach: Skip Johnson. **Telephone:** (405) 325-8354. **Baseball SID:** Eric Hollier. **Telephone:** (405) 325-6449.
Assistant Coaches: *Clay Overcash, Clay Van.
Home Field: L. Dale Mitchell Park. **Seating Capacity:** 3180. **Outfield Dimensions:** LF--335, CF--411, RF--335.

OKLAHOMA STATE COWBOYS

Conference: Big 12.
Mailing Address: O'Brate Stadium, 815 N Washington, Stillwater, OK, 74078. **Website:** okstate.com.
Head Coach: Josh Holliday. **Telephone:** (405) 744-7141. **Baseball SID:** Wade McWhorter. **Telephone:** (405) 744-7853.
Assistant Coaches: *Marty Lees, Rob Walton.
Home Field: O'Brate Stadium. **Seating Capacity:** 7000. **Outfield Dimensions:** LF--330, CF--402, RF--320.

OLD DOMINION MONARCHS

Conference: Conference USA.
Mailing Address: 4500 Parker Ave, Norfolk VA 23508. **Website:** odusports.com.
Head Coach: Chris Finwood. **Telephone:** (757) 683-4230. **Baseball SID:** Rebecca Gaona. **Telephone:** (757) 683-3395.
Assistant Coaches: Mike Marron, *Logan Robbins. **Telephone:** (757) 683-4230.
Home Field: Bud Metheny Baseball Complex. **Seating Capacity:** 2500. **Outfield Dimensions:** LF--325, CF--395, RF--325.

ORAL ROBERTS GOLDEN EAGLES

Conference: Summit.
Mailing Address: 7777 S. Lewis Ave. Tulsa, OK 74171. **Website:** oruathletics.com.
Head Coach: Ryan Folmar. **Telephone:** (918) 495-7639. **Baseball SID:** Jon Opiela. **Telephone:** (918) 495-

6616.
Assistant Coaches: Wes Davis, *Ryan Neill. **Telephone:** (918) 495-7132.
Home Field: J.L. Johnson Stadium. **Seating Capacity:** 2418. **Outfield Dimensions:** LF--330, CF--400, RF--330.

OREGON DUCKS

Conference: Pac-12.
Mailing Address: 2727 Leo Harris Parkway, Eugene, OR, 97401. **Website:** GoDucks.com.
Head Coach: Mark Wasikowski. **Telephone:** (541) 346-5235. **Baseball SID:** Todd Miles. **Telephone:** (541) 346-0962.
Assistant Coaches: Jake Angier, *Jack Marder. **Telephone:** (541) 346-5768.
Home Field: PK Park. **Seating Capacity:** 4000. **Outfield Dimensions:** LF--335, CF--400, RF--325.

OREGON STATE BEAVERS

Conference: Pac-12.
Mailing Address: 114 Gill Coliseum, Corvallis, OR 97331. **Website:** osubeavers.com.
Head Coach: Mitch Canham. **Baseball SID:** Hank Hager. **Telephone:** (541) 737-7472.
Assistant Coaches: Darwin Barney, *Rich Dorman/Ryan.
Home Field: Goss Stadium at Coleman Field. **Seating Capacity:** 3587. **Outfield Dimensions:** LF--335, CF--400, RF--335.

PACIFIC TIGERS

Conference: West Coast.
Mailing Address: 3601 Pacific Avenue, Stockton, CA 95204. **Website:** www.pacifictigers.com.
Head Coach: Chris Rodriguez. **Telephone:** 209-946-2163. **Baseball SID:** Chris Fortney. **Telephone:** 209-946-3150.
Assistant Coaches: Garrett DeGallier, Daniel Jaffe. **Telephone:** 209-946-2386.
Home Field: Klein Family Field. **Seating Capacity:** 2500. **Outfield Dimensions:** LF--317, CF--405, RF--325.

PENN STATE NITTANY LIONS

Conference: Big Ten.
Mailing Address: Medlar Field at Lubrano Park. **Website:** gopsu.com.
Head Coach: Rob Cooper. **Telephone:** (814) 863-0239. **Baseball SID:** Kris Peterson. **Telephone:** (814) 865-2497.
Assistant Coaches: Sean Moore, *Josh Newman. **Telephone:** (814) 865-8605.
Home Field: Medlar Field at Lubrano Park. **Seating Capacity:** 8500. **Outfield Dimensions:** LF--330, CF--400, RF--325.

PENNSYLVANIA QUAKERS

Conference: Ivy League.
Mailing Address: 235 S 33rd Street, Philadelphia, PA 19104. **Website:** www.pennathletics.com.
Head Coach: John Yurkow. **Telephone:** (215) 898-6282. **Baseball SID:** Mike Mahoney. **Telephone:** (215) 898-9232.
Assistant Coaches: *Mike Santello, Josh Schwartz. **Telephone:** (215) 746-2325.
Home Field: Meiklejohn Stadium - Murphy Field. **Seating Capacity:** 850. **Outfield Dimensions:** LF--330, CF--380, RF--330.

PEPPERDINE WAVES

Conference: West Coast.
Mailing Address: 24255 PCH, Malibu CA 90263.
Website: pepperdinewaves.com.
Head Coach: Rick Hirtensteiner. **Telephone:** (310) 506-4404. **Baseball SID:** Ricky Davis. **Telephone:** (310) 506-4333.
Assistant Coaches: Jim Lawler, *Danny Worth. **Telephone:** (310) 506-4199.
Home Field: Eddy D. Field Stadium. **Seating Capacity:** 1800. **Outfield Dimensions:** LF--330, CF--400, RF--330.

PITTSBURGH PANTHERS

Conference: ACC.
Mailing Address: 4200 Fifth Ave, Pittsburgh, PA 15260. **Website:** www.pittsburghpanthers.com.
Head Coach: Mike Bell. **Telephone:** (412) 383-9078. **Baseball SID:** Korey Blucas. **Telephone:** (412) 648-0000.
Assistant Coaches: *Ty Megahee, Matt Reida. **Telephone:** (412) 648-8556.
Home Field: Charles L. Cost Field. **Seating Capacity:** 900. **Outfield Dimensions:** LF--325, CF--405, RF--330.

PORTLAND PILOTS

Conference: West Coast.
Mailing Address: 5000 N. Willamette Blvd., Portland, OR 97203-5798. **Website:** www.portlandpilots.com.
Head Coach: Geoff Loomis. **Telephone:** 503-943-7707. **Baseball SID:** Adam Linnman. **Telephone:** 503-943-7707.
Assistant Coaches: Jake Valentine, Connor Lambert. **Telephone:** 503-943-7732.
Home Field: Joe Etzel Field. **Seating Capacity:** 1300. **Outfield Dimensions:** LF--325, CF--388, RF--325.

PRAIRIE VIEW A&M PANTHERS

Conference: Southwestern.
Mailing Address: PO Box 519 - Mail Stop 1500, Prairie View, TX 77446. **Website:** www.pvpanthers.com.
Head Coach: Auntwan Riggins. **Telephone:** 936-261-9121. **Baseball SID:** Ed Bailey. **Telephone:** 936-261-9140.
Assistant Coaches: Brian White. **Telephone:** 936-261-3955.
Home Field: Tankersley Field. **Seating Capacity:** 512. **Outfield Dimensions:** LF--330, CF--404, RF--330.

PRESBYTERIAN BLUE HOSE

Conference: Big South.
Mailing Address: 105 Ashland Ave. Clinton, S.C., 29325. **Website:** gobluehose.com.
Head Coach: Elton Pollock. **Telephone:** (864) 833-8236. **Baseball SID:** Greg Hartlage. **Telephone:** (864) 833-8095.
Assistant Coaches: Blake Miller, *Gil Walker. **Telephone:** (864) 200-7134.
Home Field: PC Baseball Complex. **Seating Capacity:** 500. **Outfield Dimensions:** LF--325, CF--400, RF--325.

PRINCETON TIGERS

Conference: Ivy League.
Mailing Address: Jadwin Gymnasium Princeton, NJ 08540. **Website:** https://goprincetontigers.com/sports/baseball.
Head Coach: Scott Bradley. **Telephone:** (609) 258-5059. **Baseball SID:** Warren Croxton. **Telephone:** (609) 258-2630.
Assistant Coaches: Alex Jurczynski, *Mike Russo. **Telephone:** (609) 258-5684.
Home Field: Clarke Field. **Seating Capacity:** 850. **Outfield Dimensions:** LF--330, CF--400, RF--315.

PURDUE BOILERMAKERS

Conference: Big Ten.
Mailing Address: 900 John R. Wooden Drive West Lafayette, IN 47904 || 1225 Northwestern Ave, West Lafayette, IN 47907. **Website:** PurdueSports.com.
Head Coach: Greg Goff. **Telephone:** (765) 494-3998. **Baseball SID:** Ben Turner. **Telephone:** (765) 494-3198.
Assistant Coaches: *Cooper Fouts, Chris Marx. **Telephone:** (765) 494-9360.
Home Field: Alexander Field. **Seating Capacity:** 2000. **Outfield Dimensions:** LF--340, CF--408, RF--330.

PURDUE-FORT WAYNE MASTODONS

Conference: Horizon.
Mailing Address: 2101 E. Coliseum Blvd., Fort Wayne, IN 46805-1499. **Website:** www.gomastodons.com.
Head Coach: Doug Schreiber. **Baseball SID:** Derrick Sloboda. **Telephone:** 260-481-0729.
Assistant Coaches: Brent McNeil, Ken Jones, Gordon Cardenas. **Telephone:** 260-481-5455.
Home Field: Mastodon Field. **Seating Capacity:** 200. **Outfield Dimensions:** LF--330, CF--400, RF--330.

QUINNIPIAC BOBCATS

Conference: Metro Atlantic.
Mailing Address: 275 Mount Carmel Ave., Hamden, CT 06518. **Website:** gobobcats.com.
Head Coach: John Delaney. **Telephone:** (203) 582-6546. **Baseball SID:** Kevin Noonan. **Telephone:** (203) 582-5387.
Assistant Coaches: *Pat Egan, Corey Keane. **Telephone:** (203) 582-6571.
Home Field: Bobcat Field. **Outfield Dimensions:** LF--340, CF--395, RF--315.

RADFORD HIGHLANDERS

Conference: Big South.
Mailing Address: 501 Stockton Street, Radford, VA 24142. **Website:** RadfordAthletics.com.
Head Coach: Karl Kuhn. **Telephone:** (540) 831-5881. **Baseball SID:** Kieran Intemann. **Telephone:** (540) 831-5211.
Assistant Coaches: Josh Reavis, *Matt Rein. **Telephone:** (540) 831-6513.
Home Field: Williams Field at Sherman Carter Memorial Stadium. **Seating Capacity:** 800. **Outfield Dimensions:** LF--370, CF--400, RF--370.

RHODE ISLAND RAMS

Conference: Atlantic 10.
Mailing Address: 3 Keaney Rd Kingston, RI 02881. **Website:** www.gorhody.com.
Head Coach: Raphael Cerrato. **Telephone:** (401) 874-4550. **Baseball SID:** Jodi Pontbriand. **Telephone:** (401) 481-6648.
Assistant Coaches: Sean O'Brien, *Kevin Vance. **Telephone:** (401) 874-4888.
Home Field: Beck Field. **Seating Capacity:** 500. **Outfield Dimensions:** LF--330, CF--400, RF--330.

RICE OWLS

Conference: Conference USA.
Mailing Address: 6100 Main Street; Houston, Texas 77004. **Website:** RiceOwls.com.
Head Coach: Matt Bragga. **Telephone:** (713) 348-8864. **Baseball SID:** John Sullivan. **Telephone:** (713) 348-5636.
Assistant Coaches: *Cory Barton, Paul Janish. **Telephone:** (713) 348-8862.
Home Field: Reckling Park. **Seating Capacity:** 6193. **Outfield Dimensions:** LF--350, CF--400, RF--350.

RICHMOND SPIDERS

Conference: Atlantic 10.
Mailing Address: 365 College Road University of Richmond, VA 23173. **Website:** richmondspiders.com.
Head Coach: Tracy Woodson. **Telephone:** (804) 289-8391. **Baseball SID:** Dan Wacker. **Telephone:** (804) 289-8365.
Assistant Coaches: *Nate Mulberg, RJ Thomas.
Home Field: Pitt Field. **Seating Capacity:** 600. **Outfield Dimensions:** LF--340, CF--400, RF--340.

RIDER BRONCS

Conference: Metro Atlantic.
Mailing Address: 2083 Lawrenceville Rd, Lawrenceville, NJ 08648. **Website:** gobroncs.com.
Head Coach: Barry Davis. **Telephone:** n/a. **Baseball SID:** Greg Ott. **Telephone:** (609) 896-5138.
Assistant Coaches: Lee Lipinski, *Mike Petrowski. **Telephone:** n/a.
Home Field: Sonny Pittaro Field. **Seating Capacity:** 3000. **Outfield Dimensions:** LF--330, CF--405, RF--330.

RUTGERS SCARLET KNIGHTS

Conference: Big Ten.
Mailing Address: 83 Rockefeller Road. **Website:** ScarletKnights.com.
Head Coach: Steve Owens. **Telephone:** (732) 445-7834. **Baseball SID:** Jimmy Gill. **Telephone:** (732) 445-8103.
Assistant Coaches: *Brendan Monaghan, Kyle Pettoruto. **Telephone:** (732) 445-7746.
Home Field: Bainton Field. **Seating Capacity:** 1500. **Outfield Dimensions:** LF--329, CF--392, RF--324.

SACRAMENTO STATE HORNETS

Conference: Western Athletic.
Mailing Address: 6000 J Street, Sacramento, CA 95819. **Website:** hornetsports.com.
Head Coach: Reggie Christiansen. **Telephone:** (916) 278-4036. **Baseball SID:** Robert Barsanti. **Telephone:** (916) 278-6896.
Assistant Coaches: Tyler LaTorre, David Flores.
Home Field: John Smith Field. **Seating Capacity:** 1200. **Outfield Dimensions:** LF--333, CF--400, RF--333.

SACRED HEART PIONEERS

Conference: Northeast.
Mailing Address: 5151 Park Avenue, Fairfield, CT 06825. **Website:** www.shubigred.com.
Head Coach: Nick Restaino. **Telephone:** 203-365-7632. **Baseball SID:** Shaina Blakesley. **Telephone:** 203-396-8127.
Assistant Coaches: Wayne Mazzoni, T.K. Kiernan. **Telephone:** 203-365-4469.

Home Field: Veteran's Memorial Park.

SAINT LOUIS BILLIKENS

Conference: Atlantic 10.
Mailing Address: 1303 Laclede Ave, St. Louis, MO 63103. **Website:** https://slubillikens.com/sports/baseball.
Head Coach: Darin Hendrickson. **Telephone:** (314) 977-3178. **Baseball SID:** Nick Retting. **Telephone:** (314) 977-3178.
Assistant Coaches: *Evan Pratte, Will Schierholz. **Telephone:** (314) 977-3178.
Home Field: Billikens Sports Center. **Seating Capacity:** 500. **Outfield Dimensions:** LF--330, CF--403, RF--330.

SAINT MARY'S GAELS

Conference: West Coast.
Mailing Address: 1928 St. Mary's Rd. Moraga, CA 94575. **Website:** https://smcgaels.com/sports/baseball.
Head Coach: Greg Moore. **Baseball SID:** Brian Brownfield. **Telephone:** (925) 631-4950.
Assistant Coaches: Riley Goulding, *Jordon Twohig. **Telephone:** (925) 631-8141.
Home Field: Louis Guisto Field. **Seating Capacity:** 1500. **Outfield Dimensions:** LF--330, CF--400, RF--330.

SAM HOUSTON STATE BEARKATS

Conference: Southland.
Mailing Address: 1905 University Ave, Huntsville, TX 77340. **Website:** gobearkats.com.
Head Coach: Jay Sirianni. **Telephone:** (936) 294-2580. **Baseball SID:** Ben Rikard. **Telephone:** (936) 294-1764.
Assistant Coaches: *Fuller Smith, Shane Wedd. **Telephone:** (936) 294-1731.
Home Field: Don Sanders Stadium. **Seating Capacity:** 1164. **Outfield Dimensions:** LF--330/375, CF--400, RF--330/375.

SAMFORD BULLDOGS

Conference: Southern.
Mailing Address: 800 Lakeshore Drive, Birmingham, AL 35229. **Website:** www.samfordsports.com.
Head Coach: Casey Dunn. **Telephone:** 205-726-2134. **Baseball SID:** Joey Mullins. **Telephone:** 205-726-2799.
Assistant Coaches: Tony David, Tyler Shrout, Brad Moss. **Telephone:** 205-726-4294.
Home Field: Joe Lee Griffin Field. **Seating Capacity:** 1000.

SAN DIEGO TOREROS

Conference: West Coast.
Mailing Address: 5998 Alcala Park, San Diego, CA 92110. **Website:** www.usdtoreros.com.
Head Coach: Rich Hill. **Telephone:** (619) 260-5953. **Baseball SID:** Rose McPherson. **Telephone:** (619) 260-4745.
Assistant Coaches: Matt Florer, *Brock Ungricht.
Home Field: Fowler Park. **Seating Capacity:** 1700. **Outfield Dimensions:** LF--312, CF--391, RF--327.

SAN DIEGO STATE AZTECS

Conference: Mountain West.
Mailing Address: San Diego, CA. **Website:** www.goaztecs.com.
Head Coach: Mark Martinez. **Telephone:** (619) 594-6889. **Baseball SID:** Jim Solien. **Telephone:** (619) 594-2576.

Assistant Coaches: *Joe Oliveira, Sam Peraza. **Telephone:** 619-594-3357.
Home Field: Tony Gwynn Stadium. **Seating Capacity:** 3000. **Outfield Dimensions:** LF--340, CF--410, RF--340.

SAN FRANCISCO DONS

Conference: West Coast.
Mailing Address: 2130 Fulton St. San Francisco, CA 94117. **Website:** www.usfdons.com.
Head Coach: Nino Giarratano. **Baseball SID:** Matt Fontenot. **Telephone:** (925) 878-5701.
Assistant Coaches: Mat Keplinger, *Troy Nakamura.
Home Field: Benedetti Diamond. **Seating Capacity:** 1000. **Outfield Dimensions:** LF--330, CF--425, RF--300.

SAN JOSE STATE SPARTANS

Conference: Mountain West.
Mailing Address: 1 Washington Sq, San Jose, CA 95192. **Website:** https://sjsuspartans.com/index.aspx.
Head Coach: Brad Sanfilippo. **Telephone:** (408) 924-1287. **Baseball SID:** Connor Pelton. **Telephone:** (408) 924-1229.
Assistant Coaches: Seth Moir, *Thomas Walker.
Home Field: Excite Ballpark. **Seating Capacity:** 4200. **Outfield Dimensions:** LF--320, CF--390, RF--320.

SANTA CLARA BRONCOS

Conference: West Coast.
Mailing Address: 500 El Camino Real, Santa Clara, CA 95053. **Website:** SantaClaraBroncos.com.
Head Coach: Rusty Filter. **Telephone:** (408) 554-4882.
Baseball SID: Dean Obara. **Telephone:** (408) 554-4690.
Assistant Coaches: *Jon Karcich, BK Santy.
Telephone: (408) 554-4680.
Home Field: Stephen Schott Stadium. **Seating Capacity:** 1500. **Outfield Dimensions:** LF--340, CF--402, RF--335.

SEATTLE REDHAWKS

Conference: Western Athletic.
Mailing Address: 901 12th Ave P.O. Box 222000 Seattle, WA 98122. **Website:** goseattleu.com.
Head Coach: Donny Harrel. **Telephone:** (206) 398-4399. **Baseball SID:** Jason Oliveira. **Telephone:** (206) 498-8595.
Assistant Coaches: *Greg Goetz, Wes Long.
Telephone: (206) 398-4397.
Home Field: Bannerwood Park. **Seating Capacity:** 300. **Outfield Dimensions:** LF--325, CF--392, RF--325.

SETON HALL PIRATES

Conference: Big East.
Mailing Address: 400 South Orange Ave. South Orange, NJ 07079. **Website:** www.shupirates.com.
Head Coach: Rob Sheppard. **Telephone:** (973) 761-9557. **Baseball SID:** Peter Long. **Telephone:** (973) 761-9493.
Assistant Coaches: *Mark Pappas, Pat Pinkman.
Telephone: 732 757-9534.
Home Field: Mike Sheppard Sr. Stadium at Owen T. Carroll Field. **Seating Capacity:** 261. **Outfield Dimensions:** LF--320, CF--390, RF--330.

SIENA SAINTS

Conference: Metro Atlantic.
Mailing Address: 515 Loudon Rd., Loudonville, NY 12211. **Website:** www.sienasaints.com.

Head Coach: Tony Rossi. **Telephone:** (518) 786-5044.
Baseball SID: Mike Demos. **Telephone:** (518) 783-2377.
Assistant Coaches: *Rob Hardy, Anthony Spataro.
Telephone: (518) 782-5044.
Home Field: Connors Park. **Seating Capacity:** 1000.
Outfield Dimensions: LF--300, CF--400, RF--325.

SOUTH ALABAMA JAGUARS

Conference: Sun Belt.
Mailing Address: 307 N University Blvd Mobile AL 36688 United States. **Website:** www.southalabama.edu.
Head Coach: Mark Calvi. **Telephone:** (251) 414-8243.
Baseball SID: Charlie Nichols. **Telephone:** (251) 414-8017.
Assistant Coaches: *Nick Magnifico, Brad Phillips.
Telephone: (251) 460-6876.
Home Field: Stanky Field. **Seating Capacity:** 3775.
Outfield Dimensions: LF--330, CF--400, RF--330.

SOUTH CAROLINA GAMECOCKS

Conference: SEC.
Mailing Address: 1304 Heyward Street Columbia, SC 29208. **Website:** GamecocksOnline.com.
Head Coach: Mark Kingston. **Telephone:** (803) 777-7808. **Baseball SID:** Kent Reichert. **Telephone:** (803) 777-5257.
Assistant Coaches: *Trip Couch, Skylar Meade.
Telephone: (803) 777-7808.
Home Field: Founders Park. **Seating Capacity:** 8242.
Outfield Dimensions: LF--325, CF--400, RF--325.

SOUTH CAROLINA-UPSTATE SPARTANS

Conference: Big South.
Mailing Address: 800 Univesity Way, Spartanburg, SC 29303. **Website:** upstatespartans.com.
Head Coach: Mike McGuire. **Telephone:** (864) 503-5135. **Baseball SID:** Codie Kuntsmann. **Telephone:** (864) 503-5152.
Assistant Coaches: *Adam Brown, Kane Sweeney.
Telephone: (864) 503-5196.
Home Field: Harley Park. **Seating Capacity:** 500.
Outfield Dimensions: LF--335, CF--402, RF--335.

SOUTH DAKOTA STATE JACKRABBITS

Conference: Summit.
Mailing Address: 2820 Marshall Center South Dakota State University Brookings, SD.57007. **Website:** Gojacks.com.
Head Coach: Rob Bishop. **Telephone:** (605) 688-5625.
Baseball SID: Jason Hove. **Telephone:** (605) 688-4623.
Assistant Coaches: Brian Grunzke, Kirk Clark.
Home Field: Erv Huether Field. **Seating Capacity:** 600. **Outfield Dimensions:** LF--330, CF--390, RF--330.

SOUTH FLORIDA BULLS

Conference: American Athletic.
Mailing Address: 4202 E Fowler Ave Tampa FL 33620. **Website:** https://gousfbulls.com/sports/baseball.
Head Coach: Billy Mohl. **Telephone:** (813) 974-2504.
Baseball SID: Tom Zebold. **Telephone:** (813) 974-4092.
Assistant Coaches: *Bo Durkac, Alan Kunkel.
Telephone: (813) 974-0567.
Home Field: USF Baseball Stadium. **Seating Capacity:** 3211. **Outfield Dimensions:** LF--325, CF--400, RF--325.

SOUTHEAST MISSOURI STATE REDHAWKS

Conference: Ohio Valley.
Mailing Address: 1 University Plaza Cape Girardeau, MO, 63701. **Website:** gosoutheast.com.
Head Coach: Andy Sawyers. **Telephone:** (573) 986-6002. **Baseball SID:** Jeff Honza. **Telephone:** (573) 651-2933.
Assistant Coaches: Matthew Kinney, Michael Cavazos.
Home Field: Capaha Field. **Seating Capacity:** 2000.
Outfield Dimensions: LF--330, CF--400, RF--330.

SOUTHEASTERN LOUISIANA LIONS

Conference: Southland.
Mailing Address: 800 Galloway Drive, Hammond, Louisiana 70402. **Website:** www.LionSports.net.
Head Coach: Matt Riser. **Telephone:** (985) 549-5130.
Baseball SID: Damon Sunde. **Telephone:** (985) 549-3774.
Assistant Coaches: *Tim Donnelly, Andrew Gipson.
Telephone: (985) 549-5130.
Home Field: Pat Kenelly Diamond at Alumni Field.
Seating Capacity: 2000. **Outfield Dimensions:** LF--330, CF--400, RF--330.

SOUTHERN JAGUARS

Conference: Southwestern Athletic.
Mailing Address: 7722 Scenic Hwy Baton Rouge, LA 70807. **Website:** gojagsports.com.
Head Coach: Chris Crenshaw. **Telephone:** (225) 771-3882. **Baseball SID:** Rodney Kircsher. **Telephone:** (225) 771-5609.
Assistant Coaches: TJ Perkins, Daniel Dulin.
Home Field: Lee - Hines Stadium. **Seating Capacity:** 2500. **Outfield Dimensions:** LF--375, CF--400, RF--325.

SOUTHERN CALIFORNIA TROJANS

Conference: Pac-12.
Mailing Address: 3501 Watt Way, Los Angeles, CA 90089. **Website:** usctrojans.com.
Head Coach: Jason Gill. **Telephone:** (213) 740-8446.
Baseball SID: Jacob Breems. **Telephone:** (213) 740-3809.
Assistant Coaches: *Gabe Alvarez, Ted Silva.
Telephone: (213) 740-8448.
Home Field: Dedeaux Field. **Seating Capacity:** 2500.
Outfield Dimensions: LF--335, CF--395, RF--335.

SOUTHERN ILLINOIS SALUKIS

Conference: Missouri Valley.
Mailing Address: 1490 Douglas Drive, Carbondale, IL 62901. **Website:** www.siusalukis.com.
Head Coach: Lance Rhodes. **Telephone:** (618) 453-3794. **Baseball SID:** John Lock. **Telephone:** (618) 453-7102.
Assistant Coaches: Tim Jamieson, Brett Peel
Home Field: Itchy Jones Stadium. **Outfield Dimensions:** LF--330, CF--400, RF--330.

SOUTHERN ILLINOIS-EDWARDSVILLE COUGARS

Conference: Ohio Valley.
Mailing Address: 1 Hairpin Dr. Edwardsville, IL 62026.
Website: siuecougars.com.
Head Coach: Sean Lyons. **Telephone:** (618) 650-2032.
Baseball SID: Joe Pott. **Telephone:** (618) 650-2871.
Assistant Coaches: PJ Finigan, *Brandon Scott.
Telephone: (515) 298-9567.
Home Field: Roy E. Lee Field. **Seating Capacity:** 2000.
Outfield Dimensions: LF--330, CF--395, RF--330.

SOUTHERN MISSISSIPPI GOLDEN EAGLES

Conference: Conference USA.
Mailing Address: 118 College Dr. Hattiesburg, MS 39406. **Website:** southernmiss.com.
Head Coach: Scott Berry. **Telephone:** (601) 543-5900.
Baseball SID: Jack Duggan. **Telephone:** (601) 266-5947.
Assistant Coaches: *Travis Creel, Christian Ostrander.
Telephone: (228) 243-2419.
Home Field: Pete Taylor Park. **Seating Capacity:** 4300.
Outfield Dimensions: LF--340, CF--400, RF--340.

ST BONAVENTURE BONNIES

Conference: Atlantic 10.
Mailing Address: PO Box G, Reilly Center, St. Bonaventure, N.Y. 14778. **Website:** www.gobonnies.sbu.edu.
Head Coach: Larry Sudbrook. **Telephone:** 716-375-2641. **Baseball SID:** Scott Eddy. **Telephone:** 716-375-4019.
Assistant Coaches: B.J. Salerno. **Telephone:** 716-375-2699.
Home Field: Fred Handler Park at McGraw-Jennings Field. **Outfield Dimensions:** LF--330, CF--403, RF--330.

ST JOHN'S RED STORM

Conference: Big East.
Mailing Address: 8000 Utopia Parkway, Queens, NY 11439. **Website:** RedStormSports.com.
Head Coach: Mike Hampton. **Telephone:** (718) 990-2332. **Baseball SID:** Andrew O'Connell. **Telephone:** (718) 990-1522.
Assistant Coaches: Danny Bethea, *George Brown.
Telephone: (718) 990-7523.
Home Field: Jack Kaiser Stadium. **Seating Capacity:** 3500. **Outfield Dimensions:** LF--320, CF--390, RF--320.

ST JOSEPH'S HAWKS

Conference: Atlantic 10.
Mailing Address: 5600 City Ave., Philadelphia, PA, 19131. **Website:** www.sjuhawks.com.
Head Coach: Fritz Hamburg. **Telephone:** (610) 660-1718. **Baseball SID:** Joe Greenwich. **Telephone:** (610) 660-1738.
Assistant Coaches: Greg Manco, *Ryan Wheeler.
Telephone: (610) 660-2592.
Home Field: Smithson Field. **Seating Capacity:** 400.
Outfield Dimensions: LF--327, CF--400, RF--330.

ST PETER'S PEACOCKS

Conference: Metro Atlantic.
Mailing Address: 2641 JFK Blvd Jersey City, NJ 07306.
Website: saintpeterspeacocks.com.
Head Coach: Lou Proietti. **Telephone:** (201) 761-7319. **Baseball SID:** Hamilton Cook. **Telephone:** (201) 761-7316.
Assistant Coaches: *Casey Aubin, Lucas Luopa.
Home Field: Jaroschak Field. **Seating Capacity:** 500.
Outfield Dimensions: LF--321, CF--410, RF--318.

STANFORD CARDINAL

Conference: Pac-12.
Mailing Address: 641 Campus Drive, Stanford, CA 94305. **Website:** http://www.gostanford.com.
Head Coach: David Esquer. **Telephone:** (650) 723-4528. **Baseball SID:** Tyler Geivett. **Telephone:** (650) 313-9338.

Assistant Coaches: *Thomas Eager, Tommy Nicholson. Telephone: (650) 725-2373.
Home Field: Klein Field at Sunken Diamond. Seating Capacity: 4000. Outfield Dimensions: LF--335, CF--400, RF--335.

STEPHEN F AUSTIN STATE LUMBERJACKS

Conference: Southland.
Mailing Address: PO Box 13010, SFA Station, Nacogdoches, TX 75962. Website: www.sfajacks.com.
Head Coach: Johnny Cardenas. Baseball SID: Kevin Meyer. Telephone: 936-468-7106.
Assistant Coaches: Mike Haynes, Caleb Clowers, Dylan Belanger. Telephone: 936-468-7796.
Home Field: Jaycees Field. Seating Capacity: 740. Outfield Dimensions: LF--320, CF--390, RF--320.

STETSON HATTERS

Conference: Atlantic Sun.
Mailing Address: 421 N. Woodland Blvd., Unit 8359, DeLand, FL 32723. Website: GoHatters.com.
Head Coach: Steve Trimper. Telephone: (386) 822-8106. Baseball SID: Ricky Hazel. Telephone: (386) 822-8130.
Assistant Coaches: *Joe Mercadante, Dave Therneau. Telephone: (386) 822-8122.
Home Field: Melching Field. Seating Capacity: 2500. Outfield Dimensions: LF--335, CF--403, RF--335.

STONY BROOK SEAWOLVES

Conference: America East.
Mailing Address: Stony Brook University Indoor Sports Complex, Stony Brook, N.Y. 11794-3500. Website: www.stonybrookathletics.com.
Head Coach: Matt Senk. Telephone: 631-632-9226. Baseball SID: Cameron Boon. Telephone: 631-632-7289.
Assistant Coaches: Jim Martin, Tyler Kavanaugh, Kyle Lombardo. Telephone: 631-632-4676.
Home Field: Joe Nathan Field. Seating Capacity: 1000. Outfield Dimensions: LF--330, CF--390, RF--330.

TARLETON STATE TEXANS

Conference: Western Athletic.
Mailing Address: 1333 W Washington St, Stephenville, TX 76401. Website: www.tarleton.edu.
Head Coach: Aaron Meade. Telephone: 254-968-1666. Baseball SID: Katy Gilmore. Telephone: (254) 968-9018.
Assistant Coaches: Ruben Rodriguez, *Jon Ubbenga. Telephone: (254) 968-9563.
Home Field: Cecil Ballow Baseball Complex. Seating Capacity: 750. Outfield Dimensions: LF--365, CF--400, RF--365.

TENNESSEE VOLUNTEERS (VOLS)

Conference: SEC.
Mailing Address: 1511 Pat Head Summitt Dr., Knoxville, TN 37996. Website: https://utsports.com/index.aspx.
Head Coach: Tony Vitello. Telephone: (865) 974-2057. Baseball SID: Sean Barows. Telephone: (865) 974-7478.
Assistant Coaches: Frank Anderson, *Josh Elander. Telephone: (865) 974-2057.
Home Field: Lindsey Nelson Stadium. Seating Capacity: 4283. Outfield Dimensions: LF--320, CF--390, RF--320.

TENNESSEE TECH GOLDEN EAGLES

Conference: Ohio Valley.
Mailing Address: 1100 McGee Blvd. Cookeville, TN 38501. Website: TTUsports.com.
Head Coach: Steve Smith. Telephone: (931) 372-3853. Baseball SID: Mike Lehman. Telephone: (931) 372-3088.
Assistant Coaches: Blake Beck, *Mitchell Wright. Telephone: (931) 372-3853.
Home Field: Quillen Field at Bush Stadium at the Averitt Express Baseball Complex. Seating Capacity: 1100. Outfield Dimensions: LF--329, CF--405, RF--330.

TENNESSEE-MARTIN SKYHAWKS

Conference: Ohio Valley.
Mailing Address: 1022 Elam Center, 15 Mt. Pelia Road, Martin, TN 38238. Website: www,UTMSports.com.
Head Coach: Ryan Jenkins. Telephone: (731) 881-7337. Baseball SID: Ryne Rickman. Telephone: (731) 881-7632.
Assistant Coaches: Matt Heath, *Hunter Morris. Telephone: (731) 881-3691.
Home Field: Skyhawk Field. Seating Capacity: 500. Outfield Dimensions: LF--330, CF--385, RF--330.

TEXAS LONGHORNS

Conference: Big 12.
Mailing Address: 1300 E Martin Luther King Jr Blvd, Austin, TX 78702. Website: www.TexasSports.com.
Head Coach: David Pierce. Telephone: (512) 471-5732. Baseball SID: Kevin Rodriguez. Telephone: (512) 471-2078.
Assistant Coaches: *Sean Allen, Philip Miller.
Home Field: UFCU Disch-Falk Field. Seating Capacity: 6649. Outfield Dimensions: LF--340, CF--400, RF--325.

TEXAS A&M AGGIES

Conference: SEC.
Mailing Address: 756 Houston Street, College Station, TX , 77843. Website: www.12thMan.com.
Head Coach: Rob Childress. Telephone: (979) 845-4810. Baseball SID: Thomas Dick. Telephone: None.
Assistant Coaches: Chad Caillet, *Justin Seely. Telephone: (979) 845-4810.
Home Field: Olsen Field at Blue Bell Park. Seating Capacity: 6100. Outfield Dimensions: LF--375, CF--400, RF--375.

TEXAS A&M-CORPUS CHRISTI ISLANDERS

Conference: Southland.
Mailing Address: 6300 Ocean Drive, Unit 5719, Corpus Christi, Texas 78412. Website: goislanders.com.
Head Coach: Scott Malone. Telephone: (361) 825-3413. Baseball SID: Morganne Lander.
Assistant Coaches: Marty Smith, Seth LaRue. Telephone: (361) 825-3720.
Home Field: Chapman Field. Seating Capacity: 500. Outfield Dimensions: LF--330, CF--404, RF--330.

TEXAS CHRISTIAN HORNED FROGS

Conference: Big 12.
Mailing Address: TCU Box 297600, Fort Worth, TX 76129. Website: www.gofrogs.com.
Head Coach: Jim Schlossnagle. Telephone: 817-257-7985. Baseball SID: Brandie Davidson. Telephone: 817-257-7479.
Assistant Coaches: Bill Mosiello, Kirk Saarloos, John

DiLaura.
Home Field: Charlie and Marie Lupton Baseball Stadium. **Seating Capacity:** 4500. **Outfield Dimensions:** LF--330, CF--400, RF--330.

TEXAS SOUTHERN TIGERS

Conference: Southwestern.
Mailing Address: 3100 Cleburne St., Houston, TX 77004. **Website:** www.tsusports.com.
Head Coach: Michael Robertson. **Telephone:** 713-313-4315. **Baseball SID:** Ryan McGinty. **Telephone:** 713-313-6829.
Assistant Coaches: Aaron Gilbreath, Ricky Urbano. **Telephone:** 713-313-7993.
Home Field: MacGregor Park.

TEXAS STATE BOBCATS

Conference: Sun Belt.
Mailing Address: Department of Athletics, Darren B. Casey Athletic Complex, 601 University Dr, San Marcos, TX 78666. **Website:** www.txstatebobcats.com.
Head Coach: Steven Trout. **Telephone:** (512) 245-3383. **Baseball SID:** Phillip Pongratz. **Telephone:** (512) 245-4692.
Assistant Coaches: *Josh Blakley, Chad Massengale. **Telephone:** (512) 245-3383.
Home Field: Bobcat Ballpark. **Seating Capacity:** 2500. **Outfield Dimensions:** LF--330, CF--405, RF--330.

TEXAS TECH RED RAIDERS

Conference: Big 12.
Mailing Address: 2901 Drive of Champions Ste. 200, Lubbock, TX 79409. **Website:** texastech.com.
Head Coach: Tim Tadlock. **Telephone:** (806) 317-5161. **Baseball SID:** Ty Parker. **Telephone:** (806) 834-2769.
Assistant Coaches: Matt Gardner, *J-Bob Thomas. **Telephone:** (806) 252-6309.
Home Field: Dan Law Field. **Seating Capacity:** 4432. **Outfield Dimensions:** LF--327, CF--402, RF--327.

TEXAS-ARLINGTON MAVERICKS

Conference: Sun Belt.
Mailing Address: 1301 S Fielder Rd, Arlington, TX 76013. **Website:** utamavs.com.
Head Coach: Darin Thomas. **Telephone:** (817) 272-9744. **Baseball SID:** Ian Applegate. **Telephone:** (817) 272-9610.
Assistant Coaches: Brady Cox, *Taylor Dugas. **Telephone:** (817) 272-7170.
Home Field: Clay Gould Ballpark. **Seating Capacity:** 1600. **Outfield Dimensions:** LF--300, CF--400, RF--330.

TEXAS-SAN ANTONIO ROADRUNNERS

Conference: Conference USA.
Mailing Address: One UTSA Circle, San Antonio, TX 78249-0691. **Website:** www.goutsa.com.
Head Coach: Pat Hallmark. **Telephone:** 210-458-4171. **Baseball SID:** Brent Ingram. **Telephone:** 210-845-8651.
Assistant Coaches: Ryan Aguayo, Zach Butler, Jordan Lucks. **Telephone:** 562-665-8714.
Home Field: Roadrunner Field. **Seating Capacity:** 800. **Outfield Dimensions:** LF--335, CF--405, RF--340.

TOLEDO ROCKETS

Conference: Mid-American.
Mailing Address: 2801 W. Bancroft Street, MS-408, Toledo, OH 43606. **Website:** www.utrockets.com.

Head Coach: Rob Reinstetle. **Telephone:** (419) 530-6263. **Baseball SID:** Chris Cullum. **Telephone:** (419) 530-4913.
Assistant Coaches: *Nick McIntyre, Tommy Winterstein. **Telephone:** (419) 530-3097.
Home Field: Scott Park. **Seating Capacity:** 1000. **Outfield Dimensions:** LF--330, CF--400, RF--330.

TOWSON TIGERS

Conference: Colonial.
Mailing Address: 8000 York Road Towson, MD. **Website:** towsontigers.com.
Head Coach: Matt Tyner. **Telephone:** (410) 704-3775. **Baseball SID:** Dave Vatz. **Telephone:** (410) 704-3102.
Assistant Coaches: Tanner Biagini, *Miles Miller. **Telephone:** (410) 704-4587.
Home Field: John B. Schuerholz Park. **Seating Capacity:** 500. **Outfield Dimensions:** LF--312, CF--424, RF--301.

TROY TROJANS

Conference: Sun Belt.
Mailing Address: 5000 Veterans Stadium Drive Troy, Alabama 36082. **Website:** troytrojans.com.
Head Coach: Mark Smartt. **Telephone:** (334) 670-3333. **Baseball SID:** Andy Stubblefield. **Telephone:** (334) 670-3229.
Assistant Coaches: *Shane Gierke, Matt Hancock, Peyton Fuller. **Telephone:** (334) 670-5945.
Home Field: Riddle-Pace Field. **Seating Capacity:** 2200. **Outfield Dimensions:** LF--340, CF--400, RF--310.

TULANE GREEN WAVE

Conference: American Athletic.
Mailing Address: Tulane University Athletics James W Wilson Jr Center New Orleans, LA 70118. **Website:** tulanegreenwave.com.
Head Coach: Travis Jewett. **Telephone:** (504) 862-8216. **Baseball SID:** Tom Symonds. **Telephone:** (504) 862-8249.
Assistant Coaches: Daniel Latham, *Jay Uhlman, Adam Core. **Telephone:** (504) 314-7203.
Home Field: Greer Field at Turchin Stadium. **Seating Capacity:** 5000. **Outfield Dimensions:** LF--325, CF--400, RF--325.

UC DAVIS AGGIES

Conference: Big West.
Mailing Address: One Shields Ave. 264 Hickey Gym Davis, CA 95616. **Website:** UCDavisAggies.com.
Head Coach: Matt Vaughn. **Telephone:** (530) 752-7513. **Baseball SID:** Eric Bankston (interim). **Telephone:** (530) 752-3505.
Assistant Coaches: *Lloyd , Brett Lindgren. **Telephone:** Acosta.
Home Field: Phil Swimley Field at Dobbins Stadium. **Seating Capacity:** 3500. **Outfield Dimensions:** LF--310, CF--410, RF--310.

UC IRVINE ANTEATERS

Conference: Big West.
Mailing Address: Intercollegiate Athletics Building (IAB) Irvine, CA 92697-4500. **Website:** https://ucirvines-ports.com/sports/baseball.
Head Coach: Ben Orloff. **Telephone:** (949) 824-6033. **Baseball SID:** Alex Roberts-Croteau. **Telephone:** (949) 824-5814.

Assistant Coaches: Daniel Bibona, *J.T. Bloodworth. **Telephone:** (949) 824-1154.
Home Field: Cicerone Field at Anteater Ballpark. **Seating Capacity:** 3408. **Outfield Dimensions:** LF--335, CF--408, RF--335.

UC RIVERSIDE HIGHLANDERS

Conference: Big West.
Mailing Address: 900 university ave riverside ca 92521. **Website:** ucrbaseball.com.
Head Coach: Justin Johnson. **Telephone:** (951) 827-5441. **Baseball SID:** Chelsea Pfohl. **Telephone:** (925) 698-0577.
Assistant Coaches: Curtis Smith. **Telephone:** (951) 827-5441.
Home Field: Riverside Sports Complex. **Seating Capacity:** 2500. **Outfield Dimensions:** LF--330, CF--400, RF--330.

UC SAN DIEGO TRITONS

Conference: Big West.
Mailing Address: 9500 Gilman Drive, RIMAC 4th Floor, La Jolla, CA 92093-0531. **Website:** www.ucsdtritons.com.
Head Coach: Eric Newman. **Telephone:** (858) 534-8162. **Baseball SID:** Kendrick Mooney. **Telephone:** (858) 534-8451.
Assistant Coaches: Bryson LeBlanc, Matt Harvey, Michael Ramazzotti. **Telephone:** (858) 246-1648.
Home Field: Triton Ballpark. **Seating Capacity:** 500. **Outfield Dimensions:** LF--330, CF--400, RF--330.

UC SANTA BARBARA GAUCHOS

Conference: Big West.
Mailing Address: UCSB Baseball ICA Building #243 Santa Barbara, CA 93106. **Website:** ucsbgauchos.com.
Head Coach: Andrew Checketts. **Telephone:** (805) 893-3690. **Baseball SID:** Daniel Moebus-Bowles. **Telephone:** (805) 893-8603.
Assistant Coaches: Matt Fonteno, Dylan Jones, Spencer Erdman.
Home Field: Caesar Uyesaka Stadium. **Seating Capacity:** 1500. **Outfield Dimensions:** LF--335, CF--405, RF--335.

UCLA BRUINS

Conference: Pac-12.
Mailing Address: 100 Constitution Ave, Los Angeles, CA 90095. **Website:** UCLABruins.com.
Head Coach: John Savage. **Baseball SID:** Andrew Wagner. **Telephone:** (310) 206-4008.
Assistant Coaches: Rex Peters, *Bryant Ward. **Telephone:** (310) 794-8210.
Home Field: Jackie Robinson Stadium. **Seating Capacity:** 1820. **Outfield Dimensions:** LF--330, CF--390, RF--330.

UNC ASHEVILLE BULLDOGS

Conference: Big South.
Mailing Address: 1 University Heights CPO 2600 Asheville, NC 28804. **Website:** uncabulldogs.com.
Head Coach: Scott Friedholm. **Telephone:** (828) 251-6920. **Baseball SID:** Andy Fisher. **Telephone:** (828) 251-6931.
Assistant Coaches: *Chris Bresnahan, Kyle Ward. **Telephone:** (828) 251-2309.
Home Field: Greenwood Baseball Field. **Seating Capacity:** 1000.

UNC GREENSBORO SPARTANS

Conference: SoCon.
Mailing Address: 1509 Walker Avenue. **Website:** uncgspartans.com.
Head Coach: Billy Godwin. **Baseball SID:** Mark Pinkerton.
Assistant Coaches: *Hunter Allen, Greg Starbuck.
Home Field: UNCG Baseball Stadium. **Seating Capacity:** 3500. **Outfield Dimensions:** LF--340, CF--405, RF--340.

UNC WILMINGTON SEAHAWKS

Conference: Colonial.
Mailing Address: 610 S. College Road. **Website:** www.uncwsports.com.
Head Coach: Randy Hood. **Telephone:** (910) 962-3793. **Baseball SID:** Tom Riordan. **Telephone:** (910) 962-4099.
Assistant Coaches: *Chris Moore, Matt Myers. **Telephone:** (910) 962-3570.
Home Field: Brooks Field. **Seating Capacity:** 3500. **Outfield Dimensions:** LF--340, CF--390, RF--340.

UT-RIO GRANDE VALLEY VAQUEROS

Conference: Western Athletic.
Mailing Address: 1201 W. University Dr. Edinburg, TX 78539. **Website:** GoUTRGV.com.
Head Coach: Derek Matlock. **Telephone:** (956) 665-2235. **Baseball SID:** Jonah Goldberg. **Telephone:** (956) 665-2240.
Assistant Coaches: *Rob Martinez, Russell Raley. **Telephone:** (956) 665-2891.
Home Field: UTRGV Baseball Stadium. **Seating Capacity:** 5500. **Outfield Dimensions:** LF--325, CF--410, RF--325.

UTAH UTES

Conference: Pac-12.
Mailing Address: 1825 E. South Campus Dr., Salt Lake City, Utah 84112. **Website:** UtahUtes.com.
Head Coach: Bill Kinneberg. **Telephone:** (801) 581-3526. **Baseball SID:** Joseph Feldman. **Telephone:** (801) 231-1329.
Assistant Coaches: *Jay Brossman, Gary Henderson. **Telephone:** (801) 581-3024.
Home Field: Smith's Ballpark. **Seating Capacity:** 14511. **Outfield Dimensions:** LF--345, CF--420, RF--315.

UTAH VALLEY WOLVERINES

Conference: Western Athletic.
Mailing Address: 800 W. University Parkway, Orem, UT 84058-5999. **Website:** www.gouvu.com.
Head Coach: Eric Madsen. **Telephone:** 801-863-6509. **Baseball SID:** James Warnick. **Telephone:** 801-863-6231.
Assistant Coaches: David Carter, Joldy Watts. **Telephone:** 801-863-8647.
Home Field: UCCU Ballpark. **Seating Capacity:** 5000. **Outfield Dimensions:** LF--305, CF--408, RF--312.

VALPARAISO CRUSADERS

Conference: Missouri Valley.
Mailing Address: 1700 Chapel Dr, Valparaiso, IN 46383. **Website:** valpoathletics.com/baseball.
Head Coach: Brian Schmack. **Telephone:** (219) 464-6117. **Baseball SID:** Brandon Vickrey. **Telephone:** (219) 464-5396.

Assistant Coaches: Casey Fletcher, *Kory Winter. **Telephone:** (614) 565-0990.
Home Field: Emory G Bauer Field. **Seating Capacity:** 500. **Outfield Dimensions:** LF--330, CF--400, RF--330.

VANDERBILT COMMODORES

Conference: Southeastern.
Mailing Address: 2601 JESS NEELY DRIVE NASHVILLE, TN 37212. **Website:** vucommodores.com.
Head Coach: Tim Corbin. **Baseball SID:** Josh Foster. **Telephone:** 205-213-5091.
Assistant Coaches: *Mike Baxter, Scott Brown. **Telephone:** 615-322-3716.
Home Field: Hawkins Field. **Seating Capacity:** 3626. **Outfield Dimensions:** LF--310, CF--400, RF--330.

VILLANOVA WILDCATS

Conference: Big East.
Mailing Address: 800 East Lancaster Avenue, Philadelphia, PA 19085. **Website:** www.villanova.com.
Head Coach: Kevin Mulvey. **Telephone:** 610-519-4529. **Baseball SID:** Dean Kenefick. **Telephone:** 610-519-6514.
Assistant Coaches: Eddie Brown, Jabin Weaver, Mitchell Bennett. **Telephone:** 610-519-5520.
Home Field: Villanova Ballpark at Plymouth. **Outfield Dimensions:** LF--320, CF--400, RF--320.

VIRGINIA CAVALIERS

Conference: ACC.
Mailing Address: PO BOX 400839 - CHARLOTTESVILLE VA, 22904-4839. **Website:** www.virginiasports.com.
Head Coach: Brian O'Connor. **Telephone:** (434) 243-5114. **Baseball SID:** Scott Fitzgerald. **Telephone:** (434) 924-9878.
Assistant Coaches: Drew Dickinson, *Kevin McMullan. **Telephone:** (434) 243-5114.
Home Field: Disharoon Park. **Seating Capacity:** 5359. **Outfield Dimensions:** LF--332, CF--404, RF--332.

VIRGINIA COMMONWEALTH RAMS

Conference: Atlantic 10.
Mailing Address: 1200 W. Broad Box 843013 Richmond, Va. 23284. **Website:** vcuathletics.com.
Head Coach: Shawn Stiffler. **Telephone:** (804) 828-4822. **Baseball SID:** Hannah Jo Riley. **Telephone:** (804) 828-8496.
Assistant Coaches: Mike McRae, *Rich Witten. **Telephone:** (804) 828-4820.
Home Field: The Diamond. **Seating Capacity:** 12134. **Outfield Dimensions:** LF--330, CF--402, RF--330.

VIRGINIA MILITARY INSTITUTE KEYDETS

Conference: SoCon.
Mailing Address: 319 Letcher Ave, Lexington, VA 24450. **Website:** vmikeydets.com.
Head Coach: Jonathan Hadra. **Telephone:** (540) 464-7601. **Baseball SID:** Mike Carpenter. **Telephone:** (540) 464-7015.
Assistant Coaches: Ray Noe, *Sam Roberts. **Telephone:** (540) 464-7605.
Home Field: Gray-Minor Stadium. **Seating Capacity:** 1499. **Outfield Dimensions:** LF--325, CF--390, RF--335.

VIRGINIA TECH HOKIES

Conference: ACC.
Mailing Address: 25 Beamer Way, Blacksburg, VA

24060. **Website:** www.hokiesports.com/baseball.
Head Coach: John Szefc. **Telephone:** 540-231-5906.
Baseball SID: Pete Moris. **Telephone:** 540-231-9965.
Assistant Coaches: *Kurt Elbin, Ryan Fecteau, Tyler Hanson. **Telephone:** (570) 295-4267.
Home Field: Atlantic Union Park / English Field.
Seating Capacity: 5000. **Outfield Dimensions:** LF--330, CF--400, RF--330.

WAGNER SEAHAWKS

Conference: Northeast.
Mailing Address: One Campus Road, Staten Island, NY 10301. **Website:** www.wagnerathletics.com.
Head Coach: Jim Carone. **Telephone:** (718) 390-3154.
Baseball SID: Brian Morales. **Telephone:** (718) 390-3215.
Assistant Coaches: *Craig Noto, Andrew Turner. **Telephone:** (718) 420-4121.
Home Field: Richmond County Bank Ballpark at St. George. **Seating Capacity:** 7171. **Outfield Dimensions:** LF--320, CF--390, RF--318.

WAKE FOREST DEMON DEACONS

Conference: ACC.
Mailing Address: 401 Deacon Blvd, Winston-Salem NC 27105. **Website:** www.godeacs.com.
Head Coach: Thomas Walter. **Telephone:** (336) 758-5570. **Baseball SID:** Ryan Sosic. **Telephone:** 336-758-5842.
Assistant Coaches: Bill Cilento, John Hendricks, Joey Hammond. **Telephone:** 336-758-5645.
Home Field: David F. Couch Ballpark. **Seating Capacity:** 3823. **Outfield Dimensions:** LF--310, CF--400, RF--300.

WASHINGTON HUSKIES

Conference: Pac-12.
Mailing Address: Washington Intercollegiate Athletics Department of Intercollegiate Athletics | University of Washington Box 354070, Graves Building, Seattle, WA 98195. **Website:** https://gohuskies.com/.
Head Coach: Lindsay Meggs. **Telephone:** (206) 616-4335. **Baseball SID:** Brian Tom. **Telephone:** (206) 949-7523.
Assistant Coaches: *Elliott Cribby, Ronnie Prettyman. **Telephone:** (425) 765-4999.
Home Field: Husky Ballpark. **Seating Capacity:** 2200. **Outfield Dimensions:** LF--327, CF--395, RF--317.

WASHINGTON STATE COUGARS

Conference: Pac-12.
Mailing Address: Bohler Addition, Pullman, WA 99164. **Website:** wsucougars.com.
Head Coach: Brian Green. **Telephone:** (509) 335-0332.
Baseball SID: Bobby Alworth. **Telephone:** 509-335-57585.
Assistant Coaches: Anthony Claggett, *Terry Davis. **Telephone:** (509) 335-0211.
Home Field: Bailey-Brayton Field. **Seating Capacity:** 3500. **Outfield Dimensions:** LF--330, CF--400, RF--330.

WEST VIRGINIA MOUNTAINEERS

Conference: Big 12.
Mailing Address: 3450 Monongahela Blvd, Morgantown, WV 26505. **Website:** WVUsports.com.
Head Coach: Randy Mazey. **Telephone:** (304) 293-4740. **Baseball SID:** Joe Mitchin. **Telephone:** (304) 293-9909.

Assistant Coaches: Mark Ginther, *Steve Sabins.
Telephone: (304) 293-4740.
Home Field: Monongalia County Ballpark. Seating Capacity: 3500. Outfield Dimensions: LF--325, CF--400, RF--325.

WESTERN CAROLINA CATAMOUNTS

Conference: SoCon.
Mailing Address: Ramsey Center - Athletics; 92 Catamount Road; Cullowhee, NC 28723. Website: CatamountSports.com.
Head Coach: Bobby Moranda. Telephone: (828) 227-2021. Baseball SID: Daniel Hooker. Telephone: (828) 227-2339.
Assistant Coaches: Andrew Cox, *Taylor Sandefur. Telephone: (828) 227-2022.
Home Field: Childress Field / Hennon Stadium. Seating Capacity: 1500. Outfield Dimensions: LF--325, CF--395, RF--325.

WESTERN ILLINOIS LEATHERNECKS

Conference: Summit.
Mailing Address: 1 University Cir, Macomb, IL 61455. Website: https://goleathernecks.com/.
Head Coach: Andy Pascoe. Telephone: 309-298-1521. Baseball SID: Matthew Hutchison. Telephone: 309-298-1133.
Assistant Coaches: Adam McGinnis, *Andy Pascoe. Telephone: 309-298-1521.
Home Field: Alfred D. Boyer. Seating Capacity: 502. Outfield Dimensions: LF--325, CF--395, RF--330.

WESTERN KENTUCKY HILLTOPPERS

Conference: Conference USA.
Mailing Address: E.A. Diddle Arena, 1605 Avenue of Champions, Bowling Green, KY 42101. Website: wkusports.com.
Head Coach: John Pawlowski. Telephone: (270) 745-2277. Baseball SID: Matt Keenan. Telephone: (270) 745-3756.
Assistant Coaches: *Adam Pavkovich, Ben Wolgamot. Telephone: (270) 745-2274.
Home Field: Nick Denes Field. Seating Capacity: 1500. Outfield Dimensions: LF--330, CF--400, RF--330.

WESTERN MICHIGAN BRONCOS

Conference: Mid-American.
Mailing Address: 1903 W. Michigan Ave, Kalamazoo, MI 49005. Website: www.wmubroncos.com.
Head Coach: Billy Gernon. Telephone: (269) 276-3205. Baseball SID: Nate Palcowski. Telephone: (269) 387-4138.
Assistant Coaches: Will Nimke, *Adam Piotrowicz. Telephone: (269) 276-3208.
Home Field: Hyames Field at Robert J Bobb Stadium. Seating Capacity: 1500. Outfield Dimensions: LF--310, CF--395, RF--335.

WICHITA STATE SHOCKERS

Conference: American Athletic.
Mailing Address: 1845 Fairmount St, Wichita, KS 67260. Website: www.GoShockers.com.
Head Coach: Eric Wedge. Telephone: (316) 978-3636. Baseball SID: Ryan Anderson. Telephone: (316) 978-5461.
Assistant Coaches: Mike Pelfrey, *Mike Sirianni. Telephone: (316) 978-3636.

Home Field: Eck Stadium. Seating Capacity: 8153. Outfield Dimensions: LF--330, CF--390, RF--330.

WILLIAM & MARY TRIBE

Conference: Colonial.
Mailing Address: 751 Ukrop Way, Williamsburg, VA 23185. Website: www.tribeathletics.com.
Head Coach: Brian Murphy. Telephone: (757) 221-3492. Baseball SID: John Moyer. Telephone: (757) 221-3344.
Assistant Coaches: *Brian Casey, Pat McKenna. Telephone: (757) 221-3475.
Home Field: Plumeri Park. Seating Capacity: 1200. Outfield Dimensions: LF--325, CF--400, RF--325.

WINTHROP EAGLES

Conference: Big South.
Mailing Address: 1162 Eden Terrace Rock ill, SC 29732. Website: www.withropeagles.com.
Head Coach: Tom Rignos. Telephone: (864) 903-9796. Baseball SID: Brett Redden. Telephone: (803) 367-1649.
Assistant Coaches: *Austin Hill, Robbie Monday. Telephone: (803) 318-1578.
Home Field: Winthrop Ballpark. Seating Capacity: 2000. Outfield Dimensions: LF--325, CF--400, RF--325.

WISCONSIN-MILWAUKEE PANTHERS

Conference: Horizon.
Mailing Address: PO Box 413, The Pavilion - Room 150, Milwaukee, WI 53201. Website: www.mkepanthers.com.
Head Coach: Scott Doffek. Telephone: 404-750-4738. Baseball SID: Cody Bohl. Telephone: 920-740-3936.
Assistant Coaches: Shaun Wegner, Cory Bigler, Mike Porcaro. Telephone: 404-750-0629.
Home Field: Franklin Field. Seating Capacity: 4000. Outfield Dimensions: LF--330, CF--408, RF--330.

WOFFORD TERRIERS

Conference: SoCon.
Mailing Address: 429 N. Church Street, Spartanburg, SC 29303. Website: www.woffordterriers.com.
Head Coach: Todd Interdonato. Telephone: (864) 597-4497. Baseball SID: Brent Williamson. Telephone: (864) 597-4093.
Assistant Coaches: Seth Cutler-Voltz, *JJ Edwards. Telephone: (864) 597-4499.
Home Field: Russell C. King Field. Seating Capacity: 2500. Outfield Dimensions: LF--325, CF--395, RF--325.

WRIGHT STATE RAIDERS

Conference: Horizon.
Mailing Address: 3640 Colonel Glenn Hwy, Fairborn, OH 45435. Website: https://wsuraiders.com/sports/baseball.
Head Coach: Alex Sogard. Telephone: NA. Baseball SID: Nick Phillips. Telephone: NA.
Assistant Coaches: *NATE METZGER, Chase Slone. Telephone: (309) 261-6170.
Home Field: Nischwitz Stadium. Seating Capacity: 1500. Outfield Dimensions: LF--330, CF--400, RF--330.

XAVIER MUSKETEERS

Conference: Big East.
Mailing Address: 3800 Victory Parkway Cincinnati OH 45207. Website: www.goxavier.com.
Head Coach: Billy O'Conner. Telephone: (513) 745-

2890. **Baseball SID:** Hayley Schletker. **Telephone:** 513-745-3412.

Assistant Coaches: *Brian Furlong, Jake Yacinich. **Telephone:** 513-745-2891.

Home Field: Hayden Field. **Seating Capacity:** 500. **Outfield Dimensions:** LF--310, CF--380, RF--310.

YALE BULLDOGS

Conference: Ivy League.

Mailing Address: PO Box 208216, New Haven, CT 06520-8216. **Website:** www.yalebulldogs.com.

Head Coach: John Stuper. **Telephone:** 203-432-1466. **Baseball SID:** Ernie Bertothy.

Assistant Coaches: Josh Schulman, Andrew Dickson.

Home Field: Yale Field. **Outfield Dimensions:** LF--330, CF--405, RF--315.

YOUNGSTOWN STATE PENGUINS

Conference: Horizon.

Mailing Address: 1 University Plaza, Youngstown, OH 44555. **Website:** ysusports.com.

Head Coach: Dan Bertolini. **Baseball SID:** Drae Smith. **Telephone:** (330) 941-8359.

Assistant Coaches: Shane Davis, *Eric Smith.

Home Field: Eastwood Field. **Seating Capacity:** 6000. **Outfield Dimensions:** LF--335, CF--405, RF--335.

AMATEUR & YOUTH

INTERNATIONAL ORGANIZATIONS

WORLD BASEBALL SOFTBALL CONFEDERATION

Headquarters: Maison du Sport International—54, Avenue de Rhodanie, 1007 Lausanne, Switzerland. **Telephone:** (+41-21) 318-82-40. **Fax:** (41-21) 318-82-41. **Website:** www.wbsc.org. **E-Mail:** office@wbsc.org. **Year Founded:** 1938.

President: Riccardo Fraccari (Italy). **Secretary General:** Beng Choo Low (Malaysia). **Vice President Baseball:** Willi Kaltschmitt Luján (Guam). **Vice President Softball:** Beatrice Allen (Gambia). **Softball Executive VP:** Craig Cress (USA). **Baseball Executive VP:** Tom Peng (Taiwan). **Treasurer:** Angelo Vicini (San Marino). **Members At-Large:** Ron Finlay (Australia), Paul Seiler (USA). Taeki Utsugi (Japan), Tommy Velázquez (Puerto Rico). **Athlete Representative For Baseball:** Justin Huber (Austrailia). **Athlete Representative For Softball:** María José Soto Gil (Venezuela). **Global Ambassador:** Antonio Castro Soto del Valle (Cuba), Meliton Sanchez Rivas (Panama). **Executive Director:** Michael Schmidt. **Softball Director:** Ron Radigonda. **Assistant to the President:** Giovanni Pantaleoni. **Marketing/Tournament Manager:** Masaru Yokoo, Laurie Gouthro. **Public Relations Officer:** Oscar Lopez, Lori Nolan. **National Federation Relations:** Francesca Fabretto, Brian Glauser, Aki Huang, Amy Park. **Antidoping Officer:** Victor Isola. **Administration/Finance:** Sandrine Pennone, Laetitia Barbey.

CONTINENTAL ASSOCIATIONS

CONFEDERATION PAN AMERICANA DE BEISBOL (COPABE)

Mailing Address: Calle 3, Francisco Filos, Vista Hermosa, Edificio 74, Planta Baja Local No. 1, Panama City, Panama. **Telephone:** (507) 229-8684. **Website:** www. copabe.net. **E-Mail:** copabe@sinfo.net.

Chairman: Eduardo De Bello (Panama). **Secretary General:** Hector Pereyra (Dominican Republic).

AFRICA BASEBALL SOFTBALL ASSOCIATION (ABSA)

Office Address: Paiko Road, Chanchaga, Minna, Niger State, Nigeria. **Mailing Address:** P.M.B. 150, Minna, Niger State, Nigeria. **Telephone:** (234) 66224555. **E-mail:** absasecretariat@yahoo.com

President: Sabeur Jlajla. **Vice President Baseball:** Etienne N'Guessan. **Vice President Softball:** Fridah Shiroya. **Secretary General:** Ibrahim N'Diaye. **Treasurer:** Moira Dempsey. **Executive Director:** Lieutenant Colonel (rtd) Friday Ichide. **Deputy Executive Director:** Francoise Kameni-Lele.

BASEBALL FEDERATION OF ASIA

Mailing Address: 9F. -3, No. 288, Sec 6 Civic Blvd.,Xinyi Dist., Taipei City, Taiwan (R.O.C.). **Telephone:** 886-227910336. **E-Mail Address:** bfa@baseballasia.org

President: Tom Peng. **Vice Presidents:** Suzuki Yoshinobu, Chen Xu, Hae Young Yang. **Secretary General:** Hua-Wei Lin. **Executive Director:** Richard Lin. **Members At Large:** Allan Mak, Alfonso Martin Eizmendi, Pervaiz Shah Khawar. **Director:** Richard Lin. **China Baseball Development Executive Director:** Tian Yuan. **West Asia Baseball Development Executive Director:** Syed Khawar Shah.

EUROPEAN BASEBALL CONFEDERATION

Mailing Address: Savska cesta 137, 10 000 Zagreb, Croatia. **Telephone/Fax:** +43 17744114. **E-Mail Address:** office@baseballeurope.com. **Website:** baseballeurope.com.

President: Didier Seminet (France). **President:** Gabriel Waage. **Members At Large:** Petr Ditrich (Czech Republic), Marco Mannucci (Italy), Roderick Balk (Netherlands), Youri Alkalay (Bulgaria), Kristian Palvia (Sweden), Mette Nissen Jakobsen (Denmark). **Secretary General:** Krunoslav Karin (Croatia) **Treasurer:** Eddy Van Straelen (Belgium).

BASEBALL CONFEDERATION OF OCEANIA

Mailing Address: 48 Partridge Way, Mooroolbark, Victoria 3138, Australia. **Telephone:** +61 394170022. **E-Mail Address:** office@wbscoceania.org.

Secretary General: Chet Gray (Australia). **1st Vice President:** Laurent Cassier (New Caledonia). **2nd Vice President:** Rex Capil (New Zealand). **Members at Large:** Innoke Niubalavu (Fiji), Ralph Tarasomo (Papua New Guinea), Hynes David (Australia), Vaughan Wyber (New Zealand).

INTERNATIONAL GOODWILL SERIES, INC.

Mailing Address: 982 Slate Drive, Santa Rosa, CA 95405. **Telephone:** (707) 538-0777. **E-Mail Address:** goodwillseries24@gmail.com.

Website: www.goodwillseries.org.

President, Goodwill Series, Inc.: Bob Williams.

ISG BASEBALL

Mailing Address: 3829 S Oakbrook Dr. Greenfield, WI 53228. **Telephone:** 414-704-5467. **E-Mail Address:** isgbaseball14@gmail.com. **Website:** isgbaseball.com.

President: Tom O'Connell. **Vice President:** Peter Caliendo. **Secretary/Treasurer:** Randy Town. **Board Members:** Jim Jones, John Casey, Ron Maestri, Pat Doyle, John Vodenlich.

NATIONAL ORGANIZATIONS

USA BASEBALL

Mailing Address, Corporate Headquarters: 1030 Swabia Court Suite 201, Durham, NC 27703
Telephone: (919) 474-8721.
Fax: (855) 420-5910.
E-mail Address: info@usabaseball.com.
Website: usabaseball.com.
President: Mike Gaski. **Treasurer:** Jason Dobis.
Board of Directors: Mike Gaski (President), Jason Dobis (Treasurer), Elliot Hopkins (Secretary); **Members:** Veronica Alvarez, Willie Bloomquist, Steve Cloud, John Gall, George Grande Chris Marinak, Richard Neely, Tony Reagins, Wes Skelton.

National Members Organizations: Amateur Athletic Union (AAU); American Amateur Baseball Congress (AABC); American Baseball Coaches Association (ABCA); American Legion Baseball, Babe Ruth Baseball; Dixie Baseball; Little League Baseball; National Amateur Baseball Federation (NABF); National Assocaition of Intercollegiate Athletics (NAIA); National Baseball Congress (NBC); National Collegiate Athletic Association (NCAA); National Federation of State High School Athletic Associations (NFHS); National High School Baseball Coaches Associatin (BCA); National Junior College Athletic Association (NJCAA); Police Athletic League (PAL); PONY Baseball; T-Ball USA; United States Specialty Sports Association (USSSA).
Events: www.usabaseball.com/events/schedule.jsp.

STAFF
Executive Director/CEO: Paul Seiler. **Chief Operating Officer:** David Perkins. **Chief Finance Officer:** Ray Darwin. **Director, Marketing:** Brittany Allen. **Senior Director, Retail:** Carrington Nicholson. **Director, Coaching Development:** Andrew Bartman. **Senior Director Baseball Operations:** Ashley Bratcher. **General Manager, National Teams:** Eric Campbell. **Assistant Director, Youth Programs:** Anthony Cangelosi. **Senior Director, Development:** Will Chriscoe. **Director, Youth Programs:** Tyler Collins. **Assistant Director, Education:** Sarah Cox. **Director, Baseball Operations:** Brett Curll. **Assistant Director, Media Relations:** Emily Fedewa. **General Manager, Sports Properties:** Jimmy Frush. **Director, Travel Services:** Monica Garza. **Director, Baseball Administration:** Allison Gupton. **Senior Director, Technology:** Russell Hartford. **Director, Baseball Operations:** Carter Hicks. **Assistant Director, Creative Services :** Jenna Hiscock. **Director, Creative Services:** Kevin Jones. **Director, Retail Operations:** Megan Kane. **Director, Baseball Operations:** Ben Kelley. **Director, Accounting & Finance:** Cicely McLaughlin. **Director, Baseball Operations:** Charles Lane. **Coordinator, Retail & Travel Services:** Alexandra Morin. **Assistant Director, Creatice Services:** Colin Pelosi. **Director, Sport Performance:** Drew Pomeroy. **Senior Director, Athlete Safety and Education:** Lauren Rhyne. **Assistant Director, Baseball Operations:** Ann Claire Robinson. **Director, 12U National Team:** Will Schworer. **Senior Director, NTC Operations:** James Vick. **Senior Director, Media Relations:** Brad Young.

BASEBALL CANADA

Mailing Address: 2212 Gladwin Cres., Suite A7, Ottawa, Ontario K1B 5N1. **Telephone:** (613) 748-5606. **Fax:** (613) 748-5767. **E-mail Address:** info@baseball.ca. **Website:** baseball.ca.
Director General: Jim Baba. **Head Coach/Director, National Teams:** Greg Hamilton. **Business/Sport Development Director/Women's National Team Manager:** Andre Lachance. **Media/PR Coordinator:** Adam Morissette. **Administrative Coordinator:** June Sterling. **Administrative Assistant:** Penny Baba. **Coach and Umpire Service Coordinator:** Michael Landriault. **Administrative Coordinator, Men's National Teams:** Nancy Dunbar.

NATIONAL BASEBALL CONGRESS

Mailing Address: 111 S. Main, Suite 600, Wichita, KS 67202. **Telephone:** (316) 977-9400. **Fax:** (316) 462-4506. **Website:** nbcbaseball.com.
Year Founded: 1931.

ATHLETES IN ACTION

Mailing Address: 651 Taylor Dr., Xenia, OH 45385. **Telephone:** (937) 352-1000. **E-mail Address:** baseball@athletesinaction.org. **Website:** aiabaseball.org. **Baseball Director of Operations/GM:** Chris Beck. **Xenia Scouts Program Director:** Dave Gnau. **International Teams Director:** John McLaughlin. **Baseball Staff:** Jason Lester.

SUMMER COLLEGE LEAGUES

NATIONAL ALLIANCE OF COLLEGE SUMMER BASEBALL

Telephone: (321) 696-6995. **E-Mail Address:** sfoggi@FloridaLeague.com. **Website:** nacsb.pointstreaksites.com

Executive Director: Stefano Foggi (Florida League). **Assistant Executive Director:** Bobby Bennett (Sunbelt Baseball League), Jeff Carter (Southern Collegiate Baseball League). **Treasurer:** Jason Woodward (Cal Ripken Collegiate Baseball League). **Director, Public Relations:** Henry Bramwell (Hamptons Collegiate Baseball League). **Compliance Officer:** Sean McGrath (New England Collegiate Baseball League).

Member Leagues: Atlantic Collegiate Baseball League, California Collegiate League, Cal Ripken Collegiate Baseball League, Cape Cod Baseball League, Florida Collegiate Summer League, Great Lakes Summer Collegiate League, New England Collegiate Baseball League, New York Collegiate Baseball League, Southern Collegiate Baseball League, Sunbelt Baseball League, Valley Baseball League, Hamptons Collegiate Baseball League.

ALASKA BASEBALL LEAGUE

League Mailing Address: P.O. Box 2690 Palmer, AK 99645. 5 teams, 44-50 league games. Season begins play June 7 and ends Aug. 4. **President:** Chris Beck. **Email:** Chris.beck@athletesinaction.org.

MAT-SU MINERS

General Manager: Pete Christopher. **Mailing Address:** P.O. Box 2690 Palmer, AK 99645. **Telephone:** 907-746-4914/907-745-6401. **Fax:** 907-746-5068. **E-Mail:** gmminers@gci.net. **Fax:** 907-561-2920. **Website:** matsuminers.org. **Head Coach:** Tyler LeBrun. **Field:** Hermon Brothers, Grass, No Lights.

ANCHORAGE BUCS

General Manager: Shawn Maltby. **Mailing Address:** 435 W. 10th Avenue Suite B, Anchorage, AK 99501. **Office:** 907-561-2827. **Fax:** 907-561-2920. **E-Mail:** shawn@anchoragebucs.com. **Website:** anchoragebucs.com. **Head Coach:** Grant Palmer. **Field:** Mulcahy Field -Turf Infield, Grass Outfield, Lights

ANCHORAGE GLACIER PILOTS

General Manager: Mike Hinshaw. **Mailing Address:** 435 W. 10th Avenue, Suite A, Anchorage, Alaska 99501. **Office:** 907-274-3627. **Fax:** 907-274-3628. **E-Mail:** gpilots@alaska.net. **Website:** glacierpilots.com. **Head Coach:** Mike Cordero. **Field:** Mulcahy Field -Turf Infield, Grass Outfield, Lights

CHUGIAK-EAGLE RIVER CHINOOKS

General Manager: Chris Beck. **Mailing Address:** 651 Taylor Drive, Xenia, Ohio 45385. **Office:** 937-352-1000. **Fax:** 937-352-1001. **E-Mail:** Chris.beck@athletesinaction.org. **Website:** cerchinooks.com. **Head Coach:** Jon Groth.

Field: Lee Jordan Field-Turf Infield, Grass Outfield, No Lights

PENINSULA OILERS

General Manager: Kyle Brown. **Mailing Address:** 601 S. Main St., Kenai, Alaska 99611. **Office:** 907-283-7133. **Fax:** 907-283-3390. **E-Mail:** tory@oilersbaseball.com. **Website:** oilersbaseball.com **Head Coach:** Larry McCann. **Field:** Coral Seymour Memorial Park-Grass , No Lights

ATLANTIC COLLEGIATE BASEBALL LEAGUE

Mailing Address: 8 Millbrook Drive, Middletown, NJ 07748.

Telephone: (215) 536-5777. **Fax:** (215) 536-5777. **Website:** acbl-online.com. **Year Founded:** 1967. **Commissioner:** Angelo Fiore. **President:** Joe Mazza. **Secretary:** Mike Kalb. **Executive Vice President:** Doug Cinella. **Treasurer:** Bob Hoffman.

ALLENTOWN RAILERS

Mailing Address: Suite 202, 1801 Union Blvd, Allentown, PA 18109. **E-Mail Address:** ddando@lehigh-valleybaseballacademy.com. **Field Manager:** Dylan Dando.

JERSEY PILOTS

Mailing Address: 11 Danemar Drive, Middletown, NJ 07748. **Telephone:** (732) 939-0627. **E-Mail Address:** baseball@jerseypilots.com. **General Manager:** Mike Kalb.

NEW YORK PHENOMS

General Manager: Rob Bass. **Telephone:** (646) 296-1720. **E-Mail Address:** radbyrob@aol.com. **Field Manager:** Anthony Ferrante. **Field:** College of Staten Island Baseball Complex, Staten Island, NY.

NORTH JERSEY EAGLES

Mailing Address: 12 Wright Way, Oakland NJ 07436. **General Manager:** Brian Casey.

OCEAN GULLS

General Manager: Angelo Fiore, afiore@fioreservicegroup.com. **Telephone:** 904-237-1468.

QUAKERTOWN BLAZERS

Telephone: (215) 679-5072. **Website:** quakertownblazers.com. **Field Manager:** Chris Ray.

TRENTON GENERALS

E-Mail Address: mrolsh@msn.com. **General Manager:** Michael Olshin.

CALIFORNIA COLLEGIATE LEAGUE

Mailing Address: 11756 Chestnut Ridge Street, Moorpark, CA 93021. **Telephone:** (805) 680-1047. **Fax:** (805) 684-8596. **E-Mail Address:** burns@calsummerball. com. **Website:** calsummerball.com.

Founded: 1993.

Executive Director: Aaron Millman.

ACADEMY BARONS

Address: 901 E. Artesia Blvd, Compton, CA 90221. **Telephone:** (424) 209-5727. **Website:** calsummerball. com/academy-barons-roster. **E-Mail Address:** darrell. miller@mlb.com. **Contact:** Natalia Reynoso. **Field manager:** Kenny Landreaux.

ARROYO SECO SAINTS

Telephone: (626) 695-6903. **Website:** arroyoseco-saints.com. **E-mail Address:** amilam@arroyosecobase-ball.com. **General Manager:** Aaron Milam/Nicholas Gorman. **Field Manager:** Aaron Milam.

CONEJO OAKS

Address: 1710 N. Moorpark Rd., #106, Thousand Oaks, CA 91360. **Telephone:** 805-304-0126. **Website:** calsummerball.com/conejo-oaks-roster/. com. **E-Mail Address:** oaksbaseball@yahoo.com. **Field Manager:** David Soliz. **General Manager:** Randy Riley.

HEALDSBURG PRUNE PACKERS

Address: Rec Park 515 Piper St. Healdsburg, Calif. 95448. **Mailing Address:** PO Box 1543 Healdsburg CA 95448. **Telephone:** 707-280-6693. **Email Address:** JGG21@aol.com. **General Manager/Field Manager:** Joey Gomes.

ORANGE COUNTY RIPTIDE

Address: 14 Calendula Rancho, Santa Margarita, CA 92688. **Telephone:** (949) 228-7676. **Website:** ocriptide. com. **E-Mail Address:** ocriptidebaseball@gmail.com. **Field Manager:** Mitch LeVier. **General Manager:** Moe Geohagen. **Head Coach:** Clemente Bonilla.

SAN LUIS OBISPO BLUES

Address: 3195 McMillan Ave, Ste. B2, San Luis Obispo, CA 93401. **Telephone:** 805-512-9996. **Website:** blues-baseball.com. **E-Mail Address:** adam@bluesbaseball. com. **General Manager:** Adam Stowe. **Field Manager:** Clay Cederquist.

SANTA BARBARA FORESTERS

Address: 4299 Carpinteria Ave., Suite 201, Carpinteria, CA 93013. **Telephone:** (805) 684-0657. **Website:** sbforest-ers.org. **E-Mail Address:** pintard@earthlink.net. **General Manager and Field Manager:** Bill Pintard.

SOUTHERN CALIFORNIA SHEPHERDS

Telephone (GM): (562) 686-8262. **Website:** shepherdsbaseball.org. **E-mail Address (GM):** borr@fca. org. **General Manager:** Ben Orr. **Field Manager:** Dan Peters.

VENTURA COUNTY PIRATES

Website: calsummerball.com/ventura-county-pirates-affiliated-team-2018-roster/. **E-mail Address (GM):** gvranau.pirates@gmail.com. **General Manager:** George Vranau.

CAL RIPKEN COLLEGIATE LEAGUE

Address: 24219 Hawkins Landing Drive, Gaithersburg, MD 20882. **Telephone:** (301) 693-2577. **E-Mail:** jason_d_ woodward@mcpsmd.org. **Website:** calripken league.org.

Year Founded: 2005.

Commissioner: Jason Woodward. **League President:** Brad Rifkin. **Deputy Commissioner:** Jerry Wargo.

Regular Season: 36 games. **Playoff Format:** Top two teams from each division plus two remaining teams with best records qualify. Teams play best of three series, winners advance to best of three series for league championship. **Roster Limit:** 35 (college-eligible players 22 and under).

ALEXANDRIA ACES

Address: 221 9th Street, S.E. Washington, DC 20003. **Telephone:** (202) 255-1683. **E-Mail:** cberset21@gmail. com. **Website:** alexandriaaces.org. **Chairman/CEO:** Donald Dinan. **General Manager:** TBD. **Head Coach:** Chris Berset. **Ballpark:** Frank Mann Field at Four Mile Run Park.

BALTIMORE DODGERS

Address: 17 Sunrise Court Randallstown, MD 21133. **Telephone:** (443) 834-3500. **Email:** juan.waters@verizon. net. **Website:** baltimoredodgers.org. **President:** Juan Waters. **Head Coach:** Derek Brown. **Ballpark:** Joe Cannon Stadium at Harmans Park.

BETHESDA BIG TRAIN

Address: 6400 Goldsboro Road Suite 220 Bethesda, MD 20817. **Telephone:** 301-229-1854. **Fax:** 301-229-8362. **E-Mail:** faninfo@bigtrain.org. **Website:** bigtrain.org. **General Manager:** David Schneider. **Head Coach:** Sal Colangelo. **Ballpark:** Shirley Povich Field.

D.C. GRAYS

Address: 1800 M Street NW, 500 South Tower, Washington, DC 20036. **Telephone:** (202) 492-6226. **Website:** dcgrays.com. **E-Mail Address:** barbera@acg-consultants.com. **President:** Mike Barbera. **General Manager:** Antonio Scott. **Head Coach:** Reggie Terry. **Ballpark:** Washington Nationals Youth Academy.

GAITHERSBURG GIANTS

Address: 18221A Flower Hill Way, Gaithersburg, MD 20879. **Telephone:** (240) 793-3367. **E-Mail:** gaithers-burggiants@gmail.com. **Website:** gaithersburggiants. org. **General Manager:** Matt Cangas. **Head Coach:** Jeff Rabberman. **Ballpark:** Criswell Automotive Field.

FCA BRAVES

Address: 8925 Leesburg Pike, Vienna, VA 22182. **Telephone:** (702) 909-2750. **Fax:** (703) 783-1319. **E-Mail:** fcabraves@gmail.com. **Website:** fcabraves.com. **President/General Manager:** Todd Burger. **Head Coach:** Chris Warren. **Ballpark:** Annandale High School.

SILVER SPRING-TAKOMA T-BOLTS

Address: 906 Glaizewood Court, Takoma Park, MD 20912. **Telephone**: 301-983-1358. **E-Mail**: tboltsbaseball@gmail.com. **Website**: tbolts.org. **General Manager**: Brian Brewer. **Head Coach**: Doug Remer. **Ballpark**: Blair Stadium at Montgomery Blair High School.

CAPE COD BASEBALL LEAGUE

Mailing Address: PO Box 266, Harwich Port, MA 02646. **Telephone:** (508) 432-6909.
E-Mail: info@capecodbaseball.org.
Website: capecodbaseball.org.
Year Founded: 1885.
Commissioner: Eric Zmuda. **President:** Chuck Sturtevant. **Treasurer:** Paul Logan. **Secretary:** Paula Tufts. **Senior VP:** Bill Bussiere. **VP:** Tom Gay, Paul Galop. **Senior Deputy Commissioner/Director of Officiating:** Sol Yas. **Deputy Commissioner:** Mike Carrier, Peter Hall. **Director Public Relations:** Ben Brink. **Director Broadcasting:** John Garner. **Director, Communications:** Jim McGonigle. **Division Structure: East**—Brewster, Chatham, Harwich, Orleans, Yarmouth-Dennis. **West**—Bourne, Cotuit, Falmouth, Hyannis, Wareham.
Regular Season: 40 games. **All-Star Game and Home Run Contest:** July 24. **Playoff Format:** Top four teams in each division qualify for three rounds of best-of-three series.

BOURNE BRAVES

Mailing Address: PO Box 895, Monument Beach, MA 02553. **Telephone:** (508) 868-8378. **E-Mail Address:** nnorkevicius@yahoo.com. **Website:** bournebraves.org.
President: Nicole Norkevicius. **General Manager:** Darin Weeks. **Head Coach:** Harvey Shapiro.

BREWSTER WHITECAPS

Mailing Address: PO Box 2349, Brewster, MA 02631. **Telephone:** (508) 896-8500, ext. 147. **Fax:** (508) 896-9845.
E-Mail Address: ckenney@brewsterwhitecaps.com. **Website:** brewsterwhitecaps.com.
President: Chris Kenney. **General Manager:** Ned Monthie. **Head Coach:** Jamie Shevchik.

CHATHAM ANGLERS

Mailing Address: PO Box 428, Chatham, MA 02633. **Website:** chathamas.com. **President:** Steve West. **General Manager:** Mike Geylin. **Email:** mgeylin@kgpr.com. **Head Coach:** Tom Holliday.

COTUIT KETTLEERS

Mailing Address: PO Box 411, Cotuit, MA 02635. **Telephone:** (508) 428-3358. **E-Mail Address:** bmurpfcape@aol.com. **Website:** kettleers.org. **President:** Andy Bonacker. **General Manager:** Bruce Murphy. **Head Coach:** Mike Roberts.

FALMOUTH COMMODORES

Mailing Address: PO Box 808 Falmouth, MA 02541. **Telephone:** (508) 566-4988. **Website:** falmouthcommodores.org. **President:** Mark Kasprzyk. **General Manager:** Chris Fitzgerald. **Head Coach:** Jeff Trundy.

HARWICH MARINERS

Mailing Address: PO Box 201, Harwich Port, MA 02646. **Telephone:** (508) 432-2000. **Fax:** (508) 432-5357. **E-Mail Address:** mehendy@comcast.net. **Website:** harwichmariners.org.
President: Mary Henderson. **General Manager:** Ben Layton. **Head Coach:** Steve Englert.

HYANNIS HARBOR HAWKS

Mailing Address: PO Box 832, West Hyannis Port, MA 02672. **Telephone:** (508) 737-5890. **Fax:** (877) 822-2703. **E-Mail Address:** brpfeifer@aol.com. **Website:** harborhawks.org.
President: Brad Pfeifer. **General Manager:** Brian Guiney. **Head Coach:** Gary Calhoun.

ORLEANS FIREBIRDS

Mailing Address: PO Box 504, Orleans, MA 02653. **Telephone:** (508) 255-0793. **Fax:** (508) 255-2237. **E-Mail Address:** bodonnell15@gmail.com. **Website:** orleansfirebirds.com. **President:** Bob O'Donnell. **General Manager:** Sue Horton. **Head Coach:** Kelly Nicholson.

WAREHAM GATEMEN

Mailing Address: PO Box 287, Wareham, MA 02571. **Telephone:** (508) 748-0287. **Fax:** (508) 880-2602. **E-Mail Address:** alang.gatemen@gmail.com.
Website: gatemen.org. **President:** Tom Gay. **General Manager:** Andrew Lang. **Head Coach:** Jerry Weinstein.

YARMOUTH-DENNIS RED SOX

Mailing Address: PO Box 78 Yarmouth Port, MA 02675. **Telephone:** (508) 889-8721. **E-Mail Address:** sfaucher64@gmail.com. **Website:** ydredsox.org. **President:** James DeMaria. **General Manager:** Steve Faucher. **Head Coach:** Scott Pickler.

CENTRAL VALLEY COLLEGIATE LEAGUE

Mailing Address: P.O. Box 561, Fowler, CA 93625. **E-mail:** j_scot25@hotmail.com, jcederquist@aol.com. **Website:** cvclbaseball.webs.com. **Twitter:** @CVCL1.
Year Founded: 2013. **President:**Jon Scott. **Regular Season:** 30 games. **2021 Opening Date:** May 31. **Closing Date:** July 26. **All-Star Game:** July 15, Fresno, Calif. **Roster Limit:** 30

BAKERSFIELD BRAVES

Mailing Address: PO Box 20760, Bakersfield, CA, 93390. **Website:** eteamz.com/bakersfieldbraves. **Field Manager:** Bobby Maitia.

CALIFORNIA EXPOS

Mailing Address: P.O. Box 561, Fowler, CA 93625. **E-mail:** exposcv@aol.com. **Website:** calibaseball.com. **Twitter:** @cvexpos. **Field Manager:** Thomas Raymundo.

CALIFORNIA PILOTS

Mailing Address: PO Box 561 Fowler, CA 93625. **E-mail:** valleystormbaseball@aol.com. **Website:** www.calibaseball.com. **Twitter:** @calistorm1. **Field Manager:** Kenny Corona.

CALIFORNIA STORM

Mailing Address: PO Box 561 Fowler, CA 93625. **E-mail:** valleystormbaseball@aol.com. **Website:** calibaseball.com. **Twitter:** @calistorm1. **Field Manager:** Kolton Cabral.

SANTA MARIA PACKERS

Mailing Address: P.O Box 144, Kingsburg, CA 93631. **E-mail:** j_scot25@hotmail.com. **Website:** cvipers .webs.com. **Twitter:** @SouthcountryV. **Field Manager:** Jon Scott.

SOUTH COUNTY VIPERS

Mailing Address: P.O Box 144, Kingsburg, CA 93631. **E-mail:** j_scot25@hotmail.com. **Website:** cvipers .webs.com. **Twitter:** @SouthcountryV. **Field Manager:** Jon Scott.

COASTAL PLAIN LEAGUE

Mailing Address: 117 Thomas Mill Road, Holly Springs, NC 27540. **Telephone:** (919) 852-1960. **Email Address:** justins@coastalplain.com. **Website:** coastalplain.com. **Year Founded:** 1997. **Chairman/CEO:** Jerry Petitt. **COO/Commissioner:** Justin Sellers. **Director of Media & Content Development:** Shelby Hilliard.

Division Structure: North—Peninsula Pilots, Tri-City Chili Peppers, Wilson Tobs. **East**—Florence RedWolves, Holly Springs Salamanders, Morehead City Marlins, Wilmington Sharks. **South**—Lexington County Blowfish, Macon Bacon, Spartanburgers, Savannah Bananas. **West**—Asheboro Copperheads, Forest City Owls, High Point-Thomasville HiToms, Martinsville Mustangs. **Regular Season:** 52 games. **Playoff Format:** Three rounds. **Rd 1/2:** One game. **Rd 3:** Best of three.

ASHEBORO COPPERHEADS

Mailing Address: PO Box 4036, Asheboro, NC 27204. **Telephone:** (336) 460-7018. **Fax:** (336) 523-1220. **E-Mail Address:** info@teamcopperhead.com. **Website:** teamcopperhead.com. **Owners:** Ronnie Pugh, Steve Pugh, Doug Pugh, Mike Pugh. **General Managers:** Keith Ritsche, Dennis Garcia. **Head Coach:** Keith Ritsche

FLORENCE RED WOLVES

Mailing Address: 520 Francis Marion Rd., Florence, S.C. 29503. **Telephone:** (843) 629-0700. **E-Mail Address:** info@florenceredwolves.com. **Website:** www.florenceredwolves.com. **Managing Partner:** Steve DeLay. **Head Coach:** Jake Schuster.

FOREST CITY OWLS

Mailing Address: 214 McNair Field Drive, Forest City, NC 28043. **E-Mail Address:** info@forestcitybaseball.com. **Website:** www.forestcitybaseball.com. **Owners:** Phil & Becky Dangel. **General Manager:** Kiva Fuller. **Head Coach:** Matt Reed.

HIGH POINT-THOMASVILLE HI-TOMS

Mailing Address: 7003 Ballpark Road, Thomasville, NC 27360. **Telephone:** (336) 472-8667. **Fax:** (336) 472-7198. **E-Mail Address:** info@hitoms.com. **Website:** hitoms.com. **Owner:** Richard Holland. **President:** Greg Suire. **Head Coach:** Scott Davis.

HOLLY SPRINGS SALAMANDERS

Mailing Address: 101 Tennis Court, Holly Springs, NC 27540. **Telephone:** 919-249-7322. **Email Address:** info@salamandersbaseball.com. **Website:** salamandersbaseball.com. **Owner:** Capital Broadcast Company. **General Manager:** Chip Hutchinson. **Head Coach:** TBD.

LEXINGTON COUNTY BLOWFISH

Mailing Address: 474 Ball Park Road, Lexington, SC 29072. **Telephone:** (803) 254-3474. **E-Mail Address:** info@blowfishbaseball.com. **Website:** goblowfishbaseball.com. **Owner:** Bill & Vicki Shanahan. **Head Coach:** Fico Kondla.

MACON BACON

Mailing Address: 225 Willie Smokey Glover Drive, Macon, GA. **Telephone:** 478-803-1795. **E-Mail Address:** info@maconbaconbaseball.com. **Website:** maconbaconbaseball.com. **Owner:** SRO Partners (Jon Spoelstra & Steve DeLay). **President:** Brandon Raphael. **Head Coach:** Jimmy Turk.

MARTINSVILLE MUSTANGS

Mailing Address: 450 Commonwealth Blvd E Martinsville, VA 24112. **Telephone:** (276) 403-5250. **E-Mail Address:** info@martinsvillemustangs.com. **Website:** www.martinsvillemustangs.com. **President:** Greg Suire. **General Manager:** Ruthanne Duffy. **Head Coach:** Jake Marinelli.

MOREHEAD CITY MARLINS

Mailing Address: PO Box 460, New Bern, NC 28563. **Telephone:** (252) 269-9767. **Fax:** (252) 637-2721. **E-Mail Address:** mcmarlins@gmail.com. **Website:** mhcmarlins.com. **General Manager:** Buddy Bengel. **Head Coach:** Jesse Lancaster.

PENINSULA PILOTS

Mailing Address: 1889 W. Pembroke Ave., Hampton, VA 23661. **Telephone:** (757) 245-2222. **Fax:** (757) 245-8030. **E-Mail Address:** info@peninsulapilots.com. **Website:** peninsulapilots.com. **Owner:** Henry Morgan. **General Manager:** Alex Ahl. **Head Coach/Vice President:** Hank Morgan.

SAVANNAH BANANAS

Mailing Address: 1401 E. Victory Drive, Savannah, GA 31404. **Telephone:** 912-712-2482. **E-Mail Address:** jared@thesavannahbananas.com. **Website:** thesavannahbananas.com. **Owner:** Fans First Entertainment (Jesse & Emily Cole). **President:** Jared Orton. **Head Coach:** Tyler Gillum

SPARTANBURGERS

Mailing Address: 1000 Duncan Park Dr, Spartanburg, SC 29302. **Telephone:** TBA. **E-Mail Address:** TBA. **Website:** TBA. **Owner:** Matt Perry. **General Manager:** Claudia Padgett. **Head Coach:** Wesley Brown.

TRI-CITY CHILI PEPPERS

Mailing Address: 901 Meridian Ave, Colonial Heights, VA 23834. **Telephone:** (804) 499-3104. **E-Mail Address:** info@chilipeppersbaseball.com. **Website:** www.chilipeppersbaseball.com. **Owner:** Chris Martin. **General Manager:** Steve Taggart. **Head Coach:** TBA.

WILMINGTON SHARKS

Mailing Address: 2149 Carolina Beach Road, Wilmington, NC 28401. **Telephone:** (910) 343-5621. **Fax:** (910) 343-8932. **E-Mail Address:** media@wilmington sharks.com. **Website:** wilmingtonsharks.com. **Owners:** National Sports Services. **General Manager:** Carson Bowen. **Head Coach:** Russ Burroughs.

WILSON TOBS

Mailing Address: 300 Stadium St. SW., Wilson, NC 27893. **Telephone:** (252) 291-8627. **Fax:** (252) 291-1224. **E-Mail Address:** mike@wilsontobs.com. **Website:** wilsontobs.com. **Owner:** Richard Holland. **President:** Greg Suire. **General Manager:** Mike Bell. **Head Coach:** Bryan Hill.

FLORIDA COLLEGIATE SUMMER LEAGUE

Mailing Address: 250 National Place, Unit #152, Longwood, FL 32750. **Telephone:** (321) 206-9174. **Fax:** (407) 574-7926. **E-Mail Address:** info@floridaleague.com. **Website:** floridaleague.com.

Year Founded: 2004.

President: Stefano Foggi. **League Operations Director:** Phil Chinnery.

Regular Season: 45 games. **2021 Opening Date:** TBD. **All-Star Game:** TBD. **Playoffs Begin:** TBD. **Playoff Format:** Five teams qualify; No. 4 and No. 5 seeds meet in one-game playoff. Remaining four teams play best-of-three series. Winners play best-of-three series for league championship.

Roster Limit: 28 (college-eligible players only). High school grads allowed with MLB approval. Part of the National Alliance of College Summer Baseball.

DELAND SUNS

Operated by the league office. **E-Mail Address:** suns@floridaleague.com. **Head Coach:** Rick Hall.

LEESBURG LIGHTNING

E-Mail Address: lightning@floridaleague.com. **Head Coach:** Rich Billings.

SANFORD RIVER RATS

Operated by the league office. **E-Mail Address:** rats@floridaleague.com. **Head Coach:** Josh Montero.

SEMINOLE COUNTY SCORPIONS

Operated by the league office. **E-Mail Address:** scorpions@floridaleague.com. **Head Coach:** Bob Rikeman.

WINTER GARDEN SQUEEZE

Operated by the league office. **Email Address:** squeeze@floridaleague.com. **Head Coach:** Terry Abbott. **General Manager:** Adam Bates.

WINTER PARK DIAMOND DAWGS

E-Mail Address: dawgs@floridaleague.com. **Head Coach:** Chuck Schall.

FUTURES COLLEGIATE LEAGUE OF NEW ENGLAND

Mailing Address: 46 Chestnut Hill Rd, Chelmsford, MA 01824. **Telephone:** (617) 593-2112. **E-Mail Address:** futuresleague@yahoo.com

Website: thefuturesleague.com.

Year Founded: 2010.

Commissioner: Joe Paolucci.

Teams (Contact): Bristol Blues (www.bristolbluesbaseball.com) (**Brian Rooney:** gm@bristolblues.com); Brockton Rox (**Todd Marlin:** tmarlin@brocktonrox.com); Martha's Vineyard Sharks (**Russ Curran:** russ.curran@mvsharks.com); Nashua Silver Knights (**Rick Muntean:** rick@nashuasilverknights.com); North Shore Navigators (**Bill Terlecky:** navigatorsgm@gmail.com); Pittsfield Suns (**Kristen Huss:** kristen@pittsfieldsuns.com); Worcester Bravehearts (**Dave Peterson:** dave@worcesterbravehearts.com)

Regular Season: 56 games; 28 home, 28 away. **Playoff Format:** Six teams qualify. First round consists of two single elimination play-in games (3 seed vs. 6 seed and 4 seed vs 5 seed), two remaining teams play a best of three semifinal round followed by a best-of- three championship round to determine league champion. Extra-inning Games are determined by Home Run Derby!!

Roster Limit: 35. 10 must be from New England or play collegiately at a New England college.

GREAT LAKES SUMMER COLLEGIATE LEAGUE

Mailing Address: PO Box 666, Troy, OH 45373. **Telephone:** (937) 308-1536. **E-Mail:** glsclcommish@gmail.com.

Website: greatlakesleague.org.

Year Founded: 1986.

President: Jim DeSana. **Commissioner:** Deron Brown. **Regular Season:** 42 games. **Playoff Format:** Top six teams meet in playoffs. **Roster Limit:** 30 (college-eligible players only).

Teams: (15 Teams)—Cincinnati Steam (Cincinnati, OH); Galion Graders (Galion, OH); Grand Lake Mariners (Celina, OH); Grand River Loggers (Grand Haven, MI); Hamilton Joes (Hamilton, OH); Lake Erie Monarchs (Flat Rock, MI); Licking County Settlers (Newark, OH); Lima Locos (Lima, OH); Lorain County Ironmen (Lorain, OH); Muskegon Clippers (Muskegon, MI); Richmond Jazz (Richmond, IN); Saint Clair Green Giants (Tecumseh, ON); Southern Ohio Copperheads (Athens, OH); Xenia Scouts (Xenia, OH).

METROPOLITAN COLLEGIATE BASEBALL LEAGUE

Mailing Address: 78 Knollwood Drive, Paramus NJ 07652

President: Brian Casey 374-545-1991

Website: metropolitanbaseball.com

Email: mcbl@metropolitanbaseball.com

MIDWEST COLLEGIATE LEAGUE

Mailing Address: 1500 119th Street Whiting IN 46394. **E-Mail Address:** commissioner@midwestcollegiate league.com. **Website:** midwestcollegiateleague.com.

Year Founded: 2010.

President/Commissioner: Don Popravak.

Regular Season: 52 games. **Playoff Format:** Top four teams meet in best of three series. Winners meet in best of three championship series.

Roster Limit: 30

Teams: Bloomington Bobcats, Crestwood Panthers, DuPage County Hounds, Joliet Admirals, NWI Oilmen, Southland Vikings.

M.I.N.K. LEAGUE

(Missouri, Iowa, Nebraska, Kansas)
Mailing Address: PO Box 367, Nevada, MO 64772.
Telephone: (417) 667-6159. Fax: (417) 667-4210.
Email Address: jpost@morrisonpost.com. **Website**: minkleaguebaseball.com
Year Founded: 1995.
Commissioner: Bob Steinkamp. **President:** Jeff Post.
Vice President: Jud Kindle. **Secretary:** Edwina Rains.
Regular season: 44 games.
Playoff Format: The top three teams from each division will qualify for the playoffs. The second and third place finishers in each division will play a "Wild Card" one-game playoff. The winner of those games will play the regular season division winner from each division in a one game playoff. The winner of each division will then play a two out of three series to determine the MINK League Champion. Championship starts on July 25.
Opening day: June 1st. **All-Star Game:** June 26th.

CHILLICOTHE MUDCATS

Mailing Address: 11 E 2nd Street, Chillicothe, MO 64601.
Telephone: (660) 247-1504. **Fax:** (660) 646-6933. **E-Mail Address:** doughty@greenhills.net. **Website:** chillicothemudcats.com. **General Manager:** Doug Doughty.

CLARINDA A'S

Mailing Address: 225 East Lincoln, Clarinda, IA 51632.
Telephone: (712) 542-4272. **E-Mail Address:** m.everly@mchsi.com. **Website:** clarindaiowa-as-baseball.org.
General Managers: Ryan Eberly, Rodney J. Eberly.
Head Coach: Ryan Eberly.

JOPLIN OUTLAWS

Mailing Address: 5860 North Pearl, Joplin, MO 64801.
Telephone: (417) 825-4218. **E-Mail Address:** merains@mchsi.com. **Website:** joplinoutlaws.com. **President/General Manager:** Mark Rains.

NEVADA GRIFFONS

Mailing Address: PO Box 601, Nevada, MO 64772.
Telephone: (417) 667-6159. **E-Mail Address:** Ryan.Mansfield@mcckc.edu. **Website:** nevadagriffons.org. **President:** Dan Keller. **General Manager:** Ryan Mansfield. **Head Coach:** Ryan Mansfield.

OZARK GENERALS

Mailing Address: 1336 W Farm Road 182, Springfield, MO 65810. **Telephone:** (417) 832-8830. **Fax:** (417) 877-4625. **E-Mail Address:** rda160@yahoo.com. **Website:** generalsbaseballclub.com. **General Manager/Head Coach:** Rusty Aton.

ST. JOSEPH MUSTANGS

Mailing Address: 2600 SW Parkway, St. Joseph, MO 64503. **Telephone:** (816) 279-7856. **Fax:** (816) 749-4082. **E-Mail Address:** kyturner@stjoemustangs.com.
Website: stjoemustangs.com. **President:** Dan Gerson.
General Manager: Ky Turner. **Manager/Director**, **Player Personnel:** Johnny Coy.

SEDALIA BOMBERS

Mailing Address: 2205 S Grand, Sedalia, MO 65301.
Telephone: (660) 287-4722. **E-Mail Address:** eric@sedaliabombers.com. **Website:** sedaliabombers.com. **President/General Manager/Head Coach:** Jud Kindle. **Vice President:** Ross Dey.

JEFFERSON CITY RENEGADES

Telephone: 630-781-7247 **E-Mail Address:** jcrenegades@gmail.com. **Website:** jcrenegades.com.
President/General Manager: Steve Dullard. **Head Coach:** Mike DeMilia.

NEW ENGLAND COLLEGIATE LEAGUE

Mailing Address: 122 Mass Moca Way, North Adams, MA 01247. **Telephone:** (413) 652-1031. **Fax:** (413) 473-0012. **E-Mail Address:** smcgrath@necbl.com. **Website:** necbl.com. **Year founded:** 1993. **President:** John DeRosa.
Commissioner: Sean McGrath. **Deputy Commissioner:** Gregg Hunt. **Secretary:** Max Pinto. **Treasurer:** Tim Porter.
Regular Season: 44 games. **2021 Opening Date:** June 3. **Closing Date:** Aug. 1. **All-Star Game:** July 19. **Roster Limit:** 33 (college players only).

DANBURY WESTERNERS

Mailing Address: PO Box 3828, Danbury, CT 06813.
Telephone: (203) 502-9167. **E-Mail Address:** jspitser@msn.com. **Website:** danburywesterners.com.
President: Jon Pitser. **General Manager:** Chris Nathanson. **Field Manager:** Ian Ratchford.

VALLEY BLUE SOX

Mailing Address: 100 Congress St, Springfield, MA 01104. **Telephone:** 860-305-1684. **E-Mail Address:** hunter@valleybluesox.com. **Website:** valleybluesox.com.
President: Clark Eckhoff. **General Manager:** Hunter Golden. **Field Manager:** John Raiola.

KEENE SWAMP BATS

Mailing Address: 303 Park Ave., Keene, NH 03431.
Telephone: 603-731-5240. **E-Mail Address:** swampbatsribby@gmail.com. **Website:** swampbats.com.
President: Kevin Watterson. **Field Manager:** Unavailable.

WINNIPESAUKEE MUSKRATS

Mailing Address: 97 Ashley Drive, Laconia, NH 03246.
Telephone: 603-303-7806. **E-Mail Address:** kristian@muskratsbaseball.com. **Website:** winnipesaukeemuskrats.com. **President:** Mike Smith. **General Manager:** Kristian Svindland. **Field Manager:** Mike Miller.

MYSTIC SCHOONERS

Mailing Address: PO Box 432, Mystic, CT 06355.
Telephone: (860) 608-3287. **E-Mail Address:** dlong@mysticbaseball.org. **Website:** mysticbaseball.org.
Executive Director: Don Benoit. **General Manager:** Dennis Long. **Field Manager:** Phil Orbe.

NEW BEDFORD BAY SOX

Mailing Address: 309 Princeton St., New Bedford, MA 02740. **Telephone:** 508-985-3052. **E-Mail Address:** tsilveira17@gmail.com. **Website:** nbbaysox.com. **President:** Stephen King. **General Manager:** Tammy Silveira. **Field Manager:** Chris Cabe.

NEWPORT GULLS

Mailing Address: PO Box 777, Newport, RI 02840. **Telephone:** (401) 845-6832. **E-Mail Address:** gm@newportgulls.com. **Website:** newportgulls.com. **President/General Manager:** Chuck Paiva. **Executive VP of Baseball Operations:** Chris Patsos. **Director of Baseball Operations:** Mike Falcone. **Field Manager:** Kevin Winterrowd.

NORTH ADAMS STEEPLECATS

Mailing Address: PO Box 540, North Adams, MA 01247. **Telephone:** 413-896-3153. **E-Mail Address:** matt.tora@steeplecats.org. **Website:** steeplecats.org. **President:** Matt Tora. **General Manager:** Matt Tora. **Field Manager:** Mike Dailey.

OCEAN STATE WAVES

Mailing Address: 875 Kingstown Rd, Wakefield, RI 02879. **Telephone:** (401) 360-2977. **E-Mail Address:** eric@oceanstatewaves.com. **Website:** oceanstatewaves.com. **President/General Manager:** Eric Hirschbein-Bodnar. **Field Manager:** Eric Hirschbein-Bodnar.

PLYMOUTH PILGRIMS

Mailing Address: 111 Camelot Drive, Plymouth, MA 02360. **Telephone:** 617-694-2658. **E-Mail Address:** KPlant@pilgrimsbaseball.com. **Website:** pilgrimsbaseball.com. **President:** Peter Plant. **General Manager:** Kevin Plant. **Field Manager:** Greg Zackrison.

SANFORD MARINERS

Field Address: Goodall Park, 38 Roberts Street, Sanford, ME 04073. **Telephone:** (207) 650-1902. **E-Mail:** aizaryk@bridgtonacademy.org. **General Manager:** Aaron Izaryk. **Field Manager:** Cejar Suarez.

VERMONT MOUNTAINEERS

Mailing Address: PO Box 57, East Montpelier, VT 05651. **Telephone:** (802) 272-8728. **E-Mail Address:** gmvtm@comcast.net. **Website:** thevermontmountaineers.com. **General Manager:** Brian Gallagher. **Field Manager:** Charlie Barbieri.

UPPER VALLEY NIGHTHAWKS

Mailing Address: 134 Stevens Road Lebanon, NH 03766. **Telephone:** 864-380-2873 **E-Mail Address:** noah@uppervalleynighthawks.com. **Website:** uppervalleybaseball.pointstreaksites.com. **President:** Noah Crane. **General Manager:** Phil Chaput. **Field Manager:** TBA.

NEW YORK COLLEGIATE BASEBALL LEAGUE

Mailing Address: 398 East Dyke St. Wellsville, NY 14895. **Telephone:** (585) 455-2345. **Website:** nycbl.com. **Year founded:** 1978. **President:** Bill McConnell. **Commissioner:** Joe Brown. **Email Address:** joebrown.nycbl@gmail.com. **Vice President:** Brian McConnell Jr. **Senior Marketing Director:** Dave Meluni. **Treasurer:** Dennis Duffy. **Secretary:** Steven Ackley. **Franchises: Eastern Division:** Cortland Crush, Onondaga Flames, Rome Generals, Sherrill Silversmiths, Syracuse Spartans, Saratoga Revolution. **Western Division:** Genesee Rapids, Hornell Dodgers, Niagara Power, Olean Oilers, Rochester Ridgemen, Wellsville Nitros. **Playoff Format:** six teams qualify and play a 1 game playoff and then two rounds of best of three series. **Roster Limit:** Unlimited (college-eligible players only).

CORTLAND CRUSH

Mailing Address: 2745 Summer Ridge Rd, LaFayette, NY 13084. **Telephone:** 315-391-8167. **Email Address:** wmmac4@aol.com. **Website:** cortlandcrush.com. **President:** Gary VanGorder. **Field Manager:** Bill McConnell.

GENESEE RAPIDS

Mailing Address: 9726 Rt. 19 Houghton, NY 14474. **Telephone:** 716-969-0688. **Email Address:** rkerr@frontiernet.net. **President:** Ralph Kerr. **Field Manager:** Joe Mesa.

HORNELL DODGERS

Mailing Address: PO Box 235, Hornell, NY 14843. **Telephone:** (607) 661-4173. **Fax:** (607) 661-4173. **E-Mail Address:** gm@hornelldodgers.com. **Website:** hornelldodgers.com. **General Manager:** Paul Welker. **Field Manager:** Justin Oney.

MANSFIELD DESTROYERS

Mailing Address: Mansfield Destroyers, 508 Gaines Street, Elmira, NY 14901. **Telephone:** (570) 335-9575. **E-Mail Address:** info@mansfielddestroyers.com. **President:** Don Lewis. **General Manager:** TBA. **Field Manager:** Brian Hill.

NIAGARA POWER

Mailing Address: P.O. Box 2012, Niagara University, NY 14109. **Telephone:** (716) 286-8653. **E-Mail Address:** ptutka@niagara.edu. **Website:** niagarapowerbaseball.com. **President:** Dr. Patrick Tutka. **Field Manager:** Stu Pederson.

OLEAN OILERS

Mailing Address: 126 N 10th, Olean, NY 14760. **Telephone:** 716-378-0641. **E-Mail Address:** Brian@oconnelllaw.net. **President:** Brian O'Connell. **Field Manager:** Unavailable.

ROCHESTER RIDGEMEN

Mailing Address: 651 Taylor Dr, Xenia, OH 45385. **Telephone:** (937) 352-1225. **E-Mail Addresses:** baseball@athletesinaction.org. **Website:** rochesterridgemen.org. **President:** Jason Jipson. **Field Manager:** John Byington.

ROME GENERALS

Email Address: Romegenerals@gmail.com. **Telephone:** (315) 542-0675. **Website:** romegenerals.com. **Baseball Director:** Ray DiBrango. **Field Manager:** Unavailable.

SHERRILL SILVERSMITHS

Mailing Address: 3 VanWoert Ave Unit 12, Oneonta, NY 13820. **Telephone:** (401)-935-1352. **E-Mail Address:** Djduffy316@gmail.com. **Website:** leaguelineup.com/silversmiths. **President:** Dennis Duffy & Mike Sherlock. **Field Manager:** Tim Bailey.

SYRACUSE SALT CATS

Mailing Address: 208 Lakeland Ave, Syracuse, NY 13209. **Telephone:** (315) 727-9220. **Fax:** (315) 488-1750. **E-Mail Address:** mmarti6044@yahoo.com. **Website:** leaguelineup.com/saltcats. **President:** Mike Martinez. **Field Manager:** Mike Martinez.

SYRACUSE SPARTANS

Mailing Address: 208 Lakeland Ave, Syracuse, NY 13209. **Telephone:** (315) 727-9220. **Fax:** (315) 488-1750. **E-Mail Address:** mmarti6044@yahoo.com. **General Manager:** JJ Potrikus. **Field Manager:** Brian Burns.

WELLSVILLE NITROS

Mailing Address: 2848 O'Donnell Rd, Wellsville, NY 14895. **Telephone:** 585-596-9523. **Fax:** 585-593-5260. **E-Mail Address:** nitros04@gmail.com. **Website:** nitrosbaseball.com. **President:** Steven J. Ackley. **Field Manager:** Tucker Hughes.

NORTHWOODS LEAGUE

Office Address: 2900 4th St SW, Rochester, MN 55902. **Telephone:** (507) 536-4579. **Fax:** (507) 536-4597. **E-Mail Address:** info@northwoodsleague.com.
Website: northwoodsleague.com.
Year Founded: 1994.
Chairman: Dick Radatz, Jr. **President:** Gary Hoover. **Vice President, Business Development:** Matt Bomberg. **Vice President, Operations:** Glen Showalter. **Vice President, Licensing/Technology:** Tina Coil. **Vice President, Technology Development:** Greg Goodwin. **Division Structure: East**—Kokomo Jackrabbits, Traverse City, Rockford Rivets, Kalamazoo Growlers, Kenosha Kingfish, Battle Creek Bombers. **West**—Fond du Lac Dock Spiders, Green Bay Booyah, Madison Mallards, Wisconsin Rapids Rafters, Lakeshore Chinooks. **Great Plains Division: East**—Duluth Huskies, Eau Claire Express, Waterloo Bucks, Thunder Bay Border Cats, La Crosse Loggers. **West**—Bismarck Larks, Mankato MoonDogs, Willmar Stingers, St. Cloud Rox, Rochester Honkers. **Regular Season:** 72 games (split schedule). **2020 Opening Date:** TBD. **Closing Date:** TBD. **All-Star Game:** TBD.
Playoff Format: First and second half sub-divisional winners are eligible for the playoffs. The two-playoff eligible teams in each sub-division will compete in a best of three sub-divisional series. The two sub-divisional series winners will play in a one-game divisional championship game. The two divisional game winners will play in a one-game league championship.
Roster Limit: 30 (college-eligible players only).

BATTLE CREEK BOMBERS

Mailing Address: 189 Bridge Street, Battle Creek, MI 49017. **Telephone:** (269) 962-0735. **Fax:** (269) 962-0741. **Email Address:** info@battlecreekbombers.com. **Website:** battlecreekbombers.com. **General Manager:** Tyler Shore. **Field Manager:** Josh Rebandt. **Field:** C.O. Brown Stadium.

BISMARCK LARKS

Mailing Address: 300 N 4th Street, Suite 103, Bismarck, ND 58501. **Telephone:** (701) 557-7600. **Email Address:** info@larksbaseball.com. **Website:** larks baseball.com. **General Manager:** John Bollinger. **Field Manager:** Will Flynt. **Field:** Bismarck Municipal.

DULUTH HUSKIES

Mailing Address: PO Box 16231, Duluth, MN 55816. **Telephone:** (218) 786-9909.
Fax: (218) 786-9001. **E-Mail Address:** huskies@duluth huskies.com. **Website:** duluthhuskies.com. **Owner:** Michael Rosenzweig. **General Manager:** Greg Culver. **Field Manager:** Marcus Pointer. **Field:** Wade Stadium.

EAU CLAIRE EXPRESS

Mailing Address: 108 E Grand Ave, Eau Claire, WI 54701. **Telephone:** (715) 839-7788. **Fax:** (715) 839-7676. **E-Mail Address:** info@eauclaireexpress.com. **Website:** eauclaireexpress.com. **Owner:** Bill Rowlett. **Assistant Managing Director:** Andy Neborak. **General Manager:** Jacob Servais. **Director of Operations/Field Manager:** Dale Varsho. **Field:** Carson Park.

FOND DU LAC DOCK SPIDERS

Mailing Address: 980 E Division St., Fond du Lac, WI 54935. **Telephone:** (920) 907-9833. **Email Address:** info@dockspiders.com **Website:** dockspiders.com. **President:** Rob Zerjav. **General Manager:** Chris Ward. **Field Manager:** Zac Charbonneau. **Field:** Herr-Baker Field

GREEN BAY BOOYAH

Mailing Address: 2325 Holgrem Way Suite, Green Bay, WI 54303. **Telephone:** (920) 497-7225. **Fax:** (920) 437-3551. **Email Address:** info@booyahbaseball.com. **Website:** booyahbaseball.com. **General Manager:** Sieeria Vieaux. **Field Manager:** TBA. **Field:** Capital Credit Union Park.

KALAMAZOO GROWLERS

Mailing Address: 251 Mills St, Kalamazoo, MI 49048. **Telephone:** (269) 492-9966.
Website: growlersbaseball.com. **General Manager:** Brian Colopy. **Field Manager:** Cody Piechocki. **Field:** Homer Stryker Field.

KENOSHA KINGFISH

Mailing Address: 7817 Sheridan Rd, Kenosha, WI 53143. **Telephone:** (262) 653-0900. **Website:** king fishbaseball.com. **General Manager:** Doug Cole. **Field Manager:** Duffy Dyer. **Field:** Simmons Field.

LA CROSSE LOGGERS

Mailing Address: 1225 Caledonia St, La Crosse, WI 54603. **Telephone:** (608) 796-9553. **Fax:** (608) 796-9032. **E-Mail Address:** info@lacrosseloggers.com. **Website:** lacrosseloggers.com. **Owner:** Dan Kapanke. **General Manager:** Ben Kapanke. **Assistant General Manager:** Chris Goodell. **Field Manager:** Brian Lewis. **Field:** Copeland Park.

LAKESHORE CHINOOKS

Mailing Address: 983 Badger Circle, Grafton, WI 53024. **Telephone:** (262) 618-4659. **Fax:** (262) 618-4362. **E-Mail Address:** info@lakeshorechinooks.com. **Website:** lakeshorechinooks.com. **Owner:** Jim Kacmarcik. **General Manager:** Eric Snodgrass. **Field Manager:** Travis Akre. **Field:** Kapco Park.

MADISON MALLARDS

Mailing Address: 2920 N Sherman Ave, Madison, WI 53704. **Telephone:** (608) 246-4277. **Fax:** (608) 246-4163. **E-Mail Address:** info@mallardsbaseball.com. **Website:** mallardsbaseball.com. **Owner:** Steve Schmitt. **President:** Vern Stenman. **General Manager:** Tyler Isham. **Field Manager:** Donnie Scott. **Field:** Warner Park.

MANKATO MOONDOGS

Mailing Address: 1221 Caledonia Street, Mankato, MN 56001. **Telephone:** (507) 625-7047. **Fax:** (507) 625-7059. **E-Mail Address:** office@mankatomoondogs.com. **Website:** mankatomoondogs.com. **General Manager:** Austin Link. **Field Manager:** Matt Wollenzin. **Field:** Franklin Rogers Park.

ROCHESTER HONKERS

Mailing Address: 307 E Center St, Rochester, MN 55904. **Telephone:** (507) 289-1170. **Fax:** (507) 289-1866. **E-Mail Address:** honkersbaseball@gmail.com. **Website:** rochesterhonkers.com. **General Manager:** Jeremy aagard. **Field Manager:** Deskaeh Bomberry. **Field:** Mayo Field.

ROCKFORD RIVETS

Mailing Address: 4503 Interstate Blvd., Loves Park, IL 61111. **Telephone:** 815-240-4159. **E-Mail Address:** info@rockfordrivets.com **Website:** rockfordrivets.com. **General Manager:** Chad Bauer. **Field Manager:** Josh Keim. **Field:** Rivets Stadium.

ST. CLOUD ROX

Mailing Address: 5001 8th St N, St. Cloud, MN 56303. **Telephone:** (320) 240-9798. **Fax:** (320) 255-5228. **E-Mail Address:** info@stcloudrox.com. **Website:** stcloudrox.com. **President:** Gary Posch. **Vice President:** Scott Schreiner. **General Manager:** Mike Johnson. **Field Manager:** Augie Rodriguez. **Field:** Joe Faber Field.

ST. CROIX RIVER HOUNDS

Mailing Address: PO Box 10, Hudson, WI 54016. **Telephon:** (651) 272-7483. **E-Mail Address:** info@scriverhounds.com. **Owners:** Klint Klaas, Robb Quinlan, Tom Quinlan, Andy Persby, Kevin McMann, Steve Fleischhacker. **President/General Manager:** Bill Fanning. **Field Manager:** TBA.

THUNDER BAY BORDER CATS

Mailing Address: PO Box 29105 Thunder Bay, Ontario P7B 6P9. **Telephone:** (807) 766-2287. **General Manager:** Dan Grant. **Field Manager:** Eric Vasquez. **Field:** Port Arthur Stadium.

TRAVERSE CITY PIT SPITTERS

E-Mail Address: info@traversecitybaseball.com. **General Manager:** Mickey Graham. **Field Manager:** Josh Rebandt.

WATERLOO BUCKS

Mailing Address: PO Box 4124, Waterloo, IA 50704. **Telephone:** (319) 232-0500. **Fax:** (319) 232-0700. **E-Mail Address:** waterloobucks@waterloobucks.com. **Website:** waterloobucks.com. **General Manager:** Dan Corbin.

Field Manager: Casey Harms. **Field:** Riverfront Stadium.

WILLMAR STINGERS

Mailing Address: PO Box 201, Willmar, MN, 56201. **Telephone:** (320) 222-2010. **E-Mail Address:** ryan@willmarstingers.com. **Website:** willmarstingers.com. **Owners:** Marc Jerzak, Ryan Voz. **General Manager:** Nick McCallum. **Field Manager:** Bo Henning. **Field:** Taunton Stadium.

WISCONSIN RAPIDS RAFTERS

Mailing Address: 521 Lincoln St, Wisconsin Rapids, WI 54494. **Telephone:** (715) 424-5400. **E-Mail Address:** info@raftersbaseball.com. **Website:** raftersbaseball.com. **Owner:** Vern Stenman. **General Manager:** Andy Francis. **Field Manager:** Craig Noto. **Field:** Witter Field.

WISCONSIN WOODCHUCKS

Mailing Address: 2401 N 3rd St, Wausau, WI 54403. **Telephone:** (715) 845-5055. **Fax:** (715) 845-5015. **E-Mail Address:** info@woodchucks.com. **Website:** woodchucks.com. **Owner:** Mark Macdonald. **General Manager:** Ryan Treu. **Field Manager:** Ronnie Richardson. **Field:** Athletic Park.

PACIFIC INTERNATIONAL LEAGUE

Mailing Address: 4400 26th Ave W, Seattle, WA 98199. **Telephone:** (206) 623-8844. **Fax:** (206) 623-8361. **E-Mail Address:** spotter@potterprinting.com. **Website:** pacific-internationalleague.com.

Year Founded: 1992.

President: Al Oremus. **Vice President:** Martin Lawrence. **Commissioner:** Terry Howard. **Secretary:** Steve Potter. **Treasurer:** Mark Dow. **Member Clubs:** Northwest Honkers, Everett Merchants, Seattle Studs, Highline Bears, Redmond Dudes, North Sound Emeralds. **Regular Season:** 20 league games. **Playoff Format:** Top team is invited to National Baseball Congress World Series.

Roster Limit: 30; 25 eligible for games (players must be at least 18 years old).

PERFECT GAME COLLEGIATE LEAGUE

Mailing Address: 8 Michaels Lane, Old Brookville, NY 11545. **Telephone:** (516) 521-0206. **Fax:** (516) 801-0818. **E-Mail Address:** valkun@aol.com. **Website:** pgcbl.com.

Year Founded: 2010.

President: Jeffrey Kunion.

Director of Communications: Travis Larner

Executive Committee: Bob Ohmann (Newark Pilots), Paul Samulski (Albany Dutchmen). Robbie Nichols (Elmira Pioneers), George Deak (Utica Blue Sox), Kevin Hinchey (Saugerties Stallions)

Teams: East—Albany Dutchmen, Amsterdam Mohawks, Glens Falls Dragons, Mohawk Valley DiamondDawgs, Oneonta Outlaws, Saugerties Stallions, Utica Blue Sox. **West**—Adirondack Trail Blazers, Elmira Pioneers, Geneva Red Wings, Jamestown Jammers, Newark Pilots, Onondaga Flames

Regular Season: 50. **Playoff Format:** Top four teams in each division qualify for one-game playoff; next two series are best of three. **Roster Limit:** 35 (maximum of two graduated high school players per team).

ADIRONDACK TRAIL BLAZERS

President: Bobby Miller. **General Manager:** Matt Burns. **Head Coach:** Michael Fauvelle. **Telephone:** (315)

542-0675. **Field**: Robert Smith Sports Complex. **Email Address:** adirondacktrailblazers@rocketmail.com.

ALBANY DUTCHMEN

Mailing Address: PO Box 72, Saratoga Springs, N.Y. 12866. **President**: Paul Samulski. **General Manager**: Jason Brinkman. **E-Mail**: jbrinkma@gmail.com. **Telephone**: 518-210-8383. **Head Coach**: Nick Davey. **Field**: Siena Field.

AMSTERDAM MOHAWKS

Mailing Address: P.O. Box 334, Amsterdam, N.Y., 12010. **President**: Brian Spagnola. **Vice President:** Dave Dittman. **Head Coach:** Keith Griffin. **E-Mail Address:** gm@amsterdammohawks.com. **Telephone:** (518)791-7546. **Field**: Shuttlesworth Park.

ELMIRA PIONEERS

Mailing Address: 546 Luce Street, Elmira, N.Y. 14904. **Owners**: Nellie Franco-Nichols, Donald Lewis, Robbie Nichols. **Head Coach:** Matt Burch. **Telephone:** (607) 734-2690. **E-Mail Address:** donspioneers@gmail.com. **Field:** Dunn Field.

GENEVA RED WINGS

Mailing Address: N/A. **Owners**: Bob Ohmann, Lesilie Ohmann. **Head Coach:** Sean O'Connor. **Email**: info@genevaredwings.com. **Telephone:** (919) 422-4323. **Field**: McDonough Park.

GLENS FALLS DRAGONS

Mailing Address: PO Box 897, Glens Falls, N.Y. 12801. **President**: Ben Bernard. **Head Coach:** Cameron Curler. **Telephone**: (518) 361-5316. **E-Mail Address**: ben bernard1@yahoo.com. **Field**: East Field Stadium.

JAMESTOWN TARP SKUNKS

Owner: Mike Zimmerman. **President**: Dan Kuenzi. **Head Coach:** Anthony Barone. **Telephone:** (716) 720-4465. **E-Mail Address:** dkuenzi@mkesports.com. **Field**: Russell E. Diethrick Jr. Park.

MOHAWK VALLEY DIAMONDDAWGS

Mailing Address: PO Box 902, Little Falls, N.Y. 13365. **Owner**: Travis Heiser. **Head Coach**: Cory Haggerty. **Telephone:** (315) 985-0692. **E-Mail Address**: travis@mydiamonddawgs.com. **Field**: Veterans Memorial Park.

NEWARK PILOTS

Mailing Address: 65 Williams Street, Lyons, N.Y. 14489. **Owner**: Bob Ohmann, Leslie Ohmann. **Head Coach**: Matt Colbert. **Telephone:** (315) 576-6710. **E-Mail Address**: newarkpilots@gmail.com. **Field**: Colburn Park.

ONEONTA OUTLAWS

Mailing Address: 291 Chestnut Street, Oneonta, N.Y., 13280. **Owner**: Gary Laing. **General Manager**: Joe Hughes. **Head Coach**: Joe Hughes. **Telephone**: (607) 432-6326. **E-Mail Address**: joehughes@oneontaoutlaws.com. **Field**: Damaschke Field.

ONONDAGA FLAMES

Mailing Address: 285 Pinehurst Trace Drive, Pinehurst, NC 28374. **Owners**: Wayne Walker & Alyce

Lee-Walker. **Head Coach:** Ryan Stevens. **Telephone: (**315) 308-0889. **E-Mail Address:** wayne@onondagaflames.com. **Stadium:** Onondaga Community College Baseball Complex.

SAUGERTIES STALLIONS

Mailing Address: 645 Rte 212, Saugerties, NY 12477. **Owner**: Kevin Hinchey. **Head Coach**: Collin Martin. **Telephone**: (845) 707-0265. **E-Mail Address**: the saugertiesstallions@gmail.com. **Field**: Cantine Field.

UTICA BLUE SOX

Mailing Address: 7179 County Highway 18, West Winfield, N.Y. 13491. **Owner**: George Deak. **General Manager**: George Deak. **Head Coach**: Doug Delett. **Telephone**: (315) 855-5013. **E-Mail Address**: George@globalgraphicsny.com. **Field**: Donovan Stadium at Murnane Field.

WATERTOWN RAPIDS

Mailing Address: PO Box 6250, Watertown, N.Y. 13601. **Owners**: Michael Schell, Paul Velte. **General Manager**: Brandon Noble. **Field Manager**: Dave Anderson. **Telephone**: (315) 836-1545. **E-Mail Address**: rapidsgm@gmail.com. **Field**: Alex T. Duffy Fairgrounds.

PROSPECT LEAGUE

Mailing Address: PO Box 84, Elkville, IL 62932. **Telephone:** (618) 559-1343. **E-Mail Address:** commissioner@prospectleague.com. **Website:** prospectleague.com.

Year Founded: 1963 as Central Illinois Collegiate League; known as Prospect League since 2009. **Commissioner:** Dennis Bastien.

Regular Season: 60 games. **2020 Opening Date:** May 28. **Closing Date:** Aug. 2. **All-Star Series:** July 22-23. **Championship Series:** Aug. 4-9. **Roster Limit:** 32.

CHAMPION CITY KINGS

Mailing Address: 1301 Mitchell Blvd., Springfield, OH 45503. **Telephone:** (937) 342-0320. **Fax:** (937) 342-0320. **E-Mail Address:** cckings@gmail.com. **Website:** championcitykings.com. **General Manager:** Ginger Fulton. **Field Manager:** John Jeanes.

CHILLICOTHE PAINTS

Mailing Address: 59 North Paint Street, Chillicothe, OH 45601. **Telephone:** (740) 773-8326. **Fax:** (740) 773-8338. **E-Mail Address:** paints@bright.net. **Website:** chillicothepaints.com. **General Manager:** Bryan Wickline. **Field Manager:** Brian Bigam.

DANVILLE DANS

Mailing Address: 4 Maywood, Danville, IL 61832. **Telephone:** (217) 918-3401. **Fax:** (217) 446-9995. **E-Mail Address:** danvilledans@comcast.net. **Website:** danvilledans.com. **League Director:** Jeanie Cooke. **General Manager:** Jeanie Cooke. **Field Manager:** Eric Coleman.

O'FALLON HOOTS

Telephone: Unavailable. **Email Address:** ofallon@prospectleague.com. **General Manager:** David Schmoll. **Field Manager:** Joe Lincoln. **Stadium:** CarShield Field.

DUPAGE PISTOL SHRIMP

E-Mail Address: info@dupagepistolshrimp.com. **Telephone:** 855-748-2457. **General Manager & Field Manager:** John Jakiemiec. **Field:** BenU Baseball Field (Village of Lisle-Benedictine University Sports Complex).

LAFAYETTE AVIATORS

Mailing Address: PO Box 6494, Lafayette, IN 47904. **Telephone:** (414) 224-9283. **Fax:** (414) 224-9290. **E-Mail Address:** zchartrand@lafayettebaseball.com. **Website:** lafayettebaseball.com. **President:** Sean Churchill. **General Manager:** Zach Chartrand. **League Director:** Dan Kuenzi. **Field Manager:** Brent McNeil.

QUINCY GEMS

Mailing Address: 1400 N. 30th St., Suite 1, Quincy, IL 62301. **Telephone:** (217) 214-7436. **Fax:** (217) 214-7436. **E-Mail Address:** quincygems@yahoo.com. **Website:** quincygems.com. **League Director/General Manager:** Jimmie/Julie Louthan. **Field Manager:** Pat Robles.

SPRINGFIELD SLIDERS

Mailing Address: 1415 North Grand Avenue East, Suite B, Springfield, IL 62702. **Telephone:** (217) 679-3511. **Fax:** (217) 679-3512. **E-Mail Address:** slidersfun@spring fieldsliders.com. **Website:** springfieldsliders.com. **League Director/General Manager:** Todd Miller. **Field Manager:** Chris Holke.

TERRE HAUTE REX

Mailing Address:111 North 3rd St, Terre Haute, IN 47807. **Telephone:** (812) 478-3817. **Fax:** (812) 232-5353. **E-mail Address:** frontoffice@rexbaseball.com. **Website:** rexbaseball.com. **League Director/General Manager:** Bruce Rosselli. **Field Manager:**Tyler Wampler.

WEST VIRGINIA MINERS

Mailing Address: 476 Ragland Road, Suite 2, Beckley, WV 25801. **Telephone:** (304) 252-7233. **Fax:** (304) 253-1998. **E-mail Address:** wvminers@wvminersbaseball .com. **Website:** wvminersbaseball.com. **President:** Doug Epling. **League Director/General Manager/Field Manager::** Tim Epling.

SOUTHERN COLLEGIATE BASEBALL LEAGUE

Mailing Address: 9723 Northcross Center Court, Huntersville, NC 28078. **Telephone:** (704) 635-7126. **Cell:** (704) 906-7776. **E-Mail Address:** hhampton@scbl.org. **Website:** scbl.org.

Year Founded: 1999.

Chairman: Bill Capps, **Commissioner:** Jamie Billings. **President:** Jeff Carter. **Treasurer:** Brenda Templin. **Umpire in Chief:** Gary Swanson.

Regular Season: 42 games. **Playoff Format:** Six-team single-elimination tournament with best of three championship series between final two teams.

Roster Limit: 35 (College-eligible players only).

CHARLOTTE GALAXY

Mailing Address: 7209 East WT Harris Blvd, Suite J #245, Charlotte, NC 28227. **Telephone:** (704) 668-9167. **Email Address:** baseballnbeyond@aol.com. **General Manager:** David "Doc" Booth. **Head Coach:** Addison Rouse.

CONCORD ATHLETICS

Mailing Address: 366 George Lyles Parkway, Suite 125, Concord, NC 28027. **Telephone:** (704) 786-2255. **Email Address:** playconcordathletics@gmail.com. **General Manager:** David Darwin. **Head Coach:** Charles Weber

LAKE NORMAN COPPERHEADS

Mailing Address: 16405 Northcross Drive, Suite A Huntersville, NC 28078. **Telephone:** (704) 305-3649. **Email Address:** dshoe@copperheadsports.org. **General Manager:** Derek Shoe. **Head Coach:** Jeremy Johnson.

PIEDMONT PRIDE

Mailing Address: 1524 Summit View Drive, Rock Hill, SC 29732. **Telephone:** (803) 412-7982. **E-Mail Address:** joe@pridebaseball.net. **General Manager:** Logan Hudak. **Head Coach:** Joe Hudak.

CAROLINA VIPERS

Mailing Address: 12104 Copper Way, Suite 200, Charlotte NC 28277. **Telephone:** 980-256-5346. **E-Mail Address:** bnichols@goviperbaseball.com. **President:** Mike Polito. **General Manager:** Blaine Nichols. **Head Coach:** Aaron Bray.

MOORSVILLE SPINNERS

Mailing Address: 2643 N Hwy 16 Denver, NC 28037. **Telephone:** (704) 491-4112. **E-Mail Address:** ploftin@ mooresvillespinners.com. **General Manager:** Phillip Loftin. **Head Coach:** Tripp Hamrick.

LINOIRE OILERS

Mailing Address: PO Box 1113 Icard NC 28666. **Telephone:** 828-455-1289. **E-Mail Address:** LenoirOilers@gmail.com. **General Manager:** Sara Wert. **Head Coach:** Ivan Acuna.

TEXAS COLLEGIATE LEAGUE

Mailing Address: 735 Plaza Blvd, Suite 200, Coppell, TX 75019. **Telephone:** (979) 985-5198. **Fax:** (979) 779-2398. **E-Mail Address:** info@tclbaseball.com.

Website: texascollegiateleague.com.

Year Founded: 2004.

President: Uri Geva.

Roster Limit: 30 (College-eligible players only)

ACADIANA CANE CUTTERS

Mailing Address: 221 La Neuville, Youngsville, LA 70592. **Telephone:** (337) 451-6582. **E-Mail Address:** info@cane cuttersbaseball.com. **Website:** canecuttersbaseball.com. **Owners:** Richard Chalmers, Sandi Chalmers. **General Manager:** Richard Haifley.

BRAZOS VALLEY BOMBERS

Mailing Address: 405 Mitchell St, Bryan, TX 77801. **Telephone:** (979) 799-7529. **Fax:** (979) 779-2398. **E-Mail Address:** info@bvbombers.com. **Website:** bv bombers.com. **Owners:** Uri Geva. **General Manger:** Chris Clark. **Field Manager:** Curt Dixon.

TEXAS MARSHALS

Mailing Address: 7920 Beltline Rd, 8th Floor Suite 860 Dallas, TX 75254. **Telephone:** (855) 808-7529. **E-Mail Address:** info@texasmarshals.com. **Website:** texasmarshals.com. **Owner:** Marc Landry. **General Manager:** Kenderick Moore. **Field Manager:** Brent Lavallee.

TEXARKANA TWINS

Ballpark: George Dobson Field, 4303 N Park Rd, Texarkana, TX 75503. **Telephone:** (903) 294-7529. **Head Coach:** Bill Clay.

VICTORIA GENERALS

Mailing Address: 1307 E Airline Road, Suite H, Victoria, TX 77901. **Telephone:** (361) 485-9522. **Fax:** (361) 485-0936. **E-Mail Address:** info@baseballinvictoria.com, tkyoung@victoriagenerals.com. **Website:** victoriagenerals.com. **President:** Tracy Young. **VP/General Manager:** Mike Yokum.

VALLEY BASEBALL LEAGUE

Mailing Address: Valley Baseball League, PO Box 1127, New Market, VA 22844. **Telephone:** (540) 810-9194. **Fax:** (540) 435-8453. **E-Mail Addresses:** cbalger@shentel.net. **Website:** valleyleaguebaseball.com.

Year Founded: 1897. **President:** C. Bruce Alger. **Executive Vice President:** Jay Neal. **Media Relations Director:** John Leonard. **Secretary:** Stacy Locke. **Treasurer:** Ed Yoder. **Regular Season:** 42 games. **Playoff Format:** Eight teams qualify; play three rounds of best of three series. **Roster Limit:** 30 (college-eligible only)

COVINGTON LUMBERJACKS

Mailing Address: PO Box 30, Covington, VA 24426. **Telephone:** (540) 969-9923, (540) 962-1155. **Fax:** (540) 962-7153. **E-Mail Address:** covingtonlumberjacks@valleyleaguebaseball.com. **Website:** lumberjacksbaseball.com. **President:** Dizzy Garten. **Head Coach:** Alex Kotheimer.

PURCELLVILLE CANNONS

Mailing Address: P.O. Box 114, Purcellville, VA 20132. **Telephone:** (540) 303-9673. **Fax:** (304) 856-1619. **E-Mail Address:** info@purcellvillecannons.com. **Website:** purcellvillecannons.com. President/**Recruiting Coordinator/Head Coach:** Brett Fuller. **General Manager:** Ridge Fuller.

CHARLOTTESVILLE TOM SOX

Mailing Address: P. O. Box 4836, Virginia 22905. **Telephone:** (540)471-0799. **E-Mail:** mpad71@gmail.com. **Website:** TomSox.com. **President/General Manager:** Mike Paduano. **Head Coach:** Kory Koehler.

FRONT ROYAL CARDINALS

Mailing Address: 382 Morgans Ridge Road, Front Royal, VA 22630. **Telephone:** (703) 244-6662, (540) 631-9201. **E-Mail Address:** DonnaSettle@centurylink.net. frontroyalcardinals@valleyleaguebaseball.com. **Website:** valleyleaguebaseball.com. **President:** Donna Settle. **Head Coach:** Zeke Mitchem.

HARRISONBURG TURKS

Mailing Address: 1489 S Main St, Harrisonburg, VA 22801. **Telephone:** (540) 434-5919. **Fax:** (540) 434-5919.

E-Mail Address: turksbaseball@hotmail.com. **Website:** harrisonburgturks.com. **Operations Manager:** Teresa Wease. **General Manager/Head Coach:** Bob Wease.

NEW MARKET REBELS

Mailing Address: PO Box 902, New Market, VA 22844. **Telephone:** (540) 435-8453. **Fax:** (540) 740-9486. **E-Mail Address:** nmrebels@shentel.net. **Website:** newmarketrebels.com. **President/General Manager:** Bruce Alger. **Head Coach:** Arthur E. Stenberg IV.

STAUNTON BRAVES

Mailing Address: PO Box 428, Stuarts Draft, VA 24447. **Telephone:** (540) 886-0987. **Fax:** (540) 886-0905. **E-Mail Address:** sbraves@hotmail.com. **Website:** stauntonbravesbaseball.com. **General Manager:** Steve Cox. **Head Coach:** Lukas Ray.

STRASBURG EXPRESS

Mailing Address: PO Box 417, Strasburg, VA 22657. **Telephone:** (540) 325-5677, (540) 459-4041. **Fax:** (540) 459-3398. **E-Mail Address:** neallaw@shentel.net, strasburgxpress@gmail.com. **Website:** strasburgexpress.com. **General Manager:** Jay Neal. **Head Coach:** Anthony Goncalves.

WAYNESBORO GENERALS

Mailing Address: 3144 Village Drive, Waynesboro, VA 22980. **Telephone:** (540) 835-6312. **Fax:** (540) 932-2322. **E-Mail Address:** contact@waynesborogenerals.net. **Website:** waynesborogenerals.com. **Chairman:** Kathleen Kellett-Ward. **General Manager:** Tyler Hoffman. **Head Coach:** Zac Cole.

WINCHESTER ROYALS

Mailing Address: PO Box 2485, Winchester, VA 22604. **Telephone:** (540) 974-4104, (540) 664-3978. **Fax:** (540) 662-1434. **E-Mail Addresses:** winchesterroyals@gmail.com, info@winchesterroyals.org. **Website:** winchesterroyals.com. **President:** Donna Turrill. **Operations Director:** Jimmie Shipp. **Coach:** Mike Smith.

WOODSTOCK RIVER BANDITS

Mailing Address: P.O. Box 227, Woodstock, VA 22664. **Telephone:** (540) 481-0525. **Fax:** (540) 459-2093. **E-Mail Address:** woodstockriverbandits@valleyleaguebaseball.com. **Website:** woodstockriverbandits.org. **General Manager:** Robert "porky" Bowman. **Head Coach:** Mike Bocock. **Assistant Head Coach:** Paul Ackerman.

WEST COAST LEAGUE

Mailing Address: PO Box 10771, Portland OR 97296. **Telephone:** 503-233-2490. **E-Mail Address:** info@westcoastleague.com. **Website:** westcoastleague.com.

Year Founded: 2005. **Commissioner:** Rob Neyer. **President:** Tony Bonacci. **Vice President:** Glenn Kirkpatrick. **Secretary:** Jose Oglesby. **Treasurer:** Dan Segel. **Supervisor, Umpires:** Dave Perez. **Division Structure: South**—Bend Elks, Corvallis Knights, Cowlitz Black Bears, Ridgefield Raptors, Walla Walla Sweets. **North**—Bellingham Bells, Kelowna Falcons, Port Angeles Lefties, Victoria Harbourcats, Wenatchee Applesox, Yakima Valley Pippins. **2021 Opening Date:** June 5. **Closing Date:** August 9. **Playoff Format:** Four-team tournament. **Roster Limit:** 35 (college-eligible players only).

BELLINGHAM BELLS

Mailing Address: 1221 Potter Street, Bellingham, WA 98229. **Telephone:** (360) 527-1035. **E-Mail Address:** stephanie@bellinghambells.com. **Website:** bellinghambells.com. **Owner:** Glenn Kirkpatrick. **General Manager:** Stephanie Morrell. **Head Coach:** Bob Geaslen. **Assistant Coaches:** Jim Clem, Jake Whisler, Boog Leach.

BEND ELKS

Mailing Address: 70 SW Century Dr Suite 100-373 Bend, Oregon 97702. **Telephone:** (541) 312-9259. **Website:** bendelks.com. **Owners:** John and Tami Marick. **Marketing and Sales:** Kelsie Hirko. **General Manager:** Michael Hirko. **Head Coach:** Alan Embree. **Assistant Coaches:** Dylan Jones, Blake Woosley.

CORVALLIS KNIGHTS

Mailing Address: PO Box 1356, Corvallis, OR 97339. **Telephone:** (541) 752-5656. **E-Mail Address:** dan.segel@corvallisknights.com. **Website:** corvallisknights.com. **President:** Dan Segel. **General Manager:** Bre Miller. **Head Coach:** Brooke Knight. **Associate Head Coach/Pitching Coach:** Ed Knaggs. **Assistant Coach:** Youngjin Yoon, Jacob Kopra.

COWLITZ BLACK BEARS

Mailing Address: PO Box 1255, Longview, WA 98632. **Telephone:** (360) 703-3195. **Website:** cowlitzblackbears.com. **Owner/President:** Tony Bonacci. **General Manager:** Jim Appleby. **Head Coach:** Grady Tweit. **Assistant Coaches:** Jason Mackey, Michael Forgione.

KELOWNA FALCONS

Mailing Address: 201-1014 Glenmore Dr, Kelowna, BC, V1Y 4P2. **Telephone:** (250) 763-4100. **Website:** kelownafalcons.com. **Owner:** Dan Nonis. **General Manager:** Mark Nonis. **Head Coach:** Bryan Donohue.

PORT ANGELES LEFTIES

Mailing Address: PO Box 2204, Port Angeles, WA 98362. **Phone:** (360) 701-1087. **Website:** leftiesbaseball.com. **E-Mail Address:** matt@leftiesbaseball.com. **Owners:** Matt Acker, Jacob Oppelt, Eric Traut, Connor Traut. **General Manager:** Ryan Hickey. **Head Coach:** Matt Acker. **Assistant Coach:** Earl Smith, Anthony Murillo.

PORTLAND PICKLES

Address: 5308 SE 92nd Ave. Portland, OR 97266. **Phone:** (503)775-3080. **Owners:** Alan Miller, Jon Ryan, Scott Barchus. **Head Coach:** Justin Barchus. **Hitting Coach:** Mark Magdaleno. **Pitching Coach:** Jim Lawler. **Bench Coach:** Jim Hoppel.

RIDGEFIELD RAPTORS

Owner: Tony Bonacci. **Partner:** Wade Siegel. **E-Mail Address:** info@ridgefieldraptors.com. **General Manager:** Gus Farah. **Head Coach:** Chris Cota.

VICTORIA HARBOURCATS

Mailing Address: 101-1814 Vancouver Street, Victoria, BC, Canada, V8T 5E3. **Telephone:** (778) 265-0327. **Website:** harbourcats.com. **Owners:** Rich Harder, Jim Swanson, Ken Swanson, John Wilson. **Managing Partner:** Jim Swanson. **General Manager:** Brad Norris-Jones. **Head Coach:** Brian McRae. **Assistant Coaches:** Ian Sanderson, Todd Haney, Troy Birtwistle, Jason Leone, Curtis Pelletier.

WALLA WALLA SWEETS

Mailing Address: 109 E Main Street, Walla Walla, WA 99362. **Telephone:** (509) 522-2255. **E-Mail Address:** info@wallawallasweets.com. **Website:** wallawallasweets.com. **Owner:** Pacific Baseball Ventures, LLC. **President/COO:** Zachary Fraser. **General Manager:** Dan Ferguson. **Head Coach:** Frank Mutz. **Assistant Coaches:** Raul Camacho, Kyle Wilkerson.

WENATCHEE APPLESOX

Mailing Address: 610 N. Mission St. #204, Wenatchee, WA 98801. **Telephone:** (509) 665-6900. **E-Mail Address:** info@applesox.com. **Website:** applesox.com. **Owner/General Manager:** Jose Oglesby. **Owner/Assistant General Manager:** Ken Osborne. **Head Coach:** Ian Sanderson.

YAKIMA VALLEY PIPPINS

Mailing Address: PO Box 2397, Yakima, WA 98907. **Telephone:** (509) 575-4487. **E-Mail Address:** info@pippinsbaseball.com. **Website:** pippinsbaseball.com. **Owner:** Pacific Baseball Ventures, LLC. **President/COO:** Zachary Fraser. **General Manager:** Jeff Garretson. **Head Coach:** Kyle Krustangel. **Pitching Coach:** Cash Ulrich.

APPALACHIAN LEAGUE

Mailing Address: 1340 Environ Way, Chapel Hill, NC 27517. **Telephone:** 919-913-4590. **E-Mail Address:** dan@appyleague.com. **Website:** www.appyleague.com.

President: Dan Moushon. **Director of Communications and Media Relations:** Brad Young. **Baseball Chapel Representative:** Craig Stout (Princeton)

Steering Committee: Chris Allen, Ashley Bratcher, Eric Campbell, Tim Corbin, John D'Angelo, Dan Hartleb, Gil Kim, Bryan Minniti, Dan Moushon, Jalen Phillips, Steve Sanders, John Savage, Bill Schmidt, Edwin Thompson.

Division Structure: East—Bluefield, Burlington, Danville, Princeton, Pulaski. **West**—Bristol, Elizabethton, Greeneville, Johnson City, Kingsport.

Regular Season: 54 games. **2021 Opening Date:** June 3. **Closing Date:** August 7. **All-Star Game:** July 27

Roster Limit: 32 active.

BLUEFIELD RIDGE RUNNERS

Office Address: 2003 Stadium Dr. Bluefield WV 24701. **Mailing Address:** P.O. Box 356 Bluefield WV. 24701. **Telephone:** 304-324-1326. Fax 304-324-1318. **Email address:** bluefieldridgerunners@gmail.com. **Website:** www.bluefieldridgerunners.com.

Ownership/management: Bluefield Baseball Club **President:** George McGonagle. **Counsel:** Brian Cochran. **General Manager:** Rocky Malamisura **Manager:** Joe Oliver. **Hitting Coach:** Angel Sanchez. **Pitching coach:** Dennis Rasmussen. **Bench coach/ Tech Coach:** Garrett Schilling. **Head Groundskeeper:** Mike White.

GAME INFORMATION
Stadium Name: Bowen Field. **Location:** I-77 to Bluefield exit 1, Route 290 to Route 460 West, fourth light right onto Leatherwood Lane, left at first light, past Hometown Shell station and turn right, stadium quarter-mile on left. **Ticket Price Range:** $6.

BRISTOL STATE LINERS

Office Address: 1501 Euclid Ave, Bristol, VA 24201. **Mailing Address:** PO Box 1434, Bristol, VA 24203. **Telephone:** (276) 206-9946. **Fax:** (423)-968-2636. **E-Mail Address:** gm@bristolbaseball.com. **Website:** www.bristolstateliners.com.

Owned by: Bristol Baseball Inc.. **Operated by:** Bristol Baseball Inc. **President/General Manager:** Mahlon Luttrell. **Vice President:** Craig Adams, Mark Young. **General Council:** Lucas Hobbs. **Treasurer:** Delma Luttrell. **Secretary:** Connie Kinkead.

Manager: TBA. **Hitting Coach:** TBA. **Pitching Coach:** TBA. **Athletic Trainer:** TBA. Strength & **Conditioning Coach:** TBA.

Stadium: DeVault Memorial Stadium. **Standard Game Times:** Mon.-Sat., 7 pm, Sun., 6 pm. **Ticket Price Range:** $4-$8.

BURLINGTON SOCK PUPPETS

Office Address: 1450 Graham St, Burlington, NC 27217. **Mailing Address:** PO Box 1143, Burlington, NC 27216. **Telephone:** (336) 222-0223. **E-Mail Address:** info@gosockpuppets.com. **Website:** www.gosockpuppets.com

Owner: Knuckleball Entertainment, LLC. **President:** Ryan Keur. **General Manager:** Anderson Rathbun. **Assistant GM:** Thomas Vickers.

Manager: Jack McDowell.

Stadium: Burlington Athletic Stadium. **Standard Game Time:** 7:00 pm. **Ticket Price Range:** $8-15.

DANVILLE OTTERBOTS

Office Address: Dan Daniel Memorial Park, 302 River Park Dr, Danville, VA 24540. **Mailing Address:** PO Box 330, Danville, VA 24543. **Telephone:** (434) 554-4487. **E-Mail Address:** danvillebaseball21@gmail.com. **Website:** www.mlb.com/appalachian-league/danville.

Operated by: Danville Baseball Club LLC. **Owners:** Ryan Keur, Brittany Keur. **General Manager:** Austin Scher. **Head Groundskeeper:** Ryan Brown.

Manager: Desi Relaford. **Hitting Coach:** Angel Berroa. **Pitching Coach:** TBA. **Bench Coach:** TBA. **Athletic Trainer:** TBA. Strength & **Conditioning Coach:** TBA.

Stadium: American Legion Post 325 Field at Dan Daniel Memorial Park. **Standard Game Times:** Mon.-Sat., 7:00 pm, Sun. 5:00 pm. **Ticket Price Range:** $5-11.

ELIZABETHTON RIVER RIDERS

Address: 804 Holly Lane, Elizabethton, TN 37643. **Telephone:** (423) 547-6443.

Owned/Operated by: Boyd Sports LLC. **President:** Chris Allen. **Vice President:** Jeremy Boler. **General Manager:** Brice Ballentine.

Manager: Kevin Riggs. **Hitting Coach:** Jeremy Owens. **Pitching Coach:** TBD. **Athletic Trainer:** TBD. Strength & **Conditioning Coach:** TBD

Stadium: Northeast Community Credit Union Ballpark. **Standard Game Times:** 7:00 pm. **Ticket Price Range:** $5-7.

GREENEVILLE FLYBOYS

Address: 135 Shiloh Road, Greeneville, TN 37745. **Telephone:** (423) 609-7400. **E-Mail Address:** contact@flyboysbaseball.com. **Website:** https://www.mlb.com/appalachian-league/greeneville.

Owned by: Boyd Sports, LLC. **General Manager:** Kat Foster. **Assistant General Manager:** Brandon Bouschart.

Manager: Alan Regier. **Hitting Coach:** TBD. **Pitching Coach/Assistant to the Pitching Coordinator:** TBD. **Bench Coach:** TBD. **Athletic Trainer:** TBD. Strength & **Conditioning Coach:** TBD

Stadium: Pioneer Park. **Standard Game Time:** Mon-Sat., 7:00 pm, Sun., 5:30 pm. **Ticket Price Range:** $5 group discount, $7 reserved, $8 premium.

JOHNSON CITY DOUGHBOYS

Office Address: 510 Bert St., Johnson City, TN 37601. **Mailing Address:** PO Box 179, Johnson City, TN 37605. **Telephone:** (423) 461-4866. **E-Mail Address:** zclark@jcdoughboys.com. **Website:** www.jcdoughboys.com.

Operated by: Boyd Sports, LLC. **President:** Chris Allen. **Vice President:** Jeremy Boler. **General Manager:** Zac Clark.

Manager: Rick Magnante. **Hitting Coach:** Cody Gabella. **Pitching Coach:** Cody Stull. **Athletic Trainer:** NA. **Strength and Conditioning Coordinator:** NA.

Stadium: TVA Credit Union Ballpark. **Standard Game Time:** Mon.-Sat. 7 pm, Sun. 5:30 pm. **Ticket Price Range:** $6-$9.

KINGSPORT AXMEN

Address: 800 Granby Rd, Kingsport, TN 37660. **Telephone:** (423) 224-2626. **Fax:** (423) 224-2625. **Website:** www.kingsportaxmen.com

Owner: Boyd Sports, LLC. **General Manager:** TBD. **Clubhouse Manager:** TBD

Manager: TBD. **Hitting Coach:** TBD. **Pitching Coach:** TBD. **Bench Coach:** TBD. **Athletic Trainer:** TBD. **Performance Coach:** TBD

Stadium: Hunter Wright Stadium. **Standard Game Times:** Mon-Sat., 7pm, Sun., 5:30pm. **Doubleheaders—** Mon-Sat. TBD, **Sun:** TBD. **Ticket Price Range:** $6 -$8.

PRINCETON WHISTLEPIGS

Office Address: 345 Old Bluefield Road, Princeton, WV 24739. **Mailing Address:** PO Box 5646, Princeton, WV 24740. **Telephone:** 304-487-2000. **Email Address:** gm@whistlepigsbaseball.com. **Website:** www.whistlepigsbaseball.com

Operated By: Princeton Baseball Association, Inc. **President:** Dewey Russell. **General Manager:** Danny Shingleton. **Director Stadium Operations:** Adam Sarver, Rusty Sarver. **Chaplain:** Craig Stout.

Field Manager: TBD.

Stadium: Hunnicutt Field. **Standard Game Time:** Mon.-Sat., 7 pm, Sun., 6 pm. **Ticket Price Range:** $5-8.

PULASKI RIVER TURTLES

Office Address: 529 Pierce Avenue, Pulaski, VA 24301. **Mailing Address:** PO Box 852, Pulaski, VA 24301. **Telephone:** (540) 980-1070. **Email Address:** info@pulaskiriverturtles.com

Operated By: Calfee Park Baseball Inc. **Park Owners:** David Hagan, Larry Shelor. **General Manager:** JW Martin.

Field Manager: TBD.

Stadium: Historic Calfee Park. **Ticket Price Range:** $5-11.

MLB DRAFT LEAGUE

Website: www.mlb.com/mlb-draft-league. **Email:** draftleague@prepbaseballreport.com.

Founded: 2021.

Operated By: Prep Baseball Report.

President, Draft League: Kerrick Jackson.

Schedule: 68 games. **Start Date:** May 24. **Closing Date:** Aug. 13. **Playoffs:** Championship game, Aug. 15.

FREDERICK KEYS

Mailing Address: 21 Stadium Drive, Frederick, MD 21703. **Email:** info@frederickkeys.com. **Telephone:** 301-662-0013. **Website: https://www.milb.com/frederick**

General Manager: Dave Ziedelis.

MAHONING VALLEY SCRAPPERS

Address: 11 Eastwood Mall Blvd., Niles, OH 44446-1357. **Email:** info@mvscrappers.com. **Telephone:** (330) 505-0000. **Website:** www.milb.com/mahoning-valley.

General Manager: Jordan Taylor.

STATE COLLEGE SPIKES

Address: 112 Medlar Field at Lubrano Park, University Park, PA 16802. **Email:** frontoffice@statecollegespikes. com. **Telephone:** (814) 272-1711

Website: www.milb.com/state-college.

General Manager: Scott Walker.

TRENTON THUNDER

Mailing Address: One Thunder Road, Trenton, N.J. 08611. **Email:** fun@trentonthunder.com. **Telephone:** 609-394-3300. **Website:** www.milb.com/trenton

General Manager: Jeff Hurley.

WEST VIRGINIA BLACK BEARS

Address: 2040 Gyorko Drive, Granville, WV 26534. **Telephone:** (304) 293-7910. **Website: https://www.milb. com/west-virginia-black-bears.**

General Manager: Matthew Drayer.

WILLIAMSPORT CROSSCUTTERS

Address: 1700 West Fourth St, Williamsport, PA 17701. **Email: Telephone:** (570) 326-3389. **Website: https:// www.milb.com/williamsport.**

General Manager: Doug Estes.

HIGH SCHOOL BASEBALL

NATIONAL FEDERATION OF STATE HIGH SCHOOL ASSOCIATIONS

Mailing Address: PO Box 690, Indianapolis, IN 46206. **Telephone:** (317) 972-6900. **Fax:** (317) 822-5700. **E-Mail Address:** baseball@nfhs.org. **Website:** nfhs.org.
Executive Director: Karissa Niehoff. **Chief Operating Officer:** Davis Whitfield. **Director of Sports, Sanctioning and Student Services:** B. Elliot Hopkins. **Director, Publications/Communications:** Bruce Howard.

NATIONAL HIGH SCHOOL BASEBALL COACHES ASSOCIATION

Mailing Address: PO Box 1038, Dublin, OH 43017. **Telephone:** (614) 578-1864. **E-Mail Address:** tsaunders@baseballcoaches.org. **Website:** baseballcoaches.org. **Executive Director:** Tim Saunders (Dublin Coffman HS, Ohio). **Assistant Executive Director:** Ty Whittaker (Eastern Technical HS, Md.). **Associate Executive Director:** Ray Benjamin (St. Charles HS, Ohio). **Associate Exectuive Director:** Paul Twenge (Minnetonka HS, Minn.). **Executive Secretary:** Robert Colburn. **Immediate Past President:** Tony Perkins (Francis Howell HS, Mo.). **President:** Tim Bordenet (Lafayette Central Catholic HS, Ind.). **1st VP:** Scott Manahan (Bishop Watterson HS, Ohio). **2nd VP:** Todd Fitz-Gerald.

NATIONAL TOURNAMENTS

IN-SEASON

INTERNATIONAL PAPER CLASSIC
Mailing Address: 4775 Johnson Rd., Georgetown, SC 29440. **Telephone:** (843) 527-9606. **Fax:** (843) 546-8521. **Website:** ipclassic.com.
Tournament Director: Alicia Johnson.
2021 Tournament: March 11-14.

46TH ANNUAL ANAHEIM LIONS CLUB BASEBALL TOURNAMENT
Mailing Address: 8281 Walker Street, La Palma, CA 90623. **Telephone:** (714) 425-3796. **Fax:** (714) 995-1833. **Email:** lions@usapremiersports.com. **Website:** lions.usa-premiersports.com.
Tournament Director: Chris Pascal.
2021 Tournament: March 20-26 (88 teams).

NATIONAL CLASSIC BASEBALL TOURNAMENT
Mailing Address: 1651 Valencia Ave, Placentia, CA 92870. **Telephone:** (714) 993-2838. **Fax:** (714) 993-5350. **E-Mail Address:** mlucas@pylusd.org. **Website:** national-classicbaseball.com.
Tournament Director: Matt Lucas.
2021 Tournament: TBD.

USA BASEBALL NATIONAL HIGH SCHOOL INVITATIONAL
Mailing Address: 1030 Swabia Ct., Suite 201; Durham, NC 27703. **Telephone:** (919) 474-8721. **Fax:** (919) 474-8822. **Email:** carterhicks@usabaseball.com. **Website:** usabaseball.com.
2021 Tournament: Canceled (Will return in 2022).

POSTSEASON

ALL-STAR GAMES/AWARDS
PERFECT GAME ALL-AMERICAN CLASSIC
Mailing Address: 850 Twixt Town Rd. NE, Cedar Rapids, IA 52402. **Telephone:** (319) 298-2923. Fax (319) 298-2924. **Event Organizer:** Blue Ridge Sports & Entertainment. **VP, Showcases/Scouting:** Greg Sabers.
2021 Game: Summer, TBD

BASEBALL FACTORY ALL-STAR CLASSIC
Mailing Address: 9212 Berger Rd., Suite 200, Columbia, MD 21046. **Telephone:** (410) 715-5080. **E-mail Address:** jason@factoryathletics.com. **Website:** baseball factory.com/AllAmerica. **Event Organizers:** Baseball Factory, Team One Baseball.
2021 Game: Summer, TBD.

GATORADE CIRCLE OF CHAMPIONS
(National HS Player of the Year Award)
Mailing Address: The Gatorade Company, 321 N. Clark St., Suite 24-3, Chicago, IL, 60610. **Telephone:** (312) 821-1000. **Website:** gatorade.com.

SHOWCASE EVENTS

AREA CODE BASEBALL GAMES PRESENTED BY NEW BALANCE

Mailing Address: 23954 Madison Street, Torrance, CA 90505. **Telephone:** (310) 791-1142 x 4426. **E-Mail Address:** baseball@studentsports.com. **Website:** AreaCodeBaseball.com.

Event Organizer: Kirsten Leetch.
2021 Area Code Games: Aug. 6-10; Los Angeles.

AREA CODE BASEBALL UNDERCLASS GAMES PRESENTED BY NEW BALANCE

Event Organizer: Kirsten Leetch.
2020 Area Code Games: Aug. 11-13; Los Angeles.

ARIZONA FALL CLASSIC

Mailing Address: 9962 W. Villa Hermosa, Peoria, AZ 85383. **Telephone:** (602) 228-1592.
E-mail Address: azfallclassic@gmail.com.
Website: azfallclassic.com.
President: Tracy Heid
Event Director: Trevor Heid,
Information Directors: Tiffini Robinson, Tiana Eves

2020 EVENTS

Four Corner Classic. . . . . Peoria, AZ, June 3-6

AZ Freshman
Fall Classic (class of 2025) . . . . Peoria, AZ, Oct. 14-17

AZ Sophomore
Fall Classic (class of 2024) . . . . Peoria, AZ, Oct. 7-10

AZ Senior
Fall Classic (class of 2022) . . . . . .Peoria, AZ, Sept. 29-Oct. 3

Senior All Academic Game . . . . Sept. 30

Junior College All Star Series . . . . TBD

AZ Junior
Fall Classic (class of 2023) . . . . Peoria, AZ , Sept. 22-26

Junior All Academic Tryout & Game. . . . . Sept. 23

Easton Fall Classic. . . . . Peoria, AZ, Oct. 21-24

BASEBALL FACTORY

Office Address: 9212 Berger Rd., Suite 200, Columbia, MD 21046. **Telephone:** (800) 641-4487, (410) 715-5080. **Fax:** (410) 715-1975. **E-Mail Address:** info@baseball factory.com. **Website:** baseballfactory.com.
Chief Executive Officer/Founder: Steve Sclafani. **President:** Rob Naddelman. **Chief Program Officer:** Jim Gemler. **Chief Baseball Officer** Steve Bernhardt. **Senior VP, Player Development:** Dan Forester. **VP, Tournament Division:** Justin Roswell. **VP, Business Development:** Dave Packer. **Executive Director, College Recruiting:** Dan Mooney. **Senior Multimedia Producer:** Brian Johnson. **Senior Director, Web Development:** Wei Xue. **Senior Director, Event Experience:** Ryan Liddle. **National Director of Player Identification:** Patrick Lawrence.
Executive Player Development Coordinator: Steve Nagler. **Senior Player Development Coordinators:** Adam Darvick, John Perko. **Senior Regional Player Development Coordinators:** Chris Brown, Rob Onolfi.

Regional Player Development Coordinators: Josh Eldridge, Patrick Wuebben, Matt Sammarco, Ryan Schwartz. **Director of College Recruiting:** Matt Richter.
Senior Director of Human Resources and Office Logistics: Danielle Lawson. **Director of Player Development:** Mike Landis.

All America Tournaments

Academic All-America. . . . . .April 16-18, Houston

Academic All-America. . . . . .Dec. 11-13, Bradenton, Fla.

Pre-Season Tournament. . . . . . .Jan. 15-17, Vero Beach, Fla.

Pre-Season Tournament. . . . . .Jan. 15-17, Houston

Baseball Factory National Tryouts/College PREP Recruiting Program: Year round at various locations across the country. Open to high school players, ages 14–18, with a separate division for middle school players, ages 12–14. **Full schedule:** www.baseballfactory.com/tryouts.

EAST COAST PROFESSIONAL SHOWCASE

Website: www.eastcoastpro.org. **Mailing Address:** Hoover Met Complex, 100 Ben Chapman Dr, Hoover, AL 25244. **E-mail Address:** info@eastcoastpro.org
Tournament Directors: John Castleberry, Rich Sparks, Sean Gibbs, Arthur McConnehead, Lori Bridges.
2021 Showcase: Aug. 2-5, Hoover Met Complex, 100 Ben Chapman Dr., Hoover, AL 35244.

IMPACT BASEBALL

Mailing Address: P.O. Box 47, Sedalia, NC 27342.
E-mail Address: impactbaseballstaff@gmail.com.
Website: impactbaseball.com. **Founder/CEO:** Andy Partin. **2020 Events:** Various dates, June-Aug.

NORTHWEST CHAMPIONSHIPS

Mailing Address: 9849 Fox Street, Aumsville, OR 97325. **Telephone:** (503) 302-7117. **E-mail Address:** joshuapwarner@gmail.com. **Website:** baseball northwest.com. **Tournament Organizer:** Josh Warner.

PERFECT GAME USA

(A Division of Perfect Game USA)
Mailing Address: 850 Twixt Town Rd. NE, Cedar Rapids, IA 52402. **Telephone:** (319) 298-2923. **Fax:** (319) 298-2924. **E-mail Address:** pgba@perfectgame.org. **Website:** perfectgame.org.
Year Founded: 1995.
President: Jerry Ford. **VP, Operations:** Taylor McCollough. **VP, Showcases/Scouting:** Greg Sabers.

PREP BASEBALL REPORT

Mailing Address: 4750 S. Vernon Ave, McCook, IL 60525. Telephone: 708-387-0500.
President: Sean Duncan. **Vice President of Operations and Multimedia:** Matt Yarber. **National Crosschecker:** Shooter Hunt. **National Supervisor:** Nathan Rode. **Director of College Scouting:** David Seifert. **Managing Director:** Cullen McGowan.

PROFESSIONAL BASEBALL INSTRUCTION—BATTERY INVITATIONAL

(for top high school pitchers and catchers)
Mailing Address: 12 Wright Way, Oakland NJ 07436.
Telephone: (800) 282-4638. **Fax:** (201) 760-8820.
E-mail Address: info@baseballclinics.com.
Website: baseballclinics.com
President: Doug Cinnella.
Director of PR/Marketing: Jim Monaghan.

SELECTFEST BASEBALL

Mailing Address: P.O. Box 852, Morris Plains, NJ
07950. **E-mail Address:** selectfest@selectfestbaseball.org.
Website: selectfestbaseball.org. **Camp Directors:** Bruce
Shatel, Robert Maida. **2021 Showcase:** TBD.

TEAM ONE BASEBALL

(A division of Baseball Factory)
Office Address: 220 Newport Center Drive, 11418,
Newport Beach, CA 92660. **Telephone:** (800) 621-5452.
Fax: (949) 209-1829. **E-Mail Address:**
jroswell@teamonebaseball.com. **Website:** teamonebase-
ball.com.
Executive Director: Justin Roswell. **Chief Program
Officer:** Jim Gemler. **Executive VP:** Steve Bernhardt.
Senior VP, Player Development: Dan Forester.

2021 Showcases:

For a full listing of showcases visit www.teamone-
baseball.com/showcases.

2021 Tournaments:

Under Armour Memorial Day Classic West . . . . . May 28-31
Yuma, Ariz. (Ray Kroc Complex)

Under Armour Memorial Day Classic East . . . . . . May 28-31
Jupiter, Fla. (Roger Dean Complex)

Under Armour 4th of July Classic . . . . June 25-28
West Covina, Calif. (Various HS)

Firecracker Classic. . . . . July 6-10. Jupiter, FL
(Roger Dean Sports Complex)

Southwest Championships 16U . . . . July 23-26
in Mesa, Ariz. (Gene Autry & Red Mountain)

Southwest Championships 17U   July 30 – Aug. 2
Irvine, Calif. (Orange County Great Park)

Jupiter Fall Classic. .September 24–26
Jupiter, FL (Roger Dean Sports Complex)

For a full listing of tournaments visit:
www.teamonebaseball.com/tournaments.

TOP 96 COLLEGE COACHES CLINICS

Mailing Address: 2639 Connecticut Avenue NW,
Suite 250, Washington, DC 20008. **Telephone:** (202) 313-
7385. **il Address:** info@top96.com. **Website:** top96.com.
Directors: Doug Henson, Dave Callum.

YOUTH BASEBALL

ALL AMERICAN AMATEUR BASEBALL ASSOCIATION
Mailing Address: 1101 Flamingo Drive, APT 3106, Altoona, PA 16602.
Cell: (814) 931-8698.
E-Mail Address: aaabaprez@atlanticbb.net.
Website: aaabajohnstown.org
President: Mike Gossner
Executive Director: John Austin
2021 Events: AAABA National Tournament August 3-8 in Johnstown PA.

AMATEUR ATHLETIC UNION OF THE UNITED STATES, INC.
Mailing Address: P.O. Box 22409, Lake Buena Vista, FL 32830. **Telephone:** (407) 828-3459. **Fax:** (407) 934-7242.
E-mail Address: tmeyer@aausports.org. **Website:** play-aaubaseball.com.
Year Founded: 1982. **Senior Sport Manager, Baseball:** Tim Meyer.

AMERICAN AMATEUR BASEBALL CONGRESS
National Headquarters: 100 West Broadway, Farmington, NM 87401. **Telephone:** (505) 327-3120. **Fax:** (505) 327-3132. **E-mail Address:** info@aabc.us. **Website:** aabc.usapremiersports.com.
Year Founded: 1935.
President: Richard Neely.

AMERICAN AMATEUR YOUTH BASEBALL ALLIANCE
Mailing Address: 3851 Iris Lane, Bonne Terre, MO 63628. **Telephone:** (314) 650-0028. **E-mail Address:** info@aayba.com. **Website:** aayba.com.
President, Baseball Operations: Carroll Wood.
President, Business Operations: Greg Moore.

AMERICAN LEGION BASEBALL
National Headquarters: American Legion Baseball, 700 N Pennsylvania St., Indianapolis, IN 46204.
Telephone: (317) 630-1200. **Fax:** (317) 630-1223. **E-mail Address:** baseball@legion.org. **Website:** legion.org/baseball.
Year Founded: 1925.
Program Coordinator: Steve Cloud.
2021 World Series (19 and under): Aug. 12-17 at Keeter Stadium, Shelby, N.C.

BABE RUTH LEAGUE
International Headquarters: 1670 Whitehorse-Mercerville Rd., Hamilton, NJ 08619. **Telephone:** (800) 880-3142. **Fax:** (609) 695-2505. **E-mail Address:** info@baberuthleague.org. **Website:** baberuthleague.org.
Year Founded: 1951.
President/Chief Executive Officer: Steven Tellefsen

BASEBALL FOR ALL
Mailing Address: 30745 Pacific Coast Hwy #328 Los Angeles, CA 90265. **E-mail Address:** girlsbaseball@baseballforall.com. **Website:** BaseballForAll.com
Providing baseball programming for girls.

CALIFORNIA COMPETITIVE YOUTH BASEBALL
Mailing Address: P.O. Box 338, Placentia, CA 92870.
Telephone: (714) 993-2838. **E-mail Address:** ccybnet@gmail.com. **Website:** ccyb.net.
Tournament Director: Todd Rogers.

COCOA EXPO SPORTS CENTER
Mailing Address: 500 Friday Road, Cocoa, FL 32926.
Telephone: (321) 639-3976. **Fax:** (407) 390-9435. **E-mail Address:** brad@cocoaexpo.com. **Website:** cocoaexpo.com.
Activities: Spring training program, spring & fall leagues, instructional camps, team training camps, youth tournaments.

CONTINENTAL AMATEUR BASEBALL ASSOCIATION
Mailing Address: P.O. Box 1684 Mt. Pleasant, SC 29465. **Telephone:** (843) 860-1568. **E-mail Address:** info@cababaseball.com. **Website:** cababaseball.com.
Year Founded: 1984.
Chief Executive Officer: Larry Redwine. **President/COO:** John Rhodes. **Executive Vice President:** Fran Pell.

COOPERSTOWN BASEBALL WORLD
Mailing Address: P.O. Box 646, Allenwood, NJ 08720.
Telephone: (888) CBW-8750. **Fax:** (888) CBW-8720.
E-mail: cbw@cooperstownbaseballworld.com.
Website: cooperstownbaseballworld.com.
Complex Address: Cooperstown Baseball World, SUNY-Oneonta, Ravine Parkway, Oneonta, NY 13820.
President: Debra Sirianni.
2021 Tournaments (15 Teams Per Week): Open to 12U, 13U, 14U, 15U, 16U

COOPERSTOWN DREAMS PARK
Mailing Address: 330 S. Main St., Salisbury, NC 28144.
Telephone: (704) 630-0050. **Fax:** (704) 630-0737. **E-mail Address:** info@cooperstowndreamspark.com. **Website:** cooperstowndreamspark.com.
Complex Address: 4550 State Highway 28, Milford, NY 13807.
Chief Operating Officer: Mike Walter. **Director, Baseball Operations:** Geoff Davis.
2021 Tournaments: June 5-Aug. 21

COOPERSTOWN ALL STAR VILLAGE
Mailing Address: P.O. Box 670, Cooperstown, NY 13326. **Telephone:** (800) 327-6790. **Fax:** (607) 432-1076.
E-mail Address: info@cooperstownallstarvillage.com.
Website: cooperstownallstarvillage.com.
Team Registrations: Hunter Grace. **Hotel Room Reservations:** Tracie Jones. **Presidents:** Martin and Brenda Patton.

DIXIE YOUTH BASEBALL
Mailing Address: P.O. Box 877, Marshall, TX 75671.
Telephone: (903) 927-2255. **Fax:** (903) 927-1846. **E-mail Address:** dyb@dixie.org. **Website:** youth.dixie.org.
Year Founded: 1955. **Commissioner:** William Wade.

DIXIE BOYS BASEBALL

Mailing Address: P.O. Box 8263, Dothan, AL 36304. **Telephone:** (334) 793-3331. **E-mail Address:** jjones29@sw.rr.com. **Website:** baseball.dixie.org.
Commissioner/Chief Executive Officer: Sandy Jones.

DIZZY DEAN BASEBALL

Mailing Address: P.O. Box 856, Hernando, MS 38632. **Telephone:** (662) 429-4365. **E-mail Address:** danny phillips637@gmail.com. **Website:** dizzydeanbbinc.org.
Year Founded: 1962.
Commissioner: Danny Phillips. **President:** Joe Chandler. **VP:** Brent Frey. **Secretary:** John Gravat. **Treasurer:** Jim Dunn.

HAP DUMONT YOUTH BASEBALL

(A Division of the National Baseball Congress)
E-mail Address: hapdumontbaseball@gmail.com.
Year Founded: 1974.
President: Bruce Pinkall

KC SPORTS TOURNAMENTS

Mailing Address: KC Sports, 6324 N. Chatham Ave., No. 136, Kansas City, MO 64151.
Telephone: (816) 587-4545. **Fax:** (816) 587-4549.
E-mail Address: info@kcsports.org.
Website: kcsports.org.
Activities: USSSA Youth tournaments (ages 6-18).

LITTLE LEAGUE BASEBALL

International Headquarters: 539 US Route 15 Hwy, P.O. Box 3485, Williamsport, PA 17701-0485. **Telephone:** (570) 326-1921. **Fax:** (570) 326-1074. **E-Mail Address:** media@littleleague.org. **Website:** littleleague.org.
Year Founded: 1939.
Chairman: Hugh E. Tanner.
President and Chief Executive Officer: Stephen D. Keener. **Senior Vice President and Chief Financial Officer:** David Houseknecht. **Vice President, Operations:** Patrick Wilson. **Senior Vice President and Chief Marketing Officer:** Liz DiLullo Brown. **Senior Vice President and Chief Legal Officer:** Karl Eckweiler.

NATIONS BASEBALL-ARIZONA

Mailing Address: 20230 Cypress Rosehill Road, Tomball, TX 77377. **Telephone:** (877) 259-1150. **Website:** arizona.nations-baseball.com. **E-Mail Address:** info@nations-baseball.com.

NATIONAL AMATEUR BASEBALL FEDERATION

Mailing Address: P.O. Box 705, Bowie, MD 20718.
Telephone: (410) 721-4727. **Fax:** (410) 721-4940.
E-mail Address: nabf1914@aol.com.
Website: nabf.com.
Year Founded: 1914.
Executive Director: Charles Blackburn.

INSTRUCTIONAL SCHOOLS/ PRIVATE CAMPS

ALL-STAR BASEBALL ACADEMY

Mailing Address: 1475 Phoenixville Pike Suite 12, West Chester, PA 19380. **Telephone:** (484) 696-2223.
E-mail Address: basba@allstarbaseball academy.com. **Website:** allstarbaseballacademy.com.

President/CEO : Jim Freeman. **Executive Director:** Mike Manning.

AMERICAN BASEBALL FOUNDATION

Mailing Address: 833 Saint Vincent's Drive Suite 205A, Birmingham, AL 35205. **Telephone:** (205) 558-4235. **Fax:** (205) 918-0800. **E-mail Address:** abf@asmi.org. **Website:** americanbaseballfoundation.com. **Executive Director:** David Osinski.

ABC BASEBALL CAMPS

Mailing Address: 1353 Lake Shore Dr, Branson, MO 65616. **Telephone:** (800) 222-8152. **Fax:** (888) 751-8989. **E-mail Address:** sandi@abcsportscamps.com. **Website:** abcsportscamps.com.

CHAMPIONS BASEBALL ACADEMY

Mailing Address: 5994 Linneman Street, Cincinnati, OH 45230. **Telephone:** (513) 831-8873. **Fax:** (513) 247-0040. **E-mail Address:** championsbaseball@ymail.com. **Website:** championsbaseball.net. **Director:** Mike Bricker.

ELEV8 SPORTS INSTITUTE

Mailing Address: 490 Dotterel Road, Delray Beach, FL 33444. **Telephone:** (800) 970-5896. **E-mail Address:** info@elev8baseball.org. **Website:** elev8baseball.org

FROZEN ROPES TRAINING CENTERS

Mailing Address: 24 Old Black Meadow Rd., Chester, NY 10918. **Telephone:** (845) 469-7331. **Fax:** (845) 469-6742. **E-mail Address:** info@frozenropes.com. **Website:** frozenropes.com.

IMG ACADEMY

Mailing Address: IMG Academy, 5500 34th St. W., Bradenton, FL 34210. **Telephone:** (941) 749-8627. **Fax:** 941-739-7484. **E-mail Address:** colbe.herr@img.com. **Website:** imgacademy.com

MARK CRESSE BASEBALL SCHOOL

Mailing Address: P.O. Box 1596 Newport Beach, CA 92659. **Telephone:** (714) 892-6145. **Fax:** (714) 890-7017. **E-mail Address:** info@markcresse.com. **Website:** markcresse.com.
Owner/Founder: Mark Cresse.

US SPORTS CAMPS/NIKE BASEBALL CAMPS

Mailing Address: 1010 B Street Suite 450, San Rafael, CA 94901. **Telephone:** (800) 645-3226. **Fax:** (415) 479-6061. **E-mail Address:** baseball@ussportscamps.com. **Website:** ussportscamps.com/baseball/.

MOUNTAIN WEST BASEBALL ACADEMY

Mailing Address: 389 West 10000 South, South Jordan, UT 84095. **Telephone:** (801) 561-1700. **E-mail Address:** kent@utahbaseballacademy.com. **Website:** mountainwestbaseball.com. **Director:** Bob Keyes

NORTH CAROLINA BASEBALL ACADEMY

Mailing Address: 1137 Pleasant Ridge Road, Greensboro, NC 27409. **Telephone:** (336) 931-1118. **E-mail Address:** info@ncbaseball.com. **Website:** ncbaseball.com.

Owner/Director: Scott Bankhead.

PENNSYLVANIA DIAMOND BUCKS

Mailing Address: 2320 Whitetail Court, Hellertown, PA 18055. **Telephone:** (610) 838-1219, (610) 442-6998. **E-mail Address:** janciganick@yahoo.com. **Camp Director:** Jan Ciganick. **Head of Instruction:** Chuck Ciganick.

PROFESSIONAL BASEBALL INSTRUCTION

Mailing Address: 1300 Route 17 North, Ramsey Square Shopping Center, Ramsey, NJ 07446. **Telephone**: (800) 282-4638. **Fax**: (201) 760-8820. **E-mail Address:** info@baseballclinics.com. **Website:** baseballclinics.com. **President:** Doug Cinnella.

2020 Batter Invitational Showcase: October 2020

RIPKEN BASEBALL CAMPS

Mailing Address: 873 Long Drive, Averdeen, MD 21209. **Telephone:** (888) 747-5368. **E-mail Address:** information@ripkenbaseball.com. **Website:** ripken baseball.com.

SHO-ME BASEBALL CAMP

Mailing Address: P.O. Box 2270, Branson West, MO 65737. **Telephone:** (417) 338-5838. **Fax:** (417) 338-2610. **E-mail Address:** info@shomebaseball.com. **Website:** shomebaseball.com.

COLLEGE CAMPS

Almost all of the elite college baseball programs have summer/holiday instructional camps. Please consult the college section for listings.

SENIOR BASEBALL

MEN'S SENIOR BASEBALL LEAGUE

(18+, 25+, 35+, 45+, 55+, 65+)
Mailing Address: One Huntington Quadrangle, Suite 3N07, Melville, NY 11747. **Telephone:** (631) 753-6725. **Fax:** (631) 753-4031.

President: Steve Sigler. **Vice President:** Gary D'Ambrisi.

E-Mail Address: info@msblnational.com. **Website:** msblnational.com.

NATIONAL ADULT BASEBALL ASSOCIATION

Mailing Address: 5944 S. Kipling St., Suite 200, Littleton, CO 80127. **Telephone:** (800) 621-6479. **E-Mail Address:** nabanational@aol.com. **Website:** dugout.org.

President: Shane Fugita.

NATIONAL AMATEUR BASEBALL FEDERATION

Mailing Address: P.O. Box 705, Bowie, MD 20718. **Telephone:** (410) 721-4727. **Fax:** (410) 721-4940.

Email Address: nabf1914@aol.com.

Website: nabf.com.

Year Founded: 1914.

Executive Director: Charles Blackburn.

ROY HOBBS BASEBALL

Veterans (30 or 35 and Over), Masters (45 and Over), Legends (53 and Over); Classics (60 and Over), Vintage (65 and Over), Timeless (70 and Over), Forever Young (75 and Over).

Mailing Address: 4301-100 Edison Ave., Fort Myers, FL 33916. **Telephone:** (330) 923-3400. **E-Mail Address:** rh_bb@royhobbs.com. **Website:** royhobbs.com.

VP and CFO: Ellen Giffen. **President:** Tom Giffen.

SERVICE
DIRECTORY

SERVICE DIRECTORY

ACCESSORIES

FRANKLIN SPORTS
17 Campanelli Parkway
Stoughton, MA 02072
Phone: 781-344-1111
Fax: 781-341-0333
Website: franklinsports.com
E-mail:
customerservice@franklinsports.com

MIZUNO
4925 Avalon Ridge Parkway
One Jack Curran Way
Norcross, GA 30071
Phone: 800-966-1211
Website: mizunousa.com

RAWLINGS
510 Maryville University Dr.
Suite 110
St. Louis, MO 63141
Phone: 866-678-4327
Website: rawlings.com

WILSON SPORTING GOODS
1 Prudential Plaza
130 E. Randolph Street
Suite 600
Chicago, IL 60601
Phone: 800-800-9936
Website: wilson.com
E-mail: askwilson@wilson.com

APPAREL

DEMARINI
6435 NE Croeni Ave.
Hillsobro, OR 97124
Phone: 800-800-9932
Website: demarini.com

BAGS

DEMARINI
6435 NE Croeni Ave.
Hillsobro, OR 97124
Phone: 800-800-9932
Website: demarini.com

DIAMOND SPORTS
PO BOX 55090
Irvine, CA 92619
Phone: 949-409-9300
Fax: 949-409-9301
Website: www.diamond-sports.com
E-mail: info@diamond-sports.com

FORCE3 PRO GEAR
45 Banner Drive
Milford, CT 06480
Phone: 315-367-2331
Website: Force3progear.com
E-mail: support@force3progear.com

GERRY COSBY & CO.
11 Pennsylvania Plaza
New York, NY 10001
Phone: 877-563-6464
Fax: 212-967-0876
Website: cosbysports.com
E-mail: gcmsg@cosbysports.com

LOUISVILLE SLUGGER
1 Prudential Plaza
130 E. Randolph Plaza
Suite 600
Chicago, IL 60601
Phone: 800-800-9936
Website: Slugger.com

MIZUNO
4925 Avalon Ridge Parkway
One Jack Curran Way
Norcross, GA 30071
Phone: 800-966-1211
Website: mizunousa.com

WILSON SPORTING GOODS
1 Prudential Plaza
130 E. Randolph Street
Suite 600
Chicago, IL 60601
Phone: 800-800-9936
Website: wilson.com
E-mail: askwilson@wilson.com

BASEBALLS

DIAMOND SPORTS
PO BOX 55090
Irvine, CA 92619
Phone: 949-409-9300
Fax: 949-409-9301
Website: www.diamond-sports.com
E-mail: info@diamond-sports.com

RAWLINGS
510 Maryville University Dr.
Suite 110
St. Louis, MO 63141
Phone: 866-678-4327
Website: rawlings.com

WILSON SPORTING GOODS
1 Prudential Plaza
130 E. Randolph Street
Suite 600
Chicago, IL 60601
Phone: 800-800-9936
Website: wilson.com
E-mail: askwilson@wilson.com

BASES

C&H BASEBALL
10615 Technology Terrace
#100
Lakewood Ranch, FL 34211
Phone: 941-462-3076
Website: chbaseball.com

BATS

DEMARINI
6435 NE Croeni Ave.
Hillsobro, OR 97124
Phone: 800-800-9932
Website: demarini.com

DIAMOND SPORTS
PO BOX 55090
Irvine, CA 92619
Phone: 949-409-9300
Fax: 949-409-9301
Website: www.diamond-sports.com
E-mail: info@diamond-sports.com

LOUISVILLE SLUGGER
1 Prudential Plaza
130 E. Randolph Plaza
Suite 600
Chicago, IL 60601
Phone: 800-800-9936
Website: Slugger.com

MIZUNO
4925 Avalon Ridge Parkway
One Jack Curran Way
Norcross, GA 30071
Phone: 800-966-1211
Website: mizunousa.com

OLD HICKORY
P.O. Box 588
White House, TN 37188
Phone: 866-PRO-BATS
Fax: 615-285-0512
Website: oldhickorybats.com
E-mail: mail@oldhickorybats.com

RAWLINGS
510 Maryville University Dr.
Suite 110
St. Louis, MO 63141
Phone: 866-678-4327
Website: rawlings.com

THE WOOD BAT FACTORY
4924 NY0 28
Cooperstown, NY 13326
Phone: 607-282-4431
Website: thewoodbatfactory.com
E-mail: chrissy@thewoodbatfactory.com

BATTING GLOVES

DEMARINI
6435 NE Croeni Ave.
Hillsobro, OR 97124
Phone: 800-800-9932
Website: demarini.com

FRANKLIN SPORTS
17 Campanelli Parkway
Stoughton, MA 02072
Phone: 781-344-1111
Fax: 781-341-0333
Website: franklinsports.com
E-mail: customerservice@franklinsports.com

MIZUNO
4925 Avalon Ridge Parkway
One Jack Curran Way
Norcross, GA 30071
Phone: 800-966-1211
Website: mizunousa.com

RAWLINGS
510 Maryville University Dr.
Suite 110
St. Louis, MO 63141
Phone: 866-678-4327
Website: rawlings.com

BATTING CAGES

BALL FABRICS, INC.
510 West Arizona Ave.
DeLand, FL 32720
Phone: 866-360-1008
Fax: 386-740-7206
Website: www.ballfabrics.com
E-mail: info@ballfabrics.com

C&H BASEBALL
10615 Technology Terrace
#100
Lakewood Ranch, FL 34211
Phone: 941-462-3076
Website: chbaseball.com

WEST COAST NETTING
5075 Flightline Drive
Kingman, AZ 86401
Phone: 928-692-1144
Fax: 928-692-1501
Website: westcoastnetting.com
E-mail: info@westcoastnetting.com

CONCESSION OPERATIONS

STADIUM1 SOFTWARE LLC
13479 Polo Trace Drive
Delray Beach, FL 33556
Phone: 561-779-4040
Fax: 561-498-8358
Website: www.stadium1.com
E-mail: ed.mullen@stadium1.com

ENGINEERED BACKSTOP DESIGN BUILD

C&H BASEBALL
10615 Technology Terrace#100
Lakewood Ranch, FL 34211
Phone: 941-462-3076
Website: chbaseball.com

WEST COAST NETTING
5075 Flightline Drive
Kingman, AZ 86401
Phone: 928-692-1144
Fax: 928-692-1501
Website: westcoastnetting.com
E-mail: info@westcoastnetting.com

FIELD COVERS/TARPS

C&H BASEBALL
10615 Technology Terrace
#100
Lakewood Ranch, FL 34211
Phone: 941-462-3076
Website: chbaseball.com

FIELD WALL PADDING

C&H BASEBALL
10615 Technology Terrace
#100
Lakewood Ranch, FL 34211
Phone: 941-462-3076
Website: chbaseball.com

WEST COAST NETTING
5075 Flightline Drive
Kingman, AZ 86401
Phone: 928-692-1144
Fax: 928-692-1501
Website: westcoastnetting.com
E-mail: info@westcoastnetting.com

FOOD SERVICE

STADIUM1 SOFTWARE LLC
13479 Polo Trace Drive
Delray Beach, FL 33556
Phone: 561-779-4040
Fax: 561-498-8358
Website: www.stadium1.com
E-mail: ed.mullen@stadium1.com

GLOVES

ALL-STAR SPORTING GOODS
17 Leominster Road
Shirley, MA 01464
Phone: 800-777-3810
Website: All-starsports.com
E-mail: Weborders@all-starsports.com

DIAMOND SPORTS
PO BOX 55090
Irvine, CA 92619
Phone: 949-409-9300
Fax: 949-409-9301
Website: www.diamond-sports.com
E-mail: info@diamond-sports.com

FORCE3 PRO GEAR
45 Banner Drive
Milford, CT 06480
Phone: 315-367-2331
Website: Force3progear.com
E-mail: support@force3progear.com

LOUISVILLE SLUGGER
1 Prudential Plaza
130 E. Randolph Plaza
Suite 600
Chicago, IL 60601
Phone: 800-800-9936
Website: Slugger.com

MIZUNO
4925 Avalon Ridge Parkway
One Jack Curran Way
Norcross, GA 30071
Phone: 800-966-1211
Website: mizunousa.com

RAWLINGS
510 Maryville University Dr.
Suite 110
St. Louis, MO 63141
Phone: 866-678-4327
Website: rawlings.com

WILSON SPORTING GOODS
1 Prudential Plaza
130 E. Randolph Street
Suite 600
Chicago, IL 60601
Phone: 800-800-9936
Website: wilson.com
E-mail: askwilson@wilson.com

MUSIC/SOUND EFFECTS

SOUND DIRECTOR INC.
2918 SW Royal Way
Gresham, OR 97080
Phone: 503-665-6869
Fax: 503-914-1812
Website: www.sounddirector.com
E-mail: jj@sounddirector.com

NETTING/POSTS

BALL FABRICS, INC.
510 West Arizona Ave.
DeLand, FL 32720
Phone: 866-360-1008
Fax: 386-740-7206
Website: www.ballfabrics.com
E-mail: info@ballfabrics.com

C&H BASEBALL
10615 Technology Terrace
#100
Lakewood Ranch, FL 34211
Phone: 941-462-3076
Website: chbaseball.com

WEST COAST NETTING
5075 Flightline Drive
Kingman, AZ 86401
Phone: 928-692-1144
Fax: 928-692-1501
Website: westcoastnetting.com
E-mail: info@westcoastnetting.com

PITCHING MACHINES

ATEC
655 Spice Island Drive
Sparks, NV 89431
Phone: 800-800-9931
Website: atecsports.com

PLAYING FIELD PRODUCTS

C&H BASEBALL
10615 Technology Terrace
#100
Lakewood Ranch, FL 34211
Phone: 941-462-3076
Website: chbaseball.com

WEST COAST NETTING
5075 Flightline Drive
Kingman, AZ 86401
Phone: 928-692-1144
Fax: 928-692-1501
Website: westcoastnetting.com
E-mail: info@westcoastnetting.com

PROTECTIVE EQUIPMENT

ALL-STAR SPORTING GOODS
17 Leominster Road
Shirley, MA 01464
Phone: 800-777-3810
Website: All-starsports.com
E-mail: Weborders@all-starsports.com

C&H BASEBALL
10615 Technology Terrace
#100
Lakewood Ranch, FL 34211
Phone: 941-462-3076
Website: chbaseball.com

DIAMOND SPORTS
PO BOX 55090
Irvine, CA 92619
Phone: 949-409-9300
Fax: 949-409-9301
Website: www.diamond-sports.com
E-mail: info@diamond-sports.com

EVOSHIELD
1 Prudential Plaza
130 E. Randolph Street
Suite 600
Chicago, IL 60601
Phone: 800-800-9936
E-mail: evoshield.com

FORCE3 PRO GEAR
45 Banner Drive
Milford, CT 06480
Phone: 315-367-2331
Website: Force3progear.com
E-mail: support@force3progear.com

MIZUNO
4925 Avalon Ridge Parkway
One Jack Curran Way
Norcross, GA 30071
Phone: 800-966-1211
Website: mizunousa.com

RAWLINGS
510 Maryville University Dr.
Suite 110
St. Louis, MO 63141
Phone: 866-678-4327
Website: rawlings.com

WEST COAST NETTING
5075 Flightline Drive
Kingman, AZ 86401
Phone: 928-692-1144
Fax: 928-692-1501
Website: westcoastnetting.com
E-mail: info@westcoastnetting.com

WILSON SPORTING GOODS
1 Prudential Plaza
130 E. Randolph Street
Suite 600
Chicago, IL 60601

Phone: 800-800-9936
Website: wilson.com
E-mail: askwilson@wilson.com

RADAR EQUIPMENT

POCKET RADAR, INC.
3535 Industrial Dr.
Suite A4
Santa Rosa, CA 95403
Phone: 888-381-2672
Fax: 888-381-2672
Website: https://www.pocketradar.com/
E-mail: tscaturro@pocketradar.com

STALKER SPORTS RADAR
855 E Collins Blvd.
Richardson, TX 75081
Phone: 972-398-3780
Website: stalkersportsradar.com
E-mail: sales@stalkerradar.com

SCOREBOARD

STALKER SPORTS RADAR
855 E Collins Blvd.
Richardson, TX 75081
Phone: 972-398-3780
Website: stalkersportsradar.com
E-mail: sales@stalkerradar.com

STADIUM GRAPHICS - WINDSCREENS, BANNERS, BLEACHER WRAPS

BALL FABRICS, INC.
510 West Arizona Ave.
DeLand, FL 32720
Phone: 866-360-1008
Fax: 386-740-7206
Website: www.ballfabrics.com
E-mail: info@ballfabrics.com

THE EMBLEM SOURCE

THE EMBLEM SOURCE
4575 Westgrove #500
Addison, TX 75001
Phone: 214-793-7250

Website: theemblemsource.com
E-mail: larry@theemblemsource.com

TRAINING EQUIPMENT

ATEC
655 Spice Island Drive
Sparks, NV 89431
Phone: 800-800-9931
Website: atecsports.com

DIAMOND SPORTS
PO BOX 55090
Irvine, CA 92619
Phone: 949-409-9300
Fax: 949-409-9301
Website: www.diamond-sports.com
E-mail: info@diamond-sports.com

LOUISVILLE SLUGGER
1 Prudential Plaza
130 E. Randolph Plaza
Suite 600
Chicago, IL 60601
Phone: 800-800-9936
Website: Slugger.com

WEST COAST NETTING
5075 Flightline Drive
Kingman, AZ 86401
Phone: 928-692-1144
Fax: 928-692-1501
Website: westcoastnetting.com
E-mail: info@westcoastnetting.com

UNIFORMS

FRANKLIN SPORTS
17 Campanelli Parkway
Stoughton, MA 02072
Phone: 781-344-1111
Fax: 781-341-0333
Website: franklinsports.com
E-mail: customerservice@franklinsports.com

MIZUNO
4925 Avalon Ridge Parkway
One Jack Curran Way
Norcross, GA 30071
Phone: 800-966-1211
Website: mizunousa.com

WILSON SPORTING GOODS
1 Prudential Plaza
130 E. Randolph Street
Suite 600
Chicago, IL 60601
Phone: 800-800-9936
Website: wilson.com
E-mail: askwilson@wilson.com

WINDSCREENS

BALL FABRICS, INC.
510 West Arizona Ave.
DeLand, FL 32720
Phone: 866-360-1008
Fax: 386-740-7206
Website: www.ballfabrics.com
E-mail: info@ballfabrics.com

C&H BASEBALL
10615 Technology Terrace
#100
Lakewood Ranch, FL 34211
Phone: 941-462-3076
Website: chbaseball.com

WEST COAST NETTING
5075 Flightline Drive
Kingman, AZ 86401
Phone: 928-692-1144
Fax: 928-692-1501
Website: westcoastnetting.com
E-mail: info@westcoastnetting.com

YOUR COMPANY NAME HERE
Make sure the baseball community can find you in 2020.
Call: 919-213-7924
E-mail: advertising@baseballamerica.com

INDEX

INDEX

ED WOLFSTEIN

MAJOR LEAGUE TEAMS

MINOR LEAGUE TEAMS

PARTNER TEAMS

OTHER ORGANIZATIONS